THE DEVELOPMENT OF INTERNATIONAL LAW

BY

SIR GEOFFREY BUTLER, K.B.E., M.A.

MEMBER OF PARLIAMENT FOR THE UNIVERSITY OF CAMBRIDGE
AND FELLOW OF CORPUS CHRISTI COLLEGE

AND

SIMON MACCOBY, M.A.

SOMETIME SCHOLAR OF CORPUS CHRISTI COLLEGE
AND WHEWELL SCHOLAR OF THE UNIVERSITY

THE LAWBOOK EXCHANGE, LTD.
Clark, New Jersey

ISBN-13: 978-1-58477-215-6 (cloth)
ISBN-13: 978-1-61619-055-2 (paperback)

Lawbook Exchange edition 2003, 2010

Printed in the United States of America on acid-free paper

THE LAWBOOK EXCHANGE, LTD.
33 Terminal Avenue
Clark, New Jersey 07066-1321

Please see our website for a selection of our other publications and fine facsimile reprints of classic works of legal history:
www.lawbookexchange.com

Library of Congress Cataloging-in-Publication Data

Butler, Geoffrey G. (Geoffrey Gilbert), Sir, 1887-1929.
The development of international law / by Sir Geoffrey Butler and Simon Maccoby.
p. cm.
Originally published: London ; New York: Longmans, Green and Co., 1928. (Contributions to international law and diplomacy).
ISBN 1-58477-215-8 (cloth: acid-free paper)
1. International law—History. I. Maccoby, Simon. II. Title. III. Contributions to international law and diplomacy.

KZ3225 .B88 2001
341—dc21 2001050211

THE DEVELOPMENT OF INTERNATIONAL LAW

BY

SIR GEOFFREY BUTLER, K.B.E., M.A.

MEMBER OF PARLIAMENT FOR THE UNIVERSITY OF CAMBRIDGE
AND FELLOW OF CORPUS CHRISTI COLLEGE

AND

SIMON MACCOBY, M.A.

SOMETIME SCHOLAR OF CORPUS CHRISTI COLLEGE
AND WHEWELL SCHOLAR OF THE UNIVERSITY

LONGMANS, GREEN AND CO. LTD.
LONDON • NEW YORK • TORONTO
1928

LONGMANS, GREEN AND CO. LTD.
39 PATERNOSTER ROW, LONDON, E.C. 4
6 OLD COURT HOUSE STREET, CALCUTTA
53 NICOL ROAD, BOMBAY
167 MOUNT ROAD, MADRAS

LONGMANS, GREEN AND CO.
55 FIFTH AVENUE, NEW YORK
221 EAST 20TH STREET, CHICAGO
TREMONT TEMPLE, BOSTON
210 VICTORIA STREET, TORONTO

Made in Great Britain

TO THE MEMORY OF

L. OPPENHEIM

AND

H. ERLE RICHARDS

PREFACE

In 1911, or thereabouts, it was suggested to me almost simultaneously by the late Professor Oppenheim and the late Sir Erle Richards that it was desirable that some one should write anew the history of the Law of Nations. Wheaton's great book was out of print: Dr. Walker's admirable first volume, published in 1899, had not been followed by a second; on the other hand, there were to be found in many countries treatises and articles by authors of deep learning—I may mention in particular the works of Dr. Nys—which could furnish material for any writer who should undertake within the covers of a single volume the compilation of a general history. After some reflection I undertook to prepare such a work for Messrs. Longmans. The longer I worked at the task the more clearly did I perceive that it was not one either quickly or easily completed. The war came, and occupations after the war, which delayed the production of the manuscript. Then with the permission of the publisher I entered into partnership with my former pupil, Mr. Simon Maccoby.

I have insisted on writing a word in analysis of the nature of our joint effort, because I am anxious that, if the book be fortunate enough to meet with approbation, the part played by my collaborator should be fully appreciated. I had accumulated notes for my lectures, but we have jointly planned the work afresh in detail and have carefully discussed together every chapter, before and after it has been written. Lastly, it was I who reduced the material to its final form in writing. But the accumulation of matter, the quest for the last or the best authority, the reduction of the text to penultimate form, have been primarily the work of Mr. Maccoby.

We had not been long at work when we perceived that our main problem was one of method. To trace separately and in due order each doctrine or practice of International Law from its appearance to the present day would have meant writing a text-book of the subject on conventional lines, which have, it may be remarked, altered very little since the days of the earliest writers. It may be presumed that a long line of authors would not have remained bound by rigidity of method if this had not been found desirable by their public. Consequently, nothing would have been gained, and some irritation might have been caused, by the production of a work in which the familiar outlines had been blurred by the mere insertion of great wads of history.

On the other hand, the solution of the problem was not to be found in writing chronologically such a history of diplomacy as would bring out in special relief the gradually expanding corpus of international jurisprudence. Even granting that an accurate picture had been obtained, the book would have been intolerable to read. As the author completed each section of his historical narrative it would have been necessary for him to retrace his steps to take up point by point, and at the stage at which he had dropped it in the preceding section, the record of the growing law. All continuity would have been lost.

We experimented, therefore, with a third alternative. Believing that changes in International Law have been ultimately an expression of changes in the state system of the world and in the practice of the nations, we have tried, as it were, to cut into the procession of history at fixed points, to select some central theme at each stage, and to treat it in the light of history and law. In this attempt we arrived at a division of history from our point of view into three major periods which we have termed respectively those of the Prince, of the Judge, and of the Concert. In the first period, the scholar is still in the age of the dissolving Holy Roman Empire: in the second, commercial and dynastic wars — above all, the long-drawn-out struggle between France and England—dominate the scene: in the third and last, it is the voice of some force other than that of pure nationalism which, whatever be the reason, reasserts itself. No division of this kind can be wholly satisfactory, but it is our belief that under one or other of these headings almost every issue which has interest for the historian of the Law of Nations can be conveniently treated. Is it possible otherwise to reconcile the need of reducing to a minimum the interruption of the narrative and that of coping with the "spill over" of legal questions from one period of history to another? None the less, it has been the adoption of this selective method of treatment which has caused us in the title of the book to substitute for the word *History* the word *Development* of International Law.

It has been an inestimable benefit to us that we have both been members of the Cambridge Schools of History and Law. The practice of those bodies has been that men of deep, if unostentatious, learning have always been ready to share their erudition with their humbler brethren. We have taken advantage of this tradition and have with great profit to ourselves submitted different portions of this book to the criticism of Dr. Arnold McNair, Dr. J. H. Clapham, Dr. J. R. Tanner, and Mr. C. W. Previté-Orton. Two other former pupils of my own have laid me under obligation to them. Captain B. H. Liddell Hart has read the chapter which concerns the growth of military forces: to Mr. Charles Smyth I owe at least one helpful suggestion. My colleague Mr. Arthur Goodhart, Fellow of Corpus, most generously found time to read the page proofs. To all of these we are grateful, although the responsibility for error must rest with us alone. I should like to conclude with a word of gratitude to Mr. R. Vere Laurence, Fellow of Trinity, who from the day that he first encouraged me to lecture on this subject has watched my attempt to teach it with friendly interest, and has never failed to proclaim his belief in the merit for educational purposes of the history of the Law of Nations.

The section in Chapter IV. on "Reprisals as a measure of redress short of war" was written by Mr. Maccoby for the *Cambridge Law Journal* in 1924, and is reproduced by the kind permission of the editors.

GEOFFREY BUTLER.

Christmas Day 1927,
NUWARA ELIYA.

CONTENTS

PART I

THE AGE OF THE PRINCE

PART II

THE AGE OF THE JUDGE

PART III

THE AGE OF THE CONCERT

SYNOPSIS

[*The notes appropriate to each chapter are printed at its conclusion.*]

PART I

THE AGE OF THE PRINCE

CHAPTER I.: THE WORLD BY LAND

Introduction: Predominant interest in the *Jus Belli*. *The right to wage war:* Public and private war, necessary authority, the independent *respublica*. The Papal and Imperial claims. *State sovereignty:* Bodin's definition. Its application. Importance of the attribute of sovereignty, Prince of Orange. Situation in Germany and in Italy. *The family of nations:* List of precedency (1504), that of the Council of Trent (1559-1560). Sully's estimate. *New Cyneas* of Crucé. William Penn. Abbé de St. Pierre. *Communities in revolt:* Difficulty in defining their position. The Netherlands and Spain. Action and theory. The Swiss and the Grisons. *Expelled and heretical rulers:* A problem in sovereignty. Elizabeth and Mary Queen of Scots. *The position of infidels:* Division of Joseph Acosta. The Turks, Franco-Turkish alliance of King Francis I., the principle of collective bargaining (capitulations). American Indians. Sepulveda, Suarez, Victoria, Las Casas. *The Hanseatic League:* Its strength and weakness. Wallenstein, French Treaty of 1716, the Holy Alliance. *Elective monarchies:* The Bohemian monarchy, the Empire, Poland, and the Papacy. *Questions of precedence and dignity:* Franco-Spanish rivalry, the *pacte de famille*. Portugal, Bavaria, Venice, Swiss confederation. Anglo-Spanish War. The Treaty of Westphalia. The *alternat* system. Utrecht. *Titles:* Ceremonial titles. The royal title. The British and Russian imperial titles. Napoleon. *Language:* Position of French. Appearance of English. Disappearance of Latin. The League of Nations. pp. 3-35.

CHAPTER II.: THE WORLD BY SEA

The *Mare Liberum* of Grotius. His concessions to actual conditions. These conditions. The claims of Venice, of Genoa. Bynkershoek. The British claims, Selden's *Mare Clausum*. The Dutch wars. Elizabeth and the Stuarts. Assertion by the British of their right, Sully's voyage in 1603, the incident of the MERLIN, Louis XIV. and Charles II. Anglo-Dutch Treaty of 1784. Cornwallis and the Peace of Amiens (1802). French claims in the Mediterranean. Scandinavian kingdoms and the Baltic. Danes, the Swedes, Wallenstein, Gustavus Adolphus. Alliance of France, England, Holland, and Denmark against the Swedes. Prussia and Russia in the eighteenth century. The Armed Neutralities. The Danish rights bought out in 1857. The Black Sea, ambition of Peter the Great. Treaty of Kutchuk-Kainardji. British support of "that ancient rule of the Ottoman Empire." The colonial seas. The navigators of Portugal. The papal confirmation, Victoria and his *De Indis*. The Spanish adventurers. Castiliano-Portuguese agreement. Columbus' discovery of Hispaniola. The attitude of the King of Portugal. The Papal Bull. The line of Tordesdillas. Magellan and the Philippines. Spanish and Portuguese partition of the New World. Hawkins, Drake, Leicester, and Hatton. French and British establishments in North America. Jamaica. The *Asiento*, Philip V.'s grant to French Guinea Company, British South Sea Company at Utrecht. Spanish claim to a right of search, the war of Jenkins' ear. The Eastern seas, the rights of Portugal. Dutch inroads, 1595-1601. Dutch United East India Company formed in 1602. English East India Company in 1600. Spanish-Portuguese offers to the Dutch and the submission in Westphalia in 1648. English negotiation with Spain-Portugal. The massacre of Amboyna. Cromwell and the Portuguese. Charles II. wins Bombay. Monopolistic pretensions become anachronistic. *The limit of territorial waters:* Bartolus and one hundred Italian miles. Baldus, Bodin, Gentilis. James I. and the Tsar Alexander. The theory of *portée de vue*, King Philip II. of Spain, Scottish and Scandinavian fishing practice. *Portée de canon*, Bynkershoek following Grotius. Varying definitions. Identification of lowest unit of maritime measurement with largest controllable area. First done by Galiani. Adoption by Washington, 1793. Lord Stowell in the TWEE GEBROEDERS and the ANNA. Old conception of the King's Chambers. Territorial Waters Jurisdiction Act, 1878. Anglo-American Treaty of 1818. Principle not unchallenged, four maritime Powers have never accepted it. Anglo-American Convention, 1924. pp. 40-58.

CHAPTER III.: INTERCOURSE: IN PEACE

Equilibrium: Ancient examples. Cinquecento Italy, Machiavelli. The balance of power, Henry VIII., Henry IV. of France, Richelieu. Louis XIV. and the alliances. The Mutiny Act and a standing army. The Peace of Utrecht. Fénelon's teaching. The partition of Poland. Napoleon III.'s doctrine of compensation. Lord Haldane's dictum. Italian irredentism. Weakness of the doctrine. *Intervention:* (*a*) for maintaining equilibrium, (*b*) religious, (*c*) humanitarian, (*d*) sanctional. The legal doctrine, Grotius, Pufendorff, Wolf, Vattel, de Martens. Gradual development of modern opinion on the subject. De Martens and the Holy Alliance. The doctrine of non-intervention. *Diplomatic intercourse:* Greek and Roman practice. Byzantine practice and the Pope. Development of a residential system. Venice and Florence. France and Spain, the Hapsburgs and England. Robert Wingfield. Elizabethan diplomacy, Sir Thomas Edmondes, the secret service, the Foreign Office. Unorthodox activities of seventeenth and eighteenth century diplomats. Immunity. *Classes of diplomatic agents:* Variety of practice up to the Congress of Vienna. *Consuls* a mediaeval office, the modern consular system. *Spread of the practice of legation, particularly in the Far East:* Grotius. Universality of practice. Western experience in China, in Japan, in Siam. Korea. *Diplomatic privileges: Droit de chapelle, droit de quartier, droit de l'hôtel.* Personal immunity of diplomats. *International negotiation:* Negotiation and ratification. Multiple alliances. Personal intercourse of rulers. Peace congresses. Münster and Osnabrück. Satow on the great congresses. The Congress of Vienna. The Conference of Paris in 1919. pp. 61-105.

CHAPTER IV.: INTERCOURSE: IN WAR

The bellum justum: The pagan and Christian position according to Suarez. St. Augustine. Thomas Aquinas. Conditions prerequisite to a declaration of war. Divided culpability. Invincible ignorance, excusable ignorance, probability. Vasquez. Victoria transitional to modern theory. Molina carries it further. Grotius. The war of rights succeeded by the war of trade and the war of might. The doctrine of nationality and of self-determination. The League of Nations and impediments to making war. The conscience of mankind. *The rights of a just belligerent:* Canonist doctrine. Cajetan's theory of execution. Victoria and the treatment of defeated princes. *Methods of war:* (*a*) booty, Lateran Council of 1179, Victoria, the practice during the "hundred" and "thirty" years' wars; (*b*) pillage, Cajetan and Victoria; (*c*) ransom, ancient and mediaeval practice, royal

PART II

THE AGE OF THE JUDGE

CHAPTER V.: TEMPERAMENTA

Introduction: Influence of the humanitarian spirit. *Declaration of war:* Different conditions by land and sea: common absence of a declaration in maritime war in the seventeenth century, the Dutch wars. The Anglo-French wars of the eighteenth century. Growth of contrary practice in nineteenth century. The Hague Convention (1907). *Enemy individuals and their property at the outbreak of war:* Perilous position of the alien before the eighteenth century. Opinion of the international lawyers. Treaties for relief, France and Savoy (1713), Russia and Naples (1787), Prussia and U.S.A. (1785), England and France (1786), England and U.S.A. (1795). Milder practice of nineteenth century. Exceptions, Danish ordinance (1807), Confederate States decree (1861). Enemy custodian in England (1914). *Enemy persons:* Practice severer, Napoleon, France (1870), Boer republics (1899), Russia (1904), Turkey (1897), belligerent practice (1914-1918). *Droit d'Aubaine:* Mediaeval position of the alien, subordination to seigneur. Grotius' condemnation of the practice. Abolition as between Holland and France at Nymwegen and Ryswick. Treaties of Louis XV. and XVI. Treaty between Russia and Naples (1787). Montesquieu and Necker and French revolutionary governments. A palpable anachronism in nineteenth century. *Right of individuals to emigrate:* Acknowledged in seventeenth century; common practice of eighteenth and nineteenth; drawbacks; *gabella emigrationis.* Modern emigration difficulties. *Freedom of coast fisheries:* French *ordonnances* (1543, 1584, 1681, 1692), challenge of British Admiralty. Stowell, YOUNG JACOB and JOHANNA. English ordinances of 1806 and 1810. Nineteenth century increasingly favourable. U.S. Supreme Court, PAQUETE HABANA, LOLA (1898). Deep-sea fishing. *Treatment of prisoners of war:* Systematisation under Louis XIV. Exchange cartels of Dutch, French, and English. Ransom in the eighteenth century, under Napoleon. Parole. Catharine of Russia. Prusso-American Treaty (1785). American prisoners in England. Napoleonic prisoners. German practice in 1870 contrasted with that in 1914. pp. 193-209.

CHAPTER VI.: THE WORLD OF COMMERCE

Mediaeval privileges to alien traders, and customs regulation of sea-borne commerce. Ordinance of the Staple (1353). Hansa merchants. Reprisal under state authority. Government negotiation on behalf of merchants. Growing organisation of mercantile community. Commercial clauses in general treaties, and finally commercial treaties. Louis XI. Anglo-Burgundian Treaty (1407). England and Castile (1403). *Intercursus Magnus* (1496). Its terms. *Intercursus Malus* (1506). Anglo-Spanish Treaty (1499). Little analogy with modern treaties of trade. Disputes over home industries, dyed cloth, rivalry between Dutch and English. Anglo-Dutch shipping controversy. The Navigation Act. Colbert's policy of protection leads to controversy with the Dutch. D'Avaux' report. Free ships free goods as between France and Holland in Ryswick (1697). Dutch policy the liberation of innocent intercourse. Anglo-Dutch Treaty of 1674 defines contraband and stipulates for free ships free goods in war. Prussian treaty with U.S.A., immunity from attack for merchant shipping. The Methuen Treaty (1703), political subinfeudation. *The old commercial systems:* Features of the British Navigation Acts in home and colonial trade. Comparison with Spanish practice, *Casa de Contratacion* at Seville, the *flota*. Portuguese practice. Dutch East India Company, massacre of Amboyna. English, French, and Imperial East India Companies. West Indian trade. British-American trade, imports and exports, "enumeration." Walpole's concessions. Colbert's Company of the West. Danish West Indies. British-African Company. A managed system. Progress towards greater liberality of concessions. English treaty with Portugal (1642). Agreements on exclusion. Treaty of Utrecht. Anglo-Spanish War of 1739. Slight progress towards opening of trade in seventeenth and eighteenth centuries. Mutual jealousy. French decision of 1756. Revolt in San Domingo (1791). Outbreak of twenty-one years of war (1793). Revolt of British colonies, United States forces British ports. Huskisson's repeal of Navigation Acts. Opening of Spanish-American and Brazilian ports. King Ferdinand VII. pp. 211-226.

CHAPTER VII.: NEUTRALITY

The maritime position: A doctrine of neutrality postulates a state system and general discard of obligation to discriminate between just and unjust war. *Consolato del Mare:* Severer codes. *Robe d'ennemy confisque celle d'amy.* French *ordonnances* (1543, 1584). Dano-Scottish agreement (1463). Letters of neutrality. No basis for a theory till eighteenth century. Even then practice unfavourable to its development. Gustavus Adolphus, Frederick of Prussia (1756), "Rule of 1756," Napoleon's continental system. Evolution of a theory, contribution of Bynkershoek, of Vattel. Leagues to defend neutrality, Suedo-Danish (1693), Choiseul's proposal (1756), Catharine II. and the First Armed Neutrality (1780), the Second Armed Neutrality (1800). Century ends with extreme assertion of belligerent position. *The right of passage :* Grotius finds an implied reservation of it at the original institution of private property. Treaty of Westphalia and roads of the Empire. Scattered dominions of seventeenth-century princes demanded it. Spanish treaty with Navarre in 1512. Simultaneous bargaining with France. Hapsburgs particularly affected. Generals in the field. Napoleon's high-handed action in Venetia (1796), Switzerland (1798). Gradual change of public and expert opinion shown in Vattel. Influence of the United States: and of geographical changes in Europe. Modern practice. *Ports, harbours, and territorial waters :* Scant respect for rights of neutrals in the seventeenth century. The scandal of the Downs (1639). The incident at Bergen (1666). Boscawen (1759) and Suffren (1781) in Portuguese waters. Increasing precaution among neutrals, Italian proclamations of neutrality during American War of Independence. The Tuscan regulations. Rules as to reception of prizes, United States (1778), England (1861), Hague Convention (1907). Prize-court proceedings overseas. English officials at Port Mahon and Leghorn. Tsaritsa's instructions to Orloff. The French *règlement* (1799). M. Genêt in U.S.A. (1793). Lord Stowell and the FLAD OYEN. U.S. Foreign Enlistment Act (1818), British Act (1819). The ALABAMA. Hague Conventions. The APPAM. pp. 229-247.

CHAPTER VIII.: THE EQUALITY OF STATES

Little pretence of equality in the sixteenth century. Theory of equality traceable to Hobbes. His analogy between men and states. Pufendorff's interpretation of equality of right, to independence, not of all rights or capacities. Question in fact feudal, not debatable *a priori*. Barbeyrac's naturalistic position. Realists not interested, J. J. Moser, Mably, de Martens. Eighteenth century, however, generally held equality existed. The Philosophes, Vattel. Wars of late eighteenth century diverted interest from controversy. England's practical attitude. The Congress Period and Concert of the Powers. The Four Powers. France admitted. Protest of Württemberg. Metternich and Italy. Successful protest of Greece. Neutralisation of Switzerland (1815), Belgium (1839), Luxemburg (1867). Status of Greece, Rumania from 1856 to 1878, Congress of Berlin, and Serbia and Montenegro, Turkey and Bulgaria. Hague Conference membership. Conference of London. The League of

Nations. Minority provisions in peace treaties (1918). Latin America. The Drago doctrine. Control imposed on Turkey (1878), Egypt (1880), Greece (1897). Naturalists in nineteenth century, Carnazza-Amari, Ruy Barbosa. Court of International Justice and of Arbitral Justice. International Prize Court. The International Unions, postal, telegraph, railways. Apportionment of expenses. Dominion status. *Assertion of equality of right between neutral and belligerent:* Increasing materialism in the objects of war led to stiffening in the neutral attitude. Neutrals demanded that their ships should go unhampered unless they trafficked in arms or attempted to enter with cargo places besieged from the sea. In return they conceded right of search. Precision of *règlement* of Tsaritsa Catharine (1778). Some international lawyers put neutral rights higher, Hübner, Galiani, Prussian lawyers in question of the Silesian Loan. Orthodox position of Albericus Gentilis and Lampredi. The right of convoy, Queen Christina's articles (1653), the Dutch negotiation with English Commonwealth (1657). Dutch and Swedes during French revolutionary wars. Lord Stowell, the MARIA (1799). Various treaties granting the right of convoy, Dutch-American (1782), Prusso-American (1785), Anglo-Danish dispute (1800). Count Bernstorff, the FREYA. Second Armed Neutrality. Anglo-Russian Convention (1801). British Crimean practice never recognised convoy. Declaration of London. English practice in the war 1914-1918. pp. 248-267.

CHAPTER IX.: MARITIME THEORY AND PRACTICE

Originally enemy property at sea capturable wherever situated. Friction produced formal agreements, Anglo-Burgundian treaties (1406-1495), Anglo-Genoan treaty (1460). Latter reminiscent of *Consolato del Mare* in tolerating neutral carriage of enemy goods but in expecting their removal by belligerents. Severe French edicts (1543-1584) probably held good prize neutral property on enemy ships, possibly neutral ships carrying enemy property, i.e. *la robe d'ennemy confisque celle d'amy*. Dutch ambassador in Paris (1653) suggests latter interpretation in announcing, as French concession to Dutch, condemnation of enemy cargo alone. From seventeenth century attempts similarly to free neutral ships carrying enemy goods, *i.e.* "free ships free goods." Temporary concession of this principle by France to Holland (1648), permanent concession (1662). Other treaties incorporate principle, Hispano-Dutch (1650), Anglo-Portuguese (1654), Franco-Spanish (1659), Portugal and Holland (1661). As if in compensation, nations adopt principle that all goods on enemy ships are capturable, Anglo-Dutch treaties (1667, 1674, 1689), Franco-Swedish treaty (1672), Suedo-Dutch treaties (1667, 1675), Franco-British treaty (1677), Franco-Dutch treaties (1678,

1697). Tendency not permanent, and, in absence of international legislative organ, law only discoverable from specific treaties merely binding contracting parties as between themselves. England's contrary practice, Anglo-Swedish treaties (1661, 1666, 1670), Anglo-Danish treaty (1670), following *Consolato*. French inconsistency shown in Hansa treaties (1655, 1716), *ordonnances* (1681, 1704, 1744). Certain countries outside all treaties. French rigidity produced by Dutch and British practice. Utrecht treaties, "free ships free goods," but only for contracting parties. General offer by France of this principle on condition of reciprocity (1778). First Armed Neutrality resisted by England. English practice in war of 1793, surprising treaty with U.S.A. (1794). Russian retreat in convention of 1801. Treaty of Amiens, start of England determination to free itself from all restraining agreements on this point. Canning and Brazil (1827). Anglo-Portuguese treaty (1842). Reversal of English policy in Crimean War, Declaration of Paris, general concession that neutral flag covers goods of enemy except contraband, Lord Colchester in the Lords, Gibson Bowles, Mr. Malkin. U.S.A. and immunity of all private property. Horsfall Commission, Cobden, Bright, and Palmerston. Position of crew on board ships visited. The war of 1812. Hague Convention. *Treatment of prize:* Conditions in the *Consolato*. French *ordonnance* (1681) and Royal decree (1756). British practice in American War. U.S. practice of destruction in war of 1812. French practice in war of 1870. Russian practice in Far East (1904). Declaration of London. German submarine warfare, effect on U.S.A. *Safe-conduct in special cases:* Voyages on scientific, exploratory, religious, or philanthropic errands.

Contraband of war: Censure by Church Councils of the export of arms to infidels (1179, 1214, 1245). Natural belligerent objection to supplying of enemy with goods likely to prolong war, *i.e.* contraband of war. Queen Elizabeth's dispute with Hansa towns. No agreement on list of obnoxious goods, *munitions de guerre* and *munitions de bouche*. Practice of pre-emption. As belligerents relinquished right of capture they desired to stop or at least pre-empt contraband. Lord Stowell's decisions in HAABET and in SARAH CHRISTINA. Naval Prize Act (1864). Criterion to distinguish contraband due first place to Grotius, whose definition foreshadows blockade. Succession of treaties progressively produce certainty, Anglo-Spanish (1604), Anglo-Dutch treaty of Southampton (1625), Franco-Hanseatic (1655), Franco-Spanish (1654), Franco-Dutch (1662), treaties of Utrecht (1713). Treaties only bound participants as between themselves. Elsewhere situation governed by proclamation of sovereign, *e.g.* decision of H.M. Commissioners of Prize (1665), Official Prize List (1744). Dutch tendency to severer practice. Nations' policy capricious and governed by temporary considerations. Even England accepted a short list of contraband articles in Russian treaty of 1766. This later quoted against England, which in maritime wars of eighteenth century was growing always more severe. Outbreak of war in 1793 freed England from several obligations. Stricter views seen in its treaty with Denmark (1780), with U.S.A. (1794), Sweden (1803). England careful to avoid recommittal at end of war, *e.g.* with Holland (1814), Portugal (1842), till Spain alone left with short list as against England. Definition of contraband owes most to Stowell after Grotius. JONGE MARGARETHA, ATALANTA. Penalty for carriage of contraband. *Traffic in arms:* Galiani. Lampredi. Jefferson. Nineteenth-century developments in doctrine of contraband. England in Franco-Austrian War, in Crimean War. Federal Government in U.S. Civil War. Continuous voyage probably not applied to contraband but only to blockade. French, Italian, and British courts have applied conception of continuous voyage to the carriage of contraband. The Hague Conference (1907). Demand for new lists. Conference of London. The war 1914-1918. Practice of England. Abolition of list of conditional contraband. Large contraband list.

Blockade: The besiegers' right of isolating a place besieged extended to sea approach in the case of a coast town. Extension by the Dutch placaart of 1584 to number of ports in no sense besieged. Dutch placaart and proclamation of 1630. Placaart against Spain of 1636. Dutch declare English coast blockaded (1652, 1666), French coast (1672, 1673). Dutch action imitated by Spain (1663) and by England (1689, 1756). By eighteenth century original justification lost sight of in mere desire generally to forbid intercourse with an enemy. Treaties attempt to prevent fictitious blockade by defining measure of force necessary to constitute a blockade. Franco-Danish treaty (1742), Dutch-Neapolitan (1753). The Armed Neutralities. England in 1793, having eluded pressure of the Armed Neutralities, had free hands. Admiralty instructions (1793). Admiral Hood in Mediterranean anticipates British decision to declare French coast blockaded (1806). Napoleon's reprisal a blockade of Britain, the continental system (Berlin, 1806). British Order in Council (1807) extends blockade to Napoleonic satellites. After Napoleonic wars various attempts to cut down rights of blockade. Treaty of U.S.A. with Sweden (1816). France and the doctrine of "the first bite." Mitigation of blockade by licence even in Napoleonic wars. British courts in Crimean War. The Declaration of Paris. U.S.A. admitted legality of "strategic" and "military," but wished to see abolished "commercial" blockade. This preceded by few years the largest commercial blockade experienced till then, blockade of Confederate States. Case of SPRINGBOK. Doctrine of continuous voyage applied, but novel distinction made between cargo and ship in awarding penalty. At opening of twentieth century demand for clarification of the law of blockade. Declaration of London. Practice in the war of 1914-1918. Position of neutrals. N.O.T. Order in Council of March 1915. Alternative of a "long-distance blockade." Punitive blockades in interventions and reprisals.

Privateering, its evils and abolition: The practice of privateering in the seventeenth century. *Ordonnance* of Louis XIV. Franco-British treaty (1677). The *règlement* of 1691. Life and conduct on a privateer. Defence of the system by Lord Grenville (1801). Neutrals deny them their ports. Marine regulations of Sweden (1804). Suedo-Danish agreement against privateers at the beginning of the Crimean War. Lord Clarendon announced British intention not to issue letters of marque, French declaration. Declaration of Paris abolishes practice. U.S.A. Spain (till 1908), Mexico (till 1909), and Venezuela did not adhere to the Declaration of Paris. Note of U.S.A. (1856). Enlistment of private ships produces difficulty. Prussian action in 1870. Present-day practice.

THE BRITISH PRIZE COURT.—*Introduction:* Proclamation of 1426 takes prize under official cognisance. Proclamation of the Council rendering prize court proceedings obligatory. Doctors' Commons. Admiralty Court. Relation to executive. Lord Stowell in the FOX, Judicial Committee in the ZAMORA (1916), judgments. Relation to legislature. Material for judgment. The standing interrogatories. Varied business before the court. Local courts. Appeals. Complaints of procedure. Frederick of Prussia, Bernstorff, the Dutch, Spanish minister Wall, Baron Ehrensward, Kleen, James Stephen, Sir Erle Richards. *The atmosphere of the Prize Court:* Lord Stowell's dictum, his scorn of international "philanthropy." The reward of naval service. *Enemy character:* Anglo-American tendency to stress domicile as well as nationality, Story and Stowell following Bynkershoek. VROW ELIZABETH, TOBAGO, United States decisions. PHOENIX, SALLY, SAN JOSÉ INDIANO, JAN FREDERICK, SECHS GESCHWISTERN, JEMMY, MINERVA. The rule of 1756. The MARIA, the VIGILANTIA. Napoleon's Milan decree (1806). *Trading with the enemy:* Lord Stowell expresses strict view in the HOOP (1799). NELLY, prize to the Crown, not the captor. Licences to trade with the enemy, JONGE AREND, COSMOPOLITE. *Presumption of enemy character:* Neutrals had onus of proof. *Colonial trade:* French *ordonnances* (1704, 1744), English Rule of the War of 1756. Lord Stowell, the IMMANUEL. Instructions of 1793, modification of 1794, instructions of 1798. The ESSEX, the WILLIAM. The Armed Neutralities. Agreement of 1801 between England, Russia, and Denmark. Napoleon's Berlin decree (1806). pp. 268-330.

CHAPTER X. : CHANGES OF NATIONALITY

Plebiscites : Clauses permitting optional withdrawal inserted in cession treaties. Grotius, Pufendorff, Vattel suggest onus of obtaining consent lay with ceding Power. French revolutionary thinkers first suggest right of self-determination. Decree of the National Assembly (1790). Smaller territories annexed by France: Avignon, Comtat Venaissin, Savoy, and Nice (1791-1793). Belgian Netherlands, Liège and Rhenish Germany, intimidation (1792-1793). Italian duchies (1848). Form of the question put in 1860. Northern districts of Schleswig (1866), Norway and Sweden (1904). Bismarck. Chili, Tacna, and Arica. Transference of territory at the end of the war 1914-1918. Plebiscite in the Saar. *Option of individuals :* Individuals emigrate from an early period and wish naturalisation. Government opposition to emigration, Philip II. of Spain, Alva, Louis XIV., Sir Leoline Jenkins, Austrian charter (1784), Russian ukase (1864). Opinion of the lawyers, Grotius, Vattel, de Martens. English practice, 1793-1814. The People *v.* Isaac Williams. *Nemo potest exuere patriam.* Napoleon's regulations. Influence of the states of the New World. Wheaton, Story. Opinion of Secretary of State (1859). Latin-American practice. Treaties with U.S.A. British Naturalisation Act (1870). pp. 333-345.

PART III

THE AGE OF THE CONCERT

CHAPTER XI. : AN EXPERIMENT IN MECHANISM

Introduction : Little international legislation before Congress of Vienna. Formation in 1814 of the coalition against Napoleon. Military agreement outside capacity of the smaller Powers. The four great Powers at the Congress of Vienna. Treaty of 20th November 1815. Agreement to hold further gatherings. *"Legislation" at Vienna Congress :* Experiments in political science, no permanent organ erected, Ionian Islands given to England as "mandatory" Power, international rivers, declaration against the slave trade. *The conference of the ambassadors :* Its origin and functions. Enlargement of its powers, achievements, succession to Duchy of Parma, Napoleonic refugees in Brussels, suppression of revolutions. South American situation. Army of occupation. Pozzo di Borgo. Castlereagh at Aix-la-Chapelle insisted on the winding up of the ambassadors' conference. *London Conference :* Slave trade and Barbary pirates. International fleet suggested by Alexander. Suedo-Danish dispute over terms of treaty of Kiel. *Frankfort Conference:* Dispute between Bavaria, Baden, and Austria over Salzburg territory. Castlereagh's views on the congress system. The Tsar Alexander's views. *Aix-la-Chapelle:* (1818) Quadruple alliance confirmed, admission of France. Russian proposal for Universal European League. Prussian proposal for a treaty of mutual guarantee. Protocol as to further meetings. Minority questions. Accomplishments of the Aix Congress. The Spanish questions. Proposal of Duke of Wellington as Spanish-American mediator. Spanish rejection. Leftward trend of French politics. Spanish and Portuguese revolutions (1820). Revolution in Naples (1820). Metternich and England, Metternich and Russia. Proposed meeting at Troppau turned into a conference. *Troppau and Laibach:* Tsar's proposals for an extended "Holy Alliance" carried. Metternich's hand forced. Castlereagh's violent objections. Conference at Laibach. Italian representatives. Stewart's attitude. Austrian successes in Italy. Conference at Florence foreshadowed. Russo-Turkish disputes. Proposed conference at Vienna. Castlereagh's suicide. Canning. Wellington goes to Verona. *Congress of Verona:* Tsar's scheme for marching a European army against Spain. The French proposal for isolated action. Wellington's rejection. Other matters not allowed to cause breach. *Abandonment of congress system:* John Quincy Adams' judgment on permanence of the system. Difficulties in varying types of government composing the alliance not met by formula of "legitimacy." Misreading of situation by the autocrats, Benthamism and the coming radicalism. Difficulty of finding room for the smaller states. Obstacles of imperfect international locomotion. Canning's views on the congress system. Metternich and Canning. Abiding interest of the period. pp. 349-377.

CHAPTER XII.: THE AMERICAS

Washington's farewell advice to U.S.A. The revolutions in South America. Possibility of the erection of a separate American system. Recognition of South American republics deferred by U.S.A. till 1822. British attitude contrasted both with that of U.S.A. and that of the other Powers. Canning's conferences with Polignac. Russian claims in North America. Monroe's message to Congress. John Quincy Adams, Canning and the Monroe doctrine. Was the Monroe doctrine a policy or a principle? The danger of the two systems. Canning's recognition of South American states. His overestimation of the potentialities of the Americas of his day. As a principle the "separateness" of the Americas had little duration. Commerce and shipping bound South America to England and Europe. Inter-

CHAPTER XIII.: ARBITRATION

CHAPTER XIV.: DISARMAMENT

CHAPTER XV.: THE CONCERT IN POLITICAL ACTION

armament. Austrian ultimatum. The idea of a congress endures. "The Pope and the Congress." Adjournment of the Congress. *The Powers and the Lebanon:* Massacre of the Maronites by Druses. Commission of Inquiry. Rival French and British schemes. Régime established. *The proposed Polish Congress of* 1863*:* National uprising in the "Congress kingdom." Notes presented to Russia by France, Austria, and England. Spread of revolt to border provinces. Gortchakoff's reply. Collapse of the Three Powers' scheme. *The Schleswig-Holstein Conference of* 1864. The treaty of 1852. Danish proclamation of 30th March 1862. Napoleon III.'s proposal of a congress. Attitude of the Powers. Military execution of the Germanic confederation. War. Armistice. Situation escapes European control. *The proposed Congress of* 1866 *and the Conferences of London of* 1867 *and* 1871*:* Tension in Austro-Prussian relations. Clarendon's offer of mediation. Napoleon III.'s proposals for a congress. Suggested programme. Clarendon's absurd optimism. Bismarck. Austrian limitations. Austro-Prussian War. French policy. French ambitions unmasked. Conference on Luxemburg. Franco-Prussian War. Russia and the Black Sea. Gortchakoff's defence. Protocol of the London Conference of 1871. Inconclusive nature of its decisions. *The Conference of Constantinople of* 1876, 1877. Near Eastern crisis of 1875. Andrassy note. Berlin memorandum of 1876. English rejection. Serbia and Montenegro enter the war. Bulgarian massacres. Conference of Constantinople. Dilatory tactics of the Turks. London protocol. Russo-Turkish War. Treaty of San Stefano. Conflict with the terms of 1856. Lord Salisbury's circular note. Big Bulgaria. Salisbury's agreement with Schuvaloff. Congress of Berlin. Its immediate and ultimate decisions. Contrast between the Congresses of Paris (1856) and Berlin. *The Powers and the execution of the decisions of the Congress:* Greece, Montenegro, Crete. *Egypt and the Conference at Constantinople:* Turkey and the Powers. *The crisis and proposed Conference of* 1908*:* Austrian obstinacy, German support, and collapse of Isvolsky and Grey. *The Congo Conference:* Colonising activity on the African continent. Anglo-Portuguese treaty. French and German protests. Bismarck's summons of the Conference. Berlin (1884-1885) and Brussels (1890) Conferences. *The Conference of Madrid* (1880)*:* Spanish and French concessions in Morocco. Extension of these to other Powers. Moroccan protests. Conference at Madrid. Anglo-French agreement of 1905. Preparations for a French protectorate. The Kaiser's speech. Delcassé's resignation. Conference at Algeciras in 1906. *The Conference of Ambassadors,* 1912-1913*:* Count Berchtold's proposals. The Balkan War. Turkish disasters. Discussions in London. The Adriatic and Albania. Treaty of London. Peace of Bucharest.

The proposed Conference of 1914*:* Austrian ultimatum to Serbia. *The Peace Conference and the Peace Treaties of* 1918-1919*:* The various armistices. The greater and lesser allies. Council of Ten and the Council of Four. The draft treaty. German delegates. The Austrian treaty. Revolt of the smaller Powers. Treaty with Hungary. Bela Kun. Rumanian invasion. Treaty of the Trianon. The Bulgarian treaty. The League of Nations. A new colonial system. International Labour Office. Plebiscites, Silesia, Schleswig, East Prussia, and Klagenfurt. Smyrna, Saar Valley, and East Galicia. Government of Danzig and the Saar Valley. Demilitarisation as a preliminary to a general reduction of armaments. The minority treaties and minority clauses. Proposed Permanent Court of International Justice. Convention of St. Germain and the general act of the Congo Conference. The liquor traffic in Africa. Traffic in arms. International air convention. The Turkish treaty. American mandate for Constantinople and the Straits. Decision of February 1920. The San Remo Conference of 1920, the Straits, French mandate in Syria, British mandates in Palestine and Mesopotamia. Meeting at Lympne. Treaty of Sèvres. Mustapha Kemal. Peace Conference of Lausanne. *The Genoa Conference:* Its convocation by the Supreme Allied Council and Belgium. Its economic character. Attitude towards Russia. Work of the financial commission, of the transport commission, and of the political commission. Breach between Anglo-Italian and Franco-Belgian interests as regards Russia. Supplementary conference of experts at The Hague. *The Lausanne Conference:* Peculiar features. Its agenda. Exchange of populations. The capitulations. Minorities. The Straits. Mosul. Thracian, Straits, and commercial conventions. Customs tariff. Frontiers. Question of the debt. pp. 427-486.

CHAPTER XVI.: THE CONCERT IN ECONOMIC ACTION

Widening of the international outlook in economic matters. Conventions on postal, telegraphic, railway, and customs matters, etc. The mechanism of the International Postal Union. Basis of contribution. *Adaptation to changed circumstances of International Law:* Subsoil of the sea, the air. Wireless convention of 1906. Varying views. Flying convention of 1919. *International river commissions:* The Rhine and the Danube. *The opening of arterial rivers to general navigation:* Principle established at Vienna. The St. Lawrence. South American and African rivers. *Inter-oceanic canals:* Suez and Panama Canals. Clayton-Bulwer and Hay-Pauncefote treaties. *Other international conventions:* Metric system (1875). Monetary conference (1892). Trade marks (1883). Copyright (1886). Phylloxera conventions, 1878, 1881, 1889. Bird protection. Seal fishery (1911).

Labour conventions: Desire for uniformity in labour legislation. Swiss initiative in 1881 and 1889. Emperor William II. invites conference to Berlin in 1890. Berne meeting of 1905. Labour conference of 1913. Projected conference at Berne, September 1914. *International Labour Organisation:* Its mechanism and record. pp. 488-502.

CHAPTER XVII.: SOME TYPES OF TREATIES IN THE NINETEENTH CENTURY

Growing number of commercial treaties in the nineteenth century. Dutch priority in making such treaties. Most-favoured-nation clause, Franco-Russian treaty, 1787. Clauses granting privileges in port or of navigation to foreigners. *Treaties with Eastern nations:* Capitulations, extra-territoriality, tariff limitation. Anglo-Japanese treaty. Agreements of 1898 and 1911. China and the Washington Conference of 1922. *Extradition treaties:* Older conception specifically political. The eighteenth century, Vattel and the Swiss practice. Development of the criminal aspect, Dano-Brunswick treaties, Beccaria. French treaties with several countries. Nineteenth century, development of general and reciprocal agreements. Anglo-American treaty of 1842 contrasted with the Hispano-German treaty of 1878. Political refugees. Fugitive assassins of rulers. Anarchists. Extradition sometimes applied to subjects as well as aliens. *Treaties of social philanthropy:* Extension of benefits to foreign labourers. *Health conventions:* Dangerous diseases. Plague in the fifteenth century. Yellow fever (1821), Asiatic cholera (1831). French sanitary law of 1822. *Cordon sanitaire.* Superior council of health established in Constantinople in 1839. International sanitary council at Tangier (1840). Maritime sanitary and quarantine council in Alexandria in 1881. Bucharest, Teheran councils. First international conference at Paris in 1851. Cholera epidemic of 1865. Prompt notification. Over-drastic quarantine regulations. Conference at Vienna, measures for research. Regulations of Venice (1892), Dresden (1893), and Paris (1894) concerning cholera. Venice regulations against plague (1897). Conference of Paris (1903) and first drastic measures. General reorganisation. Pan-American Sanitary Conference (1905). Post-war measures. *The slave trade.* Treaties of 1841. Congo Conference of 1885. International offices. Abyssinia and Burma. *North Sea fisheries. White-slave traffic. "Rebus sic stantibus":* Earlier practice unlimited duration. Insertion of time clauses. Modern practice. The problem unsolved. Russia and the Straits in 1871. Article XIX. of the Covenant of the League of Nations. pp. 503-525.

CHAPTER XVIII.: THE LEAGUE OF NATIONS

Important position of the Concert of Powers in the nineteenth century. Lesser Powers and arbitral tribunals. The Hague Conferences. The war of 1914-1918. Establishment of a League of Nations. Its preventative functions in the case of war. The composition of the Assembly. The structure of the Council. "Equality" in the Council. Rival claims of the great and smaller Powers to representation. Formation of groups. Withdrawal of Spain and Brazil in 1925. Change of balance in the Council. The rule of unanimity in 1919 and 1927. Solution of a proved difficulty in calling and forming international congresses in time of crisis. Matters solely of internal jurisdiction. The League and non-member states. Arbitration and judicial procedure. The Supreme Court of International Justice. Its composition. Skilful avoidance of the controversy as to the equality of states. Contractual obligations between states to refer matters to the decision of the Court. The "optional clause." Courses open to the League in an attempt to decide disputes. Sanctions, joint action against delinquency. Possible military obligations of the League. Discussion of Article X. in 1922. Reluctance of the Powers to undertake automatic obligations. *Non-political activities of the League:* The Finance Committee; the Economic Committee; the "World" Economic Conference and its report; the Committee on Communication and Transit. Conclusion, primary necessity the creation of confidence. Two views of the League. An automatic organ or mediatory machinery. League's treatment of minority questions and of mandates. Failure to reduce armaments. Successful performance of its normal duties only method to make it trusted and effective.

PART I

THE AGE OF THE PRINCE

Das liebe heil'ge Röm'sche Reich,
Wie hält's nur noch zusammen?

CHAPTER I

THE WORLD BY LAND *

INTRODUCTION. THE RIGHT TO WAGE WAR. STATE SOVEREIGNTY. THE FAMILY OF NATIONS. COMMUNITIES IN REVOLT. EXPELLED AND HERETICAL RULERS. INFIDELS. THE HANSEATIC LEAGUE. THE ELECTIVE MONARCHIES. QUESTIONS OF PRECEDENCE AND DIGNITY. TITLES. LANGUAGE.

Introduction.—He who would study the history of International Law must call upon his imagination for an effort if he is to think himself back into the sixteenth century. In particular is this the case, if he should ask himself just what it was which formed the chief preoccupation of those who in that age thought about the external relations of states. Men and women and governments change less than is sometimes imagined, but at different periods they are apt to lay emphasis on different questions. To-day in a period of change men ask what new unity in Europe, or in the world, events foreshadow. Four hundred years ago it was exactly the reverse. Also acutely conscious of a change in progress, men wondered at what stage the dissolution of European unity would stop. To-day the activities which thrive in peace seem full of promise: in those days war as an agent of change seemed both more frequently at work, and more powerful, than at perhaps any previous epoch of the history of the Christian West. Thus during the sixteenth century the study of the *Jus Belli*, the Law of War, predominated. It is the theme alike of theologians such as Franciscus a Victoria (died 1546 or 1549) and Covarruvias (1511-1577), of lawyers like Albericus Gentilis (1552-1608) or Bodin (1530-1596), and of soldiers like Ayala (1548-1584) and the Prince of Orange [1] (1533-1584). The approach in each case may be different, the interest according to the writer's idiosyncrasy predominantly theoretical or practical, but they all ended by investigating the same problems. Was war legitimate under any circumstances for Christian peoples? Under what conditions and for what ends might suitable wars be

* Notes will be found throughout at the end of each chapter.

CHAP. I. waged? And, when the treatment descended to detail, the unsettled problems were innumerable. Had heretical or infidel communities a right to immunity from unprovoked aggression on the part of Christian states? Could one assume as permissible full and friendly communication with races sunk in heathen ignorance or error? Were acts of armed rebellion against princes, still more their deposition, justifiable, and, if so, in what conditions: and how, if it were pronounced legitimate, did such legitimate rebellion affect the relation of the rebel community to neighbouring states? All this it was which gave meaning to the speculation, vital then if academic now, as to what authorities had unquestionable right to wage a war. It will be well to deal with this last question first.

The Right to wage War.—Everywhere in the feudal kingdoms of the Middle Ages private warfare had existed. In the Empire and in France it had been authoritatively regulated till it was finally prohibited, in the former in 1495 and in the latter at the end of the fourteenth century. By solemn agreements, and by acts of an almost constitutional character, war between vassals was recognised; and some went so far as to include a war between vassals and their sovereign. *Magna Carta* permitted in cases of royal delinquency twenty-five baronial "observators" to proceed to arms against the king. The Aragonese *Privilege of Union* made a similar provision in Aragon, while in Castile public recognition was given to the right of the nobles to withdraw their allegiance by a *diffidatio*.

A distinction, however, was made between public and private war even in the Middle Ages. If war between the vassals of the same prince, or between the vassals of different princes, was private war, what was considered a public war? The definition of public war most generally agreed upon by the commentators,(2) especially if, after the habit of the day, the phrase be expanded into solemn public war, was a series of acts of armed force exercised against one another, after the observance of certain forms, by two sets of combatants, each possessing the direct authority of the supreme power inherent in a Commonwealth or Respublica. A Respublica might assume many different shapes, and the word had a wider connotation than our modern word, a State. Accordingly the ascription of a right to wage public war (solemn public war, to use the language of the large majority of writers) was narrowed down to include only the supreme authorities in those Respublicae which were distinguished from other Respublicae by the acknowledgment of no external domination. Even in stating this definition one is conscious that there remain a number of traps for the unwary, traps logical, constitutional, historical and theological, and even the most learned must needs walk, like Agag, delicately.

Quite apart from the controversy of those who held that the supreme power within the borders of a Respublica must take a monarchical or an aristocratic or a democratic form exclusively—and in the sixteenth century states like France or Scotland were convulsed by these contentions—the claim of even the largest and most important Respublicae to lawful independence of external domination could be challenged. First there was the claim of the Popes to be the Vicars of Christ, Lords of the World, the Superiors to all sovereigns and states on earth. Protestant states refused the claim, sometimes with abuse, while Catholic states were apt only to admit that the Pope was *orbis dominus ad ordinem spiritualem* (Lord of the World so far as spiritual regulation was concerned), and then only with certain reservations. None the less the undoubted fact remained that the Papacy had, at one time or another, secured a confession of supremacy from almost all monarchs or rulers, and had made itself the suzerain of some kingdoms like Naples, Aragon and England, compromising, sometimes but for a brief period, sometimes for very long, the perfect and uncontrolled independence of the states involved. Then there was the Imperial pretension, weightily advanced by civil lawyers, not merely to a supremacy of dignity over all lordships in the world, but to a legal supremacy, with all which that implied. Frenchmen in particular were not slow to rebut this contention. A favourite line of argument traced the succession of their monarchy to that of Charlemagne, King of the Franks ; but on occasions they could ransack Biblical or literary genealogies in efforts far more fantastical than this,(3) while, when they were particularly provoked, they could retaliate with spirit by an appeal to common sense. Thus Alciat (1492-1550), the famous Roman lawyer, having maintained that the King of France was still subject to the Emperor, "the Lord of all the World," the better known Bodin (died 1596) gave him flat denial, "seeing that the Roman Empire, when it was at its greatest, contained scarce the thirtieth part of the world, and that the German Empire is not now the tenth part of the Roman Empire." (4) The

CHAP. I.

monarchs of the different states of the Iberian peninsula based their freedom from Imperial control on the ground that they had won their territories afresh from the Infidel: while Edward II. of England, abjuring argument, contented himself with the statement that the kingdom of England was wholly free from Imperial control (" Regnum Angliae ab omni subjectione imperii esse liberrimum ").[5] Kingdoms like Denmark, Bohemia, Poland and Hungary had in difficult times been made to acknowledge the supremacy of powerful Emperors, an acknowledgment which had involved the presence of well-disciplined German armies, but by the end of the sixteenth century only the kingdom of Bohemia was still retained within the Imperial System.

It is hard then not to conclude that the effective admission of Imperial supremacy in the legal sense came only from the princes and cities of Germany and Northern Italy; Venice forming always an exception, for until the tenth century it had looked rather towards Constantinople than to Rome and, after that epoch, had begun a long independent career of its own. Yet even among these, while in the exceptional cases a technical legal suzerainty in the Empire had to be admitted, so large a number had figured with prominence on the European stage and had ruled their particular territories or dominions with such obvious absence of superior control that the claim to sovereignty was in the case of many only with difficulty withheld. Italian lawyers, for example, claimed sovereignty for the Duke of Savoy: and, in point of fact, there was no appeal from his courts, he did no military service, and he organised his territories exactly as he wished. Yet technically his highest legal position was that of the Emperor's vicar for his own fiefs and some enclaves corresponding roughly to Savoy and Piedmont,[6] and, as Bodin not illogically asserted, it was not easy to claim for a vicar independence of his principal. The Genoese republic acted almost always in complete detachment from the Empire, sometimes even putting itself under the protection of the King of France; but when a Marquis of Finale, in danger of territorial absorption by the republic, appealed to the Emperor in the middle of the sixteenth century to adjudge him an immediate Imperial vassal, Genoa, after a threat of the Imperial ban, was forced to admit the jurisdiction of the Empire. Belli (born 1502) claimed sovereignty for the duchy of Milan though it was an Imperial fief, investiture with which was obtained from the Emperor. In Germany the process of imperial decentralisation had not gone so far as it had gone across the Alps. None the less lawyers had asserted the sovereignty of the Duke of Lorraine, the Dukes of Burgundy had organised in almost complete sovereignty large portions of the North-West, better known as the Low Countries, the Electors of Saxony and Brandenburg judged without appeal, and the Elector of Bohemia bore the kingly title. The dignitaries next below these in strength, the greater feudal families, the princes of the Church and the cities, all had been known to raise armies or fleets, to collect taxes for that and other purposes, to make leagues and to fight wars both domestic and foreign. They had established effective systems of control over the territories in which they were interested. Even in the sixteenth century a Lübeck burgomaster like Wullenweber could dominate the Baltic and dethrone a king of Denmark. The Count Palatine John Casimir was able to interfere with effect in the French wars of religion: and this was equally true of second-class princes like the Duke Wolfgang of Zweibrücken and the Margrave Philibert of Baden.

State Sovereignty.—Europe, then, at the dawn of modern history is hardly an object of congenial study for the systematically minded. When in the eighteenth century Goethe wrote with respect, using the common phrase, of the "Public Law of Europe," he was writing of something both more and less than International Law. He was referring to an amalgam of formulae, jurisprudence, political speculation and recorded practice which did somehow in two hundred years make Europe geographically and politically less suggestive of a maze and more suggestive of a chess-board. Herein lies the importance of the work of Bodin, one of the earliest workers in this field. The ideas which his contemporaries entertained concerning the apparatus of government appeared to him chaotic, ideas unrelated by theory or related only by antiquated or inapplicable theory. In the *de la République* he sought to introduce some system and order. Finding the term "souverain" used in French legal terminology to describe various courts like the Parlement of Paris and the Cour des Aides, from which there was no appeal, he introduced the term into political theory and even into international politics.[7] The sovereign Power, distinguished by the possession of all the vital political prerogatives, was the head and motive force of each completely separate political system; and in each completely

CHAP. I.

separate political system there was, or should be, a sovereign Power distinguished by the possession of all the vital political functions. Sovereignty was the absolute, and perpetual, power of a state, unlimited alike in capacity and time: no state, properly speaking, could exist without it, and to divide it was to establish anarchy. The sovereign Power possessed the right of making laws, waging war, naming officials, levying taxes, sitting in ultimate judgment, pardoning and receiving oaths of allegiance or obedience, though it might adopt fixed agencies, principles or methods for exercising any of these functions. Applied inwardly within the sphere of influence of an already preponderant authority, this theory acted powerfully to forward centralisation and to end local and provincial autonomy. Applied outwardly in the tangled public system of Europe, it had profound importance, though it was not always helpful if employed without suppleness and elasticity. Thus, examining the states of Italy, Bodin, on the grounds of an occasional trace or vestige of Imperial influence, questioned the sovereignty of Savoy, Milan, Genoa, Lucca, Mantua, and Florence. Moving northward he reached scarcely more helpful conclusions with regard to Germany. He had once, he said, been of opinion that the princes and cities of the Empire were sovereigns bound not by alien commands and laws, but only by the terms of their own federation and society. He had, however, departed from this opinion and had decided that sovereignty lay with the Diet, for he had observed that it had dethroned Emperors and had punished princes with exile and cities with proscription.

If the world had to wait some decades for the much needed clarification of the German situation he is indeed foolish who is unable to appreciate the signal value of Bodin's survey of the international field. The vigour with which he brushed aside Imperial pretensions has been already noted. Though he handled the papal claims more tenderly, he gave them but little serious consideration. He established nine different classes of princes and he showed his touch with reality by allowing sovereignty to the tributary prince, to the protected prince, and to the prince who recognised a measure of inferiority to an ally of greater power. Did not the Emperor himself pay tribute (disguised somewhat as *libera pensio*) to the Turk, in return for non-molestation, in his capacity of King in Hungary? On the other hand, he was a ruthless critic of the pretension to sovereignty of those smaller states which lay on distant and doubtful boundaries far from the centre of power. All round France he pointed to a chain of such states. Béarn and Dombes could rightfully be claimed as fiefs by the Crown of France, as had been Brittany prior to its absorption. Lorraine, Lumes, Aspremont, East Friesland, the abbey of Gozen (lord of twenty-one villages), and the lordship of Beaulieu could be claimed as Imperial fiefs. Bodin was to a marked degree a tidier-up of Europe, but states of this type are still represented in the family of nations, despite the legal weaknesses pointed out by Bodin and the upheavals of three hundred and fifty years. Monaco, Andorra, San Marino and Lichtenstein, not to mention Luxemburg, still exist to give joy to the youthful philatelist, and to witness to the tenacity in international affairs of the thing which is, in the face of the thing which the learned say should be. According to Nys there were in the sixteenth century some two thousand sovereigns in Europe, if sovereignties of this class were to be reckoned.

We must beware of reading our ideas into the past, for the existence of states of this character produced results of great legal and political importance. The first important armed resistance to Alva in the Netherlands, and the first Dutch warfare by sea, were by virtue of commissions issued by the holder of one of these small sovereignties. The principality of Orange had once been a fief of the kingdom of Arles, but it was not thought strange that the Prince of Orange by God's grace could, in virtue of his sovereignty in Orange, raise an army of thirty thousand men for a campaign against the Duke of Alva. In his capacity of sovereign prince in Orange he commissioned sea-faring persons to cruise against the Spanish commerce, appointed an Admiral, issued articles of war, and promulgated prize regulations. He possessed, it is true, enormous estates in the Low Countries, but for these he was subject to Philip, Count of Flanders, King of Spain. He was head of the German princely family of Nassau, but this made him vassal of the Emperor. That he was something more than this, and that this something more enabled him to issue his commissions by land and sea, was an invaluable asset to the Dutch, who not for some years were able to lay claim, and to exercise, a *de facto* territorial sovereignty of their own in Holland and in Zeeland. Is it too much to say that a technicality altered the course of history?

Italian statesmen found themselves confronted by conditions at once equally trivial and equally momentous.

CHAP. I. What was to be the future of such petty states as the Marquisates of Saluzzo and Montferrat? Was a separate existence to be continued for the republics of Lucca and Siena? Was absorption to be the fate of the Duchy of Urbino, familiar territory to the readers of *John Inglesant,* of the Lordships of Piombino and Elba, and the Duchy of Ferrara? These again were not trifling questions. The Marquisate of Saluzzo, having been a bone of contention between the rival suzerains, the King of France and the Duke of Savoy, gave rise finally to the hard-fought Franco-Savoyard War lasting from 1588 to 1600. The succession to Mantua and Montferrat led to hostilities between France, Spain and the Empire which lasted from 1628 to 1631. The Duke of Florence won Spanish consent to his annexation of Siennese territory, but the thwarting of his designs upon Lucca and Piombino provides material for a not uninteresting chapter in the history of diplomatic intrigue; and the papal absorption of Ferrara in 1597, and of Urbino in 1631, can be reckoned among the major political questions of the day.

As regards Germany, one may well believe that not a little of the bitterness with which the Thirty Years' War was fought to a conclusion, can be traced not so much to the religious enthusiasm evoked, as to that little studied, but none the less fierce, struggle for survival among the nine hundred authorities so many of which claimed practical independence within the Empire. Actually, according to Dupuis, five hundred and fifty in the end succumbed. In the sphere dominated by the thirteen cantons the sovereignty of Geneva, their ally, was contested by its Bishops, as also by the Dukes of Savoy who, as late as 1602, made a determined attempt upon it. A demand by the Imperialists during the Thirty Years' War that Basle should fulfil the terms of the Edict of Restitution affected another neighbour to whose fate the Swiss were always sensitive. East of the Swiss was the singular Confederacy of the Grisons, or Grey Leagues, whose anomalous international position, and whose imperfect control of subject territory, led to Spanish and Imperial encroachment which, during the first half of the seventeenth century, had to be resisted by Venetian diplomacy and French arms.[8] Even the French monarchy could be seriously inconvenienced for many years because a subject was also Duke of Bouillon, " Prince souverain de Sédan, Jametz, Raucourt."[9]

CHAP. I.

The Family of Nations.—One has but to look at the history of its growth to observe that the state system of Europe, as it has been known to recent generations, is of no great antiquity and retains, often in unexpected ways, the traces of its origin. It is a fascinating task to attempt to construct a view of Europe at different epochs as it would have appeared to an individual living at each stage. Some indication of what were considered to be the "powers," and what was their order of importance, is to be obtained from contemporary documents. Before the rise of Protestantism the various princes and states found it necessary to be represented, either permanently or occasionally, at the papal court. The papal officials therefore had the thankless task of establishing an order of precedence among these emissaries. In 1504 on the occasion of the reception of a solemn embassy of obedience from England, the master of ceremonies drew up the following list.

Order of the Christian Kings.

The Emperor.
The King of the Romans.
The King of France.
The King of Spain.
The King of Aragon.
The King of Portugal.
The King of England (in dispute with the preceding three as to dignity).
The King of Sicily (in dispute with Portugal).
The Kings of Scotland and Hungary (in dispute).
The King of Navarre.
The King of Cyprus.
The King of Bohemia.
The King of Poland.
The King of Denmark.

Order of Dukes.

The Duke of Brittany.
The Duke of Burgundy.
The Duke of Bavaria (Count Palatine).
The Duke of Saxony.
The Marquess of Brandenburg.
The Duke of Austria.
The Duke of Savoy.
The Duke of Milan.
The Duke of Venice.
The Dukes of Bavaria.
The Dukes of France and Lorraine.
The Duke of Bourbon.
The Duke of Orleans.
The Duke of Genoa.
The Duke of Ferrara.

This list, drawn up for a particular occasion, was not exhaustive, and there are some important omissions. There is naturally no mention of the Papacy; but no place is found for the clerical electorates of Cologne, Treves and Mayence, for the great German bishoprics or abbeys, for the important Italian republic of Florence, for the cantons of the Swiss federation, and for the non-electoral magnates of Germany. The Papacy in issuing invitations to the third series of sessions

CHAP. I. of the Ecumenical Council of Trent in 1559 and 1560 provided valuable evidence as to contemporary conditions. To the list of kings was added the King of Sweden, a kingdom re-established by revolt from Denmark, and, oddly, the Emperor of Moscow. Among the lesser powers the Pope made efforts to include the German electors and the Swiss cantons; while the non-electoral magnates, such as the rulers of Brunswick, Lorraine, Württemberg, and Baden, the German bishops, and free cities such as Strassburg, Nuremberg, and Augsburg, were also exhorted to send representatives.(10)

Sir Ernest Satow has collected evidence of the official views of governments as to their own and others' status during the last four hundred years. A careful study of four idealistic schemes is almost equally informing. The Grand Design of Sully was a very different thing from what it has sometimes been represented, but, although in one sense it is unhistorical, it has subjective value in that it gives an idea of the opinions of one experienced in public affairs; and, read intelligently, a notion can be formed from it as to the relative value of the Powers in his judgment. He proposed a redivision of Europe into fifteen states, a redivision to be carried out chiefly at the expense of Austria and Spain, in other words the Hapsburgs. There were to be first of all six hereditary monarchies, those of France, Spain, Britain, Denmark, Sweden and Lombardy (Savoy). Next there were to be six elective monarchies, the Papacy, the Empire, Venice, Hungary, Poland and Bohemia, the nomination to the thrones of which was to be mainly controlled by the senior hereditary monarchs, though the Pope and Emperor, once enthroned, joined them. Lastly, there were to be three Republican Confederacies, the Helvetian, the Italian (composed of the smaller states of Italy), and the Belgic, that is the Low Countries. The fifteen states were to be bound in a confederation, possessing a system of local councils and a central council, on which they were to be represented in rough proportion to their individual importance. One of the Federation's tasks would be to drive the Turk from Europe. Personally, Sully would seem to have been in favour of driving the Tsar of Muscovy back into Asia, as being a barbarian and no true Christian, but he does not press the point. The scheme had its origin in the traditional anti-Hapsburg policy of France. In a sense it was an expansion of the famous anti-Hapsburg League of Halle, formed by the German princes under French inspiration in 1610. Yet in spite of its disregard of the growing importance of the greater German states, it bears the trace of being the handiwork of an experienced diplomat, and, in its recognition of the status of the Dutch and Swiss, it anticipated the recognition given to those peoples at the Treaty of Westphalia.(11)

In comparison with Sully, Emerich Crucé, who wrote his book *The New Cyneas* in 1623, appears pitifully academic. He proposed a federation of all rulers, and his table of precedence shows an undenominational breadth of view. The Pope, the Sultan ("especially as he holds the city of Constantinople which is the twin equal of Rome"), the Emperor, the Kings of France and Spain, the Kings of Persia and China, Prester John, the Precop of Tartary, and the Grand Duke of Muscovy, the Kings of Great Britain, Poland, Denmark, Sweden, Japan, Morocco and the Great Mogul—this was to be the order; and after these "all brave princes who maintain themselves and do not depend upon any one"; and, "if any potentate be displeased at this order he will do well to lay his case for arbitrement before the general assembly." A council of the delegates was to hold periodical meetings at which all differences were to be adjudged, and it was to anticipate trouble rather than to meet it after it had once arisen. Republics, however, were only to have a vote in the necessarily rare event of an even division among the monarchs on the council. The value of the book is to be found chiefly as illuminating the surer touch of Sully and of William Penn.

William Penn's scheme of 1692 shows remarkable approximation to reality, and gives a fairly accurate view of the Powers at the end of the seventeenth century. There was to be the familiar federation, with its council; but the number of delegates from the component nations was to be proportioned to the annual income of each state or the figures of its foreign trade. The suggested apportionment was as to the Empire 12, France 10, Spain 10, Italy 8, England 6, Portugal 3, Swedeland 4, Denmark 3, Poland 4, Venice 3, the seven Dutch provinces 4, the thirteen Swiss cantons and their neighbours 2, Holstein 1 and Courland 1. Penn was in favour too of embracing the whole of Europe by the inclusion of the Russians and the Turks, allotting them ten places in addition. His essay testifies to the doubt still entertained in Europe as to the inclusion of Russia among the European states. Soon it would be impossible for any one to ignore the work shortly to be accomplished by Peter the Great. That monarch, by his policy of clutching out towards the Black

CHAP. I. Sea and the Baltic, was about to form the gigantic tweezers by which the Russian monarchs nipped into, and held on to, Eastern Europe. With the inclusion of Russia in the European state system a totally new character was given to the problem of the expulsion of the Turks from Europe, a problem round which, as may be surmised from Sully's partial acquiescence in it as an ideal, all former schemes of international organisation centred. The crusading aspect of the Eastern Question had ended. An aspect of it more familiar in the last two centuries was to begin.

Penn's list of the Powers still manifests deficiencies as grave as the inclusion in the Empire, of states as important as Bavaria, Brandenburg-Prussia, Saxony and the Austrian dominions; in Italy, of principalities as different as Savoy, the Papacy, Genoa and Florence. The Peace of Westphalia (1648) had given a new status, a *Landeshoheit*, to the German states which meant in practice a liberty to grow. How far that growth had progressed is indicated by the list of the Abbé St. Pierre published in 1717. As secretary to the plenipotentiary of France at the Treaty of Utrecht (1713) he had acquired an eye for political values, and his list, with the single exception formed by the omission of Brandenburg-Prussia, avoided the defective vision of his predecessor. In speculating on the federation of Europe he reckoned his component states as follows: France, Spain, England, Holland, Savoy, Portugal, Bavaria and its associates, Venice, Genoa and its associates, Switzerland and its associates, Lorraine and its associates, Sweden, Denmark, Poland, Muscovy, the Austrian dominions, Courland and its associates, Hanover and its associates, the ecclesiastical electors and their associates. For the purposes of representation on the central European body the smaller secondary states were to be placed at the head of local groups of petty sovereignties. In passing from the Design of Sully to the project of St. Pierre the observant must have detected the gradual change towards the map of Europe which was embodied in the Treaties of Westphalia and Utrecht, a map organically connected with the map of present-day delineation.(12)

Communities in Revolt.(13)—The problem of assigning a position in international society to communities in revolt from their overlord was raised in the sixteenth and seventeenth centuries by the eighty years' struggle between the Crown of Spain, heir to the Burgundian possessions, and the seven Dutch provinces. In the strictest theory these provinces were part of the Empire and they had, it is true, together with other Burgundian territories been organised into an Imperial circle in 1548. Nevertheless, their territorial lord, the King of Spain, comported himself in the fullest independence. In his attempt to curb a proud and military nobility, to dominate a rich and exigent citizenry fanatically attached to local privileges, and to extirpate a growing number of heretics by the introduction of Spanish methods in Church and State, he provoked a dangerous insurrection. After a period in which the insurgent party in the provinces affected still to respect the authority of the King of Spain, his rule was renounced and sovereignty offered to England, to France, and even to the Empire. England and France, until the moment at which war broke out between them and Spain, affected not to recognise the independence of the revolted provinces, and maintained that they were only engaged in negotiations with the Netherlands for the purpose of inducing them to come to terms with Philip. In truth, however, secret help and encouragement was given, for the Duke of Anjou, brother of the French King, and the Earl of Leicester, favourite of the English Queen, were allowed to make armed attempts upon the "protectorate," and even upon the sovereignty. After the French, the English and the Austrians had discovered that the Dutch, in offering sovereignty, meant to confer nothing but a barren title, and the privilege of fighting Philip to the verge of bankruptcy and exhaustion, these were left to their own resources under the leadership of the house of Nassau Orange, although they received some subsidies from Henry IV. of France and loans from the thriftier Elizabeth. In 1598, partly in the hope of conciliating Dutch opposition and partly to secure at least the formal dissociation of England and France from the rebel cause, Spain set up its Burgundian possessions as an independent state under the sovereignty of a married pair of Hapsburgs. France was detached from the Dutch in 1598 and England in 1604. Two last campaigns were undertaken by the great general Spinola in the vain hope of achieving a decisive result before the archducal pair, and Spain, should be driven to undertake negotiations, in which a totally fresh approach would have to be made to the question of the international position of the United Provinces. In 1607, after much wrangling, an eight months' truce was arranged to facilitate negotiations. To obtain this truce the archducal combatants were compelled to make a private declaration that they were treating with the

CHAP. I. United Provinces as with sovereign states. Even when the two parties had met on this basis there was the greatest difficulty in obtaining an agreement. The two sides were at cross purposes, for the Hispano-Belgic negotiators were not really prepared to concede sovereignty. They had in mind something which fell far short of this, some considerable formal concession in return for a long truce at the end of which the struggle might be resumed. They dared not show their real hand, but aimed at contriving that objections to the proposed bases for permanent peace should come from the Dutch side. Finally after two years of strained negotiation, in which diplomats from England, Denmark, the Palatine, Brandenburg and France played an invaluable part, a twelve years' truce was arranged, the Archduke and his consort treating with the Dutch "in the quality of free states over which the Archdukes made no pretensions." The war was renewed in 1621, but by 1633, when the Burgundian possessions had again fallen to Spain on the death of the ruling Archduchess, it became clear that this country was no longer so much concerned with questions of technical sovereignty in the Netherlands as with Dutch encroachments on its colonial empire. As the stadholder, Frederick Henry of Orange, remarked on seeing the draft of the Spanish terms in 1633, Spain and the Dutch, if they could agree about the Indies, would soon settle their difficulties in Europe. It was not, however, until 1648 that, after fifteen further years of fighting, Spain recognised for good and all the independence and sovereignty of the United Provinces. This it did without any limiting conditions whatsoever. It even confirmed their colonial holdings. At the same time the last links were snapped which attached the Provinces to the Empire.

As step by step this war of arms proceeded there had developed too a war of theory. The Dutch had started by enumerating their constitutional grievances, and, as is the fashion in rebellions, their manifestoes claimed that they were opposing not the King of Spain but rather his oppressive and tyrannous agents, whose actions were unknown to their master and whose withdrawal and disavowal they implored. Later the rebels introduced religious changes in the territory under their control, and the King of Spain, who had grown weaker, made the tactical offer of returning to the constitutional system of his predecessor. This would have allowed him to suppress the religion of his opponents, not perhaps so thoroughly as he might wish, but none the less effectively.

No choice was now left to his rebellious subjects in declining this proposal except perhaps to take the high ground "that it was their duty to abandon the King as a tyrant who sought to oppose and to destroy his subjects; and that consequently it behoved them to seek another protector." Many resolutions of this character had to be taken in Holland and Zeeland, many an attempt had to be made to confer upon foreign rulers an expensive protectorate wholly devoid of privileges, before the rebellious Provinces were at last emboldened to face the world as an independent and confederated state. CHAP. I.

The orthodox Spanish position, in opposition to that of the Dutch, can clearly be seen in Balthazar Ayala's treatise on the Laws of War.[14] A tyrant, he says, may legitimately be resisted, and even killed, but under no circumstances can a sovereign be dubbed a tyrant. However grievous be the burdens which a lawful prince may inflict upon his subjects, these have no right to rebel. There would always be available other remedy against a king who abused his position. The Pope had various means of restraint and of compelling a monarch to deal justly: where the interests of the Christian commonwealth demanded it the Pope would be able to depose. Therefore, till the time arrived for recourse to such a remedy, subjects should support their prince against all rebels, whose crime was just as detestable as heresy, and who could in no way claim to be treated as lawful enemies. The revolt of the Netherlands occupies so prominent a position in the history of government, and to it so many beneficial consequences can be justly ascribed, that it is well to be on guard, lest, dazzled by the philosophy of the successful side, Ayala's point of view be seen only as the utterance of obstinacy. Closer acquaintance with the circumstances suggest that both governors and governed shared the predisposition to approach the matter of dispute in terms of feudal law rather than in the terms of a scarcely yet thought of doctrine of self-determination. That the Dutch were in the end reduced to claim, and to make good, a total severance from Spain provides a noteworthy incident in the history of freedom; but it is also the first of several revolutions which, considered in retrospect, are not free from features which suggest both the limitations of mere nationalism and the negative character of mere separation. That Ayala used the argument which he did use, that he could count on a respectful reception in at least some quarters for it, are testimony both to the tenacity of Europe in resisting change and to the reality of those

CHAP. I.

forces, never wholly destroyed, which were in protest against the indefinite subdivision of the continent.

Along with the revolt of the Netherlands it is apposite to note that full international sovereignty was conceded to two republican federations, border states of the Empire also, the Swiss and the Grisons. The ten original Swiss cantons had in 1499 extorted from the Hapsburgs the admission that they were no longer liable to the military service of the Empire, to Imperial jurisdiction and Imperial taxation. This agreement did not include, however, various "allies" of the Helvetic cantons, men like the Abbot of St. Gall, the Bishop of Basle, and the Count of Neuchâtel. Nor could it include, of course, the three cantons which were added early in the sixteenth century. In the course of the Thirty Years' War, the revival of Imperial power, alluded to above, brought under definite question the claim of the Swiss that their "allies," and the added cantons, were entitled to the immunities secured by the peace of 1499. The ultimate failure of the Catholic and the Imperial party to dictate a peace to Germany rendered easier the task of the Swiss representative at the negotiations of Westphalia. He was successful in securing all that was desired by a clause which provided that "the town of Basle and the other cantons of the Helvetians do possess what is tantamount to complete freedom and exemption from the Empire." In the case of the Grisons their very existence was threatened by the upheavals of the period. They were composed of a confederacy of three leagues based on the territory of Ilanz, Chur and Davos, and formed a rich prize in that they held in subjection rich, Italian-speaking, and strategically important territory, especially the Valtelline. First the Spaniards from the Duchy of Milan attempted to secure and organise this vital spot as a semi-independent principality: shortly afterwards the house of Austria revived long dormant claims upon a large portion of the Grisons' territory proper. After the French had in two sets of campaigns helped to defend the independence of the Grisons, they in their turn showed a disinclination to leave the Valtelline, and had to be expelled by a coup arranged in collusion with the Spaniards and Austrians. In 1639 the Hapsburgs accepted the *status quo* as final, and in 1652 relinquished in sale their last rights.(15)

Expelled and Heretical Rulers.(16)—It was ultimately as a problem in sovereignty that the mind of the sixteenth century saw the question of the position of expelled and heretical rulers. As regards the expelled sovereign, the case of Mary Queen of Scots raised all aspects of the difficulty. Forced to abdicate under the threat of death, Queen Mary escaped from the hands of her captors, renounced her abdication, gathered a party and fought for her crown. Defeated, she fled to the Queen of England, whose heir she was, and begged for shelter, the recognition of her rank, and help against her rebels. Queen Elizabeth recognised her as Queen, but before giving her assistance asked her to clear herself of the charge brought against her by her subjects. The varied nature of the proposals as to the composition of the quasi-tribunal, before which the exiled Queen was to justify herself, are evidence enough of the international difficulties inherent in the case. The English Privy Council made a suggestion that the ambassadors of the great Powers should be present, and there was even some talk of allowing them a voice in the proceedings. The commission, however, was not allowed to take on a wide scope. Evidence tending to discredit the moral character of Queen Mary was tendered by her subjects. Then the Queen of England closed the investigation, asserting that neither side had been discredited, but that she could not undertake to restore the Queen of Scots by force of arms until she had more conclusively cleared herself. For the next eighteen years the Scottish Queen, legitimate heir be it remembered to the English crown, was detained in England as a prisoner of state or something very like it. Her attempts, and those of her agents, failing to secure permission for her to leave the country, she turned to conspiracy, in which she gave consideration to the assassination of Queen Elizabeth, the provocation of an armed revolt against her, and to the invocation of foreign powers to invade the land. The agent of the Scottish Queen, the Bishop of Ross, was found to be concerned in practices of this nature, and was in turn arrested. When charged he claimed to possess a diplomatic character by virtue of his mistress's commission. The English government declined to admit his claim on the double ground, taken under legal advice, that his mistress had been lawfully deposed and that he himself had abused ambassadorial privilege. When Mary Queen of Scots was herself brought to trial before an English tribunal, she denied its jurisdiction in her capacity of an anointed queen responsible to God alone. When she protested against her death sentence on these grounds, she had the support of by far the greater part of official Europe.

CHAP. I.

With regard to the sovereignty of heretical rulers even the more moderate Catholic sovereigns and theologians admitted that the Pope, in fulfilment of his spiritual duties, might be compelled, in the event of the continued persecution of the faithful by their lawful sovereign, *de facto* or even *de jure*, to relieve the persecuted subjects of their allegiance, and to call the next Catholic heir to the throne. In 1570, for instance, Pope Pius V. declared Queen Elizabeth cut off from communion with the Holy Roman Church, released her subjects from their obedience to her and forbade them to recognise her any longer as their sovereign. In 1588, Philip of Spain, encouraged by the Pope's promise to recognise him as King of England, took upon himself the dethronement of Elizabeth. In 1589 and in 1590 there were determined efforts on the part of many Catholics in Europe to induce Pope Sixtus V. formally to depose Henry IV. of France and to give recognition to a Catholic successor. The Papacy declined to commit itself, and was justified when Henry IV., after "instruction," perceived the Catholic verities and sued the Pope for a pardon, which was gladly given. Almost the last dramatic employment of the papal prerogative on an international scale may perhaps be said to have taken place when the Pope, despite the important part which his representatives had played in the negotiation of the Treaties of Westphalia, declared the final form of those treaties "null and void," as legalising within the Holy Roman Empire the existence of heresy.

Infidels.—Contact with the Saracens and the Turks had first raised the problem of communication between infidels and members of the Society of Christian States. Later, after the Spanish discovery of America and the Portuguese establishment of direct sea-trade with Africa, India and China, there arose the added problem which was provoked by the necessity of intercourse with American communities in varying stages of culture, as also with monarchies, in some cases of long standing, in India, China and Japan. One writer, the Spanish professor, Joseph Acosta,(17) was quick-sighted enough to classify the barbarians in three divisions. First, he pointed out, there were those non-Christians who were organised in stable and orderly states possessing some degree of civilisation, such as the Turks and the Chinese. Then there were organised communities, in which stability and order did indeed exist, albeit that it rested on other foundations than those of justice. In this class were the Peruvians and Mexicans. Lastly, there was need to reckon with mere herds of Caribs among whom existed nothing which could be properly termed social order. Although Acosta came near to the root of the matter and established distinctions, hardly improved upon by the framers of the constitution of the League of Nations when they laid down the future of mandated areas, he pursued the matter no further but passed to the subject which he was immediately treating. CHAP. I.

Islam in theory perhaps is always at war with unbelievers. A reciprocal obligation, phrased generally as an obligation to rescue from paynim hands the Holy Sepulchre, is at the back of the crusading sentiment which endured, though with rapidly diminishing force, long after the Middle Ages. Practice, however, on both sides did not coincide with precept. Moderate Christian opinion in justifying war against the Turks and Saracens was apt to state its aim as the recovery of lands which had at one time been in Christian hands rather than as the propagation of the Faith. But if Christian opinion could tolerate disregard by a Christian sovereign of a papal, or imperial, appeal for assistance in a holy war directed at the Turk, it looked very much askance at a Christian sovereign's alliance with the Turk, even if entered into in a time of danger. Such an alliance always contained in it the risk of a further Turkish advance into Europe and the loss of more territory from Christian control. As such it was not a legitimate means of defence. France has always sought an anvil in Eastern Europe upon which, if necessary, to hammer out its immediate eastern neighbours: and an alliance with the Sultan formed a permanent part of the equipment of French diplomacy in its long contest with the house of Hapsburg, since the eastern dominions of that house marched for many hundreds of miles with the Turkish Empire and were dangerously exposed to Turkish attack. Francis I. in the sixteenth century, Louis XIV. in the seventeenth, and his successors later made use of this policy and were exposed to a storm of obloquy in consequence. It was this more than anything which lies behind a recurrent charge, to be found in imperial writers, of the special lack of scruple in French diplomatic methods. So true it is that every nation has in the armoury of its diplomatic practice some weapon which renders it an object of traditional suspicion to the others. The French to excuse themselves took refuge in accusing the remaining Powers. Francis I. indeed, with an impudence which was characteristic, went further. In a letter to the Pope in justification of his Turkish alliance, formed by the Treaty of

CHAP. I. Belgrade (1536), he adopted the humanitarian pose, asserting that " the Turks are not outside the pale of human society to such an extent that we are permitted more contact with dumb beasts than with the infidel." (18) Vienna's comment on such dicta was not unlike the comments of Victorian Toryism upon the political practices of Mr. Gladstone. The danger involved in an alliance with the Turk could no longer be asserted after the beginning of the eighteenth century, for by that time the Turkish menace was at an end, much Christian territory had been recovered, and there was a reasonable prospect, despite spasmodic symptoms of Turkish recovery, that the Sultan would be driven out of Europe.

Writing to-day, moreover, it is possible to see that Francis I., by a diplomatic innovation which shocked his contemporaries, was in reality a benefactor of European civilisation. The Treaty of Belgrade in its famous " capitulations " (or chapters of agreement) contained the first worked-out scheme of " extra-territoriality." This has formed a model ever since for a system which ensures a *modus vivendi*, mutually beneficial, for the intercourse of nations living at totally different stages of civilisation. Such arrangements provide that those Westerners who have dealings in the East, dealings impossible apart from a background of western civilisation, should not, though far from home, lose all the benefits of that civilisation: that commerce, for example, should not be subjected to a system of justice, or the jurisdiction of courts, which have grown up in utterly different conditions. The details governing the structure of extra-territorial courts (provided to regulate the mutual intercourse of indigène and foreigner) have varied, and will vary, with the particular conditions of each subsequent constituent agreement. The principle remains the same, and is the creation of Francis I. and his advisers. It applies to the clash of irreconcilable conditions of life the notion of collective bargaining. Extra-territoriality as a piece of diplomatic machinery has been subjected to some criticism in recent years. It has been represented as the result of high-handed action upon the part of advanced communities, the bullying of the weaker by the strong. It is instructive therefore to remember its origin, a treaty clutched at by Francis I. in that abject decade which succeeded the battle of Pavia (1525) and the Paix des dames, the nadir of the French monarch's fortunes, and signed by Solyman the Magnificent at the highest moment of Turkish power in Europe.

As regards infidels other than the Turk the discussion was left almost entirely in the hands of Spanish theologians, who were concerned to define the moral duty of their nation toward the peoples which it had encountered in America. They asked, and the question has perpetual interest, whether Spain had the right to go to war with inoffensive infidel communities and to deprive them alike of possessions and of sovereignty. Could it be found in the Papal Bull issued by Alexander VI. in 1493, which divided the new world between the Spanish and the Portuguese? Could it be drawn from that Imperial authority held by Charles, King of Spain, from 1519 to 1556? The harder natures, men like Sepulveda (1521-1572), were inclined to maintain that, alike as heathens and as savages, infidels had no rights against the Christians, armed as these were with the delegated powers of Pope and Emperor. The more generous breathed a humaner air and expressed sentiments of the purest charity. The attitude of these is best seen, as regards international relations generally, in Suarez (1548-1617), as regards the specific American question, in Franciscus a Victoria (died 1546 or 1549). "The human race," says Suarez,(19) "however much divided into various peoples and kingdoms, has always retained not only its unity as a species but also a certain moral and quasi-political unity, indicated by the natural precept of mutual love, a love which extends to all, even to foreigners of any nation. Wherefore although every perfect state, whether it be a republic or a kingdom, is in itself a perfect community composed of its own members, still each state, viewed in relation to the human race, is in some measure a member of that universal unity. For those communities are never singly so self-sufficing but that they stand in need of some mutual aid, society and communion, sometimes for the improvement of their condition and their greater commodity, but sometimes also for their moral necessity and need, as appears by experience."

The Spaniards, said Victoria,(20) could in the beginning have had no other rights in America than those of Gospel-preaching and unmolested trading. Only if freedom of trade had been refused, or if there had arisen violent opposition to the preaching of the Gospel, would the Spaniards be entitled to use force; and existing Spanish title to territory, if legitimate, must be traced back to one or other of these sources or to the free choice of the original inhabitants. Jews were tolerated inside Christian society, and Muham-

CHAP. I.

madan states, at least when not established on previously Christian soil, were recognised as legitimate, on the ground that those who had not been by baptism admitted into the Christian community could not be proceeded against by violence when they had given no offence. So it was with the heathen Indians. As to the Spanish claim to a title by "discovery," that might have been considered valid if the land had been vacant, and it might give greater authority to Spain than to other European nations, but it could not be held good against the Indians, who had been already living in the lands "discovered" by the Spaniards. This attitude was based on firmer ground than that of Las Casas (*c.* 1510),[21] who reached much the same conclusion as to the Indians' right to friendship, good treatment, and religious education, but based it on a series of arguments which had as their basis a papal grant of sovereignty to Spain on the condition of a missionary obligation.

The Hanseatic League.[22]—From the fourteenth to the sixteenth century a considerable part was played upon the international stage by the union of German commercial towns near the North Sea or the Baltic, which was led by Lübeck and was known as the Hanseatic League. It had no executive organs. Lübeck summoned the meetings, called Hansetage, and seemed always willing to spend time and patience in the effort to bring about common action in matters which affected these two stretches of water. But the leadership of Lübeck and the obvious common interest in the preservation of an open passage through the Sound between the North Sea and the Baltic were not the only forces which kept this league together. The Hanseatic towns, some seventy in all, had joint interest in the special Hanseatic privileges at foreign commercial centres and at the league's headquarters. The most important of the foreign komtors were at Bruges (at Antwerp after 1540), at London, and at Bergen. The league was not easily kept together, as the Lübeckers learned despite their statesmanlike efforts. Towns as far apart as Cologne and Riga always had local interests to pursue, and these at any moment were apt to appear more vital than adherence to some general policy dictated by the league. Moreover, schemes of high political policy did not flourish in the timid and sceptical commercial atmosphere of German burgher government. Despite these handicaps a good deal was accomplished. A successful war was waged against Denmark in the fourteenth century, and a victor's peace obtained at

Stralsund in 1370. In the fifteenth century England was forced to a regrant of privileges to the Hansa, while the rising commercial power of the Dutch was strenuously contested. The sixteenth century saw renewed efforts directed against Denmark. When, after the defeat of the Armada, Elizabeth took special contraband measures against Spain, it was the Hanseatic League which voiced the neutral attitude. There can be little doubt but that if, say in the sixteenth century, a strong national power had arisen in Germany, particularly in north Germany, the Hanseatic towns might have figured much more prominently than they ever did in the maritime and colonial history of Europe.

In the seventeenth century Wallenstein dreamed for a moment of harnessing to the Imperial chariot the prestige and maritime power of the Hanseatic League. After Wallenstein's defeat before Stralsund, and the decay of German commerce which followed the Thirty Years' War, the three towns, Lübeck, Hamburg and Bremen, were left together as the sole free representatives of the ancient Hanseatic tradition. Though they were mentioned at times in Imperial treaties—the Treaty of Nymwegen in 1678 secured them the return of their commercial rights as they had enjoyed them before the war—they also undertook for themselves the negotiation of independent treaties to safeguard their maritime interests. Such a treaty was the Franco-Hanseatic Treaty of 18th September 1716. By the terms of this it was agreed that men of the Hansa should, in France, pay the same import and export duties as did Frenchmen, and that, conversely, the French should be in an analogous position when they were in Hansa towns. The Hansa men were only to pay the French tonnage dues of fifty sous for port to port traffic in France. The French were to be relieved of the Hamburg tax of Lastgeld. Various hypothetical conditions were made for the eventuality of war. Beside the regulation of such details as the type of ship and crew which would be reckoned Hanseatic should the French king be at war, or the amount of caution money to be deposited by privateers before clearing port, it contained the interesting feature that the French consented, in the case of a war between France and the Emperor, that Hanseatic cities should be deemed to be neutral provided that French ships in Hanseatic ports received similar treatment. As late as the third decade of the nineteenth century the Holy Alliance dreaded the conclusion of a commercial treaty between the

CHAP. I. Hanseatic towns and the South American communities. Such a treaty, it was thought, would appear to break the unanimity of European non-recognition. The last buildings owned by the league in foreign towns were finally sold, that at Bergen in 1775, that at London in 1852 and at Antwerp in 1863. The Hanseatic towns were of course incorporated with the North German Confederation 1st July 1867. The British Mission to them was abolished three years later.

The Elective Monarchies.[23]—There are disadvantages in the familiar terminology which speaks of the states of Europe as "subjects of international law," if it be held to suggest that the states form a community of which the components though they may differ in wealth and grandeur have none the less an original equality. States were no more originally equal than were the simple savages of the social contract theory. As far as Europe is concerned, it is roughly true to say that the states are the *disjecta membra* of the Roman, or the Holy Roman Empire, that all members have not the same uses or the same glory, and that the fabric of the states, be it a matter of diplomacy or of the law of nations, is charged with the electricity of previous history. It makes all the difference, alike to the historian and to the international lawyer, that for instance certain monarchies were elective. Up to the end of the eighteenth century two important units in the state system of Europe threw that continent into continuous confusion by the recurring event of an election to their thrones. It seemed indeed at one time that this special cause of international perturbation would spread from the Empire and Poland to other states. In the fifteenth century Bohemia and Hungary were added to the list, and during the sixteenth and seventeenth centuries the Hapsburgs had always to face the danger of a revival of the claim by these kingdoms to elect their ruling prince. It was, in fact, the Bohemian claim in 1618 to elect as king one who was neither Hapsburg nor Catholic, which provided the spark which set the world ablaze for thirty years. For a part of the second half of the sixteenth century it seemed not fanciful that the claim to elect might be put forward in France. The Papacy was always an elective monarchy but in a different sense, and the frequent elections to their kingship by Balkan powers in modern times, though so frequent as almost to constitute a system, never has in fact become so.

The Imperial election had been a danger to European peace almost from the beginning of the Holy Roman Empire.

Even after the Hapsburg family had established a strong presumptive claim to the Imperial throne, the French monarchy throughout three centuries never wearied of organising German or European opposition to these pretensions. A few French monarchs, Francis I. and Louis XIV., for example, dreamed of their own election as Holy Roman Emperor. Almost all of them encouraged the major German rulers, those of Saxony, Bavaria and Prussia, to aspire to the candidature against the Hapsburgs. The lack of a male candidate among the Hapsburgs, apart from the husband of the heiress of that house, enabled France in 1740 to organise a Bavarian election and an onslaught upon the Hapsburg dominions by Bavaria, Saxony and Prussia which led to eight years of European war. When in 1806 the Holy Roman Empire was abolished, one at least of the political dangers and the legal anachronisms bequeathed by the past had vanished for ever from Europe.

The Polish kingdom also was a disturbing factor. It was the field, not the only field, upon which already in the sixteenth and seventeenth centuries Bourbon and Hapsburg played out their rivalry. In the eighteenth century it was a centre of interest or a bone of contention for all Europe. At the beginning of the century the electoral house of Saxony had secured the throne by election and endeavoured to employ it as the basis for formidable schemes of expansion. Sweden, the power against which these schemes were in part directed, replied by the invasion of Poland and the enthronement of a rival elected king, Stanislas Leczinski, who for a time received the recognition of France. The new Polish election of 1733 provoked a European war. Stanislas was now the father-in-law of the King of France. Backed by French money and helped by the fact that he was a Pole, he secured election in September. Against him there came into the field the united influence of Russia, Austria and Saxony, which proved strong enough, with the aid of Russian troops and Saxon bribes, to secure election for the Elector of Saxony in October 1733. A fresh war between Bourbon and Hapsburg then broke out, and against the Emperor were ranged France, Spain, and Sardinia.

The vacancy which occurred in 1763 again produced grave European complications. These were the more dangerous in that the neighbours of Poland, Russia, and Prussia were vastly more strong and more designing than ever before. By November 1762 Russia and Prussia had come to agreement

CHAP. I.

on the necessity of a native Pole as king. After the period of the vacancy had begun in November 1763 the Russian and Prussian courts in March 1764 made an additional arrangement by which they ruled as out of the question the establishment of an hereditary and absolute monarchy. This would have put an end to foreign influence within the kingdom. Finally, in 1764 the presence of a Russian army secured the election of Stanislas Poniatowski, the last king. France had endeavoured to promote an attack by Turkey on the Russians in retaliation for their interference in Poland. This war came finally in 1768 after the world had witnessed a ludicrous spectacle in which Russian troops, taking their orders from the ambassador of Russia, put down " rebellion " against the Polish king undertaken by Catholic confederations of Poles financed by Austria and France. It was the Russo-Turkish War which proved to be the end of the kingdom of Poland. In 1772 came the first partition. The Poles made an eleventh-hour effort to secure both independence and stability through the establishment of a new constitution which provided for an hereditary monarchy with considerable powers. This led to the partitions of 1793 and 1795 which ended the existence of the state. Even so, the view has been widely held that Russian, Austrian, and Prussian rule over the divided Poles was on the whole less of a menace to the peace of Europe than the survival of the old anarchic and elective monarchy.[(24)]

Questions of Precedence and Dignity.—When certainty had gradually emerged as to the status of European communities the way became open for dispute as to precedence among sovereigns and states. The papal list of 1504, quoted above, indicates uncertainty as to the relative position of England, Portugal, and Sicily. There were indeed many similar controversies. Philip II. of Spain, mindful of the fact that his royal house had held the Imperial dignity and ruled many realms beyond the Spanish border, was restless in the face of the French claim to a traditional precedence. A long and bitter controversy began between the Crowns of France and Spain which was carried on at many capitals and involved their diplomatic representatives in acrimonious squabbles. The first public exhibition of the struggle was provided at the Council of Trent in 1562 when the Catholic world was all but rent asunder by it. Readers of the *Diary* of Samuel Pepys will remember the entry for the last day of September 1661 :—

"This morning up by moon shine, at five o'clock, to Whitehall, to meet Mr. Moore at the Privy Seale, and then I heard of a fray between the two Embassadors of Spaine and France; and that, this day, being the day of the entrance of an Embassador from Sweden, they intended to fight for the precedence. Our King, I heard, ordered that no Englishman should meddle in the business, but let them do what they would. . . . So I went to the Spanish Embassadors and the French, and there saw great preparation on both sides; but the French made the most noise and ranted most, but the other made no stir almost at all; so that I was afraid the other would have too great a conquest over them. Then to the Wardrobe, and dined there, and then abroad and in Cheapside hear that the Spanish hath got the best of it, and killed three of the French coach horses and several men, and is gone through the city next to the king's coach; at which it is strange to see how all the City did rejoice. And indeed we do naturally all love the Spanish and hate the French. . . . At last at the Mewes, I saw the Spanish coach go, with fifty drawn swords at least to guard it, and our soldiers shouting for joy. . . . So then I went to the French house, where I observe still that there is no men in the world of a more insolent spirit where they do well, nor before they begin a matter, and more abject if they do miscarry, than these people are; for they all look like dead men, and not a word among them, but shake their heads. The truth is, the Spaniards were not only observed to fight most desperately, but they also did outwitt them; first, in lining their own harnesse with chains of iron that they could not be cut, then in setting their coach in the most advantageous place, and to appoint men to guard every one of their horses, and others for to guard the coach, and others the coachmen. And, above all, in setting upon the French horses and killing them, for by that means the French were not able to stir. There were several men slain of the French, and one or two of the Spaniards, and one Englishman by a bullet which is very observable, the French were at least four to one in number; and had near one hundred case of pistols among them, and the Spaniards had not one gun among them; which is for their honour for ever and the others disgrace. So having been very much daubed with dirt, I got a coach, and home; where I vexed my wife in telling of her this story, and pleading for the Spaniards against the French."

Thus, characteristically, the most human of all eye-witnesses indicates the serious light in which the rivalry was regarded. The difference was not settled until the Spanish crown passed by inheritance to a junior branch of the French reigning house of Bourbon. Then the Bourbon *pacte de*

CHAP. I.

famille arranged the seniority of ambassadors between them on a family basis. At the courts of the Bourbon family the French ambassador was always to be senior : at other courts whichever ambassador from the two courts had been first accredited. The Council of Trent brought to light other grounds for friction. The Portuguese king challenged the high place in seniority allotted to the kingship of the Romans,(25) a mere high-sounding title devoid of actual sovereignty, so he alleged, and indicative only of a succession right to the Imperial dignity. More important still was the challenge of a German prince to the international position of republics. The ambassador of the Duke of Bavaria refused to allow precedence to the Venetian envoy on the grounds that his master, whose family had once provided emperors, would only allow kings and electors to rank before him. The papal officials had to explain that the Venetian republic might claim a royal title—that of Cyprus—before the storm could be abated. But this excuse was not available for the Swiss confederation when their position was challenged by the Dukes of Florence and Bavaria. Considerations of reality triumphed in the end, for the Swiss established their claim to follow next after the Venetians.

Modern writers upon International Law have begun from the postulate of an equality of states before the law, even if they have been prepared to allow, both at the present time and in former generations, the existence of some conditions which in a minor degree seem inconsistent with it. If that equality of states has ever existed it was assuredly at a period subsequent to the seventeenth century. Perhaps its existence at any time has been too readily assumed, for the terminology, and the ideas of Europe in 1600 were rooted in reality, the history of Europe is a record of an organic growth, and every epoch is the legatee of its predecessors. Egalitarian conceptions have impregnated the political thought of the present generation. Considerations of sentimentality have coloured its phraseology. The interests of convenience in a business age have reconciled the public to such habits as that of allotting precedence at international gatherings by the alphabetical order of the names of states in the French language, a habit which in practice seats Albania above Germany and Costa Rica above the United States. Three hundred years ago such a practice was unthinkable, and that it was unthought of, is significant. The public law of Europe to those who reflected must have appeared as the expression of the European state system, and a deceptive over-simplification is likely to result in the views of any one to-day who regards either the system or its expression as starting from too many generally accepted postulates. The common assumption of the inequality of states was often fateful. Thus an Anglo-Spanish war was drawn out for four years because, when in 1600 the combatants had been drawn together by the mediation of the King of France, the English advanced a claim to precedence which the Spaniards as "the holders of twenty viceroyalties" were unwilling to concede, and this although the war was bringing frightful loss upon their Crown and nation. Contemporary opinion accepted as unfortunate but comprehensible the fact that, after innumerable difficulties, a compromise was reached by which the Treaty of Westphalia was made in two sections, the one at Münster and the other at Osnabrück. The Crown of Sweden refused to allow precedence to its ally, the French, and the French Crown refused to allow complete equality to its ally the Swedish. Accordingly, the conferences between the Imperial party and its opponents were divided into two, with two sets of mediators; the French negotiated with the Imperialists at Münster, while the Swedes did the same at Osnabrück.

It is only necessary to recount the catalogue of such disputes to make it quite obvious why the *alternat* system of treaty signature was gradually adopted, for if quarrels of this nature had been pushed to their logical conclusion the transaction of international business would have had to cease. When a document was drawn up which registered agreement between states, the plan was selected of preparing as large a number of original documents as there were signatories, each one of whom retained an original on which the place of his signature conformed with his idea as to the position of his state. A Franco-Swedish incident is pertinent. In a treaty made between France and Sweden in 1631, Cardinal Richelieu insisted on the right of the French King to sign both originals first. A controversy then opened with the Swedish court which, to the discomfiture of Richelieu, produced a decisive precedent, one in which Francis I. and Gustavus Vasa had in the previous century each signed first his own original of a treaty. Richelieu was thus forced to allow the Swedish Crown the right of *alternat*. Down to the end of the eighteenth century statesmen are found disputing as to whether or no one state "had the *alternat*" with another. France, for example, denied the *alternat* to the monarchs of

CHAP. I. the reigning houses of Savoy and Brandenburg, whose monarchies were first recognised by Europe in the Peace of Utrecht (1713), and maintained this attitude up to the French Revolution. The *alternat* was only accorded Russia by France in 1779. Among the German principalities disputes of this kind consumed an especial amount of energy. In documents involving many signatories it was sometimes found easier to record agreement by a wholesale exchange of originals signed only by one Power. At the Utrecht preliminaries, according to one authority, this was the method pursued.

Titles.—Closely akin was the question of the claim of sovereign Powers to specific titles. The titles of honour granted by the Pope do not seem to have caused much trouble, such titles as *Filius primogenitus Ecclesiae* which had been granted to the French monarch, or the English king's title *Fidei Defensor*. Even these, however, have played their part in history, sometimes by unexpected means and by unjustifiable processes, for sentimental associations cling about the fabric of history. French piety of the nineteenth century was to justify a claim to protect the Latin Places by arguments in which the old king's title was to play by no means the flimsiest part. In the long ceremonial titles, secular in origin, and in use only on occasions of solemnity, there lurked the seeds of war, especially of course where those titles laid a claim to territory in the possession of another Power. The title "King of France," which the kings of England bore, was even in the sixteenth century a constant reminder of the exploits of Edward III. and the Black Prince. Henry VIII. was certainly sensitive to this. The claim disputed between Denmark and Sweden, later in the same century, to wear the three crowns of the Scandinavian kingdoms envenomed their intercourse for at least a hundred years. The epic of Swedish domination of the Baltic opened with the irritating refusal of a line of Polish kings to give up the title "King of Sweden." The Austrian royal house clung steadfastly to the "Kingship of Hungary" from 1526 till 1699, when their victories over the Turk at length made good their hard-won aspiration. As near to present times as 1814 there was a possibility that the Hapsburgs' Alsatian title would be used to justify a claim for the ending of French dominion in Alsace; while as late as 1856 Prussia and Switzerland found themselves in sharp antipathy over the conditions which should govern the Prussian king's retention of the personal title Prince of Neuchâtel.

CHAP. I.

The titles which the heads of states assumed might differ in their origin, even the royal title. That of Naples was Papal: those of Bohemia and Poland were Imperial. The Sforzas found the ducal title necessary for the enhancement of their prestige in Milanese territory and were compelled to sue for a grant of it from the Emperor. Charles the Bold of Burgundy made the most strenuous efforts to persuade the Emperor Frederick III. in 1473 to give him the royal dignity, and was at first so successful that he bought a crown and robes and prepared a coronation ceremonial. His chagrin was correspondingly great when the cautious Emperor, fearing that his already over-mighty vassal would be still more formidable as King of Burgundy, withdrew from the negotiations. In the next century Mary of England secured the papal title of Queen of Ireland although that title had been assumed *motu proprio* by Henry VIII. before her; while Cosimo de' Medici, who needed a dignified new title to weld together his Sienese and Florentine dominions, but foresaw complications should he even request the royal rank, accepted with gratitude papal elevation to the dignity of the Grand Dukedom of Tuscany. Even this title caused a crisis, for the Dukes of Ferrara, Mantua, and Savoy protested furiously, and the Emperor worked strenuously to have the grant revoked. The almost contemporary efforts of the Dukes of Savoy to gain a royal title were somewhat ludicrous. Charles Emmanuel, in particular, hardly concealed his passionate desire for a kingdom to which should attach, either the old name Arles, or a new epithet Allobrogian (Dux Allobrogum was a pompous neo-classic version of Dux Sabaudiae). A determining factor in the Thirty Years' War was the Imperial grant of an electorate to the Duke of Bavaria. The Imperial cause in Hungary, and on the Rhine, was given indispensable help between 1680 and 1714 as a result of the Emperor's sanction of the assumption by the Duke of Brunswick-Lüneburg in 1692 of the rank of an Elector, and of the title "King of Prussia" by the Elector of Brandenburg in 1700. A larger part than is sometimes admitted by those who disregard the "antiquarian" study of International Law must be allowed to the effect of the kingly titles of the houses of Prussia and Savoy (recognised by all Europe in 1713) in securing that the unification of Germany and Italy respectively came through those two dynasties. Recently rulers in Serbia, Rumania, Bulgaria, and Montenegro changed their titles with a view to winning more respect for their position; and no one will suggest that the alteration had not its signi-

CHAP. I.

ficance.[26] The twentieth-century Briton wonders why the Briton of the nineteenth century sneered at the Queen's assumption of the Imperial title in India and took no steps to press a project, definitely mooted, for the creation of a kingdom of Canada. Perhaps if British statesmen had been more widely read in the history of the public law of Europe, the British Empire might to-day have been equipped with more ideas with which to meet its chief imperial problem.

The Russian Imperial title has a singular history. When in the early eighteenth century Russia forced its way into the full circle of European Society there were natural difficulties in connection with the Tsar's title and his precedence. In the Treaties of Westphalia the Tsar had been described as the Grand Duke of Muscovy. Ivan III. had married Sophie Palaeologus in 1472, taking the double-headed eagle, the emblem of the Byzantine Emperors, for his standard. This double action furnished to the Russian rulers a shadowy claim to be the successors of the Eastern Emperors: it was tenderly preserved, and was ready for use by Peter the Great, who in 1721 adopted the title of Emperor by *ukase*. Trouble had already arisen with Austria in the seventeenth century on the occasion of the reception of Russian embassies and the signature of treaties, trouble which was intensified by the Russian demand for the recognition of their Imperial dignity, together with the ascription of Majesty, a word hitherto carefully preserved for the Emperor. In 1717, in the course of the negotiation of a treaty of alliance, there had been interminable wrangling between the Russians and the French because of the latter's refusal to write "Majesté Czarienne." It was not indeed till 1744, in a difficult moment for French diplomacy, that the head of the Russian state was accorded the full title Tsaritsa. Even then French diplomacy, always intent on reserving for its sovereign the second place in the international world, made it clear that despite this concession no question would be admitted as to the seniority of the King of France.

The assumption of tendentious political titles has been a fruitful source of trouble in the affairs of nations. The first Napoleon, to take no other example, was a master in this war breeding art, and his method of procedure deserves some mention as giving an apt illustration of the dangers which are at all times latent in the practice. In 1809 Napoleon's official title was "Empereur des Français, roi d'Italie, protecteur de la Confédération du Rhin, médiateur de la Suisse."

Oliver Cromwell's mere protectorship seems modest in comparison.

Language.—The language of diplomatic intercourse has sometimes been a matter of negotiation. By the seventeenth century French rather than Italian or Spanish, as had at times seemed possible, was becoming marked out as a successor to mediaeval Latin. Under Louis XIV. French diplomats seem usually to have managed to carry on negotiations, written and spoken, in their own tongue. The language used in the preliminary discussions and in the majority of the Treaties of Utrecht was French, and the Anglo-French commercial treaty of 1713 and the Franco-Imperial treaty of 1714 must be two of the last important examples of Latin instruments. Eighteenth-century negotiations (except on occasions those between the German powers and Russia) were held almost exclusively in French. At Vienna the victors employed it not only with the vanquished French but among themselves, and finally drafted the treaty in that language. The victorious Powers, however, took the precaution, already practised at Aix-la-Chapelle, Paris and Versailles, of laying it down that the use of French was *pro hac vice* and that it committed them to nothing. The rise of nationality in the nineteenth century had a curious effect on treaty-making. In treaties between two countries there began to appear parallel texts in the languages of the contracting parties, though these were sometimes accompanied by a third text in French for the greater security of the participants in the agreement. Treaties in which many nations were concerned continued to be written for the most part in French. Not till 1919 did English obtain some measure of equality. In that year the business of the council of three at the inter-allied negotiations was transacted in this language. The Treaty of Versailles was printed in both French and English, both texts being allowed validity. Provision was made also for the transaction of League of Nations business in both languages. In view of the susceptibilities of some of the representatives, especially the Spanish-speaking, the matter is not yet *chose jugée*.

NOTES

(1) The Prince of Orange, though not an author, was responsible for several state papers, notably the *Justification* of 1568 and the *Apology* of 1580. The defence of his resistance to Philip turned on such matters as "tyranny" and justifiable "rebellion," subjects

considered in any study of the *Jus Belli* in the sixteenth century and even much later. Motley notices Orange's minute directions to his fleet concerning the exercise of acts of war, discipline and prize. (*Rise of the Dutch Republic*, vol. 2, pp. 319-320.)

(2) "Ut bellum solenne sit ex jure gentium, duo requiruntur; primum ut geratur utrimque auctore eo qui summam potestatem habeat in civitate: Deinde ut ritus quidam adsint de quibus agemus suo loco. Haec quia conjunctim requiruntur, ideo alterum sine altero non sufficit." (Grotius, *Law of War and Peace*, bk. I. cap. iii. 4.)

(3) The well-known Guillaume Postel (1510-1581) advanced claims as fantastic as any for the French monarchy. In one of his works, claiming a special position for the French king in temporal affairs, he alleged that Japheth, Noah's son, had been appointed the instrument of divine purpose. The French monarchy had inherited Japheth's task, the Gauls or Gomerites being the descendants of Japheth's son Gomer. (Butler, *Studies in Statecraft*, pp. 49-50.)

(4) This sentence is from Knolles' English translation of Bodin's *De la République*, published in 1606.

(5) Bryce in his *Holy Roman Empire* (p. 185, ed. 1913) quoted this phrase from Selden's *Titles of Honour*.

(6) See Borrelli, *Editti antichi e nuovi*, 77, 80.

(7) Bodin (died 1596) published his famous work the *De la République* in 1577. From the point of view here being treated, bk. I, cap. 8, entitled *De la Souveraineté*, bk. I, cap. 9, entitled "Du Prince tributaire ou feudataire," and bk. I, cap. 10 "Des Vrayes marques de Souveraineté" are most important. Bodin's influence was important in fortifying the central power in every community, and completing the buttress-work of theory round the independent sovereign prince. Mr. C. W. Previté-Orton has pointed out that Marsilius of Padua came somewhat near to formulating a doctrine similar to that here outlined in his conception of the 'legislator humanus superiore carens.' Bodin's incisive ideas forced the German theorists of the next century on to the defensive. The Germans, who had once been wont to deny that there could exist any real political independence of their Emperor, now had to admit that that potentate was not even sovereign, if by sovereignty were denoted the sum of all the "marks" which Bodin required. A representative sentence from the German theorist Arnisaeus (*Doctrina Politica*, lib. I, cap. 8) will display their reluctance to accept Bodin's conclusion: "Non sunt autem jura majestatis ad eum modum dividenda quem fingit Bodinus. Nam singulis partibus talia jura concedit quae trahunt secum universam majestatem quod fieri non posse paulo ante diximus." Any theory acceptable to Germans had to take into account the special position of their princes and estates. "Plura enim sunt capita et jura, quorum concursus efficit majestatem perfectam, quam quidem totam et universam pluribus communicari impossibile est sed partes ejus nihil prohibet disjungi et pluribus attribui, ita quidem ut in singulis sit particula majestatis in toto vero corpore summa et plena majestatis."

(8) See Oechsli's *History of Switzerland*, published by the Cambridge University Press.

(9) The importance of the Bouillons may be gathered incidentally from seventeenth-century works of the type of the *Mémoires du*

Cardinal de Retz. Their stronghold of Sédan was an important consideration in the minds of plotters against Richelieu in 1641 and 1642.

(10) Cardinal Pallavicini's monumental *History of the Council of Trent*, produced to refute Sarpi's work of genius, is a mine of international political history in the seventeenth century. It is to be obtained in three large tomes in the French editions of the Abbé Migne. The account of the oral and written invitations of the third series of council sessions is to be found in book 15.

(11) For the most recent discussion of Sully's Grand Design see Butler, *Studies in Statecraft* (Camb. Univ. Press).

(12) A very useful summary of the most important plans for international organisation is that of Dr. Ter Meulen, published in German at The Hague in 1917 under the title of *Der Gedanke der Internationalen Organisation in seiner Entwicklung*, 1300-1800. See also Butler, *Studies in Statecraft* (Camb. Univ. Press).

(13) Motley's work on the rise of the Dutch republic, though influenced by the author's prejudices, is still the best book on the opening stages of the Dutch struggle. The diplomatic negotiations later referred to may be found treated in English works like Edmundson's *History of Holland* issued by the Cambridge University Press.

(14) Balthazar Ayala's treatise was entitled *De Jure et officiis bellicis et disciplina militari*. As was fitting in one who was a Military Judge in the army of the Prince of Parma, his observations on the qualities necessary for military command, the duties of him appointed to exercise it, and finally the problem of military discipline, were preceded by a very important and pithy discussion of the Law of War. His most important chapter from the present point of view is the second of bk. 1. Ayala's opinion stands out in such section-headings as "Principis auctoritas semper sequenda contra rebelles; nulla justa causa rebellandi; rebellis gravissimum crimen; legitimus princeps tyrannus dici non potest."

(15) For an account of the Grisons see the special chapter on the Grisons in Oechsli's *History of Switzerland*. There is a useful chapter in the *Cambridge Modern History*, vol. iv. chap. II., entitled the Valtelline.

(16) Froude's very considerable volume of writing on Elizabeth in his *History of England* (1529-1588) has brought together much information concerning the political history of Western Europe during the latter half of the sixteenth century. The struggle of the "heretic" queen against the more conservative forces in England and in Europe is studied, and Mary of Scotland's history between 1569 and 1587 secures attention. The activities of Spain, the Papacy, and the League against Henry of Navarre are treated in the volume on the Wars of Religion in the *Cambridge Modern History*. See *Letters and Papers of Sir T. Edmondes* (Roxburgh Club) Introduction.

(17) Jose d'Acosta (1539-1600). The work quoted was the *De Promulgatione Evangelii apud barbaros*.

(18) Gentilis devoted a chapter of his *De Jure Belli* to a discussion of the question "Si foedus recte contrahitur cum diversae religionis hominibus." Commercial treaties he did not consider illegitimate, but military treaties negotiated between Christian states and infidel on equal terms appeared to him improper, even if the forces of the alliance were to be directed against other infidels: much more so

CHAP. I. if they were to be turned against Christians. Though Gentilis apparently would have approved the capitulations he found it impossible to justify the Franco-Turkish League.

(19) Suarez was the last of the great Iberian theologians of the sixteenth century. The very famous passage quoted here is from bk. II. cap. 19 of the *Tractatus de legibus ac Deo Legislatore*, a work which after its first publication at the author's place of residence, Coimbra, was speedily republished at Antwerp and Mayence (Walker's *History of the Law of Nations*, p. 155). The clarity of Suarez's vision may be seen in another remarkable phrase defining the *Jus gentium* strikingly as the law "quod omnes populi et gentes variae inter se servare debent."

(20) Francisco di Victoria. This now famous Navarrese, after an education in Paris, became Professor of Theology in Salamanca. A decade or more after his death there appeared from the press at Lyons a collection of thirteen *Relectiones* or lectures, of which the fifth and sixth were occupied with the rights and duties of the Spaniards in their dealings with the native Indians (1557). His calm, balanced, and wonderfully just analysis of the legal and moral elements of the situation assures him growing fame as the continent of America takes an ever-increasing share in the shaping of human destiny.

(21) Las Casas. One of the heroic figures of the sixteenth century is that of Las Casas, the Spanish ecclesiastic, who devoted great effort to enlisting the Spanish Crown for the protection of the natives of America. Unlike Victoria, he had a thorough knowledge of the Indian question at first hand. He had made his first voyage to the Indies within the decade following Columbus, and from 1510 was active in opposition to the greed and violence of the Spanish colonists which were depopulating Hispaniola. In 1515 he returned to Spain to urge the cause of the natives upon the Crown. In 1542, after the Spanish system had been extended to the extensive continental areas of Mexico and Peru, he made another assault upon the royal conscience by placing the manuscript of his *Destruction of the Indies* before Charles V. To the Council of Valladolid, held in the same year for the purpose of drawing up a system for the American colonies, he reiterated his arguments pointing to the Indians' claim to personal freedom and the protection of the Crown.

(22) *The Hanseatic League.* The league belongs to a class of political construction which played a very considerable part in the Europe of the sixteenth and even the seventeenth century, but which has not survived in the modern international world. It was the only federation of its class active in maritime affairs, though parallel organisations were formed for action on land among the German cities. In ultimate analysis, of course, the Swiss Cantons and the Grisons were of the same type of political construction. In these cases, however, direct connection by land, without the intervention of foreign territory and common interest in the control of subject lands—a more vivid interest than common rights to certain types of chartered privilege abroad—permitted the evolution of veritable *respublicae*. The decisive political epochs in the history of the league were 1370, 1471, when the restoration of the Yorkist house in England was promoted, the Wullenweber years in the 1530's when new enterprises against the Danish monarchy were undertaken, and the

fateful turning-point of the Thirty Years' War when it declined to second Wallenstein's maritime ambitions. There does not seem to be a special work on the league in English which is readily accessible. An interesting German work is *Die Blütezeit der deutschen Hanse* by E. R. Daenell, 1905.

(23) The later weak and effeminate members of the Valois family who ruled between 1559 and 1589, and whose efforts were paralysed by the Wars of Religion, were certainly not of the type to inspire respect. Theoretical discussions of popular rights began on the Protestant side with such works as the *Francogallia* of Francis Hotman, chapter 7 of which is headed "De Summa populi potestate in regibus causa cognita condemnandis et abdicandis." With the ascent of the Huguenot Henry IV. to the position of legitimate French king, it was the Catholics who began to entertain the idea of proceeding to "popular" choice of monarch. It must be remembered that a Europe, all or a considerable proportion of whose monarchs were elective, could not have developed on the same lines as a continent largely controlled by a small number of hereditary families.

(24) The late Lord Salisbury was one who approached very close to this attitude.

The circumstances of the Imperial and Polish elections discussed in the text must be followed in a good diplomatic history. It should be noticed that a great "Positivist" international lawyer like J. J. Moser was so persuaded of the part which the Imperial election played in the Public Law of Europe, that he included a considerable number of documents turning on the circumstances of the vacancy of 1740 in his great collection the *Versuch*.

(25) Pallavicini's *History of the Council of Trent* or Paolo Sarpi's will be found to devote much space to the precedence struggles here recited. Precedence occupied an altogether bigger place in sixteenth-century diplomacy and international relations than the modern mind can easily grasp.

(26) In this regard the titles assumed during the last fifteen years in Egypt, the Hejaz, Iraq, and Nejd, are also apposite.

CHAPTER II

THE WORLD BY SEA

DOMINIUM MARIS: THE PRESENT LIMIT OF TERRITORIAL WATERS.

CHAP. II. **Dominium Maris.**—The sixteenth century did not subscribe to the modern doctrine that the High Seas are the property of no nation. The *Mare Liberum* was written by Grotius to establish that doctrine. The Dutch cast covetous eyes at the Portuguese spice trade with the Moluccas, so the treatise could be certain of a favourable reception. The author's knowledge of the Civil Law furnished him with more than one trite maxim to justify its central thesis. Ulpian had written that the sea was by nature open to all and that therefore, like the air, it belonged to all. A passage in the Institutes claimed as common to all men by natural law the air, flowing water, the sea and the seashore. If any one had pointed out, and no one as a matter of fact did do so till long after, that the Roman jurisconsults in their opinions considered maritime navigation solely from the point of view of private law, or of the internal public law of the Roman state, there was still left in the erudition of Grotius a formidable armoury for attack upon the Portuguese. He even drew assistance from the camp of the enemy, quoting the Spanish theologians and lawyers, despite the fact that Spain's interest was coincident with Portugal's, both nations quoting the Papal Bull of 1493. Indeed, the two nations were at the moment united in allegiance to the same prince. None the less it was Grotius who was the innovator. A glance at the map, or the history, of Europe indicates that his innovation amounted almost to paradox. Indeed, there are passages in his other writings which indicate that he modified his position.(1) Perhaps he was conscious of the contrast between his more extreme contentions and the practice of states. He seems himself to have conceived as possible the renunciation by treaty of general navigation rights, to have allowed that the possession of a fleet, or of a strong point on land, might impose maritime jurisdiction along with it, and to have tolerated the impropriation of the seas in parts not yet governed by the law of freedom. Let it be assumed that these were concessions made by common sense to actual conditions. What then were these conditions?

"The Doges of Venice are lords of the Adriatic just as the King of England is lord of the English sea." (2) So writes an English Franciscan, a pilgrim to the Holy Land, in 1344. He was describing conditions which lasted for several centuries. The Venetian claim was supported by lawyers, by Julius Pacius (1550-1635), for example, in his *De dominio Maris Hadriatici*, which was published in 1669. The claim as paraphrased by Bynkershoek, an opponent though a moderate one, ran somewhat as follows. The Venetians, though they do not completely encircle the Adriatic with their dominions, can rightly claim sovereignty over it, provided a small part is left near the shore for other princes who have territory washed by its waters. The justification is that no one but they has ever occupied it; none other frequents it or has territory on its shores; they have already been in possession for centuries by universal consent; they came into this possession without using force on the fall of the Roman Empire, and their authority has been acknowledged without envy by all neighbouring lands, islands, castles, kings and fleets, so that mere proscription would now give them a title—this last to meet the objection based on Roman law that the sea could not be impropriated from *occupatio*—and finally there are the confirming facts of continuous navigation, naval victories, and the Doges' annual marriage to the sea. Almost exactly similar claims were advanced by the Genoese to the dominion over the Ligurian Sea; and they, too, found legal support, as for example that of Pietro Battista Borgo in the *De dominio serenissimae Genuensis Reipublicae in mari ligustico* which appeared in Rome in 1641. A main contention of the Genoese lay in the claim that they actually dominated this sea with their fleet which did indeed protect their subject islands—Corsica was Genoese—which did drive off Barbary pirates and whomsoever else they chose to drive off, and which strategically could determine the destiny of Italy in so far as they were able at will to permit, or to prohibit, the transportation by sea of French or Spanish military forces. The Venetians in the thirteenth century had fought a successful war with Bologna and Ancona to compel acknowledgment of their supremacy and the right

CHAP. II. to levy duties. The precedent once established here was followed elsewhere.

Bynkershoek (1673-1743)[(3)] writing in the eighteenth century was then confronted with an established and long-standing practice. Indeed, he never adopted the highly theoretical standpoint of Grotius. In his treatise *De dominio maris* one chapter is summarised as follows: " There is nothing in the Law of Nature or in the Law of Nations or even in the Roman Law which stands in the way of sovereignty over the sea." He inquired not so much whether the maritime republics of Italy could hold dominion of the seas, as whether they did hold it. Thus combating the Genoese contentions he pointed out that the republic might have all the triremes which it claimed, but that, as they were mostly in port, they could confer no right to a dominion of the seas, for this could only be secured by constant occupation. In the case of a Barbary inroad he observed that both papal and Venetian galleys were called on to undertake the task as well as Genoese. The contentions of the treatise of Grotius were made to look even more academic by the maritime position of the British. Their claim to control their seas could not be dismissed by Bynkershoek quite so playfully as could those of Genoa and Venice. To begin with, that master of erudition, Selden (1584-1654), had with the encouragement of two kings disembowelled his classical and theological library and the muniment chambers at the Tower, to produce the British vindication, *Mare clausum*. More important, however, Englishmen were prepared to bombard foreign ships which did not strike their flag and lower their topsails in salute to the king's flag. In the seventeenth century three wars moreover had to be fought with the Dutch, and in the *casus belli* no little part was played by the British anxiety to extort from their opponents the utmost consequences of the " Britishness " of British seas. The " free sea " policy of Elizabeth led to the " shut sea " policy of the Stuarts. This is but another way of saying that we passed from an offensive policy against the Iberian Powers to a defensive one against the Dutch.

Selden's book may seem almost grotesque to modern readers unaware of the disproportionate importance attached in his day to an erudition which expanded itself upon Holy Writ, classical poetry, mythology and history in an unending search for analogies, even those remotely relevant. Even then perhaps there may have been detected something a little ludicrous in the piling of Ossa on Pelion in the matter of alleged evidence. Thus to prove that the sea, and even the most open ocean, could be appropriated he brought into play Biblical quotations, the example of Neptune, the history of seventeen peoples of antiquity, the statement of Dionysius of Halicarnassus that Rome was mistress not only of the Mediterranean but also of whatsoever parts of the ocean were navigable, and lastly, the observation that many modern nations were advancing claims to sovereignty over seas even if these claims were based on untenable arguments. He met the possible objection drawn from Queen Elizabeth's opposition to the Portuguese pretensions by affirming that she had not denied that the sea was patient of dominion, that her denial was only that King Sebastian had established such dominion. The objection of Grotius that the flowing and shifting waters of the sea were impatient of boundaries Selden met with the sensible observation that meridians were quite as good as hedges. He then proceeded to mark out the four parts of the British ocean. The outer boundary of the southern part was the north coast of Spain, and that of the eastern part the west coast of Germany. To the northern and western portions of the British seas, bounded the one by Greenland, Iceland and lands yet unknown, the other by America, Selden assigned no precise outer limits, but insisted that, even when portions of the total western and northern oceans fell outside the full legal dominion of the King of England, this monarch nevertheless retained the largest rights. The Arctic, for example, was claimed by virtue of the navigation of the Muscovy Company to Archangel. In a later section of his work Selden explained methodically what he considered to be the historical basis for these gigantic claims, bringing forward the Romans, Britons, and Saxons in succession as masters of the northern seas, and emphasising among other matters that curiously misleading Roman title, Count of the Saxon shore. Lastly, came his array of "modern instances." Was there not the title given to the Lord High Admiral of England, which was *praefectus classium et marium nostrorum*, in contrast with a title which might be held to bestow jurisdiction alone over the fleet. Was this not clear proof of England's sovereignty over the British seas? Further, did not Queen Elizabeth refuse permission to Danes, Swedes, and men of the Hanseatic towns to carry corn to Spain, her enemy? And did not French fisherfolk before they caught sole for the table of Henry IV. ask British permission first, in default of which they rendered themselves liable to capture? Selden

CHAP. II.

for the British seas had perforce to make the all-important concession of the right to innocuous passage for merchants and travellers—that fatal bridge over which the hardiest defenders of maritime sovereignty were ultimately to be forced, destined to find on the other side no stopping place possible until they reached the hurly-burly and promiscuousness of "the freedom of the High Seas." Lest Selden's admission might be thought to imperil British sovereignty he made the obvious parallel of the use of a field for passage, pointing out that in both cases passage did not affect the owner's rights.

Though Selden's [(4)] book won not only the approval of English kings but also of the Long Parliament which ordered its translation, its greatest interest to the student of history is as a mirror in which to read the determination of the British seamen, the crown, and the nation to maintain a position which ministered alike to their interest and to their pride. Sully in his *Memoirs* recalls an almost incredible incident which took place as he was sailing to England on his mission to King James in 1603, an incident which deeply offended French *amour-propre*, and which was to furnish Cardinal Richelieu with the text for a warning to Louis XIII. as to the necessity for strengthening French naval power. De Vic, Vice-Admiral of France, soon after he had cast anchor in Dover roads (at which place he had landed part of the retinue of Sully), sailed thence on his return to Calais, and passing by the British royal ship on board of which Sully then was, he ordered his—that is the French—flag to be hoisted, and gave him a salute; soon after which the flag was again taken in. The English captain of the ship, wherein Sully was, seeing the French flag hoisted, commanded his men to fire on the Vice-Admiral of France, swearing he would suffer no flag to be seen in these seas but that of England. A gun was immediately fired upon De Vic's ship, who, having demanded the reason of it, prepared to defend himself. Sully complained of it to the English captain . . . who answered him only with rage and fury: he was therefore forced to submit, and made a sign to the Vice-Admiral to take in his flag, which he did. De Vic, thinking himself injured, demanded satisfaction of the English Admiral, who answered him that the King of England did not permit what the captain had presumed to do, desired that he would excuse his indiscretion, and promised that nothing like it should occur again. This reply appeased and quieted all parties. So runs the most comprehensible account of an incident which is thus minimised into a lamentable excess of zeal on the part of an English sea-captain to assert a right at a singularly inappropriate moment. That it was the inappropriate nature of the moment, rather than the singularity of the claim, which was in question is shown by the fact that in 1652 England and Holland went to war after the English government understood that the Dutch had refused to salute the British flag. When peace was made in 1654 the Dutch were compelled to undertake to salute the British flag in "British seas," an undertaking the renewal of which was insisted on in 1667 at the end of a second Anglo-Dutch war. The third Dutch war of 1672-1674 was precipitated all but deliberately by another incident which arose over a salute. A small British yacht, the *Merlin*, sailing by the Dutch Admiral's squadron, fired into the fleet because she had not been saluted. The Dutch sailors took up the attitude that, although the British right to a salute might be admissible, a petty British vessel could hardly demand it of a whole Dutch squadron. Downing, who was British minister at The Hague, envenomed the dispute by a demand for reparation. Nevertheless, at the peace of 1674 [(5)] the Dutch undertook to recognise as British all those seas between Cape Finisterre and Staten, and to order even whole squadrons to salute, "content," as Bynkershoek said, "with the use and fruit of the sea and making no difficulty of ceding to another's ambition that which was not useful to themselves." There promised to be similar difficulties with the French when Charles II. in 1662 ordered his ships to make the same claims from them as from the Dutch, but a famous letter of remonstrance from Louis XIV. through D'Estrades, his ambassador in England, which declared that those contemplating his humiliation could only see his actual naval forces, not his royal heart, appears to have induced greater caution. None the less it was still possible for William of Orange, very insecurely seated on the English throne, to win support by issuing in 1689 a proclamation mentioning among other matters Louis XIV.'s refusal to acknowledge the British position in the British seas. Even a century later the Anglo-Dutch treaty of 1784 repeated, as regards the right to a salute, the terms of that of 1674; while Cornwallis at the Peace of Amiens (1801-1802) refused to surrender it.

Although it is possible to find evidence that the French made claims, rather half-heartedly, in the Mediterranean, which were serious enough to be considered worthy of re-

CHAP. II. futation by Bynkershoek, the Baltic was the scene of hotter and more real contention. The Kings of Denmark [6] and Norway, especially in the course of that period during which they united the Swedish with their other dominions, were a standing menace to all those whose ships had business in that sea. In earlier days they aroused intense hostility on the part of the Hanseatic League, at a later time on the part of the Dutch confederation. The Danes were in a special position, for they were so situated as to control from the land the three channels of communication between the North Sea and the Baltic—the two Belts and the more important Sound, from which an immense revenue could be drawn through the instrumentality of a high toll charge. The seventeenth century produced other pretenders to the *dominium maris* in this quarter after the Danish Power, curtailed as it had already been by the defection of Sweden and overshadowed by Sweden's vigorous dynasty, committed the decisive error of an inept intervention in German affairs at the very moment at which the Imperial Power by land was at a most formidable height. Christian IV. was decisively defeated by Tilly and Wallenstein who acted in concert, was pursued through his territories on the mainland, and was driven to his islands. When the Imperial forces reached the Baltic coast the design was formed of wresting for the Emperor from the non-German Powers the maritime supremacy of the Baltic. To this end co-operation was to be sought from the German Hanseatic cities and their fleets. Kinship would justify an appeal to the Spanish monarchy for ships, and the price to be paid to both would be the closing of the Baltic to the Dutch, whose marine materials, timber, hemp, pitch, tar and sails, were imported from the coasts of that sea. The Imperial commander Wallenstein took the title, General of the Oceanic and Baltic Seas, an old Imperial title having been *rex oceani*, and with the help of the Emperor endeavoured to persuade the Hanseatic towns to fall in with his plan. They showed, however, great reluctance, and the scheme collapsed when Wallenstein's attempt to master the German Baltic coasts failed before Stralsund.

Stralsund's resistance gave time for the intervention of a new and even more formidable candidate for the *dominium maris*, the Swedish King Gustavus Adolphus. He broke into Germany like an avenging angel. The Swedish coasts were already in his control. Finland and Ingria had been wrested from Russia and Livonia, while much of the West Prussian coast had been torn from Poland. He showed himself capable of raising in 1621 a fleet of one hundred and fifty-eight vessels, in 1630 an army of seventy thousand men. His dramatic success changed his objective and destroyed his moderation. He passed beyond his earlier aim at establishing the Baltic coast as the outer ring of his country's defences. Extravagant phantasies changed his ambitions into German. According to Oxenstierna, his chancellor and collaborator, he formed the idea that he might become Emperor of Scandinavia with all the Baltic rulers as his vassals. After his death Sweden was still capable, under energetic kings, of amazing feats of arms. It was still within its power to seize further large portions of the Baltic coast-line from Germany and Denmark and to force its shipping free from Danish tolls, but the *dominium maris* had to be relinquished. A new opposition had arisen, and in the dangerous form once more of coalition. Part of the Swedish success in 1645 had been due to Dutch anger at the Danish Sound tolls. In 1645, however, the Danes agreed to reduce greatly the tolls on Dutch shipping, by something more than half the total. Charles x. of Sweden underestimated the effect of this concession, and in 1659, after humbling Denmark in the dust by requiring that the Sound should always be closed to fleets of nations hostile to his country, he found that the Dutch had joined the Danes against him. More important, however, was the fact that they were joined by France and England, which nations were nervous lest the entire resources of north-eastern Europe in shipbuilding materials and mining enterprise should be concentrated in the hands of Sweden, and lest their trade with Danzig and Russia should be interrupted. The formation of this alliance saved the independence of Denmark and proved a decisive event in the history of the Baltic. By the beginning of the eighteenth century the growth of the Prussian power and the Russian entry into Baltic politics had made any attempt at Swedish or Danish domination unreal. Later, of course, the four Baltic Powers were to contrive a considerable measure of amity in opposing to the British conception of the right of maritime belligerents, the principles of the Armed Neutralities. Denmark continued to exploit her geographical advantages by collecting the Sound dues till the middle of the nineteenth century. By that time the United States of America, protagonists for the Grotian maritime contention, had more than any other Power grown impatient at the manifest disproportion between the services of the Danes to navigation and the Danish charges. On this score alone could its Belt and Sound tolls be justified in the eyes of the government at Washington, which, in the absence of case proven, was threatening not obscurely to take action. The solution was reached peacefully. In 1857 the principal maritime Powers of Europe bought out the Danish rights as against themselves by a payment of £3,000,000. The United States paid in the following year £79,757; and other Powers followed later.

The history of the Black Sea furnishes some interesting features. In the seventeenth century it was a Turkish territorial sea, approached as it was through the narrow Dardanelles and Bosphorus and bordered entirely by Turkish territory. Peter the Great at the end of the century made an attempt to gain possession of coastal territory. He failed and Russia gained nothing in this direction, till the Treaty of Kutchuk-Kainardji in 1774 opened the way to its domination of the northern coasts, and further legally permitted Russian navigation. When Russian ambition came to embrace Constantinople and the Aegean a new phase of the Eastern question opened. Then it was that strangely enough a vicarious assertion of the *dominium maris*, or something very like it, was seen, for England was found repeatedly insisting on the survival of some part of the Turkish domination of the Black Sea, "that ancient rule of the Ottoman Empire," that both the sea and the straits giving access to it should be closed to the entry of non-Turkish vessels of war.

The colonial seas, the Atlantic, Pacific and Indian Oceans never knew in the early days of modern history a general right of innocuous passage to the ports on their shores. Colonial trade was strictly reserved to the nationals of the sovereign Power; and among the nationals there was often a particularised licence to special individuals or companies, just as the licence was sometimes restricted so as to include only particular ports. The origin of this system must be traced to certain phases of Castilian-Portuguese history. Under the inspiration, and with the support, of the royal house Portuguese navigators at the end of the fourteenth, and at the beginning of the fifteenth, century began to push down the West African coast. A little later, using the magnetic needle and the ancient astrolabe, adapted to serve the uses of a quadrant, they struck out into the open ocean, where they discovered, conquered and settled the Azores, the Madeiras and the Cape Verde Islands.(7) The Kings of

Portugal now deemed it prudent not to neglect elementary precautions to secure their position beyond all risk of easy challenge. Accordingly, they sued the Pope for confirmation of their exclusive rights to these discovered territories. The request was granted on the assumption that the Pope, as Vicar of Christ, had authority to dispose of heathen countries to princes who were Christian: nor was the assumption seriously challenged until the Spaniard Victoria, more than a century later, raised his voice in his famous university lecture, the *De Indis*. Meanwhile, however, Spanish adventurers from Biscay had as early as 1393 possessed themselves of one of the Canaries. Their lead had been spasmodically followed, in particular by Andalusians who had sailed from Seville: and the Crown of Castile completed the conquest by two expeditions fitted out, the one in 1480 and the other in 1495. If a serious clash was to be avoided an agreement was essential between Castile and Portugal. Accordingly, on the occasion of the signature of a treaty of peace between these countries in 1479, the Castilians recognised a Portuguese monopoly of traffic and commerce on the west coast of Africa in return for Portuguese recognition of the Castilian position in the Canaries.

A further adjustment became necessary after Columbus, sailing with the commission of the Castilian Crown, had discovered Hispaniola. Columbus on his return in 1493 was forced to run into the Tagus for shelter. He was hospitably received by the Portuguese king at Lisbon. The latter admirably suppressed his chagrin at having refused, where Castile had accepted, the original application of Columbus. He declined the advice of some courtiers who would have had Columbus quietly done to death. But he could not refrain from venting his anxiety lest the latest discoveries had been made in " the seas and boundaries of his seigneury of Guinea." On being assured by the explorer that his orders had been to sail due west from the Canaries the king expressed the hope that the Spaniards would always sail due west, in that to sail south would be to violate the rights of Portugal, a decidedly new claim. The Portuguese did ponder for a time a sudden attack upon the Spanish discoveries, but in the end opened negotiations with Castile. This Power anticipated a decision by negotiation, for it obtained Papal Bulls, dated 3rd and 4th May, which conferred upon it all territories " discovered or to be discovered" south and west of an imaginary line drawn from pole to pole one hundred leagues to the west of the Azores

CHAP. II. and Cape Verde Islands. At Tordesdillas, however, in June of the following year commissioners of the two Crowns finally signed an agreement stipulating a revision of the papal line, which, it was agreed, was unfair to the Portuguese. The new line was to run 370 leagues west of the Cape Verde Islands, beyond which boundary the Spaniards secured exclusive rights of navigation and discovery. Arrangements, never carried out, were agreed to for a meeting of experts with ships who should proceed to the stipulated line, carefully ascertain its longitude, and even erect a system of beacons if any land should fall under the meridian.[(8)] The Papal Bull had made no provision for the possibility of the Spaniards by sailing west reaching the same sea as that which the Portuguese attained by sailing east. This came about when the disappointed Portuguese Magellan, voyaging west under Castilian commission, did in 1521 reach the Philippines and the Moluccas. The Spaniards maintained themselves permanently in the former, but after long and involved cosmographical negotiations resigned their claims to the latter on a Portuguese payment of 850,000 ducats.

After this agreement exclusive areas at sea were marked out by the two countries, the Spaniards claiming the Gulf of Mexico and the Pacific between Mexico, Peru and the Philippines, the Portuguese, the Atlantic south of Morocco and the Indian Ocean. When Hawkins in the course of his first two voyages approached a Spanish city it was always with the statement on his lips that he had been driven off his course by storms. When he persisted in disregarding the prohibition of the Spaniards his fleet was battered by a Spanish flotilla, his enormous wealth was seized, his men were captured and he himself, with the young Drake, only just managed to escape. In 1580 Leicester and Hatton decided to take as their legal ground for their refusal to surrender the piratical, if lovable, Drake and his treasure to Spain, the fact that no Anglo-Spanish treaty provided for the prohibition of English trading and cruising in the South Seas, so that, although the Spanish king could work his will on the English seamen whom he captured, he had no case for extradition against those whom he did not. Spain made no decided objection to the French and British colonial establishments in North America founded at the opening of the seventeenth century, but showed much greater reluctance to recognise the foreign occupation of footholds in the Gulf of Mexico (the modern Caribbean). Yet it might have paid her to do so, for much damage was inflicted on her by buccaneers, acting under letters of marque from French and English governors in the West Indies. When Spanish recognition was won in 1670 for the British possession of Jamaica, in 1697 for the French possession of a portion of Hispaniola, the old doctrine of exclusive navigation had to yield place to the more tenable position of an exclusive mercantilism for the remaining possessions of Spain. Even here events forced a departure from the absolute exclusion of foreign commercial intercourse. By the close of the seventeenth century Spanish navigation had already reached a low ebb, and, in order to supply the Spanish colonies with negro slaves, a monopoly was granted to a Portuguese company. When Philip v., the grandson of Louis XIV., ascended the Spanish throne, this *Asiento* was transferred to the French Guinea Company and further trading privileges were accorded to French merchants. In 1713 the British South Sea Company became possessed of the *Asiento* under the Treaty of Utrecht, and there was added the additional, and highly prized, privilege of sending one ship of 500 tons to the annual fair at Cartagena. Under cover of this legal provision a most extensive illicit trade grew up which the revived Spanish monarchy of the early Bourbons endeavoured to suppress by the extensive use of the right of search. English agitation rose to a height with the story of Captain Jenkins' ear, and Walpole's pacific government was compelled to insist on a conference and to demand at that conference the total abolition of the Spanish right of search. It was in truth the last fragment of the Spanish maritime *dominium*. When Spain refused to surrender "a right which was its only defence against British buccaneers," war was declared amid the mob cries for "a free sea or war."

On the Portuguese (subjects of the King of Spain between 1580 and 1690) rested the burden of the defence of the *dominium* theory in Eastern waters. They were even more interested in its maintenance than the Spaniards because, apart from the captaincies of the Brazilian coast, they owned no very large land areas comparable in any way with the Spanish viceroyalties of Peru and Mexico. Their empire consisted of a continuous chain of fortified trading posts along the shore and in the islands all the way from North Africa to the Moluccas. This chain was vulnerable to attack from European marauders. The native rulers were always potential allies for these marauders, for they hated the supremacy of Portugal, which constrained their trade by the issue

CHAP. II.

of passports to their vessels and which kept them obedient by superiority of armament. The attack on the Portuguese position came when Philip, King of Spain and Portugal, in pursuance of his attempt to subdue his Dutch rebels forbade them the port of Lisbon whence they had been able to distribute over Northern and Eastern Europe the Portuguese importations from the East. After some attempts to open an independent way to the East by the north-eastern passage through the Arctic Ocean, Dutch companies of merchants, braving Portuguese hostility, began a trade with the East themselves. After despatching sixty-five ships in fifteen voyages between 1595 and 1601 the Dutch finally formed their United East India Company in 1602, with a capital of just eighteen times that of the English East India Company, which had been founded for similar purposes in 1600, while England too was at war with Spain and Portugal. The Portuguese exhausted themselves in their efforts to defeat the Dutch incursion, but gave up the attempt in 1661, retaining but a fragment of their Eastern empire. The Crown of Spain, which, while it represented Portuguese interests, had repeatedly made attractive offers to the Dutch, suggesting European compensation for a relinquishment of their East Indian policy, had at length resigned itself to the Dutch contentions at the Peace of Westphalia in 1648. The Portuguese had in analogous manner refused to admit the legal presence of the English in the East Indian seas. The consequence was a series of treaties between England and Spain, as representing Portugal, and these were often couched in most ambiguous terms. Thus in the peace treaties of 1604 and 1630 there were clauses permitting free commerce for the two nations "where commerce was held before the breaking out of the war." According to the Portuguese this excluded England altogether from the East Indian trade: according to the English the only places which could be governed by the implied prohibition were those in actual control of the Portuguese. Owing, however, to a common detestation of the Dutch who in 1623 finally succeeded in expelling the English from the Moluccas, with the barbarity of the judicial murders of Amboyna, hostilities between the Portuguese and English were rare. In 1642 a treaty confirmed a temporary understanding arrived at locally by the Portuguese viceroy and the English president, and plans were considered for a joint effort to expel the Dutch from Eastern seas. It was Cromwell who finally extorted formal acknowledgment of

British trading rights from the Portuguese; and a few years later as the dowry of his queen Charles II. obtained Bombay, the first territorial foothold in the Indian seas to be held by the British in sovereignty. Thenceforward the growth of British interests in the East forms a well-known story, which culminated in the establishment of the Indian Empire and the absorption of the Dutch colonies during the Napoleonic wars. Ceylon was retained but Java and Sumatra were returned. Far distant were those conditions in which the British had to struggle for their foothold in the East. For, as the world shrank, monopolistic pretensions broke down; they vanished not in obedience to any abstract theory, nor in the twinkling of an eye, but gradually, as nation after nation estimated the effort necessary for the maintenance of each particular claim and, openly or tacitly, threw up the sponge. The mercantilist theory and Navigation Acts made it possible for governments to do this without violence to economic orthodoxy. Vast tracts of land became open to exploration, and the spirit of adventure found an outlet upon continents quite as much as on the seas. The point of saturation, of a clash between the nations, in colonial enterprise was still far distant. The claim to an exclusive lordship of the seas became meaningless, but few, it may be suspected, who have traced the history of that claim will dogmatically assert for the doctrine of the Freedom of the Seas either a universal or a perpetual validity.(9)

The Present Limit of Territorial Waters.—Lawyers began early to discuss the extent from the land into the sea to which the authority of a prince or state might be deemed to reach. The weighty opinion of Bartolus of Saxoferrato (1313-1359) could be quoted as judging the distance to be one hundred miles or two days' journey. He clearly had in mind piracy as a danger against which a prince had a duty to provide protection, for he observed that, just as the head of a province ought to purge the territory of bad men by land, so ought he to do so on the sea. The hundred (Italian) miles there proposed was destined to make an appearance in later international discussion when Alexander I. issued his *ukase* of 1821 which forbade foreign vessels to approach for fishing purposes nearer than one hundred miles to his Alaskan shore. Baldus (1327-1400), another famous lawyer and a pupil of Bartolus, proposed sixty miles as the same limit, or one day's journey. Bodin (1530-1596) accepted the distance proposed by Baldus, but Gentilis (1552-1608) reverted to the choice of Bartolus, in-

CHAP. II.

creasing it even when the proximity of another state did not interfere *vel etiam ultra si non propinquant alteri provinciae.* The hundred-mile limit had been present in the mind of Salisbury, the minister of James I., when he sought to defend his master's fishery proclamation of 1609 against the objection of the Spaniards, for he declared that King James's authority extended " at least one hundred miles into the sea."

Meanwhile, Philip of Spain had already adopted a different limit, one which for its part was destined to obtain international currency. In an Admiralty code, designed for the Netherlands and issued in 1563, he had given instructions that no hostile act on account of war or any other cause should be done his subjects, allies, or travellers within sight of land or port. This coincided with an old Scottish fishing practice which claimed as exclusively Scottish all fishing which lay within a land-kenning or sea-line from which land could be descried from the foremast-top. This distance was defined as fourteen miles by King James VI., both in the proposed Treaty of Union with England (1604) and in a letter written in 1618 to Dudley Carleton at The Hague in which the Dutch states were requested to command their subjects to stay without that limit should they wish to fish. The King of Denmark and Norway in 1691 took up a similar position as regards the right to fish in those seas which he did not regard as exclusively his. This standard of measurement came to be called the *portée de vue*, and it entered into treaties and proclamations of neutrality during the eighteenth century. Thus in the treaty between Naples and the Porte, which was signed in 1740, it was agreed " that neither party would permit vessels to be pursued or molested on their coasts within a distance at which ships can discern land." Similarly, in a proclamation of neutrality by Tuscany and Venice in 1779, the *portée de vue* was taken as the limit beyond which belligerent vessels which left port were free to attack incoming ships, though, and this is interesting, the *portée de canon* marked the more general limit for ordinary hostilities.

The principle of *portée de canon* was generally adopted in the eighteenth century owing to the authority of Bynkershoek. Grotius had already in the *De Jure Belli et Pacis* indicated that the lord of the shore could assume authority over those who were upon an adjoining portion of the sea " as far as they were coercible from the land to no less a degree than if they had been upon the shore." Bynkershoek's opinion, therefore, did not fall strangely upon the ears of his contemporaries. They had been already familiarised with the gun-shot limit for such objects as the salute to fortifications which even Molloy, an extreme exponent of British rights, writing in 1676, allowed British ships to render within this distance. Neutrals, moreover, had long been wont to regard belligerent commerce as immune from attack while it was within the range of the guns of the forts of their nationals. In principle the extension was merely one from authority derived from armament actually *in situ* to authority derived from the certainty of quickly available armament.

The *portée de canon* was left undefined in terms of linear distance or is found so undefined in many proclamations of neutrality throughout the eighteenth century. Theorists, however, though often unwilling to accept the *portée de canon* as marking the limit of all dominion from the land, began to attempt to define it. The Spaniard Abreu y Bertodano (1746) preferred the hundred-mile limit for jurisdictional purposes, but was prepared to accept a two-league or six-mile limit for the conditions of neutrality. Valin, the Frenchman who in 1760 wrote a treatise on Louis XIV.'s *Ordonnance* of 1681, was hesitatingly prepared to define gun-shot as two leagues. G. F. de Martens in his *Précis of International Law* of 1789 allowed the lord of the shore three leagues as a normal limit to his authority, but did not exclude the possibility that the state might acquire an extension of authority. Even Azuni (1795), who defined the cannon-shot as three miles, obviously thought that the *portée de vue* made a better limit for belligerent activities off a neutral shore. Mr. Fulton in his learned book, *The Sovereignty of the Seas*, has fully described the extensive debate and the conflicting practice which centred round the problem of definition during the sixteenth, seventeenth and eighteenth centuries. Successively (but with continuous eddies of opinion), five alternative criteria for decision of the larger question of control had been put forward. The range of navigation, the range of vision, the range of cannon, the *Thalweg* or maritime mid-line, and the essential "leaping-off ground" control of which might be postulated for a proper enjoyment of the *fructus* of the sea, all these deserve examination in minuter treatment of the subject; and all, with the possible exception of the fourth, the *Thalweg* theory, have left their mark somewhere in subsequent practice. Although there is no necessary connection between a claim to terri-

CHAP. II. torial waters and the historic claim of certain countries to sovereignty over whole seas or part of them, none the less shrinkage of these latter claims, a process which has been described in the previous section, did undoubtedly produce an atmosphere conducive to the substitution of exact definition for the more vague pretensions put forward by some nations to the control of their home waters. The inclination of Bynkershoek towards a view based on the *portée de canon* was very powerful but by no means unchallenged. It was easy also for convenience' sake to fix upon the lowest unit of maritime measurement—the league. There need be no surprise that in course of time writers should tend to identify the two. The first to do so was, according to Fulton, the Italian Galiani, who in 1782 published a vindication of his master's, the King of Sicily's, adherence to the Russian Armed Neutrality. It is this which gives an interest to the instructions given by Washington in 1793 to the executive officers of the United States that they should consider for the time being the limit of the nation's territorial waters to be a line " one sea league or three geographical miles " from the shore. Still more important in the history of the Law of Nations are the decisions of Lord Stowell. The way for these had been prepared. The English Admiralty Court in the seventeenth century had declined to regard as lawful belligerent operations carried out in bodies of water lying within lines, drawn from headland to headland, traditionally regarded as national and known as the King's Chambers. The claim to the King's Chambers, however, had been allowed gradually to lapse, was deliberately omitted in the later proclamations of King Charles II., and had become by the Napoleonic wars merely a memory. " Long before the end of the eighteenth century," writes Fulton, " it was well established that a vessel, captured by one belligerent from another belligerent in the port of a neutral state or within the actual reach of cannon, was not good prize. The next step was to give effect to the same principle, whether the place was within the range of a fort or not. The decisions which introduced the three-mile limit into English jurisprudence were those of Sir William Scott (afterwards Lord Stowell)." The classic cases of the *Twee Gebroeders* and the *Anna* are in point. The first arose from the seizure in 1799 by the boats of a British man-of-war, in the Groningen-Watt, between East Friesland and the island of Borkum, of certain vessels which it was believed were bound from Hamburg to Amsterdam, a place at that time blockaded by the British. It was claimed by the King of Prussia that the capture had been made within the territorial waters of his state. There were two cases of the *Twee Gebroeders*, the first (Alberts, master) was tried on 29th July 1800, the second (Northolt, master) was tried on 27th November 1801. Lord Stowell said :— CHAP. II.

> "The capturing vessel was lying within the limits to which neutral immunity is usually conceded. She was lying in the eastern branch of the Ems, within what may, I think, be considered as a distance of three miles, at most, from East Friesland. An exact measurement can not easily be obtained; but in a case of this nature, in which the Court would not willingly act with an unfavourable minuteness towards a neutral state, it will be disposed to calculate the distance very liberally; and more especially as the spot in question is a sand covered with water only on the flow of the tide, but immediately connected with the land of East Friesland, and when dry, may be considered as making part of it. I am of opinion, that the ship was lying within those limits in which all direct hostile operations are by the law of nations forbidden to be exercised."

In deciding the second case, in which circumstances were much the same, Lord Stowell said that "in the sea, out of the reach of cannon-shot universal use is presumed." He made no reference to three miles as an equivalent distance. A few years later, in 1805, in deciding the case of the *Anna*, which was captured at the mouth of the Mississippi by a British privateer, and in which the question of the violation of American waters had to be considered, he said, quoting Bynkershoek :—

> "We all know that the rule of law on this subject is *terrae dominium finitur ubi finitur armorum vis*; and since the introduction of fire-arms, that distance has usually been recognised to be about three miles from shore." *

This decision of Lord Stowell profoundly influenced the opinion of subsequent governments. It is not quite true, however, to regard it as having finally disposed of all conflicting theories. In Great Britain the Territorial Waters Jurisdiction Act of 1878 (41 & 42 Vict. c. 73) gives general expression to his contentions, though, unlike Lord Stowell,

* We have throughout used Mr. Fulton's words in describing the decisions of Lord Stowell and their significance.

CHAP. II.

it measures the three-mile limit from the coast-line at low-water mark, and makes claims as to jurisdiction over foreign ships which pass through territorial waters such as the general practice of nations has not yet countenanced. The adoption of one league as equivalent to the range of a cannon-shot had reference at first solely to questions of neutrality, *e.g.* the capture of prizes. It was soon extended to other purposes. Thus under the Anglo-American Treaty of 1818 American fisherfolk were forbidden to operate within three miles of all but certain specified portions of the British North American coast. This extension of the principle has not gone unchallenged, partly by Russia, partly by the Scandinavian nations, and partly by those of the Iberian Peninsula. The view of Bynkershoek and the view of Stowell appear moreover far less easily reconcilable in the light of the development of modern long-range cannon. It is well to remember that no fewer than four of the maritime states of Europe make no pretence to regard the three-mile limit as sacrosanct, and that experts in all countries have shown dissatisfaction with it as a solution of the question which it was designed to meet.[10] At the same time, despite the prophecies of some it has survived the greatest war of recent times as normal Anglo-American practice. The convention of 1924 between Great Britain and the United States, which gave the latter country, in its desire to enforce its "Liquor Laws," the right to visit British ships within a much extended limit, is quite definitely admitted to be a treaty-based deviation from the general rule, the validity of which is unaffected. The limit fixed in the Anglo-American Convention of 30th January 1924 shows a return to older and less rigid principles of measurement than that of accurately defined distance. The United States may seize vessels attempting the breach of its liquor legislation at any point between its coast and the sea-line which they could reach by an hour's navigation. The United States, too, did not receive this concession as a right but as a privilege purchased by the grant of a privilege in return. The "proper" limit of territorial writers, expressly asserted to be three miles, was safeguarded perhaps more by this necessity of making a counter-concession than by the mention of three miles as the "proper" limit.

NOTES

(1) Professor Magoffin published in 1916 a parallel Latin and English edition under the auspices of the Carnegie Endowment for International Peace. It appears that the young and brilliant Grotius had been employed by the Dutch East India Company to justify the capture of a Portuguese galleon made in 1602 by one of their ships. This warlike act against the Portuguese was little to the taste of some of the members of the Company, and Grotius was apparently asked to expound the law of prize. This he did in a work which did not fully see the light until 1868 in the *De Jure Praedae*. The twelfth chapter, however, was published separately in 1608 as the *Mare Liberum*. It should be noted that the first British reply to the Dutchman was not from the Englishman Selden, but from the Scotsman Welwood, professor of civil law at Aberdeen. In 1613 he produced a small volume entitled an *Abridgement of all the Sea-Lawes*, and in 1615 the Latin work *De Dominio Maris, Juribusque ad Dominium praecipue Spectantibus Assertia Brevis et Methodica*.

(2) See Corpus Christi College, Cambridge, MS. No. 370.7.

(3) Bynkershoek (1673-1743) published the treatise *De Dominio Maris* in 1702, while still under thirty years of age. Though it was the work of a young man it provided a clear-sighted and moderate approach to the subject different alike from the legalism of Selden and the sanguine expansion of the young Grotius. It was Bynkershoek's *via media* which was in the end to prevail. Still stronger traces of Bynkershoek's caution and conservatism may be found in his *Quaestiones Juris Publici* of 1737.

(4) Selden's book was not published to the world till 1635, but was already written in some shape by 1617 or 1618. James I., who had Selden's first draft in 1618, did not publish it, apparently because he feared to provoke a controversy with Denmark, which had extensive claims of its own in the North Atlantic. Charles I. was a different man from his father, and his publication of Selden's work in 1635 was the fortification by theory of a maritime enterprise whose scope was intended to be extensive.

(5) Complete accounts of the circumstances surrounding the Anglo-Dutch maritime disputes in the seventeenth century are given in the *Sovereignty of the Sea* by Thomas Wemyss Fulton (pp. 378-516). Cap. xi., for example, in which the peace negotiations of 1653 and 1654 are recounted, will impress the most sceptical reader with the reality of the pretensions to maritime sovereignty. The British negotiators proposed to use their maritime sovereignty to tax the Dutch fisheries, and even to limit the size of Dutch war-fleets. The final treaty contained the clause which provided for a salute in Art. xiii.: "Item quod naves et navigia dictarum Foederatarum Provinciarum tam bellica et ad hostium vim propulsandam instructa, quam alia, quae alicui e navibus bellicis hujus Reipublicae in maribus Britannicis obviam dederint, vexillum suum e mali vertice detrahent et supremum velum demittent, eo modo, quo ullis retro temporibus, sub quocunque anteriori regimine, unquam observatam fuit."

(6) The Danes, besides their Baltic claims, put forward pretensions in the North Atlantic, where the waters between Norway on the one

CHAP. II. hand and the Shetland Islands, Iceland, Greenland, and Spitsbergen on the other, were claimed for the Norwegian crown. This desert of waters lacked the importance of traffic lanes such as the Channel or the Sound ; but claims to its sovereignty were made to justify the attempt to impose restrictions upon cod-fishing off Iceland and taxation upon whaling off Greenland or Spitsbergen. The seventeenth century was marked not only by the Dutch assertion of freedom of navigation, but also by the extension of their fisheries to new areas of water.

(7) The life of Prince Henry the Navigator and the history of the expeditions sent out by him, almost as private adventures, deserve attention.

(8) Some curious information with respect to the Spanish-Portuguese negotiations will be found in the chapters dealing with Columbus in Prescott's *Ferdinand and Isabella*.

(9) Little help could be found for this section in works of the type of Hautefeuille and Cussy. The penetrating observations of Ortolan were more useful.

(10) Mr. T. W. Fulton's *The Sovereignty of the Sea* (Blackwood) is a mine of information. It ends with a strong protest against regarding the "three-mile limit" as settled doctrine.

CHAPTER III

INTERCOURSE: IN PEACE

EQUILIBRIUM. INTERVENTION. DIPLOMATIC INTERCOURSE: DIPLOMATIC OFFICIALS—CLASSES OF DIPLOMATIC AGENTS—CONSULS—SPREAD OF THE PRACTICE OF LEGATION—SPECIAL DIPLOMATIC PRIVILEGES—NEGOTIATION OF TREATIES AND AGREEMENTS.

CHAP. III.

Equilibrium (1).—It is to Italy of the fifteenth century that the student of International Law must look for the adoption of the Balance of Power as a political principle for the guidance of states in the conduct of their foreign relations. Here, as elsewhere, it is possible to find the prototype in earlier ages. Polybius, for example, describes the balance maintained in the Sicilian Wars by Hiero of Syracuse for his own preservation between the Carthaginians and the Romans; and it is but one instance of an equilibrium which must have been struck repeatedly and almost unconsciously by monarchs in a similar position. A policy directed to that end is a recurrent theme in the history of Judah and Israel. Yet there were several causes which combined to make *cinquecento* Italy the natural ground for the modern appearance of the phenomenon. In the first place the Italian Powers, though wealthy judged by contemporary standards, were not territorially large; and the process of concentrating authority in a single centre was more rapidly accomplished than was the case elsewhere. When once the internal sovereignty of the various states had been asserted, the communities, gathered in the relatively modest area of the Italian mainland, were bound to be brought into close and constant contact. It was otherwise with the non-Italian communities of Europe. The establishment of full internal sovereignty was a process slower and far more laborious: the governments, preoccupied with establishing their unquestioned authority within their boundaries and separated from their neighbours by vast land distances, were only secondarily conscious of questions in the sphere of external relations, except when their attention was directly called thereto by

CHAP. III.

frontier disputes or by the machinations of their disaffected subjects at foreign courts. Here, then, no need would be felt for the institution of permanent embassies. If during the fifteenth century even the greater Powers could still manage their relations with their fellows through the despatch of special *ad hoc* missions when the need arose, the Italian states for their part found that they needed much more constant representation at one another's capital cities, alike for political as for commercial transactions. Especially with the five greater states of Italy, Milan, Venice, Florence, the Papacy and Naples, this close and constant contact led to the establishment of an equilibrium of power and influence so delicately poised that the utmost watchfulness was felt to be necessary (especially against the Papacy and Venice, more securely placed and so more restless than the others), lest some sudden accession of force to one, or more, of their number should throw the whole of the peninsula into disorder and threaten the territory or the independence of the remaining states. The most astute Italian of his day, the great Lorenzo de' Medici of Florence, had already converted the aim at balance from a rule of thumb into a political postulate. Guicciardini in his *History of Italy* says of Lorenzo that he " understood with the Florentines that it was necessary to oppose the aggrandisement of the principal Powers of Italy, and to maintain an exact equilibrium among them, as much for the safety of the Republic of Florence as for the guarantee of his own authority."

There were moral reasons also for the emergence in Italy of the doctrine of a Balance of Power. The scepticism, the more extensive sophistication, of Italy had, at least partially, helped to prepare it for a principle which based the security of its states on " real " sanctions, such as those apparently promised by a policy of Equilibrium, rather than on treaties, of reciprocal guarantee or of security, which experience seemed to prove rather lulled states into a foolish and unjustified tranquillity than served for protection in the moment of danger. It was only in the Italy of this day that the Machiavellian mistrust of treaties could be elevated into a theory: and the Machiavellian counsels of " the Prince," which profoundly affected contemporary international practice, further promoted a movement which aimed at security by means of a constant watchfulness over the equilibrium of states. At the very end of the fifteenth century the delicate equilibrium in Italy was upset, not after all by the Papacy or Venice, but by Milan. The Milanese ruler *de facto* called in the French and helped to launch them against Naples, the Power which had professed the greatest solicitude for the Milanese duke *de jure*. When thereupon the Spaniards, the English, the Empire and most of the Italian Powers were called in to retrieve Italy from the effects of the French irruption, that close contact of the leading European states was accomplished which was the prerequisite of a permanent doctrine of equilibrium, no longer confined to Italy but extended to the European field.

At this stage it is well to have before the eyes the characteristic portions of the Machiavellian doctrine. Machiavelli asserted that an unvarying adherence to treaty stipulations would be unwise for the prince, because he could not be certain that the other parties would stand by their undertaking after it had ceased to be convenient to them to do so. Accordingly, " a well-advised prince should not fulfil his promises when the fulfilment would be hurtful, and when the reasons which induced him to promise are no longer present." This is a frank statement of the view which holds that every treaty is signed under the tacit reservation, *rebus sic stantibus*. Machiavelli continued in condonement that this would not be good had all men been created honest, but " as they are wicked, and as they assuredly would not keep their word to you, why should you keep your word to them ? " All down the ages, in their outlook upon foreign policy, statesmen have ranged themselves beneath the standard either of Grotius or Machiavelli. This is not the place in which to enlarge on the antipathy between them. Rather it is appropriate to point out that, however negative the teaching of Machiavelli may seem in its denial of moral progress in the human race, it was, like the teaching of Hobbes, whom he resembles, constructive in a sense. By locating and describing the well-springs of human action it forced upon the attention of his generation the necessity for a theory with which to meet the changing circumstances in which they found themselves. By depicting these circumstances with pitiless intelligence it did force men into the adoption of methods based on a principle where, till then, they had proved themselves empiricists. It does not detract from this feat to show that his analysis was partial, or that he ignored motives which in his day, or shortly after, were manifestly operative. His contentions have eternal validity even if they may need supplement : and an age which conceived of a Balance of Power as productive of stability in the changes and chances of a dissolving Empire

CHAP. III.

was intellectually better equipped than one without that vision. Later ages, more richly equipped, have sneered at the "balance doctrine." The best of contemporary opinion welcomed it. To disparage men like Machiavelli, who prepared for it by pioneer work, is to ignore the fact that the attainment of wisdom is by stages.

From whatever combination of causes the doctrine of the Balance of Power became firmly fixed in European policy, Henry VIII. of England, proud of his power to turn the scale in the contentions between the Emperor and the King of France, adopted as his device the vaunting motto *cui adhaereo praeest*. Later, Francis Bacon remarked upon the jealousy with which these Powers watched each other's slightest movement. Henry IV. of France, in the years immediately before his death, was without doubt evolving a scheme for a joint attack with other Powers upon the Austro-Spanish Hapsburgs, whose might threatened the security and freedom of the rest of Europe. In this he hoped to rely upon the co-operation of Elizabeth and James I. Richelieu gathered together against a *bloc* consisting of Spain, Austria and Bavaria an alliance sufficiently strong to shake off the old constitution of Europe, which had allowed the Hapsburgs too much power. As a result France, after Westphalia, could claim the merit of having secured to the greater part of Europe the possibility of living free from fear of Imperial or Spanish domination. Twenty years later the whole structure of the European balance had to be altered to meet the situation produced by the growth in power of a France freed at last from the final echoes of religious war, internal unrest, and the antiquated feudalism of the Fronde. The extent to which Louis XIV. dominated the imagination of his contemporaries and of immediate posterity has been described but cannot be too often emphasised. There is pregnancy in the wit who said that it was not so much a case in those days of speaking of the king as one might speak of God, as of speaking about God as one might speak about the king. Thus Louis XIV. grasped at nothing less than the control of Europe. A claim to annex the Spanish Netherlands, based on an alleged right of his wife, foreshadowed even greater claims and brought into being, under the aegis of Sir William Temple, an alliance between England, Holland, and Sweden in 1667. The alliance of 1667 was followed by the further European groupings of 1672, the League of The Hague; of 1686, the League of Augsburg; of 1689, "the Grand

Alliance"; and that of 1702. The names of William of Orange and of Marlborough recall negotiations and campaigns which, stretched over forty-seven years, have as their common feature united opposition to the ambition of Louis which seemed in turn to threaten the liberty of Holland, the Empire, Spain, and Protestant England. By this time the Balance of Power had become a prime maxim of the public policy of Europe. When England resolved on a serious constitutional innovation in taking the royal army under parliamentary control, the justification for this step, as outlined in the preamble to the Mutiny Act, ran as follows :— CHAP. III.

> "Whereas it is adjudged necessary by His Majesty and the present Parliament that a body of Forces should be continued for the safety of the United Kingdom, the defence of the possessions of His Majesty's Crown and the preservation of the Balance of Power in Europe."

In the interests of this same balance, France, England, and Holland twice took it upon themselves to regulate the succession to the Spanish dominions and organised a partition of that which the Spanish nation and king so fervently desired to keep united. No great international war was ever fought so directly on the basis of a political principle—so it would seem—as the War of the Spanish Succession (1700-1714), which arose out of the breakdown of these Partition plans: and no peace ever enshrined more fundamentally a political principle than that Peace of Utrecht which ended the major part of these hostilities. The treaty clause justifying the renunciation by French princes of succession to the Spanish throne and by the Spanish king of that to the French throne ran :—

> "Since, indeed, the war, to which an end has happily been set by God in this treaty, was in the beginning undertaken and was afterwards waged so long and with such supreme efforts, immense expenditure and almost infinite loss of life in order to avoid the peril overhanging the Liberty and the Security of Europe from the too close union of France and Spain: accordingly for the end that all care and suspicions may be removed from the minds of men and that the Peace and Tranquillity of the Christian World may be ordered and stabilised in a just Balance of Power (which is the best and most solid foundation of mutual friendship and a lasting general concord) the Catholic and most Christian kings have wished to make provision by fit precautions that the kingdoms of Spain and France should never come under one rule or be united."

CHAP. III.

It is a singular commentary upon the limitation of human intelligence directly it be exclusively dominated by a single principle that the historian can not but reflect that the Crowns of Spain and France, even apart from the prohibition of the Utrecht Treaty, would in all likelihood never have been united; and that the very candidate to the Spanish Succession, who was supported by all the Powers which expressed their concern for the balance, did in fact repeat in his person that junction of the Imperial, Austrian, and Spanish titles which had proved so dangerous to "European liberties" in the person of Charles v.

Even accepting the position of those international lawyers who would refuse to allow the Balance of Power, like the Monroe Doctrine, treatment in any formal treatise upon International Law, these doctrines would still find entrance through the gateway of the chapters which deal with Intervention. Truth to tell, it has never been the narrower lawyer who has been the best exponent of these semi-political doctrines. In the seventeenth century by far the most representative exposition of the political and legal implications of the "balance doctrine" was made by an ecclesiastic, director of conscience and tutor to the young Duke of Burgundy, then heir to the French throne, the saintly Fénelon. As an example of the noblest judgment of the day upon a much abused doctrine the two following quotations are significant:—

> "Whatever destroys the just balance or tends to set up a universal monarchy can be no other than unjust, however it may be founded on the written laws of a particular country, which can never be placed in opposition to the sovereign and universal law of Nature for the common security and Liberty engraven in the hearts of all the Nations of the World."
>
> "When a Power is grown to such a pitch that all its neighbours are hardly a match for it, they have an undoubted right to unite for the restraining of the increase which, were it suffered to proceed, would become too great to be opposed in its attempts on the common Liberty. But that such confederacies for restraining the growing power of a state may be lawful the danger from it must be real and pressing; the League defensive or no further offensive than a just and necessary defence requires; and such bounds must be set to it as it may not entirely destroy that Power which it was formed only to limit and moderate."

Fénelon, who was born six years after Grotius died and who died nearly two hundred years after the death of

Machiavelli, has in this passage incorporated something of the outlook of both of these his predecessors. He admits the motive of self-interest in the policy of states, but, even allowing it to be the main or only motive, he is not prepared to rest content that the resultant condition should be one of international anarchy.

The inadequacy of the Balance of Power as a diplomatic conception became definitely clearer when a somewhat novel turn was given to its application in the later eighteenth century. The advancing military power of Russia was threatening the territories of both Turkey and Poland. Austria and Prussia formed thereupon a so-called "German system" and demanded compensation in the event of any increase of Russian territory, in order that their relative influence in the tale of nations might suffer no diminution. Accord was finally established by the complete extinction of the badly organised Polish state and its absorption by the three eastern monarchies, in a proportion resting upon the principle of balance. No country has been more fortunate in its historians than Poland, and the doctrine of the Balance of Power has never shaken itself free from the odium which has attached to this the most dramatic example of its operation. The doctrine has had a clinging smell in history. That Napoleon III. had recourse to it has blinded the opinion of the world to much that was altruistic, and the reverse of narrow nationalism, in his foreign politics. It was enough that when his ambitious neighbours, the kingdoms of Sardinia and Prussia, advanced their respective pretensions to unite Italy and Germany, he took his stand on this principle, more popular and more easily defended before than after the French revolutionary philosophy had made dogmas of international policy fashionable which took no count of nations. Greater certitude, greater promptitude, less hesitation in the face of inevitable risk, might have brought him some Rhenish districts or even the coveted Belgium. It was not failure, as often, which brought him condemnation, and the same methods had won Nice and Savoy for France; he had placed his whole reliance during a great transaction in the nineteenth century on a formula which no longer retained the authoritative charm which it had had for the eighteenth. He had made an over-simple analysis of the public opinion of his age, and the judgment of that age has dealt with him over hardly in return. The Balance of Power, faced from the beginning of the last century by that more fruitful conception

CHAP. III. —the Concert of the Powers, maintained some sway none the less over the minds of statesmen up to the outbreak of the war in 1914 and has still a place in international relations. Lord Haldane, for example, is on record as having told the German ambassador to the Court of St. James, the Prince Lichnowsky, that "the theory of the Balance of Power is an axiom of British foreign policy and has resulted in our *rapprochement* with France and Russia." A more recent instance of a demand for compensation, out of regard for the maintenance of balance, is to be found in the Italian request to Austria in the year 1915. Even if Austrian troops were established, precariously indeed, in various points of Serbia, Russian armies at the same time stood deep in Austrian territory. Yet, to compensate Italy for her worsened position in the Adriatic, extravagant demands were made for compensation in the Trentino, Venetia Giulia and at Trieste. So far had mankind moved from the lofty conceptions of the Abbé Fénelon.

Although some of the ablest lawyers of every generation have acquiesced in the view that the doctrine of the Balance of Power is a necessity, if the whole fabric of international rules is to be safeguarded, others have been quick to join statesmen and moralists in pointing out its dangers. It has been termed dangerous, because in effect it jeopardises the independence of states, and because it can be quoted to justify a general right of all the states mutually to interfere in each other's affairs. "If the equilibrium were ever realised nothing could be more terrible than the enslavement of every state with regard to its neighbours—it would be necessary to recognise in every state the right to intervene in the domestic affairs of the others—it would be better indeed to have a universal monarchy, for to be subject to several states at the same time would be much harder than to be dependent on the one." (2) The collapsible nature of the equilibrium and the pretext which it affords to states for a meddlesome intervention in the affairs, or the actual government, of their brother states, lie at the back of all attacks upon the system. The Concert system and the system of the League of Nations have arisen to secure for the peace and independence of states a security less perilous than an ever-changing balance could have afforded. These do not avoid a tendency to intervention, but it is a tendency better safeguarded. To that subject, or rather to some aspects of it, for it arises to prominence again later in this treatise, it is due that attention should be directed. CHAP. III.

Intervention.(3)—History provides types of intervention other than that alleged as necessary for the maintenance of the Balance of Power. Intervention for religious reasons was frequent in the sixteenth and the seventeenth century. Though the restoration of the equilibrium was in part a motive, religious considerations were present when Spain on various occasions intervened in France during the long Guise drama. Out of his duty to the Church a Spaniard appears among our English monarchs. To save the faith of England we made demonstrations in the Netherlands, and, when it appeared that the Catholic League, or the Austrian Hapsburgs, would carry all before them in Germany, it seemed to Protestants that, in answer to their petitions, the Lord God aroused himself and brought down the Danish and the Swedish armies from the north. By faith, or rather for the faith, Oliver Cromwell made his effort on behalf of the Duke of Savoy's Protestant Vaudois. It does not alter the case that, since he could bring no direct pressure on the Duke, the more immediately effective influence of the French Cardinal Mazarin was procured and proved successful. Although religious intervention practically ceased in Western Europe after the Treaty of Westphalia, in Eastern Europe, where the writ of Westphalia never ran and religion remained a more important criterion than state allegiance, it was destined to endure as a very real factor. The Tsaritsa Catharine's first intervention in Poland was, ostensibly at least, produced by concern for the position of those Polish subjects who were Orthodox in faith. Her Turkish policy was largely affected by her claim to exercise a guardianship over the Greek Orthodox subjects of the Sultan, a claim which, conducted from Kutchuk-Kainardji through Unkiar-Skelessi, led to the war in the Crimea of 1855.

With the advent of the nineteenth century the religious interventions of previous centuries tended to broaden into what may be called humanitarian interventions; and the Russo-Turkish wars of 1827-1828 and 1877-1878 were fought on the broad issue of the right of the Christian subjects of the Porte to practical independence and advanced political institutions. The nineteenth century also saw the inauguration of collective humanitarian intervention. Throughout the century the Concert of Europe was compelled, partly by Russian exigency, partly by the desire to forestall Russian

CHAP. III. territorial expansion, but partly also by its own humanitarian sentiment, to intervene repeatedly in the affairs of the Turkish Empire. The first intervention was marked by the battle of Navarino and the protocol which turned Greece into an independent kingdom: the last was the Macedonian administrative intervention between the years 1903 and 1908,[4] which came to an end with the constitutional revolution in Turkey in 1908.

Other types of intervention have been discussed by the theoretical writers. Thus Bluntschli was concerned to establish the right of intervention by a third Power, if two sets of combatants in a civil war were violating the traditional war usages; and the Belgian Arntz made a similar claim in the case of two analogous departures from conventional behaviour: the first, when a state lying across a route common to other Powers should refuse communication by railway or telegraph to its neighbours; the second, when a government, turning tyrant, should suddenly relapse into mediaeval notions and forms of justice. A practical example of a limited form of modern humanitarian intervention may be found in the official English criticism of the treatment of its native subjects by the Congo Free State Administration. In the years from 1903 to 1905 not only did Lord Lansdowne entrust his consular representative, Roger Casement, with a special mission of inquiry and publish his report, but he made persistent efforts to interest the co-signatories of the Berlin Act in the alleged conduct of King Leopold's authorities.

The older theorists discussed humanitarian intervention of a sort, but contrived almost always to think of abuses in political terms. Grotius, for instance, refused to allow oppressed subjects to take up arms for themselves, but permitted a prince to intervene for them, making the remarkable observation in justification, "quod uni non licet alteri pro eodem licere potest." Pufendorff (1632-1694) was even more cautious, and finally from excess of caution involved himself in a contradiction. "I could not," he wrote, "approve the statement of the famous Bacon, Chancellor of England, that a custom like that which the Africans possess of sacrificing men to their false divinities, and eating their flesh, is a sufficient cause for a declaration of war upon such peoples and prescribed by Nature herself." Yet he lamely ended his argument thus: "The surest way in my opinion is to say that this [intervention] is only permissible where tyranny has mounted to such a height that the subjects can legitimately take up arms." Wolf (1679-1754), who in one sense marks the transition between the seventeenth and the eighteenth century, is important, for it is he who took up for the first time the later widespread attitude, that of an absolute proscription of intervention. "To intervene," he wrote, "in the internal affairs of others, in whatever way it may be, is to oppose the natural liberty of nations, a liberty which exists independently of the will of other nations. States which behave in this way do nothing but employ the right of the strongest." Vattel (1714-1767) began by condemning intervention, but forthwith proceeded to allow a large latitude for foreign intervention in the case of constitutional disputes between a prince and his people. Vattel's doctrine was old-fashioned even for his day. De Martens (1756-1821) brought a keener instinct to bear upon problems which were to be distended by the events of the revolution of 1789 and the monarchical counter-attack. In different editions he takes different views, but he undoubtedly visualised, while he sometimes deprecated, the new "legitimist" interventions.

Vattel had of course not yet envisaged the possibility that the people should attack the constitutional prerogative of a prince. The constitutional struggles of England in the seventeenth century were probably as remote from the ideas of Neuchâtel as were the writings of the purely philosophical authorities. As a true Neuchâtelois at any rate he was still thinking in the traditional terms of the violation by a prince of a fundamental charter. "But if the Prince," he declared, "attacking the fundamental laws gives his people a legitimate cause of resistance, and, if the tyranny become unsupportable, raises the nation to rebellion, every foreign Power is entitled to succour an oppressed people which demands its aid." This much right to intervention was still not enough for Vattel. He must needs add, "further, whenever matters come to a civil war, foreign Powers may assist whichever of the two sides seems to them to have the right." This was dangerous teaching. It had already brought the untold horrors of the second half of the Thirty Years' War upon Germany, which had received the benefits of Swedish and French intervention for the maintenance of its liberties. The eighteenth century was, as has been pointed out above, to see it used similarly by Catharine of Russia in her successful effort to prevent the Poles securing for their country an administration fitter for the times than their elective monarchy, their rebellious and undisciplined confederations and the

CHAP. III.

liberum veto of a single noble. Intervention killed old Poland. It was always based, however, on the fundamental laws, the constitution and the privileges of the republic. Sometimes invoked by the king, sometimes by a pro-Russian confederation of nobles, it ended the independence of the country first of all and then destroyed the country after three partitions.

As has been said, G. F. de Martens restated Vattel's views and adapted them to the European system of his day with a pertinent reminder of their possible implications. He is an author less studied now than formerly, but it is not too much to say that an intelligent understanding of the Congress period is impossible apart from a knowledge of his teaching. Let only one passage be taken for example :—

> " When a nation be divided in opinion and in will, it is impossible to refuse a foreign nation (1) the right to offer its good offices, (2) to lend all kinds of help to that of the two parties which is authorised to ask it and has effectively claimed it, (3) to intervene *motu proprio* in such a dispute when a right, specially and individually acquired, or care for self preservation, authorises it thereto . . . so that there is hardly a civil war anywhere in which foreign powers do not find a pretext for taking part when they think fit, without thinking that they are departing thereby from the independence and free will of nations." (5)

Martens' text could provide the Powers of the Holy Alliance with a legal defence for the political interventions which they exercised, or threatened to exercise, in the numerous constitutional disputes which took place between sovereigns and their peoples in the Europe of the early nineteenth century. (6) The interventions in Italy of 1822, 1831 and 1848-1849, that in Spain of 1823, or of Russia in Hungary in 1849, are the most noteworthy. Metternich could infect the allied Powers with the fear that the defeat of absolutism and the triumph of constitutionalism in any one place would by contagion affect others (as was indeed proved in 1848), and that in the public excitement thrones would be shaken and Jacobinism reintroduced. So far as Italy was concerned he could usually have quoted in his favour the violation of some treaty clause, but it is significant that he rarely failed to take the wider ground, that of a general duty of self-preservation. The " liberal " Powers in opposition developed their challenge to a general right of intervention for the preservation of existing institutions. It was from their line of conduct that the doctrine of non-intervention took its familiar form. To-day as a principle it seems clear-cut, unshakable. Behind it, however, there is a hinterland in which good, but forgotten, lawyers move, men who might not have understood it and who certainly would not have believed in it, because the conditions which make it both understandable and cogent had not yet arisen.

The discussion of intervention has of recent years left the familiar fields of political, religious and humanitarian intervention. Nations, powerful commercially and in their trading activities, have during the last century asserted their right to intervene in other states, subject to revolutionary movements, in order to protect the lives and property of their nationals. Conversely, states which dread the possibility of such intervention have united in defence of the doctrine of non-intervention. Acute differences on this subject disturbed the harmony of the Pan-American Conference of 1928, and form a standing menace to the existence of the Pan-American Union.

DIPLOMATIC INTERCOURSE

Diplomatic Officials.—The origin of diplomatic intercourse is older than recorded history. The tablets of Tel-el-Amarna indicate that it existed among the monarchies of the Ancient World. Between the Greek city states it had reached a high point of development. The Greeks were great travellers and traders: they were also keen politicians. Commercial questions therefore became questions of state, and the ubiquitous struggle between oligarchy, democracy and tyranny caused the citizens of one city to fix their eyes upon the next one, for its fate might influence their own. What would now be called a diplomatic code of some complexity appears to have been developed, but the development was due more to internal custom or domestic regulation than to systematisation and understanding among the states. While there were no permanently resident embassies after the modern fashion, a careful examination of Greek texts has enabled a painstaking scholar to distinguish between four types of diplomatic officers: heralds (Κήρυκες), ambassadors proper (Πρέσβεις), heads of embassies ('Αρχιπρεσβευταί), and plenipotentiaries ('Αυτοκράτορες), which last did not need to refer back to their principals specified points of

CHAP. III. negotiation.[7] A distinction in style and form seems to have distinguished between (*a*) religious missions sent out by a state (Θεωροί), (*b*) missions sent to demand redress (Ἔκδικοι), and (*c*) embassies to a congress (Σύνεδροι). State envoys proceeding on legitimate business, even where they lacked specific guarantee of protection from hostility, were immune from violence by general understanding.

Republican Rome, too, had a municipal code of diplomatic practice which in its case was closely intertwined with its traditional state religion and its war customs. After an insult had been offered Rome, or a wrong inflicted on it, several of the twenty sacred heralds, members of the College of Fecials, proceeded to demand reparation. If they failed in their mission they tore their garments, returned to Rome and made their report to the Senate. Then debate arose, and if war were decided, a second deputation of fecials was nominated upon whom was placed the symbolic duty of discharging a javelin into the enemy camp. This part of the procedure had obvious difficulties, and, after resorting to the fiction of performing it at an enemy camp in Rome, the fecials finally adopted an appropriate ceremony at the temple of Bellona. The fecials also had religious functions at the conclusion of a peace. It was the oath taken by the chief fecial which sanctified a treaty entered into with, or by, the Roman people.

So much is worth repeating of the methods of the Greeks and Romans, not because any feature of the modern diplomatic system is traceable to them, unless it be the sacrosanctity of envoys, but because they illustrate some of the conditions necessary if an elaborate diplomatic practice were to be developed. For this does postulate a group of powerful and independent states, free externally from grave danger of barbarian conquest and internally secure from the establishment of any universal monarchy. It postulates also a similarity of religion, institutions and language, together with political and commercial relations of the closest kind. Only in such an environment could arise and flourish such characteristically modern diplomatic institutions as the resident embassy and the international conference. The Roman Empire, a universal dominion with a barbarian fringe, had not such an environment.

The necessity of intercourse between the different Powers of the Dark Ages produced diplomatic missions of a kind, which, whenever there was sufficient learning in their midst, took Roman form and titles. When negotiations of any delicacy were undertaken, such as required record, it was almost inevitable that they should in the earlier days be in the hands of officials trained in the Roman tradition, and at a later date in the hands of the only educated class to be found, the men of the Church. The relations of the Roman Emperor at Byzantium with the rulers of the Burgundians, the Franks, the Lombards, the Visigoths, the Ostrogoths and Vandals probably furnished the barbarian chieftains with useful lessons in the conduct of intercourse among themselves. These lessons would have been reinforced by the Bishop of Rome, who had one time or another to approach most of the barbarian kings, were it for the propagation of the Faith, to obtain mercy for their Roman subjects, or for the maintenance of Church discipline or doctrine. When Charlemagne united a considerable portion of Western Europe under him to form a state, which brought to men's minds the image of the Empire, he sent embassies to Rome, Constantinople, Spain and the Arabs of the Eastern Caliphate. The act appears to have taken place without any effort of special improvisation. For permanent missions there was no call.

The rapid rise of the Papacy to a position of European control and the subordination to it of the local Churches of Western Christendom forced the Popes, even those most other-worldly by inclination, to take up control of the most important institution in this. Ecclesiastics, often members of the College of Cardinals, which elected the Pope, were sent to represent him personally for definite, or indefinite, periods to the various national Churches. These representatives exercised great power and sometimes exacted heavy and unpopular ecclesiastical taxation. They are the ancestors of the modern legates *a latere* and legates *missi*, of nuncios and internuncios. Reciprocally to the growth of this practice lay rulers began to find it indispensable to have representation of their interests in the Curia at Rome. Church dignitaries and Church institutions became great landowners and Churchmen came to play a vital part in the internal life of kingdoms, either as prelates or as the clerical estate, which possessed peculiar ecclesiastical privileges. Princes found it essential to influence the nomination of their subjects to high positions in their lands and to ask, at least temporarily, for the abatement of certain clerical privileges, such as exemption from taxation. They learned by experience that a fairly satisfactory *modus vivendi* could be established by agreement with

CHAP. III. Rome, and the necessity for constant negotiation over a wide variety of subjects led to the eventual establishment of permanent missions in that city. These last do not as a matter of fact antedate the permanent missions at other centres, but they had been preceded by a system in which the efforts of *ad hoc* missions had been supplemented by the activities of resident Roman clerics, often of exalted rank. These national protectors were recognised at Rome as representing the different national and national-ecclesiastical interests and they laid suitable communications before the Pope and the Sacred College. It must be remembered that even in the second half of the seventeenth century the struggle between the Papacy and Louis XIV. opened with a dispute concerning the diplomatic privileges of one of the cardinals, protectors of the French nation.

Venice, ruled by a peculiarly methodical and far-sighted oligarchy and possessed of vast commercial interests in a number of relatively distant lands, was the first state to pay marked attention to the creation of an orderly diplomatic service. Representation of all but a permanent character had become obligatory at Constantinople long before the close of the fifteenth century. In the sixteenth century the republic had accredited ambassadors to the Pope, the Emperor and to the Kings of France and Spain. It had envoys in Switzerland, at Naples, Turin, Milan and in London. Careful accounts were sent home by the Venetian representatives,[(8)] accounts which were preserved in the archives and have proved a peculiarly important source of material for the writers of sixteenth-century history. The diplomatic art was highly developed in other parts of Italy also. Machiavelli,[(9)] while employed by that department of the Florentine republic which dealt with war and foreign relations, was constantly despatched on temporary foreign missions, in which he appears to have exercised patience and skill. Twenty-three times was he thus employed and was involved in four journeys to the King of France, two to the Pope and at least one to the Emperor. Temporary envoys of this itinerant type, men usually of no exalted birth and of but moderate status at home, must have found their missions anything but a sinecure. A man sent in this way was cut off from the home authorities by the primitive nature of communications so that a sudden turn of affairs might completely invalidate the instructions given before his departure. Such conditions demanded decentralisation, but so far from finding his authority thereby increased, he could rely upon no general recognition of an envoy's powers: and indeed few such were credited who had not a definite and limited piece of business to transact and full powers in good form to carry it through. There was little place as yet for what was later to become the principal work of diplomacy—the creation of a favourable atmosphere and the subtle task of gradual, yet persistent, suggestion. Indeed envoys without obvious and definite missions might, even though accredited, come to be regarded with considerable hostility as little better than authorised spies. Finally, funds provided at the opening of a mission were apt to become exhausted, and an envoy might be left for long in a state of want and despondency, either because at home there were no funds to spare for him or because chaotic conditions in the government prevented attention to his needs. Machiavelli, for example, seems to have derived but little profit from his many missions, and indeed mentions the fact that he had to consume his private substance in the course of his employment. There is history behind the insistence upon the possession of a private income which, till recently, confronted the would-be attaché in the diplomatic service.

Close on the heels of Venice the then great monarchies of Europe, France and Spain established continuous representation at the leading political centres. The Austrian Hapsburgs were backward in so doing. They were poorer; and a considerable danger of losing their non-Austrian dominions should they not rivet their attention at home, gave them more reason to look eastward to the Turk than to play high politics in Western Europe. England under Henry VIII. paid marked attention to foreign affairs. Wolsey, Pace, the Wingfields, Gardiner, Foxe, Bishop Tunstall, Thomas More, Cranmer, Bonner, the Earl of Wiltshire and the Duke of Suffolk are all among the envoys and ambassadors who were despatched on different occasions for special negotiations. The nearest of these missions to approach the modern conception of a resident embassy was perhaps that of Robert Wingfield,[10] who was at one period, between 1511 and 1517, almost continuously with the Emperor Maximilian. He served also in the Netherlands between 1522 and 1526. As regards finance he presents a too often repeated spectacle. He wrote to appeal for money in 1512: he begged for it once more in 1514, asking to be recalled from Vienna. In 1517 he flatly refused to accompany Maximilian back to Germany.

CHAP. III. He was unpaid and his servants refused to remain. Later, he implored the King and Wolsey to pay a merchant who had lent him money on his word as an ambassador.

Queen Elizabeth developed the system which she had inherited. She preserved almost continuous representation at Paris where she kept an ambassador, who, however, was often absent from his post, leaving his work to be done by an agent. The most famous of these agents was Sir Thomas Edmondes, whose despatches, preserved among the Stowe manuscripts at the British Museum, throw a flood of light on the activities of Henry IV. throughout the Wars of Religion and after. At one period he wrote almost daily despatches to Lord Burleigh. His position was not merely vicarious as his appointment was independently made. As Edmondes during a brilliant career became successively secretary to the queen for the French tongue, a clerk of the Council, ambassador, first to the Archduke at Brussels then to the French king at Paris, comptroller of the royal household and a Privy Councillor, it is possible to regard the post of agent as a post *de carrière* in the Tudor Civil Service, still quite unsystematic, which was available for young men of merit among the gentle rather than the noble families. Altogether more professional than any ambassador, long residence abroad might make an agent indispensable. Knowing what to look for, and where to look for it, their posts afforded them unrivalled opportunities for every experience which a diplomatist covets. Only the pomp and exalted station of a full ambassador was denied to them, their work was wholly similar. Perhaps the minor diplomatic posts at the smaller courts in Germany before the war furnish a modern, if inexact, analogy. Financially they were no better off than their superiors. In 1593 Edmondes wrote that he had not "the means to put a good garment on my back to appear in honest company." Beside these acknowledged agents there were continuously secret agents who were practically spies. As far as Madrid, the Netherlands, Germany and Rome were concerned Queen Elizabeth got very much of her information from these. An attempt to establish an embassy at Madrid on a "diet" of £3, 6s. 8d. a day broke down in 1568 owing to religious difficulties between the English ambassador and the Spanish authorities. The truth is that the vast increase of foreign business was almost necessarily producing a modification in the machinery of state. This was the case in all countries. In England from the fifteenth century onward the office of Secretary of State had been growing in importance. In 1433 indeed a second secretary had been appointed, a foretaste of that bifurcation, due three centuries later, between the Home Office and the Foreign Office. The fitful appointment of two secretaries ceased in the reign of James I. when the practice became permanent. In 1640 one secretary was charged with all business to be transacted with Spain, Italy and Flanders; the other took charge of French, German, Dutch and Baltic matters: the one with Roman Catholic, the other with Protestant, issues on his hands. In France four secretaries of state were in office for a time sharing between them home and foreign business. Later there arose specialisation and the foreign department was divided on a territorial basis and placed under a single secretary of state. In Spain a constitutional reform of 1480 established a Council of State as the authority for the public forces and for foreign affairs, but Charles V. and his son Philip II., who together controlled Spain's destinies for eighty years, worked, the one with a secret committee, the other with secretaries of state, and deprived it of all real initiative. And the history of other countries differs hardly sufficiently for comment. The personal element of course always counted, and the Prime Minister or Minister President on the one hand, the active favourite upon the other, might always, and may always, supersede the normal and official chief.

Envoys and ambassadors were to be found throughout the sixteenth and even later centuries in what seem to-day curiously unorthodox situations, and it is recidivism, rather than mere abnormality, which should have been brought in accusation against the recent behaviour of the Soviet republic's emissaries to other countries. The lavish promises, the actual expenditure, on behalf of their king, made by French agents in preparation for the German Imperial election of 1519, have their parallel in the efforts made by French and Austrian agents at the time of elections to the Crown of Poland. Monluc, the French representative at Warsaw in 1573, was successful in securing the crown for his prince, the Duke of Anjou, after the expenditure of vast sums of money had helped him to form and to inspire a "praetorian" band of Masovian noble electors prepared to stick at nothing, not even civil war. In 1575 the Austrian mission and the papal nuncio spared no effort to secure a Hapsburg election. The speeches made to the Polish electoral diets of the sixteenth century by the French, the

CHAP. III. Hapsburg, the Swedish, the Russian and the Transylvanian ambassadors would make strange reading for the *corps diplomatique* at Warsaw in 1928. No less alien to the spirit of modern diplomatic institutions were the functions undertaken by the ambassadors of the European states at the meetings of the Council of Trent. The French representatives used strong, and even scandalous, language in exposing ecclesiastical abuses; and, in opposition to their Imperial and Spanish *confrères*, who by manipulation of clerical forces endeavoured to carry or to block decisions, organised anti-Spanish and anti-Italian forces for analogous purposes. Where a government was thought unfriendly, or likely to become so, ambassadors were often instructed to encourage the elements of opposition. In Elizabethan England the Spanish delegate to the Court of St. James assumed the leadership of the pro-Catholic party and permitted the organisation of rebellion and assassination plots. For this the Spanish envoy, D'Espes, was expelled in 1572, to be followed by the full ambassador, Mendoza, in 1584. Even in the eighteenth century diplomatic history has numerous cases to show in which the fomentation of resistance, and even of revolt, was still an ambassadorial occupation in countries whose government was chaotic, unpopular or unauthoritative. Beside well-known instances in Sweden, Poland and Russia, a Spanish ambassador plotted against the regency of Orleans in France in 1715 and a Swedish envoy against the Hanoverian dynasty of England in 1717. The action which these incidents did as a rule provoke should be taken as evidence not so much that a contrary convention existed as that the conception of correct procedure was the fruit of gradual growth.

The distribution of money or pensions to influential persons constituted a familiar means whereby a diplomatic mission might interfere in affairs which were properly domestic. Under an absolute regime the Crown's immediate advisers or the royal favourites were obvious objects for approach. Where effective authority was distributed between the Crown and a system of Estates, as in seventeenth-century England or eighteenth-century Sweden, the possibility of ambassadorial finesse in the distribution of money became even greater. In England in 1675 home politics were troubled by the rivalry between the Crown and a powerful faction, and the restoration of unity could only have been sought on the basis of a foreign policy which aimed at France. In these circumstances the French ambassador, Ruvigny, entered into close relations with the opposition leaders and stimulated their attacks upon the king. This did not prevent a simultaneous offer to the king of a pension of £100,000 should he dissolve the Parliament, action which would undoubtedly have postponed the likelihood of Anglo-French hostilities. And Ruvigny's Dutch and Spanish colleagues, representing states at war with France, spent money to promote among the "Parliament men" bad blood which might be profitable. The meeting of the Swedish Diet in 1769 saw similar attempts upon the part of foreign envoys to control the course of Sweden's policy. The French ambassador, de Modène, provided the "Hat" party with six million livres on the condition that the constitution should be altered: while the Russian ambassador, Osterman, spent £11,500 in a single attempt to carry, as he wished it, an election to the marshalship of the Diet. In autocratic Russia there may be found a parallel to these intrigues. Prior to the Russian break with Austria in 1744 Frederick the Great instructed Mardefeld, his ambassador at St. Petersburg, to spend up to five hundred thousand crowns in bribing the pro-Austrian vice-chancellor.

Before turning to another aspect of the question it is well to recount two incidents without parallel in European diplomatic annals—instances of the murder of envoys by officials of foreign governments, who had been authorised at least to seize their papers by violence. In 1541 Francis I. of France had accredited Rincon to the Sultan of Turkey and Fregoso to the republic of Venice. It was common knowledge that they were to endeavour to engineer a combined attack on the dominions of the Emperor Charles V. Near Pavia, in the Duchy of Milan, which belonged to Charles V., they were murdered by Spanish soldiers who acted, so it was suspected, with the knowledge of the Spanish governor, and in the hope of securing the papers of the envoy. A much later incident of the same type occurred in Rastatt in 1799. Bonnier, Roberjot and de Bry were French plenipotentiaries bound for an international congress convened at Rastatt in 1797 for the purpose of redistributing territory within the Empire. War broke out, however, in 1799 between the Emperor and the French. On 8th April the Emperor, who was indignant that the smaller German Powers continued to bargain with the French, declared with the appropriate formalities the dissolution of the conference. The French delegates protested, held their ground, and persisted in their German negotiations. Austrian troops arrived at Rastatt and requested the French delegates to leave. On their refusal, and after an interval of several days, the Austrian commander, who was eager for their papers and who wished to punish them for their insolence, ordered them to depart within twenty-four hours, declining to furnish them with a safe-conduct. Almost as soon as the Frenchmen most unwillingly set out—for it was in direct contradiction to their orders from the Directory—they were treacherously stopped by Austrian hussars, Bonnier and Roberjot were killed, de Bry, left for dead, escaped only with his life, and all the papers of the mission were confiscated.

Classes of Diplomatic Agents.—All text-books on the Law of Nations describe the process by which a *cadre* of officials unsystematically, if at all, organised became divided into a number of recognised grades. During the seventeenth century diplomatic officers were or tended to be classed in two ranks. The ambassadors were of the higher order, enjoyed greater social prestige, and, being appointed from among persons of distinguished birth in their own country, carried much greater weight in the capital in which they discharged their duties. The expense of maintaining an embassy was considerable. Governments, therefore, became reluctant to send, and individuals to undertake, ambassadorial missions unless there were compelling reasons for, or overwhelming advantages to be gained by, so doing. Accordingly, a more modest class of diplomatic officer came to be nominated. He was styled variously Envoy, Minister Resident, and a little later Minister Plenipotentiary. In 1651, for example, the Great Elector of Brandenburg-Prussia had accredited ministers resident to Paris, Cologne, Stockholm, Brussels, The Hague and even Vienna. The practice seems to have indicated a certain modesty, or absence of pretension, in the accrediting authority. It is noteworthy that the United States of America till 1893, up to what may be termed her emergence as a conscious World Power, declined to nominate, even to the most important states, any representative of higher rank than envoy.

There was, then, a greater lack of uniformity in the practice of earlier centuries than some writers have been ready to admit. The precise system of terminology is not important for the present purpose, since the admitted confusion, and the survival of old difficulties as to precedence, combined to produce situations of acerbity and to demand a remedy. The Congress of Vienna, as is well known, resolved to provide it. The committee, which sat to discuss the question of precedency, both among sovereigns and their diplomatic representatives, failed to reach agreement so far as that of the sovereigns was concerned. This was unfortunate, for a decision in this matter would have lightened their secondary task. They divided the diplomats however into three classes :— CHAP. III.

(*a*) Ambassadors, legates and nuncios.
(*b*) Ministers plenipotentiary, envoys, etc.
(*c*) Chargés d'affaires accredited to foreign ministers.

Precedence among envoys of the same rank was fixed by seniority, except in the case of such nuncios as enjoyed traditional precedence at certain courts. Ministers from such Powers as allowed one another the *alternat* were to decide by lot the order in which an instrument embracing several Powers was to be signed. At the Congress of Aix-la-Chapelle a further class was provided for, that of ministers resident. These ranked below ministers plenipotentiary but above the chargés d'affaires.

Consuls.—The student of mediaeval literature, in particular that class of it which records the experience of travellers to the Holy Land, will not infrequently encounter a mysterious official known as consul. The Consular Service as it is known in modern countries is the creation of the nineteenth century, yet the consuls of to-day have their prototype in the consuls maintained over eight hundred years ago in the Levant, Constantinople, Palestine, Syria and Egypt by Genoa, Pisa, Florence, Venice and possibly other communities. The habit of appointing consuls dates from the end of the eleventh century, and its origin has been described by antiquarians as follows. The towns of Southern France, of Provence and Languedoc, were about the year A.D. 1000 ruled by magistrates—as were some towns in mediaeval Italy—to whom the title " consuls " was applied. In the twelfth century the word *consulat* appears to represent the body, or college, of these magistrates, among whom the functions of a certain number seem to have been specialised into the settlement of disputes concerning trade by land or sea (*consules mercatorum, consules artis maris*). Now it was of common occurrence in the Middle Ages that foreigners, whether near or far comers, lived by themselves in special quarters of the city in which

CHAP. III. they settled: in "reservations," to choose a word with modern associations. Moreover the citizens' law, being personal rather than territorial in its operation, was hardly supposed to run in matters which concerned men of alien birth and speech. Primitive notions would have reckoned it too good for them, and would have preferred that foreigners should "stew in their own juice." That was an idea doomed to early disappearance, but, in disappearing, a trace was left behind. This conception, added to the practical convenience which arose from the existence of officials who could judge the strange community and represent it, led to the appointment by the early commercial and seafaring states of *consules in partibus ultramarinis*. It was an arrangement welcomed on all sides, by citizens, by foreigners, and not least by travellers, for these consuls are found acting to strange pilgrims in very much the fashion of the modern travel agencies as guide, philosopher, and friend conjointly. The practice grew after Provence and Languedoc had lost their identity and the habits of the Italian towns had ceased to interest their larger neighbours. The French had consuls in the thirteenth century; curiously enough, until quite a late date they were appointed in Mediterranean countries for the most part. The Hanseatic cities never took kindly to the idea, and a consular system was left to be one of the first boons which a United Germany, in the shape of the North German Confederation, conferred on the German states in 1867. So far as England is concerned, "consuls" were indeed appointed in Turkey from 1675, but the modern organisation of the Consular Service dates from 1825.

The guns of Admiral Narborough's squadron in 1675-1676 were employed to extort in Tripoli the conditions essential for the exercise of consular activity. The fascinating Henry Teonge gives in his diary the two following treaty clauses:—

> "That the English Consull now or any time hereafter living in Tripolys shall be there at all time with entyre freedom and safety of his person and estate: and shall be permitted to chuse his own draggarman and broaker, and freely to goe on board any ship in the road as often and when he pleaseth; and to have liberty of the country; and that he shall be allowed a place to pray in; and that no man shall injure him in word or deede."

And again:—

> "That the English consull here shall have full liberty to hoyst the English flagg at his pleasure on his house-topp."

CHAP. III.

The Spread of the Practice of Legation, especially in the Far East.—Legation and the reception of ambassadors date back to an early age. Permanent embassies unknown to the ancients could, according to Grotius, be declined for sufficient reason. The tide, as he wrote, was turning against any tendency to do so. In 1614 Holland and Sweden bound themselves by treaty to the exchange of ministers; and in the same year a similar treaty was made by Holland with the German principalities of Brandenburg, Baden, Württemberg, Anhalt and Ottingen. These were models for the other Powers; and, though the practice in many cases rests on no discoverable treaty regulation, it was a common act to find stipulations, providing for the establishment of resident representatives, in the texts of treaties with Oriental states, as in those made by Christian states with Turkey.

Determined hostility to the reception and despatch of ambassadors, especially of the resident kind, was first encountered in the Far East, in China, Japan, Korea and Siam. The British and British Indian authorities endeavoured to open relations with the Chinese Empire through the Macartney Mission of 1793, the Amherst Mission of 1816, and the Napier Mission of 1833-1834, but never with success. To Western eyes it seemed monstrous that in a world of expanding commerce any one country should form as it were an isolated vacuum. Lord Amherst's mission, therefore, was designed to put the East India Company's China trade "on a secure, solid, equitable footing, free from the capricious, arbitrary aggressions of the local authorities and under the protection of the Emperor [of China] and the sanction of regulations to be drawn up by himself." On the other hand, the stiffness of etiquette in the court of Imperial China, the Chinese disdain of foreigners as barbarian inferiors, the Chinese mistrust of their representatives as spies, presented innumerable obstacles not merely to the establishment of friendly relations upon a permanent basis between the Emperor and the King or any other Western potentate, but even to such tentative steps towards that end as were exemplified in the three missions mentioned above. Lord Macartney was indeed received in person by the Emperor after some "kotow" difficulties, but the Chinese resolutely refused a treaty. Lord Amherst refused the "kotow" and never saw the Emperor. Lord Napier accomplished nothing, for he had aroused the hostility of the Viceroy of Canton. The relation between the British merchants at Canton and the Chinese authorities

CHAP. III.

became increasingly strained when the Imperial Commissioner, undertaking a campaign for the suppression of the opium trade, received the surrender of very large stocks from the British merchants and yet persisted with a policy which virtually blockaded them in their factories. The British official in charge of relations with the Chinese officials at Canton, despite a real attempt at conciliation, proved helpless to effect an improvement and finally withdrew with the merchants to Hong-Kong. As a result of his representations to the British government armed operations were undertaken on a considerable scale with the definite intention of putting Anglo-Chinese commercial dealings upon a satisfactory footing. The Treaty of Nanking which in 1842 closed the operations, and which was followed shortly afterwards by Sino-French and Sino-American agreements of almost exactly the same bearing, opened the modern history of China. It provided, amongst other points, for correspondence between Chinese mandarins and British officials of the same rank on a footing of equality. The British superintendent and the consuls, however, still found that the Chinese officials paid inadequate attention to their representations or complaints.

The intractable nature of the Imperial commissioner at Canton, and the bad terms which, owing to his disregard of foreign interests, had arisen between him and the Governor of Hong-Kong, led to a naval demonstration against the town in 1856. When the news reached London Lord Palmerston, who had long been desirous of insisting on the establishment of regular diplomatic relations between London and Peking, determined that establishment should form part of the eventual peace. A clause in the instructions to Lord Elgin when he went out as British plenipotentiary in 1857 was to obtain

> "the assent of the Chinese government to the residence at Peking, or to the occasional visit to that capital, at the option of the British government, of a minister duly accredited by the Queen to the Emperor of China, and the recognition of the right of the British plenipotentiary and Chief Superintendent of Trade to communicate directly in writing with the high officers at the Chinese capital, and to send in communications by messengers of his own selection, such arrangements affording the best means of ensuring the due execution of existing treaties, and of preventing misunderstanding."

After armed operations, carried out jointly by England and France, high Chinese officials were sent to Tientsin to negotiate treaties with the English, French, Russian and American plenipotentiaries. Four treaties were signed in June 1858, in each of which provision was made for diplomatic relations.

There was still to be trouble however. The Chinese were determined that envoys when in Peking, even temporarily, should submit to Chinese ceremonial. The English and French governments were equally resolute that they would rather undertake renewed armed action than allow the hitherto unsatisfactory basis for Sino-European relations to persist. The Chinese were again defeated in 1860, and British, French and Russian Legations were established in Peking in 1861, an American Legation in 1862, and those of other Powers at later dates. It was at last obtained that the representations and complaints of European Powers should be carried to the central authority at Peking, the Imperial capital. Frequently enough the control of the Imperial officials at the centre failed to make itself effective with the local mandarins, but no one can contemplate the subsequent history of business transacted between China and the West without being conscious of the immense advantage gained. That it was not to be permanent was due to causes which could not have been foreseen in the middle of the nineteenth century, and arose out of the action of forces which were operative not in China alone but in the whole of Asia.

The history of the establishment of foreign missions in Japan is not such a troubled one. By a treaty negotiated more or less unwillingly with Commodore Perry in 1854 the Japanese allowed the establishment of a consul-general from the United States at Shimoda. Mr. Townsend Harris arrived as Consul-General in 1856 and began to press for leave to visit the Tycoon at Yedo in order to communicate a letter to him from the President. The Tycoon, or hereditary acting ruler, was erroneously thought by the Americans to be the Emperor himself. In 1857 he gave audience to Mr. Harris at Yedo, the modern Tokio. Mr. Harris argued to such good effect that it was resolved that a treaty should be made with him, who at least had come unarmed, rather than that by a negative attitude at the present juncture armed Western intervention should be provoked, and a more unfavourable treaty should befall the Japanese. The treaty was ready at the beginning of the following year. It made provision for diplomatic representation at Yedo. It was duly signed by

CHAP. III.

the Tycoon, despite the objections of the Mikado, who was moved by religious scruples and a dread of the revival of Christianity in the Empire. This treaty formed the model for the treaties which were made shortly afterwards by many of the other Powers. None the less the position of foreign diplomats was not really assured until the Mikado's ratification of the treaties was secured by the demonstration of an armed squadron in November 1865. In 1868 the Mikado, who was definitely setting about the modernisation of Japan, publicly took up the position that the ostracism of foreigners as barbarians must be abandoned, and invited the foreign diplomats to an audience, an invitation accepted by the English, French and Dutch ministers.

To Siam the East India Company appointed an envoy extraordinary as early as 1822, even before a treaty had been negotiated to establish a basis for his relations with the British authorities. A second envoy came in 1826 and an American arrived in 1833; but both British and American attempts to negotiate treaties, which it was hoped might be comprehensive, met with a rebuff. Not till the English mission in 1855 under Bowring were difficulties cleared out of the way. As a result a British consulate was established at Bangkok.

Korea was opened up to diplomatic intercourse by the Japanese. As the result of an incident in 1875 the Korean government consented to sign a treaty, which *inter alia* stipulated for the presence of a Japanese minister at the Court of Korea. The principal Western Powers followed this example some years later, and by 1884 a number of diplomatic and consular agents were in residence in Seoul.

Diplomatic Privileges.—The privileges nowadays accorded to diplomatic representatives, together with a discussion of the conditions and the limits under which it is usually considered proper to exercise them, have been repeatedly set out in the various authoritative treatises on International Law. Diplomatic immunity, as it was regarded in the sixteenth century, is most compendiously summed up in three general phrases: *droit de chapelle, droit de quartier,* and *droit de l'hôtel.* The principles upon which these ideas rest can furnish with little alteration a guide to diplomats in the exercise of their functions under modern conditions.

As Roman Catholicism, once the religion of the Western World, was replaced in certain countries by other forms of obedience—Lutheran, Calvinistic, Anglican and others—

liberty in the choice of adequate representatives could only be secured to states by a mutual exemption of the diplomatic corps from an obligation of conformity to the state religion. This practice grew slowly and was not established till men had begun to think as naturally in political as they did in religious terms, for until this stage was reached the conception of mutual representation between sovereign states could not become clear-cut. The ambassador of England accredited to Madrid early in the reign of Queen Elizabeth, a certain Dr. Marr, had serious difficulties with the Spanish authorities. He had been indiscreet, it is true, in speaking sharply of the Pope, and, the matter having been reported to the Spanish government, he had first been excluded from the court, then banished to a country village. There the local authorities appear to have compelled the embassy staff to attend Catholic worship. The English queen made a sharp demand for an immediate and full concession of religious liberty, and the incident closed with the withdrawal of the mission. It had still to be understood that in all forms of human intercourse, not least in the Law of Nations, privileges may arise for reasons of convenience, but are never free from corresponding obligations. A long series of cases stretching from Elizabethan days to the present was needed to make this clear, and to establish a tradition in which law and common sense should be found to coincide. Even, however, where the full *droit de chapelle* was conceded there was always the possibility that it might be extended so as to become an abuse. The seventeenth century saw many instances in which an ambassadorial chapel, to the disgust of the government, was openly frequented by recusants from a national and prescribed religion.[(11)] Two of the last occasions on which there was some difference as to the *droit de chapelle* are mentioned by Holtzendorff as occurring in the years 1781 and 1846 respectively. In the former year the Emperor Joseph, having conceded liberty of private meeting to the Protestants in Vienna, endeavoured to procure the closing of the ambassadorial chapels which, he contended, had thereafter lost their *raison d'être.* In the latter year the Pope declined to allow Italian services in the Prussian legation chapel.

The *franchise du quartier*, a diplomatic institution for which a pedigree of considerable antiquity has been established, gave rise to a serious dispute toward the end of the seventeenth century. More extravagant claims to diplomatic immunity

CHAP. III. seem to have been tolerated at Rome, Madrid and Frankfort than at any other centres. At Rome the missions claimed not merely the usual *franchise de l'hôtel* but, among other claims, the right to exclude the papal police from the whole vicinity of the ambassadorial residence. At Rome in 1660 the Cardinal d'Este, *comprotecteur des affaires de France* and therefore diplomatically privileged, quarrelled with the Vatican over the arrest of a trader who lived near the cardinal's quarters. The dispute, which was most undignified, ended in a brawl between the cardinal's men and those of the chief of police, Don Mario Chigi, who was brother of the Pope. The cardinal had to apologise, and the dispute might never have taken place but that the cardinal was hypersensitive as to his position, because he was engaged at the time in an independent series of family intrigues for the Dukes of Modena and Parma. Indeed to the modern eye it seems absurd that ambassadors should be privileged to prevent the arrest of persons residing in the vicinity of their embassy. It is not without significance that it was in Rome that this franchise was most hotly pressed for and most hotly resisted. In Rome diplomats of every grade trod one upon another, so large was the diplomatic *corps* and so incessant were the changes in its composition. Moreover, the dual character of the papal power produced a unique complication alike for the negotiator as for the authority on etiquette. The secularising policy of the Renaissance Papacy becomes more than ever comprehensible in the age of the Enlightened Despots. In the great monarchies religion tended to be reduced to a department of the state and prelates to become court chaplains. Such a position can be challenged in two ways. The way of Hildebrand was not suited to the eighteenth century: to a governing class, which thought in terms of the public law of Europe, it was more impressive, because more realistic, than any Hildebrandine claim, that Louis XIV. in dealing with the Pope was dealing with a sovereign prince, with such a sovereign, moreover, as had acted as mediator at the Congress of Münster. Louis XIV. came into violent conflict with the Pope when his ambassador, the famous Duc de Créqui, who had been urged to assert the prestige of France in Rome, obeyed his instructions by turning into a major incident the brawl which arose between his suite and a Corsican regiment of papal guardsmen. Relations were severed between Paris and the Vatican, preposterous demands were made by the King, war was declared, and the Pope in 1664 was forced to make a humiliating treaty at Pisa. But it was as a monarch that he was humiliated, and the Papacy retained for future use a position among the sovereign princes of Europe which an exclusively spiritual policy would not have safeguarded. The sovereign prince could never become a royal chaplain—not even in 1804—and all Bossuet's teaching as to the immediate nature of the royal authority, important as its political implications were, never dislodged the Papacy from this legal pinnacle. Can it be wondered therefore that the Popes made up for their actual weakness by a nice discrimination in diplomatic formalities? Successive Popes negotiated with the various countries for the resignation of their swollen ambassadorial privileges. France resisted with more tenacity than any other country; and finally the Pope took up the position that he would in future receive no new ambassador unless he had previously renounced the *franchise du quartier*. It was not till 1693, and during the pontificate of Innocent XII., that the French king consented formally to abandon this diplomatic privilege. Perhaps the claim may be said to have been finally smothered in laughter when in 1759 the French minister raised it to defend an attack made, as it turned out later, under a misapprehension, by his servants on the sbirri who gave annoyance by passing continually to and fro before the French Legation house at Genoa. The legation "quarters" at Peking recall a famous phrase, but, being protected by treaty agreement, they belong, as has been shown, to a different order of ideas. The *franchise du quartier* has also been claimed to exempt from octroi-tax supplies brought into the residence of a mission ostensibly for the use of its inhabitants. In the seventeenth century the Spanish government was at pains to buy out this right by a bargain with the individual ambassadors accredited to the King of Spain. As less became heard of this *franchise* this particular application of it vanished: at least it became merged in the various ambassadorial rights which were based on the more important *franchise de l'hôtel*.

The *franchise de l'hôtel* was to have a much longer history in the record of diplomacy. It was by an easy transition that the notion of extra-territoriality was extended from the person of the ambassador to his domicile; and, as the slow process described above established the immunity of the person, so a still slower, but quite definite, process established the immunity of the thing. The process was slower because the possibilities for abuse were so tangible that the

CHAP. III. need for admitting the exceptional position of an ambassador's house might well be regarded as anything but axiomatic by unprejudiced opinion. The ambassadorial residence might, and did, become the refuge of political fugitives. Ambassadors, acting from humanitarian motives or from a purely fictitious conception of the extra-territoriality of their embassies, did sometimes refuse to surrender the political fugitives. In 1726 Stanhope, the English ambassador at Madrid, declined to surrender Ripperda even though that adventurer had taken refuge without his knowledge. A similar incident took place in 1747 at Stockholm in regard to Springer. In both cases the governments concerned after some natural hesitation overrode the plea of extra-territoriality and by display of force secured their will. Nevertheless the British government protested both to Spain and to Sweden, and as regards the latter broke off negotiations for a period.

The revolutionary movements in the various capitals of Europe during the nineteenth century were bound to produce "incidents" for a country like England which was so often found, in word particularly, a patron of liberalism wherever it showed itself. In Spain, for example, during the constitutional struggles ex-ministers and ex-officials were only too glad to seek the shelter of a friendly embassy, nor was this generally refused. In the South American states, owing to political conditions which were even more disturbed than those which reigned at Madrid, ministers driven from power, or defeated revolutionaries, were again and again admitted to shelter by sympathetic diplomats: nor in the then condition of those countries can the sympathetic action be dismissed as unreasonable. As a result of incidents which occurred during a Lima revolution in 1866, the French envoy to Peru made an attempt to get solemnly formulated by the local diplomatic corps a special Latin-American international law of legation refuge. An American minister, Egan, played a conspicuous, and in the eyes of some contemporary diplomats an unjustifiable, part in sheltering the refugees of the following of ex-President Balmaceda of Chili at the American Legation in 1891. During the last few years the *franchise de l'hôtel* has been reduced to, and stabilised at, a justifiable point. It consists in little more than freedom from police entry and a courtesy exemption of the embassy building from most types of local and national taxation, often on a basis of reciprocity. The old claim to be relieved from octroi-duty emerges perhaps in the modern courtesy exemption from import duties of articles destined for the *chef de mission* and his staff.

The personal immunity of diplomatic agents and their suites has been equally a bone of contention and produced a succession of incidents and a mass of argument. That the personal immunity of an ambassador did not protect him, should he conspire against the state to which he was accredited, was proved by a long line of cases which began with the English expulsion of the Spaniards D'Espes (1572) and Mendoza (1584), included the confinement by Queen Elizabeth of the Frenchman l'Aubespine (1587) and ended with the French expulsion of the Spaniard Cellamare (1718) and the English arrest of the Swedish Gyllenborg (1716-1717). At Constantinople, Christian envoys, instead of being given their passports and being escorted over the frontier when the Porte went to war against their masters, were arrested and lodged in prison by a Turkish Imperial custom which was still maintained as late as the eighteenth century. Apart from these exceptions states did not allow the use of compulsion against the diplomatic representative of a foreign power. When the envoy of Peter the Great was arrested for debt the English government of Queen Anne was profuse in apology and caused the passage of legislation—a famous Act (12) in the history of diplomatic immunity—to obviate the recurrence of such action in the future. Thus not only is his residence and its effects safeguarded, but a minister's person is no longer subject to debt procedure. More than this, the courts will not *subpoena* him, nor accept jurisdiction over him in civil cases, except in a limited number of special instances. In matters of police administration, major and minor, no criminal jurisdiction is exercised over a diplomatic agent, but he is expected to accommodate himself voluntarily to the general stipulations of the criminal law, to such obligations also as traffic rules and sanitary regulations. No personal taxation is levied from an ambassador. These privileges are extended from the ambassador to his family, his official staff and that part of his domestic staff not subject to the territorial power. Once an ambassador could judge his own staff and punish them. Such an exercise of jurisdiction is now utterly out of date. Recent occurrences suggest that an ambassador would now refer a criminal offence of any gravity back to his home government, which would decide whether the criminal should be surrendered to

CHAP. III. the territorial jurisdiction for trial or a demand be submitted for his return with a view to trial in the home state. There are instances of the adoption of both courses of action within the past few years.

The truth is that despite the suggestion of Grotius [13] that the immunities of a diplomat rest upon a principle—that of extra-territoriality and of a diplomat's identity with the accrediting authority—they do in fact rest upon the more shifting consideration of convenience. Before a certain stage in the development of Europe there was no conceivable reason why there should be ambassadors at all, still less that they should be cloaked with extraordinary privileges. Before Grotius' view was to be justified by actual conditions many storm-tossed states had to reach political stability and to win through to national pride. The world of diplomacy had to appreciate the full consequences of the sovereign independence of states, even those deranged by civil war. Finally there had to be manifested a decline of vindictiveness in the treatment of their political enemies on the part of warlike political factions. All this is but to say that there had to be solidification in the viscous condition of European politics: that geography and politics had to change, as they did change in Europe between the sixteenth and the nineteenth century, from a dynamic into a comparatively static human interest.

International Negotiation.—The earlier type of special ambassador was entrusted with a definite mission or perhaps a set of missions. He had to carry with him documents showing, first, that he had been appointed in due legal and constitutional form the representative of the prince for whom he was acting, and, secondly, that he had full authority to negotiate an agreement on a specific number of topics. These documents were inspected, and were proved, in order to obtain the assurance that negotiations carried on with the bearer of them would be authoritatively honoured by the prince whom he was representing. This inspection of credentials was considered the more important, because "ratification," as it has come to be called, that is a formal and later confirmation of the agreed terms, was in the earlier days of modern diplomacy apparently not considered an essential part of a morally binding agreement. Gentilis,[14] Grotius,[15] Pufendorff [16] and Vattel [17] all seem confident that a plenipotentiary acting without constraint and within his written powers, inspected by his fellow negotiators, quite definitely bound his prince. In more modern times there has been a sharp distinction drawn between the executive and legislative departments of government. A tendency has shown itself therefore to regard the negotiation of treaties as a function of the executive, their ratification as the function of the legislature, this last because the terms of treaties have frequently involved the passing of subsequent laws. This is not to admit the contention of some that the making of treaties has ceased in England to be part of the prerogative of the Crown, an opinion as false as it is dangerous, but merely to indicate that even in England the organ of government concerned, the responsible Cabinet, has wished to retain the ceremony of ratification as a useful reality, in that it affords an eleventh-hour control which may prove serviceable in exceptional conditions of irresistible popular disapprobation. The most recent public discussion of the desirability of the so-called "open diplomacy" took place in the House of Commons on 11th March 1925.

In the sixteenth and seventeenth centuries the resident minister in like manner produced the official documents which appointed him the authoritative agent for his prince in the foreign capital. He was normally sent out with written instructions to guide him in his policy, and he occasionally received from time to time a special authorisation to open specific negotiations with the local government. When his home government sought to innovate a striking change in the relations between the two states, his activities were supplemented, or he might even be replaced, by an ambassador extraordinary, often a noble of high rank or of the Blood Royal, one in far closer and more confidential touch with the latest tendencies in policy at the seat of the home government. An exceptional mission of this type is of course still employed, but mainly for matters of high ceremony. The publicity which attaches to an imposing mission is a disadvantage, rather than a help, in the transaction of normal business. When it is necessary to stimulate, or add to, the activities of a local embassy a prominent statesman is still sometimes sent, but as often as not he is found seeking to disguise the importance of his mission. Indeed, it is more often the despatch of technical or expert officers, rather than the accrediting of a plenipotentiary, which modern diplomatic situations require.

An important epoch opened in the late fifteenth and early sixteenth century with a feature the novelty and importance of which has been sometimes overlooked. Then it was that

CHAP. III.

between a number of states what may be called conjoint negotiations, and conjoint agreements for offensive and defensive purposes, attained a hitherto unknown significance. The first prominent agreement of this type, for one does not count the crusading expeditions, was probably the League of 1495, which was alike a triumph for the new diplomacy and an admirable indication of its potentialities to subsequent investigators. To meet the threatening power of France, which had just overthrown the kingdom of Naples, an alliance was negotiated at Venice between the King of the Romans, the Spanish sovereigns, the Pope, Milan and Venice, a league later joined by the King of England. As was revealed in discussing the history of the Balance of Power, many similar alliances were joined in the years immediately following, these mainly arising out of the then condition of Italian politics. Notable instances were the League of Cambrai (1508), the Holy League (1511) and the alliance, against the Empire, of France, the Papacy, Florence, Milan and Venice in 1526. Alliances of this nature were sometimes more imposing than real. Powers undertook, often knowingly, more than they were able, or indeed intended, to perform, and, though occasionally there can be found efforts to restrain the allies from treating for peace except conjointly, the diplomacy of the day was still of too amateur a character either to hold together an alliance which it had created, or to bring it as a united force to peace negotiations. In 1596, for example, Elizabeth of England, Henry IV. of France and the Dutch signed an offensive and defensive alliance. Henry IV., an architect of some dexterity in the formation of alliances, had undertaken not to make peace with Spain, the common enemy, except with the consent of his allies. He violated this agreement by signing the Peace of Vervins in 1598. By any one who remembers the record of the various alliances against either Louis XIV. or Napoleon, this will not be treated as curious or the perfidious practice of a dead departed age. Alliances have yet to be constructed which will withstand the fatigue engendered by war, lack of money, jealousy of an ally's success, intolerable danger or the enemy's offer of specially advantageous terms. The frailty of the new nation states in conjoint action however must not blind the observer to the emergence of a new phenomenon in international politics.

Efforts, it was written above, were made to overcome the inherent weakness of the alliances negotiated through the new diplomacy. One effort deserves attention. It was that of bringing rulers face to face, of allowing them to supplement in personal interviews the preliminary work of their diplomatic agents. Monarchs had met before, but there was something more formal than heretofore had been the case in the systematic succession of personal interviews between Henry VIII. of England on the one hand and on the other the Emperor and the Regent of Flanders in 1513, the King of France in 1520 and 1532, King Charles of Spain in 1520 and 1522. Francis I. of France and Charles of Spain similarly sought personal interviews at critical moments. The Pope met the Emperor and the King of France at Nice in 1538: the Emperor met the King of France at Aigues-Mortes a month later. In 1536 King James V. of Scotland came in person to Paris.

The new diplomacy, beside creating conjoint alliances for war, endeavoured also to promote conjoint congresses for peace. One of the first notable instances of such action was the Peace Treaty of London in 1518. It is true that it was negotiated only between a special French mission and the English Privy Council, but special provision, on which the English government insisted, was made for later adhesion on the part of England's allies, the Emperor, the King of Spain and the Pope. In connection with this comparative innovation in diplomacy an interesting survival from an older age must be mentioned. The day after the treaty was signed the King of England and the French representatives went in person to St. Paul's Cathedral to swear to it. It is said that the treaty of alliance between France and Switzerland, signed on 28th May 1777, and solemnly sworn to in the cathedral at Solothurn, was the last treaty in Europe to be publicly confirmed on oath.(18)

A peace congress which closed for a time an era of general European war, and which illustrated well the close personal relation of royalty to the new diplomacy, was that of Cambrai in 1529. Charles V. had given full powers (and elaborate instructions) to his aunt, Margaret, the ruler of the Netherlands. Francis I. sent his very able mother, Louise of Savoy, who had shown herself a most intelligent regent of France during his captivity. Henry VIII., who had intended to send his *alter ego* Cardinal Wolsey, sent Thomas More and Bishop Tunstall. Between themselves the royal ladies negotiated the very satisfactory *Paix des dames*,(19) which covered a number of disputed questions in the Netherlands, France and

CHAP. III. Italy. Separate treaties were made by the English plenipotentiaries with each party.

A more significant congress than that of Cambrai was that of Cateau-Cambresis in 1559, since it covered an even wider range of European interests. Negotiations, begun in 1558, were transferred to St. Pol in October and back to Cateau-Cambresis in February 1559. Here an equilibrium was struck for Western Europe which endured substantially unchanged until the days of Richelieu. It was at this conference that England acquiesced in a nominally temporary retention of Calais by the French. Another survival of an older time is here worth passing mention. As security for the fulfilment of the clauses of the treaty an exchange of hostages was arranged. The later to be famous William of Orange, who had been a plenipotentiary with Alva, Egmont and Aerschot in negotiating the peace on behalf of the Crown of Spain, proceeded after its signature as a hostage to Paris. The last exchange of hostages to insure a treaty is said by Crandall [(18)] to have taken place in 1748 over the conclusion of the Treaty of Aix-la-Chapelle. Great Britain then undertook to deliver to France two persons of rank as hostages for the return of Cape Breton and of possible captures in the West Indies. Even the above-mentioned Treaty of Vervins in 1598 can not be altogether excluded from this same general type. Henry IV. began by endeavouring to persuade the English and the Dutch to avail themselves of the possibility of adhesion, a possibility which he had extorted in his terms with the Spaniards. Though he failed in this and, as pointed out above, in so doing split up an alliance in the new diplomatic tradition, he did nevertheless represent the allies' point of view very successfully in securing the separation of the Spanish Netherlands from the Crown of Spain and their conversion into an independent state, an anticipation of the modern kingdom of Belgium. The inclusion among the signatory parties of the Swiss and of Savoy gave, moreover, a certain international air to the treaty.

Towards the end of the Thirty Years' War (1618-1648) the most terrible, devastating and widespread struggle in which the modern nation states of Europe had been yet engaged, preparations were made for the gathering of a peace conference of a much more advanced type than that of those which have been hitherto examined. Pope Urban VIII. had as early as 1635 proposed a peace congress. He on the Catholic, the King of Denmark on the Protestant, side were eager to offer their services in the very difficult work of bringing a general congress together, and of organising and vitalising its proceedings when it had assembled. The Pope took the initiative in 1636 by sending to Cologne a papal legate who began not unhopefully to collect a conference. Imperial and Spanish representatives arrived, and for a time it seemed that Cardinal Richelieu, who was in control in France, would find it difficult to avoid complying with the papal desire for an assurance that France would participate. Fortunately for the development of Richelieu's policy the Austrians and Spaniards decided to refuse passes to representatives from the Dutch and Swedes. They were allies of France, but Sweden possessed no legal German status, and the Dutch no universally recognised international status at all. The Swedes thereupon refused to come to a congress held in a Catholic city under the auspices of the Pope. Despite an attempt of the Venetian government, practical as ever, to save the peace gathering by an offer of mediation, the congress accomplished nothing, failing even to promote a truce. Thus the traditions of a passing Europe were still strong enough to prolong by twelve years a war which men had come to loathe, and to deal yet another blow to the diminishing prestige of the Papacy, which left a mark upon that august institution apparent for two hundred years. The international lawyer does well not to be premature in tidying up his Europe. Another papal attempt in 1638 broke down also. It was no fault in diplomacy, but traditionalism and a lack of will which produced these results. In the first case the French government had never desired peace, although it had disguised its sentiments in formal deference to the Holy See. In the second case the Swedish government had declined even a truce unless its armies, living on French subsidies or on the country, were financed during the cessation of hostilities. In 1638 an English attempt to negotiate an agreement for a Brussels conference died still-born.

Meanwhile, Swedish and Imperial diplomats at Hamburg were negotiating as to conditions for a conference, and the pourparlers were extended to include the Frenchman d'Avaux. In 1640 the growing importance of these proceedings was held to justify the despatch of the Imperial Councillor, Von Lützow. Discussion appeared interminable, the French and the Swedes vying with each other in the raising of difficulties over such questions as the form of safe-conduct, the representation of the states in the Empire, and the place of

CHAP. III.

meeting. The Swedes demanded from the French an annual grant of one million livres to be paid them so long as the truce should last. Finally, a preliminary treaty was signed on 25th December 1641 which provided for the opening of a congress on 25th March 1642. This was to assemble and to sit in two separate sections. At Münster discussion was to take place between the Emperor and his allies on the one hand and the King of France and his allies on the other, mediation being undertaken by the Pope and Venice. At Osnabrück, a city within the easily traversible distance of some thirty miles, the discussion was to be conducted between the Emperor and his allies on the one hand and the King of Sweden and his allies, mediation being undertaken by the King of Denmark. The Emperor for his part undertook to supply safe-conducts to the representatives of all Swedish and all French allies.

There was some delay in the ratification of this preliminary compact because it was abhorrent to the Emperor that he should grant safe-conducts to certain of the German Protestant states who had become the protégés of Sweden. Contemporary opinion was sceptical as to the possibility of success in the proposed type of congress, which in many particulars was without a precedent. So experienced and skilful a statecraftsman as Maximilian of Bavaria still believed in a separate arrangement with France as the surest way to restore a general peace: while the Imperial government made difficulty over the question of "full powers" and experimented with the offer of a separate peace with Sweden. The historian must still read of these vacillations with bated breath. After a long delay the Emperor and the King of Spain ratified the preliminary treaty, the date for convening the congress being correspondingly retarded. The representatives did not as a matter of fact get together till the spring of 1644 or begin real business till 1645. In an assembly which included twenty-six Diet votes at Münster and forty at Osnabrück, the number of disputes over precedence can be easily imagined. Then grave defects were found in the powers of the negotiators. For example, examination revealed that the powers of the French representatives gave authority to negotiate but not to sign, and were made out in the name of the King of France, a minor, without any reference to the Regency. Amendments dealing with these and other points had to be sought from home.[20] Grotius has been termed the father of the Law of Nations, the Treaty of Westphalia the foundation of International Society. The foundations were not laid precipitately. CHAP. III.

Finally at long last, on 1st June 1645, the French in their own language at Münster, the Swedes in Latin at Osnabrück, brought forward their proposals for peace. At Münster there were no joint sittings. Memoranda and notes were exchanged through the mediators Fabio Chigi and Contarini, who represented the Pope and Venice respectively. At Osnabrück, where it had been arranged that a Danish representative should mediate, Dano-Swedish hostility prevented such action, and the Danes departed before the congress began business. Accordingly, in that city direct delivery of notes took place between the negotiators. The diplomats of the Westphalian settlement were perhaps in their day the most skilled in Europe. The admiration of intelligent Europe went out to men like Trautsmandorff, chief plenipotentiary for the Emperor, Peneranda representative of Spain, Servien and d'Avaux who came from France, Salvius of Sweden, Wetstein the Swiss, and the Dutchman Adrian Pauw. The electoral college deputed the Bishop of Osnabrück, various German states sent Adami, Wittgenstein and Lampadius. These men were the honour of their generation and they made the peace in 1648.

Sir Ernest Satow in his admirable book on *Diplomatic Practice* [21] describes and discusses the great congresses which took place at Oliva (1660), Aix-la-Chapelle (1668), Nymwegen (1676-1679), Frankfort (1681), Ryswick (1697), Carlowitz (1699) and Utrecht (1712-1713). It is unnecessary to repeat what has been well done already. From the more general point of view, which is proper to this survey, it is especially interesting to observe that the same forces which drew certain powers together in order to fight down the bellicose ambition of Louis XIV., these very forces which found expression in the equilibrium which was aimed at in the Partition Treaties governing the Spanish Succession, were operative also in producing, and were invoked to bring about, the peace settlements. This is noteworthy, but it is also observable that, during the seventeenth century, there took place an extension of the method of negotiation by congress to new portions of the world and to nations outside the European state system. Poland, Venice, Austria and Russia sent representatives to the Congress of Carlowitz in 1698 for the purpose of negotiating a peace with the Sultan of Turkey. It proved a complicated task to compose the preliminary difficulties, but

CHAP. III. in the end three peace treaties were signed on 26th January, while a fourth, that between Turkey and Russia, had already provided for a two years' truce. It is a common place of the text-books of the Law of Nations that Turkey did not become a member of the Concert of Powers till the Congress of Paris in 1856. It is impossible all the same to leave unnoticed the change which in this respect a century and a half had made in the outlook of Europe. In 1535 Francis I. was the object of general execration, because France had made an alliance with a Muhammadan government. In 1698, although there was no question of allowing Turkey to intrude itself into a grouping of the European countries, there does appear definite recognition of the reality of Turkey as a negotiating Power, and even of a certain obligation toward it in the comity of nations. Lastly, the absence of a common treaty, which all the Powers could sign, is, and remained, characteristic of the diplomatic methods of a former age. Even at the Peace of Utrecht in 1713 there were still separate treaties between France, England and all participating countries individually and reciprocally.

The Congress of Vienna of 1814-1815 is a landmark in the history of international negotiation. It did not meet to create peace *de novo*, but to carry out the terms of a preliminary agreement, which was embodied in no less than seven treaties, between France and its various allied opponents. Though there were very many states which claimed to be represented in a national gathering which met to liquidate the Napoleonic wars, the first plenipotentiaries of the four great Powers, Great Britain, Austria, Prussia and Russia, in a series of meetings during the third week of September attempted to assume the management of the business of the congress without further ado. This premature attempt to bring into being what was afterwards a feature of nineteenth-century diplomacy—an inner council of the Powers—was defeated by Talleyrand, who secured perhaps the greatest triumph of his career. Business was to be divided up into General European and German. German affairs were to be discussed by a committee appointed from the five important German states, Saxony, which was suspected of Napoleonic leanings, being excluded. As for general European affairs—especially the disposition of territories in Poland, Italy and Central Europe—the Allied Powers, it was suggested, should reach an agreement among themselves and later admit France and Spain and other Powers to make objections.

Talleyrand opposed this from the first and utilised the jealousy of the excluded Powers to gain his point. If, he argued, the signature of the preliminary Paris treaties, above referred to, constituted a claim to direct the subsequent congress, then no logic or justice could exclude all eight signatories—France, Great Britain, Austria, Russia, Prussia, Spain, Portugal and Sweden. Surely it must be necessary for the congress as a whole, not any part of it however dignified, to authorise its proceedings. By 8th October he had won his case, and the committee of the eight Powers constituted itself the preliminary committee of the congress. On 30th October it elected Metternich President and Gentz Secretary: on 1st November it gave notice that a specially appointed committee of three would begin an examination of the powers of the plenipotentiaries. The committee of eight appointed special committees to deal with particular topics. On subjects other than territorial there were committees on the abolition of the slave trade, on the free navigation of international rivers, and on precedence among princes and diplomats. A statistical committee was appointed to guide the five Powers (France, Great Britain, Russia, Austria and Prussia) in the complicated question of the redistribution of territory. For Swiss and for German affairs there were special committees: the former committee was exceptionally strong and did lasting work; on the latter the divergent aims of Austria and Prussia prevented in the end the adoption of a constructive policy. It was proposed to establish a committee which should deal with Italian affairs, but Metternich blocked this proposal. None the less, at one time a committee was sitting on the affairs of Tuscany, Parma, and other Italian duchies, while yet another dealt with the title to the old Duchy of Bouillon. At different stages, and round different subjects, discussion went on in the sessions of the committee of eight, the committee of five and, be it noted, in the committee of four (the five with France excluded). Finally, on 12th March, the escape of Napoleon having led to his outlawry and the speeding up of business, the committee of eight appointed a special drafting body with three secretaries to summarise the work of the congress in a single and authoritative text. This text, the historic *Acte final*, was signed on 9th June by the plenipotentiaries of seven out of the eight Powers, Spain holding aloof on the ground that only a small proportion of the decisions found in the *Acte* had actually been taken in the committee of eight.

CHAP. III.

The succession of meetings between the Powers of the Holy Alliance between 1818 and 1822 (Aix-la-Chapelle, Troppau, Laybach, Verona) have resulted in the attachment to this epoch of history of the phrase " The Congress Period," and it is not easy to agree with those who treat the title as a misnomer. There was direct continuity with that method of diplomacy, no longer new, of which the cardinal feature is the conjoint action of several Powers. Judged from the political standpoint the field of action was restricted in comparison with that of the Congress of Vienna. The difficulty vanishes if this point be realised. Judged from the standpoint of the historian of international negotiation there are no features which call for comment. The same may be said of the Congresses of Paris (1856) and Berlin (1878). The former promoted, though it did not originate, the use of international gatherings for the purpose of reaching agreement concerning, even, one might add, of codifying, particular branches of the Law of Nations which had till then been the subject of international dispute. The practice was to be strikingly developed in the nineteenth and the twentieth centuries, as witness, for example, the conferences held at The Hague.

The most notable change of method shown in the liquidation of the European War of 1914-1918, which took place at the Peace Conference of Paris in 1919, was shown in the conduct of the entire proceedings under agreements of armistice rather than under the terms of a treaty of peace. To this must be added the diminished consideration shown to the defeated Powers, an attitude accounted for perhaps by a desire to retaliate upon the rough methods of Bismarck at the conclusion of the Franco-Prussian War of 1870. Lastly, the management of the congress by the greater Powers in the victorious alliance was autocratic to an extent unknown before. This may have been due to the effect of the acute strain of war in the victorious countries, as also perhaps to the discredit which had attached to the impractically democratic organisation of international gatherings such as the second Hague Peace Congress. The proceedings in 1919 were organised and managed without any participation by the defeated Powers, who were merely summoned separately at considerable intervals to consider the draft which had been prepared by the Allied and Associated Powers, and to submit objection in writing. The proceedings in connection with the German treaty were naturally the most severe. The Allied draft treaty being almost ready towards the end of April, the German government was told to send plenipotentiaries. When these arrived they were not, like Talleyrand, made free of the conference, but found that they were expected to stay almost entirely in their quarters shut in behind closed doors. On 1st May credentials were exchanged: on 7th May the draft treaty was handed to the Germans, who were given time to prepare their observations. These were summed up in a note of 30th May, which was answered in a general allied note of 16th June, in which only a few minor concessions were allowed. On 28th June the practically unchanged treaty was signed together with a supplementary protocol. After the signature of the treaty with Germany many of the more important personalities left Paris, but machinery was left behind to prepare the Austrian, Hungarian, Bulgarian and Turkish treaties, and to obtain signature of them from the appropriate delegates.

Theory and practice by no means always squared in the organisation of the conference. It was composed of five plenipotentiaries from the great Powers and two from the smaller. Eight plenary meetings were held before the delivery of terms to the Germans. The chairman, the secretary-general, the vice-presidents and secretaries were elected, and many committees were set to work. Yet the effective control rested at first with a council of ten selected from the five great Powers, then with a council of four and finally with a council of three which was composed of the Prime Ministers of Great Britain and France and the President of the United States. It was this council which assumed the real responsibility for the first draft of the German treaty and for the later exiguous concessions made. After the signature of the German treaty consideration of the terms of the remaining treaties was taken over by the Foreign ministers of the five great allied Powers.

NOTES

(1) For treatment of the theory and practice of equilibrium see Dupuis, *Le Principe d'équilibre et le concert européen*, and Donnadieu, *Essai sur la théorie de l'équilibre*. It is unfortunate that in these and analogous works the authors quickly become absorbed in the diplomatic history, and are diverted from following up the political idea, which is admittedly elusive. This has produced on legal circles an

CHAP. III. impatience with such studies of the Balance of Power for which the aegis of international law is sought.

(2) The quotation is taken from a work entitled *Die Chimaere des Gleichgewichts von Europa*, published in Altona in 1758 under the name of von Justi.

(3) Ellery C. Stowell, author of the *Diplomacy of the War of 1914*, in his work on *Intervention in International Law* has collected a bibliography of European and American books on the related doctrines of Intervention and Non-Intervention. Among such may be cited Mamiani, *Rights of Nations* (English translation from the Italian, 1860); Strauch, *Zur Interventionslehre* (1879); and the important article by Rougier in the *Revue générale de droit international* (1910) entitled "La Théorie de l'intervention d'humanité." Stowell gives a complete account of the subject. See also a doctoral thesis of H. Hodges, *The Doctrine of Intervention*. This is less complete.

(4) For details see G. P. Gooch's *History of Modern Europe*, and vol. 3 of the *Cambridge History of British Foreign Policy*. Such detailed financial and police administration as the intervening Powers undertook on territory fully Turkish was unprecedented in the history of independent states.

(5) De Martens, *Précis*, § 74.

(6) In 1821 there was issued by Kamptz a formal treatise which justified intervention by the great Powers in the internal constitutional affairs of independent states: *Völkerrechtliche Erörterung des Rechts der Europäischen Mächte in die Verfassung eines einzelnen Staats sich zu mischen*.

(7) Egger, *Études historiques sur les traités publics chez les Grecs et chez les Romains*. This was extensively used by Pradier-Fodéré.

(8) E. Alberi, *Le Relazioni degli Ambasciatori Veneti al Senato*.

(9) See his own accounts in his *Legazioni*.

(10) Richard Wingfield's diplomatic career is interesting. In 1513 he was at Malines and Brussels. Between 1514 and 1515 he was serving in the Netherlands. In 1515 he was sent to France: in 1516 to Brussels. In 1520 he was ambassador at Paris at £1 a day. In 1521 he was sent to Germany to negotiate between the Emperor and the King of France, and in 1525 to Spain, where he died.

(11) Protestant services in the houses of Dutch consuls became a difficulty in France after the Revocation of the Edict of Nantes.

(12) Statute of 7 Anne, c. 12.

(13) Whewell's *Grotius*, ii. 209.

(14) *De Leg.*, iii. 14.

(15) *Op. cit.*, ii. 11.

(16) *De jur. Nat.*, iii. 9, § 2.

(17) *Op. cit.*, ii. 12, § 156.

(18) Crandall, *Treaties*, p. 11.

(19) The early Peace Congress of Arras (1435), which attempted to arrange a Franco-English peace, had still shown strong traces of mediaevalism in comparison. Michelet states that, in addition to the directly interested parties—the Emperor, the Pope, the Council—Castile, Aragon, Navarre, Naples, Sicily, Milan, Cyprus, Poland and Denmark were represented.

(20) Garden, *Traités de Paix*, vol. i. p. 140.

(21) Chapter xxv.

CHAPTER IV

INTERCOURSE: IN WAR

THE BELLUM JUSTUM: THE RIGHTS OF A JUST BELLIGERENT. METHODS OF WAR: BOOTY, PILLAGE, RANSOM, HOSTAGES, STRATAGEMS OF WAR. MILITARY SERVICES, I.: ARMIES (CONTRIBUTIONS AND REQUISITIONS, FORCED LABOUR BY CIVILIANS, TREATMENT OF THE WOUNDED). MILITARY SERVICES, II.: NAVIES. LEVIES AND SUBSIDIES FROM NEUTRAL POWERS. MILITARY SERVICES, III.: AIR FORCES. REPRISALS AS A MEASURE OF REDRESS SHORT OF WAR.

Bellum Justum.[(1)]—Until nations have reached a highly advanced stage in their development it is war which is the most potent instrument of change. It distinguished the Christian theologians from their pagan predecessors, the philosophers and the lawyers, that they initiated a discussion of the question as to how far, and within what limits, war might be regarded as a moral proceeding. The discussion was destined to last long. The fundamental difference between the pagan and the Christian position is put clearly by Suarez (1548-1617) :— CHAP. IV.

> " It was the error of the pagans to believe that the rights of states rested on force of arms and that it was possible legitimately to undertake wars in order to acquire glory or riches."

And again,

> " The Romans believed that the wars undertaken against the enemies of the Republic were just on both sides. In effect they wished to fight with them under conditions such that the conqueror by virtue of a tacit agreement should become possessed of the goods of the conquered."

He is as characteristic when he demolishes the pagan attitude by what is in his eyes *reductio ad absurdum* :—

> " If the titles of war which the ancients admitted, ambition, cupidity, pride or the desire to prove one's courage, were sufficient to make war legitimate, each state would have the right to invoke them and . . . war would then of itself be lawful . . . on both sides."

CHAP. IV.

In view of some specific texts in the New Testament Christian writers were bound to start the discussion of war with a consideration as an initial question of the legitimacy of war even in self-defence. There was the Sermon on the Mount, and throughout the Gospels scattered exhortations to an attitude of non-resistance. Escape from the dilemma lay for the theologians in the parallel which they drew between the forcible execution by a judge of justice upon a resisting criminal and warlike operations conducted by a state against its foreign enemies who had wronged its citizens and had refused redress. It was obviously fit and proper for Christian magistracy to defend honest citizens against wrongdoers by force: in the same way force might be applied to culpable strangers, non-citizens and even the prince of another state. The canonists and theologians of the fifteenth and sixteenth centuries were faced with the existence of a number of independent political authorities and, in their anxiety to approximate war as closely as possible to a legal execution, they insisted that an otherwise independent prince, responsible perhaps to none but God, was yet justiciable *vis-a-vis* the prince upon whom he had inflicted a wrong, either directly or vicariously through the persons of his subjects. The wronged prince, after he had in vain demanded redress, they held justified in executing justice upon his enemies.

With similar breadth of view were handled the texts of Holy Writ which enjoined non-resistance to evil and the turning of the other cheek. St. Augustine,[2] for example, gave a lead to subsequent Fathers of the Church by a statesmanlike exposition of the passages in question. He pointed out that it was in the dispositions of the heart that it was necessary to fulfil the Christian precepts of patience with wrongdoing, the will never being allowed to depart from sentiments of charity. How could this obligation interfere, he asked, with the necessary imposition upon the wicked of many things which must displease them, of punishment in a temper of charitable severity such as would look rather to the ultimate good of the wrongdoer than to his fleeting pleasure. Thomas Aquinas nearly a thousand years later took up a closely similar attitude. The attitude of the Christian mind, according to his interpretation, must always be that of a man who is ready not to resist and not to defend himself if, as was to be expected, such conduct on his part produced no evil consequences. On occasions, however, it was certainly necessary to act differently for the general good or even for the good of those with whom one battled. St. Augustine [3] was evidently of the opinion that the whole military machinery of Rome had been sanctioned, at least by implication, in the New Testament. CHAP. IV.

> "If the teaching of the Gospels had condemned absolutely all sorts of wars, St. John the Baptist would have needed to give no other advice to the soldiers who consulted him on what it was necessary to do to secure salvation than to bid them renounce their profession. However he did say, 'do violence to no man, defraud none and be content with your pay.' As soon therefore as he asks them to be content with their pay it becomes clear that he did not forbid them to carry arms."

As Christian intelligence established the possibility of participation in war without a breach of the moral code enjoined by Christ, and as, following St. Augustine, it sanctioned for individuals the profession of arms, Christian theorists developed their teaching by dividing wars into two classes, the offensive and defensive. After making it clear that in certain cases an actually offensive war might be justifiable, the doctors of the Church devoted attention to a consideration of the *criteria* of a just war. Aquinas produced a definition which is a model of sound judgment. He held that a war to be just must conform to three conditions. In the first place there must exist sufficient authority in him who declares it, in the second place there must be a just cause of offence by a guilty party, and thirdly there must be present a just intention to make war solely for the establishment of peace, the repressing of the wicked or the assistance of the good. In laying down these *criteria* Aquinas, as often, was taking a far more practical line than many of the later canonists. These indulged in distinction and sub-distinction reaching at the most complicated stage a division into at least seven classes, upon each one of which hung an *a priori* judgment.

1. War against infidels—just.
2. Judicial war, against rebels—just.
3. Presumptuous war, by rebels—unjust.
4. Legitimate war, in virtue of a right (*i.e.* a just cause)—just.
5. Temerarious war, against the right—unjust.
6. Voluntary war, undertaken by vassals without the authority of their lords—unjust.
7. Necessary war, in pure self-defence—just.

By the end of the Middle Ages some general agreement had

CHAP. IV.

been reached in three directions at least. The authority of an independent prince was almost universally held indispensable before armed operations of offence could be rightly undertaken, although a minor authority might undertake defence against direct aggression. A just cause was held to postulate a preceding refusal of redress for injuries done; and a just aim, or intention, in a declarant of war could be thought of as including the attainment of a speedy peace on terms which redressed the injustice and made provision for such matters as the cost of the armed proceedings. It might include even the provision of future security against the repetition of aggression.

The cardinal objection to all the earlier scholastic theory lay in the fact that it assumed that in most given conjunctions of political circumstances plain and patent injustice, visible to all the world, would exist on the one side, and that plain and patent justice would exist on the other. In such cases, no doubt, the contentions of the theologians and canonists would be formidable. The declarant of an unjust war would have been guilty of a mortal sin, his killing would have been murder, his booty stolen goods. To the wager of a just war, on the other hand, it was but moral justice to allow the incidental right to kill those who impeded directly or even indirectly the establishment of justice. Further there was the custom of allowing certain types of private property to be appropriated as booty. If a majority of wars could have been simply denominated just or unjust, as these philosophers assumed, the Church would very quickly have established control of the situation. Even supposing that a prince had been godless enough to have envisaged without dismay the commission of mortal sin in the waging of an unjust war, subjects, allies and mercenary soldiers, tempted to take part in the operations, would have been forbidden to engage in his wrongdoing on pain of incurring the penalty of mortal sin notwithstanding considerations such as their pay, their oaths of allegiance, their unconditional undertakings and the like.

It must not be supposed, however, that the *jus belli* of these theologians would permit subjects, each for himself, in the stress and danger of the opening of a war to engage in a prolonged examination of the justice or injustice of their prince's war. Most of the theologians and canonists had a sense of political realities and were little inclined to encourage the subject of delicate conscience to the scrutiny of every step of high policy undertaken by his ruler. Such an attitude would have led direct to anarchy.[4] Accordingly most of them were inclined to follow the lead of St. Augustine, who took up the strong line that the subject should obey orders "if it be certain that that which is commanded him is not contrary to the law of God, or at least, if it be not certain that it is contrary to such law." The difference is so marked between certainty that a war is not contrary to God's law and absence of certainty that it is contrary, that St. Augustine in using the distinction went no little way towards meeting the necessities of the state. In cases therefore of wars "not certainly contrary to God's law," wars which permitted the subjects of a prince to harbour some hope of their prince's justice, the subjects were not excused from the binding duty of allegiance although the prince and his immediate counsellors might still in very fact be guilty of mortal sin. In any such case there could be no question as to the moral innocence of his subjects. They were only guilty of mortal sin if they followed their prince in a war which was certainly and patently unjust. If there were any element of doubt as to the war's injustice, an element which persisted after the inquiry of learned men, the subject might innocently fight on the ground of the duty owed to his prince. Here, however, a distinction was made between the case of a subject and that of mercenary soldiers, allies and friends. A subject had to be certain of his prince's injustice before he could decline the duties involved in his allegiance. Allies, friends and mercenaries who harboured a doubt as to the justice of the war undertaken, were not allowed to leave the final moral responsibility with the belligerent prince. They were considered, at least by some authorities, as guilty of mortal sin if, while entertaining a doubt, they should take part in fighting.

The serious character of the sanctions for just war which were thus established ought not to be underrated even though they rested almost entirely on the moral authority of the Church. What made them ineffectual was the utter inability of men to establish in the ordinary type of international war a party wholly unjust and a party wholly just. The mediaeval theory rested on the assumption that such sharply contrasted justice and injustice existed in the normal case; and it is common to all authorities to refuse to admit that there could be a war in which there was justice on both sides. Such an assumption would indeed have destroyed the

CHAP. IV.

characteristically Christian approach to the employment of force, for in a war waged justly on both sides there would be no guilty party, the adversaries on both sides would be perfectly innocent and the killing of them would be inadmissible. Two lines of thought indicated for those under the influence of scholastic philosophy a path out of the dilemma, at least in practice. In the first place canonical theory provided for the case of "invincible ignorance" on the one side, that is for the case in which extraordinary circumstances did not permit one side to learn of, or know, the justice of the claims of the other side. This type of case was, in earlier theory at least, assumed to be rare. It was when "invincible ignorance" was expanded to "excusable ignorance" that the breach in the stricter canonical theory was made. Simultaneously, although the theologians refused to admit the breakdown of their theory of war, which involved in every war the presence of one party in the wrong who was *ipso facto* guilty of mortal sin, they admitted from an early date that the identification of the guilty party might be most difficult, and accordingly made most sensible adjustments in their conception of the moral duties of individuals.

The sixteenth and seventeenth centuries, epoch-making in other branches of International Law, proved here also the breeding-time of a great change. The theologians and canonists made a real attempt to grapple with the difficulties which arose out of controversies between princes in which there was equality of right between the contending parties or serious doubt as to the relative merits of their competing claims. Their first effort was to bring under their censure those princes who went to war when they or their councils were not absolutely certain of the justice of the proposed war, but had merely "probable" opinions to match against the "probable" opinions of their opponents. War undertaken under these conditions they adjudged unjust. Vasquez (1551-1604) is worth quoting at length on this subject. A voice from the sixteenth century has special interest owing to the innumerable claims and counter-claims to kingdoms, duchies and principalities which were advanced during that period, especially on behalf of the Crowns of France and Spain.

> "It happens frequently in cases which concern the title to kingdoms that opinions are divided. Some affirm that probably the right to such a kingdom belongs to such a king, others that it belongs to such an other. The usual result is that the two kings declare war upon each other, and each

attempts to secure the kingdom against the wish of the other. Since the king in such circumstances acts in the quality of judge, it is necessary to determine if his 'probable' opinion that the kingdom belongs to him is sufficient to justify him in declaring war . . . even in the case in which another is already in possession. In my opinion the matter is worthy of the greatest attention of the theologians for from it more than from anything else depend the issues of peace and war among Christian princes. Every one sees clearly the importance of the question but few doctors have given much heed to it and those few have written little." (5)

CHAP. IV.

It was one of the vicious features of the whole probabilistic casuistry that it never provided any precise standard of measurement in probability.

When once the approach by the method of probability had been admitted the casuist had the whole situation cut and dried. The claimant in possession, seeing that it was forbidden by morality to contest his claim by arms on the basis of another equally "probable" claim, had incumbent upon him the obligation to examine the case of his adversary with care. If doubt were to persist after an honest and conscientious examination, the possessor was considered to have a perfect right to remain, and the smallest measure of doubt by the possessor as to the validity of his opponent's claim was apparently sufficient to permit him to refrain from an offer to compensate or to partition his possessions. In the case in which neither claimant was in possession a partition might be proposed, which the more powerful had no right to refuse, even though his claim were as strong as that of the weaker claimant whom he could have defeated in war. In place of partition one claimant might offer compensation elsewhere to the other. Further, arbitration by arbiters might be employed, though Suarez (1548-1617) said that this was but rarely adopted. The ultimate authority of the Pope was mentioned by some writers as a resort of the last instance, but it was not obscurely indicated that it had become almost unemployable in this type of case and that, if invoked, it might seriously embarrass the Holy Father.

Thus did the commentators, and the commentators on the commentators, tithe intellectual mint and cummin in the endeavour to meet a situation which was slipping from their grasp, but already the basis was being laid for the later attitude towards war which came to regard the average class of hostilities as not without justification on either side. In

CHAP. IV. Victoria (d. 1546 or 1549) there are pregnant sentences out of which a bridge could have been constructed from the ancient to the modern. He was discussing the hypothetical case of a clash between Spaniards and American Indians, the latter opposing the just claims of the Spaniards to trade and settle in their country. He took the attitude that the Spaniards in the last resort would be justified in fighting, but that the Indians for their part might, as the result of terror at the coming of a mightier people, be reduced to the canonical condition of "invincible ignorance," in which they could not *ex hypothesi* perceive the justice of the Spanish claim. In such a case, he pointed out, hostilities upon the Indian side would be just also. Then by a rapid transition Victoria widened the whole basis of discussion by expanding the canonical "invincible ignorance" into a novel "excusable ignorance," a step which widened out of all knowledge the number of wars which could be regarded as just upon both sides. Victoria himself gave an example in the struggle for the Duchy of Burgundy which was being waged in his day between the Crowns of France and Spain.

> "If for example the French occupy Burgundy believing as a result of an excusable ignorance that it belongs to them, and if our Emperor (Charles v.) has a certain right over the province, he (the Emperor) may take it back, and the French defend it, by force."

Molina (1535-1600) pushed to their logical conclusion the consequences of Victoria's admission.

> "If the two parties are of different opinions and each one believes without doubt that the object of the strife belongs to him, obviously one of the two parties is deceived; but if his error be invincible in that he has applied the proper diligence and has followed the advice of experienced men, the war will be just on both sides. . . . It would be an excellent thing then to end the controversy by a compromise or by the choice of arbitrators. . . . Nevertheless I do not think this always obligatory."(6)

Molina here not only parted from the traditional Christian theory which saw in war a form of execution on wrongdoers, but surrendered a substantial part of the ground which had still been maintained by Victoria and Suarez. Compromise, arbitration, avoidance of war became merely "excellent things," and were no longer moral duties the departure from which is mortal sin.

That Grotius was still very largely under the influence of the theological discussions in respect to war is proved, for example, by his reproduction of the whole argument which had raged round the Christian attitude to fighting. A curious result of his inheritance of the doctrine of just war is to be found in his attitude towards a neutral Power in a war wherein the probability indicates that one side is waging war unjustly. He writes :—

> "The duty of those who keep themselves outside hostilities is to do nothing which renders stronger him who maintains an unjust cause or may impede the movement of him who is waging a just war . . . but in doubtful cases to maintain an equal attitude towards the two (belligerents), as far as concerns permission for the passage (of troops across territory), for provisions furnished their regiments and the refusal of succour to the besieged." (7)

One anomalous feature can be observed throughout the more than one thousand years of Christian discussion of the just and unjust war. No duty is enjoined upon princes who are not parties to the dispute to intervene in aid of the just belligerent or even to protect him from the worst consequences of an unfortunate battle. All that is suggested is that the just claimant refrain from war in the absence of confidence in a victorious and profitable outcome. Victoria in connection with this point wrote :—

> "It is clear, indeed, that if the King of France for example had rights over Milan but that the war would be, both for the kingdom of France and the province of Milan, the source of intolerable ills and great calamities, he is not permitted to secure his rights by war. This can only be made for the good of France and of the province of Milan. When on the contrary the war would result in great calamities for both it could not be just."

It has been said that the Peace of Westphalia ended the era of religious wars, and certainly the men of the seventeenth century witnessed a new attitude towards a new type of war. The great continental wars, it is true, were still the result of competing dynastic claims to provinces. The wars of the various coalitions against Louis XIV. saw both sides produce their "probable" cases, each from its own point of view, and decline to admit the good faith of their adversaries. Peculiarly pettifogging in their conception were the claims of Louis XIV. to the Spanish Netherlands in 1667 and to the various Imperial territories upon the ownership of which the

CHAP. IV. Chambers of Reunion passed judgment in the years which followed 1679. The Hapsburg claims to the whole of the Spanish Succession were perhaps as regards their moral validity hardly preferable. Side by side with wars like those which Louis XIV. waged there began to appear in increasing number a sort of war in which neither side appeared to insist on the existence of a legal claim the denial of which led to its vindication by armed force. The three Anglo-Dutch wars of the seventeenth century (1652, 1664-1666 and 1672) were characteristic wars of this type. The true reason for these wars is to be found in the British determination to win to themselves the Dutch carrying trade and to establish a colonial Empire, this notwithstanding the fact that upon the essentials of Anglo-Dutch rivalry was superimposed the antique framework of an alleged Dutch refusal to salute the British royal ships. The first Dutch war was really the result of the Navigation Act, a British legislative attempt to divert from Dutch to British bottoms a formidable amount of their then carrying trade. The second war was marked by the conquest from the Dutch of the present American New York and New Jersey; the third was launched amid deliberate and conscious cries of "*Delenda est Carthago*." The Anglo-Spanish hostilities initiated by Cromwell were an even more extreme example of this kind of war. Spain was deliberately singled out by Cromwell as an enemy which offered the opportunity of ample colonial plunder, and though Oliver Cromwell "the Empire builder" is the imaginative creation of writers, like Lord Rosebery and Theodore Roosevelt, who were seeking an ancestry for liberal or democratic Imperialism, the war did in fact add to the British Empire Jamaica and Dunkirk. These wars, largely commercial, colonial and naval in aim, were fought almost avowedly on the old pagan basis that war was a not illegitimate way of increasing national colonial possessions, national wealth and trade and national well-being of every kind. It was one of the results of Renaissance thought, particularly in Italy, that among other notions of the ancient world it had given renewed life to this. The Anglo-French hostilities of 1756-1763 are instructive from this point of view. The innovating mind of Pitt the elder saw in a war which had broken out on an Austro-Prussian issue, a war of the passing type, an occasion for an ambitious expansion of the British Empire.

In Europe, however, it is primarily with the name of Frederick the Great that there is associated the contention that mere force, ambition and ability make grounds for extensive interference with well-established territorial or dynastic arrangements. With him goes Catharine of Russia, and the descent from Machiavelli has oftentimes been pointed out. With the filching of Silesia from Austria Europe moved a definite stage further from the notion that a Power was only justified in making war if it had been afflicted with weighty grievances long unredressed. A number of dynasties, the Bavarian, the Saxon, the Prussian, the Russian and the Austrian, began a series of busy manœuvres to extend their territories, their holdings and their armies. Any move—from war or even armed invasion without a proper declaration of war down to the bribery of royal paramours—became permissible. Failure alone became inexcusable, failure like that of the Emperor Charles VII. of Bavaria against the house of Austria or that of the Emperor Joseph against Turkey. In the course of these manœuvres Austria, Bavaria, Saxony, Poland and Turkey were threatened in turn. In a sense the Napoleonic era with its ruthless disregard of traditional boundaries and reigning families was but a continuation on a grander scale of the era initiated by Frederick the Great. It must be remembered none the less that the practices of Frederick never had the field entirely to themselves. Even Frederick found it necessary to employ state lawyers to make out a case for him in order to temper, at least in part, the hostility of the conscience of contemporary opinion against those who tampered with its deep-seated, because inherited, conception of "just war." He had the ability to see, and the wit to express (but only in private) the idea that if the issue could be at least in part confused in the public mind by manufactured, or largely irrelevant, pleas, interest in the misfortunes of an aggrieved Power would markedly lose in intensity. When in 1740 his minister Podewils took up the matter of right with Frederick the answer which he received was "the matter of right is the affair of the ministers, that is your affair. It is time to work in secret, for the order to the troops has been given."

England from first to last refused to admit the Napoleonic arrangements with the Spanish and Portuguese dynasties or the negotiations which resulted in the practical absorption in the French Empire of the Dutch and German provinces. The Peace of Vienna brought a restoration of orthodoxy in the principles which determine the justice of war. Much effort was made in the nineteenth century to elevate the

CHAP. IV.

principle of nationality to the position of a dogma, and an effort was made in recent years to do the same for the principle of self-determination. When Napoleon III., Cavour and Bismarck had all employed the sentiment of nationality to suit their ends, and after the unification of Germany and Italy had disposed of the most pressing questions of nationality with which the men of the last century were confronted, the former attempt broke down. It is too early to predict the future of the latter effort. It can only be noted in passing that the prominence given in the work of the League of Nations to the study of "Minority questions" is some indication of a serious attempt to mitigate the evils inseparable from the application of the rights of self-determination. Orthodoxy after 1870 rested on an all but tacit agreement between the rulers of Austria, Russia and Prussia to insure that the pressure of ethnic groups, whom the retirement of Turkey from Europe had fanned into self-consciousness, did not shatter first the structure of their states and then the state system of Europe. In other words they had determined, separately and jointly, that nationality, whether in Central Europe, in the north or in the Balkans, though it might complicate the political life of all three Empires, should never be allowed in the main European arena to figure as the cause of a *bellum justum* directed by one of the three Empires against any of the others. The Austrian Empire, more delicately placed than either the German or the Russian, allowed itself to be drawn into the situation from which the war of 1914 resulted. Austria saw a new Piedmont in Serbia and feared for Bosnia and Herzogovina the fate of Lombardo-Venetia. An Austrian ultimatum which was intended either grossly to humiliate the Serbian government or to provoke a war with it, but in either case to end the danger which lay in South Slav nationality, found the Tsar ready to play for Serbia the part which the Emperor Napoleon III. had played for Piedmont. The Allied and Associated Powers by various declarations during 1918 adopted formally a limited vindication of nationality as the main principle of their "just war." Some of them were soon to suffer from the application of their principles in other areas and in different ways from those originally intended. At the end of the war the League of Nations does not profess indeed to put all war under its ban, as some have vainly said, but by prescribing an elaborate ritual as obligatory on all nations before recourse is had to war, and by resting this obligation on the sanction of international outlawry in cases of its neglect, it has both given to the world a fresh suggestion as to the true definition of "just war" and has revived a conception which gives new interest to the musty tomes of Fathers and canonists and scholastic moralists. It is not dynastic right, nor the principle of nationality, nor the sanctity of self-determination which the agreement of the League of Nations has enthroned. It is rather a decent respect for the opinion of mankind which has received embodiment in the machinery which the founders of the League have enjoined upon the member nations. The conscience of mankind, some men would call it and end not far from the point at which the doctors of the Church began. It is good for us from time to time that we should remember our ancestors.

The Rights of a Just Belligerent.—The canonists allowed the wager of a "just war" extensive rights over the person and the property of his "unjust" opponent. Their assumption that war consisted in the legal execution by an aggrieved prince of decisions reached by him in his capacity of judge coloured their outlook and led them to explain existing practices of war in the light of that assumption. The steps to be taken should an offending prince offer redress was a primary point of discussion. All agreed that the offer of redress ought to be accepted if it should come before the military expedition set forth. If battles had been fought and victories won it was held more doubtful whether an offer even of complete redress should be accepted. Cajetan, the cardinal, who dealt with Luther in 1518, took on this point a strong line. He held that when once military proceedings had begun, the prince who was waging a "just war" had entered on a course of judicial execution which he was under no obligation to stay. The "unjust," in his opinion, had passed from the stage at which they could offer satisfaction to that at which they must undergo punishment.

The punishment of those who waged "unjust" war was severe as judged by modern standards. The first penalty was the relinquishment of the object the seizure of which had been the original cause of dispute. Further, they must be prepared to relinquish property till the cost of the expedition, and the amount of damage done in the campaign, had been covered. In addition the "just" belligerent might take security against the renewal of the war in the shape of hostages, disarmament, the destruction of fortresses and the despatch

CHAP. IV.

of a garrison of occupation. These measures having been completed, proceedings, it was held, might be taken against the persons of the guilty enemy. Involved as they had been in "injustice" they might have deserved the penalty of death. The theologians could only strive to temper the sternness of their doctrine by refusing to countenance the wholesale slaughter of defeated combatants. While Victoria thought this permissible in the case of defeated Saracens, from whom no equitable peace could ever be hoped, he thought it abhorrent among Christians. Approving the death penalty for the responsible perpetrators of "injustice," he recommended more merciful action as regards the minor combatants. "It is necessary," he said, "to conform to the *jus gentium* in the measure to which good men are accustomed. By custom and the *jus gentium* prisoners are not put to death unless they attempt flight. Those who surrender usually stipulate for the safety of their lives." Victoria's manifest puzzlement in the face of the mediaeval notions as to unilateral justice in war is clearly brought out in his discussion of the treatment of the defeated prince and soldiers :—

> "It is not to be forgotten that the punishment must be proportioned to the guilt of him who is punished. Now it can happen that princes, even those who have not just causes, make war in such good faith that they cannot possibly be treated as guilty. Consequently it is not permitted to punish, to take anything above a just compensation, or to put to death. Further it is obvious that the case of good faith, even in the case of unjust war, must be particularly frequent for soldiers."

The political consequences of a *bellum justum* were also discussed extensively. Beside the rasing of fortresses, the occupation of others on enemy soil as security, territorial cession, tribute, deposition of the ruling prince, and the annexation of kingdoms were all subjects which were treated from the first; and moral limits to such practices defined. The general effort of the theologians was to impress upon the victorious prince that his rights arose not from the fact that he was a victor, but from his position as a magistrate in process of execution. Accordingly, it was held that the results of a victory must not be proportioned to the extent of that victory, but rather to the degree of criminality of the actions which had made the war necessary. It was not hidden from the theologians of the sixteenth century that war threw into the melting-pot the relation of all states engaged in it, that it might begin as a minor affair yet end in the suppression of the independence of some of the participating states. In his discussion of the Spanish title to sovereignty in America Victoria makes some significant remarks :—

> "When the barbarians make war among themselves, and one side, victim of injustice, has the right of declaring war, it can call the Spaniards to its aid and give them part of the advantage obtained from the victory. It was principally by this procedure that the Romans increased their Empire, lending, as they did, their help to their allies and friends, and thus acquiring new provinces by the right of war which they made justly in this wise."

Methods of War : (*a*) Booty.—The authorities allowed the soldiers to become owners of movable property seized from the guilty enemy. In practice, owing to a number of admitted exceptions, this came to mean the personal property of the embattled army after its defeat. Churchmen, pilgrims, strangers, those engaged in agricultural pursuits, had been specifically exempted from this liability by a Church canon adopted by Pope Alexander III.'s Council of the Lateran in 1179. Victoria with his keen sense of the realities of war allowed the belligerent to take even from these classes material which might serve for the purposes of war. Further, it was held that in order to prevent the prolongation of a war a "just" belligerent might proceed to such extremities as the burning of houses and the annihilation of resources. In actuality, before the organisation of the regularly paid, well maintained, thoroughly disciplined and elaborately inspected state armies which were to become a common feature of the seventeenth century, the feudal army or mercenary band, called together on the occasion of single campaigns, were not in the slightest degree to be relied on to observe the nice distinctions of the theologians. The havoc perpetrated in France by the small English bands during the Hundred Years' War, the black record of Mansfeld's forces in Germany during the opening stages of the Thirty Years' War, are clear enough indications of the insecurity of the peasant's life and property in the open countryside in the face of careless, unscrupulous or disorderly invaders who lived on the country. Wallenstein's better discipline was offset by his extremely heavy requisitions.

(*b*) Pillage.—Armies assumed the licence of pillage if they

CHAP. IV.

succeeded in entering a besieged city not after a negotiated surrender but in the actual course of assault. After a difficult, dangerous and exhausting siege, one in which the defence had been prolonged beyond what was ordinary, and, in the opinion of the besiegers, uselessly and costfully prolonged, the pillage was likely to be accompanied by wholesale slaughter and licence. Notable instances of such sackings of a city were those of Rome in 1527, Haarlem in 1572, Magdeburg in 1630 and Badajoz in 1812. In nearly all cases of prolonged resistance, or in cases of capture by assault, the generals were in no position to stay the first fury of the soldiers even if they would have really liked to do so. In numerous instances it is recorded that in order to train the soldier to endure the hardships and final dangers of the assault it was held necessary to keep vividly before him the prospects of sack and pillage. Cajetan held that it was lawful for a prince to order the sack of a city as a punishment. The prince, according to him, was not even obliged to distinguish between the guilty and innocent in such a case, for all subjects of the state were to be presumed enemy and guilty. Victoria says with equal coolness :—

> "It is not in itself unlawful to allow soldiers the pillage of a city if it be necessary for the plan of a campaign to frighten the enemy or highly excite the courage of the soldiers. Similarly it is permissible to set a city on fire. Nevertheless as such authorisations entail many inhuman acts of cruelty and savagery it is a great iniquity to deliver a city to sack without absolute necessity."

In a case of pillage the lives even of those citizens willing and eager to surrender were at the mercy of the soldiers, who could refuse quarter with almost complete immunity.

(*c*) Ransom.—In the Middle Ages the classical conception that a beaten man's life is his captor's lingered on though it was frowned on by theological authority. Victoria held that Saracen prisoners might always be put to death. In the Anglo-French wars of the fourteenth and fifteenth centuries English soldiers spared the gentlemen and nobles who were presumed to be capable of paying ransom, but they sometimes slaughtered in heaps the poorer serfs who in classical times would have been reserved for the slave market. Harsh as this sounds it is well to keep the right perspective. Ashur-nasir-pal III. of Assyria boasts of the capture of the city of Isla in these terms :—

> "I captured many of their soldiers alive. I cut off the hands and feet of some: of others I cut off the noses, the ears and the fingers. I put out the eyes of many soldiers. I built up a pyramid of the living and a pyramid of heads. On high I hung up their heads on trees in the neighbourhood of the city."

It must be remembered that armies possessed little or no means of caring for prisoners who fell to the individual charge of their captors. These only cared to be burdened with prisoners who would yield a handsome sum in ransom. Instances of royal prisoners held to state ransom were Richard I. King of England and John and Francis I. the Kings of France. The last was later replaced by his two sons. When the Lord-Deputy of Ireland, Grey de Wilton, received the surrender of eight hundred men, Spaniards and Italians, who had been landed at Smerwick on the Irish coast he put them to death, having no means of guarding them, though he held their officers to ransom. They had sailed under Spanish and papal auspices in 1580, but had no commission to wage war. He therefore classed them as pirates.

(*d*) HOSTAGES.—When a truce or a peace was concluded it was the earlier custom for one side, or for both, to surrender hostages as a security for maintenance of faith. It was early asked, therefore, what should befall these hostages were the agreements violated by one side in the opinion of the other. Victoria would have allowed the execution of hostages, if they had been taken from among the guilty, but held that, if they had been taken from among those innocent of the guilt of war, no right existed to put them to death.

(*e*) STRATAGEMS OF WAR.[8]—The theologians did not leave the discussion of the subject of war before devoting attention to the permissibility of the use of ambuscades and such other stratagems as involved the misleading of an enemy. Aquinas established clearly the distinction between telling the enemy a lie, or refraining from the fulfilment of a promise, and the act of allowing him to draw wrong conclusions from the objects which he observed or the messages which he intercepted.

> "This dissimulation enters into the category of the stratagems which can be employed in a just war. War devices of this kind do not, properly speaking, merit the name of frauds. They are opposed neither to justice nor to the properly regulated will. On the contrary it would be a disorder of the will to wish that others should conceal nothing from us." [9]

CHAP. IV.

MILITARY SERVICES—I.

Armies.—It goes without saying that the laws of war are in some sort conditioned by the character of the forces which at any epoch belligerents put into the field, the measure of control which the commissioning authority is able to retain over them, and such factors, difficult to estimate, as the professional military opinion of a generation as to the legitimate extent of interference in time of war with the normal processes of civil life.

The last step on a long road had been taken when the Congress of Paris in 1856 adopted the principle that " letters of marque " should no longer be issued. To do this was to lay it down that no part of the belligerent's war right of search and capture at sea should thenceforward be deputed to armed forces not under the direct and immediate control of the belligerent state and professionally officered and trained. So great had been the growth of humanitarian sentiment that governments no longer chose to undertake responsibility for the conduct of forces which they had not themselves organised, drilled and disciplined. Privateers were in origin sometimes nationals of, and sometimes strangers to, the Power which commissioned them. If the national mercenary, interested in war capture as a gainful profession, was thus banished in 1856 from the seas, still more severity had already been threatened to the foreign mercenary who chose to be dependent on prize operations for a livelihood. When weak states, lacking a maritime population, engaged in hostilities with other states which possessed important shipping interests, and sought to damage their enemy by offering letters of marque to foreign shipowners, strangers to the dispute, the threatened state had frequently taken up the position that it would treat as pirates these alien seamen. Thus the opinion of the world gradually expelled from the law of war the last relics of the mediaeval civilisation which had produced so luxuriant a crop of feudal armies, mercenary companies, condottieri and mercenary fleets, over whose conduct in war the commissioning state exercised an imperfect control. Hot controversy was to rage up to the present day over one relic of the older order. The modern soldier, a servant of his state from adolescence, has wished to banish from the field of legitimate warfare all military activities not professionally controlled. The *franc-tireur*, therefore, more especially in occupied countries, has been condemned as an unauthorised combatant, in that he has been held to have imperilled the law and practice of civilised war, only executable under modern conditions by professional soldiery. The *levée en masse* of a whole population under the immediate threat of an invasion has also been widely condemned and indeed only legitimised under specially defined conditions.

The armed land forces of states during the Middle Ages were originally raised on a feudal basis. A king, or a greater vassal, could summon his tenants to his service, and they had perforce to supply a stipulated number of armed and horsed followers, or risk the forfeiture of the estates which they held on the condition of such service. But at an early date the system proved unreliable and the feudal host unwieldy. Kings began to depend more and more on paid mercenaries to supplement the feudal service, especially in cases where quick and efficient offensive action was essential. Mercenaries, however, were often foreigners, both politically unreliable and as dangerous to the people and the property which they were called in to protect, as to the enemy and his property. An innovation was the light-armed and national armies of mercenaries which Edward III. of England employed in his long-drawn-out continental wars. He apparently recruited his rank and file from among his own subjects, English, Welsh and Irish. Indentures were made between the king and the nobles, or gentlemen, who undertook to raise, and to take charge of, a stipulated number of men.(10) The king sometimes paid a sum of money in advance, and of course became responsible for the pay of the troops. Commissariat arrangements were usually defective, especially where no special order had been taken in anticipation of a long campaign, and discipline was but loosely kept. The character of the armies was such that to bring them into the rich and prosperous districts of agricultural France in the fourteenth century was to invite devastation and calamity of a fearful kind. The barbarous Irish, still in the tribal stage, the fierce Welsh mountaineers and some of the most reckless of the English—Edward III. for the campaign of 1346 had invited even criminals to enlist—were hardly of the temper to feel those restraints which the laws of chivalry imposed on their leaders in their conduct of war. Even the restraints of chivalry, while they established a high standard of correctness between the opposing nobles and

CHAP. IV. commanders in the field, allowed much too great freedom to individual caprice and violence of temper when the question at stake was merely that of plebeian life and property.

The great expedition of 1346 may be taken as typical of the later mediaeval warfare on a large scale. The army landed at La Hogue in Normandy and began to plunder and to burn from the very beginning of the campaign. Spreading over a broad line of country the army quickly pillaged Cherbourg, Barfleur, Harfleur, Valognes, Carentan, St. Lo and Caen. The soldiers plundered, violated and finally destroyed what they could not carry away in peasants' carts, filled to the brim with spoil. Michael de Northburgh, a contemporary who was with the army, says of their progress, "They of the host rode on, pillaging and laying waste five or six leagues around each day and leaving many places in ashes." Carentan, "a town as large as Leicester and abounding in wine and food," was burned, and St. Lo was pillaged, while many of the inhabitants were reserved for ransom, despite the efforts of the king to save it. At Caen Froissart makes incidental mention of "the English archers slaying the people without mercy and without resistance," and of the rescue from violation by British soldiers of nuns and ladies. He sums up thus :—

> "The slaughter and pillage were too horrible to record. . . . At the two extremes of this good town were two great and rich abbeys, one inhabited by monks, the other by nuns of noble birth ; and of these latter a large number were violated and the two abbeys along with the great part of the town burned down. At which the king was sore displeased, but prevent it he could not, for his soldiers dispersed all over the town in quest of booty and no man could restrain them." (11)

The spoil taken up to date, and many of the prisoners, were sent back to England in the fleet. During the later progress, therefore, it was vain for the English soldiers to attempt to carry off bulky articles from the houses and farms. Only the smaller and more valuable articles were suitable for booty, but bargains would be struck with the peasants, by which the soldiers abstained from destruction at a price. Of the conduct of the army at Creçy it is known that but scanty quarter was given during the fighting, and that the Welshmen especially struck down French gentlemen without mercy for the sake of the plunder furnished by their arms, accoutrements and clothing. Only after the battle was over came a humaner note. Honourable burial was accorded to the French nobles.

One lesson the French had learned from the Creçy campaign, a lesson which during the next thirty years induced them to do nearly as much damage to the countryside as the English. The armies of Edward relied nearly entirely on the country for their maintenance and might be lamed by its devastation. Accordingly, when in 1355 Edward III. tried to repeat his exploit of 1346, the French themselves burned up the land behind their rearguard and in front of his advance. But there were still riches to spoil and great cities to plunder in France, as was proved by the Black Prince when he made his daring marches in 1355 and 1356. Great and unspoiled cities were burned, like Carcassonne and Narbonne: flourishing provinces were plundered, such as Armagnac, "one of the finest and fattest countries in the world." A participant in the raid of 1355, Sir John Wingfield, wrote :—

> "There has no where else been wrought such havoc as during this raid. For the lands and towns which we have laid waste brought in the French more revenue than was furnished by half his kingdom, which I could prove to you by the accounts found in the various towns and in the houses of the receivers-general." (12)

It seems to have been regarded as a just and suitable means of war that a combatant should completely waste the territories of the enemy because there was not sufficient strength to occupy them. To the end that treasure might not flow in taxation to an enemy war chest, a whole province might be wasted, even though the destruction had no relation to any specific military operation, either undertaken or planned.

An example of warfare, as it could be waged, not by the canaille in King Edward's army but by so chivalrous a knight as the Black Prince himself, is to be seen in the sack of Limoges in 1370. When this town, whose defection from the English had especially angered the Black Prince, had been taken, women and children, who threw themselves before the Prince's litter begging for mercy, were coldly disregarded and the savage butchery of thousands inspected with pleasure. Church privilege secured the sparing of the Bishop, who had been the main promoter of defection, and chivalry demanded the immunity of the French garrison, which had made a gallant defence.(13)

The fifteenth century saw the foundation in France of the first standing and national army of professional soldiers in

CHAP. IV.

the west of Europe, the francs archers and the *compagnies d'ordonnance*, who were paid from the produce of the land tax known as the *taille*. The Crown of France, however, when it was engaged, as it was in Italy, in war on a large scale, had to take into the ranks of its army hosts of domestic and foreign mercenaries in addition to these. Thus when Charles VIII. entered Italy in 1494 on a campaign which ushers in modern history, he took with him 3600 *gens d'armes*, 20,000 French and 8000 Swiss infantry. These French armies were most difficult to discipline, though they contained a stiffening of the French nobility and the new professional soldiery, and although they were fighting on territory which their king claimed as his own, fighting frequently under his very eyes. An event took place in 1501 during Louis XII.'s expedition against Naples, which illustrates what might be possible the moment the soldiers got really out of hand. During a parley for the surrender of Capua the French troops burst into the town, butchered seven thousand men in the streets and committed the greatest outrages against women and children. Caesar Borgia, who was with the French, improved the occasion by selecting forty beautiful women whom he sent back to Rome to await his pleasure.

The Italian wars which opened at the very end of the fifteenth century produced the famous professional soldiery of Spain which, together with the professional soldiery of Germany, the Lanzknechts and the Reiters, bequeathed to posterity no small portion of what is now known as the military spirit. Gonsalvo de Cordova, the great captain, who laid the foundations of Spanish power on the mainland of Italy, managed during the course of his remarkable campaigns against the French in the kingdom of Naples, to train an army of hard-marching, hard-fighting foot which proved invincible in battle for nearly one hundred and fifty years. When eventually Spanish diplomacy, no less able than Spanish arms, brought Naples and Milan into the Empire of the Spanish crown (in addition to Sardinia and Sicily already held), the Spanish soldiery who garrisoned Italy acquired many of the qualities of a "crack" military formation. The Spanish *tercios* were officered by some of the proudest of the nobility of Spain, who not only had adopted the regular service as a career but who sometimes, if they had lost their companies in consequence of a reduction of the strength, were ready to shoulder the pike as simple foot soldiers.(14) In these companies there was alike a loyal devotion to the Spanish crown and the Catholic religion, as also a keen sense of the military ideal. The professional *esprit de corps* was fostered by the care which was taken to train recruits thoroughly in the military depots at home before despatching them to their foreign stations and by the very great pride taken by the veterans in the reputation of their units. This force, when it was paid with regularity and commanded with the proper authority, was one on which the state could rely for obedience and discipline.(15) The Duke of Alva displayed its mettle to an admiring Europe when he undertook his classic march from the Italian coast to Brussels.(16) Crossing from Spain to Genoa with the principal part of his forces he mustered an army of some ten thousand men after disembarkation. The four infantry regiments of Lombardy, Sardinia, Sicily and Naples, which numbered in all nearly nine thousand men, were the best troops of Spain. Dividing his forces into three he organised a triple line of march, the second a day's march behind the first and the third a day's march behind the second. Without mishap, having crossed the Alps, he passed through Savoy, skirted Geneva, traversed Burgundy, and received permission to cross Lorraine on condition that he paid for everything he needed. For a considerable part of his march he was watched by a French force on the one side and a Swiss force on the other, but no objection could be taken to any of his movements. Until he reached the territory of the Spanish crown in the Netherlands, the only fault that could be found with his army was an incident in which three of his men turned aside to chase some Lorraine sheep. It needed special intercession to prevent all three being sent to the gallows. The more assuredly to prevent "incidents" with the country population, Alva had marched the camp women in military formation behind his troops. Even Spanish discipline gave way completely when ten years of strenuous fighting had left the ranks hungry, ragged and long unpaid. The soldiers discovered a way of paying themselves after they had broken into mutiny. In 1576 they seized and plundered Antwerp, slaying all those who opposed their attempt thus to recoup themselves.

An important stage in the history of the practice of war on land is marked by the Thirty Years' War.(17) Anarchy in Germany, and the intensity of Protestant animosity against certain aspects of the counter-Reformation, allowed to appear for the last time in European history condottieri chiefs of the type of Mansfeld, Christian of Halberstadt and even

Bernard of Weimar or Wallenstein. These generals raised their own armies and fought for their own hand. They aimed ultimately at carving out for themselves independent principalities. The unpaid and ruffianly hordes of Mansfeld and Christian, uncontrolled by any political authority and impervious to any political considerations, proved the ruin of any country upon which they were quartered, whether that of nominal friend or foe. It is fairer perhaps in estimating the conduct of war in the early seventeenth century to take for examination the behaviour of the forces of responsible generals such as Tilly and Wallenstein who acted under legitimate authority.

Tilly, a soldier of high reputation and unimpeachable correctness, one who had served with the Spaniards in the Netherlands and with the Austrians against the Turks in Hungary, held a commission from Maximilian of Bavaria as Lieutenant-General of the Catholic League, and, at certain epochs, combined with it the Emperor's commission. A characteristic example of the methods of Tilly is to be seen at the opening of the Catholic League's first campaign against the Estates of Upper Austria. When the Estates submitted he immediately drafted into his service the troops which they had raised. This at the same time increased his forces and avoided the burden of prisoners. It was a device which appealed to other commanders. Wallenstein, on the capitulation of six thousand Swedes at Steinau in 1633, allowed a large number to enlist with him. Gustavus Adolphus after Breitenfeld wrote: "We have so many prisoners that we shall not only be able to fill up the gaps in our old regiments but even to create new ones." In the circumstances of the Thirty Years' War the practice was humane. The captured men were not unwilling, for the best fate which could overtake them, were they not enlisted, was to be discharged naked and penniless into a hostile world. There was less to be said for this practice in the next century when Frederick the Great compelled the Saxon Elector's rank and file to serve in his armies against their master. It had by this time become the plain duty of a belligerent to maintain prisoners, at the expense of the enemy state, until a cartel of exchange had been arranged, or, failing that, until the end of the war. If this course were not adopted, by alternative procedure it was reckoned legitimate for a belligerent to discharge his prisoners after extorting from them promises not to serve against him for a given length of time.

Tilly's methods with regard to plunder were orthodox for his age. When in 1622 Heidelberg was captured after a long siege an honourable capitulation was allowed to the garrison, respect for which Tilly enforced in person. The town itself, however, which had been taken by assault, was regarded as belonging to the soldiery. To them Tilly allowed the accustomed three days' plunder. At Heidelberg in 1622 there were savage excesses; but what the system could become at its worst was not seen until the fall of Magdeburg in 1631. This was an important city. It had a garrison of three thousand which, along with the thirty-six thousand inhabitants of the place, had been invested since November 1630. By the beginning of May Tilly, then in possession of the outer defences, prepared for the final assault. On 4th May, 12th May and 18th May Tilly, who had undertaken the preparatory bombardment, summoned the defending authorities to surrender. The Town Council hesitated too long. On 29th May the attacking forces broke in. Wholesale slaughter began of the garrison and citizens, who were protected by no capitulation agreement, and fire was added to the other horrors of the sack. Only on the third day, when nearly the entire city had been burnt, did Tilly issue the order to spare the survivors; and not till the fifth day was the order given to stay the plunder. Pappenheim, one of Tilly's generals, put the number of the slain at twenty thousand. This has been deemed a serious under-estimate.

Tilly's attitude to quarter was clearly shown at Neu-Brandenburg in 1630. When, on 19th March of that year, he took the place by storm, he put to death the Swedish garrison of three thousand persons. He held that a garrison which, after surrender became demonstrably unavoidable, still prolonged resistance, prolonged it on its own responsibility. The besieging commander was thereby freed from any obligation to allow quarter. The fact that officers in command of besieged garrisons undertook sometimes a form of agreement with those who besieged them that they would surrender on certain conditions unless they were relieved by a certain day, indicates that military men felt that it was not safe to spin out resistance too long unless by agreement with their future captors. This was the attitude shown even up to the days of Napoleon. Nevertheless Tilly's action at Neu-Brandenburg seemed needlessly brutal to the Swedes, who resolved on reprisals for this "Neu-Brandenburg quarter." Accordingly, when Frankfort on the Oder was stormed by the

CHAP. IV.

Swedes in April two thousand Imperialists were refused quarter.

The relation of Tilly's armies to the civil population of enemy territories seems never to have attained the stage of smoothly ordered, if heavy, oppression which was characteristic of Wallenstein in his dealing with civilians. This, if correct, would warrant the assumption that Tilly lacked something of Wallenstein's organising genius. It was in 1625, in which year Tilly began the invasion of the Lower Saxon Circle, then definitely determined to fight the Emperor, that Tilly's relations with the Protestant populations reached their worst point. His reputation was so frightful that, as he approached, the countryside emptied. On the march his forces gave Lower Saxony an experience of wasting and pillage the like of which it had not known before. The peasantry rose against the intolerable violence done by the troops to person and property, only to be put down with pitiless efficiency.

Wallenstein was a soldier of considerable experience when in 1625 he received the Imperial commission to command an army of twenty-four thousand men. He had campaigned in Hungary, where he had won his company by his courage, had made a wealthy marriage and, when the Bohemian troubles broke out, had raised a regiment for the Emperor. He performed important service at a critical juncture in the battle of Zablat in 1619 and was rewarded by being allowed to accumulate a vast fortune from the confiscated Bohemian estates. This fortune he had employed to raise an army which he had been appointed to command. As the Emperor's general it was only fit that he should endeavour to give to his force a better disciplined temper towards the civil population than was possessed by the other armies in the field. His methods may be followed from his very first campaign. When in 1625 he marched into the Göttingen district, the theatre of war in that year, he established a system by which heavy requisitions were made of the country, while the towns were allowed to redeem themselves by large money payments from his right of quartering troops upon them. Resistance he punished with relentless severity. A village in which even a single soldier had been killed, was fired. Even great and famous towns accommodated themselves to these methods with understandable rapidity. Thus Nuremburg paid him one hundred thousand florins in 1625. Even on the Baltic, despite the protests of the Hanseatic League, Wismar was compelled to take an Imperial garrison which extorted large sums of money from the city. Rostock had to buy immunity from similar treatment at a heavy price, and Stralsund was told to furnish one hundred and fifty thousand dollars. When Wallenstein was in enemy territory proper, in which he might have been held to possess the war rights of the conqueror beside those arising from his position as Imperial commander-in-chief, his demands from the subjects of defeated Protestant princes for what has come to be known in the law of war as a "war-contribution" became all but intolerable. How heavy must have been the burden imposed upon such conquered districts as the bishoprics of Magdeburg and Halberstadt may be judged from the complaints which reached the Emperor, not from conquered districts but from the states of his allies, the Catholic princes, whose resources Wallenstein did draw upon, but, in contradistinction to his action in enemy territory, with real consideration. Levies of troops, the raising of money by contributions of war, heavy billeting demands, an occasional military "atrocity"—these formed the burden of an unceasing stream of complaint which was in the end to drive Wallenstein from his first command in 1630. At the beginning of 1632 when, in the Emperor's extremity, Wallenstein undertook to raise and arm a new Imperial force of seventy thousand men, he made it a condition that he was to be left unhampered in his military conduct by Imperial directions from Vienna and was to have the right of confiscation in all territories conquered by his forces. He made it clear that, if the state were unable itself to conduct its military business, it could not expect to impose conditions upon the *entrepreneur* which made it impossible for him to carry it on efficiently and on a satisfactory financial footing.

One of the worst features of the warfare was the harrying of fertile territory, not primarily as a war operation, but as revenge for the political conduct of its ruler, and as an inducement to him to change it. This was the habit of both sides. Thus Wallenstein sent Holk into the Electorate of Saxony in 1632 and 1633 with a raiding and harrying commission which was only too well executed. In 1645 the same electorate was harried by a Swedish force which, by the threat of reducing the Dresden district to a desert, compelled the Elector to sign a truce. Bavaria in 1647 underwent terrible experiences until the Elector undertook to withdraw his support from the Emperor under a temporary truce. When

CHAP. IV. Bavaria in the final months of 1647 declined to renew the truce and took up the Emperor's cause once more, Swedish and French forces devastated the Electorate with special thoroughness.

After Wallenstein's death the house of Austria took over his army, which in this way formed the foundation of the standing army of Imperial Austria, a service destined to play a glorious part in the history of European warfare. It was not the Austrian army, however, nor the powerful force of the British Commonwealth—an efficient army of sixty-five thousand which had absorbed the lessons of the three great Protestant captains, Maurice, Gustavus and Oliver—which were destined to become the force on the pattern of which all states were to organise their land troops. This glory was reserved for a totally remodelled army of the King of France.

The army of Louis XIV. must be reckoned as being in essentials the first modern army. Administratively it was controlled by a Minister of War, who had under him a service of commissaries for such matters as the issue of equipment, supplies and the making of returns. There was also a service of inspectors, who supervised the training and general efficiency of the regiments. In 1670 each regiment was ordered to be distinguished by the colour of its coats and by different marks, and much effort was expended in achieving a more decorous and finished appearance for the soldiers of the different units.(18) Great magazines of supplies were accumulated at the border fortresses, so that the problem of finding food might no longer impede the mobility, and limit the operations, of armies which crossed the borders into foreign territory. Considerable attention was given to the wounded and disabled. For the incapacitated veteran the *Hôtel des Invalides* made provision, while for the wounded on the battlefield the solution finally arrived at was a permanent medical service "à la suite des armées et dans les places de guerre." This was organised under a decree of 1708. Finally, although the proprietary right of colonels in their regiments, and of captains in their companies, was not set aside, care was taken that efficient soldiers should be in control as *lieutenant*-colonels and *lieutenants*. Cadet schools made provision for youths who were prepared to devote themselves to the career of a professional soldier. By 1678 that extremely able organiser, Louvois, the Minister of War of Louis XIV., had no less and probably far more than 230,000 men under arms.(19) So smooth, however, and so thorough was the administration, so secure the discipline and so firm the control of the central authority, that barbarities against the civil population were no longer tolerated, so far as the soldiers were concerned, while on the part of the generals semi-independent action, such as was associated with the name of Wallenstein, was now totally out of the question. An army was no longer an instrument which a ruler called out to punish his enemies, often to find he had but imperfect control of its operation. It was an instrument completely responsive to his will.

The army of Louis XIV. still contained an element composed of foreign mercenary troops which prevented it becoming a perfectly homogeneous national force. The Swiss guards were destined to serve the monarchy up to the Revolution, while a considerable rôle in the armies of the later years of the reign of Louis XIV. was played by the Irish regiments which Sarsfield brought over from Limerick. If the armies of Louis XIV. contained strong foreign elements it was not from real necessity but for traditional reasons, for reasons of policy and, in the Irish case perhaps, from magnanimity. Other princes were not always so fortunate. The Dutch republic, even for defence, had long been partially dependent on its English and Scottish regiments, while in 1700 it had to enlist 11,200 Swiss. In that same year, beside the 25,000 Swiss in the French armies and those serving with the Dutch, there were 6000 with the Crown of Spain, two regiments of 4800 with the Austrians on the Rhine, and two regiments of 4000 with the Duke of Savoy.(20) During the war of the American Revolution England found it necessary to enlist Hessians, and Swiss troops played a part in our conquest of Ceylon in 1795. Mercenary service of this type did not survive the nineteenth century. It was an age in which the sense of nationalism was intensified, so that nations like the Swiss no longer regarded soldiering as an honourable industry, and native citizens had progressively a less friendly eye for the alien military. There remained the papal force which became a kind of Yeomen of the Guard after the defeat of Lamoricière at Castelfidardo. There were to flicker into history a few last specimens of the condottiere type, Dundonald in South America, or in Egypt Slatin Pasha; but the individual adventurer is but faintly reminiscent of those vigorous soldiers of fortune who at the dawn of modern history hawked themselves round together with their companies of men. Governments which could assemble ample forces by

CHAP. IV.

the method of conscription had little need of the mercenary from abroad, but it is interesting to notice that as late as 1824 to 1828 the kingdom of Naples was busy with the Swiss in an attempt to arrange for the maintenance of four Swiss regiments of six thousand men as part of the Neapolitan service.

By the eighteenth century then European armies can be regarded as being normally under the perfect control of their state, which had now acquired an administrative perfection, and a solidity of financial position, sufficient to handle forces with an ease which would have astonished past generations. Sully might have trembled before the task of financing or administering the armies of Louvois, while King Charles I. would have declared the land and sea forces of Cromwell as beyond the capacity of the English state. Further, the growth in the humanity of war had been decided. This was due, partly to the more perfect control established by the state over its soldiers and its generals, partly to the stilling of religious passion, partly to a noticeably rising tide of humanitarianism which was before long to culminate in the *philosophe* and the benevolent despot of the eighteenth century. The horrors of Magdeburg would seem abhorrent to an Imperial commander like Montecuculi, nor would imitators be found, even in the most bitter moments of Anglo-Irish hostility, for the refusal by Cromwell of quarter to thousands at Drogheda and his special desire for the massacre of priests.

The practice of war, however, in some points remained callous. As regards devastation, for example, the French in 1689 could still order a systematic ravaging of large sections of Rhenish Germany, which involved the Palatinate and portions of neighbouring territory and necessitated the ruin of such towns as Heidelberg, Mannheim, Speyer and Worms. The military purpose of the measure was to prevent the Imperial and Austrian armies from using these districts as a base of operation against France, whose army was in process of evacuating them in order to concentrate for action in other theatres of war. Louvois attempted to justify the devastation on the ground that custom permitted it in cases of military necessity. He meant of course "military convenience," since there was no case of a real "necessity," for Louis XIV. was fighting aggressively in several fields. Marlborough, after the Elector had decided to desert the French alliance, undertook ravaging operations which in their day won notoriety—the harrying of parts of the Bavarian Electorate in 1704. It was another instance of a convenient rather than a "necessary" movement, and it was political rather than military in its inspiration. CHAP. IV.

The question of devastation has not even yet vanished from the international scene. The Hague Convention in a veiled way alludes to it, when it forbids the destruction or seizure of enemy property "unless such destruction or seizure be imperatively demanded by the necessities of the war." Sherman's notorious policy of devastation was one of the decisive factors of the Civil War in the United States of America. The British government undertook devastation on a wide scale in South Africa in order to bring Boer resistance to an end in the first two years of this century. Some provision for the affected population was sought by providing maintenance for it in concentration camps and three million pounds was voted as a grant in aid, under the terms of the Treaty of Vereeniging in 1902, towards the re-establishment of the devastated farms. The German army undertook a very thorough devastation of a limited area when in March 1917 it withdrew from threatened positions to new and powerful positions in the rear. Their object being to delay the allied advance, and the actual measure of loss being small relative to the total interests at stake, it is possible to wonder whether the indignation which it aroused at the time was not a little over-strained.

Throughout the eighteenth century then the practice of war was growing steadily milder. In Goethe's *Dichtung und Wahrheit* there is an incidental account of the behaviour of the French quartered in Frankfurt during the Seven Years' War. It leaves a good impression.(21) Similarly, his *Kampagne in Frankreich* and *Belagerung von Mainz*, accounts of his campaigns with the German armies in 1792 and 1793 in the suite of the Duke of Saxe-Weimar, throw a not unfavourable light upon the relations established between the invading armies and the civil population. The French revolutionary armies undoubtedly had a lower standard in this respect than the old royal armies. Their conduct in Belgium, Italy and the German Rhenish country was, despite the pose which they assumed as the saviours of the poor *roturier*, unprincipled, harsh and oppressive. At one stage, when the Convention gave the order for no quarter to the English and the Spanish, an order which the soldiers tacitly declined to execute, there seemed real danger of a relapse into primitive warfare.

CHAP. IV.

The fact is that with the French Revolution a new phase in the history of war was opened. This was not due so much to changes in tactics, as has sometimes been supposed, for the French revolutionary generals and Napoleon were not innovators in this respect to any large extent. De Broglie invented the division as a self-contained military unit, and Napoleon accepted it and added thereto the Army Corps, a far less original step in organisation. But the army of the eighteenth century was something of a precious tool, not to be wasted unnecessarily, not to be brought into violent opposition to the civilian inhabitants among whom it campaigned except as a last resort. It was fed from home by elaborate systems of supply train. The sensational innovation of the revolutionary epoch lay in the fact that armies were henceforward expected to live on the countryside. Modified, the system has lasted till the present day. Often the new armies were to find themselves starving. In 1796 Napoleon held out as an inducement to the soldiers, who were on the verge of starvation, the prospect of campaigning in the rich plains of Italy.

Western Germany [22] may be taken as an example, and not perhaps the worst, of the methods adopted by the French revolutionaries. Custine began with good intentions and the mild but characteristic motto "war on the palaces, peace with the cottages." Accordingly he directed that in Speyer and Worms the money contributions imposed should fall in the first place on the rich. In Frankfurt, occupied for a space by Jourdan, an attempt was made to mitigate the effect of an enormous imposition of two millions by ruling that only fortunes over a certain sum should be assessed. When, however, extensive requisitions of corn, flour, fodder, shirts, trousers and shoes began to be made—some part of which rotted and the rest was sent to France—grumbling grew loud, nor was it silenced when Custine, still with the best intentions, asked for specifications of the quantities of food-stuffs and straw available, in order, as he said, that he might be able more justly to apportion the army's demands. Meanwhile the conduct of the soldiers had the effect of wasting much of the material wealth of the country which was not requisitioned. Thus too frequently fruit-trees were used for firewood, horses were given hay for straw, and great hayricks were left unprotected from the weather. When the army paid for its supplies it was with depreciated *assignats*.

All this however was as nothing when compared with the

work of a special requisition, or evacuation commission, set up by the Convention in January 1794, one of whose tasks was to arrange that nothing of use to the enemy should be found by him in case he broke in again. Accordingly not only was the war to be made to pay for itself through requisition, but provision was to be made for the despatch into France, in case of emergency, of all cattle, corn, food-stuffs, clothing, copper, iron, lead, etc., for the destruction of bridges and the spoiling of roads. These new requisitions became nothing short of downright plunder and were aggravated by the private exigencies of unscrupulous officers and soldiers. Thus in Cologne immediately upon the entry of the troops two hundred thousand three-pound loaves were requisitioned within forty-eight hours. For the Cologne principality a heavy regular daily requisition was declared for rye, wheat, oats, straw and animals, all to be delivered to three stipulated military magazines. Further twenty-five thousand pairs of shoes were required within fourteen days from the Cologne Bezirk. More drastic methods still were employed to clothe the French soldier out of the German wardrobes. Thus even before the above-mentioned requisitions were put into operation every inhabitant of the left bank of the Rhine had been required to furnish within twenty-four hours a pair of boots or shoes and a coat or mantle. In Coblenz an ingenious French agent had hit upon the idea of summoning the citizens to the castle square, barring the exit with troops and requiring the honest burghers there and then to put off their shoes and walk home in their stockings. By the end of October 1794 the Equipment Department of the French army had already demanded on pain of death not only all arms and ammunition but iron in every shape, files, all tools of service to an army such as anvils, bellows, hammers, tongs, work-tables, picks and chains, hemp, anchors, rope, copper, brass, wire, tin, lead, pewter, saltpetre, potash, sulphur, coals, turf and construction timber. To crown this embracing demand came the contributions in money. Treves was asked for three million livres, Coblenz was assessed at one million and a half, and, when the whole area between the Maas and the Rhine was asked for twenty-five millions, two millions was imposed on Cologne. It is hardly necessary to say that it proved impossible to collect these sums, and the armies had to content themselves with more moderate levies. The support of armies by a system of levy must be treated merely as a feature of military administration in any account of

CHAP. IV. the gradual development of the military machine as it is known to-day, and it is a phenomenon so curious in itself that it must be described in its economic aspect more fully elsewhere. It is only one feature in the practice of war. It was by no means the most burdensome to civil populations.

An even more oppressive stage was reached during the hostilities in the Iberian Peninsula between 1808 and 1814. The French seizure of the kingdom was fiercely resented by the population, which took to arms and to guerilla warfare even when not organised by the "patriot" Spanish government. Stern attempts were made to put down the guerillas who continued hostilities after the Spanish field armies had been driven from the district. Thus in Catalonia Augereau issued the following typical manifesto in December 1809 :—

> "Every Catalan taken with arms in his hand twenty-four hours after the present proclamation shall be hanged without form of trial as a highway robber. Any house in which resistance is offered shall be burned." (23)

It is but fair to point out that the Duke of Wellington took much the same line himself in 1813 from his winter quarters in France, when he threatened stern measures against the Basque guerillas who would not either remain quiet or openly join Soult. The guerillas could hardly be trusted to observe such features of the laws of war as the obligation to offer quarter and to treat prisoners with humanity. Yet, as always, drastic measures in the then bitter feeling of the country made that feeling still more bitter and inaugurated a long series of atrocity and counter-atrocity. As a matter of fact, the distinction between official and independent troops was during the Peninsular campaign still somewhat academic. Even the enrolled and authorised troops of the Iberian governments were not to be trusted. Thus Wellington upon receiving the surrender of a French garrison of two thousand men in the Madrid Retiro in 1812 sent them to Portugal under a Portuguese escort. The prisoners were robbed, maltreated, and even murdered on the way.

Even the discipline of the English army was affected by the difficult and strenuous conditions of the Peninsular campaigns. Wellington personally tried hard to put down vagabondage and plunder in his army. The incident at Leiria in 1810 is well known : three soldiers and a Portuguese were hanged for plundering a chapel. The English officers were inspired to look with severity on such habits, common among the French, as using doors, window frames, and shutters as firewood. When on the retreat from Burgos in 1812 soldiers continually broke away to plunder, the droves of swine having proved an especially alluring temptation, courts-martial were not likely to take a lenient view. A Judge-Advocate-General was appointed in the autumn of 1812 to relieve Wellington of the burden of courts-martial. Despite the correct views of the commander, however, it proved impossible always to maintain discipline. Of the personnel of his army even in 1813, when the tide of victory was flowing high, Wellington was capable of saying, "It is desirable that any reinforcements of infantry which you may send to this army may come to Santander notwithstanding that I am very apprehensive of the consequences of marching our vagabond soldiers through the province of Biscay in the state of discipline in which they generally come out." Under great stress the authority of the officers was apt to prove unavailing. The victory of Vittoria produced so complete a breakdown of discipline that Wellington wrote: "We started with the army in the highest order and up to the day of battle nothing could be better, but that event has as usual totally annihilated all order and discipline." The worst breakdown of discipline in the army of Wellington occurred on the occasion of the storm of Ciudad Rodrigo, Badajoz and Saint Sebastian. "At Ciudad Rodrigo," wrote Napier, "intoxication and plunder had been the principal object; at Badajoz lust and murder were joined to rapine and drunkenness: but at Saint Sebastian the direct, most revolting cruelty was added to the catalogue of crimes." At Badajoz the soldiers were incensed by what they considered treacherous firing upon them from the houses, and, in retaliation, undertook extensive pillage and worse with tipsy and uncontrollable ferocity. At Saint Sebastian Wellington had foreseen the possibility of trouble, but his precautions proved unavailing, owing to the unusually high proportion of the officers who were lost in the successful storming of the breach. His attitude towards the whole question of pillage in the case of places taken by assault is summed up in a despatch in which he defended his own conduct as regards Saint Sebastian:—

"In regard to the plunder of the town by the soldiers I am the last who will deny it because I know it is true. It has fallen to my lot to take many towns by storm and I am concerned to

CHAP. IV.

add that I never saw or heard of one so taken by any troops that it was not plundered. Notwithstanding that I am convinced that it is impossible to prevent a town in such a situation being plundered, I can prove that upon this occasion particular pains were taken to prevent it." (24)

In the campaign of Waterloo we learn from the fascinating journal of Mercer that Wellington was so rigorous in exacting a high standard of conduct towards the local inhabitants from his much-tried army that it all but threatened to break up their moral.

It is a common assumption that there has been a progressive development towards an ever-humaner conduct of war. Such an assumption shares, with all explanations of human history which start from a teleological basis, the fact that it is difficult either to prove or to disprove. It is safer perhaps to leave the grand philosophy alone and to be content with indicating that the determining factor in the conduct of war has been the extent of the dependence upon the home authority of the military force conducting the campaign. It may ultimately be a matter of the ethical view taken by the nation in the home county, or of the troops and their commander in the field : it is immediately a matter of organisation. The feudal host made way for the mercenary army. This in turn was replaced by an army of professional soldiers. To that army was given permanent form which in due course became traditional. It was as if combatant nations had selected their champions in the old fashion of chivalry, and, for their battle *à l'outrance,* had endeavoured to clear a ring. Indiscriminate licence in plunder, an immoderate and penal practice of the requisition, were, it might be said, distracting to the troops on the campaign. The revolutionary armies of France, Wellington's armies in the Peninsula, seem in their conduct of war reminiscent of an earlier age, but the government in Paris was rendered abnormal by domestic anxieties, and by its half-digested theories on the Rights of Man. The British War Office was showing the strain of the long-drawn-out Napoleonic war. And, as has been shown above, the theory of war was changing. It is significant that the commander-in-chief apologised because the machine with which the home authorities supplied him fell short of the standard which he would have wished to see maintained. Later in the nineteenth century armies were to become less compact, but in a sense not less professional, because the control over them strengthened rather than weakened. In the wars of the nineteenth century a new feature appeared, that of the nation under arms. The comparatively small professional army disappeared, but it disappeared not in order to make room over again for the soldier of fortune or the leader of condottieri. The bigger the force the greater was the need for a perfectly trained Great General Staff. General headquarters in the field were always attached to the end of the telegraphic wire. Then control and organisation, matters formerly left for unscientific, half-amateurish treatment by the field commanders, became systematised and treated by the methods of "Big Business." Transport, the care of wounded and of prisoners, the commissariat, these, and all similar activities of an army, were to undergo this process. It must be the next task to trace in this connection the transformation both in the practice and in the theory of war.

Contributions and Requisitions.—There has been previous occasion to remark upon the contributions in money levied in hostile territories by the commanders in the Thirty Years' War. If Wallenstein acquired notoriety by his exactions, other commanders, whom history regards more favourably, were capable of making excessive demands. Thus Gustavus Adolphus imposed the enormous sum of over three hundred thousand dollars upon Munich, which had not even attempted to make resistance, and he was in fact compelled to remit part of it. The contribution in its origin was patently the commutation of the rights of pillage, bought from a victorious commander by a population which had reason to fear the total destruction of its property, if the commander after a military success either gave his force permission to pillage, which was always eagerly sought, or did not restrain it by the imposition of firm discipline. Thus Gustavus Adolphus remitted his right of pillage over Mayence, which had been held against him, for eighty thousand dollars. The citizens of Mayence would undoubtedly have lost far more than eighty thousand dollars had the soldiers been given a free hand. There would have been a wasteful destruction of valuables which the soldiers in the circumstances could not have put to use, and the military chest of Gustavus Adolphus would probably have been but little fuller.

The Englishman Molloy (1676), a strong advocate of English maritime claims, in his work the *De jure maritimo* had a singular chapter which provides an early attempt to find a place in International Law for contributions and did it

CHAP. IV.

by rationalising this consideration. His twelfth chapter mentions the demands made by invading Powers on the governments of the neighbourhood for contributions. Incidentally he was concerned for the position of those "neuters" who lived on the confines of two belligerent Powers. He was concerned at the possibly criminal position, *vis-à-vis* the municipal law, of those who paid contribution to the invader, and he attempted to justify them as follows:—

> "If some number of men, able to take what they ask, demand, (with an armed power) the payment of a certain sum to be employed in war, then in such a case the man, whom we suppose, must pay it in ransom for his life, or give it as a man doth his purse, when he is surprised in the highway, because to this man it is as much as to the whole country with an armed power. So several dutchies and Seignories, dependent on the Empire, did in the war between them and the Crown of France pay contribution. . . . But where a man or a city is fully possessed by an invading power (be the same just or unjust) from whom they can not fly nor remove their substance, most certain it (*i.e.* the contribution) is no gift."

Finally on the same ground of overwhelming necessity he allowed those that lived on the confines of two belligerents to pay contributions to both to avoid worse things.

In the wars of Louis XIV. the practice with regard to contributions grew much milder.(25) Vattel mentions the fact that at the beginning of hostilities treaties were sometimes made which provided for the levying of contributions on a reasonable basis. The territories on which they were to be levied, the amount of the contributions and the conduct to be observed by those collecting them, were then often defined. Vattel justifies both the exaction and the payment of contributions on a rather different ground from that chosen by Molloy. Contributions, he said, were justly exacted by the just belligerent to regain part of that which was owing to him. They were rightly paid by the subject to preserve his property from harm.

> "Whosoever carries on a just war has the right to make the enemy's country contribute to the support of his army and to all the expenses of war: he thus obtains a part of what is due to him, and the subjects of the enemy, by submitting to the contributions imposed, have their property protected from pillage and their country saved from harm."

Frederick the Great of Prussia did not err on the side of lenity. Yet, compared with that of Napoleon, his practice seems agreeably mild and gives evidence of the definite growth of international amenity since the worst days of the seventeenth century. Frederick the Great expected that his troops, when they lay in winter quarters, would receive from the enemy country in which they were stationed bread, meat and beer, and without payment for them. Further, he held that horses for the artillery, munitions, provisions and sums of money for the replenishment of deficiencies in the military chest might, if needed, be drawn from the countryside. There are several striking examples in the eighteenth century of the way in which the Austrian armies in particular forfeited success through their extreme scrupulousness in abstaining from any demand on the civil population. In the general theory of the eighteenth century contributions, either in money or in kind (now called requisitions), seem to have lost practically all connection with the idea of the commutation of pillage. When the Duke of Brunswick invaded France in 1792 with an Austro-Prussian force he issued some requisition receipts in the name of the *King of France.*

J. J. Moser in his *Versuch* has a number of documents connected with the levy of requisitions made in Poland by Prussian, Russian and Austrian forces during the epoch which followed the agreement between these three Powers to carry out the First Partition. Especially noteworthy is a communication from the three ambassadors to the delegation of the Polish Diet. The date is 22nd July 1773, and in it the following conditions are given. In each Polish palatinate the commanders would give to the Polish authorities a list of their troops and of the food necessary for them. Food would only be taken for the troops scheduled and actually present in Poland. No magazines would be formed to be subsequently transported abroad and sold. Food, that is corn and oats, would be carefully measured according to stipulated measures. Finally, nothing extra was to be given to the soldiers, who were already provided for by eating at the tables of those with whom they were billeted. Even more noteworthy is the arrangement made between the Russian ambassador and the Polish authorities later in 1774. It was on the avowed basis of payment for supplies. There had been Polish complaints of non-payment for goods which had been requisitioned for the use of the Russian army. The Russian ambassador, Stackelberg, took up the position that it was impossible that each load of forage or provisions should be paid for separately to each individual. He believed that proper entries had been made in the books of the Russian army, which were open to inspection, but that no doubt it was possible that in the days of disorder there had been against the enemies of Russia some discrimination. It was necessary for the Poles to appoint commissioners to deal directly with the Russian military authorities if abuses were to be avoided. As a result there were appointed two Polish general commissioners, one for the kingdom and one for the Lithuanian Grand Duchy, and under them was arranged a service of local commissioners. The Russian general remitted notes of his requirements to the General Commissioners who divided them up among the local commissioners. As these delivered the goods they were paid for.

From an early date the French methods during the revolutionary wars were severe. It is curious to find that the civilian Cambon demanded from the Convention decrees which should " permit the liberation of the peoples " to pay for itself, while the soldier Dumouriez protested that the ill-will of the plundered if liberated peoples had been the chief cause of military disaster. Dumouriez, that is to say, belonged to the older, Cambon to the newer school of military organisation. The French levy of contributions and their requisitions reached their most tyrannous height in Prussia after the battle of Jena in 1806. The day after the battle contributions of one hundred and sixty million francs were imposed on North Germany. When the treaty and the convention for evacuation were signed with Prussia in July 1807, it was decided that the French should evacuate Prussia on the payment of the outstanding contributions of war from Prussian territory the amount of which was left undefined. Napoleon himself estimated the sums due from Brandenburg and Silesia at one hundred and twenty millions of francs and urged the extraction of all that was possible. He even approved the raising of the sum to two hundred millions. When the sum due from Prussia was finally fixed at one hundred and twelve millions in March 1808, it became the settled policy of the French to refuse any conditions which should ease for Prussia the task of payment. While payment was deferred large portions of the French army could be quartered in Prussia to live on the country. Altogether the sums actually extorted have been estimated by one authority at six hundred and one million francs, and by another at not less than one thousand million.

The generals of the early nineteenth century seem to have

decided that there was danger in the requisition of food and fodder by the actual armies engaged in a military campaign. Napoleon felt the inadvisability of attempting to supply his huge army of 1812 in this way, and had made special commissariat arrangements accordingly. When these broke down, as they partially did break down, the system of requisition, to which he resorted, proved detrimental to discipline. Halleck says of the French armies which were operating in Spain, that those occupying favourable districts, in which it was possible to open a market, endeavoured to pay for their supplies, while those which operated in districts unfavourable in this respect resorted to the practice of requisition, and caused much of the bitter anti-French feeling. Wellington during his Peninsular campaigns abstained from requisitions, as did the American soldiers in Mexico and the English and French in the Crimea.

The growing size of armies through the nineteenth and twentieth centuries made it certain that the country through which they passed could only be relied on for a diminishing share of the provisioning of them, the main burden of which would increasingly have to be borne by the home commissariat service. Even in the Franco-Prussian War of 1870-1871, in which requisitioning and the levy of contributions played a larger part than had for some time been customary, the total part played by such means in provisioning the armies, or in filling the military chest, must have been relatively small. It remains an indispensable military right to requisition for the supply of food, and the like, to such forces as advanced detachments and skirmishing parties. It must also be regarded by soldiers always as a necessary reserve when the commissariat arrangements, even for the main body, have broken down, wholly or in part. Contributions can be justified as a means of sharing the burden of such exactions between the urban and the rural population. The inhabitants of a town may have little or nothing of which the military force stands in need, a country population may have what they desire to a sufficient extent, but not be in a position to lose it all simultaneously for such immediately unremunerative objects as certificates of requisition. A military force by levying a money contribution on the town may be in a position to pay in cash for at least a part of its requirements from agricultural districts.

The habit of the modern belligerent is to give receipts for such requisitioned or contributed articles which he receives.

CHAP. IV. Accordingly, the private citizen who has made an individual surrender of valuables to the belligerent has at the end of the war evidence of his claims. At the peace it is usual for one government or the other to assume the burden of the requisitions and contributions. Thus the British government at the end of the South African War redeemed all its own requisition certificates, allowed those of the Boer government to figure as evidence of the war losses sustained by those to whom they had originally been given, and made similar provision for certain types of notes which had been issued by the enemy. Germany in 1919 was forced to undertake payment for the damage it had inflicted upon the civilian population in the form of levies.(26)

Armies and Forced Work by Civilians.—The army of the twentieth century is, as has been pointed out, much more than a mere collection of warriors. It endeavours to contain within its own organisation all the activities necessary to keep the actual combatant units at the highest point of military efficiency. Thus there are essential transport and fortification sections ; but, nevertheless, the modern army must often have recourse to the requisition of the machinery of transport and still more of human labour. Indeed it is not yet certain that a belligerent in occupied territory of the enemy could not require, above and beyond such things as work on roads, both labour on entrenchments and service in erecting fortifications, for the wording of the Hague Conventions merely forbids a commander to require participation in " military operations."

The attitude of the seventeenth-century soldier, unequipped with army service corps, engineering units or labour battalions, was that work which he could not do for himself he could require from the civil population of the vicinity. Even in the territories of his own prince he was not, neither did he need to be, over gentle. A Spanish viceroy of Catalonia could write of his own master's civilian subjects (27) :—

> " Do not allow a single man in the province able to work to absent himself from the field, nor a woman capable of carrying a bundle of fodder on her back. This is no time to beseech but to command. The Catalans are naturally fickle ; sometimes they will, sometimes they will not. Make them understand that the welfare of the nation and the army must go before all laws and privileges. . . . Seize their beds for the troops, even from the highest in the province if necessary, and let them sleep on the ground. . . . If pioneers are wanted and peasants refuse to go, force them to do so, and if necessary carry them

bound. Do not spare force, no matter how loudly they cry out against you." CHAP. IV.

Nevertheless, civilians have largely been protected from forced labour on the battlefield and in entrenchments by the logic of the normal situation if not by International Law. The effort needed to gather any considerable body of unwilling labour to a needed point, the enormous difficulties of achieving any work from it, even when so gathered, and the military dangers incidental to the whole process are obvious to all. Commanders and soldiers have practically always resigned themselves, therefore, to the necessity of doing their entrenching though they have found it possible to get much indispensable transport service done for them by requisitioned materials, animals and labour.

The Treatment of the Wounded.—In the sixteenth century armies in the field were not accompanied by doctors or hospital services. The only surgeons present on the battlefield were attached to the personal staff of the commanders or of men of high station accompanying the army. The seventeenth century saw considerable development of the medical services with campaigning troops,(28) the French army under Louis XIV. being especially well equipped with hospitals. It was in the seventeenth century accordingly that arrangements were first made between commanders in the field which extended to such questions as the reciprocal care of the wounded. In 1689, for example, a convention was signed between the Elector of Brandenburg, commander for the league of Augsburg, and the Count of Asfield who commanded the French forces. It provided for a mutual respect towards both hospitals and wounded. Another example often quoted is the convention made, in June 1743, between Lord Stair on behalf of the Pragmatic army and the Marshal Noailles for the French during the Dettingen campaign. This bound both sides to treat hospitals and wounded with consideration. Noailles, when he felt that his operations might cause alarm to the inmates of the hospitals at Techenheim, went so far as to send word that they should rest tranquil as they would not be disturbed. A fuller, and more highly developed, type of agreement was that signed at L'Ecluse in 1759 by the Marshal de Brail, who commanded the French, and Major-General Conway the British general officer commanding. The hospital staff, chaplains, doctors, surgeons and apothecaries were not, so it ran, to be taken prisoners; and, if they

CHAP. IV.

should happen to be apprehended within the lines of the enemy, they were to be sent back immediately. The wounded of the enemy who should fall into the hands of their opponents were to be cared for, and their food and medicines should in due course be paid for. They were not to be made prisoner and might stay in hospital safely under guard. Surgeons and servants might be sent to them under the general's passports. Finally, on their discharge, they were themselves to travel under the same authority and were to travel by the shortest road.

The French military surgeon of the revolutionary wars, Percy, induced General Moreau to send a proposal to the Austrian commander, Krug, which contained novel features. The roads leading up to hospitals were to be marked by special signs which would indicate the presence of wounded in the vicinity. Troops were to avoid these roads wherever possible or, in passing along them, were to abstain from disturbing noises. Hospitals were to remain the property of the belligerent even after he had evacuated the country. The belligerent in occupation was, under proper security, to furnish or requisition materials for the hospitals. Those soldiers who recovered were to be allowed to rejoin their former units. When it was decided to evacuate the entire hospital, the occupying belligerent was to provide an escort for the convoy of the waggons. These proposed arrangements were rejected by the Austrians.

Belligerents without a doubt were eager where possible to hand over the wounded of the enemy or to allow them to depart at the first convenient moment. A defeated belligerent who left his wounded on the field was providing a conscientious enemy with a serious embarrassment. When eighteenth-century armies, therefore, proposed very liberal arrangements for the evacuation of wounded, the reason was not entirely philanthropic. "Philanthropy" forbade the abandonment of the enemy wounded, but good policy required that the main burden of their nursing should still be thrown on the enemy.

The need for a general and international convention, which should put the treatment of the wounded on a permanent basis and which should secure safety for hospitals, had been felt as early as the eighteenth century. Chamousset in the year 1764 referred with regret to the thousands of lives which had been sacrificed when, as a result of military operations, the forced and hurried evacuation of hospitals had become necessary in order to save the wounded from falling into the enemy's hands. Péyrilhe in 1780 proposed international recognition of the principle that the wounded should not be made prisoners of war and should not enter into the balance of exchanges. Opinion was crystallised by the well-known pamphlet *Un souvenir de Solférino* published by Monsieur Dunant who had seen the lot of those who had fallen on the battlefield in Northern Italy.(29) CHAP. IV.

When the Geneva Convention was drawn up in 1864 the positive duty was imposed on signatory states to collect the wounded of the enemy, to care for them and to return them on recovery, provided that they were unfit for further service with the armies. Hospitals, ambulances and medical staffs, duly marked with the cross of Geneva, were to be "neutralised" and made exempt from hostilities. Provision was made for special privileges to be accorded to the inhabitants who, living near a battlefield, succoured and sheltered the sick. The Geneva Convention of 1906 was designed to bring the older convention into harmony with newer methods of war. The co-operation of local inhabitants in the care of the wounded was still invited, and place was even made on the battlefield for voluntary aid societies, both of belligerent and neutral nationality. It was arranged that the dead should be, if possible, identified before burial, and that their property should be returned. Lists of sick and wounded, with information as to their subsequent fate, were to be exchanged. A definite departure from the milder practice of the eighteenth and nineteenth centuries was provided when it was agreed that the sick and wounded of the enemy might be detained as prisoners of war. The duty was imposed on the defeated belligerent of leaving sufficient of his medical staff and material to provide for his own wounded. His opponent could require the enemy medical staff to remain as long as their services were essential. He would be bound to pay them at his own customary rates, and to send them back when they had finished their duties. "Mobile medical units," including apparently even such things as field hospitals, would not be in future subject to capture under the "laws of war," though they might be diverted by the capturer to immediate and pressing medical uses. Convoys for the evacuation of the wounded, it was agreed, might only be broken up in the case of military exigency—in which case apparently the wounded could be detained as prisoners, together with all material for transport not specially designed

CHAP. IV.

or adapted for medical uses, which would fall under the ordinary rule of capture. Fixed, and stationary, hospitals which fell into the hands of the enemy did so under the proviso that they were not, except in cases of emergency, to be devoted to other than medical uses.

In 1907 international regulation of the treatment of the sick and wounded in warfare upon land was completed by a convention which extended the principle of the Convention of Geneva to warfare on the sea.

MILITARY SERVICES—II.

Navies.—Every expert has his own date for the beginning of modern history. The student of naval history will choose 1571 as the dividing point, the date of the battle of Lepanto. For Lepanto was conspicuously the last naval engagement fought on the old Mediterranean model, which had remained essentially unchanged since the days of the struggle between Rome and Carthage. It is the old world, not the new, which is called up by the pictures which historians of Lepanto have given: the Turkish and Christian galleys arranged in three divisions on a calm sea, the Christian admiral Don John of Austria rowing from ship to ship on a mission of exhortation, the crowd of soldiers on the decks in keen expectation of the boarding operations, man, in the shape of galley-slaves, as motive power, the dogged resolution of the Christian fleet to free the Mediterranean from the Sultan's stranglehold. It was not on this sea, but on the outer ocean, that there were to be developed a new model, new instruments, new organisation and new methods, of maritime contention between states. In this development the naval authorities of England were to play a typical and continuous, if not always a pioneering,(30) part; and it is therefore permissible to describe with some precision the construction, training and control of the British naval service together with the theory of war at sea which it adopted.

The English kings of the Norman and Angevin lines had large continental possessions, between which and England they had constantly to be passing. In such circumstances it is in the highest degree likely that the Crown always possessed ships for the transport of persons, goods and treasure. For the transport of a whole military expedition in time of war much more than a few royal *esneccae* (snacks) would be essential. Some idea of the method by which a force of transports was raised by the Crown is given in the accounts of Richard Cœur-de-Lion's preparations for the Crusade. Royal agents were sent to the principal ports of the country. Some ships were bought at full price; some were obtained at half price; some were provided at the expense of the Crown. Captains and sailors were taken into the king's service and paid a wage. The united fleet from all the dominions of King Richard was assembled at Dartmouth and set sail in April 1190. Five sea justices were appointed and severe disciplinary regulations were published, of which the following typical examples may be quoted. A murderer on shore was to be punished by being buried alive with his victim, a murderer at sea by being lashed to the corpse and drowned. A blow which drew blood was to be avenged by the loss of a hand, one not so serious by a threefold ducking in the sea. At the Tagus in July 1190 the fleet numbered one hundred and six vessels, each ship carrying a captain, a crew of fourteen, forty men and horses, and supplies for a twelve-month. The only naval battle took place off the Syrian coast in June 1191, when a great Saracen ship was encountered and rammed by an English ship. The accounts tell how men to the incredible number of one thousand three hundred were refused quarter, the rest of the crew of this enormous barge-raft, some fifty-five Saracens only, being spared.(31)

The English kings John, Henry III. and Edward I. all had need for fleets of transports overseas. A great part of such fleets would be collected for short expeditions by feudal methods applied to maritime affairs, the king requiring the merchants of the ports to furnish him with a fixed number of ships at a fixed rendezvous at a fixed date. For a Poitevin expedition Winchelsea was asked in King John's reign to furnish ten good and large ships: on another occasion twenty. Similarly Dunwich and Ipswich were asked for five each. Again, King Edward III. in the thirteenth year of his reign asked the Cinque Ports among others to furnish him with thirty ships, half at their cost, half at his own.

Internal discipline was not always an easy thing to maintain in a fleet which was gathered in this way. On one occasion when, in the course of the almost ceaseless Anglo-French hostilities, Edward I. had caused an expedition to be transported to Sluys in Flanders, desperate fighting broke out

CHAP. IV. between the Yarmouth and the Cinque Ports' squadrons during the course of which the Yarmouth ships were burnt. When forces from a fleet effected a landing in hostile territory the inhabitants had little consideration to expect from men of so violent a type under so imperfectly maintained a discipline. When the French landed at Portsmouth from galleys, as in 1337, or at Southampton, as in 1338, the tale is always of the town sacked and burned. The English expeditions against Normandy in 1337 and against Boulogne in 1339 repeat the story.

The reign of King Edward III., full of hostilities as it is with the French, was remarkable for the gathering of enormous fleets and for the development of highly important military contests on the sea. The figure of 738 ships, seven hundred of them British, is given as the strength of the English blockading force before Calais. These ships are said to have contained 14,956 mariners. These numbers, if correct, bear striking testimony to British maritime power, which was here engaged on the task of preventing relief by sea from reaching Calais. Henry V. on the other hand, when faced with the problem of conveying across the Channel his army of six thousand men-at-arms and twenty-four thousand archers, had to procure the greater part of his shipping from Holland and Zeeland. The first real squadron fighting in Western seas dates back only to 1340, with the famous Anglo-French naval battle of Sluys. A French fleet of one hundred and ninety ships manned by thirty-five thousand Normans, Picards and Genoese mercenaries had been prepared with a view to the prevention of the landing of Edward III. in France. Edward with two hundred and fifty ships attacked. The English battle-fleet was arranged in two lines and on a carefully-thought-out plan. A hard-fought combat of singular ferocity resulted in French losses which Edward III. himself gave as thirty thousand. The beginnings of a royal navy are hinted at in the accounts of the recapture of such ships as the *Christopher* and the *Edward*, royal ships lost to the French in 1338, and by such entries in the list of English losses as "One great ship and galley belonging to the king's royal wardrobe." [32] Two great Anglo-Castilian contests, the first in 1350, the second in 1372, the former in the Channel, the latter off Rochelle, brought another nation into the lists of Atlantic belligerents. [33]

The naval power of the English kings sank almost to nothing after the death of Edward III. [34] Henry IV., for example, found himself unable to keep the sea clear from pirates and was himself nearly captured in 1407,[35] during a voyage from Queenborough Castle to the Essex shore. At one period he was compelled to adopt the device of allowing the merchants of the ports to levy duties on the various imports and exports, the money raised by which was to be devoted to defence. He was further forced to permit them to nominate admirals of the north and south with powers to organise naval action. In the reign of Henry V. there was a remarkable revival. Oppenheim in his book, *The Administration of the Royal Navy*, goes so far as to say that under this king's rule "the Crown navy was increased till in magnitude it exceeded the naval power of any previous reign," and that the character of the ships showed "that they were provided for sea-going purposes rather than the mere escort of transport of troops which had been the object of preceding kings." Under Henry VI. the bulk of the navy was sold and the country again depended on hired ships. Five peers were appointed to keep the seas, tonnage and poundage being assigned for their expense; but this experiment, like that of Henry IV., was not long continued. Lawlessness and violence were not confined to pirates.[36] The most powerful nobleman in England, the Earl of Warwick, Governor of Calais and Lord High Admiral, seems to have made reckless and indiscriminate attacks with his own ships upon the Channel traffic on one occasion when he was crossing to Calais upon the business of his governorship. Though he sold his prizes for ten thousand pounds to the great profit of the Calais citizens, the Lübeckers protested to the king, and the Genoese undertook reprisals. Finally, the king set up a commission of inquiry to decide whether there was force in the contention of his "over-mighty" subject that these friendly states were in reality sheltering the commerce of enemy Spaniards and Frenchmen. Even so late as 1512 when the notorious Andrew Barton, on the pretext of Scottish letters of reprisal against the Portuguese, was plundering all commerce indiscriminately on the English coasts, it was an English nobleman who suppressed him at his own personal expense. "The narrow seas," said the Earl of Surrey at a meeting of the King's Council, "should not be so infested while he had estate enough to furnish a ship." With Edward IV. a beginning was made towards the restoration of a Crown navy, a movement which Henry VII. sustained but did not intensify.[37]

Henry VIII. was the monarch to whom the Tudor navy

CHAP. IV.

owed the origin of its power. Already in the beginning of his reign he showed marked interest in maritime questions, even interest of a technical character. In 1512 he fitted out a powerful fleet of forty-five ships which proceeded to Brest to fight a French fleet collected there. Two of King Henry's ships were enormous for that age, the *Regent* of one thousand tons with a crew of seven hundred, and the *Sovereign* of eight hundred tons. In the battle great guns were extensively used at sea for the first time. The expedition was repeated in the next year with forty-two ships. King Henry's interest in matters maritime was stimulated in the latter part of his reign by his Protestant attitude and the consequent danger of attack from the Continent. Considerable attention was directed to coast fortification and dockyards. In 1545 when a powerful French fleet appeared near Portsmouth, in which harbour an English fleet was preparing for sea, King Henry hurried down personally to give the order of attack.

Queen Elizabeth inherited her father's navy and dockyards —those of Chatham and Portsmouth were already notable— and added considerably herself to English naval strength. In ordinary times, it is true, the English navy consisted of one or two second-raters which acted as a police force for the narrow seas, and a crew of officers and men who were recruited *ad hoc*. Nevertheless when the moment of danger came in 1588, the ships which she had inherited or added to the force, though they had been lying mostly in dock under the care of shipwrights, clerks and watchmen, were manned by eager volunteers and rendered admirable service. The dockyards had been in charge of a capable sailor, John Hawkins, who had kept the ships in readiness and had in good condition both them and supplies such as timbers, ropes, anchors, cables, lighter cordage and canvass. Good work, too, had been done by a naval commission appointed in 1583, which had appropriated a fixed sum for dockyard expenses, and had adopted a policy of building at least one royal ship a year. When the Spanish attack came, the royal navy with its total of thirty-eight ships and, above all, with its thirteen heavy ships of over four hundred tons apiece, furnished the indispensable background to the national resistance at sea. The help of individual subjects and of corporations was, of course, indispensable. Campbell, the historian of the admirals, has given the force which engaged with the Spaniards in the following table :—

CHAP. IV.

Royal men-of-war . . .	17	(34, or 15 over 400 tons, according to Oppenheim)
Ships hired for this service	12	
Tenders and storeships .	6	
City of London ships . .	16	(double the number asked)
City of Bristol	3	(large)
Barnstaple	3	(converted merchantmen)
Exeter	2	(with tender and pinnace)
Plymouth	7	(equal to men-of-war)
Furnished by Nobility, Gentry and Commons . . .	43	(The Howards alone had ten small ships)
The Merchant Adventurers	10	
Under Lord Henry Seymour	16	(Partly royal ships)

Crews of excellent sailors were easily obtained. They had been trained either in the merchant service or in the semi-piratical operations which had been extensively carried on against Spanish shipping for some years by the sailors of Devonshire. The trouble was not to hold them but rather to prevent the Queen, who was frightened by the unprecedented expense of maintaining at her charges many thousands of sailors, giving orders for at least a partial discharge when she found that the Spaniards were not immediately at hand.

The Spanish crown had a much larger royal navy than the English. The service of the American colonies would in any case have made necessary a fleet of considerable magnitude. The Armada of 1588, however, contained Portuguese and Italian elements as well as Spanish. There were sixty-five large ships, divided into six squadrons and ranging from seven to thirteen hundred tons in burden. Beside further royal vessels of the galley type there were fifty-six strong armed merchant vessels. King Philip had encouraged the building of such ships by offering, half as a gift, half as a loan, four ducats a ton for ships of over three hundred tons and six ducats a ton for ships of over five hundred tons.

Of the character of the fighting the student of the practice of war will need a brief indication. It consisted largely of vain attempts on the part of the Spaniards to fight the kind of boarding action to which they were accustomed; and, on the English side, of a successful attempt to avoid military action of this kind, which did not give them scope for their superior seamanship, and to concentrate on manœuvre and gunnery. Fighting, when it became hand to hand, was savage. Thus, when the *San Matteo* was boarded off the Belgian coast by forces sent from Flushing by Lord Willoughby, the crew was butchered and flung into the sea, only a few officers being reserved for ransom. Sidonia's household

CHAP. IV. servants landing in Tralee to surrender were executed in Tralee Castle. Several hundred other prisoners, who had been cast ashore on the west coast of Ireland and who had been gathered together into Galway, were there shot or hanged, with the exception of ten officers who were kept for ransom. Beyond this slaughter on the part of the responsible English authorities, more extensive massacre was undertaken by the savage population of native Irish upon whose coasts ships had been wrecked.(38)

Between the accession of King Charles I. and the Revolution of 1688 much was to be done to the British navy. Ship money has occupied so prominent a place in English constitutional history that other important aspects of it have been sometimes overlooked. The levying of ship money can always be associated with a most important development in English naval history. The adjuncts to the fleet in the shape of merchantmen take, after the formation of the second ship-money fleet, an entirely subordinate place. Homogeneity was the first step on the road towards the adoption of serious naval tactics. It is difficult to trace the exact progress of these, but it is probably true to say that, but for the organisation by Charles of the ship-money fleets, there would have been no "Fighting instructions" of 29th March 1653: and that, but for the "Fighting instructions," there would have been no adoption of that English invention, the formation of a fleet in "line ahead." But there were other features of the Commonwealth and Restoration period which are not less important. A new organisation took the place of the old, and one that smacked more of the sea and a council of war than of the Court. In 1649 the Council of State took over the functions of the Lord High Admiral, and, although the old parliamentary committee on the navy was not to disappear for some years, it was the council, or rather the body of commissioners on which it devolved its authority, which was completely to remodel the force. Between 1649 and 1660 there were added to the navy no fewer than two hundred and seven ships, while the personnel rose from under four thousand to sixteen thousand men. The substitution of the Dutch for the Spaniards as the enemy at sea, and the long-drawn-out wars which ensued, brought home to those in authority the need to professionalise the service. The royalist raids upon commerce were to introduce a novel feature in British naval policy, the organisation of systematic convoy to the Mediterranean in 1650.

Indeed the naval struggle between the royalist and parliamentary forces foreshadowed a type of warfare hardly known before, but destined to last up to the introduction of steam. In 1648 part of the fleet remained faithful to the royal cause. Prince Rupert, appointed admiral, concentrated on the destruction of commerce and obtained considerable success. The parliamentary fleet attempted to blockade the royalists in their ports or, failing that, to pursue and capture them at sea. Prince Rupert was blockaded in Kinsale by Blake from May till October 1649, when the blockading force was driven off by adverse weather. The prince seized the opportunity, broke out, made further captures, but was forced at last into Lisbon harbour. The Portuguese accepted the situation and soon had a war with England on their hands. Prince Rupert again broke out, but had to make for Toulon after suffering losses. In 1651 his squadron harried English and Spanish commerce off the Azores, and in 1652 it was operating first off the west coast of Africa and then in the West Indies. Losses, mutinies, lack of seaworthiness, and the attacks of the rebel fleet brought this squadron to an end in 1653.

Meanwhile war had been declared between the English Commonwealth and the Dutch Federation. The British had inflicted on the Dutch much loss and annoyance by their insistence upon the search of Dutch ships under letters of reprisal against the French. They had captured Dutch ships as a punishment for their indulgence in trade with British colonies of royalist allegiance. There had been renewed difficulties over the question of the salute at sea. There was the Navigation Act. Fighting began in May, and the declaration of war followed in July. Both belligerents had combatant navies, but both reinforced their fighting ships heavily with merchantmen, going back temporarily on the tendency of policy in Holland as well as England. Both combatants were anxious to save their homeward bound trade from the ravages of the enemy and to inflict the utmost possible loss on enemy commerce. To neither country did it as yet appear desirable to hit at the commerce of the enemy by meeting and beating his fleet of fighting ships at sea. It was the Dutch who first stumbled upon, or were forced to, this conclusion. After some indecisive actions the need to protect Dutch shipping took Tromp out into the North Sea in May 1653. There in the beginning of June a stronger British fleet beat him in a stubborn battle and forced him home with great loss. Thereafter, a situation was set up which was to be repeated frequently in naval warfare. A powerful English fleet soon appeared in Dutch waters, commanded by Monk, and brought to a standstill the commerce of that nation of manufacturers, middlemen and merchants. The beaten Dutch fleet was refitted in one harbour and a new squadron was collected in another. The problem was to reunite them in the face of a blockading force stronger than either of them separately. Tromp accomplished this part of his task successfully, but even his united fleet was beaten by the English, who were themselves however so battered that they were compelled to withdraw in order to be refitted. The sea was thus once more open to their enemies' commerce.

The second and the third of the Anglo-Dutch wars contain incidents of far greater dramatic interest than does the first, as witness the Dutch victory in the four days' battle, the raid in the Medway, the two battles in Southwold Bay; but it is for the present purpose perhaps permissible to have dealt at disproportionate length with the first war, because to the historian there appeared in it novel features, alike in the size and power of the fleets—compared to the total resources of the states concerned—as in the wide range of their action, the length of their stay at sea, and the continuous nature of their service. For the historian of the Law of Nations it is hardly necessary to emphasise the effect on the economic life of nations of the organised destruction of commerce and the blocking up of harbours. These were unparalleled in the past and prophetic of the future.

Although the employment of merchant or privately owned ships was, as a practice, on the wane, it was by no means a dead letter. Nor is it possible to speak of even the official ships as manned by a distinct professional class. The unworthy behaviour in battle of certain captains of "hired" ships was to produce the determination, in 1652, that thenceforward the government authorities would appoint the captains of such vessels and approve their officers. Between 1660 and 1688, moreover, several important steps were taken towards the organisation of a well-found royal navy. The administration system was overhauled in 1667, 1671, 1673, 1686 and 1688. For much of this work Samuel Pepys was responsible, and the fruits were investigated and applauded by a parliamentary commission in 1692. Delay in the payment of wages was still at times a matter of serious complaint, but it cannot be denied that the condition of the officers and seamen was progressively bettered, even though it was but slowly and with frequent eddies. A "Chirurgeon-General," for example, was appointed in 1674, who not only was charged with the permanent duty of the care of the health of the service, but had some control over the distribution of relief and compensation for disabled seamen out of the chest at Chatham. In 1666 a revised scale of pay was established for flag-officers; and pensions for their services in the second Dutch war were granted in 1668. As Dr. Tanner has pointed out, this was a notable move towards the modern system of continuous employment. In 1674 half-pay benefits were extended to several ranks below that of flag-officer. In 1672 came the adoption of the principle of pensions on superannuation by age; and in 1673 this was extended to officers wounded at sea, to volunteers "borne by particular order of the Lord High Admiral," and to "officers of the land soldiers serving on board any of His Majesty's ships." This was to be effective "both as to their own relief in case of wounds, and their widows and orphans in case of death." The Admiralty Commission of 1679, after the failure of several previous attempts to tackle the abuses in victualling, abandoned contract in favour of a state victualling department. In 1677 regular provision was made for the examination of candidates for the office of lieutenant in the navy. Strenuous but not wholly successful attempts were made to improve the discipline of the service. The carrying of passengers was forbidden, save under royal warrant, and captains were charged with the duty of furnishing "a particular account of their proceedings to the Admiralty" as they touched at foreign ports. With these additional demands upon the commanders of ships came an increase in their emoluments. Table allowances were established. A larger number of ships were kept in commission, at least as regards those of greater size. It is becoming the fashion to realise the debt of England to the Stuart kings and the better knowledge of the record of the navy has contributed towards this tendency. By 1688 naval officers as a class were more numerous and enjoyed greater advantages. There was some corresponding growth in the prestige and popularity of what was now quite definitely to be reckoned as a profession. It may be attributed to the almost ceaseless naval warfare, destined to be prolonged fairly continuously till 1815, and the national choice of the sea as the area of battle, and of the navy as the instrument of war. (39) So long, however, as pay was either normally

CHAP. IV.

CHAP. IV.

in arrears, as during the seventeenth century, or too low, as in the eighteenth, and discipline was harsh, the navy was almost bound to be manned, apart from the officers, by rough material even in peace time. In war time, during which the number of ships in commission was increased, and the press gang was used, sometimes with little discrimination, the naval crews were apt to present a very doubtful appearance.[40] The nature of the private sailor, however, never had the same international importance as did the temper of the soldier. This was due to the character of naval warfare, which was almost entirely confined in its scope to the sea, and furnished but little contact between the sailors and the ordinary civil population of countries, either neutral or enemy. In the nature of things governments get a grip on their navies long before they make their land forces responsive to their will. Thus China was ready to sign international agreements with regard to conduct in naval warfare long before it could undertake obligations of a similar nature in regard to war by land: and for this reason only. Between belligerent navies themselves a moderately satisfactory practice of war took place at a comparatively early date. This was in large measure accomplished in the seventeenth century, and subsequent epochs saw little modification.

Levies and Subsidies from Neutral Powers to Belligerents.—To an historian there are few subjects of study more interesting than the provision of assistance to belligerents from Powers ostensibly neutral. To the student of International Law it furnishes valuable sidelight on the conception of neutrality held in the fifteenth, sixteenth and seventeenth centuries. The practice of these centuries is incomprehensible, as has been already pointed out, apart from a realisation of the ideas which underlay the conception of the *bellum justum* or, to put it in another way, the conception of neutrality as reached by a progressive process. The notion of the state was itself in formation; and the prince of the sixteenth century had to hand few rigid rules of international conduct, applicable either to his own state or to the states of contemporary princes. There was war no doubt, but short of war there were quieter, safer, cheaper means of weakening a rival. Elizabeth of England protested her friendship for Spain for many years before the outbreak of open hostilities. During those years volunteers in thousands were permitted, and at times encouraged, to fight in the armies of the Dutch against Spain, while the

Queen, despite her itch for economy, made the Netherlands large loans at critical moments. It may be urged, and rightly, that the Queen had an unusual reputation for double dealing among her contemporaries, but the case crops up again under Henry IV. of France and Charles I. of England. The subsidies given by Henry IV. of France and Richelieu to the Dutch while France was still at peace with Spain, the enemy of the Dutch, were notorious. Such facts as the presence of the English and Scottish regiments in Dutch service while their king was at peace with Spain, or the Marquess of Hamilton's enlistment of six thousand Scotsmen in Swedish service in 1631 while Charles was at peace with the Emperor, bear witness to the phenomenon that it was still considered legitimate to permit enlistment in the interest of one belligerent while the claim was undiminished to be in a state of friendship with the other.

Treaty provision was made in the seventeenth century for unilateral levies, as in Franco-Swiss Agreements, which made provision exclusively for French levies in Switzerland. There were bilateral levies sanctioned, however, as in the Anglo-Swedish Agreement of 1655. In 1677 enlistment was indiscriminately permitted in England to both hostile parties in the war between France and Holland, but this agreement in fact seems to have operated only in favour of the French.(41) In the seventeenth and eighteenth centuries the position of the Swiss cantons is noteworthy. They claimed to be considered neutral, though they were willing to negotiate treaties, which allowed various European belligerents to enlist a specified number of Switzers: and for this position they obtained very wide European recognition. Thus, during the campaign which broke out in 1700 there were twenty-five thousand Swiss in the French service, and simultaneously two Swiss regiments were with the Austrians on the Rhine, beside very many Swiss units with the allies of Austria, Holland and Savoy. None the less both the Emperor and Louis XIV. signed declarations which undertook to respect the neutrality of Switzerland. Subsidies, of course, were paid in return for the treaty which permitted the levy.

The first agreement of the Swiss to provide mercenaries for France was signed in 1474. A typical treaty, that of 15th May 1521, covered the lifetime of Francis I. and three years after. It provided that, if the King of France should be attacked in his own territory, he was to be allowed to recruit anything from six to sixteen thousand men in the territories

CHAP. IV.

of the Swiss. During the existence of the treaty each canton was to receive an annual pension of six thousand francs, and the Swiss "allies" were to receive proportionate, but smaller, sums. In the event of an attack upon them the Swiss were promised the aid of two hundred French lances, twelve guns and quarterly grants of twenty-five thousand crowns. When the Catholic cantons in 1587 made an agreement with Spain, the King of Spain was offered facilities for the recruitment of three to thirteen thousand men on the condition of a money payment to each canton of a settled sum, and the promise of help in the event of an attack upon his Swiss assistants. The last Franco-Swiss arrangement before the French Revolution is to be found in the Treaty of 1777. In this the Confederation gave the French permission to recruit for the French official regiments of Swiss. Even after the upheavals of the Revolution and the Napoleonic era capitulations were made with the Swiss, for four regiments of Swiss for service in the Netherlands (1814-1816), for two guard and two line regiments in the French service (1816), and for four regiments, to a total of six thousand men, in the Neapolitan kingdom (1824-1828). This was still not felt to imperil the neutralisation of Switzerland laid down by the great Powers at the Congress of Vienna.

There is no more illuminating author in this connection than Vattel. He made a famous defence of the Swiss position in regard to the whole question of enlistment for the service of foreign Powers. Faced with the problem as to whether a sovereign could properly allow his subjects to serve foreign Powers indiscriminately as mercenaries without forfeiting a neutral or independent position, he was satisfied with this "simple reason," that there could be nothing illegitimate in a practice which allowed a sovereign to send his soldiers abroad to learn an art which, from the point of view of the state, was both useful and necessary. The export of mercenary soldiers, perhaps the primary export of the Swiss, appeared to Vattel legitimate, as it also appeared a condition of Swiss prosperity. His rage was rather turned against such foreign recruiting agents as operated without permission. These might "be hanged without mercy and justly so." Vattel cogently pointed out that during the wars of previous centuries the Swiss, relying upon already existing treaties, had granted belligerents permission to recruit, and that this had never been taken by rival belligerents as an excuse for an attack upon the cantons. He even went so far as to bless the conclusion of unilateral engagements. He refused to consider it a grievance should the Swiss grant a licence to recruit to one only of two belligerents. They might well have reason to prefer to trust their men to one side rather than the other. With Vattel hesitation seems to have arisen in quite a different quarter. To him the test was the existence or non-existence of a treaty permitting recruitment before hostilities broke out. There he looked forward, though in a partial sense only, to more modern conceptions of unneutral service. He looked backward, and was the child of the conceptions of preceding centuries, when he observed, in justification of his position, that the Swiss ordinarily only granted permission for enlistment in the case of defensive wars, and that Swiss troops in the French service had always been forbidden to take part in wars against the Emperor or any of the German states of the house of Austria. So lasting were the conceptions of the just war and the Holy Roman Empire, unless his latter observation has tacit reference to the vital part played by the Emperor in the preservation of the Balance of Power.

It is not easy to be sure whether the permission of the prince, or its absence, was the determining factor in Vattel's judgment on the practice of the enlistment of mercenaries. It sometimes seems so in connection with war on land. As regards sea warfare he took a totally different stand. It was in his opinion shameful for foreigners to seek a commission from a prince in order to prey upon the vessels of a nation with which their nation had no quarrel. Such action was based solely on a thirst for gain; and the prince's commission, though it might secure immunity for the offender, did not remove the stain of infamy. Those privateers were alone excusable who assisted a nation whose cause was unquestionably just, or which had taken up arms only to defend itself from oppression. The inconsistency is remarkable; but it illustrates the lag in the conventions which governed land warfare behind those which governed warfare on the sea, a reflection of which concrete example has been afforded by previous passages. As regards naval practice he backed the dominant tendency. His contentions were speedily translated into international treaties. The French *ordonnance* of 1681 may have set a partial precedent, in that it provided that privateer captains and officers were to be treated as pirates should they sail the seas bent on the destruction of com-

CHAP. IV. merce, armed with commissions from two or more states at once. But from 1778, the year of a treaty between France and the United States, treaty after treaty assimilated to piracy the crime of any national who, when his state was neutral, accepted a commission to privateer against the commerce of the contracting party. Provision against neutral privateering under belligerent commission sometimes assumed a less extreme form, for states expressly undertook that, when neutral, they would never authorise their nationals to accept letters of marque against the other. The French Treaty of 1852 with the Dominican republic provided :—

> " S'il arrive que l'une des parties contractantes soit en guerre avec un pays quelconque, l'autre partie ne pourra, dans aucun cas, autoriser ses nationaux à prendre ni accepter des commissions ou lettres de marque pour agir hostilement contre la première ou pour inquiéter le commerce et la propriété de ses citoyens." (42)

On two occasions in the first half of the nineteenth century the Mexican republic gave to the Power with whom it was engaged in hostilities reason to apprehend that it designed to embark on a campaign for the destruction of commerce through the agency of neutrals, who might be naturalised *ad hoc* in order to give a more legitimate appearance to their activities. On the first occasion Admiral Baudin of France in 1839 threatened to treat as a pirate ship any Mexican privateer the crew of which were not Mexican born as to two-thirds. On the second, when it was known as regards Havana that the Mexican government had despatched in blank to that city commissions to privateer and declarations of naturalisation, both to be sold or distributed to neutrals, and when it was suspected that it had sent similar papers to London, the President of the United States, in a message to Congress on 8th December 1846, recommended the passage of a law which should declare to be piratical acts the accepting, or the fulfilment, of such offers.

The existence of a treaty, which had been in existence before the outbreak of hostilities, justified in the eyes of Vattel the practice of the enrolment of mercenaries. The King of Denmark in 1788 took up a similar position. Under a treaty signed between himself and Russia in 1761 he was pledged to furnish that country, should a war break out, with a certain number both of troops and ships. In 1788, during the war between Sweden and Russia, at the Russian request, he fulfilled his obligations, but at the same time proclaimed his neutrality. Sweden strongly objected but did not meet the situation with a declaration of war against Denmark. Words of Vattel are curiously apropos :—

> "If a defensive alliance has not been formed expressly against me, nor concluded at a time when I was openly preparing for war, or had already begun it, and if the allies have merely stipulated that each of them is to furnish a definite amount of help to the one that is attacked, I can not require that they should set aside a solemn treaty which they could certainly conclude (*i.e.* in the first instance) without doing me an injury."

A neutral, according to this doctrine, could claim to furnish part of his own state army and navy to aid his ally against even his friend, provided there could be pleaded only a treaty of defensive alliance, made in advance of hostilities and directed against no specific Power. This was obviously to go further than merely to permit levies to be made for an ally, as in the case of the Swiss treaties described above. The Danish regiments which fought with the Russians in 1788 did not, however, fight under Danish colours. They were regarded as Russian troops of an auxiliary character. In such a case as this Vattel only allowed the belligerent a legitimate cause of war if the whole state forces of the ally, or the greater part of them, became involved in the hostilities.

On yet another point Vattel proved himself the upholder of an older form of neutrality. He thought it permissible for a neutral state to make a loan to another state at war, provided that the loan was made at interest and as a normal commercial investment. In this judgment there is no trace of the distinction afterwards to be drawn between the neutral state and the neutral private subject. An even stranger example of the latitude which existed in eighteenth-century practice in the sphere of neutral conduct is to be found in the story of the Anglo-Dutch intervention in aid of Maria Theresa from 1740 to 1744. The incident, which, as regards the Dutch resistance to France, is commented on by Vattel (but incidentally), arose out of the undertaking by England in the Treaty of Vienna in 1731 to guarantee the succession of the Hapsburg heiress. This treaty stipulated that the British should send to the defence of the Austrians, and conversely if necessary the Austrians to the British, a force of ten thousand foot and four thousand horse soldiers. Were these to prove insufficient, the auxiliary party agreed to declare war

CHAP. IV. on the enemy and to co-operate with livelier vigour. The Dutch acceded to the treaty in February 1732. It was in virtue of this treaty that England and Holland provided Maria Theresa with help and even ventured to despatch the pragmatic army into Germany against the French. This army, commanded by the English king, gained a signal victory over the French forces at Dettingen in 1743. France, however, did not declare war on England until 1744, nor against Holland till 1745.

MILITARY SERVICES—III.

Air Forces.—"Wars have for many centuries been conducted both on land and on sea. A third and larger theatre has now been found for them. The air flows over both land and sea: more than either land or sea it is the place of vision, and of speed and freedom of movement. What we of this generation are witnessing is a process whereby the air shall come into its own. It will become the great highway for the traffic of peace, and in war . . . the forces of the air will be, not a late-found timid auxiliary to the forces of the land and of the sea, but their overseer and their director." So wrote Sir Walter Raleigh, the historian of *The War in the Air*; and in that war the British started with perhaps two hundred, but ended with twenty-two thousand, aeroplanes. And such expansion was not confined to them among the belligerents, though at the time of writing they only, with the Italians, have created a wholly separate Air Force, and have furnished it with the power to think out problems of offence and defence as air problems, by providing it with a general staff separate from that of the Navy or the Army.

The history of flight, the development in all countries of some sort of air force, cannot be matters of indifference to historians of International Law. It is a romantic story. In it there figure heroic personalities like Roger Bacon and Leonardo da Vinci; the stout Scot, John Damian, who broke his leg in experimenting from the walls of Stirling Castle in 1507; lovable Fellows of the Royal Society of the seventeenth century; courtiers of the Grand Monarch and adventurous spirits of French revolutionary times. Despite this, too little has been written about it. Of the five great English pioneers not one is mentioned in the *Dictionary of National Biography*.

Yet Sir George Cayley, the Yorkshire squire, by publishing in 1809 a paper in *Nicholson's Journal* on aerial navigation became the father of British aviation; John Stringfellow in 1848 constructed the first engine-driven model aeroplane which flew; Francis Herbert Wenham brought out in 1866 a classic treatise on aerial locomotion, in its original form a lecture to the first meeting of the Aeronautical Society; James Glaisher in that same year made the highest recorded balloon ascent, and Percy Sinclair Pilcher lost his life in 1899 in a series of dramatic and instructive gliding experiments. Lilienthal of Berlin, Hargraves of Sydney, Langley of Washington, and a score of others all faced neglect or ridicule from contemporaries, but were men of genius, whose work found its reward when on 17th December 1903 the Wright brothers were the first men to fly successfully. Nor will the name of Count Zeppelin ever be forgotten in the world of aeronautics.

Militarily the practice of flight was in England the creation of the Royal Engineers, a corps whose tantalising fate it has been to inaugurate so many movements in the military art, only to see them removed from its capable management to that of others at the very moment in which success had been secured. The Air battalion of the corps, responsible for heavier and lighter than air machines, gave way in 1912 to the Royal Flying Corps organised in military and naval wings. In 1918 these two were recombined in the Royal Air Force directed by an Air Ministry and led intellectually by an air general staff. It was the British navy which for a time handled the lighter than air machines but, proving an unkindly parent, relinquished them to other hands.

Six squadrons fought in the Retreat from Mons. At first the work of military or naval flying units was conceived of primarily as reconnaissance, a function which daily grew to be more specialised, as inventions in photography or wireless telephony gave to the airman eyes and ears. But it became obvious that the duties of the Air Force were to extend beyond reconnaissance. In a year or two under the stress of necessity the flying units went through as many stages and undertook as many functions as the two other services had passed through in centuries. Reconnaissance machines were challenged. Hence arose combat in the air and fighting 'planes armed ultimately with machine-guns. Again to assist the slow advance of infantry after preliminary bombardment, and to protect them from the deadly effect of

CHAP. IV. misdirected covering fire, contact patrols were formed to act with ground troops. At sea, for coast defence and for detection of the submarine, a different type of activity was demanded from the pilots. Great carriers also have been built for transport of troops in savage warfare. And the list might be extended. Yet in the public eye one function of the Air Force gradually eclipsed the rest, bombardment from the air of hostile forces and resources. It was this development which has given to the international lawyer a problem not of a mere technical change, but of a new order of ideas, in war. For warfare is setting out upon a wholly novel road; and it is too early yet to make accurate prediction of the consequences. A talented writer on the subject, Mr. J. M. Spaight, has shown that our notion of war needs readjustment. Gone are the cumbrous and gigantic hosts, the nation in arms, the bulky contests of professional combatants; or, where these features of the old warfare still endure, it is likely to be as smaller and secondary factors in the clash of belligerent wills. The problem of the nation at war is, as always, to break down the will of the nation which is its enemy: but in the force of bombing squadrons it will have henceforth a tool infinitely more simple to manipulate and infinitely more deadly in its immediate possibilities. "Henceforth," because in the last European war the weapon was never fully forged, or rather never fully used. The independent Air Force, acting apart from troops or ships, would have been used in 1919 had the collapse of Germany not come. Had it been used, a different history indeed would have had to be written of the efforts of international lawyers to comprehend the law of air warfare in their subject. As it is, the present state of the law reveals the indecision which reigns in the minds of those who think about the matter. And it is right that it should be so, for an elaboration of law, without experience of the conditions with which it has to deal, is dangerous.

The present condition of the law bears traces of its incomplete and, one might almost say, of its makeshift, character. It is true that in 1919 the Air Navigation Convention was signed, but, as its Article 38 made clear, the convention is only applicable in time of peace. In 1923 a code of air warfare was elaborated at The Hague, but it is a code which looks backward to the decisions of the two Hague Peace Conferences which it endeavoured to incorporate over large fields. That of 1907 did indeed draw up a series of "regulations for land warfare," and in the fourth of the "vœux," which it appended to its more definite conventions, it did express the hope that these regulations should be applied so far as were possible to the case of warfare on the sea. The attempt to do for the sea what had been done for the land, at least in some respects, broke down with the rejection of the Declaration of London. In the circumstances the code of air warfare, drawn up in 1923, both rests on no very certain foundation of analogy with other forms of warfare and lacks the reality of individual experience. Good work was done, which will not be thrown away, but that a final stage of certitude has even been approached will be held by no one who knows the rapid development of technical invention, or the ever-increasing specialisation of functions in the Air Force. To emphasise the point it is only necessary to enumerate a few of the headings of the chapters in Spaight's book: bombing, special ammunition, lawful and unlawful ruses, enemy casualties and prisoners, aircraft and enemy populations, belligerent entry of neutral jurisdiction, neutral volunteers and supplies, operations against merchant vessels. To have read any of the few books which have described the actual conduct of air operations, or to have visited a Royal Air Force station, is to be convinced that the principles, still less the detailed application, of the regulations of warfare as conducted by the older services, are not readily adopted for the air by direct analogy.

It is the value of Spaight's work that the author is not content to chronicle but is prolific of suggestion. It is his thesis that to attempt to condemn wholesale the operations of air warfare, as they have been evolved professionally, is to court the failure of the Lateran Council of 1139, which solemnly condemned the cross-bow. It may be possible, however, that the *jus gentium*, almost as old as war itself, can, if it recognise the legitimacy of these operations, impose restrictions on them. In particular, he points out the abuse or misuse of the term reprisal in the late war, and shows how, when things seemed dark or the enemy proved most obnoxious, the cry again and again went up for "reprisals in the air." Once it has been admitted that air operations on the part of bombing squadrons can legitimately be applied merely "in reprisal" and independently of an immediate military object, the way is laid open to an indiscriminate and ultimately unlicensed employment of air power. It is this reflection which explains the presence of the fourth of Spaight's tentative suggestions

CHAP. IV. for an agreement between the Powers. All four are worth recording :—

An agreement

(1) to remove from all cities all military objectives ;

(2) to recognise that certain kinds of non-military property, even if it be situated within cities, are liable to bombardment also, but only under conditions which eliminate, or minimise, loss of life—that is, in effect, when they are unoccupied [he has in mind the night hours particularly] ;

(3) to agree to treat railways, railway junctions, termini, and bridges within cities as property referred to in the preceding paragraph, and not as military objectives ;

(4) to ban the air bomb as a weapon of reprisal.

These are suggestions more easily made than carried out ; but they have about them the feature that they are obviously made by one who has visualised clearly what war in the air may be. They have, however impracticable, the touch of reality which no code of regulations has yet attained. They prove that, though the time has not arrived to dogmatise about the law of war, considerations have arisen which international lawyers cannot afford to overlook.

The importance of air combat even in 1918 may be suggested by some statistics. At the close of the war England possessed a highly organised Air Ministry with five main departments, 14,000 serviceable machines, a monthly output of 3500 more, and a total Air Force personnel of 295,000, of whom 24,000 were trained flyers—so vast was the organisation which the need and opportunity called forth. France possessed 12,000 machines, a monthly output of some 2700 new aeroplanes, 16,000 trained flyers, and a total Air Force of 150,000. America had a nominal total of 10,000 machines, a monthly output of 2000 more, 13,000 flyers, and a total Air Force personnel of some 225,000. Germany, from whom air superiority had been wrested, had 11,000 machines, a monthly output of up to 2000 new ones and 12,000 trained flyers. Finally, the almost equal efforts of Austria and Italy were not to be despised.

The numbers of machines, engines, flyers and troops in the various national Air Services were, of course, vastly reduced with the advent of peace, but it would be a mistake to imagine that the Air Departments have neglected to provide themselves with the means quickly to make their arrangements for a large increase of strength surpassing the levels of October 1918. Even at their present comparatively low numerical levels the Air Forces of to-day must be vastly more effective agents of combat than the rapidly gathered numbers of 1918. Not only have the flyers been more carefully selected and trained and the mechanical personnel on the ground more efficiently prepared and equipped, but the manufacturing mistakes of the period 1914-1918 have been scrutinised and checked, scientific advance has been obtained in construction, equipment and weather-calculation and military experimentation has been carried out in fleet manœuvres of whole squadrons. In a war between great Powers it is certain that air combat will play a wholly different part in the decision to that which it played during the war of 1914-1918.(43)

REPRISALS AS A MEASURE OF REDRESS SHORT OF WAR

Reprisals under Letters of Marque and Reprisal.—Reprisal is a mediaeval term which is first met with in the thirteenth century.(44) Lawyers, who wrote in Latin, knew it as *Repraesaliae* or *Repressaliae*, an almost exact rendering of the French *Représailles* and the Italian *Ripresaglie.* They tried hard to identify the usages it represented with practices they knew in the Civil Law. Especially did they try to identify it with the Roman *pigneratio.*(45) It was not till the early eighteenth century that the essential uniqueness of reprisal was categorically asserted by Bynkershoek in forceful terms: " Operam ludunt qui rem apud Romanos incognitam Latino vocabulo conantur exprimere."

During the thirteenth century the best organised of the rudimentary states of the Europe of that day were trying to put down the primitive measures of alleged self-redress, which led to so much internal turbulence, in order to substitute for them a legal, or at least a state-authorised, process. Among the forcible measures of self-redress which they attempted to suppress was reprisal. In the *Constitutiones Siculae* (46) is to be found the following command:—

> " Ut nullus auctoritate propria de injuriis et excessibus factis vel faciendis in posterum se debeat vindicare nec Praesalias seu Repraesalias facere, vel guerram in regno movere."

CHAP. IV.

Reprisals here clearly mean forcible seizure of goods, and in exceptional cases of persons, from those who have made similar seizures unprovoked.

But the practice was not confined within the borders of the state. It was a mode of redress for injuries inflicted by the citizen of one state upon the citizen of another, and was employed in time of peace. The mediaeval theory, very firmly held, of the joint responsibility of all citizens for their prince, and for one another, would singularly affect this type of reprisal, making all the fellow-citizens of one who had done injustice liable to reprisal. The hardship which might be inflicted on innocent persons did not fail to arouse some protest. A Church Council in Paris made a pronouncement in 1314 which contains the following :—

> "Pignerationes quas vulgaris elocutio Repraesalias nominat in quibus alius pro alio praegravatur, tamquam graves legibus et aequitati naturali contrariae, civili sint constitutione prohibitae. . . .(47)

Practical men, however, felt that the only way to achieve a substantial measure of justice between men who had not a common prince to supervise the right conduct of their relations, was to interest the whole community in which they lived in the suppression of their wrongdoing. The practice of reprisals certainly did this, and it could still be defended even in later ages on this ground. Grotius and Bynkershoek, while allowing the imperfect equity of reprisals, as sometimes punishing innocent persons for the wrongdoing of the guilty, maintained that the practice was necessary in the last resort. Moreover, even if injustice were done to an individual in the first place, the very practice of reprisals left a high degree of probability that it would be corrected. As Grotius says,(48) "et spes erat facilius membra ejusdem societatis a se mutuo jus consequi posse, et indemnitati suae consulere, quam externo, quorum multis in locis exigua habetur ratio."

Reprisals, however, even to work rough justice would need to be steadily controlled. Lawyers would be impressed by the appalling abuses possible in a system which allowed individuals, without hindrance, to take reprisals from all the citizens of a state, one member of which they alleged had done them a wrong. Princes would see that reprisals undertaken privately by the subjects of one of them against the subjects of another would be likely to lead from outrage to outrage into a state of war. This was in fact the case when the Cinque Port sailors undertook reprisals against the French Channel sailors in 1292.[49] Princes felt it to be necessary that their subjects should ask them for authorisation.[50] Only in this way could they examine the justice of the demand and know the extent of their political commitments if they resolved to approve of its enforcement. Subjects on the other hand would find it advisable to have authority for forcible seizure in order to protect themselves from the charge, and possibly the penalty, of piracy. CHAP. IV.

Already in 1295 Edward I. was writing [51] "Bernardus nobis supplicavit ut nos sibi licentiam marcandi homines et subditos de regno Portugalliae et bona eorum per terram et mare quousque de sibi ablatis habuisset restitutionem." It was not till 1353, however, that Edward III. is found speaking as though reprisals could only be authorised by him. The Statute of the Staple of 1353 reads in cap. 17 as follows :—

> " Item qe nul marchaunt estraunge soit emplede ou empeche pur autri trespas ou par autri dette dount il n'est pas dettour plegge ou meinpernour : purveu totes voies que si noz ligez gentez marchauntz ou autres soient endamages per ascuns seignours *destraunges* terrez ou leur subgitz et les dites seignours duement requis faillent de droit a nouz dites gentz, nous eions le lei de mark et de represailles come ad este use devaunt cez heures saunz fraude ou mal engin.[52]

Finally Henry V. went so far as to appoint special officers to punish what he considered piracy, but what the average sailor of the day would probably have regarded as legitimate reprisals.[53] In 2 Hen. V. st. I. cap. 6 is to be read :—

> ". . . Qe en chescun port de meere soit fait et assigne un loial homme appele conservatour de trieues et saufconduitz de roi . . . que le dit conservatour eit . . . le poaier de punir toutz ceux que sount ou serront enditz . . . sibien a suyte de Roi quome a suyte de partie chascune chose affaire encountre les trieues et saufconduitz de roi sur le haut meere. . . .[54]

Some injustice [55] appears to have been done by the King's wholesale suppression of violence against foreigners, for very soon the legislation was altered and provision made for reprisals even in time of peace. Reprisals were only to take place after *lettres de requête* had been sent out under the Privy Seal and disregarded. The aggrieved party was then to obtain letters of marque under the great seal which would authorise him to make reprisals until he had recovered property equal in value to that which had been violently

CHAP. IV. taken from him.[56] Princes not only restrained the reprisals of their subjects by requiring them to obtain special authorisation, but also limited their own power of issuing such authorisations by treaty provisions. Many treaties [57] of peace from the fifteenth century onwards contain the condition that no reprisals shall be authorised until the prince of the subject despoiled shall have applied officially for redress to the prince of the alleged despoiler. For example, the treaty of 1550 between the monarchs of Spain and Scotland contains the following provision :—

> " nec debebunt litterae repressaliarum debitis admonitionibus et requisitionibus non praecedentibus decerni : admonitiones fiant per expressum Nuncium quem Princeps Partis quae de jure sibi denegato contendet mittet ad alterum Principem. . . . Post ejus Legati vel Nuncii *reditum,* si constat clare et aperte jus denegari aut indebite retardari aut plus justo differri reppressaliae concedi poterunt." [58]

Treaties containing this type of provision persist very long in European history. De Martens in his *Essai concernant les Armateurs* can quote several in the eighteenth century which allow reprisals only in the case of *déni de justice*.[59] A favourite question of theory especially concerned this term *denegata justitia* or *déni de justice*. Did it merely include those cases which the courts had refused to consider, or might it cover the far wider class of instances where it seemed to aggrieved parties that the plainest notions of justice had been neglected? All the lawyers [60] urge great caution before reprisals are undertaken in any instance falling within the second class. There is a presumption that a court has done justice if it has considered a case, and only the strongest proof ought to be sufficient to defeat it. The grant of reprisals being nearly always made by the prince, the legislation of some states sought to make certain that the application for the grant would be heard in the proper atmosphere and examined with the suitable precautions. In England, as has been seen already, the grant would only be made after the plaint had been examined both by the Keeper of the Privy Seal and the Chancellor. In the Italian cities, to judge from John of Legnano,[61] the process seems to have been even more judicial. Where statutes laid down an order, that order was to be followed. Where they did not, a statement of claim was to be delivered, the party cited and proceedings taken as the laws ordained. There were allowed to appear to oppose the declaration of reprisals not only the delegates of the people against whom they were to be directed, but any member of that people even without instructions, and finally any citizen of the state meditating reprisals, since he might be injured by the retaliation provoked by an unjust grant. Methods of proof of the alleged injustice and pleas for the defence were laid down. In France those petitions for reprisals which had gone before the *Parlement* had been examined judicially. When in 1485 the Crown by decree assumed the monopoly of grants of reprisal it undertook to grant them only after "great consideration and complete knowledge." The *Ordonnance de la Marine* of 1681 definitely established a procedure. The Admiralty was to examine and assess the claim, half the amount of the claim was to be deposited as security, and the prizes made were to be judged in the same manner as war prizes.

Obsolescence of Reprisals under Letters of Marque and Reprisal. Reprisals undertaken by the State.—At the end of the seventeenth century the old type of reprisal was already obsolescent. The decay was due to a variety of factors. The sea was better kept and piracy almost negligible in European waters. Justice was better administered everywhere, and foreigners not markedly discriminated against. These results were largely due to the increasing part played in all spheres of national life by the central Power, *l'état* proper. Such a state of things was bound to reinforce the movement for the definite abolition of reprisals, especially in a trading community of the type of Holland, the merchants of which always possessed large stocks of goods in foreign ports and at sea; in both cases goods particularly exposed to seizures. Bynkershoek [62] examining a succession of treaties [63] made by Holland with foreign Powers commented on the progressive attempt to oust reprisals altogether from the sphere of international relations. His own opinion, however, was that, while a restriction of the use of reprisals might be advisable, their total abolition was impossible. He considered useless the attempted abolition of reprisals provided for in such a treaty as that between the Emperor of Morocco and the States General of 1710. Reprisals had always to remain the ultimate sanction for honest dealing between two persons or bodies of persons who were not subject to the same prince. "Sed cui bono ejusmodi conventio," he wrote, "quid enim si non administretur! utique tunc alter princeps ad Repressalias recurret et aiet, earum usum rebus ita exigentibus, necessarium esse coepisse."

CHAP. IV. Bynkershoek was right. Even with the growing power of the state individuals might still injure foreigners, and their governments might show themselves unable or unwilling to punish the offenders and force them to make redress. Moreover, it was quite possible that a government itself might take steps with regard to foreigners which their state would regard as a manifest injustice. While, therefore, it might always be necessary in the last resort to proceed to measures of force, the methods of its exercise were likely to change. States were becoming fully conscious of their rôle as the representatives of their subjects' interests abroad. Any injuries inflicted upon their subjects would increasingly be regarded as direct injuries to the state. Accordingly, states were now far less likely to confine their efforts to obtain redress to a mere authorisation to take reprisals allowed to the aggrieved. They would proceed to action themselves, and their subjects, accustomed to the greater ability and readiness of their governments to act in their interests abroad, would ask for nothing better.

Two typical cases might be quoted in proof. During Cromwell's Protectorate, an English Quaker's ship had been seized on the coast of France. He could get no remedy and appealed to Cromwell. Cromwell gave him letters to the Chief Minister of France, Cardinal Mazarin, and asked him to come again if he could get no satisfaction within three days. The Quaker could get no redress from the minister within the time stipulated. He returned and reported the facts. Cromwell despatched two ships of war with orders to bring in French ships and goods. These he ordered to be sold until the extent of the Quaker's loss had been covered. The command was executed and the Quaker indemnified.(64)

During the war of the Austrian Succession (1740-1748), at a period when Prussia was neutral, Prussian merchants complained bitterly to Frederick II. of the treatment they had received at the hands of the British navy and the British prize courts. Frederick's diplomatic efforts on behalf of his subjects, continued for many years, did not meet with success. He appointed a committee presided over by Cocceius, a famous lawyer, to report as to whether the British seizures and condemnations had been justified; and, if not, the amount of compensation due. This commission reported that the Admiralty and courts of justice in England had acted in violation of the Law of Nations and even of a particular declaration concerning contraband made to the Prussian minister in London by the Secretary of State. It would be just to indemnify the merchants who had suffered. They had made an examination of the claims and had reduced them from 239,840 crowns to 156,846 crowns, but added 33,283 crowns as interest. The king was justified in using the money, which he had bound himself to pay over to British subjects, to indemnify his merchants for losses undergone as a result of the unjust conduct of the navy and courts of the British king. Frederick acted on the report of the committee, but the difference was settled in 1756 by a compromise.(65)

Despite the advent of the newer type of reprisal, undertaken by the state itself, the older type under "letters of marque and reprisal" was not yet quite extinct. The last instances of letters of reprisal granted to private persons occur at the end of the eighteenth century. France made a grant of letters of reprisal to two of its subjects, shipowners, who had had ships seized by the British in 1778 (66) before a declaration of war. Formal war intervened and prevented action from being taken on the grant of reprisals pure and simple. In 1793 there was a grant of reprisals to certain Marseillais against Genoa.

The significance of the advent of a new type of reprisal, destined quickly to oust the old, was not immediately remarked upon by the publicists. Vattel, for instance, discoursed eloquently on the subject of reprisals, but did not draw attention to what was of cardinal importance. In different paragraphs (67) he mentioned state-authorised reprisals under letters of marque executed by private citizens and reprisals undertaken directly by the state; but he did not remark that the one was a dying practice while the other was growing in importance. G. F. de Martens,(68) the greatest publicist in Europe of his day, had a clearer view of what was happening. "L'état préfère user lui-même de représailles en faveur de ses sujets," he says in his discussion of the subject, while in his *Causes célèbres du Droit des Gens* he goes into the full history of the Prussian reprisal already referred to. Klüber begins his discussion on modes of redress short of war with the phrase, "un état se fait droit à lui-même." He seems already to consider a wrong done to private individuals exclusively from the public point of view as a wrong done to their state.

Modern Reprisals, Cases, a Definition, an Examination of their Utility.—Reprisal as between states has lost none of its

CHAP. IV.

importance since the late eighteenth century. It has been continuously employed for the redress of alleged grievances down to the present day. Two very modern instances may, perhaps, be fitly given here.[(69)] In July 1922 the German government, owing to the rapid depreciation of the German exchange, applied for relief from some of the obligations which it had undertaken under the Treaty of Versailles and subsidiary agreements. Among other things it requested the allied governments to grant a reduction of the monthly payments to the allied clearing offices from £2,000,000 to £500,000. France was one of the Powers principally interested, but the French government, mistrustful of German allegations of inability to pay, returned an emphatic negative to the request for a reduction of the clearing payments and threatened reprisals if Germany did not give guarantees by 5th August that it would carry out its obligations under this head. These reprisals consisted in the expulsion of five hundred Germans from Alsace and Lorraine, the confiscation of the income and property of German companies in Alsace, and the non-recognition of German clearing claims. They were actually effected by the French government, but countermanded when the business classes of the districts concerned pointed out the effect on industry. The difference was successfully settled by subsequent negotiation.[(70)] In July 1925 some Frenchmen, alleged by the German police to be smuggling, were arrested near the boundary between territory occupied by the French and territory left unoccupied. They were detained at Barmen but subsequently released. As a reprisal Barmen was occupied by the French forces for several hours, many arrests were made, and finally the whole occupied area was shut off from the unoccupied area for ten days.[(71)] It is necessary to go back for fifteen years to find an instance of as serious a reprisal as the last. In 1908 Holland had long had to complain of the treatment of Dutch ships by the Venezuelan authorities. When in this year the Dutch representative, M. de Reuss, was dismissed by the President and virtual Dictator, de Castro, the government of Holland resolved to take steps for the redress of its grievances. Dutch warships were sent into Venezuelan waters and captured the entire Venezuelan navy. De Castro had meanwhile fallen, and, when his successor had completed negotiations to Holland's satisfaction, the ships were restored to Venezuela.[(72)] This reprisal, however, may be said to have been taken with perhaps less precipitation than the French measure just quoted, and after a longer exploration of the possibilities of negotiation. It is certainly more typical than the French. CHAP. IV.

The examination of cases which has been undertaken should facilitate a definition of reprisals. When a state by patient diplomacy has failed to secure redress for a legal wrong inflicted upon it by another state and, with praiseworthy restraint, desires to refrain from war, it is permitted to take against the delinquent state exceptional measures called reprisals. These must inflict a not disproportionate injury and be designed to compel consent to a just and satisfactory settlement. In many cases, of course, what the one state alleges to be a justifiable reprisal, the other state will call an illegal act of aggression. Measures of reprisal, moreover, are to be distinguished from those of retortion which are justified not by the illegality of another state's action, but by the harsh and oppressive bearing of its legislative enactments or administrative ordinances.

Prima facie it would seem that the existence of the right to undertake reprisals is an unqualified gain to international society. The extreme step of a declaration of war, with its possibly fateful complications, has not necessarily to be taken in order to bring material pressure to bear to secure the redress of a wrong which may be small in itself. The history of the nineteenth century, however, has revealed the possibility of so much abuse of the method as to make several theorists doubtful of its desirability.(73)

The great point which can be made is that in modern times the effective use of reprisals is confined to the greater Powers in their relations with the smaller. This was not the case in the eighteenth century. These reprisals were in fact practised against the greatest Powers without necessarily implying war. Frederick II. of Prussia, for example, practised reprisals against both Russia and England, while England undertook reprisals against Spain, then a first-class Power. Since the middle of the nineteenth century, however, formal reprisals against a great Power are universally felt to be impossible.(74) Reprisal, then, is only practised against small or weak Powers by others which fear little harm from the utmost step they can take. So confident, indeed, are they of the superiority of the force they can bring to bear, that they take it for granted that the state against which they have proceeded will quickly bow to the logic of facts and, not making a difficulty of its wounded dignity, will hurry on to concessions in order to secure relief from the measures of coercion.

CHAP. IV.

It is obvious that measures like these may be abused. The Pacifico reprisal [75] was not honourable to the British name. The reprisals practised by France against China in 1884 [76] were a cover for what appears to have been a carefully considered plan to secure the control of a Chinese province. Accordingly, Calvo and Despagnet are perhaps not altogether wrong in looking upon reprisals as a method which does not always tend to the triumph of justice. Calvo says, referring particularly to the Pacifico reprisal and a British reprisal against Brazil in 1862, "Nous nous bornerons à citer ces exemples qui ont eu le plus éclatant retentissement et qui ont d'ailleurs excité une réprobation unanime." Despagnet says, "Au point de vue du droit des gens une grande puissance abusant de sa force envers un pays incapable de résistance se donne tous les avantages de la guerre sans assumer les responsabilités que celle-ci entraîne soit à l'égard du pays attaqué, soit à l'égard des États neutres." Despagnet was thinking mainly of instances of pacific blockade.

In some cases, indeed, it would seem that a system which necessitated a declaration of war before action in every case would be an actual advantage from the point of view of weaker Powers. In nearly all countries a declaration of war can only be made with the approval of the legislative chambers. This is not necessarily true of reprisals, which could be undertaken by an unscrupulous government thus unchecked, and in the hope of facing its legislature with a successful *fait accompli*. Again, the very publicity which always attends an outbreak of war serves to arouse world opinion to an examination of the justice of the conduct of the belligerents. The will, therefore, as well as the opportunities for intervention, are created. This is not true to nearly the same degree in the case of reprisals.

Reprisals and the League of Nations.—The signing of the Hague Convention regulating the opening of hostilities (1907) had already caused inquiry as to how the opening of reprisals was to be distinguished from the opening of hostilities.[77] Reprisals of the more serious type, such as those undertaken by Great Britain against Greece on the occasion of the Pacifico dispute, or by France against Germany in 1923, are differentiated in the first place from measures of war by the hope of the executing government that its actions will not be taken by the other as having produced the legal state known as war. But the fact of war or no war does not depend on the hope of the government which undertakes the reprisals, but on the intent of either party to the dispute. It seems hardly doubtful that legally a Power can accept any positive measure of aggression such as the seizure of ships, subjects or territory, whether called a measure of reprisal or no, as tantamount to an opening of war.

The bearing of these remarks becomes obvious when we turn to consider the Covenant of the League of Nations. According to its provisions no member may declare war against another except in very special circumstances fully set out in Articles 12, 13 and 15 of the Covenant. No mention of reprisals, however, is made in any of the articles. Does this mean that a Power can proceed to exercise reprisals with the old liberty? What, then, if the Power against which these steps have been taken chooses to regard them as marking the opening of hostilities? All the provisions carefully made to block the avenues to war would have been defeated, and each belligerent would be able with some show of reason to fix the blame for the outbreak on his opponent. It must be taken for granted, therefore, that war can only be waged under the conditions foreseen in the Covenant, and that acts of reprisal cannot be treated as acts of hostility entitling the state against which they have been directed immediately to claim the full rights of war.

But are acts of reprisal themselves permitted, and if permitted, under what conditions? (78) The wording of the Articles is important in this respect and should be examined with some care. Article 11 says that any war, or threat of war, is a matter of concern to the whole League, which has the right to take any action that may be deemed wise and effective under the circumstances to safeguard the peace of the world. In addition it is declared to be the friendly right of members of the League to draw the attention of the Assembly, or of the Council, to any circumstances affecting international intercourse which threaten to disturb international peace or the good understanding between nations upon which peace depends. Quite obviously under Article 11 members have not bound themselves to abstain even from serious measures of reprisal though they are given the alternative of drawing the attention of the League to their grievances. A serious measure of reprisal, however, would either itself fall into the category of "threats of war," or would lead to such threats. It would, therefore, immediately come under the cognizance of the League, which possesses an uncircumscribed choice of action for meeting the danger.

CHAP. IV. Article 12 is perhaps more directly concerned. The relevant portion reads:—

> "If a dispute should arise between them (the Members) likely to lead to a rupture, they will submit the matter either to arbitration or judicial settlement or inquiry by the Council."

Is a dispute in which one party has threatened the other with reprisals a dispute likely to lead to a rupture? A plausible case can be made for excluding altogether from the scope of the Article disputes which have only reached the stage of a threat of reprisals for some alleged wrong. The mere fact that only reprisals are threatened, and not more serious steps, might be said to show that there was no likelihood of danger for the time. Moreover, even the execution (and not merely the threat) of reprisals need not always have a very grave significance. Measures of reprisal are sometimes undertaken for small, but very irritating, breaches of International Law, and in such cases there is not the least need to fear extreme developments. Just on occasions of this kind states would not like to submit their actions to long and futile examination. It might be argued that a sharp reminder by positive action would end the difficulty and secure redress quickly. The necessity of submitting to the delays of the processes mentioned in the Article, with all the petty chicaneries for which they give so convenient an opportunity, would encourage unwarranted action by unscrupulous Powers, confident that no direct measures would be taken against them for some time.

There is a good deal of force in these arguments. There seems no good ground in the Covenant for necessarily submitting to the processes of Article 12 such comparatively minor reprisals as those exercised, for instance, by Frederick the Great against England, when, neither before nor after the reprisals, did the dispute seem likely to develop into war. It would be advisable, however, to provide that the Power undertaking this type of reprisal should report its grievance to the Council and the action which it has taken to secure redress. This could well be done under the latter section of Article 11. A state which has made reprisals with a good conscience need not fear investigation, while the Power against which they have been directed could also report and demand an inquiry.

The case is different, however, when such major reprisals as "pacific blockades" or wholesale expulsions are in question. A dispute during which such steps are threatened is obviously an embittered one, and the mere threat will have done much to aggravate the matter to the point of bringing it within the category of "disputes likely to lead to a rupture." In such a case it would seem that under Article 12 the parties to the dispute have bound themselves to seek arbitration or judicial settlement or investigation by the Council. It would seem to be the duty of the Power which has made the threat to refrain from acting upon it as soon as it is satisfied that one of the processes provided for in the Covenant has been set in motion. Only in a case where vital damage has wrongfully been done to it, and redress, instantly necessary, is alone to be obtained by immediate action, can a state rightfully proceed to the serious measures of reprisal it has threatened. In such a case it may be suggested that the Council should be notified at once in order to be able to deal immediately with the threatening situation. Such instances of real necessity could only be rare, and it would be the duty of the Council to satisfy itself that the state which had pleaded necessity had acted in good faith. Serious measures of reprisal would on the whole, therefore, be held in reserve till after the report of the arbitrators, court, or council. They could be used as the milder alternative to war against the state which stubbornly refused to accept the findings of the body which had investigated the dispute. The question of the position of reprisals under the Covenant was raised in practice when Italy, as a reprisal for the murder of Italian soldiers on Greek territory, and after an offer of satisfaction by Greece which the Italian government alleged to be insufficient, occupied Corfu (August to September 1923). The Council of the League decided to appoint a Committee of Jurists to report upon the legal issues raised by the incident.

NOTES

(1) Vanderpol's exhaustive treatise entitled *La Doctrine scolastique du Droit de Guerre* has collected practically all the relevant texts in a French translation. Vanderpol's versions have here been accepted without question as authoritative. His deductions and conclusions, however, have not always been followed.

(2) *Ep. v., Ad Marcellinum.* (3) *Ibid.*

(4) Nevertheless, even in 1794, the Tory moralist Gisborne, in his *Duties of Man,* vol. i. pp. 287-8, could write: "Every individual officer who is called into active service is bound to investigate the

justice of the war in which he engages to the utmost extent of his abilities and information."

(5) *Comm. in Summ. Sanct.*, tom. ii. disput. 64, cap. 3 (quoted by Vanderpol).

(6) *De Justitia et Jure*, vol. i. disp. 103 (quoted by Vanderpol).

(7) Bk. iii. cap. xviii.

(8) The question of the legitimate bounds of stratagem has, of course, descended from the mediaeval doctors to the soldiers and sailors of every generation. On the naval side the flying of false colours has presented theme for argument so late as the last war, and a subtle distinction may perhaps be drawn between their use as a protective device and their abuse as a means unfairly to establish a treacherous advantage in battle. Two commanders, Lord Peterborough on land and Lord Dundonald on the water, have been noted as masters of the art of inducing the enemy to deceive himself. Peterborough, the brilliant British commander in Spain in 1705 and 1706, undoubtedly approached the forbidden limits on occasion.

(9) *Summa Secunda, Sec. Quaes.* 40, De Bello.

(10) In Oman's *Essay on War*, in H. W. C. Davis's collection called *Mediaeval England*, the details of a typical indent are given. The Earl of Kent undertakes in 1360 to raise a force of sixty men-at-arms (of whom ten are to be knights) and of a hundred and twenty bowmen—the whole properly equipped and provided with horses. Service is to be for three months at the accustomed wages of war.

(11) Quoted by Mackinnon in his *History of Edward III.* from Lettenhove's *Froissart*, iv. 405-19.

(12) Robert of Avesbury, *De Gestis Edwardi Tertii* (ed. Thompson), gives letters from Wingfield and the Prince of Wales, pp. 432-5.

(13) The main authority used for Edward III.'s warfare was Mackinnon's *History of Edward III.* Froissart's *Chroniques*, which cover the military life of the period 1325-1400, are the necessary reliance of all commentators. Froissart (1338-1404) was not only an assiduous contemporary collector of facts, but knew many of the heroes whose exploits he described. The warfare of kings and princes, however, was not the worst. The almost uncontrolled *Grandes Compagnies* were without any politic considerations whatsoever. Froissart makes Aymerigot Marcel, a captain of one of these bands, say: "Combien étions-nous réjouis quand nous pouvions trouver sur les champs un riche abbé, ou un riche prieur, ou un riche marchand, ou une route de mulets de Montpellier, de Narbonne—Tout était nôtre."

(14) Charles V. himself was ordered out of the ranks on one occasion by the Marquis de Vasto (Fortescue, *History of the British Army*, i. 98).

(15) Charles V. always saluted the gallows.

(16) One of the best-known contemporary sources of information on the exploits of the Spanish infantry is Brantôme's *Vie des Grands Capitaines*. Brantôme had not only been in Spain and Italy, but had accompanied a Spanish expedition against the Moors.

(17) The volume on the Thirty Years' War in the *Cambridge Modern History* was the principal source of the facts immediately following. Monro's *Expedition* is a valuable account by a contemporary Scottish soldier of the exploits of Scottish troops in Danish and Swedish service. Readers of Scott will remember the inimitable Dugald Dalgetty in the *Legend of Montrose*.

(18) Uniform, the subject of a not unimportant chapter in the modern Law of War, has an obscure history. Though before the seventeenth century there had been isolated attempts to dress whole armies in one colour, the soldiers of the earlier part of that century were still wrestling rather with the problems of regimental uniformity. Thus the six regiments of the London trained bands of the Civil War wore red, white, green, blue, buff, or orange (G. F. Townshend, *Siege of Colchester*, p. 170). The "New Model" army of 1645 was apparently the first English army to be clothed entirely in scarlet, a colour which was inherited by the later standing army. At Malplaquet it is already not illegitimate to talk of British red-coats, Austrian white-coats, and Prussian blue-coats. The need for uniformity in dress was not acutely felt at sea, so that even in Nelson's time it is impossible to speak of a "uniform" among the common sailors (John Masefield, *Sea Life in Nelson's Time*, cap. v.).

(19) Duruy estimates the French corps under arms during the War of the Spanish Succession as 450,000.

(20) The figures are from Oechsli's *History of Switzerland*.

(21) There are, however, much worse accounts of French conduct in territories directly hostile to them like Hesse and Brunswick.

(22) The account is from Conrady, *Die Rheinlande in der Franzosenzeit*.

(23) The authority is Halleck.

(24) The standard histories for Wellington's Spanish and Portuguese operations are Napier's and Oman's, which may, however, on occasion be profitably supplemented by General Foy's *Guerre de la Péninsule*. The collected volumes of *Wellington's Dispatches* contain much information concerning the indiscipline rife among his troops. Sir Herbert Maxwell's *Life of Wellington* (2 vols.) has much information valuably concentrated. Mercer's *Journal of the Waterloo Campaign* gives striking insight into contemporary behaviour.

(25) The levying of contributions, however, still played an enormous part in warfare. When temporary entrance into France was possible immediately after Ramillies, Marlborough was quick to levy on French Flanders, and one of the first consequences of Oudenarde was the despatch of detachments to forage and raise contributions.

(26) Treaty of Versailles, Art. 244 (Annex 1).

(27) *Cambridge Modern History*.

(28) Gustavus Adolphus's regiments already possessed four surgeons, while the Armada had sailed with a quite respectable surgical personnel. The famous Ambroise Paré (1517-1590), who has left us some idea of the state of the wounded on sixteenth-century battlefields, was taken to Italy by Montjan, Colonel-General of the Foot (1536), and was specially summoned to Metz by Guise (1552). On this last occasion he helped Guise to succour the abandoned wounded soldiers of the enemy and to make arrangements for their transport back to their army.

(29) How the small Geneva society which gathered behind Dunant circularised governments, called international conventions, and finally procured the full diplomatic conference of 1864, is well told in Lueder's *Genfer Konvention*.

(30) It is one of the features of M. Halévy's work, *Histoire du peuple anglais au 19e siècle*, tom. i., that he shows how in many particulars, especially that of the design of ships in the eighteenth century, it was

the French service which led and the British which followed. Metternich in 1817 hazards the opinion that the United States of America built better ships than England but manned them less well.

(31) Kate Norgate's *Richard Cœur de Lion.*

(32) Cunningham's *English Industry and Commerce.*

(33) Facts of the type narrated in the preceding paragraphs were collected by such old-fashioned naval historians as Campbell.

(34) The distinguished historian of the Tudor Navy, Mr. Oppenheim, has clearly pointed out that the period 1415-1422 formed an exception to the general story of the naval impotence of the Lancastrian monarchy.

(35) Campbell's *Lives of the Admirals,* vol. i.

(36) A very full documentation of piracy charges under Henry VI. as extracted from early proceedings in Chancery is printed as an appendix to Kingsford's *Prejudice and Promise in Fifteenth-century England.* Chapter IV. of this work deals with piracy in the West Country.

(37) Campbell's *Lives of the Admirals,* vol. i.

(38) Froude's *Elizabeth,* cap. xxxvi.

(39) J. R. Tanner in the *Cambridge Modern History,* vol. iv. cap. xvi.; vol. v. cap. viii. See Dr. Tanner's many other works upon the Navy; also *Dict. Nat. Biog.* under Blake, Rupert, Monk; and D. Hannay, *A Short History of the Royal Navy.* An account of other contemporary navies than the British is contained in E. B. Powley, *The English Navy in the Revolution of* 1688.

(40) The temper of the English naval officer during England's greatest naval war is well described in Fitchett's *Nelson and his Captains.* John Masefield's *Sea Life in Nelson's Time* deals admirably with the general life and tone of the men of the fleet.

(41) A curious class of diplomatic dispute, well represented in the seventeenth century, is that between the national government of mercenary troops and the government which they serve concerning certain types of order given to them. Thus the Swiss government ordered its officers serving with the army of Louis XIV. not to participate in the invasion of the United Provinces undertaken in 1672—an order which compelled Condé to surround the Swiss troops and threaten them with death. James II. gave the Dutch much trouble with regard to the six English and Scottish regiments in Dutch service. He recalled them during Monmouth's rebellion, and after their subsequent return began to press for Catholic officers. He recalled them again early in 1688, and when the Dutch declined to release them, ordered them to return.

(42) Ortolan's *Diplomatie de la Mer,* vol. i. bk. ii. cap. xi.

(43) The bureaucratic organisation of the national Air Forces on lines historically parallel to the English organisation of the Navy in the sixteenth and seventeenth centuries, or to Louvois' organisation of the French Army, has been studied by J. M. Spaight in his work, *The Beginnings of Organised Air Power.*

(44) The word "reprisals" is always found in close connection with the Low Latin *marca* throughout the mediaeval period. Mediaeval kings speak in the fourteenth century of granting letters of marque and reprisals. *Marca* and *marcare,* however, occur already in the twelfth century. See Ducange under "marca."

(45) The Council of Paris said in 1314: "Pignerationes quas vulgaris elocutio repraesalias nominat." CHAP. IV.

Ayala says: "Pignerationes hae, quas repraesalias vocant."—*De Jure et Officiis Bellicis,* lib. i. cap. iv.

(46) Lib. i. lit. 8.

(47) In Martenius, tome vii.; *Ampliss. Collect,* quoted by Ducange.

(48) Lib. iii. cap. ii., *De Jure Belli et Pacis.*

(49) Moore's *Digest,* vol. 7, p. 131; quoting Ward's *Law of Nations.*

(50) Philip the Fair's decree (1313), quoted in De Martens' *Essai concernant les Armateurs,* is typical.

"Ut de requisiti in reddenda justicia defectu constet illi qui marcham indicere voluerit per literas regias vel alia publica instrumenta antequam ad dictam marcham procedat."

(51) Rymer's *Foedera,* vol. ii. p. 691.

(52) *Statutes of the Realm,* printed by command, 1816, vol. i. p. 339.

(53) See opening paragraph of Stat. Hen. v., 4, cap. 7, *op. cit.,* vol. ii. p. 198.

(54) *Statutes of the Realm* in *op. cit.,* vol. ii. p. 178 ff.

(55) See opening paragraph of Stat. Hen. v., 4, cap. 7.

(56) Stat. Hen. v., 4, cap. 7:—Et à la greindre consolation de ses ditz foialx lieges au fyn qu'ils pourront pluis prestement et sanz longes delaies avoir remede en ces cas voet mesme nostre seigneur le Roi que cellui ou ceux qui se sentira ou sentiront grevez encountre le teneur et fourme de tielles trieues dedans le roialme d'Engleterre ou sur le meer ou es parties pardela compleindra ou compleindront au gardien du prive seal qi pur le temps serra qui tiel compleint oiee et entendue entferra pur la partie compleignante lettres de request soutz le prive seal en due fourme. Et si apres tiel request faite la partie requise ne ferra dedeins temps convenable due restitution ou satisfaction a la partie grevee adonques le chanceller d'Engleterre fera faire a tiel partie grevee si le voet demander lettres de marques desoutz le grande seal en due fourme. . . .

(57) *E.g.* Treaty between Spain and Scotland, 1550, quoted in the text Treaty between Spain and France, 1489.

(58) Dumont, *Traités,* tome iv. partie ii. p. 12.

(59) France and United Provinces, 1739, Art. 33. France and Denmark, 1742, Art. 44.

(60) *E.g.* Grotius, lib. iii. cap. ii., *De Jure Belli et Pacis*: "Jus denegatur—verum etiam si in re minime dubia (nam in dubia re praesumptio est pro his qui ad judicia publice electi sunt) plane contra jus judicatum est."

Bynkershoek, c. xxiv., *De Repressaliis*:

"Ne quis autem temere de justitia denegata conqueratur variis gentium pactis prospectum est," quoting the Hispano-Dutch treaty, 1648 and Franco-Dutch treaty, 1662.

(61) His work is entitled *De Bello, de Represaliis et de Duello.*

See especially caps. cliii.-clviii. Holland has an excellent edition issued by the Carnegie Endowment.

(62) *Quaestiones Juris Publici,* cap. xxiv., *De Repressaliis.*

(63) Especially treaties between England and States-General, 1654, Art. 16 (though Art. 24 mentions reprisals), and between Morocco and the States-General, 1710, Art. 9.

(64) Villemain, *Histoire de Cromwell,* vol. ii. p. 256.

CHAP. IV. (65) All the documents are given in full in De Martens' *Causes Célèbres du Droit des Gens.*

(66) De Martens' *Essai conc. les Armateurs*, quoting the "Code des Prises."

(67) Paragraphs 346 and 347, *Droit des Gens.*

(68) In his text-book on *International Law.*

(69) The policy adopted by France against Germany of the seizure of "productive pledges" in the Rhineland and the Ruhr must in its total aspect be regarded as a case of reprisal, though the French use the term "sanction," and claim to be acting under the Treaty of Versailles. The matter cannot be profitably discussed here owing to its intimate connection with current international politics.

(70) *Annual Register*, 1922. Also the *Times* from 13th July onwards to the middle of August.

(71) *Daily Chronicle*, 17th July 1925: Message from Cologne correspondent.

(72) *Annual Register*, 1908, under "Holland" and "Venezuela."

(73) *E.g.* Calvo and Despagnet.

(74) In 1834 President Jackson had recommended reprisals against France on account of the reluctance of the French Chambers to vote an appropriation for the settlement of American claims. The French government replied by withdrawing its ambassador. Serious results might have followed, but for the pacific inclinations of the French government and the tactful mediation of the British government. Moon's *Digest*, vol. vii. pp. 123-6.

(75) During an Athens riot in 1847 the house of Don Pacifico, a Gibraltar Jew and a British subject, was plundered. Instead of going to a Greek court for redress in the first instance, he appealed to the British government, which after long negotiations ordered a powerful squadron into Greek waters with instructions to seize Greek vessels leaving Greek ports. These were to be held until justice had been done Pacifico. The Greek government was compelled to accept the British terms, though it held that Pacifico had much over-estimated his losses. *State Papers*, 1850, pp. 332-932.

(76) See *Annual Register*, 1884, under "China."

(77) Westlake's *Collected Papers*, pp. 590-606.

(78) See Pollock's *League of Nations* (2nd ed.).

PART II

THE AGE OF THE JUDGE

"The seat of the judicial authority is locally here in the belligerent country, according to the known law and practice of nations, but the law itself has no locality."

CHAPTER V

TEMPERAMENTA

INTRODUCTION. DECLARATION OF WAR. ENEMY INDIVIDUALS AND THEIR PROPERTY AT THE OUTBREAK OF WAR. THE DROIT D'AUBAINE. THE RIGHT OF INDIVIDUALS TO EMIGRATE. THE FREEDOM OF COAST FISHERIES. THE TREATMENT OF PRISONERS OF WAR.

Introduction.—It has been the aim of the first part of this book to convey an impression of International Law as responsive to the successive changes which civilisation underwent in Europe in the gradual formation of the modern state system. Political and geographical considerations can help the international lawyer to a far clearer conception than he might otherwise obtain of the principles, the rules, and even the detailed stipulations of the Law of Nations. And yet that law, just as it cannot be wholly explained in terms of jurisprudence, cannot be explained purely in terms of geography or politics. There are, beside all these, other factors. One always present, progressively important from the sixteenth century onwards, yet difficult to define, is to be found in what has been termed humanitarian sentiment. The reluctance among human beings to press home to the full conclusions justified by logic has been so common as to become systematic. It has tempered obligations, reduced rights, protected the indefensible, and mollified harshness. Grotius went to the Law of Nature to find in it principles which should overrule the crude and at times inequitable enactments of positive law. He called these principles *temperamenta*. If the name be adopted, though with an alteration in its connotation, and applied to the operation of the humanitarian spirit, it is possible to find that from the earliest days there were at work upon the public law of Europe *temperamenta*; and that to the operation of these much was due in the practice of the European nations. It is convenient to draw attention in turn to some of them which, producing for the first time in the eighteenth century their

CHAP. V.

full effect, form an appropriate introduction to that part of the work particularly devoted to that century, an age in which sentiments of humanitarianism play so conspicuous a part.

Declaration of War.—War at its worst was usually preceded by a declaration. This might take the shape of a formal pronouncement to the enemy or a public announcement at home which enumerated the grievances and declared the decision to seek a remedy for those grievances by act of force. In land warfare it was comparatively difficult for a state to conceal its belligerent intentions, and the majority of the subjects of the enemy power would have some opportunity to prepare for invasion, if they lived in border provinces, or to decamp, if they were resident subjects of the invading nation. During the seventeenth century the lot of individuals began to be ameliorated. It became increasingly understood that a formal declaration of war was *more Romano* obligatory, and treaties were signed which stipulated that enemy subjects should normally enjoy a period of time in which to settle their affairs and to withdraw. At sea conditions were different. Ships would start from home in ignorance of the impending hostilities or even of strained relations. Some might be actually in the ports of the enemy, some might be navigating thither, some might be far out at sea engaged in distant trade. Had maritime hostilities been preceded by a declaration of war in every case, it would not have made the exercise of the strict rights of capture any the less harsh to such mariners, shipowners, or consigners of cargo as had trusted their vessels to the sea in reliance upon the peaceful atmosphere which delusively had seemed to reign about them. But the condition of affairs was worse indeed than this, for the tradition still lingered that the legal act of war dated from the commission of the first act of violence.

Grotius had held the opinion that a declaration of war ought to precede acts of hostility, while Bynkershoek, even more of a conservative, agreed that a declaration was called for from "greatness of mind" if not from actual law. None the less, maritime practice followed the old ways. When rupture threatened in the relations between one state and another, despite the fact that the point of rupture had not been reached, nor war formally declared, states in their ports put an embargo on the ships of the possible enemy, and frequently gave for immediate use letters of reprisal to ships of their own fleet putting out to sea. As Molloy said, "The two nations are not therefore in a perfect state of hostility though they take from each other as enemies and many times these general reprisals grow into a formal war. Such was the Dutch war of 1664." The Dutch war referred to arose from the despatch of a fleet without a declaration of war, first to Africa and then to America, to avenge on the Dutch treatment which they had meted out to the Africa Company. Further, unpremeditated incidents at sea sometimes led to the outbreak of a general war. Thus the difficulty over saluting between Tromp and Blake led to the first battle of the Anglo-Dutch war of 1652, a war which had never been declared and concerning the waging of which, and even the question as to whether it should be waged at all, neither admiral had been given precise instructions. An admiral might leave port with orders to capture foreign merchantmen and even men-of-war, yet the government which sent him might mean no more than that it was ready for hostilities if the state which suffered these indignities chose to retaliate with a declaration of war. Molloy's comment is as ingenuous as it is pertinent: "A general war is either solemnly denounced, or not solemnly denounced; the former, when war is solemnly declared, or proclaimed, by our king against another state. Such was the Dutch war of 1671. An unsolemn war is when two nations slip into a war without solemnity: as ordinarily happeneth among us."

The French were particularly angered by British measures on the sea in 1755 and 1778.(1) In the former year Admiral Boscawen captured two French ships-of-war and some English privateers took about two hundred and fifty French ships without a declaration of war. The French made especial efforts in 1761 to obtain from Pitt a promise that the private ships, which had been taken before the declaration of hostilities, should be restored. They failed. On 17th June 1778, after formal diplomatic relations had been broken but before war had been declared, British naval units attacked French frigates off the coast of France. Napoleon in 1803 was so incensed when he learned that the English had captured two French vessels in the Bay of Audierne, anticipating a declaration of war, that he took the drastic step of keeping as prisoners of war ten thousand Englishmen who were in France. He defended this action as reprisal for England's breach of International Law.

The sentiment that the declaration of war should precede acts of hostility, a sentiment which can be traced to the seventeenth century and beyond it, became increasingly strong

CHAP. V.

during the nineteenth century. The justification made by the Japanese of their attack on Russian ships in Far Eastern waters in February 1904, which began even before the withdrawal of their ambassador in St. Petersburg, was at the time very generally felt to be weak. The Russians naturally made no attempt to restrain the exhibition of their indignation. It arose in part from this incident that the Hague Conference of 1907 laid down the necessity of a previous and unequivocal warning in each case before resort to hostilities. This warning might take the form either of a declaration of war, giving reasons, or of an *ultimatum* with a conditional declaration of war. It was the latter to which England had recourse at the beginning of the war with Germany in 1914. The sentiment which had induced Choiseul to plead so hard for the return of the French ships of 1755 was based on the consideration that there had been deception by the captors of the captives, which latter were pursuing their lawful vocations in full confidence of the friendship of such ships as they encountered. The Hague Conference in condemning the old hard practice took the same attitude. Ships actually in the enemy's port at the declaration of war, or those entering without knowledge of its declaration, were henceforward to be allowed to depart. Enemy merchantmen, met on the high seas, if they could establish their ignorance of the outbreak of the war, were no longer to be confiscated, though they could be detained until the war had ended. [Convention 6.]

Enemy Individuals and their Property at the Outbreak of War.—At the beginning of the eighteenth century the customary law of states was usually harsh to the individual alien who had become an enemy through the outbreak of hostilities between the state of his residence and that of his allegiance. It was a common thing for treaties of commerce in the eighteenth century to attempt to regulate as between the contracting parties the position, should war be declared between them, of citizens of the one in territories of the other. And it was necessary, for frequently enough the stranger, placed in this ambiguous position, enjoyed no sort of protection, might be imprisoned or violently expelled, his property, personal, real, or mercantile, might be confiscated, his debtors freed from their obligations, his *locus standi* in the eyes of the civil courts removed.

The enemy alien, if unprotected by the stipulations of a treaty, would find but little comfort in reading the classical commentators. "Hostium actiones et credita quae apud nos invenientur an exorto bello recte publicentur": so runs the question of Bynkershoek, and he answered it by pronouncing confiscation legal. Vattel thought that alien property in land, as having special claims on the protection of the sovereign, ought at the outbreak of the war to be exempted from seizure, but he was in favour of confiscation when it was a case of debts or money due to a foreigner. On the other hand, as regards the expulsion of alien residents Bynkershoek admitted that the law was seldom applied in its full rigour; and, as did Vattel, commented with approval on the practice of an allowance of delay to the foreigner to order his affairs. In the treaty of 1713 between France and Savoy the new attitude found expression, and confiscations effected during the preceding war were reversed. When Spain made peace with France, and Russia signed an agreement with Denmark in 1814, provision was made for the abolition of sequestration upon enemy incomes and debts.[2]

The latter part of the eighteenth century produced several treaties of commerce and navigation which protected more fully the person and property of enemy aliens at the outbreak of war. For example, the treaty between Russia and Naples, signed 6th January 1787, agreed mutually to allow enemy subjects a year to wind up their affairs, and undertook that there would be no interference with the removal of their property. Similarly in 1785 the United States had agreed with Prussia that their merchants on both sides in such circumstances should be allowed nine months to collect their debts, settle their affairs, and carry off their effects. A still further development is to be seen in such treaties as that between England and France of 1786, or that between England and the United States of 1795. Under these agreements it was contemplated that the enemy alien should have permission to pursue his calling unmolested by the government of the place of his domicile except in such cases as those to which suspicion attached. Even then twelve months was to be given to prepare for departure. In the American treaty there figured as further protection the pledge that debts, shares, bank accounts and government securities were to be exempt from seizure. This concession embraced non-resident enemies as well as resident. Even before such treaties are encountered governments had not infrequently in their actual proclamation of war permitted enemy subjects to continue peaceful residence. England permitted such residence to French subjects on the outbreak of war with

CHAP. V. France in 1756, and to Spanish subjects in 1762. In the United States residence was permitted to enemy subjects by an Act of Congress passed in 1798.

During the nineteenth century the milder practice with regard to enemy property held almost exclusive sway, the only two prominent instances to the contrary being a Danish ordinance of 1807, which provided for the sequestration of all British goods and debts in Denmark, and a decree in 1861 of the Confederate States of America which confiscated all alien enemy property except public stocks and securities acquired since 1st May 1861. During the war of 1914-1918 the practice was more severe. In England, for example, enemy property was placed under a custodian, and very often liquidated at great loss. On the other hand, to quote Dr. Arnold McNair, "it is doubtful whether alien enemies in many other belligerent states enjoyed greater procedural capacity than those in the United Kingdom. In fact, the exceptions to the English rule were, or became, such, that the disability to sue attached practically to non-resident aliens alone, and not even to them in all cases." (3)

As regards the persons of enemies the tendency was not so predominantly towards leniency as in the matter of their property. Napoleon I., as has been pointed out, refused, in reprisal for English measures, to allow ten thousand Englishmen, resident in France, to leave that country in 1803. France in 1870 undertook the removal of Germans from the department of the Seine. The Boer republics in 1899 expelled many British subjects, and Russia in the war of 1904-1905 undertook a partial expulsion of the Japanese from her Far Eastern provinces. Turkey in 1897 went to the length of a total expulsion of Greek nationals.(4) In the war of 1914-1918 a general internment of resident enemy aliens was adopted sooner or later in most belligerent countries. This course was taken in part no doubt as a safeguard against the activities of spies and sabotage, but the progressive embitterment of national sentiment against enemy individuals made it in fact an act in part beneficent to the victims. Total expulsion of enemy subjects, with the exception of men of military age, who were detained, was adopted by Portugal and by some of the British colonial governments.(5)

The Droit d'Aubaine.—Among the survivals of the past which the eighteenth century endeavoured to remove from International Law and practice was the *droit d'Aubaine*. It was a frequent theme in the treaty provisions of the seventeenth and eighteenth centuries, for it offended the egalitarian and humanitarian sentiment which was growing in that age. Under feudal conditions of life a stranger who entered the domains of a seigneur and dwelt there, became that seigneur's serf: and the serf in strict legal theory had but very imperfect capacity to own property as against his lord. In France by the fourteenth century the legal capacity of the stranger was to some extent defined. It was allowed that he might acquire and possess, but that he might not inherit or transmit his succession either by testamentary disposition or by intestacy. By letters-patent of 5th September 1386 the Crown of France assumed the seigneurial privilege of *droit d'Aubaine*, which, at least in its origin, included more than the mere inheritance of the stranger's property.

Grotius in the seventeenth century already criticised the right as barbarous in the following words:—

> "If in any country a stranger be not allowed to make a will, that prohibition does not take place in virtue of the law of nations but in virtue of the particular laws of that state: and, if I am not mistaken, comes in epochs in which strangers were treated as enemies [Grotius appears to have missed the feudal origin]. Accordingly it has been abolished with good reason among the most civilised peoples." (6)

The Dutch were successful in obtaining from the French the abolition of the *droit d'Aubaine* in the interests of their nationals by the Treaty of Nymwegen and again at the Peace of Ryswick. Under Louis XV. and Louis XVI. it was a very frequent provision to find in a treaty that the *droit d'Aubaine*, or the levy on a stranger's succession of a less violent form of it, 10 per cent. by the *droit de détraction*, had been reciprocally abolished by the contracting parties. In the treaty between Russia and Naples which was signed on 6th January 1787, there is an article which, while it stipulates that neither party would have recourse to this right, is noteworthy because it expressly mentioned that in neither country had the right or any analogous custom existed.

Montesquieu and Necker were among those opposed to the exercise of the *droit d'Aubaine*, and its unconditional abolition became practical politics in the heyday of the *Rights of Man*. Louis XVI. by an edict of 18th January 1787 had abolished without reciprocity or reserve the *droit d'Aubaine* as against subjects of Great Britain, and this notwithstanding the rigour of British laws which forbade the acquisition of real

CHAP. V.

property by strangers. But the Constituent Assembly went further. Finding that the exercise of the right "is contrary to the principles of fraternity which should bind all men, whatever be their country or government; that this law, established in barbarous times, should be proscribed in a nation which has founded its institutions upon the rights of men and citizens, and that for this reason should open its bosom to all the peoples of the earth, inviting them to enjoy under a free government the sacred and inviolable rights of humanity," it abolished in August 1790 both the *droit d'Aubaine* and that also of *détraction*. A further law of 8th April 1791 permitted strangers to succeed to the property of French relatives. The Napoleonic code reverted to a position based on an arrangement of reciprocity, but this attitude in turn was relinquished by an enactment of 19th July 1819. By this date the *droit d'Aubaine* may be said to have become a palpable anachronism. In 1812 Napoleon had abolished it from the kingdom of Italy *vis-à-vis* Switzerland; and Austria had confirmed this by abolishing it altogether as regards Lombardy in 1815. The first twenty years of the nineteenth century saw much movement in the same direction; sometimes it took the form of a specific agreement such as that between Electoral Hesse and the two Sicilies in 1818, sometimes the proclamation of a general offer of reciprocal action such as was taken by the Swiss cantons between 1803 and 1809.

A typical treaty clause abolishing the *droit d'Aubaine* may here be quoted :—

"*Treaty of Navigation and Commerce between France and Russia, 31st December 1786/11th January 1787.*

"Les nations qui sont liées avec la France par des traités de commerce étant affranchies du droit d'aubaine dans les états de S.M.T.C. elle consent que les sujets russes ne soient pas réputés aubaines en France et conséquemment ils seront exempts du droit d'aubaine ou autre droit semblable sous telle dénomination qu'il puisse être; ils pourront librement disposer par testament, donation ou autrement, de leurs meubles et immeubles en faveur de telles personnes que bon leur semblera et les dits biens délaissés, par la mort d'un sujet russe seront dévolus sans le moindre obstacle à ses héritiers légitimes par testament ou ab intestat, soit qu'ils résident en France ou ailleurs . . . Ils seront également exempts du droit de détraction aussi longtems qu'il n'en sera point établi des pareils dans les états de S.M. l'Impératrice de toutes les Russies."

The Right of Individuals to Emigrate.—The latter half of the seventeenth century saw introduced into the public law of Europe the conception that it was legitimate for the inhabitants of a province or district which was changing hands, to leave the district rather than to become citizens of a new régime. To opt for the former nationality was not provided for in name but rather in fact. An early example of this is seen in Article 17 of the Treaty of Ryswick (1697). This runs:—

> "That all the inhabitants of the city (*i.e.* Strasbourg) or of its dependencies of whatever condition they be, who desire it, be permitted to transfer their domicile wherever they please, and to remove their effects free of toll, within a year of the ratification of the peace." (7)

Article 14 of the Treaty of Utrecht allowed a year to French subjects who had lived in territory ceded to England, during which time they might remove themselves and their effects if they would. At Campo Formio the inhabitants of former Austrian territory who gave notice of their intention within three months, were to be allowed three years to sell their movable and real property and to withdraw. The Treaty of Amiens (1802) made similar provision for the inhabitants of ceded districts. More generous yet was the arrangement made in 1814, in which year the Napoleonic Empire was dismantled and France restored to the limits of 1792. In all those lands which were to change masters, six years were to be allowed to all inhabitants to dispose of their effects, if they so wished, and to choose another domicile. Treaties of this type had the important effect of making easier the way for the withdrawal of intransigent opponents to a new régime, a distinct alleviation of what is known to-day as the question of minorities. Those who remained might not unfairly be assumed to have given at least a partial consent to the alteration in their national allegiance. The natural indisposition of individuals to move made the concession less of a genuine alleviation in practice than it was in theory, nor did it prevent the infliction of great misery, such as will be readily conceived by readers of Goethe's poem *Hermann und Dorothea.* It does not, however, detract altogether from its importance to point out that it was but a timid step of conservative prudence on the part of dynamic geographers of the eighteenth century when it is compared with the later project of the *plébiscite,* which was to permit, not individuals, but whole populations,

CHAP. V. to decide, when their past political connections had been sundered, what their new régime should be.

There were disadvantages in the practice of emigration from the point of view of a state which had no mind to see its population drift away in driblets.[8] So much was this the case that, even while the right of special individuals to emigrate freely with their property figured in international agreements, many governments took steps to check by financial barriers the liberty of the subject to remove his person, and his taxable capacity, beyond the boundaries of the state. The *gabella seu census emigrationis* was imposed to this end. But it became an object of reciprocal agreement between states, and the subject sometimes of municipal *ordonnance*, to abstain from the levy of such an imposition. Martens records several instances of treaties to this effect between German states in the second decade of the nineteenth century.

The twentieth century has seen a rather curious reversal of the attitude between the governments of immigrant and emigrant states. Almost up to the middle of the nineteenth century no European government was really desirous of losing population and no American government of refusing it. In the second half of the nineteenth century, however, states like Italy had been convinced that emigration provided an outlet for the energy of young men who were almost insufferably cramped at home, and whose adventure might become a profitable enterprise even to the nation losing thereby some population. Did not Italian economists ascribe the improvement of Italian finances at the opening of the twentieth century in some measure to the stream of remittances from America, and was not the "dollar stream" of importance to other European financial systems? While European states, however, convinced themselves of the wisdom of allowing uncontrolled departure to those elements of the population which desired it, the American states, whose first thirst for population had been appeased, began to question the wisdom of indiscriminate admission. The problem was precipitated by the experience of the United States and of certain British colonies with immigrants from the Far East, especially from China. It was found that the continued immigration of Chinese from the Further East threatened to put a dangerous strain upon the social and economic framework of the localities in which they had obtained any footing; and as early as 1880 China was persuaded to sign a treaty with the United States by which the Americans were permitted to "limit" Chinese immigration. CHAP. V.

The international problems involved in discriminating between "desirable" and "undesirable," between "low standard" and "high standard" immigrants became plain when the United States proposed to extend from the Chinese to the Japanese an "insulting" exclusion. Whereas the Chinese government was powerless against foreign states, the Japanese government was in a different position. President Roosevelt wisely resolved to avoid a dangerous situation by throwing the task of keeping the Japanese at home upon the Japanese government, thus safeguarding the theoretical equality of the Japanese race with other races whose entry into American society was not yet to be discouraged. It has been doubted whether the United States Congress was wise in departing later from the "Gentleman's Agreement" and in taking full Japanese exclusion into the framework of its legal system of immigration statutes in 1924.

It was the American immigration law of 1921, however, which was notable as being the first statute to introduce a highly organised, though somewhat disguised, discrimination among European immigrant nationalities. Though the Latin-American states and the British dominions have not yet adopted measures which have given so much offence to powerful European communities, their present tendency to admit only obviously "profitable" types of immigrant may in the future be developed into forms which may prove galling to certain states exporting their manhood.[9] It is, perhaps, fortunate that the intra-European immigration immediately after the war relieved the pressure for the time, and that a voluntary limitation of numbers may be reckoned on more and more to appease for the future a nascent controversy between European countries and the United States. It should be pointed out, of course, that no immigration law adopted anywhere is intended to interfere with the obviously fruitful human intercourse promoted by commercial travellers, merchants, artists, tourists, and students engaged in activities which necessitate their temporary stay in a foreign country.

The Freedom of Coast Fisheries.—By an ancient tradition, even during the progress of a war between their respective countries, English and French fishermen left one another unmolested in the English Channel. The earlier French *ordonnances* of 1543 and 1584 respected this tradition by

CHAP. V.

allowing the French admiral to grant fishing truces (*trèves pêcheresses*) to subjects of the enemy on reciprocal conditions. Under Louis XIV. the practice grew less lenient. The *ordonnances* of 1681 and 1692 made fishing-boats liable to capture. Writing in 1760, Valin remarked that fishing truces, even for the daily catch of fresh fish, had not been made for a century. He ascribed this to the bad faith of the enemies of France who, abusing the confidence of the French, had habitually carried off French fishermen. The French crown at the outbreak of the war of American Independence once more renewed immunity for fishing-boats, and the English fleet apparently respected the French boats. The earlier stages of the war of the French Revolution also passed without trouble in this respect. The English Admiralty, however, on 24th January 1798 issued an express order against the French and Dutch fisheries, an order to which Lord Stowell gave effect from the bench in the cases of the *Young Jacob* and the *Johanna* [1 C. Rob. 20]. The French protested, through the medium of their commissary for the exchange of prisoners in London, and secured the final withdrawal of this order after some difficulty, in May 1800. Napoleon had had to hint not obscurely at an embitterment of war to obtain the grant of this grudging concession. The British Admiralty held the view that the liberty accorded to the fishing fleet of France was a pure concession on its part, and did not embrace the deep-sea fishery or oyster fishery. The English ordinances of 1806 and 1810, however, did respect the coast fisheries. During the course of the century, however, changes took place which indicated that what had been but a local arrangement was becoming incorporated into world practice. After the decisions by the Supreme Court of the United States in the cases of the *Paquete Habana* and the *Lola* (1898), it could be held that fishing-boats were by the Law of Nations exempted from all the operations of war; and this view was formally ratified at the second Hague Conference, which included with fishing vessels such small boats as plied in purely local trade. It is well to remember that deep-sea fishing vessels and the larger ships employed in local trade were never exempted from the chances of war, as also that the Germans did not in the Great War regard even small fishing vessels as immune.

The Treatment of Prisoners of War. (10)—Notable improvement was established in the condition of prisoners of war during the late seventeenth and the eighteenth century.

Louis XIV. undertook responsibility for the ransom of such French officers and men as in a war fell into the hands of the enemy. There was some attempt to discriminate between honourable and dishonourable surrender. The commanding officer whose capture could be attributed to cowardice was left to make his own arrangements for liberation. The punctilio which dated from the age of chivalry left long and still leaves, to the observant vision, its mark on International Law. In 1666 the Dutch opened negotiations with the English for an official exchange of prisoners. In time an elaborate technique was established. Commissioners for the exchange of prisoners were appointed to reside in the country of the enemy. These made lists of the numbers at each detention centre, with their ranks, supervised to some extent their treatment, and prepared rotas for immediate exchange. In suitable cases there was organised a service of cartel ships [(11)] for the transport of exchanged prisoners of war, which ships were entitled to immunity from the law of prize on the immediate journey and on return.

A good example of an exchange cartel is to be found in the Anglo-French Agreement of 13th September 1798. Its provisions ran as follows :—

> "An exchange of prisoners of war will be opened at once between the two Powers, man for man and rank for rank. The French government will begin by sending into England on a French *parlementaire* a certain number of English prisoners, five officers to go with each hundred men. On their arrival in England the British government will despatch without delay in an English *parlementaire* an equal number of prisoners of the same grade. . . . The two governments will continue the exchange from side to side in this manner until they deem it advisable to cease."

But the establishment of a system of exchange did not completely displace the system of ransom. Most cartels still put a money value on the liberation of a prisoner and the value varied with his rank. Thus in the Anglo-French cartel of 12th March 1780 the value of prisoners, fixed at one pound for a private, rose in an arranged ascending scale. A system which proclaimed a commissioned officer the worth of several privates could not be stomached by such egalitarian bodies as the National Assembly or the Convention. The former on 16th September 1792, the latter on 25th May 1793, resolved upon the abolition of all pecuniary tariffs in exchange, which thenceforward must proceed on the blameless, but in

CHAP. V. reality not very different though less merciful, principle of man for man and rank for rank. One defect in this was that it made no provision for an exchange in the case of a rank which had no exact counterpart, either in the Army List or the detention camp, of the opposing army. In practice the exchange of such a prisoner had to be effected by an estimation of worth in terms of so many units of the enemy.

It is worth noting an obstinate contention on the exchange value of different types of prisoners which raged between Napoleon and the English government. During the Peninsular War there were at one stage some fifty thousand French prisoners in English hands. Napoleon had not captured any comparable number of English, but was able to make up the number if he reckoned his prisoners taken from the Spanish and Portuguese armies which were fighting in the allied cause. The English began by desiring only to exchange French soldiers for English: Napoleon was firm in maintaining that for three thousand French he had the right to exchange one thousand English and two thousand Spanish or Portuguese. It was finally agreed that this ratio should be established, but that in this case the English prisoners should obtain priority; yet in the end Napoleon, fearing that England would break off the exchange directly it was in possession of the liberated Englishmen, preferred to discontinue negotiations.

During the eighteenth century there was, it may be maintained, an attitude of extreme liberality towards the lot of prisoners of war.(12) Vattel, before he took up in his third book the question of exchange and ransom, noticed the custom of release upon parole. He had good cases to bring forward, that of the Dutch garrisons released by the French on condition of their abstention from hostilities for a year's span, and that of the French garrison of Linz, which was allowed by the armies of Maria Theresa, Queen of Hungary, to return over the Rhine on similar conditions. Parole which was actually given by commanders in the field was usually honoured by their governments at home. Vattel, in commenting upon the system of parole, waxed sentimental:—

> "By a custom which brings out equally the honour and humanity of Europe an officer prisoner of war is sent back on his parole and has the consolation of passing the time of his confinement in his own country and in the bosom of his family."

At the beginning of the French revolutionary wars the garrisons in their entirety of Longwy, Mayence, and Valenciennes were allowed to march away on condition of not serving against the allies for a stipulated time. In the case of Mayence it was for a year, but as a matter of fact the troops were transferred to serve against the internal enemy, the Vendée. The Germans in 1870 allowed such French officers as surrendered at Sedan, Metz, Soissons, Strasbourg and Verdun to offer their parole, a parole which the French authorities wherever possible were anxious to interpret narrowly.

The attitude of the "philosophe" in the eighteenth century towards prisoners is clearly shown in Article 7 of the *règlement* of Catharine of Russia issued for the Mediterranean armament of 1778:—

> "The Turkish prisoners of every captured vessel shall be treated with great humanity, provided with provisions and against every other need and not be allowed to lack for anything. Their clothes shall not be taken from them and not any more rigour be used with them than the inspection and safety of the vessel shall require. If there be wounded among them efforts shall be made to cure them and to furnish every help as the duty of humanity requires. Finally, it is completely forbidden to hand them over or to sell them to any other country."

The same spirit is shown in the Prusso-American Treaty of 1785, which in its Article 24 lays down that prisoners made by one party from the other were not to be sent to the distant continents of Africa, Asia, or Australia, but were to remain in Europe or in America. There was to be no crowding in noxious places, in dungeons or in prison ships. Prisoners were not to be manacled. Officers were to be allowed parole "within convenient districts," while the rank and file were to be placed in cantonments "large enough to permit of exercise and containing barracks as convenient as those of the captor soldiers." The food of captive officers and soldiers was to be as good as that which they saw enjoyed by those around them. Commissaries were to be allowed to visit the camps to distribute such articles as might be sent to the prisoners from home. These commissaries were to be allowed free access and privileged correspondence. Accounts for the maintenance of prisoners were to be settled at the end of the war and without reference to other claims and counter-claims. It is possible that the mutual dissatisfaction felt by English and Americans at the treatment by the other side of their prisoners may have been responsible for the terms of the Prusso-American Agree-

CHAP. V.

ment of 1785, especially the clause in it forbidding the transport of prisoners to foreign lands, for in 1782 there were about one thousand American prisoners in England. One English prison ship became especially notorious, the *Jersey*.

> "Let the dark Scorpion's hulk relate
> The dismal tale of English hate.
> Her horrid scenes let Jersey tell
> And mock the shades where demons dwell."

The English complaints are equally sustained. Prisoners were not usually placed in the hulks unless they had been guilty of some misconduct.

The vast numbers of prisoners which were often involved made it impossible for a state to live up to such doctrine. During the Napoleonic wars England was sorely taxed to deal with the quantities of French prisoners. More than fifty thousand had been taken altogether. Of these three thousand were on parole, under somewhat restricted conditions, in small English towns. Six or seven thousand were in Dartmoor prison. Many were confined on hulks at Portsmouth, Chatham and Weymouth. The condition of French prisoners in Spanish hands was, in view of the Spanish bitterness against their invaders, much worse than that of their comrades in English keeping. The prison ships at Cadiz and, later, confinement at Majorca and Cabrera, played havoc among the French. Payrat, for instance, says that of the seventeen thousand French who surrendered at Baylen in 1808, not more than two thousand were surviving in 1814. Even in England the mortality was considerable; and pathetic memorials in the shape of a "prisoners' cemetery" tell their story of the deadly effects of apathy and banishment in more than one unsuspected corner of England, as any one can testify who knows the Roman road at Norman Cross. The administrative capacity of states showed, in no quarter more than this, a vast improvement during the nineteenth century. An exhaustive body of regulations was drawn up at The Hague. Germany managed her quarter of a million French prisoners in the war of 1870 without inflicting noticeable hardships. Her record in the war of 1914-1918, during which some two million prisoners had to be handled, has certain dark pages which it will take some time for her enemies to forget. Similarly there were dark pages in the record of the Confederate and the Union governments' treatment of prisoners in the Civil War in America. On the other hand, many of the German prison camps were commanded by enlightened officers, and it is true to say that both in Germany and the other countries there was no sign of a complete collapse of either national or international machinery, though the strain was of course unparalleled. In at least one respect the lot of prisoners in the recent Great War was marked by worse features than before. As Vattel saw, considerations based upon military necessity or advantage can always lead a belligerent to refrain from the practice of exchange. The fate of prisoners may be adversely influenced by mutually embittered or suspicious belligerents, as was shown by the hard bargaining which was drawn out to great length between Napoleon and England. The war of 1914-1918 was a struggle in which the theory of attrition was pushed on the Allied side as never, save possibly in the American Civil War, it had been pushed before. This in itself ruled out the feasibility of more than limited exchanges, and those chiefly of the disabled or the elderly.

NOTES

(1) Many Continental commentators in the nineteenth century, like Hautefeuille, Cussy, and Kleen, forgetting the old naval spirit and even the old legal spirit exemplified in authorities like Bynkershoek, Valin, and Stowell, found it impossible to speak in measured terms of incidents of this type.

(2) The authority relied upon here is Hall.

(3) Even then in most cases the expropriated interests could obtain nothing from the liquidating government, but were left to find it after the peace from their own. Only the United States of America seem belatedly in 1928 to be ready to make restitution for the seizures which had taken place in 1917. The fact that the Allies in the peace of 1919 put the burden of compensation upon the enemy would seem a departure from the improving practice of a century. There are still many Germans, particularly colonists, who have not settled their accounts with their government.

(4) The authority used here is Pitt-Cobbett.

(5) Oppenheim, ii. 206, ed. 1926.

(6) Pradier-Fodéré has a very good historical note in his edition of Grotius. Klüber paid special attention to instances of the abolition of the *droit d'Aubaine*.

(7) It was natural that the first international recognition of political emigration should be connected with the Empire, the scene of so many forced emigrations on account of religion.

(8) The subject of attempts by government to check emigration is treated in the second part of Chapter x.

CHAP. V.

(9) The complicated and dangerous problems connected with emigration and immigration have already formed the subject of two international conferences—that of Rome in 1914 and that of Havana in 1928. The difficulties between the Japanese and the United States are discussed in the *International Survey* of 1924.

(10) Payrat's book, *Le Prisonnier de Guerre* (Paris, 1910), is an authority of high value. The American, H. C. Fooks, in his *Prisoners of War* (1924), has gathered interesting material.

(11) Cartels are conventions between belligerents concluded for the purpose of permitting certain kinds of non-hostile intercourse between them which would otherwise be prevented by war.

(12) A very famous instance of this, mentioned by Goldsmith in his *Citizen of the World*, was the collection of subscriptions among the British public to provide food for the twenty thousand French prisoners in England, who were in danger of starvation owing to their government's neglect to remit funds for their upkeep (1758).

CHAPTER VI

THE WORLD OF COMMERCE

THE COMMERCIAL COMITY OF NATIONS: THE OLD COMMERCIAL SYSTEMS

The Commercial Comity of Nations.—Among the first steps taken by states to intervene in the transactions of commerce overseas were the accord of protection and the grant of privilege to alien traders who dwelt under, or came into, their jurisdiction: there was also the imposition of a form of customs regulation upon sea-borne commerce which entered or left their ports. Richard I. of England bestowed great advantages upon the men of Cologne in 1194. They were allowed to trade freely in all the fairs in the country, to be exempt from the London tolls, and to pay but two shillings annual rent for their guild-hall in London.(1) As regards sea-borne commerce Edward I. seems to have made a great advance by putting the imposition of custom duties upon a national basis with special "customers" as officials; but the work cannot be deemed completed until Edward III.'s Ordinance of the Staple in 1353. A characteristically mediaeval feature of this was the differentiation between the payment of denizens and aliens. Customs disputes soon arose, and long continued, between English and foreign merchants. Thus early in the fifteenth century the Hansards complained of the illegal exactions of the customs officials. Simultaneously the English merchants and officials denounced an extensive leakage in the customs, due to the sharp practice of the merchants of the Hanse who passed through as their own the goods of other aliens, and obtained thereby the special rebate and privileges allowed to their community.

CHAP. VI.

A second stage was reached when the Crown undertook to authorise retaliation for such violence and wrong as was inflicted upon its subjects who, abroad or at sea, were engaged upon their commercial vocations. This has been fully discussed in the section which dealt with the subject of

CHAP. VI.

reprisals. Contemporaneously with this, and as an alternative to an endless chain of reprisal and counter-reprisal, the state was found to be conducting negotiations with foreign communities for the redress of all such wrongs. To this it was generally impelled by the petition of the aggrieved. Thus in 1403 Henry IV. and his parliament of Coventry initiated a long discussion with the Hanseatic League which aimed at no less a goal than the settlement of all claims on account of illegal violences which had been offered, or undergone, in recently preceding years. There were taken into consideration by the English representatives claims from Hamburg, Bremen, Stralsund, Lübeck, Greifswald, Kampen and the Livonians, while they urged in return against the citizens of Wismar and Rostock claims from such a variety of English cities as Newcastle, Hull, York, London, Colchester, Yarmouth, Norwich, Clee, Wiveton and Lynn. The balance in the end appears to have been established against the English, for their king undertook to pay the considerable sum in settlement of over five thousand nobles.[(2)]

There followed further stages in the growing interest of the state in commerce. English traders who were engaged in foreign commerce organised themselves with the king's approval in several new areas, though never in such intimate connection with the state as were the first group of merchants organised for the export trade—the Staplers, whom, after some perilous experiments with the Staple, the English government had fixed at Calais in 1363. Thus the state inserted in treaties of general political interest clauses which dealt with the details of trade. And finally the treaties between states concerned themselves almost exclusively with commerce. In 1391 the king confirmed the appointment of a "governor" who had been elected by the English merchants trading with Prussia and the Hanseatic cities. In 1407 "governors" were set up with similar authority to procure agreement among the English merchants in cases of dispute, to arrange differences between them and the foreign traders, and to apply for redress of injury on their behalf for the British trade in Holland, Zeeland, Brabant, and Flanders. In 1408 the same was done for British trade in Norway, Denmark, and Sweden. When in a previous section the position and functions of the mediaeval consuls were under discussion, it was but to record the opening of another chapter in the story of state interest in commerce. In 1485 a Florentine "consul" was appointed in Pisa, in 1513 a

Genoese in Scio and the Archipelago, and in 1530 an Englishman in Candia.[3] CHAP. VI.

It is less easy to trace the stages in the evolution of the commercial treaty. Pradier-Fodéré failed to find a French document which would in any way answer to this description until the reign of Louis XI. (1461-1483).[4] Various English documents are to be found from the early part of the fifteenth century onwards in Rymer's collection which may perhaps be reckoned as commercial treaties. Thus there is a commercial arrangement with the Duke of Burgundy in 1407, ancestor of a long line of Burgundian treaties in connection with trade in the Netherlands: there is an agreement with Castile negotiated in 1403 under the terms of which English and Castilian merchants could come with their goods into one another's country, stay for trading and depart once more with safety. Later in the century treaties appear of an even more definitely commercial type, although it was still common for them to be accompanied by clauses which arranged for political or even military alliance, or arranged for the extradition of "rebel" refugees. The famous *Intercursus Magnus* of 1496 negotiated between England and the house of Burgundy, then in control of the Low Countries, may be taken as a typical specimen of politico-commercial treaty; and it may profitably be compared with the later *Intercursus Malus* negotiated at a time when the Burgundian ruler, the Archduke Philip, was by an accident of the sea put into English power. Further, interesting examples of the blending of political and commercial motives, with a consequent half-political, half-commercial result, are to be found in such treaties as the Anglo-Spanish of July 1499, or that between the Duchy of Saxony and England in 1505.[5]

A summary of the *Intercursus Magnus* is worthy of record:—

(1) Liberty was assured to the subjects of both contracting governments to enter their dominions mutually, to stay, to buy necessaries and to depart.

(2) English and Flemish merchants might enter each other's countries with their merchandise, might move about, sell and buy freely, and occupy houses and warehouses. Their ships laden or unladen, armed or unarmed (provided they were not piratical) were to be admitted into the ports and harbours of each country, and were to be allowed to moor, though proper dues and tolls were to be paid and, in the case of a shortage of foodstuffs, export of victuals might always be proscribed.

CHAP. VI.

(3) Merchants might be armed on board ship and carry arms ashore until they reached their hostelry. Arms were then to be laid aside.

(4) Fisherfolk were to be suffered to move freely everywhere on the sea without necessity for a safe-conduct. If they were forced by stress of weather into a port they were to be amicably treated.

(5) Pirates were to find no shelter. Proclamations were to be made that no subject of either prince was to buy goods seized by pirates from subjects of the other; and officers were to be appointed with power to seize such goods, which were to be restored to the party, which had been robbed, on no other proof than oath if necessary. The property of the pirates also was to be taken and used as compensation.

(6) Ships sailing from the ports of either prince were to give him surety to the extent of double the value of the ship and cargo, unless the ship proceeded by royal or archducal licence, in which case the prince himself should be regarded as responsible for the misconduct of the ship to the extent of any damage her crew should do.

(7) Ships were to help one another with supply of stores at sea. For these the proper payments were to be made.

(8) As regards ships of nations not party to the contract, they should not be molested in sailing to the ports of either of the contracting parties.

(9) Although ships of one party forced by storm into the ports of the other party were to be assured of a friendly reception, the landing of merchandise or the transfer of goods was not to proceed without the authority of the port officers.

(10) The goods of any nation at war with the one country were not to be carried under any pretext or "colour" by the subjects of the other contracting country. If such goods were carried, or were suspected of being carried, and interrogation were made by subjects of the belligerent contracting power, a true and entire declaration as to the nature of the cargo carried was to be made by the non-belligerent, and this was to be regarded as ending the necessity for any further search. If events should however prove that a false declaration had been made, the carrier was to be liable to the belligerent to the extent of the value concealed.

(11) Wrecked goods were to be freely restored to their owners within a year and a day, suitable charges having first been made for salvage and custody.

(12) The officers of the customs were to do no damage to boxes, packages, etc., and to make no exactions and to compel no sales.

(13) Good weight was to be given to foreign merchants.

(14) English merchants in the Low Countries, and Flemings in England, having reason to suspect the flight of debtors,

were to have the right of securing their arrest notwithstanding any local privileges. CHAP. VI.

(15) If wrongs were done to the subjects of one prince by those of the other, innocent fellow-subjects of the guilty were not to be molested under letters of reprisal before diplomatic efforts had been undertaken to arrive at a settlement. Existing letters of reprisal were to be suspended, and no steps were to be taken in connection with outrages recently alleged, unless a specially convoked diet should declare otherwise.

(16) English merchants were to be allowed to export bullion on producing a certificate from the authorities in the city, where the purchase was made, that the need for it was genuine.

(17) A meeting was to be held between the merchants of the Calais Staple and the Flemings to compose their difficulties.

The *Intercursus Malus* of 1506, being negotiated while the Burgundian ruler was in England and possibly under some measure of English pressure, attempted to alter, in certain respects, the arrangement of 1496, of course to the English advantage. For example, while English merchants were confirmed in their right to anchor, to remain and to tranship their goods in Flemish ports without the payment of certain harbour and port dues, Flemish merchants were to remain liable to the regular charges. The unqualified liberty of trading in Flanders gained by the English was balanced by a reciprocal liberty which the Flemings gained, but this was qualified by the mention of "the liberties and privileges of the English merchants." (6) Further, it was specifically agreed that English cloth was never to be excluded from the Netherlands, and that a tax was never to be placed on its sale.

It is clear that clauses of this type which entered into the details of everyday commercial life are an innovation in the intercourse of states. They have in their totality vital importance for the merchant classes, and in their general character they differ in no essential point from the provisions of a modern treaty of commerce though they make no mention of such essentially more modern developments as "most favoured nation" treatment or the interchange of consuls. That they belong to a past age, that in their interpretation it would be a mistake to find features only possible under conditions of industry and exchange as they are known to-day, is shown rather by the clauses with which they are associated than by the contents of the clauses themselves. This consideration stands out in the Anglo-Spanish Treaty of 1499: there political clauses find a place, side by side with the

CHAP. VI. commercial, and differentiate the treaty from those of a commercial type. They run in effect as follows :—

(1) There shall be friendship and alliance between the monarchies. Each shall defend the other in the possession of its territories.
(2) If the one ally claim help from the other, it shall be given by the latter and at his expense.
(3) No rebel against the one prince shall be harboured by the other or permitted to remain in his territory. If found, rebels shall be arrested and extradited.

In these cases it was as if an alliance between states was regarded as a perfect blending of their national life, in which all activity, including the interchange of goods in commerce, was included.

This does not lessen the significance of such agreements in the eyes of the historian. It is noteworthy that the *Intercursus Magnus* of 1496 adjusted the commercial relations of the two parties so satisfactorily that the Dutch were still attempting to secure its adoption as the basis of an English treaty which they contemplated at the end of 1651. The feeling between the two countries in that year was bad, not so much owing to political rivalry, as on account of commercial jealousy. The commercial jealousies of the seventeenth century fall into two classes, those which concerned the development of the new world east and west, which are treated elsewhere, and those produced by normal development in the home lands. Of these there were more than one example. There was the dispute over the dyed cloth industry. Beginning in 1608 James I. of England quarrelled with the Dutch about the importation of English dyed cloth into Holland, the central mart for that commodity. England had long woven cloth for export into Holland, but the material had not been dyed and was unfinished, so that its dyeing and preparation for the market had given employment in the Low Countries to many who were bound to suffer by King James' project for the establishment of a dyeing industry in England. The Dutch sought to protect themselves by prohibiting the importation of dyed English cloth,[7] and were successful in bringing about the collapse of the king's policy, to his indignation.

More serious than this was the shipping controversy between the two countries in the middle of the century. The English Commonwealth had since the execution of the king been obsessed by the illusion of a close confederation to be established between the two Protestant and maritime republics. After this suggestion had been repulsed and the mob at The Hague had given cause for legitimate grievance, the Navigation Act was proposed to the English parliament. It was intended to deal a formidable blow to the Dutch carrying trade, the importance of which can be gauged from the fact that several years later it was still possible for Colbert [8] to estimate that the Dutch owned more than fifteen thousand of the twenty-five thousand ships which he reckoned to be afloat. " No goods or commodities whatever of the growth, production or manufacture of Asia, Africa or America " were to be brought into England, Ireland or other possessions of the Commonwealth in any other ships than those owned, commanded or chiefly manned by English subjects; and this under pain of forfeiture of ship and cargo. Moreover, no European commodities were to be brought from any country in any ship not owned by Englishmen or by subjects of the country which produced the merchandise. This with other causes led to the Anglo-Dutch war of 1652-1654.[9]

Much of the Dutch feeling against Louis XIV. must be ascribed to the formidable protective policy which he adopted at the advice of Colbert. Tariffs on certain manufactured articles were raised to heights insurmountable by the Dutch importer, while some goods were excluded by law altogether.[10] Some Dutch interests were more impressed by the heavy cost which attached to a policy of opposing the designs of Louis on the continent than they were by the cogency of their prince's arguments in favour of establishing a Balance of Power. The council of the great city of Amsterdam, always a nerve-centre of commerce, was only very reluctantly persuaded to withdraw opposition to an extreme measure like William's expedition against King James II. Macaulay, who examined the correspondence of D'Avaux, the able representative of France at The Hague, found that the French government had had ample warning of the grave political consequences that would attach to such measures as the prohibition by King Louis of the importation of Dutch herrings into France. D'Avaux pointed out, for example, that sixty thousand Dutchmen were dependent on the herring fishery, and that, should the prohibition be enforced, grave reprisals might be expected. When peace was finally concluded with France after nine years of war one of the important concessions on the French side was a commercial treaty favourable

CHAP. VI.

to the Dutch and designed to last twenty-five years. Under this treaty Dutch shipping was relieved of the heavy French impost of fifty sous per ton, and the general principle of "free ships free goods" was established as between France and Holland at Ryswick in 1697.

It had already been for some time almost the conventional Dutch policy to negotiate treaties of trade and navigation such as should put on an assured and definite basis the "natural" right to innocent intercourse, commercial and other. When the Dutch at length won from the Spaniards at Münster their hard-won recognition their first step was a supplementary treaty of trade and navigation. It is noteworthy that the new type of commercial treaty followed as a rule previous examples which had been isolated and attempted to define in advance the practice which should be obligatory in naval warfare upon the one contracting party as belligerent towards the other as neutral. The Anglo-French Treaty of St. Germain-en-Laye (1677), for example, stipulated the principle of "free ships free goods"—that is to say, the immunity of enemy goods intercepted in neutral bottoms—and made a list of various articles which it should be under no circumstances permissible to class as contraband. The Anglo-Dutch Treaty of 1674 provided that the Dutch should traffic with the enemies of England in war just as in peace time provided no contraband should be carried: also that privateers before obtaining their commission should provide ample security. Later commercial treaties went a step further by attempting to define in advance the conduct of the contracting parties in the event of an outbreak of war between them. A notable measure of philanthropy informed the treaty between Prussia and the United States in 1785. Clauses assured for one another's prisoners humanitarian treatment, and allowed to their merchants reciprocally nine months after the declaration of war to wind up their affairs. Literary men, farmers, women and children were permitted the right of indefinite and unmolested stay. Moreover, and it is a significant event in the record of American practice, merchant shipping was promised immunity from attack. The mutual grant of preferential tariffs provided in another case for what was not very remote from political subinfeudation, as is seen from the very special tie which bound Portugal to England after the famous Methuen Treaty of 1703. In return for duties on British cloth much lower than those imposed on foreign cloth, Portuguese wines were admitted to

England on the payment of duties far lower than those imposed upon the wines of France. CHAP. VI.

The Old Commercial Systems.—The English Navigation Acts are better understood if they be compared with those principles which had previously governed maritime commerce and which they were intended to replace. Commercial treaties, or commercial clauses in treaties, of the seventeenth century usually made fairly liberal provision for general European trade. The policy of the British Navigation Act of 1651 was more illiberal. Under it foreign ships were in effect permitted to bring to England goods only which had been produced in their particular territories; (11) while it apparently assumed that English ships would import foreign goods from their ports of origin except in stated cases. An exception, it is true, was made for the goods of the Levant, which might be handled at any Mediterranean port. The Restoration Act of 1660 went even further. Thus foreign shipping was then prohibited from undertaking any export trade from England save for a direct home destination. In peace time, therefore, a friend carrier would be treated almost as though he had been a neutral who was undertaking the transport of contraband to an enemy, in that both his ships and his goods were forfeited for any violation of the Act (12 Car. ii. cap. 18). In the treaty of Breda Holland was successful in obtaining some slight modification of this attitude, for exemption was given to German goods which had been brought in, overland or up the rivers, specifically for transportation; and Denmark received a similar concession.

Colonial (12) trade, and indeed all non-European trade, was in much tighter bonds, for it was usually closed by the home countries to all strangers; and beside being confined to nationals was often the subject of narrow restrictions and monopolies. It is not always realised that the colonial trade of England in America was, within these narrow national limits, comparatively free from impediment. It is true that only English subjects (in view of Scottish (13) experience the word British must be avoided) and English ships were allowed to trade with the plantations, that no European goods (with certain exceptions) for America could be imported direct but only through England (Act of 1663), and that "enumerated" colonial cargoes had to be brought to England and unladen there (Act of 1661). But there were no restrictions on the port or time of sailing, nor gild or company monopoly. This system was free indeed compared to the practice of Spain

CHAP. VI.

with her *Casa de Contratacion* established in 1503 at Seville. A board was set up in the old *Alcazar* of Seville. It was composed of a treasurer, a factor, and a comptroller. It granted licences, provided for the equipment of fleets, determined their destination, and furnished their sailing instructions. Merchandise for exportation was deposited in the *Alcazar*, return cargoes were brought there, and contracts for their sale were arranged. Supervision was exercised over all ships which left Cadiz and Seville or the American ports, on their return; and it should not be forgotten that in the total catalogue of Spanish colonial trade the Pacific galleons from Manila to Acapulco brought in their contribution. It was, therefore, to Cadiz that the ships of European nations were compelled to come for many generations in order to sell goods for exportation to Spanish America, or to buy goods from that dominion for export to their own lands. English ships, despite the famous " Asia, Africa and America " clauses of the Navigation Acts, had permission to go to Cadiz and to bring back Spanish-American goods from that port to England. Spanish America for its part was left to depend for European goods upon the tenuous stream of the *flota* from Seville. The Portuguese trade with the colonies was almost as much concentrated in the port of Lisbon as was the Spanish in Cadiz and Seville, so that it was through Lisbon that there took place the extensive trade of England with Brazil.[(14)]

Dutch colonial trade was for long the monopoly of the East India and West India Companies. The Dutch East India Company established itself strongly in the Spice Islands where, after uneasy rivalry with the British East India Company, it acquired sole control of the trade, for the massacre of Amboyna resulted in the evacuation of the British. The East India Company had factories in India, has left a permanent mark upon Ceylon, and was later established in South Africa. It owned also forts, factories and suzerainties in the East Indian Islands. England had, of course, the East India Company, which possessed the exclusive right to do trade with India and the lands of the Indian Ocean. France too had her East India Company, and there was a last belated attempt in the eighteenth century by the Emperor to set up a similar body with headquarters in his Netherlands port of Ostend. This the commercial jealousy of the Dutch and the English set itself to suppress, and the Emperor at the Treaty of Vienna in 1731 withdrew from the contest. The Dutch West India Company, beside its Caribbean factories and the Guiana territories, had African stations for the gold and slave trades. At one moment it had all but effected the conquest of Brazil. The English held islands, including the important Jamaica and great continental tracts, but had no exclusive company. Direct trade in non-enumerated commodities between the British-American colonies and the foreign West Indian holdings was not restricted, provided it took place in British bottoms, and did not result in the illegal importation of return cargoes of European manufacture.(15) The Dutch and English in 1700 were alarmed by the advent of Philip v. to the Spanish throne, which seemed to suggest that the French would be admitted to the Spanish-American trade. Yet, if they had not merely opposed the French admission but had insisted on sharing, the opening of Hispanic America to the full currents of trade might not have been so long delayed. Further, one of the intra-American direct trades—the British-American import of sugar from the foreign West Indies—attained such importance that the West Indian interest induced the British legislature to hamper it by the discrimination of the Molasses Act of 1733. In the matter of export, however, the principal British-American products, which were destined for the European markets, were "enumerated" between 1720 and 1750, so that they had to pass through a British port and pay the dues on the way to their ultimate destination. New England was hardly affected by the early "enumerations" after 1661, but was given a grievance in the reign of Queen Anne when "naval stores" were added to the list. The weakening of England's naval enemies, which was effected in Europe by the operation of the Law of Contraband, was pursued in America even in peace time under the Navigation system.(16) Thus England tended to become the entrepôt between British colonial products and their foreign consumer. Tobacco, indigo, dyeing woods, rice, molasses, sugar, furs, and copper ore were all "enumerated" commodities. Yet a more liberal attitude was taken towards two of these articles when Walpole permitted the planters of Georgia and Carolina to send rice direct to European ports south of Finisterre, and later made even broader concessions to the sugar planters of the British West Indies. The French in the West Indies held Guadeloupe and Martinique. Between 1664 and 1674 Colbert attempted to put the entire French colonial trade into the hands of the gigantic Company of the West, which was to

CHAP. VI.

possess a trading monopoly. It was to embrace Canada, Acadia, Newfoundland, the Antilles, Cayenne, land round the Amazon and in Africa, Cape Verde, the Cape of Good Hope, and Guinea. Protests were immediately forthcoming from the French West Indies, and Colbert abandoned the attempt in 1674, throwing the trade open to all French subjects, and confining it of course to them. The Dutch took up the same attitude on their West Indian trade in the same year. The Danes meanwhile had effected a lodgment in the Virgin Islands, and did a small trade through their nationals. All the West Indies depended for their labour on slaves imported from the west coast of Africa, where there was rivalry between the Portuguese, English, French, Dutch and Danes. The English for a long period endeavoured to control their African interests through an exclusive African Company.

Thus far it has been apparent that, when within the various states trade ceased to be merely municipal, governments in each of them came upon the scene almost at once with fostering solicitude. Of the colonial trade this was true from the very first in all countries, the only variation arising in the degree of administrative management in which that solicitude found expression. Nothing could be more foreign to the spirit of the sixteenth and the seventeenth century than the remark of a well-known shipping magnate of the twentieth: " It is not for us to interfere in politics except where politics interferes with us." (17) The development of a managed system of oversea trade into a system which approximated to one of *laissez faire* was the work of the seventeenth and eighteenth centuries and demands attention next.

The seventeenth and eighteenth centuries witnessed an ever-increasing number of commercial treaties, many of which concerned a wider apportionment of colonial trade. In 1642 Portugal and England signed a treaty by which the English sought a foothold in part of the Portuguese-African trade. Under the thirteenth article the English were to be allowed to trade with the lands, places, castles, ports and coasts of Africa, Guinea and the Isle of St. Thomas, " and wheresoever it shall be proved that they trafficked in the times of the kings of Castile." No higher duties were to be imposed on them than on the allies of Portugal—an early example of the guarantee of most-favoured-nation treatment. When the Dutch in 1661 finally brought themselves to admit the defeat of their attempt to found an empire in Brazil, they acquired by the Treaty of The Hague the right, later relinquished, to trade freely with Brazil (except in Brazil wood [Article 3]), and similar rights to those of the English in West Africa [Article 4]. The Treaty of Münster in 1648 had this important feature. There the Dutch and the Spanish mutually recognised their exclusive trading spheres and undertook not to interfere in them. The Spaniards were all the same to retain their right of navigation to the East Indies, so the agreement was to that extent conciliatory, but they were to advance no further. The Dutch for their part undertook not to frequent the Castilian harbours in those seas which were chiefly in the Philippines. Further, the Dutch undertook not to navigate or traffic in any of the Spanish harbours outside Europe whether fortified or unfortified, the Spaniards in return abjuring trade with the Dutch ports in the Indies and in America, including those Brazilian ports of which the Dutch were actually in possession. About the same time England and Spain came to an understanding about their exclusive spheres. In the Treaty of Madrid of 1667 the English were allowed to import into Spain East Indian goods from their Indian factories, but as regards the sale of such goods to America were little more successful than the Dutch and obtained no privileges. In the Treaty of Madrid of 1670 provision was made for mutual abstention from one another's American ports. The Treaty of Utrecht was noteworthy for a very slight opening of the barriers in Spanish America. The English nation was to be given the monopoly of importing 144,000 negroes in the course of thirty years at the rate of 4800 per annum, though during the first twenty-five years an even larger number might be permitted by arrangement. This so-called "Asiento" contract was put into the hands of the South Sea Company, an organisation composed of holders of the British debt. It probably desired greater privileges, and would have paid heavy bribes to get them. In the mad "bubble" of 1720 the rumour was circulated, probably by interested persons, that the British government might be ready to consider the retrocession of Gibraltar and Minorca in return for new trading privileges in Peru. The "Asiento" Company was to have the additional privilege of loading one ship of 500 tons each year for South America, in which land the cargo was to be sold along with the goods brought from Spain by the *flota*. Difficulty arose out of English attempts to exceed the measure of this privilege and to ignore the exclusion of their trade, which was otherwise complete. It was exasperation on the part of the British

CHAP. VI.

public with the exercise of the right of search which Spain claimed for her *guardacostas* that led in the end to the Anglo-Spanish war which began in 1739.

The West African coast, the source of slaves for the American trade, figured prominently in treaties of the period. The Anglo-Portuguese Treaty of 1642, the Dutch Treaty with Portugal in 1661, made provisions which have already received notice. The second Anglo-Dutch war of 1664-1666 took its origin from the despatch of the squadron of Holmes to take reprisals from the Dutch for the treatment of the English-African Company. When the Suedo-Dutch Treaty of 1667 was signed at The Hague the Swedes undertook not to traffic to Cabo Corso and the Guinea coast. When the Danish-Dutch Treaty of 1666 was concluded the Danish king was pledged to withdraw his claim to Cabo Corso, Tacquoray, and Anemabo. He was compelled also to surrender Christiansborg to the Dutch West India Company as soon as the privileges granted to the Danish West India Company expired, which event was due in 1680. In 1727 by the convention of The Hague the Dutch Company agreed for a consideration to grant to the French the exclusive right of trading between the fort of Arquin and Porto Darco or the river Sierra Leone. The Dutch were not to enter French ports on that coast nor even those occupied by other nations. In the peace negotiation of 1761 France bargained for the retention at the least of Goree on the West African coast, and was rewarded by its restoration in 1763, though the British retained Senegal.[18]

In other words, the seventeenth and the early eighteenth centuries saw some slight loosening of the tightly regulated trading system of the world. Commercially trade routes were in a flux. Exclusive pretensions to the control of the trade centres were challenged by exactly the same forces as those which had challenged, and had finally sapped, the claims to dominion of specific seas. The perfect simplicity of nationally controlled and geographically demarcated areas of trade was slowly spoiled by an increasing number of concessions made by one nation to another after bargain. The progress towards a condition of *laissez faire* might have been quicker perhaps, but for the operation of the force of mutual jealousy in an ever-changing European state system. In the historic Eastern Question jealousy between the nations lest Constantinople should become the reward of the activity of any one country ended in treaty agreements which made the affairs of the Turk a matter of joint and co-operative interest to the signatory Powers. That solution as applied to colonial trade was far outside the compass of commercial thought in the eighteenth century. The volume of trade was vast, but in the end mutual jealousy was to throw it open to unrestricted competition, that is, by the process of catch who catch can, to the control of the more powerful states. Yet the powerful states were unable to monopolise its conduct for reasons which will shortly be apparent. Hence the conditions of the nineteenth century, an age of the dominance, but not the exclusive dominance, of England.

The mutual jealousy of the trading nations was soon demonstrated, for the exclusion of all nations equally from the Spanish-American trade was shown to be a point not merely of Spanish, but of general European, interest. No commercial nation wished this vast new field to be opened to a rival on exclusive terms. That explains why in the Treaty of Utrecht the Dutch, the English and the Portuguese insisted on an undertaking by Spain that the Spanish-American trade would remain closed. In the Portuguese treaty Spain ceded the colony of Sacramento on the south side of the Plata to Portugal, but the Portuguese undertook not to trade in Spanish America and not to favour such strangers as wished to ship merchandise thereto.[(19)] Similar reciprocal undertakings were signed between Portugal and France. France engaged that her subjects in Cayenne and elsewhere should not trade in the Marañon (Amazon), in the estuary of the Amazon, or beyond the river Vincent Pinson, while the Portuguese promised that their subjects would not trade in the Cayenne colony.

A partial surrender of the old commercial system was made when France in 1756 admitted as a war measure neutral shipping to her colonial ports. The pillar of the French colonial system was fractured in 1791 by the black revolt of the colony of San Domingo. The system was almost necessarily abandoned with the outbreak of the war of 1793. The collapse was a feature of the passing of the old colonial empires of England, Spain and Portugal. The revolt of the North American colonies did more than open for the future to the ships of all nations the most promising harbours of the New World. The balance of British intercolonial trade in America was destroyed, the sugar islands were left in a weak economic position, and the attempts made after 1815 to hold upright the old navigation policies in the Caribbean

CHAP. VI.

was shattered by the determined American retaliatory measures. The obvious readiness of other nations to attack still other parts of English navigation policy led to the British resolve to sound the first note of permanent retreat in the Acts of 1822, a retreat which was to end only with the opening to all of even such trade between British possessions as was not coasting trade.[20] The Brazilian ports were thrown open to British ships on the arrival of the Prince Regent with the Portuguese navy in his flight from Portugal before the forces of Napoleon in 1807. Portuguese discontent at the loss of a profitable monopoly rendered possible the partial reversal of this measure, but when in 1822 Brazil proclaimed its independence the Brazilian ports were opened once again. As regards the colonial trade of Spain the opening in 1808 of Spanish-American ports to British ships was not the official measure of the legitimate Spanish authority so much as the only possible result of the weakened hold of the Spanish administration over its transatlantic possessions. Official Spain, whether it were the constitutional regency of 1808-1814, the legitimate rule of Ferdinand or the new constitutional government of 1820, regarded the admission of foreign shipping into Spanish-American harbours with irreconcilable dislike. It might be ready to consider such a concession in return for help, diplomatic or military or both together, in its efforts to secure once again dominion over the Spanish colonies. King Ferdinand's decree in February 1824 which proclaimed freedom of commerce to these parts, which were by then very largely outside his control—was a desperate attempt to bribe England into a European conference convoked to consider means for the suppression of the revolutions in Spanish America.

NOTES

(1) Cunningham's *Growth of English Industry and Commerce*, i. 91.

(2) Cunningham's *Growth of English Industry and Commerce*, i. 419-21—an account based on Hakluyt's *Voyages*, i. 154-74, and for the money settlement on Rymer's *Foedera*, viii. 601.

(3) The immediate authority for nearly all the facts cited here is Cunningham's *Growth of English Industry and Commerce*. Cunningham is careful to base himself, whenever he can, on Rymer's *Foedera* —that invaluable collection of English documents of state which the would-be historian of International Law must use not in this chapter alone. Thus the document concerned with the confirmation in

1391 of the English "governor," of the merchants trading to Prussia, and the Hanseatic cities is printed in Rymer, vol. viii. p. 360, the document of 1530 in vol. xiv. p. 389.

(4) Some authors have seen the first mediaeval Mediterranean treaty of commerce in a Siciliano-Venetian document of 1140; the first Netherlands treaty in a document signed by Brabant and Holland in 1203; the first Northern treaty in an arrangement between Riga and Smolensk in 1229; and the first English commercial treaty in an agreement of 1217 between Norway and England.

(5) The *Intercursus Magnus* may be found in Rymer's twelfth volume, in Latin. The treaties of Henry VII. mentioned in the text may also be found in vol. ii. of Pollard's *Documents of Henry VII*.

(6) One of the foremost obstacles to international trade in the Middle Ages and beyond, was the claim put forward by the merchants, natives of the locality or of the state, to special privileges in all branches of trade and to an exclusive monopoly of certain types of transaction. Even in 1697 the Swedish government was still imposing heavy disabilities upon resident English merchants (Ashton's *Iron and Steel in the Industrial Revolution*, p. 109).

(7) Heaton, in his work *The Yorkshire Woollen and Worsted Industries*, has shown that the Belgian government of the Archduke Albert also refused to take dyed cloth from England, p. 186.

(8) Duruy's *History of France* quotes the following from Colbert's message to Arnold de Pomponne, the French ambassador at The Hague (21st March 1669):

"The sea-borne commerce of Europe employs some 25,000 vessels; in the natural order of things each nation would possess a share of this tonnage proportionate to its power, its population, and the extent of its coasts. But the Dutch have from 15,000 to 16,000, the French five or six hundred at most."

(9) Even Scotland was treated as a foreign country for navigation purposes from 1660 to 1707. It needed the Jacobite menace to persuade English merchants to take up a kindlier attitude towards Scottish shipping.

It must be remembered that there were still further weapons in the Navigation Act armoury than those described in the text. No navigation enactment in any country could, of course, contemplate the total exclusion of foreign shipping, and even the drastic English Act allowed a foreign country to send its own produce in its own ships. It was still possible, however, to promote the national shipping even against this foreigner, by allowing lower duties on imports brought by the national ships or lower port charges. A charge of this latter type was introduced in France in 1659, by which foreign shipping in French ports was to pay fifty sous per ton (Duruy's *History of France*).

(10) The Dutch replied to Colbert's famous tariff of 1667 by adopting surtaxes on French wine, brandy and manufactures.

(11) Even so the foreign ship, laden with its own national produce embarked at the usual port of trade, was handicapped as compared with the English (or Irish) ship.

(12) For the English colonial system of trade Beer's classic work on the *Old Colonial System* may be consulted. Sections of Guttridge's *The Colonial Policy of William III*. will reveal at once English official

CHAP. VI. determination to enforce navigation policies, and the evasion attempted by the colonists.

(13) Individual Scotsmen, however, could settle in the plantations and trade as English subjects.

(14) There was an important trading "factory" at Lisbon. The Navigation Act had permitted the import of Brazilian goods through Portugal.

(15) Cf. G. L. Beer's *The Old Colonial System and English Colonial Policy, 1754-1767.*

(16) See Alboin, *Forests and Sea-Power* (Harvard Ec. Studies).

(17) Sir Frederick Lewis at the 36th Annual General Meeting of Furness, Withy & Co. Ltd., 27th July 1927.

(18) Many of the treaty clauses given above are extracted from the extremely Positivist *Droit Public de l'Europe,* written by the Abbé de Mably (1709-1785).

(19) This treaty clause—also quoted by de Mably—seems sufficient evidence that all parties were aware of the extremely heavy smuggling trade which went on with Spanish America. A large degree of illicit traffic was a usual feature of eighteenth-century trade even in Europe. It was thus that Ireland evaded the worst consequences of subjection to England (cf. Gill's *Rise of the Irish Linen Industry,* p. 218, for the smuggling out of woollens).

(20) In 1816 the American government had obtained a treaty with England which established complete reciprocity of treatment for British vessels in American ports and American vessels in British (home) ports. As England, however, persisted in not allowing American ships into colonial harbours, America in reprisal closed her harbours to British ships from the colonies—a reprisal which compelled England, in view of consequent colonial distress, to open her colonial harbours to the American flag.

In the end the British system was to become more "liberal" than the American, which came to regard trade between New York and Alaska, between Porto Rico and Hawaii, as "coasting trade" reserved to the national marine.

CHAPTER VII

NEUTRALITY

NEUTRALITY: THE MARITIME POSITION—THE RIGHT OF PASSAGE—PORTS, HARBOURS, AND TERRITORIAL WATERS.

The Maritime Position.—It is untrue to say that the conception of neutrality was unknown throughout the Middle Ages. There was certainly no philosophy of neutrality comparable to that developed by Europe in the eighteenth century. For such a philosophy to arise it was first necessary for the principle to be firmly established that states were independent and that they enjoyed an absolute right to non-interference from their neighbours. Further it was essential to consign to the grave the obligation upon states to discriminate between the just and unjust belligerent, for this necessarily bestowed upon a state which was not party to a dispute the position of a judge over its peers, the belligerent communities. If philosophy had not yet permitted the neutral an assertion that he was the friend of both sides, that he insisted on being treated as such and must be allowed to assume that rôle, there was undoubtedly made in the war practice of the Middle Ages a clear distinction between the friend who was not allied for the purposes of the war and the enemy waging war. Thus the *Consolato del Mare* provided that the friend's goods should be respected wherever they might be found. Even if the friendly merchants (who usually in the Middle Ages accompanied their goods) refused to ransom the captured ship, the captor was still bound to surrender their goods when he arrived at his home port. The sole condition was a payment to the captor of the freight which would have been earned by the enemy had he completed his voyage. Similarly ships of the friend which carried goods of the enemy were to be respected, and freight charges were to be paid him for the carriage of the enemy goods. Yet belligerent convenience was again to be consulted in the matter of the voyage. Just as the friend who had his goods on an enemy ship was com-

CHAP. VII.

pelled to receive them wherever the captor might land them, so the friendly boat which carried the goods of an enemy might be required to alter the course of the voyage and to unload the enemy's cargo in a safe place. And the friend who refused such instructions was liable to be sunk.(1)

The *Consolato del Mare* aimed then at giving as much protection to the interests of the friendly merchant as was consistent with the belligerent's prime purpose of hurting his enemy. But it could be argued that the mere act of commercial intercourse with the enemy was in fact to give him aid and comfort, while to trade with him in arms, horses or munitions of war was directly to help him in his hostile movements. Accordingly, rules much more severe than those of the *Consolato del Mare*, a code based largely on the practice of the Mediterranean, were also widely current and especially outside the Mediterranean. Thus the old French rule, *robe d'ennemy confisque celle d'amy*, punished the friend even for normal association in commerce with the enemy, apart altogether from the trade in arms or the attempt to relieve places which were besieged. By the *ordonnance* of 1543 it was laid down that a friendly ship which carried enemy goods would be forfeited, and that friendly goods carried in an enemy ship would be confiscated. In 1681 special rules were issued condemning all military goods bound for an enemy destination, even though these should be carried in a friendly ship and be the property of friends. Nevertheless, both under French practice of the sixteenth and seventeenth centuries the distinction between friend and enemy was still important enough to have permitted the return to the friend of everything except the military stores, that is the ship and the rest of the cargo. This is remarkable, for later ages punished him and his associates with the confiscation of all the cargo and the ship. Under the *ordonnance* of 1584 further indulgence was granted to the friend in that the appropriation of the military stores was to be offset against payment. Often there were specific understandings, as in the agreement made in 1331 between England and the cities of Castile and Biscay or that made in 1353 between England and Portugal, in which the belligerent allowed to the friend who should be involved with his enemy, amicable and reasonable discrimination both in respect to goods and shipping. It is evident then, both from such transactions as these and from the rules of the *Consolato del Mare*, that the belligerent even in the Middle Ages was prepared to admit that the princes and states which were his friends might claim not to suffer unnecessarily from the effects of his hostilities. Not to have conceded such a claim would have led in most cases to an addition to the ranks of the enemy. Further, states recognised a condition of abstention from hostilities, whether these were deemed justly or unjustly undertaken, as a possible position for other states to adopt in such cases as were covered by the signature of an *abstinentia guerrarum* on their part with other contractants. Such contracts as the treaty of 1463 between Scotland and Denmark may be cited as containing instances of the *abstinentia guerrarum*. Further, a belligerent might be willing to concede immunity from hostility to a particular territory or area, either from the desire not to extend the area of war or for other reasons. Francis I. of France, for example, gave in 1542 letters of neutrality to the bishopric of Cambrai, the county and town of Cambrésis.(2)

Until the eighteenth century, however, there was lacking any real basis in theory to support a state should it demand to remain neutral when a belligerent firmly asserted the justice of his cause and declined to accept anything except co-operation. A state so placed had to fight or to give way. When George Frederick, the Elector of Brandenburg, pressed upon his brother-in-law Gustavus Adolphus the claim to remain neutral in the war between the King of Sweden and the Emperor this impasse was exemplified. "Was ist das für ein Ding? Neutralität, ich verstehe es nicht. Es ist nichts damit," was answered by the Prussian monarch's "Que faire? Ils ont des canons." An even better known example of belligerent intransigence taken from the middle of the eighteenth century is shown by the demands which Frederick of Prussia presented to Saxony in 1756. He overran the Electorate without a declaration of war. He refused to accept an offer of Saxon neutrality though it were guaranteed by hostages and admission to the three Saxon strongholds of Pirna, Wittenberg, and Torgau. He demanded nothing less than the transfer to himself of the administration of Saxony and the use of its army against Austria. The "continental system" of Napoleon was but a dramatic denial of the right of continental Europe to adopt a neutral attitude during his war with England. He invaded Portugal when that country begged to be allowed not to confiscate the goods of British merchants, while he annexed the Papal States when the Pope attempted to keep his ports open to the enemies of France, and to refuse a French alliance menacingly offered.

CHAP. VII.

So much for practice. It was Bynkershoek who made the first real advance in the work of establishing a tenable theoretical position for neutrals against the *soi-disant* just belligerent. His opinion is couched in momentous words.

> "If I do not deceive myself, the justice or injustice of the war does not affect a common friend. It is not for him to place himself as judge between the two belligerents who are, the one and the other, his friends; nor, on the ground that their cause is the more just or less, accord or refuse more or less to this one or that. If I am neither on one side or the other, I can not aid the one in such a way as will hurt the other."

Vattel is far less sound. He took up two incompatible lines of argument in his attempt to reconcile the old quasi theological theories of the just war with the practical necessity for the provision of a theoretical basis for the practice of legitimate neutrality. He admitted without reserve the discarded theological theory that a war could not be just on both sides, that the unjust belligerent assumed a terrifying responsibility, and that the belligerent unjust through invincible ignorance or error was not morally guilty. But to the list of the possible causes of a just war he added the preservation of the Balance of Power. Against the unjust belligerent he was prepared to discriminate by holding it wrong to furnish him with aid under a treaty of alliance or to concede him passage. Finally he maintained that it was the duty of every state to assist the just belligerent.

> "It is lawful and praiseworthy to assist in every way a Nation which is carrying on a just war, and such assistance even becomes a duty for every nation which can give it without injury."

After this interesting development of the doctrine of the *bellum justum* Vattel proceeded to withdraw from the resulting position all practical effect by establishing the contention that regular war must as to its results be accounted just on both sides, so that whatever is permitted to one belligerent must be permitted to the other. Further, immunity had been conferred upon the unjust belligerent by the voluntary Law of Nations. The implication of his not very lucid arguments is that the neutral, except perhaps in the act of granting passage, had owing to the risk of error no right to discriminate between the two belligerents. It was precisely this, despite admitted difficulty in coming to a decision as to the merits of the case, which the neutral wished to do.

More decisive than the theoretical position which the publicists attempted to establish were the measures taken by the statesmen of would-be neutral countries to shake themselves out of particular wars. A single Power was in a weak position, especially if it were disinclined to fight for its conception of neutral rights against an oppressive belligerent. This was true of a number of neutral Powers acting simultaneously but in isolation. During the course of the hostilities of 1756-1763 the complaints of Holland, Denmark and Spain had been long and loud concerning Britain's treatment of their shipping, but little was done by Great Britain to meet their grievances. There was precedent for united neutral action. In 1693 Sweden and Denmark had leagued together in opposition to the Anglo-Dutch attempt to forbid all trade of neutral Powers with their enemy, the French. Consequently, Choiseul now attempted to induce both the Dutch and the Swedes to form a neutral league of maritime powers. What he then proposed, a belligerent in the Seven Years' War, became the actual policy of the very able head of a powerful neutral government in the war of 1778-1783. In 1780, Catharine II. of Russia organised the Armed Neutrality of Russia, Sweden and Denmark on a basis of support for an advanced neutral position. She was successful in obtaining the adhesion of Holland, Prussia, Austria, Portugal and Naples. In 1800 Russia, which in 1793 had completely abandoned the position which she had adopted in 1780, took the initiative by inviting Prussia, Sweden and Denmark to co-operate in action against the belligerent conduct of England. The second Armed Neutrality went even further than the first. The members undertook military measures to enforce their views. The Tsar Paul sequestered English property in Russia, Denmark laid an embargo on British ships in Danish ports and closed Hamburg, Lübeck and the Elbe to British commerce, Prussia closed the Weser and the Ems and occupied with troops the English king's Electorate of Hanover. These measures were temporarily effective and resulted in the compromise arrangement reached in the Maritime Convention made between England and Russia in 1801, to which Denmark and Sweden afterwards acceded. But the compromise did not last. When, in 1807, war between Russia and England again broke out, Russia in its declaration of war annulled the Maritime Convention, and Great Britain immediately returned to those principles against which both Armed Neutralities had been directed.

CHAP. VII.

The Berlin decrees of Napoleon were the signal for a general assertion on the part of both belligerents of the extremity of belligerent power. The times were hardly ripe for development in a contrary direction. Thus, although by the eighteenth century the notion of neutrality had projected itself sharply into the minds of statesmen and of writers on International Law (Bynkershoek, who did much to focus the idea, never himself employs the word), there were yet a large number of questions upon which a final equilibrium was to be obtained in that balance between neutral and belligerent interests which it was clear by 1800 was to be and to remain the determining factor in the definition of neutrality.

The disputes between neutrals and belligerents during the eighteenth century tended to concern themselves overwhelmingly with the single subject of the treatment of neutral shipping which was engaged in commerce with the enemy and which encountered on the high seas, or upon the enemy's coast, the armed ships of the belligerent. There were, however, several other spheres of international action which were likely to be affected by the increasing emphasis which came to be laid upon the rights of neutrals—rights which, however, could only be logically justified by neutrals accepting obligations which in turn were likely to be more and more onerously defined. The right of a neutral Power to have his territorial waters kept free from the armed operations of belligerents would conversely be matched by the obligation not to admit privateers and their prizes, by the obligation to take due precaution against the abuse on the part of a belligerent fleet of the claim to shelter, by the obligation to exercise due diligence in preventing any reinforcement of the belligerent from being obtained in his ports. Indeed, the cry of the belligerent was often not so much for an extension of his privileges as one to have his obligations more accurately defined. This comes out most clearly in the history of the law of blockade. It is to questions other than those which concern maritime capture that it is now opportune to turn.

The Right of Passage.—Grotius in a well-known paragraph expressed the attitude of the belligerent of his day on the question of a right of passage :—

> " Thus it is that the territories, the rivers, and the parts of the sea which perhaps have become the property of a people must be open to those who have need of passage for legitimate purposes ; for example, because expelled from their own

> country they seek unoccupied lands, or because they wish to traffic with a distant nation, or even because they go to take back that which belongs to them in a just war. The reason is the same as that given above: it is because the institution of property was introduced with such a reserve, useful to those who avail themselves of it and not harmful to those who permit it. The founders of property must therefore be regarded as having preferred it so."

That is to say, Grotius founded a right of passage on those imagined rights reserved by the human race when, by an imagined mutual contract, they instituted, or permitted the institution of, the ownership of property in land. Grotius was the child of a generation which in the sphere of politics was beginning to think in terms of contractual philosophy. In current phraseology, he was engaged on "rationalising" action which for centuries had been, and incidentally would be, the general rule. At Westphalia it was one of the sanctioned inheritances of the Holy Roman Empire that the roads of the Holy Roman Empire through whatever territory they might pass should be open to every component state or sovereign. But whether or no that were good German doctrine, the practice was very much wider than Germany itself. Indeed, in a Europe in which princes saw their territories scattered, as it had been from a pepper-box, any other practice was necessarily unsatisfactory. Grotius declined to believe that a prince had a right to refuse passage through his country. It was, in his view, no legitimate excuse to urge that he was fearful of the action which might be taken by a mass of men in marching through the countryside. A prince had no right to plead his apprehensions that he might, by opening his roads, become entangled with the belligerent who was not so benefited. It was futile in him even to point out an alternative route, for a just belligerent asking in good faith the shortest and most commodious way might under no circumstances be refused. Some protection, indeed, a would-be neutral might expect. He could demand that the troops on their journey should proceed in convenient detachments; he might require the right of posting protective garrisons at the invader's expense, or demand to be given hostages for the good behaviour of the troops. The doctrine of Grotius was full-blooded, as indeed was the common practice of the age. There was but scant comfort in either for the weak or apprehensive neutral state:—

> "One can infer from this [the law of necessity] how it is

CHAP. VII.

permitted to the just belligerent to occupy a territory situated in a land outside the area of hostilities. This can happen if there is a danger, not imaginary but real, that the enemy will invade that place himself, and cause in that way irreparable damage. The occupation, however, is on condition that the occupant takes nothing that is not necessary for the defence, availing himself, for example, only of the topographical advantages of the country, and leaving intact jurisdiction and property : and that he has the intention of restoring the occupied place as necessity ceases."

It is not without interest to examine the negotiations which preceded the Spanish annexation of a large part of the kingdom of Navarre in 1512, in that they concern a bargain, struck in the manner of the sixteenth century, over an army's right to passage through alien territory.(3) Navarre lay between France and Spain, Powers at war, and had long endeavoured to maintain, both in this and previous wars, a strict neutrality between them. In May plenipotentiaries from Navarre had been despatched to the French court, but early in June the situation had been changed by the arrival by sea of an English force destined to co-operate with a strong Spanish force collected for the purpose of invading southern France. The projected invasion was out of the question except by the violation of Navarre. To this King Ferdinand was opposed, fearing exposure to retaliation, for the forces of Navarre, such as they were, were in a strong strategic position whatever route might be chosen. Accordingly the Spaniards requested a free passage through Navarre, but insisted, as prudence suggested, that six of the strongest Navarrese fortresses should, by way of hostage, be handed over for the duration of war to six subjects of Navarre who should be nominated by the Spanish Government. Alternatively they offered Navarre a Spanish alliance. At once a second deputation was sent from Navarre to the King of Spain charged with securing either the modification of the Spanish conditions or the delay of negotiations pending the conclusion by the first delegation sent to Paris of a defensive arrangement with France. On 17th July the latter signed with the French a treaty of mutual defence, the terms of which, by a singular series of accidents and through treachery, were made known in Spain before the termination of negotiations in that country. France and Navarre both undertook to refuse passage to the enemies of either of them. Navarre in addition agreed to declare war upon the English, now close to the Franco-Navarrese borders, and upon any troops co-operating with them. The Spaniards held Navarre to a previous treaty by which the Navarrese had undertaken to refuse passage to the French; and on 21st July the Spanish commander began the invasion of Navarre, which he quickly overran. Although it had been originally the proclaimed Spanish intention that the occupation of the country should not outlast the expedition against France, and although the occupation had originally been regarded as in the nature of a surety for the pacific behaviour of Navarre, the estates of that country were forced to tender an oath of allegiance to the Spanish king in 1513, while the conquered portions were incorporated into the kingdom of Castile on 15th June 1515.

It has already been pointed out that the Spanish monarchy, in order to transfer troops from Spain to the Netherlands in 1567, had first to make sure of the goodwill of Genoa, Savoy, and Lorraine. The Austrian Hapsburgs in the seventeenth century were faced with the perpetual problem of defending their anterior lands from French attack although these south-western possessions were separated by the whole breadth of Germany from the main Austrian *bloc*. This was especially true of Upper Alsace, for it must be remembered that the Hapsburgs did not withdraw from South-Western Germany until 1815. When the two branches of the Hapsburg house, which reigned in Spain and Austria, attempted to co-operate in defence against the French, they found communication between Spanish Milan and the Austrian Tyrol quite indispensable. Venice, almost alone of the Italian states, refused a passage to the Spaniards, so that it was necessary for Hapsburg troops to pass over the fifty miles between Lake Como and the Stelvio Pass. These fifty miles were under the jurisdiction of the Grisons, with whom Spain attempted to negotiate an agreement to let the Spaniards pass. French and Venetian agents bestirred themselves and defeated the attempt. In retaliation Spain in 1618 imposed a bar on the trade between its duchy of Milan and the Grisons, and encouraged a movement for independence in the vitally important Valtelline. From 1618 to 1639, the year in which the Grisons accepted an alliance with the Hapsburg Powers, that confederation was the scene of disorder, revolution, and armed military intervention by France on the one hand and by Austria and Spain on the other. The Hapsburgs twice made passages which have as feats of arms passed into history. In 1629 forty thousand Imperialists marched into

Italy against the French: in 1634 twelve thousand Spaniards led by the Infante Ferdinand marched into Germany.(4)

By 1713 Austria had, like the British Empire of to-day, its permanent problem of communications. Connection was essential between the mass of provinces centred round Vienna, Prague, or Buda and the outlying portions such as the Netherlands or the Breisgau on the one hand or Milan, Naples, and Sicily on the other. Nor was Prussia more fortunate. The Mark lands were equally remote from the Rhenish territories of Cleves, the North Sea district of East Friesland, the central Minden, and the Baltic kingdom of East Prussia. Prussian history down to the nineteenth century is the record of the successful completion of a jig-saw puzzle.

Grotius maintained that passage could be demanded of right quite apart from any previously signed treaty assuring it or regulating the details of its assertion. States nevertheless found it advisable to stipulate in advance, wherever it were possible, either for the accord of passage to themselves or for its denial to their opponents. A reciprocal undertaking was reached on 12th May 1587 between the Catholic cantons of Switzerland and Philip, King of Spain. The king was offered the rare privilege of passage for such of his troops as he wished to march northwards, and promised in return to offer no obstacle to the movement of Swiss mercenaries from the cantons to the Pope, the Duke of Savoy, or the French League. Phillimore cites Swiss treaties with France extending over a long period, under the terms of which the Swiss undertook to refuse a passage to French enemies.

Treaties of passage were frequently arranged by generals in the field, as was the case in the French agreements for passage in 1796 with Sardinia, Parma, the Pope, Württemberg, Baden, and Bavaria. When Napoleon on 28th April 1796 forced the court of Sardinia to sign an armistice, he secured, beside Sardinian neutrality, the possession of certain strategic points and the right of passage through Valenza. Similarly, when it was a question of operating against the Austrians in Mantua (who themselves claimed, and exercised without treaty, passage across Venetian territory to and from Mantua), Napoleon, after a preliminary entry into Venetia without one, was successful in obtaining a treaty. Two Venetian officers were cajoled into signing a secret treaty, later confirmed by the Signory, which allowed the French to pursue the Austrians over Venetian territory or to besiege them in any citadels of Venice. The French undertook to pay three million francs for any damage caused. When the old order was overthrown in Switzerland in 1798 the Swiss were compelled by treaty (19th August) to accord to the French the use of two roads leading to South Germany and to Italy. Even when after the Act of Mediation of 1803 Napoleon compelled the Swiss to accept the position of "absolute" neutrality, he was capable of saying, on the outbreak of an Austrian war in 1809, "If I have need to march into Switzerland I shall do it. I can always find a pretext: the most insignificant pamphlet aimed at me will serve my purpose."

That Napoleon took these steps aroused, of course, much hostile comment among contemporaries, but it is not fanciful to find behind such comment rather a protest of disgust at a conventional exhibition of ὕβρις upon the part of a tyrant than the outraged sentiments of defenders of the Law of Nations. Yet this judgment may well be wrong, for opinion was forming, or about to form, against the view that passage was either a right or even desirable. Vattel's attitude was representative of eighteenth-century theory, and looked beyond it in some respects. According to him a sovereign was required to grant innocent passage to bodies of troops, as well as to individuals; and such a grant included in his eyes the right to exercise military discipline and to buy provisions. But he held that the permission should always be requested, and that it might be refused for good reason. The passage of troops in numbers could never be completely harmless, and he instanced the damage which had been done to Venetian and papal lands during the war of the Austrian Succession. Further, it did not escape him that the political intentions of him who demanded passage might well be doubtful. On this Vattel based his concession to the neutral of a right to refuse passage or to exact every reasonable security. He expressly contradicted the opposing view of Grotius on this point, only observing that obligation lay on a neutral to display impartiality as between the two belligerents both in regard to the concession and the refusal of the right to pass. Vattel did not lose contact with reality. He contemplated circumstances (though they were regarded by him as exceptional) in which a passage might lawfully be forced. Where no inconvenience was involved to any man, when passage was indispensable to a belligerent either as an anticipatory or as a counter-move in the face of an opponent, he regarded the refusal of passage as indefensible obstinacy and the imposition of over-nice conditions as unlawful.

CHAP. VII.

Apart from the previous treaty of guarantee, the German demand upon Belgium for passage in August 1914 might have been regarded as not inadmissible in the eighteenth century. The effort nowadays necessary to conceive this as possible is the measure of the strength of those forces which have been at work a hundred years. Upon no branch of the Law of Nations has the influence of the United States of America been so formative as on the conception of neutrality. The attempts of the French representative Genêt in 1793 to enlist the citizens of that country for active operations against Great Britain, which was at war with France but on peaceful terms with the United States; the trial and acquittal of one of these enlisted citizens, Gideon Henfield; the realisation by the United States of deficiencies in its law of neutrality; the series of attempts to amend that law which culminated in the Foreign Enlistment Act of Congress of 1818: all these produced profound effect all over the world both upon governments and students of the law. In Europe the process of mediatisation, the absorption of the smaller units of the Holy Roman Empire, after its end at Austerlitz, into the tessellated pavements of United Prussia, United Germany, or United Italy, the disappearance of anachronisms like the independence of Geneva or the dynastic links which connected the King of England with Hanover or the King of Prussia with Neuchâtel, in a word the emergence of the modern simplified map of Europe, made the necessity for a right of passage less likely to arise. Simultaneously, as the price of freedom from the manifold disadvantages of war, a more complete abstention from every connection with the interests of belligerents has been in part assumed by, in part imposed on, neutrals. The strong neutralist sentiment which was a feature of the nineteenth century allowed weak neutral states like Belgium and Switzerland, quoting the guarantee of their neutralisation, to impose respect on powerful belligerents such as were France and Prussia in the war of 1870, during the course of which Switzerland even assumed the internment of the last field army of France under Bourbaki in February 1871. With the twentieth century new conditions arose, the discussion of which must for the moment be postponed. It can only be pointed out here that in 1900, during the Anglo-Boer War, Portugal, to comply with a treaty obligation *vis-à-vis* Great Britain, allowed the landing at Beira of a contingent of that country which was on its way to Rhodesia; while in 1915, during the Great War, British and French troops were landed at Salonika, a portion of the territory of a neutral power, Greece, which protested but took no action. Lastly, under the conditions of the League of Nations any signatory Power must give free passage to any other signatory Power which is co-operating in the protection of the covenants of the League. Fauchille has suggested that the effect of Article 16 of the Covenant of the League is to bring about, in the cases to which it refers, a reversion to the older conception of neutrality. Dr. Arnold McNair discusses the question with shrewdness in the fourth edition of the second volume of Oppenheim's *International Law*.

Ports, Harbours, and Territorial Waters.—Two well-known incidents taken from the seventeenth century will suffice to show the scant respect felt in that age by a belligerent strong at sea for the sovereignty over territorial waters claimed by the neutral. In 1639 a large Spanish fleet of sixty-seven sail, commissioned to land ten thousand men at Dunkirk to serve against the Dutch, was pursued in the Channel by a Dutch armament. The Spanish ships took refuge in the Downs, anchoring alongside the English squadron of Vice-Admiral Pennington. The English king and the vice-admiral were imperative in requiring from the Dutch abstention from hostilities in waters which were admittedly under English jurisdiction. The Dutch Admiral Tromp contented himself with a blockade pending reinforcement from Holland. Then, seizing upon a pretext, he attacked the Spanish fleet and almost completely destroyed it. The feeling at the English court was bitter against the Dutch for flouting the English requests, and almost as bitter against the Spaniards for having thrust themselves uninvited under English protection. Nevertheless, no English declaration of war followed.

In this case of the "scandal of the Downs" a neutral sovereign had claimed the right of giving indefinite shelter to a belligerent fleet in a place perilously near its final destination. Less exceptional was the position of the King of Denmark and Norway in 1666. Owing to the Anglo-Dutch hostilities the Dutch East Indiamen were avoiding the Channel and attempting to reach the home ports by sailing round the north of Scotland. A fleet being despatched to these waters under the Earl of Sandwich, the Dutch merchantmen took refuge in the Norwegian port of Bergen. There the earl attempted to attack them, but was driven off by the forts. The King of Denmark contented himself with a remonstrance.

CHAP. VII.

Both these incidents can be paralleled from the history of the eighteenth century, when neutral Portuguese waters were twice made the theatre of belligerent attack. In 1759 Boscawen made an attack on a French squadron between Sagres and Lagos, and in 1781 Suffren made his attack on the ships of Commodore Johnston. For the former the British government made some amends. And yet without question during the eighteenth century neutral Powers grew at once more careful of their obligation to impartiality and more insistent on the fullness of the sovereignty over their ports, harbours, and territorial waters. Noteworthy are the proclamations of neutrality made during the American War of Independence by Tuscany, Genoa, Venice, the Pope, and Naples.(5) These contained a general prohibition of all hostilities within cannon-shot range of the port or land; and detailed regulations were laid down to impose order and pacific behaviour on belligerent ships within the neutral jurisdiction. Thus in the Tuscan regulations belligerent ships were forbidden to cruise about in search of enemies within a cannon-shot of ports or harbours, such conduct being held to be in prejudice of public commerce and an impediment to free departure from the port by others. Further, belligerent ships were forbidden to stay in port in order thence to proceed forth against ships which entered or departed. If a belligerent ship were at anchor and the port signal were given that a ship was arriving, it was forbidden to leave port. Even if it were already sailing but were still within the limits of the port it was to be summoned back by cannon-shot. Similarly, if it were arriving and already within the limits of the port it was forbidden to turn back on the announcement of the arrival of another ship. If a belligerent ship were in port together with other ships the choice of leaving earlier or later was to be with that ship which had arrived first, but a belligerent ship was not to leave before twenty-four hours had elapsed after the departure of a ship of any other nationality. In order to avoid the delay which this practice might occasion at such busy ports as Leghorn, the captain of a war vessel for himself, or the commodore for a squadron, was to be permitted to depart at any time on giving his word of honour to refrain from attacking any vessel which had departed within the twenty-four hours prior to his own departure, and any others which were signalled or in view at the time at which he had sailed. Captains or owners of belligerent merchant ships were to give suitable guarantees for similar behaviour if they desired to depart without observing the twenty-four hours restriction. It was provided in addition that all capture of prizes taken contrary to such regulations was to be null and void.

In order to win belligerent consent to such restrictions upon their action, it was necessary for the neutral state to adopt an attitude of the strictest abstention from all taint of belligerency, and further to impose such an attitude upon all its citizens or subjects. Tuscany and the other Italian communities forbade their subjects, as well as the denizens of, and even the aliens temporarily resident in, their countries to fit out ships for privateering, or to play even the smallest part in the fitting out of such ships though it were done outside the state. Enlistment in any capacity for service on a belligerent ship was also forbidden. Venice thought it worth while to couple with this stern attitude towards enlistment for sea service an injunction against enlistment for service in the army of any belligerent state. The Italian states prohibited the ships which flew their flags to take as passengers belligerent soldiers or sailors. Venice (9th September 1779) and Naples (14th September 1778) went so far as to stop all ships of their flags from carrying or loading contraband for belligerent countries, a measure which was made applicable to all subjects, residents and temporary visitors.

All the four states on the other hand permitted the admission of prizes without restriction. While the Tuscan proclamation made no narrow examination into the conduct of a belligerent with his prize, the Venetian was careful, before permitting the sale and conversion of the ship or cargo, to presume that there had taken place a proper sentence of good prize from the competent belligerent tribunal. This impartial hospitality towards prizes was sounder than the more partial conduct which some states were prepared to assume in advance by treaty. Thus in the treaty made by the United States of America with France in 1778 the United States undertook to admit French privateers with their prizes, but to refuse entry to prizes taken from the French. The practice of admitting prizes has been thought in modern times in some sense to compromise the perfect neutrality of the admitting state. England since 1861 has excluded prizes altogether, other states have admitted them, but for twenty-four hours only, and have forbidden their sale. The Hague Convention of 1907 adopted exclusion as the formal rule, but permitted a Power to allow entry when a prize should be

CHAP. VII. brought in simply for sequestration, pending the decision of a prize court.

Tuscany appears to have allowed a belligerent warship to reinforce its crew in the Tuscan port, and only Rome forbade reinforcement beyond the need of navigation in the case of merchantmen. No Tuscan subjects, however, were to be enrolled, and no belligerent nationals were to be taken by force even from other boats of the same flag. Such a provision as to reinforcement was general, and in its modern much modified form, which restricts it to the number of sailors necessary to navigate the ship to a home port, seems unobjectionable. Yet it was banned by the Hague Convention in 1907. None of the Italian communities seems to have objected to the making of repairs on a belligerent ship of war. Naples indeed in its proclamation specifically mentions the practice with approval. In the twentieth century such a provision would be deemed to give the belligerent too much use of the neutral port. The modern rule limits the repairing process to the making of a ship seaworthy, and has generally imposed limits on the provisions or fuel which may be taken aboard.

The cruisers and privateers of the eighteenth century had a vast range of action for they often made their prizes several thousand miles away from a home port. In these circumstances it might prove most difficult either to take a prize home expressly for purpose of condemnation, or even to take it to a neutral port and let it await there the dilatory proceedings of a home tribunal. In any such case documents and witnesses would have to be sent home and heavy claims for damage would be maturing in the event of an unjustified detention. It is obvious, therefore, why Powers which had no convenient ports for the establishment of prize tribunals endeavoured to make use of neutral harbours. Even England, which in the Western Mediterranean long possessed Port Mahon, had officers appointed at Leghorn, in the Duchy of Tuscany, who were charged with making a preliminary examination of witnesses and documents in order to decide whether to release a ship or to send it on to the court of prize. To this measure of jurisdiction the Grand Duke of Tuscany did not object, especially as the activities of the officers appointed did in fact result frequently in the release of ships. Powers other than England had even more reason to desire the setting up of a complete jurisdiction on neutral territory. Thus when Catharine of Russia despatched the famous expedition of Orloff from the Baltic ports to the

Mediterranean in 1778 her instructions to the admiral in connection with his practice as to the treatment of prizes, pending the erection by himself of a prize commission, and to the smooth working of that body, were as follows. The Russian vessels were to take such ships as they should capture before the Russian minister plenipotentiary at Naples, Skavronsky, or his colleague at Venice, Mordvinoff, "if the government of the republic interpose no obstacle." These diplomats were to investigate and judge in matters of prize until the arrival of the fleet and the erection of the commission. The French *règlement* of 1779, "concernant les prises qui seront conduites dans les ports étrangers et les formalités que doivent remplir les consuls de S.M. qui y sont établis," gave French consuls in neutral ports every duty of the prize court in connection with the captured ships except the act of condemnation, which had to be performed at home on the basis of the papers, affidavits, and documents despatched or prepared by the consul. During the revolutionary wars, however, French enemies were given reason to complain of the fullness of the jurisdiction set up by French consuls in neutral countries. Thus in 1793 the French consul at Charleston in the United States—on the authority of M. Genêt, so it appears—proceeded to condemn British prizes brought into that port by illegally equipped privateers, while in 1799 in the case of the *Flad Oyen* (6) Lord Stowell had reason to reject the legality of the authority which the French consul at Bergen in Norway assumed in the matter of prize condemnation. He cogently tore asunder the pretext that because the French claim, as voiced by the Danish merchant Mr. Krohn, had reasons based on general principle to support it, it was therefore valid. He quoted with approval the decisions of the United States government, and he denied that because vessels were taken by the British to Lisbon and Leghorn for examination they were *condemned* by any other court than the Court of Admiralty in Great Britain. He defended the British practice with regard to these two ports by alleging the special treaties which existed between the Portuguese, or Tuscan, governments on the one hand and the British government upon the other. "To make the ports of Norway the seats of the French tribunals of war is to make the adjacent sea the theatre of French hostility. The coasts of Norway could no longer be approached by the British merchant with safety, and a suspension of commerce would soon be followed by a suspension of amity."

CHAP. VII.

CHAP. VII.

The various activities, referred to above, of Monsieur Genêt in the United States, who claimed to act by virtue of the provisions of a treaty of 1778, put the development of the theory of neutral duties to a decisive test, the more so in view of the feeling against the British rampant among large numbers of the citizens of the republic. The United States administration, owing to the influence of Washington, declined to allow the legality of Genêt's commissions, which were issued on the territory of the United States, and, in its judgment, violated their sovereignty. Further the administration took the view, which was important, "that if the United States have the right to refuse permission to arm vessels and raise men within their ports and territory, they are bound by the laws of neutrality to exercise it." Accordingly, the French prize courts were closed, steps were taken to restore British ships taken by such vessels as carried M. Genêt's commission, or were illegally manned by American crews. The subsequent events, which led up to the passing by Congress of the Foreign Enlistment Act of 1818, have been already described. It was followed by the British Act of 1819. Thus by the end of the second decade of the twentieth century it may be asserted that a high standard of abstinence from belligerent service had been set for neutrals by two of the great maritime Powers. They even went so far as to assume the duty of punishing their individual subjects who enlisted in the service of belligerents. When lack of "due diligence" on the part of the Liberal government in 1862 permitted the *Alabama* to leave Liverpool, and this ill-fated ship, in the service of the Confederate government, had done its worst in a destructive cruise against the shipping of the Union, an international body of arbitrators, which met ten years later, awarded damages of fifteen and a half million dollars to the United States.(7) The incident marks further progress in the process by which sharper endeavours were demanded by belligerent of neutral Powers in preserving the virginity of their neutrality. It did not serve the British government to point out that its legal powers to stop the ship had been defective, or that it had acted with the same diligence which it usually displayed in domestic affairs.

Eighteenth-century proclamations laid down no limit for the length of stay permissible to belligerent ships of war in neutral harbours. England in 1862 adopted the rule of limiting the stay to twenty-four hours in ordinary cases. Its wide adoption by other Powers has made it authoritative.

Nor was there any general rule as to the number of belligerent vessels which might be together admitted to a harbour. A Hague Convention has fixed the number at three where it is not otherwise determined by municipal law. Neutral Powers have for the most part followed the lead of the United States in 1793, and have carefully limited the right of belligerents to bring prizes into their harbours. A Hague Convention has given unseaworthiness, stress of weather or want of fuel and provisions as the sole excuses under modern conditions for the intrusion. In the well-known case of the British ship the *Appam*, captured by the Germans off the west coast of Africa and brought by them into Newport News, the Supreme Court of the United States upheld the court of first instance in holding that as the *Appam* had not been brought to America under any one of the three conditions given in the Hague Convention, the ship had to be returned to its owners.

NOTES

(1) The "Consolato" was printed—together with other old collections of sea-laws—by Pardessus in his *Collection des lois maritimes antérieures au xviiime siècle*.

(2) Nys, *Le droit international*, vol. iii. p. 536: "Neutralité; Quelques indications touchant l'histoire de la neutralité."

(3) The story may be found in Prescott's *Ferdinand and Isabella*.

(4) See the chapter on the Grisons in Oechsli's *History of Switzerland* (Cambridge University Press), or the chapter on the Valtelline in vol. iv. of the *Cambridge Modern History*.

(5) These declarations were printed by Lampredi in his *Del Commercio dei Popoli Neutrali in Tempo di Guerra*, and were translated into French with the rest of the book by Jacques Peuchet, 1802.

(6) 1 C. Rob. 135.

(7) See below, p. 394.

CHAPTER VIII

THE EQUALITY OF STATES

THE EQUALITY OF STATES: ASSERTION OF EQUALITY OF RIGHT BETWEEN NEUTRAL AND BELLIGERENT.

CHAP. VIII.

The Equality of States.[1]—An examination of the state system of the sixteenth century will discover little or no sign of a claim by smaller states to an equality, either of dignity or of right, with larger states. Princes disputed among themselves for dignity or precedence and on such grounds as their relative position in the Holy Roman Empire, the antiquity of their lineage, the glory of their ancestry, the duration of their dynastic rule, the size, the wealth, the population, and the power of their respective territories. Republics, moreover, were sometimes hard pressed to keep a reasonable precedence in international affairs. And yet how large a part was played in the development of International Law by the theory that somehow or other there did exist equality among the states. The spark which for the modern world set ablaze the long train of this doctrine is to be found in the theory of Thomas Hobbes, that there was in the supposed state of nature an equality of right among all men, and in the few casual references of the same author to the fact that princes and states lived together in the state of nature and were therefore governed by the principles of the Law of Nature. His leading remarks must be quoted textually :—

> "The Right of Nature, which Writers commonly call *Jus Naturale,* is the Liberty each man hath, to use his own power, as he will himselfe, for the preservation of his own Nature; that is to say of his own Life; and consequently, of doing any thing, which in his own Judgement, and Reason, hee shall conceive to be the aptest means thereunto."[2]

Here is a liberty, equal for all, merely of undertaking all things necessary for self-preservation without any reservation expressed as to individual capacity for performance. It is translatable into the international sphere very readily.

But the ideas of Hobbes as to this equality among natural men went much further than their mere equality in a right to endeavour to preserve themselves.

> " Nature hath made men so equall in the faculties of body, and mind ; as that though there bee found one man sometimes manifestly stronger in body, or of quicker mind than another ; yet when all is reckoned together, the difference between man, and man, is not so considerable, as that one man can thereupon claim to himselfe any benefit, to which another may not pretend, as well as he. For as to the strength of body, the weakest has strength enough to kill the strongest, either by secret machination, or by confederacy with others. . . . And as to the faculties of the mind . . . I find yet a greater equality amongst men, than that of strength." (3)

This equality of capacity in men to do one another harm in the condition of nature seems to have a very close connection with Hobbes' theory of their equality of right.

> " The question who is the better man, has no place in the condition of mere Nature ; where (as has been shown before), all men are equall. The inequality that now is, has been introduced by the Lawes civill. . . . If Nature therefore have made men equall, that equalitie is to be acknowledged : or if Nature have made men unequall ; yet because men that think themselves equall, will not enter into conditions of Peace, but upon Equall termes, such equalitie must be admitted. And therefore for the ninth Law of Nature, I put this, *That every man acknowledge other for his Equall by Nature.* The breach of this Precept is Pride." (4)

Hobbes' theories as to the state of nature and the origin of the commonwealth rested on his assumption of a state of continuous war. That states were in the condition of nature he proved from this continuous attitude of belligerency.

> " But though there had never been any time, wherein particular men were in a condition of warre one against another ; yet in all times, kings and persons of Sovereigne authority, because of their Independency, are in continuall jealousies, and in the state and posture of Gladiators ; having their weapons pointing, and their eyes fixed on one another ; that is, their forts, garrisons, and Guns upon the Frontiers of their Kingdomes ; and continually Spies upon their neighbours ; which is a posture of War." (8)

Hobbes' analogy between men in the state of nature and states was incomplete ; it was only half an analogy. An integral part in Hobbes' theory of " natural men " had been their

CHAP. VIII. essential equality, at least in their equal capacity to do one another harm ; and it had been this which had given a justification for the universal mutual recognition of equality which Hobbes reckoned as the Ninth Law of Nature. This equality, which might be assumed in men with some superficial appearance of reality, because all men were more or less of the same height, weight and physical capacity, was not to be assumed so easily of states. Had Hobbes been pressed, even he could hardly have produced a brilliant paradox in defence of the essential equality of say the King of France with the Prince of Sedan, the Emperor with Count Függer, the King of Spain with the Knights Hospitallers of Malta. Accordingly, when in a bold phrase Hobbes came to transfer the application of his principle of equality to the sphere of international relations, his argument was vitiated from the beginning.

> " Again natural (law) can be divided into the natural law of man which has come to be called the law of nature and the natural law of states which can be called the *Lex gentium* and is commonly called the *Jus gentium*. The precepts of each are the same, but because states, once instituted, put on the personal properties of men, the law which we call natural, in speaking of the duties of individual men, we call *jus gentium* when applied to whole states, nations and peoples. And those elements of Natural Law and Right, which have hitherto been discussed, translated to states and whole peoples, may be reckoned as the elements of the Law and Rights of peoples." (5)

It is obvious from this passage how Hobbes' anthropomorphic conception of the state (" because states, once instituted, put on the personal properties of men ") had made easy his slip from sound logic, his omission of even a passing phrase of caution or reserve.

It was Pufendorff (1632-1694) who revealed the significance which the doctrine of "natural equality" might assume. Hobbes' position had been in essence sceptical. As he detected a capacity for mutual harm in all men, so he assumed them to be equal, or at least to require themselves so to be regarded. The paradox was forced in part by his irritation at the super-simplicity of the Aristotelian division of men on the basis of natural endowment into slave-owners and slaves. Pufendorff viewed the matter less paradoxically.

> " So under this regulation of Nature, how much soever a man may surpass his neighbours, as to bodily or intellectual endowments, he is still obliged to pay all natural duties as

readily and as fully as he expects to receive them : nor do those advantages give him the least power or privilege to oppress his fellows. . . . Nor on the other side does the bare unkindness of nature, or of fortune, set a man in a worse condition than others, as to the enjoyment of rights . . . and this equality may be called an equality of rights." (6)

Here the Law of Nature, by the difference in emphasis, has been stated in such a way as, when applied to the international sphere, will with apparent justification allow the Prince of Sedan to claim equality of right with the King of France. Pufendorff's own statement, however, is more cautious. He preferred to introduce the idea of equality on the side of precedence and then gradually to extend the thought to cover merely completeness of internal sovereignty. He was still concerned with safeguarding the internal independence of small states against the larger. He did not venture to assert equality of right, or of capacity, in undertaking international functions :—

> " (From all of which) it is sufficiently clear that there is no perfect obligation which presupposes proper right in another by which a Prince, really possessed of sovereign power, is bound to yield precedence to any other King or Prince as more honourable . . . however superior in the particulars before mentioned (ancient lineage, wealth, power, territory). . . . Nor indeed is a state governed by the populace inferior in Dignity to a state governed by a Prince, though in a Democracy there is no particular person to be compared to a King."

Further he wrote, and more boldly :—

> " If a King finds himself strong enough to defend his crown easily, I do not see why he should allow precedence to another from whom he has nothing to fear, and whose protection he has no need to seek. All those who are free are free equally ; and superiority of strength or wealth gives no prerogative. A Prince whose lands are only one hundred miles in length is as much sovereign in his own territory, and as capable of exercising the acts necessary to the end of civil societies, as another whose jurisdiction extends over six hundred miles of country."(7)

The framework of all such declarations of independence is feudal and imperial. In the attempt to shake free from the inherited restrictions of the past the ideas of the philosophy of the *Social Contract* played the greatest part. Succeeding generations, forgetful of the historical setting of the problem, made use of *a priori* methods in the formation of general

CHAP. VIII.

principles of equality which had little or no reference to any former threat to that equality. This was the work of the great age of enlightenment, the eighteenth century. Yet in the passage quoted above Pufendorff took up a strong position. Transferred from general terms to the particular case, the Elector of Brandenburg was equal to the King of France because he had nothing to fear from him and because he could provide for the political and civil needs of Brandenburg-Prussia every bit as efficiently as could the French king for his state. Even so far as this had reference to internal economy within a given political area, this statement, applied by Pufendorff to areas which were in fact largely self-sufficient, ceased to have relevance in the nineteenth century, the age of world commerce and of such movements as those of federation and the Zollverein. It is to be noted, moreover, that in matters of international organisation, confined in his day to such business as the making of treaties or the gathering of peace conferences, both of which activities have enormously increased in the last two hundred years, Pufendorff had nothing to say. The initiative in such matters, however, and in the signature of treaties tending to the establishment of new international custom, was almost always with the greater Powers. There may well have been an equality of right to conclude such treaties between the greater and the smaller Powers, but there was certainly no comparison between the authority enjoyed by a treaty provision signed between England and France and one signed even by such considerable, but minor, Powers as Savoy and Genoa. Aptly enough, Barbeyrac, a translator and annotator of Pufendorff, who was a convinced disciple of the Naturalist school, refused to allow any binding force to mere international custom or to agree that a treaty provision almost universally adopted bound that state which had not formally entered into the agreement which contained it.

> " Since the peoples are all equal one to the other, even if all, save one, should agree to establish certain rules, that Power, though alone, could refuse to submit to them." (8)

The stretching of the claims of independence and equality to the point of imposing a bar to all effective international action has always been the great obstacle to the effectiveness of international institutions.

The realists, who approached International Law not as part of a universal philosophy but as students of the actual behaviour of states, the contents of state papers, the dicta of authorities and statesmen, did not pay much attention to the theory of the equality of states. The great J. J. Moser in his *Versuch* drew up a list of European states and divided them lawyer-like into the categories of sovereign states, states whose full sovereignty was in dispute, and half-sovereign states. Mably, who thought of states overwhelmingly from the point of view of their actual participation in the international life of the day, divided states into three classes—Powers of the first rank (England and France), Powers of the second rank (Austria, Spain, Russia, etc.), and Powers of the third rank. De Martens even spoke of the possibility of dividing the states of his day, viewed from the political angle, into four classes, and further mentioned that nations had sometimes been induced for various reasons to depart from the reciprocity of rights established for all nations by Universal Law.

Nevertheless, it was during the eighteenth century that the doctrine of equality thoroughly established itself. The fashionable Vattel, for example, committed himself wholeheartedly to the metaphysical obscurantism of the doctrine.

> "Since men are by nature equal, and their individual rights and obligations the same, as coming equally from nature, nations which are composed of men and may be regarded as so many free persons living together in the state of nature, are by nature equal and hold from nature the same obligations and the same rights. Strength or weakness in this case counts for nothing. A dwarf is as much a man as a giant is ; a small republic is no less a sovereign state than the most powerful kingdom." (9)

It is difficult to imagine a closer-packed bundle of fallacies. This was to go ludicrously far in the naturalistic direction, though ultimately it was not really the superior arguments of either side in the controversy which prevailed. That stormy period of war which ended the eighteenth and began the nineteenth century saw the creation of much International Law. And it saw the dissolution of much international theory and the side-tracking of much controversy as unreal. Barbeyrac, as has been already indicated, refused to admit that a well-nigh international custom, or an almost universal provision in international treaties, could bind a state against its will. This view he had rested on the inherent equality of states. It was England which first of all conspicuously displayed an example of solitary opposition to the recognition

CHAP. VIII.

as International Law of a number of propositions concerning the law of maritime capture which had been adopted by every other state which was important on the sea except itself. This was not to proclaim that the authorities in England were naturalists. The First and Second Armed Neutralities attempted to impose upon England recognition of the formula "free ships, free goods," the limitation of the designation "contraband" to actual instruments of war, the necessity for a blockading force to be *in situ* before the rights of blockade could be exercised, the right of neutrals to navigate "from port to port and on the coasts of the nations at war." The attempts, however, broke down before England's persistence, and, one must add, the lapse from their own doctrine of members of the Armed Neutrality themselves when they became belligerent. When it was proposed that the laws of war at sea should be discussed at the Peace Congress which had been summoned to Vienna to liquidate the Napoleonic adventure, Castlereagh secured the relinquishment of the project. Englishmen desired no international limitation of their war rights at sea, which they found it more profitable to deduce themselves from historic practices than to allow an international Congress to define in advance. It was a similar sentiment, joined to a necessary realisation that a blockade can be a weapon of offence—a weapon of which England may often find herself in need—which with other apprehensions led to the rejection by the House of Lords of the Declaration of London.

But the liquidation of the Napoleonic adventure brought on to the European stage for the first time what came later to be known as the Concert of the Powers. Russia, Austria, England, and Prussia claimed, by virtue of their sacrifices and exploits in ridding Europe of Napoleon, the right to take the principal part in the reorganisation of the European system. By agreement among themselves they were able in all but certain respects to override the protests which arose against their management of the Vienna Congress. The monarchy of France, which under Talleyrand led the opposition to the dictation of the great allied Powers at Vienna, was conciliated by admission into the close councils of the inner ring. Thereupon the Four Powers were able to face with equanimity the sullen illwill of even so considerable a state as the Spanish monarchy. They carried through the reallotment of the extensive Polish, German, and Italian territories which the downfall of Napoleon had left without definite ownership.

When Napoleon returned from Elba the Four Powers took the initiative in drawing up a solemn treaty of alliance to which they invited the adhesion of the rest of Europe. All this constituted a noteworthy challenge to notions of an equality among the states. Still more was this the case when, in the first quarter of the nineteenth century, there was formed the habit among the great monarchies of endeavouring to act together in the control of new revolutionary movements disturbing to the peace of Europe. Political equality, it may be said, was denied by the larger to the smaller Powers even if no actual challenge was made to their juridical authority. The smaller states, fearing this challenge, were passionately averse to the acceptance of a permanent state of political inferiority. Behind any sort of challenge they detected a threat to their independence as a final stage in logical deduction. Dickinson in his work on the doctrine of the equality of states has collected a number of instances of protests made by small states against their relegation to a position of inferiority. The protest of Württemberg in 1823 against its exclusion from the Congress of Verona was due in part to a reaction from the policy of Metternich in German affairs, but was made on the general ground that there was legitimate reason to fear for the independence of the small communities if the great Powers attempted by themselves to supervise the common interests of Europe. Though Württemberg had little direct concern with the issues discussed at Verona, and though its monarch was compelled to retract his protest, the mere fact of protestation was not altogether without effect. Similar protest had some success throughout the century. When, after Greek affairs had in 1869 occupied the attention of the Powers, a conference was held to settle the affairs of the Near East, Greece successfully refused to participate except upon terms of complete equality. Again, when in 1883 a conference was called to arrange for the regulation of navigation on the Danube, Rumania took up an analogous position.

None the less, it is impossible to avoid the consideration that throughout the nineteenth and twentieth centuries many of the smaller states had special conditions imposed upon their international existence by acts of the greater Powers. These sometimes acted unanimously, sometimes with dissentients. Thus Switzerland was declared a neutralised state in 1815, Belgium in 1839, Luxemburg in 1867. The international character of Greece was after hesitation fixed as that

CHAP. VIII.

of an independent constitutional kingdom, and guaranteed as such by England, France, and Russia. The status of Rumania from 1856 up to the final recognition of its independence in 1878 was decided at a conference at Paris in 1858. The Congress of Berlin admitted further Balkan states into the European family. Rumania, Serbia, and Montenegro were forced as the price of their independence to establish full equality of rights for all their subjects, whatever their religion. Further they undertook to impose no obstacles on the internal organisation of religious bodies or on the communication between these and their religious chiefs. Bulgaria, though not yet independent, undertook similar obligations, and Turkey voluntarily adhered to the same policy. Rumania, which interpreted very narrowly its obligation to the Jews resident within its jurisdiction, was to feel much international pressure to amend its ways, though its Jewish policy compared at least favourably with that of one of its mentors, Russia. The Hague Conferences, and in particular the Second Conference of 1907, saw an attempt to establish its proceedings upon the basic position that all states were equal. The lack of success which resulted may have had some effect on the opinion of the participant nations; for, when it became a question of an attempt to draft a code of maritime practice, it was but a gathering of the great maritime Powers which assembled in 1908 for the conference of London. The United States of America in the twentieth century has in practice succeeded in imposing very special conditions upon the international life of Cuba, Hayti, San Domingo, Nicaragua, and Panama, although there have been among the political leaders in Washington and among the publicists of the Republic the stoutest upholders of the doctrine of juridical equality among states. The provision of the League of Nations with two organs, the Council and the Assembly, is based on the realisation of the political inequality of states, although the method adopted for the composition of the former pays tribute to the notion that juridically an equality may be held to be in existence. The formation of a League of Nations in itself gave formality to an inherent existence of inequality among the states: it regularised that inequality by ensuring that the controlling power was not usurped by any group which cared to seize it. The safeguard of minorities, no longer of merely religious, but thenceforward of political, minorities, was taken over from the European Concert big or little, and assumed by the League. This was done by the act of the allied and associated Powers themselves in establishing the League of Nations, and the recognition of the independence of the new Powers (Poland, Czecho-Slovakia, the enlarged Jugo-Slavia, Greece, and Rumania) was made dependent on their acceptance of the "minority conventions." "Minority" provisions were also inserted in the treaties with those states which had formerly been hostile. Some of the new states were successful in objecting to a régime dictated by such minority treaties, a régime which they maintained could lead only to external interference in their domestic affairs and a perpetual turbulence among their subjects. Esthonia and Latvia, for example, escaped with the signature of a mere "minority declaration," and Esthonia in particular reduced to a minimum the supervisory authority of the League. States which had had their independence limited by the liability to such supervision could not but reflect with envy upon the lot of Powers which were free from such harassment. Thus Italy has Slovene and German minorities, while Jugo-Slavia has Italian, Bulgarian, and German. Yet Italy was left free to proceed as she thought fit, while Jugo-Slavia was bound by the terms of the "minority treaties" and the supervision of the League of Nations.

The Latin-American states throughout the nineteenth century contended that the great Powers, and even smaller European states, declined to treat them on a footing of equality; nor did they find in the terms of the Monroe doctrine anything but a protected subordination to the United States. The limits even of this little esteemed protection were not easily defined. When internal disorder produced damage to European persons and property, or when there was a failure in the payment of loans to the subjects of the European Powers, the Latin-American communities found themselves subjected to pressure or coercion. The Drago doctrine, put forward by Dr. Luis Drago in 1902, was an attempt to state the right to equality of treatment by other Powers of the Latin states of the American continent. "All states," wrote the distinguished Argentinian statesman to the minister of the Republic at Washington on 29th December 1902, "whatever be the force at their disposal, are entities in law, perfectly equal to one another and mutually entitled by virtue thereof to the same consideration and respect." This message to the minister was afterwards worked up by the Third Pan-American Congress, held at Rio de Janeiro in 1906,

CHAP. VIII. and by the Argentinian representatives at the second Hague Peace Conference, into a demand for a general ban on all attempts to collect public debts as between countries by the use of force. This proposal was not carried, a somewhat colourless compromise being substituted for it, on the motion of the United States. On the other hand, the mere presence of the South American delegates at the second Hague Peace Conference is not without significance in any attempt to appreciate the steady progress towards the universal recognition of the importance of Latin America which was the ultimate end of patriots like Drago. At the first Peace Conference no state from South America had been represented. It is one thing, however, to reverse a policy of under-appreciation, quite another to lay down a general principle of equality among the Powers.

At the present day he who would assert this equality is confronted by an overwhelming number of considerations which forbid it. He will be faced by the extra-territorial rights enjoyed by the subjects of many Western states in the Nearer and the Further East; and by the fact that these Eastern countries have in many instances had a limitation on the free operation of their customs imposed and accepted in a large number of international agreements. Similar control applied to their respective budgets had, in consequence of faulty financial administration, been imposed on Turkey in 1878, on Egypt in 1880, and on Greece in 1897. A limitation of armaments was imposed on the defeated Central Powers in 1919, not to mention other restrictions upon the freedom of their action. Again, certain international rights, even when no formal bar existed, have never been enjoyed to an equal degree by the greater and the smaller states. In the Turco-Italian War even so powerful a state as Italy was prevented from exercising its full belligerent powers at sea by the illwill of France. In the Turco-Greek War between 1919 and 1922 both France and Italy paid scant regard to Greek belligerent claims. In the two international conferences at The Hague, at which all states, large or small, met on a footing of nominal equality, the invitations were issued by a great Power which planned the programme and order of business in consultation with its fellows. In the committees of the conferences the opposition of even a single great Power was sufficient to cause delay and to provoke attempts at compromise. Finally, when the drafting of the Conventions was undertaken, the influence of the great Powers was predominant. To the

London Naval Conference of 1908-1909, as has been said, and to the Washington Conference of 1921, great Powers had the unquestioned *entrée*, secondary Powers being admitted only by the special grace of the convener or by reason of a special direct interest in the matter under discussion. In the League of Nations the great Powers were made permanent members of the Council, while a dividing line was proposed among the others in 1926, which does in fact admit the emergence of a new category of second-class Powers.

Despite the general drift of tendency in the nineteenth century, the theoretical supporters of natural equality were still active. Carnazza-Amari perhaps represents an extreme type. "All men," said he, "have the same origin, the same type, are physico-spiritual beings. . . . States and nations resulting from the gathering of a great number of human beings have the same traits which appear in their members. If men are equal in their types and in their rights, states which are collective personalities, composed of men, are similarly beings juridically equal." Nowhere, perhaps, was the doctrine of natural equality so widely held as among the representatives of the South American states who were present at the meetings of the second Hague Peace Conference. Before this gathering lay the task of constituting two International Courts which it was proposed to establish—an International Prize Court and one of Arbitral Justice. The struggle between the "egalitarians" and the "realists" was sharply joined. In the matter of the International Prize Court some of the leading "egalitarians" like Ruy Barbosa were prepared to allow that, as only the maritime interest of states was in question and not their position in totality, the doctrine of natural equality did not forbid an arrangement whereby all states should enjoy the equal right of appointing judges, but that those appointed by Great Britain, Germany, Italy, Japan, Russia, Austria, France, and the United States should always be members of the court, while seven others appointed by the remaining Powers, or some of them, should sit by rota. The more rigid egalitarians refused any whittling down of their theory even in the matter of the International Prize Court. When, however, discussion passed to the composition of the Court of Arbitral Justice all the South American representatives closed their ranks, and they were joined by some of the smaller European Powers. The delegates from the United States, Choate and Scott, tried to show the South Americans that the equality of states

CHAP. VIII.

was sufficiently safeguarded by the fact that the judges nominated by the smaller Powers would be of equal status with, and chosen for the same twelve-year period as, those selected by the larger Powers. The fact that the judges from the great Powers would actually sit for the full time, while those from the smaller Powers would only sit for various periods, arranged in gradations from ten years to one year, according to the importance of their nominating state, would not affect the equality of their rank, according to this view, or consequently that of the Powers which nominated them. These arguments did not in fact remove the opposition ; but the project did not reach the stage even of presentation for signature, largely for other reasons, chief among which was the general feeling that before an International Prize Court or a Court of Arbitral Justice could be erected there was need for greater agreement among the nations as to the law which these organs should administer. The whole controversy none the less is pertinent to the subject under discussion.

In the various International Unions which came into being during the nineteenth century the greater Powers were on the whole more ready to drop into a position of equality with the smaller Powers. But these unions were concerned with less controversial matters, such as the universal postal, the international telegraph or railway service. In such questions the interests of all Powers were largely the same, and it was less likely that there would arise great differences of principle among the great Powers themselves or between these on the one hand and the lesser Powers on the other. Nevertheless, even here it was impossible to keep out all manifestations of inequality, since separate representation was allowed to the dominions, colonies and dependencies of the colonial states and, when schemes were adopted for apportioning the payment of expenses, it was usually arranged on the basis of the establishment of a rough proportion between the capacity to pay, or the services received, and the contributions actually imposed. In some of the more recently formed unions the principle of equality was abandoned from the outset, even in the matter of voting, care being taken scrupulously to avoid the giving of offence. Thus in the International Office of Public Hygiene five classes were established to each of which were assigned one, two, three, four or five votes and one, two, four, eight or sixteen units of assessment respectively. Each Power was allowed to choose its own class, but would, according to its choice, become responsible for the appropriate contribution. The allotment of contributions to the League of Nations was similarly based upon a classified and an ascending scale. CHAP. VIII.

Assertion of Equality of Right between Neutral and Belligerent.—It was not due to any stiffening of belligerent practice, or at any rate to this predominantly, that trouble between neutrals and belligerents became sharper in the eighteenth than in previous centuries. On the contrary, there is reason to suppose that neutral ships or sailors or goods which fell into belligerent hands were more likely to get just treatment in that period than formerly. The trouble was rather that the general character of war in the eighteenth century worked to deprive the Power at war of the justification based on righteous belligerency. Wars by land arose very frequently out of designs to partition the neighbour's territory, or to remake the map of Europe in accordance with a scheme of balance. By sea, the interests of nations led them to aim at spoiling their neighbours of their colonies, their trade or shipping. War was essentially the means to grow rich and great. In these circumstances there was validity in the plea of the neutral to be left alone peacefully to pursue innocent trade free from the barbarities which war would involve for the participants. Neutrals might readily concede that there was no colour of innocency in contraband trade, in the carriage of munitions of war or the attempt to bring succour to besieged places. But the neutral Power often found itself faced with inflated notions of the nature of contraband, blockade and unneutral service, notions conceived solely to the advantage of the belligerent and lacking that moral justification alluded to above. Privateering and naval interests grew fat on the plunder of private merchandise; and Admiralty courts lost few opportunities of stretching old doctrine to cover new cases, such expansion generally being made favourable to the belligerent interest. The diplomatic correspondence of the eighteenth century reflects the resultant exasperation of neutrals; and colour was given to this by the realisation that the privation and loss, humiliating in itself, was inflicted upon them by states wrestling for no lofty principle, but only for material advantage or, in the case of privateers, solely for gain. It was at once to assert neutral dignity and neutral independence of hostilities, as also to safeguard from injury and annoyance the most valuable part of a nation's commerce, that neutral states began increasingly to insist that ships which carried their flag should

CHAP. VIII.

pursue unhindered all but illegitimate trade: and the taint of illegitimacy became in definition restricted to a traffic in arms and to attempts to enter with cargo places besieged from the sea with stationary ships. Belligerent rights against neutral merchant ships came to be confined to the official visit for the ascertainment of nationality and the discovery of the presence of contraband on board. The procedure fixed for such visits was most careful of neutral dignity. Thus the Tsaritsa Catharine of Russia, who throughout her reign was steadily identified with an expression of the neutral position, in her *règlement* of 1778, instructed the Russian ships to send only a small boat to any neutral vessel which it was necessary to visit. From this only one man was to come on board. He was to examine the ship's papers and to hear what the crew had to say. Only under the most glaring evidence of a suspicious character was there to be an opening of the "écoutilles" and hold.

There were even more extreme upholders of this doctrine. Writers like Hübner and Galiani put forward in far more drastic terms the claim of neutrals to immunity from belligerent operations. Hübner (10) took up the position that a neutral ship at sea was part of the territory of that neutral. The belligerent, according to him, enjoyed no sort of jurisdiction over her, for that was the prerogative alone of the home state. And this position had already been advanced by the Prussian lawyers against England during the famous dispute known as that of the Silesian Loan. In this the point had been made that the neutral ship was neutral territory, and that to seize enemy goods from it was equivalent to a violation of neutral land in order to make booty of enemy goods. It was one stage in the controversy which raged round the phrase "free ships, free goods" which will have to be treated elsewhere. Here it must be recorded that Hübner passed on to a formal denial that the prize courts of a belligerent could have jurisdiction over neutral ships. Such jurisdiction could not, according to him, be a matter of right, nor one of consent, and was an attack upon the independence of the neutral state to whom the judgment was due even in the case of the carriage of contraband property. It would be not only vicious in form but it made for injustice to give jurisdiction to a belligerent prize court, for it was to constitute the interested party a judge in his own cause. This is strong meat, but it would be difficult to deny the contention a certain logicality, unless one were to take into consideration the overwhelming and historic contrary practice of nations.

Finally Hübner advanced the ingenious proposal that the prize court should be composed of representatives of the two states concerned, belligerent and neutral. CHAP. VIII.

Galiani (11) to a considerable extent repeated the propositions of Hübner. He did, however, allow the belligerent to have jurisdiction over cases of the nationality of ships in which false ascription might be alleged. In other cases jurisdiction over neutral captures belonged properly to the neutral. He explained that it would be simple, if the prize were taken into a belligerent port, for powers to be given to the consul of the neutral state concerned to set up a court of prize which could consist of the consul himself and assessors. Lampredi (12) reverted to the position which had been taken by Albericus Gentilis. In this the necessity of collision between neutral and belligerent rights was taken as granted. He was perhaps not quite so ready to subordinate the neutral to the belligerent as was the Italian doctor whose phrases still ring sonorous and arresting down the ages. He was speaking of the Anglo-Hanseatic controversy :—

> " Est *aequo aequius*, et favorabili favorabilius et utili utilius. Lucrum illi commerciorum sibi perire nolunt. Angli nolunt quid fieri quod contra salutem suam est. Jus commerciorum aequum est, at hoc aequius tuendae salutis est ; illud gentium jus, hoc naturae est ; est illud privatorum, hoc est regnorum."

However, Lampredi took his stand firmly on the customary habits of belligerents. The floating ship was not to be regarded as a piece of national territory entitled to the neutral's immunities. The belligerent had always assumed the right to judge in prize certain types of neutral commerce which inflicted harm upon him, unless of course he had resigned the right by treaty. Finally he considered that for a neutral to judge cases in which its own nationals and their property were involved was just as objectionable in theory as it was for the same responsibility to be assumed by the belligerent. If a belligerent might be presumed to be biassed towards condemnation of the prize, a neutral might be equally biassed towards acquittal. There were, moreover, practical objections to neutral jurisdiction. If the belligerent captor was assumed to have made for his home port, perhaps at great distance from the neutral state, how were prize proceedings to go on ? Were the captors to undertake the tedious and costly process of securing legal representation at the neutral court and of despatching papers and witnesses thither to give the neutral judges means of

CHAP. VIII. judgment? If on the other hand it were assumed that the consul of the neutral in the belligerent country was to set up a court, would not this involve a greater violation of the sovereignty of an independent nation than the traditional capture on the high seas of neutral ships?

The dilemma could not be easily answered. Practice endeavoured to dissolve it. Neutrals attempted at once to protect their commerce from visit and search, to safeguard their dignity and to deprive belligerent prize courts of jurisdiction. The means were easy. Let them organise their vessels in groups and convoy them with a government ship of war. Let the neutral government assume the duty of eliminating contraband of war from the cargoes carried, and let it authorise its naval officers to submit to the belligerent right of search no further than to give their word that the cargoes under their protection were inoffensive. But a belligerent like Great Britain, pressed to the uttermost, would not be likely to countenance this innovation in the laws of war. It might well question the care exercised by the officer commanding the convoy or might regard as inadmissible the neutral's definition of contraband. Further there was the insuperable barrier to agreement presented by Great Britain's claim, wherever treaties presented no obstacle, to take enemy goods, even those inoffensive in character, from neutral ships.

The government of Queen Christina of Sweden first claimed immunity for convoyed ships and did so in 1653 during the Anglo-Dutch hostilities. Article 4 of the Instructions to Ships of the Royal Swedish Navy, dated 16th August 1653, runs as follows:—

> "They shall in all possible ways decline that they, or any of them, be searched. For seeing that they are only sent to prevent all inconveniences or clandestine dealings, it is expected that they may be believed and suffered to pass and proceed on their course unmolested with all such things as may be under their care." (13)

The Dutch during the Commonwealth Wars with Spain endeavoured to negotiate with the British Admiralty for the immunity of convoyed ships. The Dutch ambassadors reported home on 21st September 1657:—

> "I acquainted their Lordships that of old all kings and states had made a difference between particular ships sailing upon their risks and adventures and ships of state and those which pass the sea under their flag and protection. That their High and Mighty Lords (the Dutch states) were of opinion that it does

strengthen the security of this state that ships of the state and officers should be responsible, as it were, for the ships sailing under their convoy." (14)

In the eighteenth century Holland and Sweden again proved the protagonists of this sanctity of convoy. Holland asked for immunity in this respect during the war of 1756 and during that of the American Revolution. In her own practice during the war of 1781 she accorded it to neutrals. When during the wars of the French Revolution belligerent practice was beginning to bear continually more heavily upon neutrals it proved to be a Swedish convoy which was the first to attract prominent attention and to come into conflict with British policy. A Swedish merchant fleet under convoy, which carried pitch, tar, hemp, wood, and iron to French and Spanish ports in the Mediterranean, attempted to resist search in January 1798. In the case of the *Maria* (11th June 1799) Lord Stowell condemned the claim of the Swedish fleet to immunity from search, and in addition penalised it for resistance by ordering the confiscation of the ships. By this time, however, there existed between states which were favourable to a modification of belligerent practice at sea a considerable number of treaties protecting convoy as a right. An early example is to be found in the Dutch-American Treaty of 1782, or the American Treaty with Prussia in 1785. Article 14 of the latter may be quoted textually.

> "If the said vessel be under the convoy of one or more vessels of war belonging to the neutral party, the simple declaration of the officer commanding the convoy, that the said vessel belongs to the party of which he is, shall be considered as establishing the fact, and shall relieve both parties from the trouble of further examination."

Accordingly, when new troubles arose over convoy in 1799 and 1800 between Denmark and England, Count Bernstorff, the Danish minister, endeavoured to take a high tone. In his note of 19th April 1800 he said :—

> "None of the independent maritime powers of Europe has ever, so far as the undersigned is aware, recognised the right to visit neutral vessels under escort of one or more war ships, and it is evident that they could not do so without degrading their flags and renouncing an essential part of their own rights."
> "The neutral government by convoying with its warships the commercial vessels of its subjects, gives belligerent Powers a guarantee that is more authoritative and still more positive than is that furnished by the documents with which the vessels

are supplied; and it could not, without dishonour to itself, admit any doubts or suspicions on this point, for they would be as injurious to it as they would be unjust on the part of those who should entertain or manifest them."

After the incident which occurred in the Channel on 13th July 1800 in the case of the ship *Freya*, Bernstorff wrote specifically :—

"Danish officers in command of convoys are held personally responsible to see that the cargoes belonging to their convoys do not contain articles prohibited by the rules of the Law of Nations or by treaties existing between Denmark and the belligerent powers."

It was the incident of the *Freya*, in which a Danish warship and convoy were detained for resisting search, which led the Tsar to issue an invitation to Sweden, Prussia, and Denmark to unite with him in the formation of another Armed Neutrality. When the agreement between Russia and the other three Powers was drawn up an article was inserted providing for the complete immunity from search of all vessels under convoy. It was Russia, on the other hand, which departed from this position in a convention made by the new Tsar with England in 1801. Russia then merely insisted on the freedom of neutral convoys from search by privateers, but expressly exempted search by commissioned ships of war. But England never agreed to immunity for convoys, though in 1854-1856, fighting side by side with France in the Crimean War, and for the purpose of bringing the maritime practice of the allies into line, it undertook for the time to respect it. Immunity for convoys was embodied in the Declaration of London in February 1909, but as this was never ratified, England entered the Great War with hands untied in this respect.

During the War of 1914-1918 neutrals bitterly protested against the aggravated practice of search which was declared by the belligerents to be necessary under the changed conditions. The practice of the eighteenth century had visualised belligerent vessels as staying outside the range of cannon and as sending a few men in a boat for the inspection of a ship's papers. Neutral captains during the Great War found themselves compelled to put into belligerent ports, often far out of their course, and there submit themselves to an elaborate search. In justification of this development several considerations were alleged: the growth in the size of vessels, the greater quantity of cargo carried, the greater ingenuity in simulating innocence, the winter weather in the North Atlantic and the submarine danger. Great delay and heavy losses were undoubtedly inflicted on neutrals. The Allied Powers developed a technique which aimed at reducing this loss and this delay to a minimum. But the inspection of the cargoes of ships in neutral ports, and the provision of a certificate of innocent character should these prove satisfactory, must appear a perilous invasion of the rights of neutral nations. The government of the United States, it is true, did not impede the British embassy's issue of letters of assurance to the ships' masters of innocent merchant vessels, but might not such a practice in the future induce neutral patriots to talk indignantly of the loss of their sovereignty and independence not only upon the sea but even upon the land?

NOTES

(1) Throughout the first part of this chapter the indications provided by the admirable work of E. de W. Dickinson, *The Equality of States in International Law*, have been closely followed.

(2) *Leviathan*, cap. xiv.

(3) *Ibid.*, cap. xiii.

(4) *Ibid.*, cap. xv.

(5) Dickinson, *op. cit.*, p. 75 (note).

(6) *De Jure Naturae et Gentium*, iii. 2, 2.

(7) *Ibid.*, viii. 4, 18.

(8) Barbeyrac's *Pufendorff*, iii. 2, 9, note 1.

(9) Vattel, *Le droit des Gens*, Introduction, §§ 18-21.

(10) Hübner's work, printed at The Hague in 1769, was the *Traité de la Saisie des bâtiments neutres ou du droit qu'ont les nations belligérantes d'arrêter les navires des peuples amis*.

(11) Galiani (1728-1787) called his work *Dei Poveri dei principi neutrali verso i principi guerreggianti et di questi verso i neutrali* (Naples, 1782).

(12) Lampredi's work was the *Del Commercio dei popoli neutrali in tempo di guerra* (Florence, 1788).

(13) J. B. Scott, quoting in his *Armed Neutralities* from Thurloe's *State Papers*, vol. i. p. 425.

(14) *Ibid.*, vol. vi. p. 511.

CHAPTER IX

MARITIME THEORY AND PRACTICE

Capture at Sea: Treatment of Prize—Safe-Conduct in Special Cases. Contraband of War: Traffic in Arms. Blockade. Privateering: Its Evils and Abolition. The British Prize Court: The Atmosphere of the British Prize Court. Enemy Character: Trading with the Enemy—Presumption of Enemy Character. Colonial Trade and the Rule of the War of 1756. Port-to-Port Trade on a Belligerent Coast.

CHAP. IX. **Capture at Sea.**—To the mediaeval mind the right of a belligerent to seize the property of his enemy, wherever it might be found, needed neither demonstration nor defence. At sea such property was thought of originally as capturable whether it were carried in the friend's ship or the enemy's. Calculations as to national advantage hardly came into the adoption of this principle: it probably seemed the one plain, reasonable, and justifiable course at a time in which conceptions of neutrality were—as has been indicated—very far from clear-cut. All the same, it may have been a course which led to friction, and from an early date Powers were attempting to reach formal agreements about it. Throughout the fifteenth century treaties were signed which allowed the belligerent to capture enemy cargoes from the ships of his friends. There were no fewer than five treaties between Burgundy and England between 1406 and 1495 in which such clauses were inserted, not to mention an Anglo-Genoan agreement of 1460. This latter was more generous to the neutral than the Burgundian treaties, in that it seems to have contemplated some form of compensation, and may be quoted because of its remarkable similarity to the relevant portions of the *Consolato del Mare*.(1)

"Nor shall they load or carry in their ships the above-mentioned goods or merchandise of any of our enemies . . . in case they should have done so, the said Genoese, questioned and interrogated by our men, must immediately and without delay (on oath, which our subjects must trust) tell the truth and declare what goods and what kinds of cargoes of our enemy or enemies they carry in their ships and deliver these over without bother to the captains or commanders of our vessels which guard the sea, or to other of our subjects who may have encountered the ships of the said Genoese—these nevertheless receiving everywhere on the sea the charges for carriage of this kind of enemy goods."

The opening of the stipulation had still provided according to the old fashion that as between nominal allies there should be no aid by the subjects of the one to the subjects of a Power at war with the other. This, coupled with the agreement that the Genoese could not be punished for undertaking the carriage of goods for the enemy of England and that the English must confine their measures to steps taken against their enemies, goes to suggest that while belligerents were expected to take their enemy's goods out of neutral ships, except where this was provided against by convention, yet the carriage of such goods by the neutral would not be regarded as an international offence.

The sixteenth century saw in France the King's authority given to far stricter rules. Article 42 of the royal edict of 1543 and Article 69 of the royal edict of 1584 ran as follows:—

"And because in the past . . . when any prize was made at sea by our subjects, sundry suits were made by our said allies to the effect that goods taken in war belonged to them as being their portion and share with our said enemy, from which resulted great condemnations against our said subjects, so that they have since been afraid to equip ships for war to do us service, and to harm our said enemies, We, to remedy such frauds, and to the end that our said subjects may regain their courage and have greater inclination and opportunity to equip ships for war at sea, wish and command that, if the ships of our said subjects be taken at sea containing the goods, merchandise, or men of our enemies, or the ships of our enemies containing the persons, merchandise, or other goods of our said subjects, allies, and confederates, that the whole be good prize, as though belonging to our enemies. Further, the said allies and confederates may without harbouring the enemy do their own traffic at sea in their own national ships and with their own sailors." (2)

It seems probable from these articles that neutral property on enemy ships was to be regarded as good prize, and that French ships carrying enemy property were good prize. The articles were, however, sometimes further interpreted to mean that neutral ships were condemnable with their whole

CHAP. IX. cargo for carriage of enemy goods. In the course of long and difficult negotiations with the French on this very subject, Boreel, the Dutch ambassador in Paris, reported in 1653 that the French were making a great merit of their willingness to depart from the condemnation of ships in the Dutch case. The French attitude was made plain in the despatch of 26th December 1653, a date at which France and Spain were at war and Holland was at peace. Boreel reported :—

> "They think here that it is a maxim favourable to their interests that their enemies should receive no defence or service from the subjects of their High Mightinesses by [the Dutch] carriage from their [Spanish] territories of merchandise, goods, and other objects on enemy account." (3)

The penalty for such carriage was to be the removal from the Dutch ships of the enemy goods, but this was a diminution "of the law which they upheld formerly and of the *ordonnances* of Kings Francis I. and Henry III.," so that, in future, Dutch ships and neutral or Dutch goods would not be confiscated, and from that moment the rule hitherto observed would lapse, that is, *la robe d'ennemy confisque celle d'amy*.

The belligerent right to impede neutral traffic at sea, whether by the milder measure of demanding the unloading of enemy property or by the severer measure of attempting total condemnation before a court, was so manifest an encumbrance on maritime trade that the attempt began early in the seventeenth century to procure its supersession. Curiously enough, the first international concession was asked for by France, the very Power which in 1681 and 1704 was to formulate the most exigent of belligerent codes. The Sultan by Article 12 of the Franco-Turkish Treaty of 1604 agreed that the goods of his enemies in French ships should be regarded as uncapturable. A similar concession was made in 1612 to the Dutch, already a great carrying people, who had every advantage to gain by the expansion of neutral rights.

The new principle was first apparent when Europe learned of the Franco-Dutch Treaty of 18th April 1646. By Article I the French were for four years to forgo their maritime rights against Dutch commerce, so that enemy goods in Dutch bottoms, even foodstuffs, were not to be confiscated. At the expiration of four years the Dutch found it impossible to gain a permanent concession of this magnitude from the French till 1662. Meanwhile, the principle had been incorporated in the Hispano-Dutch Treaty of 1650, the Anglo-Portuguese

Treaty of 1654, the Franco-Spanish Treaty of 1659, and the treaty made by Portugal with Holland in 1661. When the Dutch and the French finally made their commercial treaty in 1662 they adopted the device of compensation which had been a feature of this series of treaties. If the neutral flag was to cover enemy goods, then it was stipulated that the belligerent should be free to seize everything on board an enemy ship, including even neutral goods. Similar provisions to these were adopted in the Anglo-Dutch Treaties of 1667, 1674, and 1689, the Franco-Swedish Treaty of 1672, the Suedo-Dutch Treaties of 1667 and 1675, the Franco-British Treaty of 1677, and the treaties signed between France and Holland in the years 1678 and 1697.(4)

But universality was denied this movement. There was in existence no organ of international legislation. Each treaty was the subject of separate bargaining, and did no more than bind the two contracting parties when one was belligerent, the other neutral. States felt free to adopt differing sets of principles in their negotiations with individual Powers, and in truth to issue domestic ordinances framed on other than treaty provisions. Thus while England adopted the Dutch principle in its Dutch treaties of 1667, 1674, and 1689, and in its French treaty of 1677, it preserved the rule of the *Consolato del Mare* in its Swedish treaties of 1661, 1666, and 1670, and in its Danish Treaty of 1670. Contrary to both principles, Article 2 of the Rules for the Prize Court, published in 1664, condemned neutral ships carrying enemy persons or goods.(5) Similarly, France felt at liberty to adopt one type of rule in the treaty with the Hansa cities in 1655, a rule which liberated enemy goods in Hanseatic ships but released Hanseatic goods in enemy ships, and quite another rule in 1716 with the same authorities, by which condemnation was proclaimed as the lot both of enemy goods in Hanseatic ships and Hanseatic goods in enemy ships; while it issued in 1681, 1704, and 1744 the extremely drastic *ordonnances* which were presumably applicable to all ships of any nation which did not have with France special treaties in a contrary sense. The truth is that in the seventeenth, and even the eighteenth, century the day had not come for the signing of commercial treaties which extended over a large international sphere. In their absence belligerents applied what they thought to be their customary rules, or even arbitrary edicts. This makes for the complication which, it has been pointed out, was the normal condition of international practice in the early stages of modern

CHAP. IX.

European history. Even in 1780 Sweden and Denmark had no commercial treaty with Spain, nor Russia with either France or Spain.(6) When Frederick the Great argued against the British seizure of his ships,(7) the long detention of them for the purpose of examination, and the lack of compensation for the consequent losses caused, he was forced to argue on general principles, for there was in existence no Anglo-Prussian treaty of commerce. He was most at ease when, as in the case of the discussion on the nature of contraband, he could point to, and argue by analogy from, existing treaties, even those not signed by Prussia.

The French *ordonnance* of 1681 provided for the capture not only of neutral property on enemy ships but of neutral ships carrying enemy property, and this was imitated in the Spanish *ordenanza di Corso* of 1715. The French *règlements* of 1704 and 1744 confiscated from the neutral ship not only enemy goods but goods of enemy origin when the vessel was not sailing directly home. By the rules of 1704 a neutral ship loading cargo at an enemy port and proceeding to another port, not a home port, was held to be confiscable with her cargo. Such provisions emanate from a strictly belligerent interpretation of neutral relations with the enemy. The neutral, in these rules, is regarded as doing the enemy's carriage and as adding to his comfort and resources. No neutral Power was the least likely to give a powerful or constantly bellicose belligerent a treaty right to exercise such privileges against her. The Dutch and English practice from 1689 to 1713 may be urged as a justification of the French rules of 1704. Thus the Danes in 1691 accepted the right of the Dutch to forbid their ships, when laden with French goods from one French port, to make a call at any other French port on their way homewards, or from undertaking trade between French and Imperial ports. Similarly, the Prussian Resident in London was informed by the English in 1711 that Prussian ships could only carry Prussian or English goods to France, and that Prussian ships which had French goods on board could not sail to French ports other than that in which they laid on board their cargo.(8) The student of international practice must not expect at too early a date the simplicity which characterises alone the latest stages of juridical development. In international as in domestic legal systems the " tidier up " is the product of advanced and sophisticated stages.

The treaties of 1713, between England and France, England

and Spain, Holland and Spain, and France and Holland, made provision for the joint principles of "free" enemy goods on neutral ships together with confiscable neutral goods on enemy ships: these to be in operation between the contracting parties. The treaties made throughout the remaining years of the century were based on the same principles. Nevertheless, the English prize court did not necessarily apply them to countries not party to the Utrecht negotiations, that is, to Sweden, Denmark, Prussia, and the Empire: and Holland, in reprisal for its conduct in refusing aid during the war of 1778, was specifically removed from the privileges assured it by the treaty. France had already taken a similar step against the Dutch on 31st December 1745, when their treaty of commerce signed in 1739 was revoked by the French and they were exposed to the rigour of the *règlement* of 1744.

In the war of 1778 France was apparently prepared to make an unconditional surrender of her right to remove enemy property from neutral ships. The treaty of commerce with the United States which was signed 6th February 1778 contained the definite provision that "les bâtiments libres assureront également la liberté des marchandises," and by the *règlement* of 26th July 1778 all neutrals were granted similar privileges. Neutrals, however, were informed that the French king reserved the right of withdrawal from this position if within six months his enemies had not accorded reciprocity. A political use of this revocation was made against the Dutch between 14th June 1779 and 22nd April 1780.

Early in 1780 the Tsaritsa Catharine of Russia began a remarkable attempt to impose a codified maritime law of war upon the world. The second of her famous five principles ran:—

> "That the effects belonging to subjects of the said Powers at war shall be free on neutral vessels, with the exception of contraband merchandise."

To her views she was successful in rallying France, Spain, Holland, and the United States, a group of belligerents hostile to England, and the neutral Powers, Sweden, Norway, Prussia, Portugal, the two Sicilies, and the Emperor. England, however, while acting with unwonted tenderness for neutral susceptibilities at sea in the endeavour not to add unnecessarily to the number of her enemies, declined to subscribe to the principle that "free ships made free goods."

CHAP. IX. In the war of 1793 England returned avowedly to her old principles. Even the United States was forced to accept a commercial treaty which made specific provision for the taking of the goods of the enemies of Great Britain from off American ships. Article 17 of the treaty, which was signed on 19th November 1794, expressly stipulates for the neutral vessel:—

> "If any property of the enemy should be found on board such vessel, that part only which belongs to the enemy shall be made prize."

Despite the threats of the Second Armed Neutrality of 1800, England in 1801 received from Russia, Sweden, and Denmark explicit confirmation of her right to remove the goods of her enemy from their ships. The Russian Convention of 17th June 1801, to which the two other Baltic Powers later acceded, expressly provided in Article 3 that

> "the effects embarked on a neutral ship shall be free, with the exception of contraband of war and of enemy's property."

In the Treaty of Amiens England did not renew with France the engagement made as late as 1786 that as between the two Powers, when one was neutral and the other belligerent, free ships should make free goods. When the Tsar Alexander tried in 1807 to withdraw from the position which he had assumed in 1801, the English reply to this attempt to wriggle out of his convention with England was singularly uncompromising. This in itself is evidence that England had determined on a policy of freeing herself from such treaty restrictions as she had accepted in the course of the seventeenth and eighteenth centuries.

> "His Majesty [the King of England] proclaims anew those principles of maritime law against which the armed neutrality, under the auspices of the Empress Catharine, was originally directed, and against which the present hostilities of Russia are denounced. These principles have been recognised and acted upon in the best periods of the history of Europe. . . . These principles it is the right and duty of His Majesty to maintain: and against every confederacy His Majesty is determined under the blessing of Divine Providence to maintain them. They have at all times contributed essentially to support the maritime power of Great Britain. . . . When the opportunity for peace between Great Britain and Russia shall arrive, His Majesty will embrace it with great eagerness. The arrangements for such a negotiation will not be difficult or complicated.

His Majesty, as he has nothing to concede, so he has nothing to require." (9) CHAP. IX.

Indeed, in 1814-1815 England conceded nothing which involved the immunity of hostile goods even under the neutral flags of France and the Netherlands, Powers with whom, prior to the outbreak of war in 1793, that immunity had been agreed upon by special treaty. In 1827 Canning refused to ratify a treaty with Brazil because it contained an article which involved the abandonment of the right to seize enemy goods on Brazilian ships. In 1842 England expressly withdrew from the allowance of those ancient Portuguese privileges in this respect, which dated back to 1654.(10) When the Anglo-Portuguese Treaty of 1842 was signed, Article 11 "notified that the licence hitherto allowed by former treaties to the ships of both countries to transport any objects of merchandise belonging to the enemies of either country is henceforth abandoned and renounced." It was no doubt with a view to retort against the policy of Great Britain that the United States, though conceding in all its treaties the general principle of "free ships, free goods," generally added a rider to the following effect:—

> "If one of the two parties is at war with a third party while the other maintains neutrality, the flag of the neutral will cover the property of enemies whose government has recognised the same principle."

Thus in a war between the United States and Great Britain the United States would have the right to take British goods from, say, Colombian ships, just as England could also take American goods from them.(11)

English policy was to undergo a dramatic reversal on the occasion of the outbreak of the Crimean War. Many factors combined to produce this. The war was fought in alliance with France, and the practical difficulty which attended joint operations of the two fleets, each enforcing different rights against neutral ships, was felt to be overwhelming. Further, before the war broke out, and during its opening stages, naval action in the Baltic was thought to be the principal weapon of the allies; and for such naval action a friendly attitude on the part of Sweden and Denmark, the leading advocates of neutral rights by sea, was judged important. Again, it was hoped, especially in France, that a mild belligerent policy at sea would have an important effect in Germany. To these more purely diplomatic reasons must be added a change of

CHAP. IX.

sentiment among the ruling classes of England since the Napoleonic epoch. Philosophic radicalism was now largely in the ascendant and openly deplored those "days of barbarism." So much was this the case that it was just at this time that the British foreign secretary, Lord Clarendon, was beginning an attempt to remove another relic of "barbarism," to wit privateering, seeing "no reason why a licence should be given for robbery by sea, any more than by land."

Accordingly, it required little pressure from the French foreign minister, Drouyn de Lhuys, and the French ambassador in London, Walewski, to produce in the London Cabinet the resolution to forgo, at least for the period of the war, its traditional policy of "seizing enemy property laden on board a neutral vessel even though not contraband of war." This determination was communicated to neutrals in a special message of 28th March, which contained also the promise that neutral goods on enemy ships would not be confiscated, this being a return concession of France to England in acknowledgment of the departure from traditional views. It was, however, a more serious matter when the plenipotentiaries of England in the Peace Congress at Paris in 1856 made together with the plenipotentiaries of France, Prussia, Russia, Austria, Sardinia, and Turkey the Declaration of Paris, the most significant clause of which was undoubtedly that one of the four which laid it down that "the neutral flag covers the goods of the enemy with the exception of contraband of war." It is important to notice that by the Declaration of Paris this new rule was established, not merely between the declarant Powers, but as between all Powers which acceded to the instrument, irrespective of their attendance at Paris. The proposal to adhere to the Declaration of Paris called forth a protest in the House of Lords. Lord Colchester moved a resolution which stated "that the most eminent jurists of all ages have accepted as a principle of International Law that the right of capturing an enemy's goods on board of neutral vessels is inherent in all belligerent Powers, that the maintenance of this right is of essential importance, and its abandonment of serious injury to a Power whose main reliance is upon her navy." Lord Derby, the leader of the Opposition, fiercely attacked that part of the Declaration which gave safety to enemy goods in neutral ships. He declared that the concession was opposed to the policy of Pitt, Grenville, and Canning, and that it deprived England of "those natural advantages which her great maritime power has given her in war, and of the exercise of that superiority, and those belligerent rights, without which she is nothing." He taunted Lord Clarendon with having been "led by the nose," and having "deliberately walked into the trap set before his face." (12) In more recent times the late Mr. Gibson Bowles has played the Elisha to Lord Colchester's Elijah. In the *British Year Book of International Law for 1927* Mr. H. W. Malkin quotes the Cabinet minutes of 7th and 8th April 1856 to show that Lord Clarendon was in reality exchanging the shadow for the substance by relinquishing an untenable practice in exchange for the abolition of privateering, a practice to which we were especially vulnerable.

The United States of America was one of the Powers which did not sign the Declaration of Paris. The four articles had to be signed together, and the United States was unwilling to give up the practice of licensing privateers, a procedure abolished by the first article, except as part of a general move to render unlawful the capture of private property at sea. On 28th July 1856, Mr. Marcy, in answer to a notification by the French minister of the signature and terms of the Declaration of Paris, offered the accession of the United States, so far as it lay within the power of the Washington executive to give it, if there were added to the words, "that privateering is and remains abolished," the words, "and that the private property of the subjects or citizens of a belligerent shall be exempted from seizure by public armed vessels of the other belligerent, except it be contraband of war." This amendment would have freed both private enemy ships and the enemy goods on such ships from confiscation by the belligerent. There was for a time a tendency among important circles in England to consider a curtailment, even to this length, of belligerent rights. Lord Palmerston, who was Prime Minister, could not help hoping that "in the course of time the principles of war which are applied to land may be extended without exception to hostilities by sea, and that private property shall no longer be exposed to aggression on either side." The Horsfall Commission on Merchant Shipping, appointed in 1860, recommended complete immunity for all merchant ships and the cargoes during war. In 1862 Cobden and Bright co-operated in support of a motion in the Commons which declared "that the present state of International Maritime Law as affecting the rights of belligerents and neutrals is ill-defined and unsatisfactory and calls for the early attention of His Majesty's Government." Lord

CHAP. IX.

Palmerston in replying showed characteristic courage in declaring that he had changed his opinion since 1856. To surrender the right of taking the ships, the property and the crews of the enemy would be, he said, an act of political suicide.

In this reference to the crews of the enemy mercantile marine Lord Palmerston was recalling an important feature of naval warfare in the eighteenth century. The sailors aboard enemy merchantmen were always regarded as the reservoir from which a belligerent could most promptly recruit his naval strength. They could be made prisoners of war; and indeed Napoleon had often protested against the British exercise of this right, even as Bismarck was later to protest against the French recourse to it in the war of 1870. This part of their right against what by a stretch may be called private property, the naval Powers were prepared to modify at the Hague Peace Conference of 1907, but no other. Neutral members of the crew of an enemy merchantman were, under the terms of the Hague Convention, to be released without question, while neutral officers were to undertake not to serve in an enemy ship during the remainder of the war. Enemy subjects, both officers and men, were only to become prisoners of war should they decline to give an undertaking to refrain from all future military service.

Treatment of Prize.—A small but interesting department of the laws of capture at sea is occupied by the treatment of prize. Cases arise in which, for some reason, it is inconvenient or impossible for the captors to take enemy ships, or neutral ships with hostile cargoes, into a port for the necessary adjudication. This case had been treated in the *Consolato del Mare*. If the captain of a neutral ship should refuse to carry his enemy cargo into a place of safety under the direction of the captor, the captor was to be allowed to sink him, but was bound to make provision for the safety of the crew. This practice was to be applied only in such cases as those in which the larger part, or the whole, of the cargo belonged to the enemy. Further, in the case of an enemy ship with the cargo of a friend, the friends on board were directed to make arrangements for the ransom of the ship. If they should decline to do this, the ship with the goods still on board might be sent on by the captor to his home port: the friends would in that case have no claim for damages and would be liable for the full amount of the carriage charges promised to the enemy. The arrangements which are contained in the

Consolato for the destruction, the ransom, and the rescue of the crew showed a very fair regard for the interests of friends. What the law might be for the treatment of enemy ships with enemy ladings and enemy crews was nowhere stated.

The French *Ordonnance de la Marine* of 1681 was claimed by Valin [13] as the first official provision made by a belligerent for allowing his ships to permit their prizes to be ransomed. A prize might have been injured by battle or by storms, so that it shipped water and sailed so slowly as to expose the privateer to danger of its own and the prize's capture. A prize too might have on board a crew who were likely to mutiny, or, again, a prize taken in distant seas might not be of sufficient value to justify the detachment of a crew to sail it. From the standpoint of the belligerent government, however, good reasons could always have been urged against the practice of ransom. A ransom was always fixed at a value much below that of the prize, and further, the enemy did not lose his sailors. Accordingly, although it was impossible to abolish the practice of ransom so long as privateering existed, belligerent Powers might, and did, make efforts to restrict the acceptance of ransom with a view to inflicting greater loss on the enemy than a privateer might, for his own purposes, be likely to effect. Thus the French Royal Decree of 15th May 1756 forbade a privateer to undertake ransoming until it had sent back home three prizes. On the other hand, conversely, Powers could forbid their nationals ever to enter into a contract of ransom. During the American War of 1776-1783 this was done in the case of British subjects by statute.[14] Further, not only might an enemy ship be ransomed, but also neutral ships and property which for any reason could have been taken into a prize court for adjudication. A late instance of ransom is to be found in connection with the *Alabama*, when the captain found neutral property on board his Federal captives.

Ransom was effected under a ransom contract. The captured ship received a passport which allowed it to sail for a prescribed port by a prescribed course within a limited period of time; and the captor received his contract and one or two hostages. If payment were not made to the captor, he could cause suit to be brought against the giver of the contract of ransom, and this was heard in the enemy's court.

A French *ordonnance* of 2nd December 1693 allowed the destruction of an enemy prize. In the days in which prize

CHAP. IX.

money was an important consideration for all sailors, and ransom an habitual custom, the destruction of prizes was not likely to be widely undertaken. In 1812, however, the naval officers of the United States began the systematic burning of captured ships. Their naval forces were not large, and they preferred not to be inconvenienced by the task of bringing them into court. The English prize court also was called upon to deal with such instances of destruction as those of the *Felicity* and the *Actaeon*. The Confederate captain Semmes of the *Alabama* burned those Federal prizes which he did not ransom because of the presence of neutral goods in the ship. In 1870 the French destroyed two German prizes with neutral goods on board, and their courts later refused the neutrals compensation. In 1904-1905 the Russians extended the destruction of ships to include those of neutrals who in that war could only have been liable for carriage of contraband or unneutral service. Though much dissatisfaction was caused by this, nations who had few or no overseas ports suited to the reception of prizes refused to accept the doctrine propounded by England that the destruction of prizes was inadmissible. Under the Declaration of London, England agreed to accept the destructibility of prizes, but under conditions which left so many loopholes that it would in fact have been the relinquishment of its position. The captor indeed had first to be certain that the ship was confiscable; but as allowance was made for the strategic difficulty of bringing the prize into a port, and as the captor was in fact made judge as to the validity of these considerations, England under the guise of a compromise did in reality see the question determined in an unwelcome direction. Insistence on the preservation of the lives of the crew, on the preservation of all documents and the assumption of an obligation to compensate for the destruction of neutral goods, were all included in the Declaration of London, which was of course never ratified. The submarine operations of the Germans, which involved the destruction of neutral ships without warning, were unprecedented, as indeed was submarine warfare. It had no countenance in the practice of nations and was justly condemned by public opinion. But the very success of the innovation, regarded from an immediate and tactical point of view, makes it difficult to suppose that, despite the condemnation it provoked, it is not to be heard of again in maritime warfare. That, on the other hand, it brought into the war against Germany the one powerful neutral is a consideration which in this respect it would be foolish to undervalue. CHAP. IX.

Safe-Conduct in Special Cases.—A pleasant addition to the international amenities of the eighteenth century was the safe-conduct granted mutually by England and France to each other's ships when they were destined for exploration in distant seas. Bougainville, for instance, obtained a safe-conduct in 1766 which protected his ships from the consequences of hostilities in the event of an outbreak of war. Later Captain Cook's expedition to the furthest waters of the Pacific was protected by the French government;[15] and in 1785 the expedition of Lapérouse received similar indulgence from the British. Flinders, however, in 1803 was held by the French to have forfeited his safe-conduct when he changed from his original ship the *Investigator*, to which the grant had been made, into the *Cumberland*. The practice was admitted into universal law by the Hague Convention No. 11 of 1907 which restricted the rights of maritime capture. Not only exploring and scientific ships but vessels bound on "religious" and "philanthropic" missions were then protected and were freed from the obligation of procuring a specific belligerent's safe-conduct in each case.

Contraband of War.[16]—The repeated promulgation by Church councils of canons which forbade Christians to export arms to the Saracen enemies of the Faith is historically the origin of those notions which lie behind the word contraband, the forbidden trade in arms. The General Council of 1179 punished with excommunication, loss of goods and reduction to slavery any one who sold to the Saracens iron, arms or ships' material.[17] The same attitude was adopted by the Councils of 1214 and 1245.[18] Canonists in later centuries devoted thought to the subject more minutely. They asked, for instance, whether a ship which carried to the Saracens a cargo, or a partial cargo, of forbidden goods was also itself confiscable: whether the taint attached to noxious cargo extended to the innocent goods and thereby rendered them liable to confiscation. Already in these questions of an early age much is anticipated of that doctrine which was later evolved by international lawyers in their treatment of the subject of contraband.

Where it was a case only of the relation in war time between Christian Powers and their friends, it was for long impossible to distinguish clearly the emergence of an agreed limitation of the belligerent right of confiscation to the case of arms.

CHAP. IX.

The belligerent was apt to require much more. Even where a belligerent was ready to limit himself at all in such measures as he might direct against the trade of a friendly Power with his enemy, he was apt to exclude from the application of such limitation a good deal more than warlike material. He was apt to include on his list along with munitions, arms, armour and artillery, food for example, the later *munitions de bouche*. The quarrel between the Hanseatic towns and Queen Elizabeth [(19)] in 1589 arose out of the detention of ships laden mostly with food for Spain, and the seizure for the Queen's use of the food so conveyed. Yet it is not easy to make positive assertions. The Queen objected apparently not only to the carriage of grain by the Hanseatic ships, but also to the fact that these were charged *apparatis bellicis et nauticis* (with military and naval goods) for a Spanish destination. It is not clear from the context whether these goods included raw naval materials from the Baltic, such as in the seventeenth and eighteenth centuries were to form frequently a subject of contention between neutral and belligerent Powers, the former anxious to keep them out of the contraband list, then a well-known feature of warfare, the latter anxious to include them.

Belligerents in earlier centuries, faced by traffic between their friends and their enemies, did not always claim to confiscate for their own purposes objects of use in war. By the French edict of 1584, to which reference has already been made, Henry III. contemplated the seizure of contraband, but undertook in return the payment of something above market-price (Article 69). Later belligerents, when neutral Powers vehemently resisted the claim to confiscate as contraband articles which, unlike arms, were only of indirect use in war, were sometimes disposed to compound with their opponents by imitating this old French royal practice with regard to arms, and to buy from the neutral such goods as they wished to keep out of the hands of the enemy. Difficulties in particular arose over the neutral export of such provisions to an enemy as were held likely to be proceeding to the provisioning of a special expedition. It was the same with the export of naval material by neutral countries. Lord Stowell in the case of the *Haabet* [(20)] took occasion to put on record his view that pre-emption of provisions was a mitigation of an old belligerent right of seizure. The cargo of provisions bound avowedly to a belligerent port was to be paid for, but only at a reasonable price and not at the famine figure which might prevail in the enemy country. The

English practice, when the neutral Sweden was forwarding cargoes of naval material to the enemies of England, was pre-emption and not confiscation. In the case of the *Sarah Christina* Lord Stowell again had the opportunity of adopting the same attitude which was, he implied, really merciful. "It has been deemed," he said, "a harsh exercise of a belligerent right to prohibit the carriage of these articles which constitute so considerable a part of its (*sc.* Sweden's) native produce and ordinary commerce." The practice of pre-emption was again provided for in the case of provisions, and of neutral stores destined for enemy ports by the Naval Prize Act of 1864 (Article 38).

A decisive point in the history of belligerent practice was reached when Grotius attempted to supply a reasoned basis for belligerent discrimination among such goods as were conveyed by a belligerent's friend to his enemy.

> "First it is necessary to discriminate among the goods themselves. There are some which have no other use but for war, such as arms: there are others which have no use at all in war, such as those which serve (only) the ends of pleasure; finally there are those which have a use both in war and apart from war, as money, food, vessels and naval materials."

With regard to the first class Grotius was prepared to consider those who supplied them to the enemy as enemies: with regard to that class of objects which, in describing as ministrant to pleasure, he probably considered as pure luxuries, such as marbles, clocks, rich costumes, pleasure-boats, he saw no harm in a neutral's endeavour to supply them to the enemy. Finally, in the case of those things useful alike in peace and war, Grotius allowed that the belligerent might intercept them in cases "of necessity," but on condition of restitution in normal cases. Such "interception" and restitution would apparently cover the not uncommon practice of pre-emption discussed above. A reservation was, however, made by Grotius which may have been intended partially to cover the nascent Dutch practice of the blockade. If a neutral owner had already carried articles of the third class to a "fortress besieged or a port closed," concerning which the hope of the belligerent was a speedy surrender or a peace, he might be mulcted in his goods for the damage caused, while if he had merely attempted such a carriage he could be required by seizure of his goods to give surety for behaviour in the future. The implication which lay in the distinction made between the furnishing of goods of doubtful

CHAP. IX.

use to an ordinary enemy on the one hand and on the other to an enemy besieged or with ports closed, was that an enemy in the latter case was much more likely in the strain of his position to put the goods in question to a warlike use. In this case, therefore, the neutral carrier identified himself with the enemy far more obviously.

Since the day of Grotius three distinct parties have carried on the controversy which sought to decide what class of goods it was proper for a belligerent to confiscate from a neutral carrier. The first party has sought to restrict the meaning of the word contraband to arms alone, the second has favoured its extension from arms to cover a wider class of objects, but has always differed within itself over the limits of the class. The third, with Grotius, has favoured the subdivision of the type "contraband" into two sections, the goods of absolute contraband and those of a conditional contraband character, goods which, though patient of peaceful usage, might be presumed, from their particular destination to enemy forces or points of military significance, to be intended for purposes of war. These, were they to be treated strictly, might be confiscated; if mercifully, pre-empted. The serious attempt to make a detailed enumeration of the articles to be considered as contraband may be said to have begun with the treaties and the proclamations of belligerent Powers in the seventeenth century.

The Treaty of Southampton (17th September 1625) (21) between King Charles I. of England and the United Provinces made an early use of the word contraband and proceeded to describe it as follows:—

> "Toutes marchandises de contrebande, comme sont munitions de bouche et de guerre, navires, armes, voiles, cordages, or, argent, cuivre, fer, plomb et semblables de quelque part qu'on les voudra porter en Espagne et aux autres pays de l'obéissance du dit Roy d'Espagne et de ses adhérens, seront de bonne prise avec les navires et hommes qu'ils porteront." (Art. 20.)

It must be noted that Charles I. and the United Provinces were both belligerents and had a natural desire to stretch as far as possible the list of goods which it should be absolutely prohibited to export to their enemy, the King of Spain. How much progress had been made with the definition of doubtful points can be indicated by a comparison of the above terms of this treaty with a previous English treaty, such as that with Spain in 1604. In this both parties had agreed to abstain from furnishing to the enemies of, or rebels against, the other "soldiers, provisions, money, instruments of war, munitions or any other help in maintaining the war." The proclamation which King Charles I. issued a year after the signature of the Dutch treaty went even further and in greater detail into the description of contraband, "wherewith His Majesty may not suffer his said enemies to be furnished." The avowed purpose of this proclamation was "to remove all pretext of ignorance or other exception which may be taken against the proceedings of his judges and officers, with any of the subjects of his friends, confederates and allies." The list embraced "ordinance, armes of all sorts, powder, shott, match, brimstone, copper, iron, cordage of all kinds, hempe, saile, canons, Dance pouldavis, cables, anchors, mastes, rafters, boate oars, balcks, capraves, deale board, class boarde, pipe staves, and vessels, and vessel staffe, pitch, tarr, rosen, okam, corne, graine and victualls of all sorte." (22)

Lists as embracing in their scope as that of the treaty of 1625 or the proclamation of 1626 were likely to be much reduced in treaties signed between parties who were not allies engaged in war but merely friends, one of whom at least was not at war, and therefore looked at the contraband list from the standpoint of a neutral trader. When neither party to a treaty was engaged in hostilities, the treaty was more likely still to show solicitude for the neutral interest by reducing the list to the lowest possible scope. Instances such as that of the Anglo-Portuguese Treaty of 1642, which omitted to penalise even the transport of arms, were rare, although the American dislike of all capture of private property at times found expression, as for example in Article 13 of the treaty between the United States and Prussia of 1785. This remarkable clause not only forbade the confiscation of arms and ammunition, but enjoined upon the interested belligerent purchase from the neutral at a full market-price, and in addition compensation to the shipowner whose vessel should be detained by the adoption of this procedure. Just as rare, however, were treaties, like that of Westminster between the English and the Dutch, signed on 6th April 1654, which prohibited the supply by one party to the enemy of the other of soldiers, arms, ammunition, money, provisions, victuals and other prohibited goods, enforced confiscation and even further penalties for contravention, and promised a joint commission to undertake the preparation of a detailed definition of contraband.

CHAP. IX.

A good example of the newer type of contraband list is to be found in Article 11 of the Treaty of Paris which was signed between Louis XIV. and the Hanseatic towns in 1655. It embraced "munitions de guerre, armes à feu, (sçavoir) canons, mousquets, mortiers, bombes, pétards, grenades, saucisses, cercles, affûts, fourdettes, bandoulières, poudre, mesche, salpestre et toutes autres sortes d'armes, comme picques, espées, morions, casques, cuirasses, hallebardes, javelots et autres armes servans à la guerre, ensembles des chevaux, des cordages, et des toyles navales, qui ne puissent servir qu'à faire voiles." The same article declared the carriage of provisions by the Hanseatic merchants to the enemy of France to be allowable except in the case of towns attacked by the King of France. The French treaty made with Spain in 1659, known as that of the Pyrenees, omitted the naval stores enumerated above, and the general nature of its list of contraband was widely adopted in other treaties such as the Franco-Dutch of 1662, the Suedo-Dutch of 1667 and the Anglo-Dutch and Anglo-Spanish of the same year. Finally, the Anglo-French Treaty of St. Germain-en-Laye, after making some additions to the contraband list in the Treaty of the Pyrenees, minor in character except for the prohibition of the transport of soldiers, proceeded to the innovation of the insertion of a list of non-contraband articles. Stuffs and manufactures of wool, linen, silk, cotton and of any other material; all kind of garments and the stuffs of which they are made; coined and uncoined silver and gold, tin, iron, lead, copper and charcoal; wheat, barley and other grains and vegetables; tobacco and spices, salted and smoked meat, dried and salt fish, cheese, butter, beer, oil, wine, sugar, salt and all which belongs to the sustenance of life—all these were included in the list, which was extended beyond materials of this kind to embrace also cottons, hemps, pitch, cordage, sails, anchors, masts, planks, beams and the worked wood of any tree which might serve for the construction or repair of ships.

The mutual engagements as to the limitation of contraband, which had been entered into by the leading maritime Powers and which might have been supposed to have lapsed, were renewed in the Treaty of Utrecht in 1713 as between England and France, France and Holland, England and Spain, and Holland and Spain. It must be remembered that maritime practice, here as elsewhere, arose out of no general principles, but looked for justification to specific treaties and existed for the most part as between particular signatories. This is what makes confusion and uncertainty the dominant feature of any picture which the historically minded lawyer may attempt to draw. Though a belligerent might have treaties with several of the leading maritime states, by which his action against the cargoes of their subjects was circumscribed by this or that definition of contraband, there might still remain many cargoes and many shipowners against which his Admiralty courts were free to apply their own, and a quite different, definition of contraband. Thus in the English prize court in the year 1765 (to take a year preceding the Anglo-Russian Treaty of 1766) Prussian, Hanseatic, Russian and Neapolitan cargoes would be treated according to the proclamation of the sovereign, while Swedish and Danish cargoes would be, from the point of view of their owners, most inadequately protected. The Admiralty prize court had committed itself definitely to the position that "sovereign princes at war may declare such and such things to be contraband and, after notice to their allies, their subjects may seize them." His Majesty's Principal Commissioners of Prizes decided in 1665, well after the beginning of the new movement for limitation by treaty of the definition of contraband, that contraband should include "canvas, masts, pitch, tar and all other navall accomodations, as also wine, oyl, brandy, fish, corn, salt fish, and all other things that tend as provisions to the support of life, as well as powder, guns or other instruments of war." And it must be remembered that at this date this definition would have been applicable as against every European state except Portugal, for the Anglo-Swedish Treaty of 1661—the only other by which England was in the circumstances bound—put provisions, money and ships on the forbidden list. In 1744 the British official list (as contained in the instructions of 18th June) still included beside horses and the orthodox catalogue of arms, "sailwork, riggings, cables, cordage, masts, lead, pitch, tar, hemp, together with all other equipage that serves for sea and land, laden in Danish or Swedish ships, or ships belonging to neutral countries and bound for the enemy's country." (23) England was then at war with France and Spain, with whom she had had commercial treaties which propounded a narrower list than this. Holland on the other hand was an ally, so that the Anglo-Dutch treaty list of contraband was not applicable in a normal way, and the Danish and Swedish treaties were deliberately interpreted by the English court in such a way

CHAP. IX.

as to put Denmark and Sweden in the category of neutrals which were without specific treaties. Accordingly, it is true to say that the British Instructions of 1744 were valid against all nations except Portugal, whose treaty signed in 1654 with England placed Portugal in a special and unique position. The historian of the seventeenth and eighteenth centuries, when his record be of war, has need to walk warily.

The historian can justly point out that there is a definite Dutch tendency to a severer practice. As late as 1709, in addition to the orthodox catalogue of arms together with horses and fodder, the Dutch contraband list contained naval materials, cast iron, steel, iron bars, large and small nails, copper, lead, tin, tallow, flax, oakum, etc., wheat, rye, barley, buckwheat, oats, spelt, starch, groats, beans, pease, rice and millet, together with other grains of whatever origin destined for France, Spain and other enemy places. Sweden on the other hand by her Dutch treaties of 1667, 1675 and 1679 had contracted out of all these provisions except as with regard to arms. Denmark was not in such a strong position, and, although she was perhaps the other leading neutral, her treaty with the Dutch of 1691, as amplified by a supplementary "specification of prohibited merchandise," prohibited that country's ships from the carriage of sails, ropes, masts, lead, pitch, tar, hemp "together with all that might serve for equipment by sea or by land." (24) A prize court could find this phrase conveniently elastic.

The novel commercial treaties of the eighteenth century illustrate the diversity of the motives which actuated the various Powers in making provisions by treaty as to contraband. The Franco-Danish Treaty of 1742 was more severe than the French *Ordonnance de la Marine* whose list of contraband confined itself to the direct instruments of war, for under the treaty tar, pitch, rosin, cloth for sails, hemp, ropes, masts and ships' timber were put into the forbidden list. In such a treaty France would obviously wish to get her price, if she were to bind herself at all, as over against Denmark in the matter of contraband, while Denmark might be supposed to have preferred a definite self-limitation on the part of France, even at a high price, to the possibilities of extreme measures should France become belligerent. In the Anglo-Russian Treaty of 1766 on the other hand, England permitted the contraband list to sink to smaller proportions even than those of the Treaty of the Pyrenees. This concession, whether made by inadvertence or out of good will to the Tsaritsa, and a desire to win her political support, did in effect prove troublesome. Later, this treaty was quoted by Russia, Spain, France, Prussia, Austria, Sweden, Denmark, Holland and Sardinia, when, in the general movement to force down belligerent pretensions over contraband, they were at one in asserting that the Anglo-Russian list of 1766 represented the true conception of contraband of war in natural law. The Tsaritsa Catharine occupied herself not a little with the question. Article 2 of the Russo-Prussian Convention of 19th May 1781 runs as follows :—

> "To avoid any ambiguity and any misunderstanding regarding what is to be considered as contraband, Her Majesty the Empress of all the Russias has declared that she recognises as such only the goods included under this head in articles 10 and 11 of her treaty of commerce with Great Britain, whose obligations, which are founded entirely on the natural law, she has extended to the Crowns of France and Spain, which countries have not hitherto bound themselves with her Empire by any engagement relating purely to commerce. Since there likewise exists no engagement of this nature between His Prussian Majesty and the Powers now at war, he declares for his part, that in this respect he also desires to bind himself with them by the obligations of the aforesaid treaty of commerce between Russia and Great Britain, with specific reference to articles 10 and 11 of that treaty."

The English government was warned by experience. When, during the critical period of 1780, it was necessary to define contraband in relation to the Anglo-Danish Treaty of 1670, "ships' timber, pitch, tar, rosin, copper in sheets, sail-cloth, hemp, cordage and generally everything that is in use in the equipment of ships, except unwrought iron and fir planks" were reckoned to be contraband, if proceeding in Danish ships to the enemy's country. Provisions, it was stated, were to be free. In 1794 the British government secured in the American treaty of commerce an admission that shipbuilding material was contraband of war, and even an unwilling assent to the proposition that "provisions and other articles not generally contraband" might conceivably become such. In return Great Britain expressed itself willing to undertake pre-emption of those articles not generally contraband. In 1803, when England and Sweden both urgently needed a modern application of their treaty of 1661, Sweden was induced to consent to pre-emption of provisions and to the inclusion of a list of naval stores. These when produced in Sweden, laden in Swedish ships and bound

CHAP. IX.

for the enemy, it was agreed, should be pre-empted at the full price plus ten per cent., or alternatively at the market-price in Sweden or England, at the option of the owner.

Events in the long wars which lasted from 1793-1815 were to release the British government from most of the treaties which tied its action in matters of contraband. The definition of contraband, agreed to anew with France in 1786, which was of a liberal nature, lapsed in 1793 at the outbreak of war and was never renewed. Contraband, as has been pointed out, had been defined by agreement between England and the United Provinces; the agreement was not renewed in 1814, when the kingdom of the Netherlands succeeded to the international position of the latter Power. The Russian treaty agreements lapsed in 1807, when the Tsar annulled "for ever all acts heretofore concluded between Russia and Great Britain." The Anglo-Portuguese Treaty of 1842 made no mention of the definition of contraband. If silence may be presumed to have been a tacit renunciation of previous agreements made by treaty, it becomes a fact that Spain, and Spain only among the Powers, retained as over against Great Britain the right to demand the operation of the shorter list of contraband, a list confined to arms and munitions of war.[(25)]

The English prize court under Lord Stowell had meanwhile assumed a line of its own with regard to contraband of war. Where the nature of naval stores was in question the Court of Appeal had in 1750 decided to condemn as contraband some loads of Swedish pitch and tar. Lord Stowell was prepared to take into special consideration the unique position of Sweden, whose exportable produce consisted very largely of naval stores. He took the line that if material of this nature, owned by Swedes and conveyed in a Swedish ship, were to be encountered on its way to the enemy it was merely to fall under the belligerent right of pre-emption.[(26)] So far as provisions were concerned, the law of contraband, in regard to which the Anglo-American treaty had declared them to be in a difficult and scarcely definable state, Lord Stowell elaborated new doctrine in the case of the *Jonge Margaretha*.[(27)] In this judgment the possibility that foodstuffs might fall within the limits of prohibited and confiscable contraband was put by the master hand in most convincing fashion. A favourable circumstance in the eyes of the prize court would be that the provisions were not the product of another country, but the production of the exporter's country; further, that they were in their native and unprepared state;

but lastly and most weightily that their destination was not to a predominantly military port—in which case there was a strong presumption of military use—but to a general commercial port. A consignment of cheeses to Brest might on the face of it be innocent, but on this occasion a powerful French fleet was lying at Brest, and there was evidence that these particular cheeses were exclusively used in French ships of war. In this case, therefore, cheeses were condemned, and biscuits (28) and wines (29) met with like treatment in suitable instances. It is the last condition—that of destination to a predominantly military port—that has figured as the touchstone for discrimination among articles *ancipitis usus* under modern conditions. Conditional contraband was the joint creation of Grotius and Stowell.

The carriage of military persons had already been put by the treaty of 1677 between France and England in that class of contraband commerce which was prohibited to neutral Powers. Lord Stowell applied the same rule in his decisions and added the carriage of enemy despatches in the case of the *Atalanta*,(30) though he made appropriate reservations in the doctrine to cover the case of despatches sent by a belligerent ambassador from a neutral country.

The traditional punishment allotted to ships which carried contraband was, as Charles I. of England declared in his proclamation of 1626, confiscation both on the way out or on return. Grotius, however, adopted a distinction and condemned the ship only when her owner had been privy to the carriage of the contraband. In 1672 the King's advocate, Robert Wiseman, was found to declare that it was only on the outward voyage, not in returning, that the ship was confiscable; and that even in such cases non-contraband goods ought to be set free. In 1713 Article 26 of the Anglo-French Treaty of Utrecht embodied this opinion, though Lord Stowell rigorously condemned the ship in such cases as those in which the carrier of contraband had been guilty of anything but perfect good faith. The ancient rule (the rule of contagion) was held to bring into the condemnation of confiscation all innocent portions of a cargo which contained contraband.

Traffic in Arms.—The end of the eighteenth century saw the origin of a famous controversy which concerned the whole basis of neutral trade in contraband with the enemy. A well-known Italian author, Galiani (1728-1787), laid it down as a principle that neutral Powers were not entitled to furnish contraband

CHAP. IX.

to a belligerent. This he interpreted to include not only the transport of arms to the enemy, but also the sale on neutral territory of contraband material to either belligerent. Galiani was combated by Lampredi (1788), who denied the principle, and it was in Venice alone of all the Italian states that the views of Galiani received some countenance in practice. Venice, always fearful of belligerent encroachment upon the neutral rights of maritime Powers, did actually during the war of 1779 prohibit to Venetian citizens all commerce, still more all traffic, in arms with belligerents. The question of the supply of arms to belligerents by neutral individuals, whether on neutral soil or by transport, has provoked doubt and aroused strong feelings on the outbreak of every war. As early as 1793 the British government protested to that of the United States against the sale of munitions of war by American manufacturers to Frenchmen. Jefferson in reply took up an attitude, familiar in the mouth of all powerful neutrals, to whom the opportunities of profitable trade are obvious :—

> "Our citizens have always been free to make, vend, and export arms. It is the constant occupation and livelihood of some of them. To suppress their callings, the only means perhaps of their subsistence, because a war exists in foreign and distant countries, in which we have no concern, would scarcely be expected. . . . The Law of Nations, therefore, respecting the rights of peace, does not require from them such internal disarrangements of their occupations. It is satisfied with the external penalty pronounced in the President's proclamations, that of confiscation of such part of these arms as shall fall into the hands of the belligerent Powers on the way to the ports of their enemies." (31)

The nineteenth century saw development in the theory and practice of the doctrine of contraband of war. In the Crimean War, England decided to class coal as an article of use both in peace and war which might become contraband in certain cases. It adopted the same position as a neutral in the Franco-Austrian War of 1859. Steam power produced by the burning of coal had now become an important element in naval strength, and merchants were advised that, "having regard to the present state of naval armaments, coal may, in many cases, be rightly held to be contraband of war." That a similar fate awaited other kinds of goods in a serious naval war was made obvious as early as 1854, when England, then practically the sole source of supply, forbade the export of "marine engines, screw propellers, paddle-wheels, cylinders, cranks, shafts, boilers, tubes for boilers, boiler plates, fire-bars . . . or any other article whatsoever which is, can, or may become applicable for the manufacture of marine machinery." In the American Civil War the doctrine of continuous voyage, which had been first elaborated in the British prize court at the end of the eighteenth century, was tentatively, as in the case of the *Peterhoff*, applied to the carriage of contraband. It had originated in an attempt to condemn indirect carriage by neutrals of goods to an enemy country from its colonial ports. How easily could the analogy have been established between this and the carriage of contraband goods by a European neutral to a neutral Carribean port, the ultimate destination, that of the Southern States, rendering the goods patently liable to treatment as contraband! The Federal government, however, had proclaimed a blockade of the Southern ports, and generally preferred to deal with the traffic by asking its court to treat the neutral carriers as in effect and in eventuality blockade-runners, a rather different application of the doctrine of continuous voyage.

Nevertheless, the French courts in the case of the *Frau Howina* (Crimean War), the Italian courts in the case of the *Delwyk* (Italo-Abyssinian War), and the British courts in the case of the German ships stopped *en route* for the Portuguese port of Delagoa Bay (Boer War) had all accepted the extension of the doctrine of the capture of contraband to cover cases in which the immediate destination of goods was a neutral port. When the Naval Conference gathered at London in 1908 the task which lay before it in defining the laws of contraband may be said to have been much more difficult than the work it undertook in reaching an agreement on the law of blockade. The constant expansion of the class of "conditional contraband" as a result of the industrial methods of the nineteenth and twentieth centuries, the possibility of a misuse of the doctrine of continuous voyage to the grievous detriment of neutral commerce, the growing impossibility of conducting an efficient search on the larger types of modern ships, were all conditions emphasised by the British delegation to the Hague Conference in 1907, when it was urging the discussion of a universal abolition of all seizure of contraband. The acceptance of such a proposal would have left to the belligerent the powers given him under the rules of blockade—the right to seize enemy ships together with the enemy goods on board of them, the right of visit and search, and the power to capture such neutral ships as,

CHAP. IX. by transporting troops or conveying information or comfort to the enemy or by any analogous act, were engaged in unneutral service. Brazil, from motives similar to those alleged by the British, had been moved to advance the less sweeping proposal of the abolition of the class of "conditional contraband." France and Germany, however, held out for the division of contraband into two classes—"absolute," which should be always confiscable if going to the enemy, and "conditional," which should only be confiscable if it was to be presumed that the enemy intended to employ it for warlike ends.(32)

The Naval Conference of London (33) was successful in producing three agreed lists. Eleven types of undeniably military goods were put into the class of "absolute contraband" of war. The list was robbed of a definite character, however, by the agreed provision that a belligerent could add to the articles upon it other goods "exclusively used for war," although notification to neutral governments before so doing was made obligatory. What this meant is shown by the fact that by April 1916 England had put two hundred and ninety-nine articles, and groups of articles, on the list of "absolute contraband." A second list of articles of "conditional contraband" was produced which included such significant articles as food, forage, clothing, money, vehicles, railways, ships and dock materials, fuel and lubricants, and lastly telephone, telegraph, and wireless material. To this list also the belligerent was to be allowed to add after due notification to neutral Powers. Important legal distinctions were made between the lists. "Absolute contraband" was made liable to instant confiscation by whatever means its transport to the enemy were contemplated, whether partly by land or wholly by sea, whether directly or indirectly. "Conditional contraband" was only to be confiscable if bound directly for the territory of the enemy and destined for the use of the armed forces of the state or for the war purposes of a government department. If the belligerent were without a sea-board, however, destination to his forces or to the warlike use of his government was to be sufficient justification for the confiscation of the goods. The ship which carried the contraband was to be liable to confiscation if the contraband, reckoned either by value, weight, volume, or freight, formed more than half of the cargo. The third list was that of those articles which might not be added either to the "absolute" or the "conditional" list. It contained the raw materials of the textile industries, yarns and textile machinery; manures and agricultural machinery; metal ores and mining machinery; paper and printing machinery; oils, seeds, nuts, and copra; rubber, resins, gums, and lacs; raw hides, together with horns and bones; raw building materials, with bricks, slates, and tiles; and other bulky prime material like bleaching powder, soda ash, caustic soda, salt, cake, ammonia, sulphate of ammonia, and sulphate of copper. Apart from these highly important prime materials, which could only be converted into objects immediately useful in war by the devotion of much expense, labour, and organisation, the list extended to cover the neutral carriage to the belligerent of certain articles of amenity or luxury which hardly rose to any importance in the economy of a nation organised for war. Raw goods like marble and ivory, and finished goods like office or domestic furniture, soap, paint and colours, clocks and watches, were all added to this third list; and it may be remarked that medical and other goods for the sick and wounded were exempted from confiscation though not from requisition in case of necessity.

The British government, as is well known, refused during the war of 1914-1918 to accept the limitations embodied in the Declaration of London, which owing to the opposition of the House of Lords had not been ratified. As early as 21st September 1914 there had been such additions to the British list of "conditional contraband" as iron ore, rubber, and hides, all of which had appeared on the "free list" in the Declaration. On 11th March 1915 "free" items such as wool and worsted yarns, and paraffin wax and castor oil, susceptible under the terms of the Declaration only of appearance in the list of "conditional contraband," did as a matter of fact appear upon the list of absolute. On 10th August 1915 raw cotton and cotton yarn appeared there also, and the same fate overtook soap and vegetable fibres on 27th January 1916. On 19th April 1916 the British government freed itself from any surviving obligation to differentiate between "absolute" and "conditional" contraband. It justified this by pointing out that a proportion hitherto unparalleled of the enemy population was directly or indirectly taking part in the war; and that the enemy government had taken control of nearly all those articles which figured on the list of "conditional contraband." By April 1916, on the eve of the abolition of the distinction between the two, the British list, as has been said above, contained two hundred and ninety-nine articles,

CHAP. IX.

or groups of articles, in the category of "absolute," seventy-eight in the category of "conditional," contraband.[34]

Blockade.—A belligerent holding his enemy besieged always claimed the right to forbid access to, and departure from, his enemy. A neutral with supplies who attempted to cross the besieger's lines on land was sternly dealt with. Ports had to be invested both on the land side and on the sea side if the possibility of relief from the sea and the land were to be prevented altogether. Accordingly, the besieger's rights on land were held to extend to his investment by sea. This conception, permissible enough perhaps in the case of a single port, broke down when it came to a declaration of intention to invest a number of places scattered along a whole coast, which claim was apparently first made by the Dutch in 1584.[35] In that year they issued a *placaart* declaring blockaded all the ports of Flanders which still remained in Spanish hands, although they were hardly in a position to besiege any one of them from the land, and were certainly not in a position to besiege all of them from the sea. This and later *placaarts* of like nature must be related rather to a survival of the belligerent's inclination to forbid all traffic with the enemy than to the notion of any partial siege by sea. Grotius seems to refer indirectly to this incident in the Dutch practice of war against the Spaniards. In enumerating the articles which it was legitimate for a belligerent to prevent a neutral Power from supplying to his enemies, he suddenly broke off his argument with these words :—

> "If the carriage of the articles has prevented the pursuit of my right, and if he who performed the carriage was in a position to know it ; if, for example, I had a stronghold besieged, or ports closed, and if surrender or peace were already awaited, he will be liable to me for the damage caused by his fault . . . the objects also belonging to him can be taken in the measure of the damage caused."

This is but a very partial justification of the Dutch measures referred to. It begins, as Bynkershoek noted with regret, by assuming peace or surrender to be imminent, and would penalise only the supply already effected, not the mere attempt to supply. This attempt to supply, also referred to *obiter* by Grotius, would be penalised sufficiently in his view by the withholding of the goods, pending the grant by the would-be supplier of security for his behaviour in the future.

It was the *placaart* of 1630 which introduced in a deliberate manner the notion of siege from the side of the sea alone. In that year the Dutch States-General obtained opinions from the various Dutch admiralties, which were probably all to the effect of that of Amsterdam, that CHAP. IX.

> "the rule which obtains in the case of towns which are properly said to be besieged, and which has with good reason been applied to camps which are as it were besieged, extends also to the enemy's ports, which when invested are deemed to be besieged." (36)

Thereupon they issued a proclamation which decreed that

> "because their High Mightinesses at great charge to the State keep the said ports [of Flanders] continually blocked with their ships of war in order to prevent transport to, and commerce with, the enemy, and because these ports and places are deemed to be besieged, which has always been an ancient custom after the example of all Kings, Princes, Powers, and States which have employed the same right on similar occasions,"

neutral ships entering the ports, or leaving them, or so close to them that it was certain that they wished to enter them, should be confiscated, together with their cargoes, by the Admiralty colleges. The liability of the ship and cargo which might desire to enter would be established from their illicit intention "even if it were encountered very far from these," the Flanders ports, unless the course had been *bona fide* changed before the ship had been encountered by the belligerent vessel. Similarly, a ship leaving Flanders was liable to capture even in the Channel or the North Sea. It was to be counted as taken in the act so long as it had not completed its voyage and had not taken refuge in a free port or neutral harbour. If, however, a ship had been chased into a port, not its home port nor that of its destination, and had been captured in leaving, it was still to be held good prize.(37)

The *placaart* of 1630 made assertions which were not exact. The blocking of the Spanish ports in Flanders was not so complete as was pretended. Nor was the fact that cruisers were merely watching the ports so generally deemed to constitute them besieged ports as the Dutch would have had it. The Dutch themselves, in a treaty signed with France in 1646, provided that ships which had thrown troops, corn, or provisions into a place besieged by French armies might be confiscated. The mention of armies may perhaps be assumed to limit the captor's rights very narrowly to places actually besieged, and not to all those which might be deemed to be besieged. The Anglo-Swedish Treaty of 1661 did not regard

CHAP. IX.

as permissible the capture of innocuous goods taken to a besieged place. Contraband under the terms of this agreement might be taken, but the rest could be sold to the besiegers or carried away. The Dutch, however, persevered in pressing for the acceptance of the stricter view. A new *placaart* was issued against Spain in March 1636. In 1652 and 1666 the whole of the English coast was declared to be blocked to neutral commerce. Against France were issued two similar decrees on 14th April 1672 and 11th April 1673.(38) It was manifestly impossible for a fleet in the seventeenth century to maintain a blockade even of any considerable section of either the French or the English coast, so that the Dutch in issuing their decrees had departed outrageously from their alleged justification as put forward in 1630, at which time their blockade was described as both continuous and costly. In effect, once more it was a return to the alternative conception, that of a general prohibition of all commerce whatsoever with the enemy, for the pretended blocking of the enemy coast amounted to no more than a public manifestation of the existence of a fleet in being.

Meanwhile the Dutch had found imitators in the Spaniards, who in 1663 attempted to declare the ports of Portugal besieged, a course of action against which it is amusing to note that the Dutch protested. In 1689 the Dutch and the English, acting together, attempted to stop all commerce with France, not so much on the ground that they had sent a fleet " to block all the ports, harbours, and havens " of the King of France, but because the restoration of a speedy peace to Christianity and the prevention of the effusion of much Christian blood made it necessary to remove from the French king and his subjects the means to carry on a war. It is a foretaste of the " starvation blockade " of later times. In 1756 England had to encounter Dutch protests against her seizure of Dutch ships laden with naval stores for French ports. The Dutch produced their treaty of 1674 with England, which permitted them to trade with the English enemy save to ports actually besieged. England after negotiation consented to the purchase of the seized cargo, but asserted that the French ports were blocked and that the ships and cargo when neutral would in future be seized and confiscated.(39)

International treaties began to take serious note of the novel belligerent practice of the declared, but fictitious, blockade. Whereas in the seventeenth century treaties like those of the

Pyrenees, Nymwegen, and Ryswyck allowed a free trade between neutrals and belligerents, except in contraband or to "places besieged, blocked, or invested," the treaties of the eighteenth century began to contain clauses which attempted to define the measure of force which it was necessary for a belligerent to possess in front of a port before it could be accepted as "blockaded." The belligerent, that is to say, was no longer trusted to furnish his own definition of that term. Thus the Franco-Danish Treaty of 1742 in its twentieth article provided that the entry to a port should, if the port were to be regarded as blockaded, be closed by two vessels at sea or a battery of cannon on shore. The treaty of 1753 between Naples and the Dutch provided in Article 22 that "no ports or cities should be deemed to be besieged or blockaded unless they were invested from the side of the sea by at least six ships of war to be stationed a little beyond cannon-shot from the shore, or from the side of the land by batteries of cannon and other works, so that it be impossible to enter without passing under the cannon of the besiegers." (40) The Armed Neutralities only permitted to belligerents blockading rights over a port before which the attacking Power had its vessels stationary, and sufficiently near to render access clearly dangerous.

England, it is well known, successfully eluded the pressure of the First Armed Neutrality, so that in 1793 she could, if she would, have had resort to the total prohibition of commerce with her enemy, having a liberty unfettered by any precise treaty stipulations as to what did, or did not, constitute a blockade. In 1793 the Admiralty gave orders to English ships to take into English ports all neutral ships carrying grain or flour in the direction of French ports. This was not exactly an exercise of rights under the law of blockade, for there was no intention at this time to confiscate. But Admiral Hood in the Mediterranean went so far as to declare that all ships which entered French ports would be considered good prize regardless of their cargo. The war began, then, with some diversity of practice, as is not infrequently the case with wars; for the Admiral by his action had put himself in a position only possible after the declaration of a blockade. Not till 1806 did the British government finally proclaim an explicit and formal blockade of several hundred miles of the French coast—from the Elbe, that is, to Brest. This action was taken despite the fact that England had determined in 1801 to humour the Russian and Scandinavian Powers by the

CHAP. IX. concession, made in treaties with them, that the belligerent, in order to secure the rights of a blockader, must have made access to the blockaded ports manifestly dangerous through the instrumentality of ships, some stationary before the port and others sufficiently close to it.

To the declaration of blockade in 1806 Napoleon replied with a counter-declaration of a blockade, in reprisal, of the whole of the British Isles. This was supported by his "continental system," which involved the exclusion of British goods from the continent of Europe, and extended the customary belligerent veto upon trading with the enemy to the European satellites of France. In his decree, issued in Berlin on 21st November 1806, Napoleon attacked the British for extending the application of blockade from strongholds to unfortified commercial ports, havens, and the mouths of rivers. Yet his contention that blockade was a hostile operation only admissible against the armed places of the enemy went further than was justifiable. Even those authorities who in the nineteenth century were most anxious to limit the right of blockade made little point out of the culpability of a desire to blockade commercial harbours, but emphasised always the inseparability between a demand for blockading rights and the means—in the shape of ships—to sustain them.

Great Britain ventured still further by the Order in Council of 11th November 1807. Not only all the ports of France but those of every other country at war with England, those of countries which, though not at war with her, excluded the English flag, and finally all the colonial ports of English enemies, were to be treated in the most rigorous way, so that ships bound thither or departing thence were to be treated as confiscable together with their cargoes. This was in fact, if not in legal theory, the answer to the "continental system." The truth is that the effects which can be procured by blockade are instruments to which recourse must always be had in war; and when the naval war is long sustained and neutrals happen to be weak, the nicer laws evolved for the conduct of this operation either find themselves wondrously "developed" or the desired effects are produced by other and side-stepping methods.

After the Napoleonic Wars were ended and the tension was relieved, a movement began—characteristically, in quarters which during that war had been neutral—to limit by treaty the blockader to the right merely to warn off the neutral blockade-runner, and to permit the exercise of confiscation only in the face of an attempt to enter the blockaded port a second time. The first treaty seriously to move in the new direction was that between Sweden and the United States of America, signed on 4th September 1816. Article 13 even permitted a neutral ship to start from home in full knowledge of the blockade merely in the hope that by the time of arrival the blockade would have been raised, for it provided that the ship in question should only be condemnable on the first attempt to enter the port if the captor were able to prove that the ship's master could, and should, have known that the blockade was still in operation when he got there.(41) This movement received some support from Powers which, though fairly formidable at sea themselves, had reason none the less to fear the effects of a blockade when it was operated by a navy more powerful than their own. France and Italy, for example, were willing to give each neutral ship an individual warning against an attempt at ingress to a blockaded port before considering that it had undertaken a formal breach of the blockade. This has been humorously termed the law of "the first bite." Another, but less important, mitigation from the belligerent point of view of the rigours of the law of blockade, found in a treaty signed by Mexico in 1828 with the Hanseatic League, provided permission for neutrals which were in port at the time of the actual declaration to depart unhindered.(42)

Belligerents themselves were at times willing to permit such mitigation, but usually only in connection with particular blockades and to their own advantage. Thus Napoleon was glad to allow the export of corn from the continent to England, which he was at the time nominally blockading. In 1809 he let through no less than ninety thousand tons of wheat and other grain from France, Holland, and Flanders. When in 1810 the English import of grain reached a total value of seven million pounds, no less than one-third of the wheat, and half of the flour, came from the empire of Napoleon under his special licence. Such measures produced a large income for the Emperor from the licensing fees, helped him to dispose of the surplus produce of his dominions, and served, in the opinion of some experts, to weaken England by forcing upon that country an adverse balance of trade. England for its part was not merely prepared to facilitate by licence this import of corn from the French territories, nominally under blockade, but undertook measures by which France and the countries of the "continental system" might be forced to take English

CHAP. IX. goods, and in addition foreign goods which had passed through British hands and would yield a profit to Englishmen if thus accepted. This somewhat singular position meant in effect that the belligerent denied the neutral the right to trade with his enemy on the ground that the enemy's ports were blockaded, while at the same time he undertook provisioning operations on a gigantic scale for the sake of the profit to government in licences and the enhanced private profit produced by this intentionally produced scarcity. This makes the Napoleonic blockade unique in history. Lord Bathurst, the President of the Board of Trade in 1812, was not far wrong in saying that France by her decrees had resolved to abolish all trade with England, but that England in return had forced France to have no trade except with England.(43)

The British prize courts during the Crimean War took up in the changed circumstances a totally different attitude. In the case of the *Franciska* the prize court held merely that the blockading belligerent was not entitled to reserve to himself, or to allow to any other belligerent, a right of trading which he did not at the same time allow to neutrals. The Court of Appeal (the Judicial Committee) went much further. It held that the right of blockade only existed for the purpose of cutting off all kind of communication, whether of ingress or of egress; and that any relaxation was as objectionable, if extended by the belligerents to the neutrals, as if it were to be confined to the belligerents themselves. This is a return to the more normal conception of blockade. The area of war was once again confined, the combatant mass restricted, the neutral mass enlarged, the weapon of blockade naturally ceased to be a bludgeon and became once more a rapier. In nothing is that made so clear as in one other feature in the case of the *Franciska*. Countenance was definitely given to a British practice of some duration which permitted a local naval authority to establish a legal blockade, on the presumption that he was empowered thereto by his government. The court noted that the neutral might, of course, in such a case have a much stronger presumption in his favour, should he wish to plead ignorance of the fact of blockade, than he would possess in the case of a blockade declared by the government at home and notified to the neutral governments. Subsequent efforts defined, by agreement between the Powers, the limits within which a locally declared blockade should be legitimate.

In 1856 the Declaration of Paris formally bound the leading European governments, including that of Great Britain, to the position that a blockade to be binding must be effective —that is, that there must exist a real danger locally in attempting to enter the blockaded port. It was during the negotiations by which it was sought to induce the United States to accede to all the conditions of this declaration that this Power took the occasion to voice its objection almost in the Napoleonic manner to "commercial" blockades. It was willing to recognise, it said, the "strategic" or "military" blockade as part of a military operation. The "commercial" blockade, having no direct military object, and being intended merely to weaken the general resisting strength of the enemy, it proclaimed its desire to have abolished by mutual and universal agreement. There are few governments in the world which have a sufficiently clear record of consistency to be able to cast the first stone against any one government for adopting at different periods differing attitudes in matters of International Law; but it is a dramatic commentary on the shortness of sight in those who rule, that the Federal government of the United States proceeded in 1861 to establish the largest commercial blockade till then known in history. Some two thousand five hundred miles of coast of the Confederate States were in that year declared blockaded, and several hundreds of vessels were employed in the enforcement of the blockade. It was during the course of the four years of hostility that an extension of the doctrine of blockade was undertaken by the Federal government. It became the habit of neutral traders to send their goods from Europe, not direct to the ports of the Southern States, but to neutral ports like Nassau, Cardenas, and Matamoras, out of which subsequent re-export to the Confederates could easily be arranged. In 1863 the *Springbok* was seized on its way from London to Nassau while it was carrying a cargo a small part of which was absolute contraband, a considerable part conditional, while the innocent portion of the cargo belonged to the same owners as the contraband. Both the District and the Supreme Courts of the United States were satisfied to the full that the cargo was intended for the blockaded coast after transhipment at Nassau. The lower court condemned both the ship and the cargo. The Supreme Court on appeal upheld the condemnation of the cargo because the voyage from London to Nassau was held to be only a part of what was essentially one longer voyage—from London to the blockaded coast; which voyage rendered the cargo liable to confiscation at any

CHAP. IX.

stage. The *Springbok* itself, however, whose papers were genuine and whose owners were not proved to have knowledge of the intended ultimate destination of the cargo, was released. To separate the cargo from the ship in the case of blockade, to condemn the cargo and not the ship, was to depart altogether from the original principle of blockade, which consisted primarily in the barring of the approach of a ship to a forbidden port or coast.

By the opening of the twentieth century considerable uncertainty was held to attach, therefore, to the practice of blockade, which was felt to be in an ill-regulated and inadequately defined condition. Powers accustomed to think of themselves primarily in the position of maritime neutrals, and those who took the belligerent view, were alike eager to introduce clarity and order. This feeling came to a head in the Naval Conference of London, which, sitting in the years 1908 and 1909, produced the ill-fated Declaration, the first twenty-one articles of which were devoted to blockade. Blockading, as against neutral, rights were in these articles subjected to much restriction. The precedent established by the decision in the case of the *Springbok* was set aside. The blockading Power would no longer have been able to bar access to neutral ports or coasts, nor to capture a ship, whatever its ultimate destination, if its immediate course were to an unblockaded port. The capture of neutral ships would have been permitted, not at any stage of the voyage, but only within the area of the operations of the blockading squadron. It has never been fully explained why the consent of the British Admiralty was obtained for the subscription of Great Britain to these measures. Lord Loreburn, their chief sponsor, and those associated with him, were so deeply impressed by the danger of blockade to a country which imported practically its whole food supply from overseas—a danger which the German submarine menace was later to prove most real—that blockade as an offensive weapon received inadequate attention. The Declaration of London was not ratified, but its decisions were so recent, and were regarded with so much respect, that when it came to the necessity of cutting off the Central Powers during the Great War of 1914-1918 from their overseas supplies, it was to legal principles other than those of the law of blockade that recourse was had. Had the Declaration of London been both ratified and adhered to with anything like strictness, a blockade of Germany conducted by its principles would have proved valueless. Germany was flanked by the neutral nations Denmark and Holland, which would have become vast re-exporting depôts for foreign goods. In the face of this condition the stoppage of commerce with the actual German ports would have been bootless. This whole chapter in the history of International Law illustrates alike the strange gaps which must always be presumed to exist in the foresight of even the most intelligent statesmen and officials; the certainty in a long-drawn and extensive war of the employment of those forces of which the historic practice of blockade is the volatile if concentrated essence; and lastly, the futility of all attempts to confine within too rigid limits, by definition and by anticipation in a time of peace, a practice which the nature of war—and one may add the nature of warriors—will in the long run for ever force to be flexible.

In the war of 1914-1918 it is true that examples of the old type of blockade, such a one as was enforced by ships in the immediate vicinity of the port or coast declared to be blockaded, were to be found in such operations as the Austrian blockade of the Montenegrin coast, the Anglo-French blockade of the Bulgarian coast, and others of the same kind.[44] Public attention was mainly directed, however, to what was known as the blockade of Germany. This was indeed never legally proclaimed a blockade at all. A legal blockade of the coast of Germany, such as would involve the proximity of British squadrons to German harbours and defences, would, in view of the development of marine mines and submarine ships, have proved, if not impossible, at least enormously costly. It would in addition have left untouched the adjacent neutral ports of Denmark, Holland, and the Scandinavian countries, which would have become on a vast scale the channels of a re-exporting trade. Accordingly, at the beginning of the war the law of contraband rather than of blockade seemed to the Allied Powers the most suitable guide to effectual action against Germany. As has been shown above, the lists of both "absolute" and "conditional" contraband were extended far beyond those included in the Declaration of London; and, in due course, the very *rationale* of the distinction between "absolute" and "conditional" contraband was abandoned, when the British courts, after having accepted without question the expanded official list of contraband, undertook to regard all articles in the list on entering Germany, whatever their nominal destination, as proceeding for the use of the German government. Finally,

CHAP. IX.

the doctrine of continuous transport, which admittedly permitted the interception of "absolute" contraband at any stage, was transferred to apply to the articles on the list of "conditional" contraband. Under this extension any goods on either of the contraband lists, which did in fact embrace all the more important articles of commerce, could be challenged even if they were bound for a neutral port. The prize court, moreover, threw upon the neutral merchant the onus of proving that the final destination was innocent. It demanded to see books, pre-war trade figures, and similar records on pain of confiscation. At the same time it permitted the British government the greatest freedom in producing evidence in its desire to convict doubtful neutrals, and went so far as to adopt the ruling of the Order in Council of 30th March 1916 which provided that enemy destination would be presumed to exist in the case of any merchant who had once been found to have forwarded imported contraband goods to territory in the hands of the enemy. It was under heavy belligerent pressure of this nature, and with the encouragement of the Allied governments, who saw the value of collective bargaining, that the associations of neutral merchants in each country were formed, of which the Netherlands Overseas Trust was typical. They were willing to guarantee that none of the imports, which were by that time strictly rationed to each neutral country by the Allies, would be transferred to Germany. Complicated as the problem was, the machinery worked better than might have been expected; and although neutral merchants were sufficiently chagrined to lose the profits which free intercourse with Germany would have provided, they had much to congratulate themselves upon in the results which their representations to London had obtained.

It is evident, from the development of the law of contraband outlined above, that the belligerent was in a position to obtain from it many of the principal benefits derivable from the proclamation of a blockade without some of the risks attaching to it, especially after the Allies compelled all ships sailing to Germany, or to countries adjacent to Germany, to come into port to submit to search, on the ground that this could not be adequately carried out at sea under modern conditions. One with so much knowledge of the issues at stake as the late Sir Erle Richards was very doubtful whether it was necessary in the circumstances to go further. However, the British and French governments proceeded, on the ground of reprisal for the German war-zone declaration of February 1915, to issue the Order in Council of March 1915. All ships bearing goods of presumed "enemy destination, manufacture, or origin" were to be taken into port, the goods unloaded and placed under the care of the prize court, but not confiscated unless already confiscable—that is to say, unless contraband. This Order prevented every article from entering Germany, and in addition did what no extension of contraband principles could ever have done—denied the exit into the world of German raw materials or manufactured products. The full effects of blockade were now obtainable, although the full punishment of ingress was not yet imposed, while no confiscation was applied in the case of egress. The execution of this totality of new measures, some derivable from the application of the law of contraband, some from that of reprisal for the violation of International Law, proved remarkably successful, owing principally, perhaps, to the favourable position of England strategically with regard to Germany.

It is essential, perhaps, before leaving the subject of blockade to notice that during the nineteenth century the idea of blockade was adapted for use in intervention or reprisals, these being measures taken without a declaration of war. The beginning of the system was seen in European waters during 1831, when a French fleet operated against Portugal, and in 1832-1833, when an Anglo-French fleet operated against Holland. In the first case the French seem to have confined their operations against ships of commerce purely to the seizure and sequestration of some Portuguese ships leaving Lisbon; in the second case a combined Anglo-French fleet co-operated with a French army in the reduction of the citadel of Antwerp, while English cruisers had apparently a special instruction to take Dutch ships into English ports unless they had a cargo which was liable to deterioration. It was after this procedure had been applied in South American waters by an English fleet in 1837 that it received its later development. In reprisal for the detention of a British consul, whose return had been persistently refused, the English Commodore Reyton on 20th January declared a blockade of the ports of New Grenada—effective only for Carthagena. The blockade lasted for twelve days, and was applied not only against ships of New Grenada but against those of neutral Powers. At the end of the blockade the ships detained were all released. As the century advanced

CHAP. IX.

the institution became part of the stock-in-trade of the greater Powers of the European Concert, and was jointly and individually employed on several occasions.[45] It has been suggested that a "pacific blockade" will be one of the principal weapons on which the League of Nations will rely for the suppression of a serious, but not vital, breach of its conditions.

Privateering.—The naval belligerent, although by the seventeenth and eighteenth century he possessed state ships of war and a permanent state naval organisation often of considerable proportions, did not contemplate the surrender of his power to license his subjects to operate against the commerce of his enemy on their own account. It is true that he was bound by a number of treaties to demand heavy caution money from his privateers before they set out, and to hold this money in readiness to indemnify such as should bring suit on account of proved illegal treatment at the hands of the privateer. Yet those who would form an estimate of the nature of the system, over which the romanticist has been able to cast some glamour, may find significant a quotation or two from measures which were designed for its regulation. Article 18 of Louis XIV.'s *Ordonnance de la Marine* runs as follows :—

> "We forbid on pain of death all captains, soldiers and sailors to sink captured vessels and to land the prisoners on islands or on distant coasts with a view to concealing the fact of capture."

There was always some trouble involved in bringing a prize into port and in securing condemnation. Moreover, there were dues to be paid to the Crown. That this trouble and this expense produced the natural consequences this quotation indicates. Article 4 of the Franco-British Treaty of 1677, to take another example, provides that no inhuman treatment shall be inflicted upon a captured crew—to elicit information such as might lead to the condemnation of the cargo. This forms, as is the case so often with treaty stipulations, a mirror which in reverse gives indication of the common practice. Yet so far was such a monarch as Louis XIV. from the contemplation of the surrender of this right that some of his *ordonnances* actually make provision for the supply of even royal ships to private individuals for the harrying of commerce. Thus the *règlement* of 5th December 1691 forbade the lending to private individuals of royal ships of over forty-four guns, but provided that frigates, fireships and ships of under forty-four guns, properly equipped, armed and munitioned, might be lent free on the condition that they were returned in a state of repair equal to that in which they had left port. CHAP. IX.

To certain temperaments life on a privateer must have appealed more strongly than that on an ordinary man-of-war. At least special steps had to be taken to guard against desertion from the naval to the privateering service. Discipline was not rigid, for each sailor apparently was deemed to have a share in the adventure, and at critical moments even to have a claim to make his voice heard in council. Then there was always the sailor's chance to become a rich man on a sudden through his ship's capture of some particularly valuable prize. It engendered the atmosphere of a Bret Harte mining camp, and privateering was often sundered by no very sharp dividing line from piracy. Thus Legge, the British minister in Berlin, wrote in 1748 to Newcastle, "The outrages committed by our privateers, who upon the apprehension of an approaching peace have degenerated into mere pirates, are, I am afraid, undeniable." An historian of the Seven Years' War, Julian Corbett, has written of the conduct of British privateers :—

> "What the King's cruisers did might possibly have been borne, but the action of our privateers was outrageous beyond endurance. Every year it had been growing worse, and it is not to be denied that at this time there were a swarm of smaller privateers in the Narrow Seas, who were not to be distinguished from pirates."

In March 1801 the Danish minister in London complained of "atrocities" deliberately committed by British privateers. A belligerent on the other hand in reply to neutral complaints on the subject of privateering was apt to assume the tone and attitude of Lord Grenville, who, speaking in the House of Lords on 13th November 1801, said,

> "and although it be true that occasional irregularities may prevail, this country ought not to renounce an important right merely because we hear some exaggerated statements of rapine and violence committed by those who exercise it. Such assertions are made with great facility, because it is almost always impossible to disprove them, unless the Neutral would pursue his complaint in those courts which are constantly open for his redress."

This speech of Lord Grenville indicates the direction in which the pressure of neutrals on belligerents was tending.

CHAP. IX.

Neutrals indeed had one way open to them by which they could demonstrate their resentment against the practices of belligerent privateers. They could deny them the use of their ports. Thus Sweden in Section 14 of its Marine Regulations, issued 21st January 1804, forbade foreign privateers to enter its ports or to send their prizes thither, except in cases of evident distress. When Sweden and Denmark on 2nd January 1854 outlined their proposed conduct as maritime neutrals to the prospective belligerents in the Crimean War they agreed in their resolution to exclude privateers from their ports and harbours. Opinion both in France and England, moreover, was at this time, to say the least of it, uneasy as regards the severity of past maritime practice. Lord Clarendon, the Secretary of State for Foreign Affairs, was able to announce to the House of Lords in March that the British and French governments "with respect to the rights of neutrals and with respect to letters of marque" were intending "to act in a measure that shall be consistent with the humanity and civilisation of the age." Which somewhat characteristically complacent utterance of the Victorian Age was in fact borne out by the British Declaration to neutrals of 28th March 1854, by which the latter were assured that it was not the intention of Her Majesty's government to commission privateers. The French Declaration published two days later took the same line.[(46)]

When the Crimean War was being closed by the agreements made at the Congress of Paris, the proposal was made by the first French plenipotentiary, Walewski, that the Powers should copy the work of the Congresses of Vienna and Westphalia by ratifying international legislation, and particularly that they should attempt to formulate some basic portions of the law of war at sea. The first article proposed by Walewski aimed at the abolition of privateering, and, in accepting it, the British plenipotentiary Clarendon described privateering as "organised and legal piracy" and as "one of the greatest scourges of war." On 16th April 1856 the Declaration of Paris was signed, and it included the famous article "privateering is and remains abolished." The engagement to invite other Powers to adhere to its stipulations was signed by the plenipotentiaries of Great Britain, France, Russia, Prussia, Austria, Turkey and Sardinia.

The United States of America, Spain (until 1908), Mexico (until 1909), and Venezuela refused to adhere to the terms of the Declaration of Paris, all apparently because they were not at that date prepared to refrain from commissioning privateers. The note of the United States, dated 28th July 1856, expressed the view that the maintenance of a large professional navy was against its policy; that consequently it would have to look to the ships of the mercantile marine for the protection of its commerce unless and until the seizure of private property at sea were universally abandoned; that privateers were not essentially more likely to disregard national rights than ships of the official navy whose crews had oftentimes enough had their cupidity aroused by the prospect of winning prize money.

Mr. Marcy, the author of this note, foreshadowed the outbreak of disputes on the question as to whether certain types of ships declared by one country to be public ships were not in reality excluded from participation in hostilities by the ban placed upon privateers. He was correct. The dispute arose first in 1870, in which year Prussia attempted to enlist the services of private ships and sailors for an attack upon French vessels of war. The owners under the arrangement were to equip and man the ships, but the crews were to be temporarily taken into the navy and to be under naval discipline. Later, when other nations attempted to make provision in advance of hostilities for the use in war of vessels and crews ordinarily employed in commerce, there was some doubt expressed as to whether this too were not a departure from the principles of the Declaration of Paris. It seems, however, to have been generally agreed that when officers and crews had some official connection with the national navy, so that their discipline and behaviour in war could be relied on, and when, in addition, the ship received such a formal belligerent commission after the outbreak of war as fully to incorporate it in the national forces, the practice lay open to no objection. But the practice of incorporating commercial ships and crews in the navy had been robbed of most of its dangers when governments like the British abandoned the practice of making in each separate instance a monetary reward to the crew of the particular ship which had made the particular capture.

The British Prize Court.[(47)]—In the Middle Ages when an English fleet put to sea against its enemies or when an English ship at sea captured an enemy ship or enemy goods, no formal provision existed for the delivery of judgment in prize. In the unsophisticated days of the thirteenth and fourteenth centuries the captor mariners would have been as astonished

CHAP. IX.

to learn that their property in the captured goods should rightfully depend on a judicial decision as would have been the soldier on land to hear similar doctrine propounded on the subject of his booty. The consent of the Admiral of the King's northern fleet and the law of the sea were justification alleged in the Court of Exchequer in 1341 by captors who had possessed themselves of a ship bound from Zeeland to Scotland. Nevertheless, the rough-and-ready decisions of captors were bound to be questioned by neutral sovereigns and subjects who had suffered injury by them. In 1357 there is a case of a neutral Portuguese ship illegally captured by the French and subsequently captured from the French by the English. The Portuguese appealed first to the Admiral and then to the King. They were heard, but obtained no restitution. From the fact that the King in advance allowed ships not belonging to him to have what they took, save two shares for the Admiral, it may be surmised that the fact of capture produced the change of property.

An important change was marked by a proclamation of 1426. Captured goods were not to be dispersed thenceforward until the Council, the Chancellor, the Admiral or the Admiral's deputy had certified whether the goods were of enemy character or not. This at least established an important principle, as did an agreement, accepting this condition, which was made between King Henry VI. and some shipowners, and was intended to safeguard from dispersal the neutral goods in a captured ship. In his instructions of 1512 the Admiral of England, Edward Howard, impressed upon his fleet his orders that only just prizes should be taken, and that no captured ship was to be removed from the fleet save after the Admiral's decision. For any definite provision for judicial procedure in prize, it is however necessary to wait until 1589, when the Council required that "prizes shall be kept safely and no part be sold, spoiled, wasted nor diminished till judgment has been first passed in the High Court of Admiralty that the said goods be lawful prize."

The lawyers engaged in suits of prize were the civilians in Doctors' Commons, advocates whose description by the iconoclastic Dickens will be familiar enough to readers of *David Copperfield* and who enjoyed the monopoly of those provinces of the legal system in which neither equity nor common law held sway.(48) In effect they were concerned with ecclesiastical matters, including the important branches of testament and marriage, and maritime matters, including the law of prize. From these lawyers were chosen the judges of the Admiralty court and their surrogates. The Admiralty judge in the eighteenth century was usually given a special warrant, based on a commission issued by the Crown to the Admiralty, to proceed to the trial of prize cases. This was done after the outbreak of war had made a prize court necessary.

CHAP. IX.

The law administered by the court was found in the collections of customary usages, such as those of Rhodes or the *Consolato del Mare*, in the provisions of particular treaties and in the text-books of the commentators upon the civil law or the Law of Nations. The Crown, however, always exercised the power of issuing orders to the court which might direct its procedure and even mould the law which it applied. Thus in 1665 nine rules, both of law and procedure, were drawn up for the prize court by the Privy Council; and that they concerned no merely trivial points is indicated by the fact that among them were instructions that in passing judgment, ship and cargo should be treated as inseparable even though either one of these were English, and, further, that spoiled or fraudulent ships' papers should result in condemnation. It was another Order in Council which laid down that if a part of the ship belonged to the enemy the whole should be condemned as prize. Executive order, as has been shown in previous chapters, formed no small portion of the law administered: along with treaty stipulations it cut in everywhere into the rulings of immemorial custom.

But beyond these statements of the executive power as to the actual law to be applied there were unofficial relations between the court and the executive. In 1665 the prize court incurred criticism from the Privy Council for laxity in the condemnation of contraband, while as late as 1745 the judge of the prize court wrote for instructions to the Admiralty as to whether pitch and tar were to be counted as contraband of war. In 1760 the judge was instructed to hold in his mind a treaty of 1667 and certain stipulations and to proceed "very carefully" in the manner expressed in a letter of Mr. Pitt. Even Lord Stowell, who had a majestically lofty notion of the prerogatives of the prize court, did not venture in his court to pass upon the legality of an Order in Council. He would not presume to judge that an Order in Council imposed upon him duties inconsistent with International Law. Orders in Council he assumed to contain applications of the

CHAP. IX.

principles of that law provided for the use of the court, or positive regulations not inconsistent with it; and it would in his judgment be indecorous to presume an actual conflict between the provisions of an Order in Council and such principles.(49) By 1916 the Judicial Committee of the Privy Council, acting as a court of appeal, assumed for the prize court a position more independent of the executive than it had ever assumed for itself.(50) The Judicial Committee asserted the right of the court to interpret International Law for itself, even though the executive authority should attempt to bind it by an Order in Council which should prescribe or declare the action which it should take, unless the Order in Council should amount to a mitigation of the belligerent rights of the Crown in favour of an enemy or a neutral. Thus an Order in Council which should prescribe reprisals, although it would be taken by the court as conclusive so far as the facts complained of were concerned, would nevertheless be subjected to scrutiny on complaint and might be held unlawful as entailing upon neutrals an unreasonable degree of inconvenience. It is important to notice, however, that despite the high degree of independence as over against the directions of the executive, the court seems always to be bound by legislative acts even supposing these were deemed contrary to International Law.(51)

The material upon which the court gave judgment was the ship's papers (52) which indicated its ownership, the ladings of the cargo, the proprietorship of the different ladings, their destination and the further orders given to the captain of the ship. Additional evidence was always obtained from the depositions of members of the crew. The instructions to the fleet of 1626 make provision for the despatch for examination by the Admiral, or his deputy judge, of the crew of the captured ship, or of at least two or three of the principal members of it. Later a fixed form of examination was set out in the so-called Standing Interrogatories which were administered by examiners who sent their completed results to the court. Captors in the less systematic days of the seventeenth century had at times proceeded to measures of violence against a crew in order to elicit confessions which would procure a condemnation, a practice which the administration at the ports of standing interrogatories would presumably check. Sir Leoline Jenkins reported in 1666 the case of the crew of a Riga ship (53) which had been barbarously treated; and the Franco-British Treaty of 1677 in Article 4 made special provision to insure the humane treatment of a captured crew.

On the basis of the ship's papers, the answers to the standing interrogatories and the arguments of the opposing advocates, the court gave its decision. This might be for acquittal with costs against the captor, or even with damages in addition thereto in the case of grossly improper capture; for the payment of these there would be resources available in the deposit money paid by privateers on obtaining their letters of marque, a regulation to which reference has already been made. A ship might be acquitted but no costs be allowed, if the court decided that the captor had sufficient justification for taking the ship in for adjudication. Again, a ship or a cargo might be condemned but costs be adjudicated, out of the proceeds of the capture, when it seemed to the court that the owners had had reasonable cause for contesting a doubtful or perhaps hitherto undecided case. Lastly, condemnation might be made with an award of costs against the owners from whom security for the costs could be required in advance of the proceedings. There is a fascinating letter, printed by Phillimore, which was written by Stowell and Nicholl to Jay the American minister in 1794. It describes fully proceedings in the eighteenth-century prize court.

Apart from the condemnation of ships and cargo, or the attendant judicial business connected with claims for freight, damages and the like, the court had other judicial functions to perform. First there was that which had the same international character as proceedings in prize. The court estreated the bonds deposited by the owners of privateers if they had acted against the requirements of their letters of marque. Then there was that which was purely national in character. The court decided disputes arising from cases of joint capture, where two or more vessels had co-operated or claimed to have co-operated in the affair. There were cases of prize salvage which involved the rescue by one British ship of another captured by the enemy but retaken from his hands. Further, there were disputes between the government and the captors over the droits of Admiralty. In the eighteenth century the work of the prize court in London was supplemented by Vice-Admiralty courts acting in British territory beyond the seas. These were given special warrants to act in prize cases by the Lords of the Admiralty. It was generally convenient for ships acting in distant waters to have a court near at hand from which a judgment could be

CHAP. IX.

obtained with expedition. In the war of 1914-1918 the Admiralty issued warrants to as many as forty-four courts overseas to act as courts of prize.

Appeals could be taken from the prize court (and later from the Vice-Admiralty courts) to a higher tribunal. The treaty signed with France in 1677 definitely provided for a special commission of nine members of the King's Council to have power to review sentences of condemnation. This was to provide a tribunal of special dignity and one uncontrolled by a preponderance of lawyers. English practice, however, had already made special provisions for appeal as early as 1628 when a commission was issued to seven Councillors to review past or present sentences in prize decisions. International considerations made it desirable to provide courts of suitable dignity for appeals in the case of every war. When in 1748 the executive attempted to expedite the hearing of prize appeals by adding to the commissioners appointed to try them a number of judges not Councillors, there was considerable doubt expressed as to whether persons outside the Council could act, a doubt which was resolved by securing an Act of Parliament which none the less provided that Privy Councillors should always be in a majority on the occasion of any sentence.

English jurisdiction in prize cases awakened especially strong antagonism in the eighteenth century. Frederick of Prussia, a neutral in the Anglo-French War of 1744-1748, conducted a long diplomatic controversy with England on the subject of the treatment at sea of Prussian ships and merchandise.[54] He was indignant that, when he complained of the capture of Prussian ships or cargoes, the British ministry declined to treat with him diplomatically on a footing of equality, but referred him to the decisions of tribunals of prize. He complained specifically of delays, amounting to two or three years, which were imposed by protracted prize proceedings on Prussian ships and on the ships of Sweden, Holland, Denmark, and Hamburg which carried Prussian goods. He deplored the absence of a grant of compensation when at long last a decision of discharge was obtained, and denounced the imposition of charges, in the shape of payment to captors and courts, which it was, in his opinion, the more usual practice of the tribunal to impose. In 1753 he proceeded to his famous reprisal in the shape of a cessation of payments on the Silesian loan. In the war of 1756-1763 neutral feeling again was outraged by some of the proceedings of the prize court. Bernstorff, the Danish minister, in 1756 wrote :—

> "No navigator of any country, however innocent may be his business, has ever obtained a just sentence before these Doctors' Commons [*sic*], whose name will descend with horror to posterity."

The Dutch, who suffered very heavily under "the rule of the war of 1756," which was applied against neutral attempts to do trade barred by British measures to belligerents, in this case that between France and her West Indian colonies, and who lost ships engaged in other commerce also, were deeply incensed against England. The Dowager Princess of Orange, a daughter of the King of England, exerted all her influence to maintain peace between the two nations. Before her death, which took place in January 1759, she had secured from her father a promise of better treatment for Dutch shipping, but the hopes built on this promise proved illusory, for seizure and condemnation continued in what the Dutch held to be innocent trade. Parliament, against the violent opposition of the privateering interest, was, indeed, persuaded to pass a Bill which allowed the owners of ships which had been seized to secure their release by the deposit of a sum of money. When a Dutch delegation, however, arrived to negotiate a settlement, delay was permitted to frustrate all hope of agreement. Spain was another nation which suffered considerably from the English measures. The Spanish minister Wall wrote to his ambassador in London :—

> "If they wish to live in accord with us, they have many occasions for the manifestation of their friendship in place of the fine phrases in which they are so prodigal, by returning to us the great number of ships which they detain in their ports, to the great detriment of our nationals." (55)

Later, when Baron Ehrensward, the Swedish minister in London, in a note to Lord Hawkesbury, justified his master's adhesion to the Second Armed Neutrality, he spoke of "the deceitful chicanery with which the proceedings of the Court of Admiralty were conducted," and of "the absolute denial of justice in many instances," as part justification. This was strong language in an age of diplomatic punctilio. Kleen, writing in 1900 a conspicuous book on Neutrality, thought fit to brand Marriott and Stowell as "advocates of booty." When he spoke of "their revolting partiality marked by professions of fairness," he was uttering a sentiment common on the

CHAP. IX.

Continent even to the present day. In 1794 the United States of America had obtained, by Article 7 of their treaty with England, a mixed commission which should be set up to decide on the claims of American citizens against the alleged illegal and irregular captures and condemnation of war vessels and other property under the authority of the British government. Even James Stephen was prepared to admit that the Vice-Admiralty courts in the West Indies were badly constituted and had, after the Order in Council of 1793, acted rashly in the condemnation of American ships. The late Sir Erle Richards, in a notable article in the *British Year-Book of International Law* for 1920, judiciously questioned the conduct of the prize court during the war of 1914-1918 in not awarding compensation to the owners of innocent neutral ships for loss caused by the long detention of their vessels pending the preparation of their case by the captors; in undertaking the condemnation of neutral vessels for the breach of regulations which were admittedly outside the range of International Law, and were the consequence only of the decision to adopt reprisal; and in adhering to the antiquated theory that the enemy was outside the law except where specific provision had been made by international agreement for his admission to the court.

The Atmosphere of the British Prize Court.—It might be well if there were to be engraven upon the walls of every prize court of the world the memorable sentences which posterity owes to Lord Stowell, and which have been held by enlightened opinion nicely to define its functions:—

> "It is the duty of a judge sitting in an Admiralty court not to deliver occasional and shifting opinions to serve present purposes of particular national interest, but to administer with indifference that justice which the law of nations holds out without distinction to independent states, some happening to be neutral and some belligerent. The seat of the judicial authority is locally here in the belligerent country, according to the known law and practice of nations, but the law itself has no locality." (56)

Yet there is another side, more realistic, which it is unwise, because it is dangerously fanciful, to overlook. The enumeration of instances and types of cases made in the last section and in the course of that which dealt with contraband, has served no purpose if it has not displayed the solicitude of the most famous of all national prize courts that International Law should not be so interpreted as needlessly to restrict, out of theoretical considerations of benevolence or humanity, the possibility of the largest amount of damage to the enemy, even if the subject, the ally, or the neutral should by his own conduct have placed himself in a position to be harmed thereby. Stowell himself was openly scornful of the international philanthropists of his own day. Speaking with especial reference to the neutral (Swedish) claim to immunity for their convoyed ships (see above, p. 264), he said :—

> " I am not ignorant, that amongst the loose doctrines which modern fancy, under the various denominations of philosophy and philanthropy, and I know not what, have thrown upon the world, it has been within these last few years advanced, or rather insinuated, that it might be well if such security (as a guarantee of the innocence of goods in an official neutral convoy) were accepted. Upon such unauthorised speculations it is not necessary for me to descant : the law and practice of nations (I include particularly the practice of Sweden when it happens to be belligerent) give them no sort of countenance ; and until that law and practice are new modelled in such a way as may surrender the known and ancient rights of some nations to the present convenience of other nations (which nations may perhaps remember to forget them when they happen to be themselves belligerent) no reverence is due to them, they are the elements of that system, which, if it is consistent, has for its real purpose an entire abolition of capture in war—that is, in other words, to change the nature of hostility, as it has ever existed amongst mankind, and to introduce a state of things not yet seen in the world, that of a military war and a commercial peace. If it were fit that such a state should be introduced, it is at least necessary that it should be introduced in an avowed and intelligible manner." (57)

In Stowell's day, moreover, it may be assumed that a severe attitude in the prize court would have been deemed the barest justice to the gallant officers and men in the Royal Navy, part of whose recompense came from prize money, and to privateersmen, who would have been left totally unrewarded apart from the proceeds of condemnation made in prize courts. To enjoy the luxury of "philanthropic" decisions at the immediate expense of the navy and privateersmen, and at the ultimate cost of the nation's effort in war, could hardly have been an ideal for an English lawyer of the eighteenth century. The events of the war of 1914-1918 indicate that, even when that immediate stimulus which arises out of a fear of doing injustice to the combatants has been removed, considerations of the possibility of damage to the national cause still weigh

CHAP. IX.

heavily against "philanthropy." As evidence of the general feeling in the England of Lord Stowell's day concerning the importance of prize condemnation, James Stephen, who practised in the Court of Prize Appeal (the Judicial Committee) may be quoted:—

> "Let us give full credit to our gallant officers, for that disinterested patriotism, and that love of glory, which ought to be the mainsprings of military character, and which they certainly possess in the most eminent degree. But it would be romantic and absurd to suppose that they do not feel the value of that additional encouragement, which His Majesty and the legislature hold out to them, in giving them the benefit of the captures they make. What else is there to enable the veteran naval officer to enjoy in the evening of his life the comforts of an easy income; the father to provide for his children; or the husband for an affectionate wife? . . . As to the common seamen and mariners, the natural motives of dislike to the naval service are in their breasts far more effectively combated by the hope of prize money, than by all the other inducements that are or can be proposed to them. The nautical character is peculiarly of a kind to be influenced by such dazzling, but precarious, prospects."

It might be feared that severity in condemning nationals, allies, or neutrals for conducting an export trade outwards mainly in British commodities to enemy colonies might result in vital damage to British trade. New enemies might declare war, and British trade end by lacking all carriers. Not so at all, asserted the confident Stephen. "The expansive force of British commerce was great enough to overcome all obstacles if neutral advantages were but removed. You might often capture the carriers of it and condemn their cargoes; but the effect would be but to raise the price upon the enemy, and the difference would go into the pockets of your seamen. The prize goods themselves would find their way from your colonies into hostile territory." Could a prize court need more encouraging assurance of the general beneficence of its acts of condemnation?

Enemy Character.—The steady pressure of the captor or privateering interest for the inclusion of as wide a range of property as possible within the circle of spoilable things is disclosed by a brief study of the phrase "enemy character." Thus Bynkershoek, followed by Lord Stowell in the case of the *Harmony*,[58] took up the position that a neutral domiciled in the enemy country had an enemy character, and that his goods therefore were capturable. Story (1779-1845), the learned American judge, advanced the principle [59] yet one stage further when he permitted the captor to possess himself of the total goods of the members of a partnership which operated from the enemy country, though one of its members were admittedly of neutral domicile. Story was of the opinion that, at least in respect of his share in the partnership, this merchant with neutral domicile was to be accounted a spoilable enemy. The eighteenth and nineteenth centuries are full of decisions which indicate that Anglo-American, in contradistinction to Continental, opinion was, in the matter of discriminating between neutral and enemy trade, laying stress upon the significance of domicile. This is demonstrated in many different ways and from several lines of approach.

In the case of the *Vrow Elizabeth,* [60] Lord Stowell refused to allow a neutral German to go behind the Dutch flag flown by his ship in order to prove his ownership, while in the case of the *Tobago* [61] he laid it down that neutral and even British liens and mortgages on captured enemy ships, though they had been executed before the war, would not be recognised as innocent. Though a neutral, and still more a British, subject was thus refused the right to go behind the enemy flag to prove his ownership or interest, the captor was later allowed to go behind the neutral flag to seize and appropriate anything of enemy taint or interest. Story went behind the neutral Portuguese flag and, having proved the owners to be of English domicile, awarded the ship to the captors; [62] while Lushington committed himself to the position that those sections of the neutral ship which belonged to the enemy could be separated from the others and awarded to the captors. [63] It is comprehensible that an observer could say that while foreign tribunals were concerning themselves with the plain fact of nationality, Anglo-American judges had noses so sensitive that they were complicating the matter beyond all understanding by ideas of domicile.

For even further extensions of enmity were recognised by the Anglo-American prize courts. Thus a neutral subject domiciled in a neutral country but with estates acquired by inheritance in an enemy colony, and seeking to import the produce of them into Europe, lost his goods, which were awarded to the captors. He was to be accounted an enemy so far as his estates were concerned. [64] Further, a neutral merchant who entered into a contract with an enemy government in pursuance of which he bought their tobacco and undertook to ship to them flour, dry goods, and money, was

CHAP. IX. to be accounted tainted with enemy character, and the goods moving in virtue of the contract were held to be spoilable, even though not actually owned by him or by the enemy government at the time of the capture. In truth, belligerents were reluctant to allow still other types of property to escape them. Especially was this the case with stuffs which, as above, were passing from the neutral to the enemy or from the enemy to the neutral, and were captured in transit; and the decision of this case, that of the *Sally*, by the British Court of Appeal in prize in 1795, was of wide-reaching application and was so applied. American merchants shipping grain to France for eventual transfer to the French government under a contract had retained ownership of the cargo, because under their contract they were only to be paid on actual delivery. The court, however, accepted the point of view of the captors, and ruled "that property going to be delivered in the enemy's country, and under a contract to become the property of the enemy immediately on arrival, if taken *in transitu*, is to be considered as enemies' property." (65) Nevertheless, when an enemy gave an opening to belligerent claims by undertaking to retain any interest in goods in course of shipment to a neutral country, it was very unlikely that the belligerent would be content to apply his own thesis and decide that the goods were neutral. He must have it both ways. Thus Story, in the United States Circuit Court of Massachusetts, in the case of the *San José Indiano*, refused to consider the remission of belligerent right in a case in which goods were being carried from an English house in Liverpool for transfer after landing to L., a neutral merchant of Brazilian domicile. And Lord Stowell in the *Jan Frederick* (66) had already condemned a Dutch cargo, transferred by the Dutch owners to neutrals, partly because the transfer had still to be completed by an endorsement of bills of lading, and partly on the more general ground that transfers, made *in transitu* by merchants from fear of imminent hostilities, defeated belligerent rights at sea.

Another class of property over which belligerents have never shown willingness to resign their rights is that of ships transferred from their enemy to neutrals either *imminente* or *flagrante bello*. Some belligerents have allowed no proof to overcome their right of capture, permitting this only to a complete and unconditional transfer effected to a neutral before the outbreak of war. This has been the case with France and Russia prior at least to the Declaration of London. British theory however was, surprisingly perhaps, not quite so strict. It allowed a transfer of merchant vessels even *flagrante bello*, provided the transfer were complete, left no enemy interest outstanding, and were not made merely *in transitu* by an exchange of papers but by the new owner taking *bona fide* possession. The greater laxity in this direction is accounted for, possibly, by the stricter view of enemy character taken as a whole by the British courts, so that what was conceded could be guarded from abuse. Thus Lord Stowell showed, in his condemnation of the *Sechs Geschwistern* (67) and the *Jemmy*,(68) that he could scrutinise such a transfer in a most penetrating fashion. British practice in the Crimean War was perhaps more considerate of neutral interests, for it allowed a neutral's cash payment of only one-third of the purchase price, and his subsequent payments made out of the earnings of the ship, not to debar the claim to neutral ownership.(69) Lord Stowell had refused to consider that any transfer at all, however good the faith, was possible in the case of the *Minerva*, an armed Dutch East-Indiaman.(70) He took the ground (which would have been equally applicable in the case of the ordinary merchant ship transferred) that the enemy could not be permitted "so far to rescue himself from the disadvantage into which he had fallen as to have the value at least (of the ship) restored to him by a neutral purchaser."

CHAP. IX.

A further extension of enemy character to the neutral was made in case of his acceptance of enemy licence to enter into any specific trade which had been closed to him in time of peace. When the French licensed Dutch ships to call at their colonial ports in the war of 1756, the English, asserting that such permission was given only that the enemy might be able the better to provision his colonies and to export from them his tropical products, condemned the ships as having become virtually incorporated in the French merchant marine. In 1806 the British prize courts finally determined upon the condemnation of the neutrals who should undertake even an indirect colonial trade for the enemy. The whole of a neutral convoy from which the belligerent had experienced resistance to his search proceedings was held condemnable in the case of the *Maria*.(71) In the case of the *Vigilantia* (72) Lord Stowell committed himself to the dictum that

> "it is a known and established rule with respect to a vessel, that if she is navigating under the pass of a foreign country, she is considered as bearing the national character of that nation under whose pass she sails."

CHAP. IX.

The acceptance of a French pass would therefore be held to condemn a ship as French even though, after the period of maritime reprisal had begun in 1806, the only safe course for a neutral ship desiring to navigate to France was to obtain in advance some assurance from the French authorities. The Danish tribunals in 1810 held that American ships in the Russo-American trade which had availed themselves of British convoy were good prize with their cargoes, although such convoy had been accepted not to invalidate Danish rights of search but to protect their ships, in no way incorporated into the English mercantile marine, against French aggression under the continental system.(73) Finally, Napoleon in the Milan decree of 17th December 1807 undertook to denationalise and to invest with English nationality—and consequently to confiscate—every neutral ship which should have submitted to British search or should have fulfilled the British requirement to touch at a British port or should have paid any tax to the British government.

Trading with the Enemy.—The range of spoil in maritime war was increased from the goods of nationals or subjects captured in course of export to or import from the enemy. In the eighteenth century the Admiralty court had, the Common Law Courts had not, held trading with the enemy to be illegal. The more lax view has been attributed by Dr. McNair to the influence of Lord Mansfield. The turn of the tide in the Common Law Courts seems to have come after 1800. Lord Stowell took the strictest stand upon this position, and quoted Bynkershoek in his support :—

> " From the nature of war it was not to be doubted that relations between enemies ceased, and that by no special declaration but from the fact of war itself."

Accordingly, subjects were prohibited from trading with the enemy. In the *Hoop* (74) the following words were uttered by Lord Stowell :—

> " It has been the established rule of the law of this court, confirmed by the judgment of the Supreme Court, that a trading with the enemy, except under royal licence, subjects the property to confiscation—and the most eminent persons of the law sitting in the Supreme Court have uniformly sustained such judgments."

In the case of the *Hoop*, though Lord Stowell allowed the existence of hardships which would be caused by the decision, he still proceeded to condemnation. In the later case of the

Nelly (75) the British prize court was urged at its discretion to decree that a subject's goods taken for trading with the enemy should not be condemned as prize to the captor but to the Crown—there being some hope of royal bounty in such a case. The court decided, however, that the subject was to be considered *pro hac vice* as an enemy, and that his goods became, therefore, condemnable to the captor in the ordinary way as though they had been enemy goods. Trading with the enemy, as has been pointed out, was nevertheless permitted under a system of licences issued by the government which in the days of the nominal blockade of the Continent reached an enormous total. Thus in the year 1809 sixteen thousand licences were granted, and in the year 1811 eight thousand. The prize court was apt, however, to scrutinise these licences very carefully. If a British subject had departed in any considerable measure from the terms of his licence he was in danger of finding his ship and goods condemned to the captors. Thus in the case of the *Jonge Arend* (76) a British subject, sailing under Prussian colours, was condemned because the holders of the licence were only entitled to trade in neutral bottoms. In the case of the *Cosmopolite* (77) goods not provided for in the enumeration for which licence was given were condemned at once, while the whole cargo, not being brought in within the three months specifically mentioned in the licence, was condemned subject to appeal. The Berlin and Milan decrees may have raised doubt in simple minds as to whether it were not positively meritorious to defy Napoleon by trading with the enemy.

Presumption of Enemy Character.—Goods found carried in enemy ships at their capture were assumed to be enemy until a neutral claimant assumed the onus of proof and defeated the presumption. In 1914 the British prize court declined to admit that a special mechanical contrivance, affixed to a ship by a neutral company and carried by that ship for a yearly rent, could be separated in law from the enemy ship and treated as neutral. Only "neutral merchandise" was protected by existing International Law from the character of enmity.

Colonial Trade and the Rule of the War of 1756.—There are certain extensions of belligerent measures which hardly fall under any previous heading. In a natural desire to injure the enemy the belligerent caught at any moral or legal justification, and had to find it wherever it could be found, for often enough, as has been shown, he might

CHAP. IX. be bound to the leading maritime nations by commercial treaties, which enjoined tenderness for the other contracting party's commerce with the enemy, except where it flagrantly violated the law of blockade or the rules which forbade the carriage of contraband. It could be argued by a belligerent that any export of his enemy's raw products or manufactured goods was of advantage to him. If a neutral Power undertook merely to satisfy his own requirements from the enemy's goods, and sent a ship to effect the transport after he had acquired the ownership of them, it was of course unobjectionable. The neutral was engaged in nothing more objectionable than the supplying of his own needs. If, on the other hand, the neutral was engaged in carrying the goods of enemy origin not directly into his own country, and for his own use, but between country and country, he was, or could be argued to be, in some measure promoting the enemy's export, and was culpable. This point of view lay behind Articles 2 to 6 of the French *ordonnance* of 1704 and the similar articles of the French *ordonnance* of 1744. Article 2 forbade the French privateers to stop neutral vessels which came from any port, even enemy, laden with goods obtained in that country and the property of neutrals—provided, however, that these vessels were returning directly home. Article 3 permitted the seizure from neutral ships of goods of enemy growth or manufacture in cases in which the ship had left an allied or neutral port in one country, and was sailing with a cargo of such goods for an allied or neutral port in another country. Article 4 permitted seizure and confiscation of goods of enemy growth or manufacture which were leaving a neutral or allied port for an enemy destination. In all these cases there was the necessary assumption that the goods, though of enemy origin, were neutral-owned. Enemy-owned goods were treated in the *ordonnance* of 1744 as confiscable without any question raised as to the port of their lading or consignment: while under that of 1704 the smallest packet of enemy goods in a cargo was held apparently to procure the confiscation of the ship and its entire cargo. Finally, where a neutral ship had left an enemy port, having put on board there its entire cargo, or part of it, and was proceeding to any other destination than that of its own country, whether that destination were that of an ally, friend, or enemy of France, the ship and cargo were regarded as good prize.

The English " rule of the war of 1756," though applied in

the colonial field, was dictated by a belligerent sentiment of a similar nature to that responsible for this significant French *ordonnance*. Mr. Mootham in the *British Year Book of International Law for 1927* has traced the previous history of this rule and its relation to the doctrine of continuous voyage. The French colonial ports, in the true spirit of the eighteenth-century colonial economy, had been closed to all but French ships. At the outbreak of the war of 1755 the maritime supremacy of England threatened to end the valuable export of colonial materials from the French colonies to Europe, and to prevent the provisioning of those colonies from Europe. In these circumstances the French Crown was prepared to admit neutral Dutch ships under limited licence to share in the West Indian trade. The British Admiralty thereupon undertook to seize, and the prize court to condemn, such Dutch ships as should engage themselves in the French colonial trade. Marriott,(78) in his *Case of the Dutch Ships Considered*, justified as follows the English action against which Holland protested vigorously :— CHAP. IX.

> " In the present war between England and France the subjects of Holland have no right to cover the property of the enemy of England, going to, or coming from, the colonies of that enemy directly ; nor indirectly to do it, through the medium of the Dutch colonies : nor to carry to the colonies of France directly, nor indirectly, any commodities, although neutral property, which have a tendency to support the enemy."

When Dutchmen at least nominally acquired the ownership of the French colonial products they " covered " the enemy's property directly : when their exports of provisions outwards, or imports of colonial products inwards, were made nominally to and from the Dutch West Indies, they " covered " the enemy's property indirectly : their provisions would support the enemies' resistance in the West Indies to the menace of English military efforts. Lord Stowell, in the case of the *Immanuel*,(79) voiced belligerent feelings especially strongly :—

> " Such colonies are dependent for their existence, as colonies, on foreign supplies : if they cannot be supplied and defended, they must fall to the belligerent, of course ; and if the belligerent chooses to apply his means to such an object, what right has a third party, perfectly neutral, to step in and prevent the execution ? No existing interest of his is affected by it : he can have no right to apply to his own use the beneficent consequences of the mere act of the belligerent, and to say, 'True it is you have, by force of arms, forced such places out of the

CHAP. IX.

exclusive possession of the enemy . . . supplies shall be sent, and their products shall be exported: you have lawfully destroyed his monopoly, but you shall not be permitted to possess it yourself: we insist to share the fruits of your victories: and your blood and treasure have been expended, not for your own interest but for the common benefit of others.'"

In 1793, when the French threw open all their colonial trade to neutral traders, the first instruction given to British naval commanders was "to stop and detain for lawful adjudication all vessels laden with goods the produce of any French colony, or carrying provision, or other supplies, for the use of any such colony." The objections, however, of the United States had to be met by the modification of January 1794, which enjoined seizure only when vessels laden with French colonial goods were "coming directly from any port of the said islands to Europe." By the Instructions of 1798 the European neutrals also were by implication permitted a direct trade with the colonies of British enemies. It was still, however, regarded as an illegal trade when one neutral carried from enemy colonies neutral-owned goods for a neutral destination not in his own country, or when he attempted carriage between the enemy colony and its metropolis. In the peculiar conditions of the colonial war of 1793-1812 between Great Britain and her enemies, the United States was in a better position than other neutrals to undertake carriage of colonial goods for European neutrals, but especially for the enemies of England. Accordingly, the device of the United States to possess themselves of this trade was to import colonial goods into the States, land them, pay customs duty even, and then to take the merchandise out of their warehouses for re-export to Europe. James Stephen [80] in his *War in Disguise* bitterly deplored the relaxation by the British of the strict rule of 1756. He drew the blackest picture of the consequences. French and Spanish colonies were prosperous despite the disappearance of the flags of those two nationalities from the high seas; the Continental was beginning to supplant the British manufacturer; the enemy, since the neutral did his carrying trade for him, had more men and ships available for his privateering; British insurance and freight rates were very high in consequence; British sailors were receiving high wages from the neutral, who was making high profits without risk, and so were deserting the British flag. Throughout Stephen's work there breathes at once the desire to injure the enemy to the utmost, mortification that British efforts should tend to neutral prosperity, and the conviction that neutrals could properly be denied any right to benefit from British efforts. Benefit should in his judgment be reserved to Great Britain alone. The trade of this character, as conducted by the United States, was speedily to be condemned. In 1805 Stephen had quoted with approval the decision in the case of the *Essex*. In 1806 the decision of the Lords Commissioners of Appeals in Prize in the case of the *William* showed firm resolve to suppress the fraudulent American re-export of the colonial goods of the enemy of England.

Port-to-Port Trade on a Belligerent Coast.—The Powers of the two Armed Neutralities had in their conventions inserted an article which, if liberally interpreted, would have abolished not merely the British claim to prevent neutrals from undertaking a colonial trade, thrown open merely for the period of the war, but even a claim on the part of any belligerent to prevent a neutral from undertaking the enemy's coasting trade. The relevant clause ran :—

> " That all vessels may navigate freely from port to port and along the coasts of the nations at war."

It is doubtful, however, whether the Baltic Powers intended under this article to press for more than the rights of their ships to call from port to port along a belligerent coast without incurring the danger of conviction in a prize court. A Danish or a Swedish ship might well for its own purposes desire to call first at Brest for some trade, then at Nantes, at Rochelle, and at Bordeaux. If it took on board at Brest some goods for eventual export to Denmark, its legal position on its course to the further French ports was in need of protection against arbitrary and even outrageous detentions. The irksome nature of belligerent restraint of neutral trade in this matter may be illustrated by two examples. In 1691 the Dutch,(81) who were at war with France, insisted that any Danish ship which had taken French goods on board should not then sail to other French ports but should make straight home for Denmark. By a later agreement of the same year Danish ships on an outward journey to France were only to proceed from one French port to another in the event of an inability to sell their whole cargo at the first port. Similarly, the British government informed the Prussian Resident in London in 1711 that Prussian ships outward bound for France were only to carry goods of Prussian or English origin ; and

CHAP. IX. that no Prussian ship would be allowed to sail from one port of France to another except in ballast. Where a Prussian ship, however, had failed to sell all its cargo at its first French port, it might go on to a second French port to sell the remainder, provided that it carried no French goods. A ship of Stockholm or St. Petersburg was very unlikely to desire to undertake a voyage from Bordeaux to Martinique or St. Domingo, whatever might be the case with a ship of Rotterdam. Further, it is unlikely that the Armed Neutrals ever desired to interpret their article so as to cover the case of a Danish ship undertaking French coasting trade—such as, say, the transport of wine from Bordeaux to Brest. Certainly Russia and Denmark in 1801 were willing to adopt in their agreement with England of that year an emendation of the clause in question, which read :—

> " That the ships of the neutral Power may navigate freely to the ports and upon the coasts of the nation at war."

This did not embrace in its scope the colonial trade. In the year 1806 the British and French reprisals and counter-reprisals began to menace more and more departments of neutral trade. Napoleon's decree of Berlin undertook simultaneously three objects : the blockade of England, the " self-blockade " of the Napoleonic *bloc* of states, and the confiscation of all goods of English origin. Belligerent venom had never been pushed further.

NOTES

(1) Hautefeuille, *Des Droits et des Devoirs des Nations Neutres*, Titre x. (ed. 1858), "Transport des Propriétés des Belligérants par les Navires Neutres et des Propriétés Neutres par les Navires Belligérants."

(2) Quoted by Ortolan in his *Diplomatie de la Mer*, bk. iii. cap. 5 (ed. 1856), from Pardessus, *Collection des lois maritimes antérieures au 18me siècle* (6 vols., 1818-1845).

(3) Ortolan, vol. ii. p. 111 (ed. 1856), from the *Lettres et négociations de Jean de Witt.*

(4) Ortolan (ed. 1858), bk. iii. cap. 5.

(5) Roscoe's *History of the Prize Court*, p. 36, based on the collection " Law and Custom of the Sea," issued by the Navy Records Society.

(6) See in Scott's *Armed Neutralities*—the Russo-Danish Convention of 9th July 1780, Art. 2, and the Russo-Swedish Convention of 1st August, Art. 2.

(7) Satow has printed some of the documents in his *Silesian Loan and Frederick the Great* (1915).

(8) Satow, *Silesian Loan*, p. 121.

(9) Quoted by Scott, *Armed Neutralities*, from *Annual Register*, 1807, p. 774.

(10) On this subject see Phillimore's *Commentaries* (ed. 1885), vol. iii. p. 354.

(11) Phillimore's *Commentaries*, vol. iii. p. 355 (ed. 1885).

(12) The whole subject of the reversal of English maritime policies in 1856 is treated at great length in Piggott's *Declaration of Paris*.

(13) In the famous *Traité des Prises, ou principes de la jurisprudence française concernant les prises qui se font sur mer, relativement aux dispositions tant de l'ordonnance de la marine du mois d'août 1681 que des arrêts du conseil, ordonnances et règlements* (1758-1760).

(14) 22 George III. c. 25.

(15) Franklin also, when he thought Captain Cook's return from his last voyage imminent, issued a circular letter to American cruisers enjoining them to do Cook no injury, but on the contrary "to afford Captain Cook and his people as common friends to mankind all the assistance in your power" (March 10, 1779).

(16) Hautefeuille's section on Contraband is of considerable importance. Twiss's chapter is one of the most useful to be found in English.

(17) Cf. Nys, *Le droit international*, vol. iii. p. 628.

(18) The nearest analogy which can be drawn to a mediaeval contraband traffic with the Saracen is the illicit supply of arms to native races in rebellion against a European Power. Alas that private traders in this age have been as ready to flout the provisions of the International Arms Convention as their predecessors were to brave the censure of the Church!

(19) Robinson's *Collectanea Maritima*, p. 136.

(20) 2 C. Rob. 174-185.

(21) Quoted by Twiss from Dumont's *Traités*, vol. v. ii. p. 480.

(22) Robinson's *Collectanea Maritima*, p. 63.

(23) Pratt's *Law of Contraband of War* (1856).

(24) Satow's *Silesian Loan*, pp. 125-128.

(25) See Twiss (ed. 1884), pt. ii. pp. 265-266.

(26) 1 C. Rob. 372.

(27) 1 Adm. Rep., p. 189.

(28) 6 C. Rob. 126.

(29) 4 C. Rob. 68.

(30) 6 C. Rob. 440.

(31) Phillipson's *Wheaton*, p. 735.

(32) A full account of the debate is given in vol. i. of Scott's *The Hague Peace Conferences*, pp. 711-716.

(33) See *Official Documents on the Declaration of London*, issued by the Carnegie Endowment (1919), with an introduction by Elihu Root.

(34) For the whole subject of the British attitude towards contraband, see Garner's *International Law during the World War*, vol. ii. cap. 32. Cf. Smith and Sibley, *International Law of Russo-Japanese War*.

(35) The section in Westlake's *International Law* dealing with blockade contains a good account of the earliest history of blockade.

(36) Reported by Bynkershoek, and translated from the *Quaestiones* by Westlake.

(37) See Robinson's *Collectanea Maritima*, pp. 158-166.

(38) Hautefeuille (ed. 1858), vol. ii. pp. 249-250.

(39) Hautefeuille on the authority of Flassan's *Histoire de la Diplomatie française*, vol. vii. p. 64.

CHAP. IX.

(40) See Hautefeuille (ed. 1858), vol. ii. p. 199, note 1.

(41) De Martens, *Recueil*, vol. vi. p. 251. (42) Art. 20.

(43) The whole subject of the system of licences is treated in E. F. Heckshers *Continental System*.

(44) See Garner's *International Law during the Great War*, vol. ii. p. 318.

(45) See Falcke's *Blocus pacifique* (Leipzig, 1919).

(46) Piggott's *Declaration of Paris* has been closely followed in parts of this section.

(47) Roscoe's *History of the English Prize Court*, largely based as it is on the documents published by the Selden Society (*Select Pleas of the Court of Admiralty*) and by the Navy Records Society (*Law and Custom of the Sea*), is invaluable.

(48) Roscoe has a life of Lord Stowell which helps to recreate the life of Doctors' Commons.

(49) *The Fox* (1811), Edwards, 311.

(50) *The Zamora*; 2 British and Colonial Prize Cases, i.

(51) *Lloyd's Report of Prize Cases*, iv.

(52) Professor Pearce Higgins in his *Droit de Visite et de Capture dans la Guerre maritime* has defined modern ship's papers (*papiers de bord*) as follows: register, muster-roll, log, charter-party, manifest, bills of lading, bill of sale, bill of health, clearance (p. 48).

(53) Wynne, *Leoline Jenkins*, vol. ii. p. 730.

(54) See Satow's *The Silesian Loan and Frederick the Great*.

(55) Hill, *History of European Diplomacy*, vol. iii. pp. 565-567. The quotation from Bernstorff is from the same source.

(56) *Maria*, 1 C. Rob. 350. (57) *Ibid.*, p. 362.

(58) 2 C. Rob. 322-342.

(59) American case, 1814, Circ. Court Mass., *San José Indiano*.

(60) 1803, 5 C. Rob. 2. (61) 1804, 5 C. Rob. 218.

(62) 1814, 2 Gall 268, 311. (63) 1854, Spinks, 54.

(64) *Phoenix*, 1803, 5 C. Rob. 20.

(65) *Sally*, 1795, 3 C. Rob. 300-303.

(66) 5 C. Rob. 128.

(67) 4 *ibid.*, 100-103. (68) *Ibid.*, 31-32.

(69) *Ariel*. Reversal of prize-court decision on appeal.

(70) 1857, 11 P.C., 119.

(71) 1799, 1 C. Rob. 340-379. (72) *Ibid.*, 13.

(73) Wheaton (6th ed.), 594-606.

(74) 1799, 1 C. Rob. 196-219. (75) 1800, *ibid.*, 219.

(76) 1803, 5 *ibid.*, 14. (77) 4 *ibid.*, 8-16.

(78) Marriott, *Case of the Dutch Ships Considered*, November 1759. In 1604 the Venetian ambassador had acquiesced in the condemnation of two ships by the Dutch for engaging in the closed trade with Spain, then at war with Holland. The first English case is that of the *Ceres* in 1744.

(79) 2 C. Rob. 186.

(80) James Stephen, *War in Disguise* (1805); Madison, *An Examination of the British Doctrine* (1805); Pinkney, *The Memorial of the Merchants and Traders of the City of Baltimore* (in Wheaton's *Life, Writings, and Speeches of William Pinkney*).

(81) Instanced by Satow in his *Silesian Loan*, pp. 127-128.

CHAPTER X

CHANGES OF NATIONALITY

Plebiscites—Option of Individuals.

Plebiscites.—Before the end of the eighteenth century it was regarded as axiomatic that states possessed complete right to acquire territory by cession or consent from those defeated, and, along with the territory, an unquestionable claim upon the allegiance of the inhabitants who continued to dwell on it. A slight modification was indeed being introduced in the international technique of annexing states by the growing habit of inserting in the treaty of cession a clause which should provide a right of withdrawal to all such as should be unwilling to assume the duties of allegiance to their new lord. The special position reserved for the French Canadians in the Franco-British Treaty of 1763 furnishes a good example of the practice. The custom did not, of course, guarantee that those who remained in the territory approved the change of rule. Still earlier historical instances are to be found in which the inhabitants of ceded territories either refused to recognise, or protested against, the cession effected by the rulers. When Louis IX. ceded some of the old Angevin lands of the kings of England to Henry III. there was a formal protest from the nobles of the ceded provinces. Similarly, the people of Guienne in the reign of Richard II. protested against their separation from the kingdom of England. When Francis I. of France, who was pledged by the Treaty of Madrid in 1526 to the cession of Burgundy to the Spanish Crown, declined to carry out the terms of his agreement, he strengthened his position by summoning the estates of Burgundy to declare the invalidity of the transaction.

When Grotius,[1] Pufendorff,[2] and Vattel[3] discussed the question of cession they did not make it inadmissible for a prince to receive a cession except with the consent of the inhabitants of the ceded territory. They put the onus of

CHAP. X.

obtaining such consent on the ceding not on the annexing prince. It was apparently the men of the French Revolution who were the first to proclaim the doctrine that annexation could only be justified by the explicit consent of the affected population. The point of departure was the decree of the National Assembly of May 1790, which sought to control tightly the executive's power over the military operations. It provided that when the executive should have undertaken an unjust aggression those responsible would be punished, the operation stopped, and a declaration made by the National Assembly that the French nation had renounced wars of conquest and attempts upon the liberty of peoples. The state to which the French first applied their new doctrine was the papal enclave of the county of Venaissin and the city and state of Avignon.

The Avignonese enclave had been papal territory from mediaeval times and had submitted to ecclesiastical government with exemplary patience until the outbreak of the French Revolution. By June 1790 the city of Avignon had resolved to shake off the last vestiges of papal authority and asked for union with France. In the same month a similar step was taken by the Venaissin revolutionaries. In France itself the more violent members of the Assembly had from 1789 been contemplating the annexation of these territories. It says much for the fairness of mind of the National Assembly that it repeatedly refused, in the course of the years 1790 and 1791, to proceed to such a step. Events, however, were to force it during the latter year. A fierce internecine feud had broken out in the papal territories which for varied reasons it was desirable to see assuaged. Thus, although the Assembly had only recently voted down a proposal for annexation by 487 votes as against 316, it resolved by decree of 25th May to despatch mediators into the disturbed districts. These arranged as one of the conditions of peace that an electoral assembly should meet to express the desire of the country as to its future political status. After approval had been obtained from Paris and the country somewhat pacified, the electoral assembly gathered at Bédarrides. The representatives of seventy-one communes out of ninety-eight were present: fifty-two, with a population of one hundred and one thousand, voted for France. In nine of these communes it may be mentioned that French garrisons were stationed. In nineteen, with a population of thirty-one thousand, a vote was obtained for the continuance of the rule of the Pope. In eleven of these places there were French garrisons. From contemporary reports it seems that communal rather than individual voting was natural to the constituencies, and that the test was a fair one. The decree of annexation passed on 14th September 1791 put repeated emphasis on the wish for annexation by the affected citizens.

These papal territories had in the first instance been occupied to impose peace upon warring factions. Savoy and Nice were occupied in 1792 during a war with a coalition of princes. General Montesquiou writing to the Minister of War on 25th September, after mentioning his enthusiastic reception in Savoy, and the predisposition there towards a revolution, asked what attitude he should assume towards such suggestions as the conversion of Savoy into the eighty-fourth department of France, or alternatively into a republic under French protection. The debate in the Convention on this letter which took place on 28th September revealed a sharp cleavage of opinion. Desmoulins was desirous of leaving the Savoyards a complete liberty of choice, Lacroix wanted to scoop advantage for France out of the situation, Danton was firm in declaiming against permission to a liberated people "to furnish themselves with new tyrants to fight against." The commissioners from the Convention to the army of the Alps on 6th October summoned the communes of Savoy to elect each a deputy "who should repair to Chambéry for a meeting on 21st October." On 22nd October it appeared that in the province of Carronge out of sixty-four communes forty-two had instructed their deputies to vote for union with France, and twenty-one had left them unfettered by any instruction. In Chablais all ninety-five communes had expressed a desire for union with France, as had the seventy-nine of Faucigny and the hundred and sixteen of Genevois; while overwhelming majorities in the same sense had been obtained in Maurienne, Savoy and Tarentaise. The Assembly forthwith proceeded to depose the house of Savoy and empowered a deputation to journey to Paris to request formal annexation, a request which was granted in the decree of 27th November. Proceedings in the county of Nice were after the same manner, and annexation was voted on 31st January 1793.

The plebiscites hitherto discussed seem to have been effected without an undue measure of French intimidation. Very different, however, was the case in the Belgian Nether-

CHAP. X. lands, Liége and Rhenish Germany, which were also overrun at the end of 1792. In the Netherlands there seems little doubt but that the populations were heartily opposed to the annexations to France except in the Liége districts. Even there eighty thousand citizens abstained, and of the nineteen and a half thousand (out of a total poll of twenty-one and a half thousand) votes given for union with France some fourteen thousand were given with a limiting condition in regard to the currency of *assignats*. In other parts of the Netherlands in which voting took place only a relatively small proportion of the citizens presented themselves at the booth, and the proceedings were dominated by French commissioners and local members of the Jacobin clubs who acted under the protection of French troops. If a free national convention had been permitted it is almost certain that there would have been no majority of delegates for annexation by the French republic.

In the case of the main Rhenish plebiscite, that of the Rheno-German people, force, in the shape of imprisonment of old office-holders and clergy, was frequently employed, and threats were made in an attempt to muster people at the polls. Nevertheless, in a town like Mayence only three hundred and forty-five people voted, in Worms two hundred and fifty, in Speyer three hundred and forty-two. The deputies chosen in these primary elections gathered on 17th March as a national convention of free Germans, and on 21st March asked for union with France. This was accorded by the decree of the convention dated 30th March 1793.

The next group of plebiscites worthy of attention occurred in Italy in 1848. There had been revolt in the kingdom of Lombardo-Venezia, in Reggio, Modena, Parma, and Piacenza, all communities under the influence of Austria. The provisional and revolutionary government in each of these was faced by the same problem, whether or not to throw in its lot with the most vigorous native Italian state, the kingdom of Sardinia, on whose army was their main reliance. The Sardinians had scrupulously to refrain not merely from annexation proceedings, but from any kind of movement in that direction. Both in the face of Europe, the settlement of which by the Congress of Vienna was bound to be disturbed, and in the face of all Italy outside the Sardinian kingdom, a valid moral title could only be established if it were shown to rest on the spontaneous suffrage of the inhabitants of the territories involved. The provisional government in Lombardy opened registers in every parish, and a vote was taken between the alternative policies of an immediate union with the Sardinian state and a delay of the decision until after the war. The voting was appointed to take place throughout seven days; and all males over twenty-one years of age were to vote under the supervision of the parish priest and two civil representatives. The result as declared on 8th June was a total of five hundred and sixty-one thousand for, six hundred and eighty-one against, immediate union with the Sardinian state. In the Venetian half of the Lombardo-Venezian kingdom departmental committees opened registers at Padua, Vicenza, Treviso and Rovigo, and forced the Venetian provisional government to convoke a special assembly of deputies, to consider whether a decision should be taken immediately as to the form of government, and if so, whether the Venetian territories were to remain a separate state or to join with Piedmont-Sardinia. On 6th July the Venetian assembly voted, by one hundred and thirty against three, for an immediate decision, and, by one hundred and twenty-seven against six, for the union proposed. In Parma the voters were allowed to express their opinion in communal assemblies, called by the mayors, not only on the question of union with Sardinia, but on such other proposals as "might seem more adapted" to Parma and to Italy. The figures, when collected from the different communes, gave thirty-seven thousand for union with Sardinia, sixteen hundred for the régime of the legitimate duke, Charles II., five hundred and thirty for union with the papal states, and one hundred and fifty-eight for amalgamation with Tuscany. The figures in the associated Duchy of Piacenza ran—thirty-seven thousand for union with Sardinia, sixty-two for union with Lombardo-Venezia, eleven for union with Parma, three hundred and fifty-two for union with the papal states, and ten for union with Tuscany. In the dominions of the Duchy of Modena the lead was taken by the municipalities of Reggio and Modena, where registers were opened for the signature of those who desired union with the Piedmontese and associated provinces. The provisional government, without publishing details of the vote taken in these and other municipalities, asserted the universal desire, as shown by the voting, for union with Sardinia and proceeded to decree it on 29th May.

CHAP. X.

The plebiscites of 1848 were honest expressions of the momentary enthusiasm produced by a national rising against the control of Italian destinies by the hated Austria. In the

CHAP. X. nature of things, however, a plebiscite hurriedly taken in time of war, and by an agitated public, did not afford scope for earnest and sober consideration of the issues at stake. There was in truth much to have been said for the delay of all decision until the hostilities against Austria had been concluded. The Piedmontese monarchy had little experience of government outside its own borders, and any monarchy was regarded with suspicion by republicans of the type of Manin, Mazzini, or Garibaldi. Further, areas traditionally independent, like those of Parma and Modena, were certain in the future to have cause to regret the sacrifice of their political individuality. Yet the issues, monarchy *versus* republic, federalism *versus* unity, were but little discussed and never subjected to a vote.

In 1860 further plebiscites were held in Tuscany, Modena, Parma, Savoy, Nice, Sicily, Naples and the papal states of Bologna, Umbria and the Marches. In Tuscany three hundred and sixty-six thousand voted for union with the monarchy of Victor Emmanuel and some fifteen thousand for the maintenance of a separate state, the only alternative offered to the voters. In Modena, Parma, Bologna, classed together as the royal Emilian provinces, four hundred and twenty-six thousand votes were cast for Victor Emmanuel's constitutional monarchy, and seven hundred and fifty-six for a separate state. In both cases voting was by secret ballot, but the governments had asked for a vote favourable to the union of Italy. In the case of the Marches, the attack on the papal government in the decree which ordered the voting was peculiarly strong, but in Umbria the proclamation was unobjectionable. The question put in these two cases and the answers given were as follows :—

Question		Yes.	No.
Do you wish to form part of the constitutional monarchy of King Victor Emmanuel, constitutional king, and his legitimate descendants ?	Umbria	97,040	350
	The Marches	133,375	1212

The Sicilian plebiscite was upon the proposition, "The Sicilian people wishes Italy one and indivisible under Victor Emmanuel, constitutional king, and his legitimate descendants." The voting showed four hundred thousand for and six hundred against. The Neapolitan voting on the same proposition showed a million and a quarter votes for and ten thousand against. In Savoy and Nice the proposition before the electors was union with the French Empire. By a treaty, made shortly before the voting, the King of Italy had ceded the provinces, so that the electors were denied a choice between France and Italy. Indeed, they were expressly told from both sides that it was their duty to confirm the treaty arrangements already made over their heads, and few pacific means were omitted by French precaution to produce a favourable result. The final figures were one hundred and thirty thousand in Savoy, twenty-five thousand in Nice, for annexation to the Empire, against which verdict there voted only two hundred and thirty-five in Savoy and one hundred and sixty in Nice. In 1866 Venetia was not formally united to Italy until a plebiscite had shown six hundred thousand votes for the union and only sixty-nine against it. In the Roman area a plebiscite on the question of union was taken in 1870, and union was carried by one hundred and thirty thousand against fifteen hundred votes.(4)

The plebiscite was so characteristic a feature of the diplomacy of the third Napoleon that its invention has sometimes been attributed to him. That this is not the case has been indicated, nor was the device to be laid aside after he had vanished from the scene. Indeed, before that, Article 5 of the Peace of Prague, signed between Austria and Prussia in 1866, had made provision for the cession by Prussia to Denmark of the northern districts of Schleswig, provided that the population of them by a free vote expressed this desire. This article, never translated into action for reasons not difficult to penetrate, was denounced in 1878. But there were other plebiscites, such as that held in Norway to adjudicate upon the union with Sweden in 1904, a transaction in which the decision to sever the tie was carried by three hundred thousand to less than two hundred votes.

On the other hand, it is not possible to point out that the hopes of the extreme supporters of the plebiscite have been fulfilled. The career of Bismarck, to take that of no other builders of empire, stood in the way of the fulfilment of the pathetic dream which would make a plebiscite the obligatory preliminary to any transfer of a population. Of such plebiscites as have taken place cynics will be found to say that the holding of them was not settled until those who were responsible for the suggestion were certain of the result. Moreover, in two instances in which nations in legal possession were bound to hold a doubtful plebiscite, both wriggled out of it. Beside the case of Prussia just recorded must be put

CHAP. X. that of Chili, which has persistently delayed the plebiscite in Tacna and Arica which had been provided for in the Treaty of Ancon. And it is not too easy to find the Power, especially since the last Great European War, which has the right to stand as her accuser. Despite the talk of self-determination the transfer of vast territory was carried out in 1919 after the old fashion. Alsace-Lorraine was thus restored to France, part of Tyrol to Italy, West Prussia to Poland, Transylvania and the Dobrudja to Rumania. Nor is this hard to understand. Though it is certain that some of these transfers did not meet with the approval of anything like unanimous sentiment among the peoples affected, only a pedant would imagine that a series of plebiscites could in the then condition of Europe have been carried out in districts of mixed population and religion without disorder, civil war and even anarchy. Even the relatively minor transactions of the kind which were arranged for taxed the diplomatic and administrative resources of the Powers. The plebiscites in Schleswig, in the East Prussian districts and those along the Austrian border, both with Hungary and the Serb-Croat-Slovene state, were only just surmounted without provoking the danger of a general war. In the case of Upper Silesia, where Polish, French, and German national feeling rose high before the settlement, there was considerable danger of such a European calamity before the actual voting took place, and again when the territorial interpretation of its results was taken in hand. A difficult factor has always been provided in the doubt easily thrown upon, and sometimes justifiably attached to, the result in view of the possibility of pressure upon the voters by the authority actually in occupation. Thus, after the war, although the Allied Powers insisted on evacuation by German forces of the districts under test, complaint was raised as to the influence exerted by the German civil servant, whose departure was impracticable if anarchy were to be avoided. The Germans conversely complained of the presence of troops of the allies, though these were often supremely indifferent to the result. The height of feeling aroused by the voting made it impossible to dispense altogether with these. The postponed plebiscite in the Saar may undoubtedly show a great improvement in the technique of the authorities charged with its conduct. But the dynamic character of international politics does not always, perhaps not often, make postponements easy.

Option of Individuals.—Until the nineteenth century

dawned there was not much movement of masses of population from the territories of one sovereign prince into those of another. What mass movement did occur was due not so much to economic as to religious causes. Thus England gained capable artisans from Flanders and France in the sixteenth century; and England, Holland, and Brandenburg gained French Protestants in the seventeenth century after the revocation of the Edict of Nantes. Again, even after 1648, there were notorious instances in which Catholic princes exercised their right of expelling Protestant subjects from their lands. The expulsion from the territory of Salzburg inspired Goethe.(5) In addition to mass movements of this kind, and those specifically provided for on definite occasions by treaty (a matter treated in a previous section), there were individual movements of merchants and others. Occasionally it did occur that a foreign merchant comfortably settled in a great commercial centre of a foreign country would resolve to sever his connection with his native land.

Governments were on principle opposed to emigration from their territories. Those of Kings Philip II. of Spain and Louis XIV.(6) of France threatened severe penalties against subjects who should make the attempt. Alva's government in 1567 forbade all persons, whether native or foreign, to depart from the Netherlands or to send away their property upon pain of death; and prohibited ship masters and waggoners by the threat of similar penalties from assisting their flight.(7) That notable lawyer Sir Leoline Jenkins put with great force the English point of view in the seventeenth century in a letter to Sir William Temple :—

> "No subject of our master's (we 'll put the case at home) can by the law go out of his dominions without his leave, whether it be expressed or by implication (as in the case of merchants and sea-faring men) granted, but there is a time always supposed for his return; I mean when the king has need of his service; and in the case of a man of quality it is always prefixed. Besides there is no doubt, and we see it is a frequent practice in England, France, etc., to call back the subject from foreign services and residences within a time prefixed, and that upon pain of death; in which case if they return not, the pain is well executed upon them . . . if they afterwards fall into the hand of their master."(8)

Even at the end of the eighteenth century in Austria a royal charter of 1784 forbade emigration and punished the unauthorised emigrant with loss of goods and civil rights,(9)

CHAP. X. while so late as 1864 (*ukase* of the 6th March) Russia forbade emigration and expatriation.

It is interesting to compare this all but instinctive objection of the governments in former times to the departure of their subjects from their dominions with the attitude of the great theoretical writers. Grotius took a statesmanlike view of the matter. He held that it was desirable to distinguish between mass emigration and the emigration of individuals. He thought mass emigration unlawful because it threatened to effect the total dissolution of society. As to individual emigration a country, unless it were deep in debt or engaged in war, might be expected to favour it "for they derive advantages from it in other ways." (10) Vattel, speaking from a purely theoretical standpoint, would have allowed the young on attaining the age of reason to quit their country, if they so desired, provided always that they should recompense for their nurture the society which they were abandoning. The basis for his permission was the fact that all men were born free. After this unfortunate beginning Vattel did make some sound observations. He saw, for example, that in the time of peace "the ends of society were best served by putting no obstacles in the way of citizens" who desired to leave the country for the sake of their business, and who had no objection to returning at their country's need. Again, he held that citizens had a perfect right to leave when subsistence was hard to obtain, the constitution had been violated, or religious intolerance erected into a system.(11) The cautious G. F. de Martens allowed that the state had a right to be informed by the intending emigrant of his intentions; but that, if he were guilty of no crime, owed no debts, and were under no specific obligation to the state, the subject had a complete right to leave it. Nevertheless, this eminent positivist went on to say that the constitutional and administrative law of each country would decide up to what point the state was authorised to restrain the emigration of its natural-born subjects.

Emigrants who left one country and settled in another could only enjoy full civil privileges in the new country after an act of naturalisation, which in general may be said to have been both difficult and costly to obtain up to the nineteenth century. The state, however, of which the emigrant was a natural-born subject was not usually ready to accept the view of the emigrant that he could transfer or had transferred allegiance. Traditionally in England opinion had always been dominated by the feudal attitude towards the question; and this country did not lightly let slip the principle, *nemo potest exuere patriam*. A natural-born subject was held to be for his whole life bound in an indissoluble allegiance, which he could not renounce by his own act; this allegiance rendered him liable to serve the Crown whenever called upon to do so. Lord Grenville, writing on 22nd March 1797 a note to the United States of America, asserted that renunciation by a British subject of his vassalage would be regarded as in high degree a criminal act. In accordance with such a view the English cruisers during the long French wars of the period 1793-1814 considered themselves entitled to remove from American cruisers which they had boarded in search of enemy goods or contraband such British-born sailors as were found, even though these were naturalised Americans.[12] Nor were they without American support in so doing, as can be seen by the case of the *People* v. *Isaac Williams* in 1799. Williams, an American, had become a French citizen and joined the French navy. On his return to the United States in 1794 he was arrested for violation of the laws of neutrality. The Federal Courts held that citizenship was indelible, and Williams was punished. Federal Courts were indeed handing down decisions to the same effect up to 1866. Again, Napoleon, in an imperial decree of 26th August 1811, forbade any Frenchman to accept naturalisation abroad save after special authorisation obtainable in letters-patent, signed by the Emperor himself, countersigned by the Secretary of State, viséed by the Arch-Chancellor, and published in the *bulletin des lois*. Those violating the decree lost all their goods and all rights of succession to property in the eye of the French law. They rendered themselves liable to expulsion if they ventured to return to France, and to rigorous imprisonment for a second attempt to return. Till 1917 the Russian penal code contained two Draconian articles aimed at unauthorised emigration and naturalisation. Article 226 punished a Russian who absented himself from Russia, and did not return on the demand of his government, by the withdrawal of all civic rights and permanent expulsion. Article 325 ordained a similar penalty for Russians who became subjects of other countries.

Just as European states, exporters of men even against their will, were interested in retaining some claim upon those who left their lands, so the states of the New World were interested in freeing them as completely as might be from the

CHAP. X. obligations which attached them to authorities in the Old World. Moreover, the protection of the United States was particularly invoked by those who had left European countries in violation of their military duties, or who did not return to perform them. With regard to these, European states were inclined to insist on the view that subsequent naturalisation in the United States could not be held to free their subjects, if these chose to return, from penalties incurred before the act of naturalisation had taken place. Against this view, which had legal support in the United States, and indeed against the opinion of such weighty American authorities as Wheaton and Story, the executive of the United States elaborated a doctrine of startling scope :—

> "The moment a foreigner becomes naturalised, his allegiance to his native country is severed for ever. He experiences a new political birth. A broad and an impassable line separates him from his native country . . . should he be taken to his native country he returns as an American citizen and in no other character."

So in 1859 wrote the Secretary of State, Mr. Cass, in Washington during a dispute with Prussia.(13)

In the case of the United States of America the persons affected by naturalisation as citizens had deliberately acquired the American national character and had later invoked the rights of United States citizenship against their former rulers. In the case of the Latin-American states there was frequently an embarrassing eagerness on the part of the government to bestow the rights (and duties), the privileges (and penalties) of citizenship upon foreign individuals who showed little active desire for naturalisation. Thus in Uruguay, by the law of 10th September 1829, foreigners married to Uruguayan women and owning land or capital or exercising a profession, industry, or craft were naturalised out of hand, while even for other foreign males three years' residence in the married state or four years in the unmarried conferred legal citizenship.(14) In Venezuela, under a special law of 1855, immigrants were to be presented with a certificate of naturalisation on arrival, and the whole foreign population seems to have been blessed with naturalisation under a decree of 1st December 1865.(15) Again, in Brazil,(16) under a decree as late in date as 1902, the possession of real property, combined with marriage to a Brazilian woman or with the paternity of Brazilian children, tacitly conferred citizenship unless express reservation was made. In most other Latin-

American states, naturalisation, though it involved a definite act on the part of the individual affected, was bestowed comparatively freely. It is possible to see in some of these provisions eagerness to free residents quickly from the possibility of invoking foreign protection, to obtain compensation for the destructive effects of civil war or to reject claims to immunity from a local American demand for military service. In the greater countries, of course, the apprehension is of so much the less force.

It was the constant pressure from the United States, and a friendly desire to meet it where reasonable, which induced the countries of Europe to accept the possibility of easy denationalisation on the part of their subjects. In 1868 and 1869 Prussia, Bavaria, Hesse, Württemberg, Baden, and Belgium signed treaties with the United States by which they undertook to recognise as American citizens such natives of their states as had been absent from home for five years at least and had acquired American nationality. These states, however, retained the right to punish their natives for any deeds done in the country of their origin prior to their naturalisation. Further, if natives who had acquired American citizenship returned and resided at home for two years, they were to fall once more under their old allegiance. The English Naturalisation Act of 1870, coming from the Power which had most trenchantly asserted the doctrine of permanent allegiance, was even more noteworthy. By Article 6 a British subject's acceptance of a foreign nationality caused him to lose his British nationality. These examples set by Great Britain and Germany were extensively copied in other countries.

NOTES

(1) *De jure Belli et Pacis*, bk. ii. cap. vi. sec. 5.

(2) *De jure Naturae et Gentium*, bk. viii. cap. v. sec. 9.

(3) *Le droit des gens*, bk. i. cap. xxi. par. 263-264.

(4) The whole history of plebiscitary procedure up to 1914 has been most carefully told in great detail and with the production of a large number of original documents in Miss S. Wambaugh's monograph on Plebiscites published by the Carnegie Endowment. Miss Wambaugh's documents, history, and discreetly expressed views are the basis of this section. Much information on the post-war plebiscites is to be obtained from the *History of the Peace Conference* (ed. Temperley).

(5) Some of the incidents were used by him in his *Hermann und Dorothea*.

CHAP. X. (6) Louis xiv.'s government after the revocation of the Edict of Nantes expelled the Protestant pastors on pain of the severest punishments. Their flocks, however, were forbidden to follow them, the government allowing even life sentences to the galleys to be pronounced against Protestants who persisted in the attempt.

(7) Motley, *Rise of the Dutch Republic*, bk. ii. cap. x.

(8) This quotation from Wynne's *Life of Jenkins* (vol. ii. p. 713) was used by Phillimore, whose sections on Naturalisation deserve attention.

(9) Zeballos, *Nationalité*, iii., pt. i. p. 71, a South American work.

(10) *De jure Belli et Pacis*, bk. ii. cap. v. sect. xxiv. 1, 2, 3.

(11) *Le droit des gens*, bk. i. cap. xix. 220-227.

(12) It was this dispute which eventually poisoned Anglo-American relations to the point of war (1812-1814). This, and the whole theme of the right of man to emigrate and to strip off the nationality of birth, especially occupied American statesmen and lawyers throughout the middle decades of the nineteenth century. It is amusing to see a state like the Mexico of the 'sixties solemnly proclaiming to its citizens that they had the right of "expatriation."

(13) Taylor's *Treatise on International Law*, p. 235.

(14) Zeballos, *Nationalité*, pp. 664-665. (15) *Ibid.*, pp. 676-677.

(16) See Sieber, *Staatsbürgerrecht*, vol. i. p. 403.

PART III

THE AGE OF THE CONCERT

"Taisez-vous. Quatre conseils valent mieux qu'un."

CHAPTER XI

AN EXPERIMENT IN MECHANISM (1)

The European Areopagus—Legislation at Vienna—The Conference of Ambassadors—Aix-la-Chapelle—Troppau and Laibach—Verona—The Abandonment of the Congress System.

The European Areopagus. Introduction.—Up to the nineteenth century there had been perhaps but one determined effort to make International Law by the nations for the nations. It was associated with the name of the Tsaritsa Catharine, who had persuaded almost the entire body of important states, with the exception of Great Britain, to signify approval of the code of maritime law which she had put forward from the neutral standpoint. It was not through a congress of the Powers that she had attempted to act. Probably it was still only practicable to convoke a congress among belligerents at a war's conclusion : at any rate, her procedure had been by the use of her diplomatic representatives at foreign courts or of those accredited to hers. The Second Armed Neutrality had at its service neither the energy nor the ability of Catharine. It never obtained the very general support or approval which had been accorded to the First, and it was speedily abandoned by its principal sponsor, Russia. International legislation, or even international administration, if the phrases be permitted, can hardly be said to have appeared on the scene until the Congress of Vienna, with the possible exception of one or two cases in which, as at Utrecht, there was recognised a change of succession or of a royal title. In order to explain its appearance at Vienna in 1814, some words of introduction are necessary.

At the opening of the year 1813 only the Tsar of Russia and the King of England were engaged in active hostilities against the power of Napoleon. The former was allied with Sweden, and pledged to wrest Norway for that country from Denmark: the latter was allied with Spain and Portugal. In February

CHAP. XI. 1813, by the Treaty of Kalisch, one of those understandings among belligerents which come home so awkwardly to roost in peace, Prussia undertook to enter the war upon the Russian side. Its price was in effect the restoration to Prussia of the status of a great Power, because it had covenanted for return to its rule of possessions and population equal to that which it had owned in 1806. After the German battles of May between the Russo-Prussian forces and the French, Metternich offered the mediation of Austria to the contending sides, and it was arranged that this should be exercised in a congress at Prague. Before the congress met, the Russians and Prussians arranged with Austria on 27th June the Treaty of Reichenbach, under the terms of which Austria undertook to join their cause, unless Napoleon accepted certain conditions as to the duchy of Warsaw, the Illyrian provinces, and the North German districts annexed to his empire in 1810. On 10th August Austria fulfilled her promise by entering the war against France ; so that by September it became clear that the allied Austrians, Russians, and Prussians had wrested military superiority from Napoleon in Central Europe. By the Treaty of Teplitz (9th September) the allies agreed to admit the princes of the Rhenish confederacy to the alliance against Napoleon, and the most important of them, Bavaria, had been secured even before the battles of Leipzig by the Treaty of Ried, signed on 3rd October. Napoleon was finally forced out of Saxony after the battle of Leipzig (18th and 19th October), and was compelled to recross the Rhine. An offer of peace was made to him from Frankfort on the condition of a surrender of all territory beyond the Alps and the Rhine. On the anticipated disregard of this overture the invasion of France was determined, and was begun by Blücher on the last day in the year.

Up to that point, British influence in the affairs of Central Europe had not been large, despite the great part played in the operations both by the British subsidies granted under treaty and the Peninsular campaigns of Wellington, leading up to the invasion of Southern France. From the moment, however, of Castlereagh's arrival at the allied headquarters, at the beginning of 1814, he was able to assume for England a position of influence equal to that of Russia, Austria, and Prussia, a position which men like Aberdeen and Stewart had naturally been unable to assert as against the personalities of the Tsar Alexander, Stein, or Metternich. All the same, England did not actually acquire a treaty position within the alliance till the congress of the allies at Châtillon, which followed Napoleon's refusal of the final offer to him of "the boundaries of 1792." By the treaties of Chaumont, signed with Austria, Prussia, and Russia, all four Powers undertook not to sign a treaty with Napoleon, save jointly and on the terms of the frontier of 1792; also to maintain among themselves a defensive alliance against France for twenty years after the conclusion of the war. This agreement was reached on 1st March 1814. The alliance foreshadowed was no vague affair. Each Power pledged itself to send in the first instance sixty thousand men to the aid of any ally who should be threatened; but, if such aid proved ineffective, to act if necessary with all its forces. The whole agreement was based upon actual experience of recent date, and it is not without interest to note that, although it had never been intended to exclude the smaller Powers at war with France from the embrace of the alliance of Chaumont, and although in fact the inclusion of Spain, Portugal, Holland, and Sweden had been definitely envisaged, it was in the end found that the military obligations involved were beyond the capacity of any of the smaller Powers.

When the first Treaty of Paris was signed with the Government of France on 30th May 1814, Spain, Portugal, and Sweden were associated with the four greater allies in the signature. Nevertheless, during the Congress of Vienna the four arrogated to themselves a special position, more particularly when it came to decisions on the question of territory, which all the ability of Talleyrand, effective though it was, and all the jealousy rampant among the lesser Powers, were unable to shake. On 25th March 1815, after Napoleon's reappearance in France, the four Powers renewed at Vienna their alliance made at Chaumont in the previous year. In addition to the defensive arrangements made before, it was agreed that Napoleon was to be reduced to impotence, and that, to this end, each Power was to keep permanently in the field a force of one hundred and fifty thousand men until this object had been attained. When, even before the overthrow of the Emperor, the *Acte final* of the Congress of Vienna was signed in which were brought together all the separate territorial agreements reached in Vienna, there was scarcely a European frontier in whose fate England, Russia, Prussia, and Austria could not claim a vital paternal interest. The second Treaty of Paris with France, which was delayed from 7th July, the date of the Allied entrance into Paris after Waterloo, till 20th

CHAP. XI.

November, was almost entirely the work of the four Powers, and the delay was due to a division of opinion as to whether France should be stripped of the conquests made by Louis XIV. or not. The treaty of 20th November finally imposed upon France only small cessions of territory additional to those of 1814, but, on the other hand, added to her burdens a payment of seven hundred million francs, beyond the financial obligations already imposed earlier in 1814, and an army of occupation of one hundred and fifty thousand men for a period not exceeding five years. In order adequately to face their new responsibilities the four Powers signed a new treaty among themselves of the same date as that of their treaty with France. A specific engagement was accepted by all to exclude the family of Bonaparte from the throne of France. In the event of another outbreak of French revolutionary principles such as to endanger the repose of other states, all four states were to concert among themselves, and with the French king, the measures necessary for the safety of their states and the tranquillity of Europe. Sixty thousand men were to be provided in the first instance by each Power in case common military action should become necessary. It was hinted, moreover, that certain emergencies might necessitate the summons, and contribution, of the whole military forces of the contracting Powers. Finally, it was arranged to hold further diplomatic gatherings, in words which must have sounded ominous to the smaller Powers of Europe. The phrasing ran :—

> "In order to assure and to facilitate the execution of the present treaty, and for the purpose of consolidating the intimate connections, which now bind the four Sovereigns, for the world's happiness, the High contracting Parties have agreed, at fixed periods and under the immediate auspices of the Sovereigns or by their respective ministers, to renew their meetings devoted to the great common interests and to the examination of the measures which at each of these periods shall be judged the most salutary for the repose and prosperity of the Nations and for the upholding of the peace of Europe."

Before pursuing the history of the European congresses convoked in virtue of this article, it is necessary to return, according to original intention, to the acts, one might almost say the legislation, of the Congress of Vienna. For there is in certain of the acts of the Congress of Vienna something more than is contained in the normal type of clause which readjusts territory in an ordinary treaty. The establishment of the German federation, the provision for a guaranteed neutralisation in perpetuity of the Swiss Confederation, the ancillary neutralisation of a zone of Savoy, the creation of the constitutional kingdom of Poland, the reunion of Belgium and Holland under one authority—it is not fanciful to detect behind each and all of these, not merely an attempt to draw anew the map of Europe, but an experiment in political science under the joint auspices of the leading nations. It was in each case an experiment important for the particular country concerned, but one which was realised as likely to have profound effect for good or ill upon that Europe which formed the background to them all.

Legislation at Vienna.—The actual legislative work of the Congress of Vienna, apart from the provisions as to territory, was not great, it is true, nor did the Powers represented at the congress deem it expedient to create any permanent international organ charged with the function of legislation for future generations, at least any organ such as would not have been covered by the provision in the treaty of 20th November 1815 for periodical meetings of representatives. Nevertheless, a great step forward had been taken in the process of international organisation and of international control. A congress of many, of all the important, Powers had covered the whole ground in more than one subject of international concern—the management of international rivers, the organisation of the diplomatic corps, the control of the slave trade. How important this was, public, and expert, opinion in Europe was not perhaps in a position fully to appreciate until the circumstances of the year 1856 presented another opportunity for international legislation by congress.

The decision as to the state character of one piece of European territory has a specially interesting significance. The fate of the Ionian Islands could not be decided in the hurried days at Vienna, and was not arranged until November 1815. They were then set up as a state, separate from, but under the protection of, Great Britain, which thus became, as it were, the mandatory Power for this area.

The way had been prepared for the handling by the congress of the question of the navigation of international rivers by the terms of the Treaty of Paris of 1814. In Article 5 of this treaty navigation on the Rhine was declared open to all from the first navigable point down to the sea. It was left to the congress about to be held to fix the dues that might be levied

CHAP. XI. by riverain states; and it was left to the congress also to extend this free system of the Rhine to all other international rivers. At Vienna, provision was made for a central commission for the Rhine, to meet annually, for an inspectorate, for a maximum total charge by weight for carriage down the whole river's length, and for a maximum number of points at which the toll might be collected. It was enjoined upon the separate states which should receive toll money that they should regard the maintenance of navigation as the primary, and in normal cases the sole legitimate charge. The congress made certain arrangements in smaller detail for the rivers Neckar, Main, Moselle, Meuse, and Scheldt, but provided that more detailed arrangements should in general follow those established for the Rhine. These arrangements for particular rivers were not inserted in the body of the *Acte final*, but were relegated to an *Annexe*. The general principles to be established for all rivers were, on the other hand, given a place among the clauses of the more authoritative part of the document, to wit in Articles 108-116. All states, it was there provided, which were separated or traversed by the same navigable river, were to arrange in common accord all regulations connected with its navigation. This was to be done at a meeting of commissioners, gathered together not later than six months after the conclusion of the congress. The principles which were to guide the assembly of commissioners were to be six in number: first, entire liberty of commercial navigation; secondly, uniformity, wherever possible, of the systems of police and toll along the river itself, and, if possible, its tributaries; thirdly, a fixed toll system whose bases were not of such a nature as to involve the detailed examination of cargo; fourthly, reduction to a minimum of the toll collecting points; fifthly, local responsibility as regards riverain states for the maintenance of towing paths and works on the river bed; lastly, the reduction to a general *règlement* of all regulations, to which central form all local systems should adapt themselves. There had been more than one attempt to find some eternal and ethical justification in principle for the opening of international rivers, notably those of the French Convention in 1792 and of Jefferson in 1783. The very fact that the question was submitted to the Congress of Vienna is clear proof that the opening of rivers rests upon grace and not on right. This view has been upheld always by England in particular, which in the Treaty of Washington, signed in 1854 with the United States, made it clear that the grant to the latter of free navigation on the St. Lawrence was a revocable privilege. The Congress of Paris in 1856, by Article 15 of the Peace Treaty, arranged for the free navigation of the Danube; and laid it down that the principle of the Vienna Congress with regard to free navigation on international rivers for merchantmen of all nations was part of "European Public Law." A special international organ for the regulation of navigation on the Danube was created in the Danube commission. The conference at Berlin on the Congo performed analogous work for the Congo and the Niger. The Institute of International Law at its Heidelberg meeting in 1888 adopted a *projet de règlement international de navigation fluviale,* which contained some forty articles. But, although all these actions indicate that the Congress of Vienna did good work, the stubborn fact remains that bitter dispute over the navigation on such important rivers as the Scheldt and the St. Lawrence was still possible in the second half of the century.

As has been shown above, it was hoped at Vienna to end once and for all the frequent disputes which had raged round questions of diplomatic precedence. In form the work of Vienna in this respect was not really legislative. The plenipotentiaries of the eight Powers, signatories of the Treaty of Paris of 1814, informed their colleagues of other nations that they had agreed on a system for the regulation of the dignity of diplomatic officers. They invited other states to adopt this system. Be this as it may, the *règlement* agreed upon was by the *Acte final* allowed exactly the same force as if it had been inserted in the treaty; and since it introduced universal, fixed, and certain principles into a mass of what before had been doubtful and involved, it must be held to constitute international legislation.

Technically the declaration made on 8th February 1815 against the slave trade was in no sense legislation. The plenipotentiaries of the eight Powers, alleging the principles of humanity and universal morality, declared that they were possessed by the sincere desire to do all they could to bring about the universal abolition of the slave trade as promptly and as efficaciously as possible. It was admitted that each Power was entitled to consider the interests, habits, and even the prejudices of its subjects, in fixing the final term for their trade in slaves. The question had been raised by England, largely at the instigation of the evangelical leaders of the anti-slave-trade movement, and was insufficiently understood

CHAP. XI.

by the representatives of the other Powers, who did actually allow English opinion to assume that they had conceded more than afterwards it was shown that they intended to grant. For the declaration was so worded as almost to encourage England to continue its steady pressure on the other Powers to fix dates for the termination of the traffic and to allow the adoption of new methods, such as a general right of search, calculated to make the supervision of the trade effective.

The Conference of Ambassadors.—After the signature of the *Acte final* of the Congress of Vienna and the second Treaty of Paris, the four great Powers found themselves jointly involved in a multitude of concerns which called for common handling. Surveillance over the Napoleonic family is a good example of the minor type of such concerns: the great immediate interest was the international army of occupation in France. It had been resolved to form such a force by a contribution of thirty thousand men from each of the four great nations, together with a fifth contingent, of the same number, contributed jointly by the smaller Powers. This force was to be placed under the command of the Duke of Wellington. As a channel of communication between the four Powers and the commander-in-chief, as also between the commander-in-chief and the French government, an ambassadorial conference was set up which was composed of the British, Russian, Prussian, and Austrian ambassadors in Paris. This body soon assumed undefined powers of supervision over the political condition of France, and, proving useful, seemed for a time likely to add to its functions. Thus the question of the succession to the Duchies of Parma and Guastalla was referred to it, and the differences, both in Europe and South America, between Spain and Portugal. Later, the conference in April 1817 proceeded to urge upon the King of the Netherlands the expulsion of Napoleonic exiles from Brussels; and, on a subsequent suggestion from Metternich, that the Paris ambassadors should assume on behalf of the four Powers the task of suppressing the revolutionaries' activities all over Europe, a circular despatch was sent to the smaller Powers of Germany and Italy and to Switzerland. Meanwhile, consideration of the disputes between Spain and Portugal soon involved an examination of the Spanish-American revolutions, for that part of South American territory seized by Portugal and held in disputed occupation would speedily have fallen into the rebels' hands if it had been abandoned by the Portuguese. Pozzo di Borgo, the Russian ambassador at Paris, was only too eager that the ambassadors should assume the task of probing the situation in the Spanish colonies. He prepared his ground so carefully that he obtained not merely the approval of the Austrian and Prussian ambassadors, but actually an invitation from the Spanish government. It was Stewart, and behind him Castlereagh, who spoiled an ingenious scheme of an ingenious man for producing united European intervention in Spanish America.

The ambassadors' conference had by this time already played some part in a first reduction of the army of occupation by thirty thousand men. This had been granted to France in 1817 in return for a payment on account of the indemnity. When the French became importunate for a further reduction, it raised the thorny question of the total of the payments to be made by the French as compensation for damage inflicted by the French armies. These payments were altogether separate from the indemnity, and had been undertaken in 1814 quite apart from any payment as indemnity. Huge sums had been claimed by the continental Powers, and the Duc de Richelieu, the French prime minister, had appealed to the ambassadorial conference for a reduction. This body, however, failed to make a united recommendation, and it had been necessary to refer the dispute for settlement to the Duke of Wellington.

When the Congress of Aix-la-Chapelle finally decided upon the evacuation of the inter-allied army of occupation, Castlereagh insisted upon the winding-up of the conference of ambassadors and the closing of its protocol, for he had always disliked the desire of Pozzo di Borgo for a continual expansion of its functions. Even so, the persistent Corsican tried to engineer a revival of the institution in 1819, at which date internal affairs in France took a threatening turn, and in 1820, at the outbreak of the Neapolitan revolution. He was to have even more success between 1820 and 1826.

Two other representative committees of the great Powers played some part in post-Napoleonic Europe—those of London and Frankfort. At London, Castlereagh organised a conference of the great and the maritime Powers to discuss means speedily to abolish the slave trade. Fourteen meetings were held between 18th August 1816 and the conference of Aix-la-Chapelle in 1818, and two meetings were held in 1819. Despite Castlereagh's efforts to obtain the mutual admission of the right of search among all the Powers concerned, the one effective measure for suppression of the trade, he failed before the persistent opposition of France and the indifference of other countries. The most he could obtain, when he took the matter up again at Aix-la-Chapelle, was an impracticable Russian proposal for the establishment of a Christian international institution, with a fleet and courts of its own, to which the right of search might be allowed without the smallest hesitation. The proposal to form an international fleet had already been made at the conference of London, but only in connection with action against the Barbary pirates who were a plague to European commerce in the Mediterranean. Castlereagh, while not enthusiastically in favour of the idea of international operation, would have been prepared to support it, if he could have obtained in return the mutual right of search in slave-trading areas. Failing to obtain this, both at London and at Aix-la-Chapelle, Castlereagh allowed the proposed international operation against the Barbary pirates to lapse. Another matter which the London conference was called upon to adjust was the Suedo-Danish dispute, provoked by the Swedish failure to fulfil the terms of the Treaty of Kiel.

The conference at Frankfort, on the other hand, turned not so much on general international subjects as on internal German difficulties. The most troublesome subject to occupy the attention of the conference was a triangular dispute over territory on the part of Bavaria, Baden, and Austria. It was produced by the Austrian resumption in 1814 of Salzburg and other territory recently in Bavarian possession. Baden for its part refused to find compensation for Bavaria, and obtained support from the Tsar. This question between Bavaria and Baden had to be referred from Frankfort to Aix-la-Chapelle, only to be referred back once more. The Frankfort conference summed up the result of its labours in a document signed on 20th July 1819 by Wessenberg for Austria, Humboldt for Prussia, Clancarty for Great Britain, and D'Anstett for Russia.

The statesmen who had co-operated so effectively at Chaumont, Paris, and Vienna could not but receive the impression from their experience that personal contact and discussion vastly expedited business, dissipated much needless suspicion, and enabled joint policies to be undertaken which would have been unattainable by older diplomatic methods. Castlereagh, Metternich, and Alexander all showed a predilection for joint conferences, a predilection which Castlereagh thus expressed in the House of Commons in February 1816:— CHAP. XI.

> "If the councils of the sovereigns had not been brought together, if they had been forced to look at their special interests through that cloud of prejudice and uncertainty which must always intervene when events are viewed at a distance . . . I am sure that the councils of Europe would have been disturbed to such an extent by doubts and misapprehensions that those great exertions whose successful issue is now before the world would never have been made."

Alexander, who had lived in the endless excitement of international discussion continuously from the beginning of 1813 to the end of 1815, had begun to hanker for a new international conference soon after he returned to Russia. Advisers of the type of Capodistrias and Pozzo di Borgo were not likely to throw cold water on this fancy. Metternich, moreover, was never unwilling to expedite business by personal conference with foreign statesmen.

Accordingly, when questions of the magnitude of the payments by France or the future of the army of occupation pressed for decision in 1818, all parties were disposed to have them, and others which had gathered, handled in a conference. There were Russian elements, which, mainly for tactical reasons, desired as full a conference as possible; one in which, beside the four great Powers, secondary nations should also be represented. Castlereagh and Metternich were united in wishing a conference which should be confined to the four alone. They carried their point with Prussia and ultimately Russia. Castlereagh was prepared to discuss at the meeting other questions than the future relations of the allies to France, though he would have had this done unostentatiously and with due regard to the susceptibilities of the smaller Powers. Were the discussion opened wide, he knew there would be those only too ready to outpace him. Aix-la-Chapelle was fixed for the *venue* of the conference in April 1818.

Aix-la-Chapelle.—By the end of September there were conferring at Aix, Castlereagh and Wellington, the Austrian Emperor, Metternich and Gentz, the Tsar Alexander, Capodistrias, Nesselrode and Pozzo di Borgo, the King of Prussia and Hardenberg, the Frenchmen Richelieu and Caraman. On 9th October a convention was signed by France and the allies, which provided for the withdrawal of the army of occupation and a French payment of two hundred and sixty-five million francs. On 12th October the four allied Powers

CHAP. XI.

secretly decided to maintain the Quadruple Alliance, but resolved to admit France into their periodical conferences as a fifth member. A far-reaching Russian proposal, evidently prepared beforehand but of which there had been no notice, had next to be discussed. A universal European league was then and there suggested, which should guarantee every European state, both as regards its territory and its existing constitutional system, and which should march against any state which indulged in revolution or aggression. Much tact had to be displayed by Castlereagh and Metternich in persuading Alexander that his scheme was too far-reaching. Towards the close of the conference the Prussians, who had been rendered nervous by the evacuation of France and the task of defending the left bank of the Rhine, produced a scheme for a general guarantee of territory in Europe, for which they secured some little attention on the part of Austria and Russia. This scheme was later changed to a treaty of territorial guarantee which should embrace the four great Powers and the Netherlands, but in view of the British disinclination to enter into any such engagement, and in view of the extreme difficulty of reducing it to a draft, it was not proceeded with any further. Accordingly, the principal result of the congress may be found in the admission of France into the gathering of the great Powers, or indeed into any such gatherings as might in the future be convoked.

As in Castlereagh's absence a section of the British Cabinet had evinced a violent antipathy to the idea of an indefinite perpetuation of international conferences, Castlereagh had been cautious enough to secure that in the protocol of the Congress of Aix-la-Chapelle all references to the future meetings of the five Powers should be as inoffensive, unassuming and unprovocative as possible. Personally he believed as strongly as ever in the advantage of the conference method, and did not consider weighty the objections which could be raised against it on the part of the smaller Powers. Alexander, who was so strong a believer in the mechanism of conferences that he even spoke of being carried to the next in a litter if it were necessary, was willing to go some way in conceding a protocol which should not arouse too many conservative and insular objections from England. Accordingly, the important section of the protocol of 15th November 1818 ran :—

"France, associated with the other Powers by the restoration of the legitimate and constitutional monarchic authority, agrees to co-operate henceforward in the maintenance and fortification of a system which has given peace to Europe, and which alone can insure its continuation. CHAP XI.

"If, the better to attain the end mentioned above, the Powers who have concurred in the present act should judge it necessary to arrange special meetings, whether between the august Sovereigns themselves or between their respective ministers and plenipotentiaries, in order at these to treat in common of their actual deliberations, the time and the place of these meetings shall on each occasion be previously arranged by diplomatic communications. . . . In case these meetings should have for object the business specially connected with the interests of the other states of Europe, they shall not take place save on a formal invitation on the part of those states concerned in the said business, and with the express reservation of their right to participate directly or by their plenipotentiaries."

Such a document, which did in fact leave intact the whole diplomatic machinery for the convoking of conferences, could be defended against that element in the Cabinet, led by Canning, which was more than a little suspicious, since it could be represented as leaving liberty to the individual states and as conceding the barest minimum to the "sacramental" point of view of the Tsar and the French constitutional legitimists.

Apart from the main tasks of providing for the evacuation of the occupying army, of securing French payments, and of admitting France into the directory of the great Powers, the conference at Aix had had, as has been hinted above, a few other matters before it. The London conference of diplomats had brought up the slave-trade question, with the proposal for a mutual grant of a right of search. They had brought up also the question of action against the Barbary pirates and the Suedo-Danish dispute. From Frankfort was remitted the question which was dividing Austria, Bavaria, and Baden. The congress sent no fewer than four notes to Stockholm, the Tsar used his private influence, and Sweden in the end consented to do tardy justice. In the German dispute it seemed at one moment that a similar success was about to be achieved, but Bavaria retained her grievance and the negotiations at Frankfort were not forwarded.

The gravest territorial problem before the Congress of Aix was not, however, the German, but that which raged between the Spanish colonies in America and their mother-country. All parties displayed some hesitation in broaching the subject openly, though it was discussed privately before it was

CHAP. XI. brought into public notice. Castlereagh opened the consideration of the question in a memorandum which advocated the choice of a single individual by the five Powers to represent them as mediator in the dispute between the colonies and Spain. He held that Spain ought to accept suitable conditions of mediation. There followed a kaleidoscope of proposal and counter proposal. The French and Russian ministers presented a second memorandum, which emphasised the risks entailed should America become entirely republican, and advocated prompt action to forestall a catastrophe so generally noisome. It was urged that the Duke of Wellington should be designated mediator by the five Powers, but that his action in Madrid should be supplemented by the conference of ambassadors. Castlereagh had regarded it as a *sine qua non* that plans of mediation should rest on the explicit disavowal of any use of force, but the counter memorandum did not regard with any favour an anticipatory limitation of this kind. The Russians next introduced the idea of compelling Spanish-American compliance to the behests of Europe by the organisation of a commercial boycott. Castlereagh again flatly refused to consider the suggestion, and pointed out that England was perfectly prepared to mediate, but not to judge, still less to enforce a judgment, between the Spanish Americans and the King of Spain. Accordingly, the congress was reduced to adopting the project of mediation by the Duke of Wellington, but only on the British conditions. These were (to select the more important only) a general amnesty for all insurgents, legal equality between the American and European subjects of Spain, and the opening of all American ports save for the reservation of a "fair" preference for Spanish traders. As Spain declined to accept these conditions, Wellington's mediation never took place.

Lastly, some minor questions came up for decision before the congress separated. The petition of the "Elector" of Hesse to assume the kingly title was refused. The remediatisation of Kniphausen (a Bentinck principality) was discussed. The complaints of the subjects of Monaco against their prince were investigated. The treatment of the German Jews in some of the smaller states was dealt with in a protocol. The treatment of Napoleon at St. Helena was approved, and the supervision of the Bonaparte family was undertaken. The old British claim to the salute in the narrow seas was finally abandoned, and complete reciprocity, with details to be elaborated in London later, was substituted. Finally, the division of diplomatic officers into three classes, which had been adopted at Vienna, was altered. A four-class division, as has been shown elsewhere, was adopted in its place.

In 1819 growing fears on the Continent concerning the increasing leftward tendency in French politics led to new proposals for the establishment of international machinery alike from France and Russia. The Russians, Austrians, and Prussians were particularly alarmed by the decline in the health of King Louis XVIII., and by the violent unpopularity of the Comte d'Artois, which presaged ill for the stability of French institutions. Pozzo di Borgo wrote to his master, the Tsar, suggesting the forwarding of joint instructions to the allied ambassadors at Paris and the taking of joint action in the event of the death of the King. In April 1819 the Tsar did actually propose the reconstruction of the allied ambassadorial conference, which had only been abolished in the previous November. Castlereagh objected strongly to such a measure as likely to worsen, rather than to improve, the French situation. Metternich thereupon put forward his own plan. The allies, he pointed out, needed some central point of contact, at which discussion could expeditiously take place without the delay of interchanging couriers. Paris, he admitted, might well not be the proper place for this, but the objections to Paris did not hold as regards London or Vienna. Vienna might be even a little better than London, for negotiations in London were too easily disturbed by the influences of party politics, and the French had particular objection to all influences which arose across the Channel. Castlereagh declined to listen to the suggestion, alleging the impossibility of Vienna, in that Cabinet authority would be obligatory for any British minister who came there, and that thus expedition would not be any more obtainable.

The Bourbon monarchy proved more robust than had been anticipated, and in 1820 international attention was diverted from it to the alarming outbreaks of revolutionary manifestations elsewhere. A military and "liberal" revolt occurred in Spain in 1820 which was able to reduce the absolutism of King Ferdinand VII. to constitutional impotence. The spread of the contagion to France was everywhere feared, and anxiety in France, Russia, and Prussia caused talk once more of French and allied conferences in Paris, and even of the summons to a new congress like that

CHAP. XI.

of Aix-la-Chapelle. Castlereagh would not consider that the Spanish revolution could constitute a danger to other countries; and insisted that the alliance had never been instituted to govern the world, and that it could not claim as a matter of course to undertake collective jurisdiction every time that a great political event threatened a possible future danger. All for which he was prepared was the issue of separate warnings in Madrid against violence to the royal family and against an attack upon Portugal. His objections served to prevent the immediate convocation of an inter-allied congress, or conference, on the subject of Spain. The Iberian situation was not bettered by the outbreak in August of a "liberal" revolution in Portugal and the proclamation of Brazilian independence two years later. But once again the attention of the Powers was diverted and confined to further revolutions in other parts of Europe.

For in July 1820 a "liberal" revolution had broken out in the kingdom of Naples to the cry of "the Spanish constitution of 1812." The monarchy was speedily compelled to surrender the substance of its power to a band of extremists, whose reputation has suffered from their lamentable failure to estimate correctly their own military weakness. The British Cabinet had not the slightest concern for the revolution, and indeed sympathised with Austrian anxiety as to its effect upon the rest of Italy. Metternich was informed that no objection would be taken by Britain to an Austrian suppression of the revolt, but that neither assistance nor open approval could be furnished. Russia and France, however, desired that the suppression should not be Austrian, but should at least have the appearance of a European character by being authorised at a European congress, the idea of which was utterly distasteful to the British. It was at least likely, so it seemed in England, that, were a congress called, the Russians would wish it to extend beyond the revolution in Naples to a discussion of South American and Iberian affairs, upon which matters the British attitude had been quite positively settled. Metternich seems to have been desirous of meeting Castlereagh's objections to a full European congress of the dimensions of that of 1818 by arranging a special Russo-Austrian interview at Troppau, and an ambassadorial conference at Vienna between the representatives of the other Powers, whereby the allies might fully be kept in touch with the policy of Austria. Russian pressure led, however, to the holding of a full conference at Troppau; and although Metternich's hope that a British plenipotentiary would be sent was doomed to disappointment, he was enabled to save appearances when the British ambassador in Vienna was instructed to attend, even if that diplomat was charged to come rather as a wary and critical observer than as a participant.

Troppau and Laibach.—The Troppau meetings began formally on 23rd October. Metternich asked for the moral support, rather than the military aid, of his allies in freeing the King of Naples. He painted a gloomy picture of the state of Italy, and insisted that intervention was legitimate for states threatened by the Neapolitan troubles. As the British and French representatives were only of ambassadorial rank, they were kept out of the intimate discussions which took place, although they were naturally admitted to full conferences between the five Powers. It was in the intimate discussions that there was evolved the preliminary protocol which was presented to a full conference on 19th November. This document advanced a number of extreme and objectionable propositions which had distinct reference to the famous document submitted by the Tsar to his allies in September 1815, to which the title of the Holy Alliance has popularly been given and far too much importance attached. The Tsar's influence had procured almost universal adhesion to this "Holy Alliance," which in exceedingly "sacramental" language had bound the signatory and contracting rulers to treat one another as Christian brethren and their subjects as children. Now by the preliminary protocol there was assumed to exist a general European alliance, and it was further implied that a state which underwent a change of régime as the result of revolution—a change which menaced other states—was *ipso facto* excluded from the alliance. The allied Powers, so ran the protocol, would refuse recognition to all such changes, as being brought about by illegal methods. Where changes of this type threatened immediate danger to neighbouring states, and where the "allied Powers" could intervene effectively, they undertook to employ first representations, and then if necessary measures of coercion. In Naples, where these principles would be applied, the King would be set free from the present deadlock, and would then be encouraged of his own free will to establish a suitable and stable system. Incidentally he would be forthwith invited to Laibach to confer with the "allied sovereigns" as to the best means of executing his plan. An army of occupation, accom-

CHAP. XI.

panied by allied plenipotentiaries, was foreseen by the shrewder observers.

In other words, Metternich's hand had been forced by the Tsar. As might be expected, the British objections to the protocol were numerous and intense. In London, Castlereagh saw in it nothing short of an attempt to erect a superstate "which would tend to destroy all wholesome national energy and all independent action, more especially within the smaller states." If the protocol were to be published he spoke even of issuing a counterblast. He objected, though less strongly, to the invitation to Laibach sent to the King of Naples. Rome or another Italian town, he thought, might have been tolerable; an Italian conference on an Italian question was a very different matter from a summons to the headquarters of Europe. Nevertheless, he consented to move to Laibach both A'Court, the British minister to Naples, and Stewart, the ambassador to Austria. A'Court never managed the journey. Representatives from all the states of Italy were summoned there.

Thus at Laibach there gathered in January 1821 another great European company. The King of Naples arrived in person in the middle of the month, and confronted the two Emperors, Capodistrias, Pozzo di Borgo, Nesselrode, Metternich, Vincent, Gentz, Blacas and Caraman, Prussian and Italian representatives, and the Englishmen Stewart and Gordon. The diplomatic *scenario* was obvious. The three Continental allies, Russia, Austria, and Prussia, were desirous of involving England and France in a common responsibility with them for the gathering Austrian expedition against Naples. Should that prove impracticable, the aim must be to cajole the British and French representatives into doing nothing which might detract from the apparent solidarity of the greater Powers of Europe. Stewart did not prove as amenable as Blacas. He spoiled the orderly development of the drama by insisting that a separate British declaration should be read at the special session, to which the Italian representatives were admitted, and by recording protests in the minutes of the subsequent meetings, at which were planned the details of the actual invasion of Naples.

In the end an Austrian invasion took place, not only of the two Sicilies but of Piedmont, in which a sudden revolution had broken out in March. The operations were highly successful. Autocratic monarchies were re-established in Naples and Piedmont under the protection of occupying

Austrian armies, which acted as the "executants of the allies." The conference at Laibach, which remained in being till May, did not dare to assume the consideration of the Spanish or Portuguese revolutions, as such a course might have meant a definite rupture in the now somewhat feverish understanding between the five Powers. A further conference was fixed for Florence in 1822. Its primary business was a reconsideration of the Italian position, but the Englishman Gordon reported home that it was probable that the Tsar would there press for allied action against Spain. The circular despatches sent from Laibach at the close of the conference showed Austria, Prussia, and Russia solid in their view as to the propriety of an assumption of supervisory powers by the alliance.

> "The three sovereigns regarded themselves and all other sovereigns and legitimate powers as more than ever called upon to watch over the peace of Europe, and to protect it not only against the errors and passions which might compromise it in the relations between state and state, but even more against those fatal attempts which delivered the civilised world to the horrors of a universal anarchy."

By the time the foreshadowed conference was approaching, England was rather more ready to think in terms of a "European alliance." Dangerous revolution was making itself felt abroad among the European Greeks of the Turkish Empire, the Tsar had been given some provocation, and the safest way to avoid a Russo-Turkish war, which might completely upset the equilibrium of the Continent, might well be an appeal to the "European patriotism" of the Tsar. And indeed that monarch was prevented from provoking a crisis by the hope that the European congress of the autumn of 1822 would deal with the Near Eastern troubles, while Metternich even staged a preliminary conference at Vienna, which embraced Prussian, English, and French representatives, in addition to the Russian special envoy Tatistcheff and himself, in the attempt to give a demonstration of European solidarity pleasing to the Tsar. As the Spanish revolution was taking an extreme form and the Russians were proposing an international army of suppression, while powerful French influences were desirous of the honour of an exclusively French expedition, it was certain that the coming conference would have on its agenda paper, beside its original Italian business, not only the Spanish problem in Europe and America, but also the Near Eastern troubles. King George IV. of

CHAP. XI.

England was desirous of appearing in person at the gathering of 1822, and the Cabinet, which dreaded the possible effect on Parliament of his mistakes, had great difficulty in persuading him to undertake a Scottish tour instead. Castlereagh, despite the objection in certain Cabinet circles to the despatch of a special British plenipotentiary, determined to be present in person and to co-operate with Metternich in an attempt to keep the five-Power alliance within bounds which were defensible in Parliament. But he was not fated to be present. He had been overworking for a long period, and the coincidence of a heavy Parliamentary session, a particularly heavy bout of work at the Foreign Office, and the task of smoothing the relations between the King and the Cabinet, taxed his strength to breaking point. After his suicide the conduct of foreign affairs passed into the hands of the very different Canning, a man who, for all his brilliance, had neither Castlereagh's deep and patient understanding of the difficulties of Continental Powers, nor his desire to keep England in touch with them, even at the cost of Parliamentary misunderstanding and popular suspicion. The break in continuity was for the time obscured by the fact that Wellington proceeded as plenipotentiary to the conference. He had been appointed and had received his instructions before Canning began work at the Foreign Office.

Verona.—Castlereagh had expected the Turkish question to rank first in importance at the conference, next the affairs of Spain, and lastly those of Italy, where the withdrawal of the Austrian armies from Naples and Piedmont had to be arranged. His " instructions " show that he was still mindful of the use of the European conference as a diplomatic clearing-house. He had intended to raise the general question of the slave trade, the specifically Anglo-Austrian question of Austria's debt settlement with England, and the Anglo-Russian difficulties caused by a *ukase* of 1821 which claimed as Russian territory a stretch of American coast outside the usually recognised limits of Alaska. Wellington on leaving England soon found that the forefront of deliberation would be occupied by the crisis in Spain, for the Tsar was pining to lead a combined expedition, and French royalists a French army, to the aid of King Ferdinand VII., at once an absolute monarch and of the French blood-royal. He found, too, that, after the preliminary conversations held in Vienna, which he did not arrive in time to attend, the allies' discussions were about to transfer themselves to Verona. And in this town there came together the most illustrious meeting of the Powers since Vienna, a meeting of two emperors, three kings, three sovereign grand dukes, a cardinal, who represented the Pope, a viceroy, three foreign secretaries, twenty ambassadors, beside a dozen ministers.

It was first necessary to persuade the Tsar out of his wild scheme of marching a "European" army against Spain. All the German Powers concerned and France, it hardly need be added, raised insuperable objections to being made a field of passage. The combined arguments of Montmorency of France and Metternich of Austria, joined to those of Wellington, were necessary to move the Tsar to the relinquishment of his pet project.

Next, consideration was given to the French scheme for a French expedition, when Montmorency presented three definite questions to his fellow-negotiators :—

(1) If France should withdraw her minister at Madrid, would the other Powers do the same ?

(2) If France should come to be at war with Spain, what moral support, and

(3) What material support would be afforded by the other Powers ?

The Tsar was immediately moved to offer the despatch of a Russian army to Piedmont, which should be held in reserve to attack either the Jacobins in France or the Spanish revolutionaries, were the fortunes of the French army to fail it. Wellington, Metternich, and, not least, Montmorency disliked a project so extreme, and discussion quickly sank in tone. Wellington as early as 30th October refused to reply to Montmorency's questions till the exact ground of complaint against Spain, and the exact cause of war, should be made clear. He was insistent that England would never be a party to interference in purely Spanish affairs. The other allies in response, drawing apart from so intransigent a statement, concerted their replies to France, which was prepared to move about the middle of November. They undertook to withdraw their diplomats from Spain and agreed to send assistance if the Spaniards stirred up revolt in France or attacked it from without, if they deposed or put on trial the royal family, or if they attempted to interfere with the law of succession. On 10th November Wellington entered a formal protest against the resolution to interfere in the internal affairs of any state. Thus French intervention under countenance of the three continental monarchies, as also the public

CHAP. XI.

and emphatic protest of Canning against it, were definitely anticipated in the proceedings at Verona. Wellington indeed departed before those proceedings were over. Formal concord, it is true, was still unbroken, as was proved in the discussion of the other questions on the programme. Even the dangerous Turco-Greek deadlock and the Spanish-American issue were proved patient of harmonious decision, and definite cleavage over these was successfully avoided.

The Abandonment of the Congress System.—The Congress of Verona was destined to be the last of the series initiated by the Congress of Vienna. The attempt to erect what was in fact a supreme government, charged with a watching brief, in the interests of the existing order, over the affairs of Europe and the world, was doomed to failure, despite the extremely close personal relations and similarity of view existing among the leading personalities in the five countries at this portentous epoch. Though the reasons for its failure seem plain enough after the lapse of a hundred years, it is wise to remember that they were concealed from contemporaries. So keen an observer, for example, as the American John Quincy Adams could write in 1820 that "as a compact between governments it is not impossible that the European alliances will last as long as some of the states which are a party to it."

The main reason for the failure of the congress system was the difference which existed in the types of the governments which engineered it. Russia, Austria, and Prussia were autocratic monarchies, responsible in no degree for the conduct of affairs, while the governments of England and France were avowedly constitutional. They were controlled by the upper classes and increasingly by the capitalist and commercial or industrial elements in the nation. The formula of "legitimacy" had ingeniously been devised at Vienna to cover this difference of type; and it was hoped by its inventors that, because each type had considerable claim to be considered customary, approved, established in its own sphere, the five governments would be able to act together in favour of "the customary, the approved, the established" in the international sphere. Ambitions of this static nature were almost bound to vanish in the inevitable march of events; and it is reasonable to doubt, though it is another question, whether the five allies, if they had acted together in perfect unison, could ever have reimposed the conditions of the eighteenth century on Latin America, to take one example only of their problems. As it was, this unison was never obtained. The British and French Cabinets had always to hold in mind the free presses and parliaments in their own countries, which looked at every question predominantly from a national standpoint. More than this, the British and French parliaments, presses, electorates, and peoples not merely demanded that the action of the alliance should run in accord with their conception of the private national interest, but also opposed the action of the alliance when it ran counter to something quite as powerful, a strong national prejudice in favour of "liberty." On questions of political arrangement, whether in Naples, Spain, Portugal, Latin America or elsewhere, the English were usually prepared, resignedly in some cases, indifferently among certain classes, to accept political change, however it might have been brought about. Thus, participation in any joint attack on "revolution" was ruled out of the question, either as impolitic and improper in itself, or as impossible to defend before parliamentary or public opinion, which was, with very few exceptions, either benevolently disposed to foreign "revolutions," or indifferent, or preoccupied with making money. Similarly, the French government repeatedly sought to take up a line of conduct palatable to the ruling classes in France, by marking out a distinction between the mere conservatism of the autocratic monarchies and such, in autocratic eyes, comparative liberalism as support of the French system of the *charte octroyée*. That was in time to fail, but it did not fail till a period later than that here discussed; and, while it lasted, its influence was always apparent in French policy. In the matter of the Spanish and Portuguese colonies, the commercial issues involved were matters of relative indifference to the autocrats. The English statesmen had constantly to bear in mind the mercantile, which was the liberal, side of the question; while the French ministers had to hold in mind the dynastic interests of the Bourbon house, a moderated liberalism, and the commercial advantages obtainable by any country which played a part on the winning side. The late President Wilson might seem then not wholly unjustified by history when, in 1917 and 1918, he repeatedly propounded the view that continuous and harmonious international co-operation was impossible between autocratically and democratically governed countries. The assumption, however, that such co-operation is more possible between democracies is a bold assumption. It is doubtful whether even a common

CHAP. XI. democratic ideology can overcome differences of interest brought about by the opposing economic claims of nations, their differing geographical position, the diverse inheritance of national traditions and prejudices, unless these differences be voluntarily subordinated to the superior claim of order in the world. Indeed, without general subordination of self on the part of democracies before the overmastering claims of order in the world, there is some reason to think that the propagation of democracy increases rather than diminishes the difficulty of world government. Popular types less readily combine, perhaps, than other types of government.

And if there were fatal divergences in the types of government among the five great Powers of the "alliance," there was something fatal in the end which it set itself, the suppression of so-called "revolution," by which was meant a recrudescence of the spirit of 1789 or perhaps of 1793. That spirit was of course a force throughout the nineteenth century and is not wholly dead to-day, but it was yielding way to novel movements, equally antagonistic to the men of the alliance, but not always clearly appreciated by them. The revolution of "the rights of man," of "Liberty, Equality, Fraternity," was the product of the contractual philosophy. Its hierophants looked backward to a social contract, none the worse for being imaginary, by which to justify their theories and their acts. The doctrines of the utilitarian philosophers, like Jeremy Bentham,[2] proposed a different test, "the greatest happiness of the greatest number." It was the source of that characteristically British form of radicalism which, individualistic in its outlook, and by historic chance parliamentary in its expression, did inspire many of the leaders of the liberals and constitutionalists upon the continent. So strong was this movement in its influence upon continental thought, that many reacted from it at a rather later date to the various socialistic theories of society. All these developments moved in an arena wholly foreign to the theoretical legitimists. They were, in fact, as Bismarck was fond of pointing out, so engaged in fighting the opponents of their own creation, that they failed to observe that attacks had developed or might develop upon them and their doctrine from a somewhat new direction. It was but another manifestation of their inability to appreciate the outlook of their contemporaries that they misunderstood the force of nationalism, no longer the pose of a few vague sentimentalists, but tempered to make an energising force in politics during the experiences which Spaniards and Prussians and others had undergone in the Napoleonic epoch.

Another reason which would have in any case contributed to the lack of permanence in this alliance of the five Powers lay in the impossibility of finding in it some standing for the smaller states. Castlereagh and Alexander had both been anxious to take the small nations into account—the first in the Treaty of Chaumont, the second in his scheme for the Holy Alliance. The world, however, still lacked experience, and the allies had had no time to permit the elaboration of a scheme which would have combined the advantages of concentrated force and universal representation on a basis satisfactory to the minor Powers. The best attained in this direction was the arrangement of the protocol of 1818, by which the smaller states themselves were to invoke the attention of the four-Power alliance to affairs which especially concerned them, and by which they were to be represented at such assemblies as considered these. Some attempt was indeed made at Troppau, Laibach, and Verona to accord a hearing to the states of Italy—but in the most important case, that of Naples, the conference denied all rights to the "revolutionary" government. Sweden had by 1818 protested against the four-Power alliance. In January 1823 Württemberg protested against its exclusion from Verona in a notorious circular letter. This the congress compelled it to withdraw. One of the acutest devices which Canning employed to kill the government by Areopagus was to pose as the champion of the smaller states. In 1823 entry was demanded for the United States into any conference on Spanish America, and the equality of Russian, Austrian, and Prussian interest in that sphere with that of the United States was formally denied. Similarly, when a conference in 1826 seemed likely to be held on Near Eastern matters, the special claims of the Netherlands were pressed, especially as compared with Prussia, which had "a smaller maritime interest."

Another real obstacle to the efficiency of government by Areopagus was, as Professor Webster has pointed out, the enormous obstacles to travel and communication involved in the elementary means of locomotion of the day. In any matter which vitally concerns a state it is difficult to confer full powers on any plenipotentiary, however outstanding. This is what gave importance to the fact that Alexander had peripatetic habits and loved to exchange the society of Russia for that of the congresses. With the Tsar Nicholas it was otherwise in both respects. It is not too much to say that the congress system would have broken down far earlier had death removed Alexander before it did. The Austrians and Prussians, being centrally situated, had a rather easier task than the Russians. But Castlereagh, as a parliamentary statesman, would have found it impossible to have attended constant congresses, even if he had desired to do so. He had to be brought back from Vienna in 1815 to defend the European settlement before the House of Commons. If the Queen had died a little earlier he would have had to be fetched home from Aix-la-Chapelle: and his parliamentary duties had so worn him out in 1822 that he took his life. The corpulent and ageing Louis XVIII. had no relish for lengthy journeys, and ministers like Decazes and Villèle thought, and perhaps rightly thought, their European importance greater if they remained in Paris. Moreover, they dreaded the loss of influence with the King and the Chambers which remoteness from Paris involved.

It was Canning who was destined to give the fatal blow to the conference system in both its forms—that is the special gatherings of crowned heads, cabinets and plenipotentiaries on the one hand, and on the other hand the more informal gatherings of ambassadors at any specially troubled moment. Canning's influence in the Cabinet had been hostile to conferences even in the day of Castlereagh. Bathurst, in reporting a Cabinet opinion to Castlereagh then at Aix-la-Chapelle, said of Canning:—

> "He thinks that system of periodical meetings of the four great Powers, with a view to the general concerns of Europe, new, and of very questionable policy; that it will necessarily involve us deeply in all the politics of the continent. . . . He thinks that all other (*i.e.* the smaller) states must protest against such an attempt to place them under subjection; that the meetings may become a scene of cabal and intrigue."

The failure, as it seemed to him, of the Congress of Verona, ending as it did with a split of the five Powers into three parts by their inability to establish unity on the question of Spain, inspired an almost indecent joy in Canning. Writing to Sir C. Bagot at St. Petersburg, on 3rd January 1823, he spoke of "the predominating Areopagitic spirit" being at last "confined" and of "things getting back to a wholesome state again, every nation for itself and God for us all."

The conference system of course was not allowed to die without a struggle. Ambassadorial conferences, especially promoted by Austria and Russia, met during Canning's tenure of the foreign secretaryship at Paris, where much attention was paid to Spanish conditions, at Madrid, St. Petersburg, and Lisbon. The Madrid conferences, intended to give guidance in detail to Ferdinand, restored in 1823, were never attended by an English representative. The English minister at Lisbon was reprimanded for the isolated attendances which he had ventured to put in at the meetings of the allied diplomats at that city: and the ambassador in Paris in a total of sixty-six meetings held by allied diplomats between 1822 and 1826 was only permitted to make five appearances, and those only for the transaction of purely formal business. In St. Petersburg the strained condition of Russo-Turkish relations may perhaps have made Canning a little less hostile to the notion of ambassadorial conferences. Nevertheless, Bagot was blamed for two attendances which he had ventured upon without authorisation, although Stratford Canning, a little later, was instructed to attend a conference "if conference there is to be." Greek and Turkish objections to the jurisdiction of such conferences gave Canning, however, a very welcome opportunity to follow his natural inclination by retreating from a commitment to joint consultation with the four Powers.

But Canning showed equal dislike of congresses on the grand scale such as those of Vienna and Aix. When, in October 1823, Polignac, the French ambassador at the Court of St. James, pressed upon Canning the convocation of a general congress on Spanish-American affairs, Canning flatly refused to enter into any joint deliberations "upon an equal footing with other Powers whose minds were less formed upon that question, and whose interests were less implicated in the decision of it." He made, moreover, a thoroughly disturbing observation when he remarked that the United States of America would have to be admitted, if Powers like Russia, Prussia and Austria, much less vitally concerned, were taken into council. When the general invitation to a Spanish-American congress was issued to the five Powers by the King of Spain in 1823, Canning ruined the prospects of such an assembly by his determined refusal to attend, a refusal justified to the French ambassador on 10th January on the general ground that "conferences are useless or dangerous, useless if we are in agreement, dangerous if we are not." The congress on Graeco-Turkish affairs, demanded by the Tsar Alexander with vehemence, could not be brushed aside

CHAP. XI.

with such easiness, for a Russo-Turkish war might well result from independent Russian action, and in due course set Europe aflame. Canning, therefore, had recourse to raising objections, and did not finally refuse the suggestion till December 1824, in which month the Greeks were told that Great Britain would not become a party to any attempt to force upon them an unwelcome pacification. Even in 1826, on the occasion of Wellington's famous visit to Russia, Canning was not yet prepared for an outright rejection of a congress on the question of Greece and Russo-Turkish affairs. Wellington was instructed to prevent a conference of the five Powers, not by a direct refusal to participate, but by making such impossible conditions as the inclusion of the Netherlands and the choice of London as a meeting place. Another proposal for a congress, this time put forward by Metternich in 1826, was doomed to failure. The envenomed relations between absolutist Spain and "liberal" Portugal threatened a dangerous situation which the ambassadorial conference at Paris had no power to control. Metternich proposed a conference, apparently without the hope of English concurrence, but fully expecting consent from his other three allies. It was now Russia, however, which, in complete contrast to all its previous behaviour as the "perfect European" Power, abruptly brought talk of such a congress to an end by a refusal to enter.

Canning had undoubtedly an honest grievance against the European alliance and its congress system, for he felt keenly not only that it was attempting the impossible task of ruling the world, incidentally in his view upon wrong principles, but also that it wronged Great Britain in not giving due weight to its interests and counsels. This grievance Canning expressed in somewhat rhetorical phrasing in a despatch to Wellesley at Vienna after Metternich had been reported as distressed that Canning should be throwing away Great Britain's place in the alliance :—

> "What is the influence we have had in the counsels of the alliance, and which Prince Metternich exhorts us to be careful not to throw away? We protested at Laibach, we remonstrated at Verona. Our protest was treated as waste paper, our remonstrances mingled with the air!"

It is not easy to answer the question. The old order was shortly to pass away; and the break with that old order, due to Canning, was undoubtedly to free England's hands in the new dispensation under which it was to find itself. But Canning on a last analysis was protesting against the abuses rather than the uses of the system. That Europe passed comparatively smoothly through the critical years which immediately followed the overthrow and removal of the conqueror, who for a generation had formed its government, controlled its policy and dictated its ideas, is testimony enough to the efficacy at the time of the areopagitic method. How could the triumphant armies and governments at Paris have separated in 1815 without retaining any kind of contact? What chance could a policy of splendid isolation have had for any one of those governments, while problems like the management of the army of occupation, or the French payment of the indemnity, were presented continually for solution? And what kind of solution was possible without mutual accommodation which depended on close touch? There could have been for Europe at the moment no policy other than that of Castlereagh and Metternich, and there is a welcome tendency nowadays among historians to do at least the former justice. If the historian go further than such a pronouncement, he ventures upon debatable ground. Has the policy of government by Areopagus bequeathed any ideas to subsequent generations, or was it a flash in the pan? In opposition, or as complementary, to the doctrine of the balance of power there had been forming the conception of the concert of the Powers, the family of nations. This conception was more sharply conceived, and there was opportunity for it to be better understood, after the epoch which has been described. There were pitfalls waiting for any who subscribed to such a conception; the concert, as all diplomatic creations, is not in itself necessarily good or evil, and it is not the last word in international political economy; but to-day at any rate its most intelligent critics will not regard as mere antiquarianism the study of a group of foreign statesmen who, as has been demonstrated, moved among such phenomena as armies of occupation, indemnity payments, ambassadorial conferences, treaties of mutual guarantee, mediation in international disputes, and even minority problems.

NOTES

(1) The chapter is based very largely on the two recent noteworthy Cambridge contributions to the history of the period 1814-1827: Dr. C. K. Webster's *The Foreign Policy of Castlereagh*, and Dr. Harold Temperley's *The Foreign Policy of Canning*.

(2) Bentham's *Principles of Morals and Legislation* was published in 1789.

CHAPTER XII

THE AMERICAS (1)

THE TWO HEMISPHERES—PAN-AMERICANISM.

CHAP. XII. **The Two Hemispheres.**—Washington, on retiring from his second term of office as President of the United States of America, gave a famous warning to the citizens of the growing republic :—

> "Europe has a set of primary interests which to us have none or a very remote relation. Hence she must be engaged in frequent controversies, the causes of which are essentially foreign to our concerns. Hence, therefore, it must be unwise in us to implicate ourselves by artificial ties in the ordinary vicissitudes of her politics . . . our detached and distant situation invites and enables us to pursue a different course. If we remain one people under an efficient government, the period is not far off when we may defy material injury from external annoyance ; when we may take such an attitude as will cause the neutrality we may at any time resolve upon to be scrupulously respected ; when we may choose peace or war as our interest, guided by justice, shall counsel. Why forgo the advantages of so peculiar a situation ? Why quit our own to stand upon foreign ground ? Why by interweaving our destiny with that of any part of Europe entangle our peace and prosperity in the toils of European ambition, rivalship, interest, humor or caprice."

There was no hint in such words of any exclusive political aspirations on the American continent. A constant attitude of neutrality in the conflicts raging in Europe was recommended—advice which had special reference, though it is sometimes forgotten, to the unnecessary and harmful complications in which the policy of the United States might have become involved if the hatred of England, rife in certain sections of the population, had been given a free hand.

When revolution broke out in the South American colonies and in Mexico, the prospects of an attempt to set up a separate American political system, under a cry of "America for the

Americans," was brought appreciably nearer. This was realised far more vividly at first by the statesmen of the European continent than by those of either the United States or England. The autocratic monarchs and their advisers felt the urgency of prompt measures which should aim at mitigating the likelihood of a concerted American movement hostile to European influences and alien to European political conditions. Simultaneously it is a little surprising to learn that the statesmen at Washington showed little eagerness to lead such a movement, deferred their recognition of the first revolutionary governments to the south of them until 1822, went so far as to contemplate the legitimacy of a mother-country's reconquering its colonies, and, even so late as 1826, minimised certain extravagant interpretations put, in Latin-American quarters, upon the Monroe declaration. Meanwhile, English politicians, familiar with the statistics both of the developing British trade with South America and of the demand in the United States for the manufactured goods of their country, took a less alarmist and on the whole a juster view of the new political situation in the Americas. Even they, however, were not free from conservative or sentimental preferences, and felt that much effort might be justifiably expended in attempts to prevent a violent rupture by the South American communities of those monarchic and dynastic ties which bound them to Spain.

CHAP. XII.

The natural attitude, then, in the legitimist circles of Russia, Austria, and Prussia towards the revolutionaries was to favour the attempt of Spain to suppress them by force. The Tsar went furthest in this direction, since, holding the revolution on the other side of the Atlantic was but an outlying manifestation of revolution upon this side of it, a judgment which his brother monarchs would probably have left unchallenged, he extended even to the distant colonies his readiness to aid the Spanish monarchy by force of arms. But beyond this he would have relished a chance of establishing a superiority of Russian prestige in America as consonant with certain peculiar interests of his country in that quarter of the world. Bourbon France in this resembled him more closely than the other Powers. It too, perhaps, cherished a secret hope of gaining once more an American colony in the confusion, and of finding thrones thereby across the seas for scions of the Bourbon house, who might thus reign in Spanish America as "liberal" and yet "legitimist" kings. Already in the case of Buenos Ayres the dictator Pueyrredon had himself offered a

CHAP. XII. throne to Louis Philippe of Orleans, while in 1820 the attempt was made to provoke a similar offer to the Prince of Lucca.

English statesmen had early reached the conclusion that it was impossible to reproduce exactly the conditions of the eighteenth century. Yet since England had been allied throughout the Peninsular campaigns with Spain and Portugal, English statesmen could not completely disinterest themselves in such questions as the determination of the Spanish government to restore its authority in America, the dispute between the United States and Spain over Florida, or the Braganza-Bourbon quarrels in South America. Englishmen did not want, perhaps because they knew they could not hope for, exclusive privileges of trade in a Spanish America which had been a Spanish preserve, but they were prepared to tolerate the normal international competition, tempered perhaps by Spanish preferences. Accordingly they wished to effect a reconciliation between the revolutionaries and the Crown on the avowed basis of the equalisation of rights between all those of Spanish race and the opening, as wide as might be, of the Spanish-American ports to all. Whether such an attempt at mediation in the hands of Castlereagh would have embraced the consideration of the permanent recognition of republican forms of government it is not easy to assert. Spanish determination prevented this British attempt to mediate, with the result that there took place a *de jure* recognition by the United States in March 1822 of the independence of several Spanish-American areas, and a British recognition of the commercial flags of several states in June of the same year.

Late in 1822, as has been seen, the French government, with the approval of Russia, Austria, and Prussia, was about to take action against the Spanish revolutionaries in Europe. The plans then entertained by the French ministry embraced more than European operations. It was hoped to furnish naval support to Bourbon princes, who should be despatched with troops to the New World, and charged "to renew the connection" with Spain.(2) When the French invasion of Spain, after the fall of Cadiz on 30th September 1823, seemed about to attain its final success, and the despatch of the expedition to the colonies seemed imminent, backed as it was by the favour of the autocratic Powers, Canning intervened decisively. Polignac, the French ambassador in London, was invited to a series of conferences at the Foreign Office, in which he was brought to declare that France had no design of acting against the Spanish colonies by force. Nor did the ambassador receive any encouragement from Canning for the proposition which his home government instructed him to lay before the Foreign Secretary, a declaration CHAP. XII.

> "that in the interest of humanity, and especially in that of the Spanish colonies, it would be worthy of the European governments to concert together the means of calming, in those distant and scarcely civilised regions, passions blinded by party spirit." (8)

If the reimposition of Spanish monarchical institutions by force was thus successfully opposed by Canning, a position of wider scope was adopted by the Administration of the United States, one indeed which denied to all European Powers the right to aspire to any further propagation of their institutions upon the American continent. So far as this country was concerned, the *ukase* of the Tsar Alexander of October 1821, which implicitly claimed the north-west American coasts from the Behring Straits to the 51st degree, had revealed the danger of European colonisation upon territories already visualised as American. It then appeared that Russian claims in North America and Franco-Russian designs in South America might very well be rebuffed together by a broad assertion of principle, the public utterance of which would reveal the United States as repelling, amid the plaudits of its own and of Latin-American public sentiment, threats from European Powers of expansion or of conquest. The form chosen for this declaration of policy was the message of President Monroe to Congress on 3rd December 1823. This made mention of the habitual abstinence of the Republic from interference in the internal affairs of European Powers, and asserted the essential difference between the political system of the European alliance and that of America. The United States, it undertook, would not interfere, as it had not in the past interfered, with the existing European dependencies in America, but it held that "the American continents, by the free and independent condition which they have assumed and maintained, are henceforth not to be considered as subjects for future colonisation by any European Powers." Further, it proclaimed that the allied Powers could not extend their political system to either North or South America without imperilling the peace and happiness of the United States, and that the Latin Americans would certainly not voluntarily adopt it. Accordingly, the United States would regard an interposition for the purpose of oppressing or controlling the other American states, recognised by it as independent, as showing an unfriendly disposition towards itself.

The truth is that John Quincy Adams had played a singularly well-judged diplomatic game. The elements in that game were three—a tradition, inherited from the fathers of American government, in favour of abstention and remoteness from the affairs of Europe; a specific disapproval of definite Russian, rumoured French, and possible areopagitic interferences in the affairs of the American continent; and lastly, the approaches which had been made by Canning to Cass, the United States minister in London, during August 1823, with a view to the discussion of the possibility of a joint Anglo-United States protest against all three contingencies, particularly that of the Areopagus. Adams shrewdly saw that Canning would never consent to this last, and under cover of the support which he judged would come, without any bargain, from England, he discharged independently the bombshell of the Monroe message. His main interest was the Russian danger: his pronouncement in fact did cover all the three.

The events which lead up to the message of Monroe form a fascinating object to the historian of diplomatic history. They figure in this work for other reasons. A glance of comparison at the pronouncements of Washington and of Monroe reveals the growth of an attitude in the United States which is of significance to the international lawyer. Was Monroe's message merely the crystallisation in words of a policy: was it comparable, for example, to Louis XIV.'s *il n'y a plus de Pyrénées*? Or was it more than this? Did it announce to the world that the future would show it to consist of two separate hemispheres, divided by an impassable gulf, two hemispheres mutually antagonistic: Europe venerable, the creation of forces and a public law built up through centuries; America full of youth and promise, with its destiny and its international law completely for itself to make? The autocrats saw and dreaded this possibility and thought it probable. Canning understood it and thought it less likely, but, with a truer insight into both the strength and the weakness of the United States, set himself by his policy towards the Americans to do nothing which would render it more probable that this unfortunate condition would be brought about.

It is certain that, if a common democratic ideology, cherished among the political leaders of the two Americas, could in itself have been a broad enough base for the erection of an American political system, one altogether separate from Europe, the ground had now been thoroughly prepared. One way of avoiding such a division between continent and continent would have been the promotion of monarchy in America; and to this plan, as has been said, Canning had had resort so long as there had seemed any possible monarchical elements upon which to build. An alternative method was to strengthen British, as opposed to autocratic, influences in the new countries. In 1824 Canning definitely reached the conclusion that an immediate *de jure* recognition of the South American governments was called for, not only in the interests of British trade but particularly as a demonstration with the object described above in view. With great difficulty he induced the King and the Cabinet to accept his policy, and on 12th May 1825 the first commercial treaty with Buenos Ayres was ratified, and on 7th November a similar treaty with Colombia. And an avowed reason for this decision at a moment at which all the other great Powers of Europe were still bitterly hostile to the new republics, and were indeed concerting with Spain the means of renewing their subjection, was, in his words,

> "the great danger of the time—a danger which the policy of the European system would have fostered—a division of the world into European and American, republican and monarchical; a league of worn-out governments on the one hand, and of youthful and stirring nations, with the Un(ited) States at their head, on the other." (4)

Like most of his contemporaries, and as a price for presenting his views emphatically, Canning can be accused of over-emphasising the immediate strength and potentialities of the American continents as compared with Europe. Even the United States was for many years to be largely dependent on Europe for many types of manufactured goods, for capital, and for man power. Latin America was for the time even less materially developed than the United States. Bolivar himself was capable of describing its population as composed of "Indians and negroes who are more ignorant than the vile race of Spaniards we are just emancipated from." (5) The government of the United States, operating, after the adoption of the Federal constitution, with a precision, method, and efficiency comparable to those of the best European models, possessing a politically harmonious population (racially harmonious also to a very large extent) and

CHAP. XII. great defensive strength, and capable of mobilising a considerable offensive naval force, imposed a real and increasing attitude of respect on Europe. Blinded perhaps by present-day experience of the rich, orderly, and cultured greater Powers of South America, it is hard to realise that not quite the same respect could be felt one hundred years ago for many of the Latin-American states. They lacked an administrative class, were a prey in many cases to constant revolution or military dictatorship, and harboured a population which, as regards all but the higher elements, appeared to live at a low material and intellectual standard. Accordingly, the tendency to treat the Latin-American states as inferior in status to the rest of the society of nations cropped up soon after their entry into it. The era of pacific blockades was not to be long delayed: even in 1899 the Latin-American states were not present at the first Hague Conference.

And yet the progress of time did not tend to bind the New World more closely into a whole, separated from Europe.[(6)] Shipping connections, when established, were rather between Europe and the separate American states than among the American states themselves; and the flow of goods and immigrants has been predominantly inter- rather than intra-continental. Again, in Europe, largely committed in 1823 to the government of despotisms, the broadening of the basis of government made steady progress, particularly after 1848, so that a separation between the continents on the ground of the difference in political theory has become increasingly less real. Even in 1826 Bolivar had recognised that the European governments of England and Holland could, as constitutional monarchies, be invited to his congress of Panama.

Territorial ambition and internecine war were not long in making their appearance upon the American continents, even though these had achieved a free and independent condition. The Congress of Panama, held in 1826, between Colombia, Mexico, Peru, and Guatemala, would have liked to found a common defensive system among the four states, to which others later might adhere. Little welcome was given to the plan, and the opportunity was lost of making, however bootlessly, a demonstration that war within the American continents would be ostracised. Perhaps even the four states themselves felt some scepticism as to the result of their labours, for the relations between the former Spanish state, the Argentine, and the former Portuguese state, Brazil, were already embittered by a dispute for the possession of Montevideo. The war between the United States and Mexico during the 'forties revealed the fact that land-hunger could produce upon the American continent wars as aggressive and peace terms as severe as those of the most reprobated European prototypes. CHAP. XII.

The declaration of Monroe and the determination of Canning to fight against any other reconqueror than Spain arrested European plans for reconquering the colonies. The growing wealth and power of the United States and its well-founded jealousy of European interference, military or diplomatic, in any part of the continent, were soon to produce remarkable developments in the interpretation of the Monroe doctrine. Polk, in his annual message of 3rd December 1845, reaffirmed that doctrine in an aggressive form. He asserted that the people of the American continent had a complete right to determine their own destinies, and that, if any part of them should decide to join the United States, European interference in the pursuit of a " balance of power " would not be tolerated. As a policy it seems impossible to criticise this pronouncement, which is only comparable to many policies directed towards an extension of influence such as are familiar enough in history. Texas was accordingly absorbed, despite the efforts of England and France, and the defeated Mexico was compelled to yield vast stretches of territory in California. That the expansion rested upon policy and not principle was clearly indicated in the determined attacks from Washington on the British positions in Central America, at Belize, and on the Moskito coasts by the Nicaraguan border. The incidents mark a further stage in the developing interpretation of the Monroe message. Washington's recommendation of abstinence from entangling alliances had been followed by Adams' ideal of the separate system. This was to be exchanged for that of a system which hinged upon the hegemony of the United States.

In 1852 a joint Franco-British proposal that the United States should join in a tripartite pact of self-denial with respect to Cuba provoked a further development. Everett, the new Secretary of State, not only proclaimed an exclusive interest for the United States in the affairs of Cuba, but announced that the " manifest destiny " of all European colonies in the Americas was to fall under the dominion of the United States. It is not to be wondered at that British statesmen began to formulate definite objections to the Monroe doctrine. Clarendon in 1854 [7] denied that the

CHAP. XII.

Monroe doctrine was an "international axiom" which ought to regulate the conduct of European states. Disraeli in a Parliamentary speech on 16th June 1856 (8) asked the British ministers to recognise the increase of the power of the United States, but at the same time to impress upon its statesmen that "instead of vaunting that they will build their greatness upon the Monroe doctrine, which is the doctrine of isolation," they should undertake the attainment of greatness by accepting the regulation of their destiny by "the same high principles of policy" as were recognised by the European governments. Far more important than such utterances came the accomplishment of Canadian confederation in 1867.

Had the secession of the Southern States been permanent, and the Union been divided into two bitterly antagonistic groups of states, not only would the knell of the Monroe doctrine have been sounded, but European influence would have been able to dominate Latin America and to immobilise North America by a balance of power. Echoes of the British reaction to the lofty language of Everett were found in the unfortunate early pronouncements of men like Gladstone, who, beside feeling some impatience with swashbuckling sentiments of the type described, detected a violation of the principles of Liberalism in the attempt of the Federals to prevent secession by force. But if unwise language led to unwise action on the part of Englishmen during the Civil War, the chief offender was not English. The third Napoleon, by importing a Catholic prince from Europe to Mexico to head the Catholic and monarchical party in that country, issued a direct challenge to the theory of American separateness. The Federal government, as soon as liberty of action had been regained by the victorious conclusion of the Civil War, insisted on a speedy termination of the Mexican adventure, which indeed ended ignominiously in 1867. It says much for the restraint of the government of the United States that, both in bringing this about, and in settling with Great Britain the claims for damage which arose out of its behaviour in the Civil War, recourse was had to peaceful methods. There were many elements in the United States which would gladly have ventured on a war with England—a war in which Canada would have been the prize of victory, and by which, if victoriously conducted, the expulsion of European influence from America would have been completed. Spain also had landed troops in San Domingo in 1861 which were not withdrawn till 1863.

Once more let it be said that American ambition and European resistance to it, as exemplified by such disputes, is a matter of interest to the historian and to the politician on both sides of the Atlantic. What is important to note is the difference between the Monroe doctrine as stated in the middle of the century, and the isolation policy of George Washington, or even the doctrine as it left the pen of Monroe. To the principle of that doctrine in its primitive form it is conceivable that all the American nations might have been rallied. Had that come about, a phenomenon would have been produced which would have profoundly affected International Law, for it might have involved the break-up of the Society of Nations into two perfectly separate groups. It was the accretions to that doctrine, added during the first half of the nineteenth century, which not only marred its primitive simplicity but also destroyed its appeal, for the successors of George Washington had turned it from a principle into a policy. To say this is not to deny the perfect right of the United States to have done so, or to attempt to do anything so foolish as to underestimate its force. The late Admiral Mahan was, as usual, near the mark when he said that the real effect of the Monroe doctrine has been to create among the people of the United States, and for ever, a specific "sensitiveness" in foreign affairs. The transformation of the doctrine is none the less a real one. As a policy of the United States it survives, and is felt by every European, every Asiatic, and every South American state; but it retains no attraction as a principle for the governments of South and Central America.

Pan-Americanism.—And it did not need the challenge of the third Napoleon: other forces were rendering unreal the ideal of American "separateness," even as they were disrupting the unity of the Americas. The advent of Blaine to the Secretaryship of State in 1881 was marked by an effort on the part of the executive of the United States to return to the special temper of American exclusiveness towards Europe which had been a feature of Monroe's address. There had been a notable falling-off in Pan-American sentiment since the days of Bolivar and Adams. Not only had German immigrants flocked to Brazil, and Italian to the Argentine, subtly affecting thereby the outlook of South America, but the United States itself had been capable in 1875 of inviting the great European Powers to undertake a joint intervention in Cuba. Blaine was jealous of any European mediation or intervention between the American nations, and tried to

CHAP. XII.

introduce the conception that such exertions were the proper province of the United States alone. He objected specifically to the contemplated Spanish arbitration between Colombia and Costa Rica. He warned France against undertaking intervention in the war between Peru, Bolivia, and Chili, a struggle which he attempted to compose by means of the diplomacy of his own country. He intervened himself, lest others might step in, during the war between Mexico and Guatemala. No less opposed was he to the ordinary operation of reprisal as between a European and an American Power. Rather than see French marines landed in Venezuela to collect a debt, he was prepared to seize the Venezuelan customs himself and to raise the money by their means to pay the debt to France.(9)

The climax of Blaine's Pan-American policy was to be the Pan-American Conference, for which invitations were issued in November 1881, and whose avowed aim was the promotion of arbitration on the American continent and the prevention of war. Blaine's successor, Frelinghuysen, recalled the invitations, however, alleging the danger of offending the non-participant governments. He thereby called forth from Blaine the stinging rebuke that he could imagine no greater humiliation "unless we should petition the European governments for the privilege of holding the congress." (10) Blaine's persistent advocacy of the Pan-American idea, and the hostility towards Europe which he fostered, were not long in producing their effect. In 1888 the Congress of the United States passed into law a bill which authorised a Pan-American conference and enumerated eight topics for its agenda—better means of communication, a customs union, uniformity of customs regulations, uniformity of weights and measures, protection of copyright, trade marks and patents, a common American silver coinage, extradition, and compulsory arbitration. If any such discussion had issued in result, America at a bound would have more than overtaken the development of technique in Europe, as concerning affairs only semi-political, so painfully and laboriously produced by half a century of negotiation and of discussion in conference. The Pan-American conferences, however, were not destined to bear any very striking fruit. Neither at Washington in 1889, at Mexico in 1901, at Rio de Janeiro in 1906, at Buenos Ayres in 1910, nor at Santiago in 1923, could results be shown equal in any sense to those attained at either of the Hague Peace Conferences.(11) Nor did any institution issue from the deliberation of the Pan-

American meetings comparable in authority to, let us not even say the League of Nations, but to the Hague tribunal. No more striking commentary on the languid evolution of human institutions could be adduced than the reflection that the fourth Pan-American gathering, for example, should have occupied itself, among other kindred subjects, with such relative trivialities as the standardisation of consular forms, the uniformity of consular fees, or the exchange of professors and college students, when the first conference had begun its labours with aims in view so much more ambitious than these.

And although the United States had hopefully initiated this novel movement, it was long before it evinced any sign of surrendering to the corporate action of the other American states its special claim to protect the American continent, a step which in some form might well be adjudged by its *confrères* a pre-requisite of any hearty impulse towards the formation of an American political league, however loosely knit. The remaining states had presumably no objection to Cleveland's defence of Venezuela against Great Britain even when it was accompanied by the pronouncement of his Secretary of State, Olney :—

> "To-day the United States is practically sovereign in this continent, and its *fiat* is law upon the subjects to which it confines its interposition."

Less to their taste, no doubt, was the extension by Roosevelt(12) of the Monroe doctrine, under which the United States was to undertake measures to compel American states in default to meet their obligations in Europe, in order to prevent direct European action against such states, a device foreshadowed by Blaine. The sound of his pronouncement cannot have been pleasant in South and Central America, when he declared :—

> "Chronic wrongdoing, or an impotence which results in the loosening of the ties of civil society, may in America, as elsewhere, ultimately require intervention by some civilised nation, and in the Western Hemisphere the adherence of the United States to the Monroe doctrine may force the United States, however reluctantly, in flagrant cases of wrongdoing or impotence, to exercise an international police power." (13)

Such "police" activities as those represented by the occupation of the free and independent republics of San Domingo and Nicaragua, or the refusal to allow Colombia to make war upon the rebellious province of Panama, were sufficiently alarming to Latin-American opinion. The forti-

CHAP. XII. fication against treaty stipulation of the Panama Canal has left its impression. When the possibility of " police action " in Mexico was suggested by the occupation by the United States of Vera Cruz in 1914, the governments of Argentina, Brazil, and Chili in alarm busied themselves at once in an attempt to create a stable government in Mexico and to mediate between it and the United States.

Attempts by other American governments to procure from their great northern neighbour the admission that the protection of the American continent was the joint concern of all the American states have so far proved unsuccessful. Never was this made more clear than in Mr. Hughes' speech at Minneapolis at the end of August 1923. Mr. Hughes denied that the Monroe doctrine was an obstacle either to Pan-American, or to world, co-operation. The doctrine, he said, was an assertion of the principle of national security, and it was to be defined, interpreted, and applied by the United States alone. He might indeed have said that the Monroe doctrine had in a sense disappeared. One portion of it vanished when the United States brought its welcome and decisive help to the Allies in the course of 1917. What the United States sees fit to do in "asserting its national security," either in France or in the countries to its south, is discussible only on a basis of foreign policy with which this chapter is not concerned. With one event of recent history it is, however, concerned—the fact that in the League of Nations there are included many American nations that are members, and at least one American nation that is not a member, of the Pan-American fraternity of states. It is not easy to reconcile this with the pure milk of the Monroe gospel, as Washington foreshadowed it and as Monroe himself pronounced it. That the League of Nations has been careful to avoid any intervention in America, although invited by Bolivia in the course of its dispute with Chili (in 1922), and by both Costa Rica and Panama in their dangerous difference over boundaries in 1921, is attributable less to the evangelistic principles laid down by President Monroe than to the Pauline interpretation of the text by his various successors.

NOTES

(1) There is now a considerable library of works devoted to the history of American foreign policy. Fish's *American Diplomacy* is an able, authoritative, and useful summary. Hart's *Foundations*

of *American Foreign Policy* and Coolidge's *The United States as a World-Power* are now oldish works. CHAP. XII.

In addition to general works on American diplomatic history, there are specialist works on its particular aspects—especially the Monroe doctrine. Thomas's *One Hundred Years of the Monroe Doctrine* (1923) is a recent example of copious American commentary. The Englishman Reddaway, several Frenchmen, and the German Kraus (1913) have contributed volumes to the discussion, and the South American Alvarez has had his volume printed by the Carnegie Endowment.

In regard to the Panama Canal, the work of H. Arias (1911) may be mentioned.

In regard to Anglo-American relations, the earlier work of Dunning and the more recent volume of Mowat make profitable reading.

(2) Temperley's *Foreign Policy of Canning*, pp. 108-109.

(3) *Ibid.*, p. 117.

(4) Temperley's *Foreign Policy of Canning*, pp. 158-159.

(5) In Temperley, p. 557.

(6) Alvarez, nevertheless, and without unanimous applause even in Latin America, attempted to prove in his *Droit International Américain* (1910) that the American states, especially in immigration, frontier, and communication questions, had laid the basis of a new and specifically American international law. Roland Usher's strikingly pessimistic *Pan-Americanism* (1915) often seems much more to the point.

(7) A. P. Newton in *Camb. Hist., For. Policy*, vol. ii. p. 273.

(8) *Ibid.*, vol. ii. p. 277.

(9) Cf. Fish's *American Diplomacy*, pp. 384-388.

(10) Thomas, *One Hundred Years of the Monroe Doctrine*, pp. 407-408.

(11) That the United States of America are still at least sentimentally attached to the idea of a special American international spirit was never shown more obviously than when in January 1928 the American President, Coolidge, resolved to attend in person the 1928 Pan-American Conference.

(12) There can be no doubt that Roosevelt's methods, and the particular Imperialist mentality among sections of the Republican party which he represented, powerfully reinforced the Spanish-American sentiment, strongly based on literature, language, and history, as opposed to the Pan-American, grounded only on a rather unreal geography and political ideology. Such works as that by the Peruvian Garcia Calderon, *Latin America* (1913), give ample proof of this. Yet after 1918, when Latin America was compelled to look very largely to New York for the capital necessary for its development, the sentiment of independence and equality was tempered by the practical need of standing well with Washington and Wall Street.

(13) Thomas, *One Hundred Years of the Monroe Doctrine*, p. 215.

CHAPTER XIII

ARBITRATION

The Practice of Arbitration.

CHAP. XIII. **The Practice of Arbitration.**[1]—Arbitration in the Middle Ages.—The thirteenth century, an age in which the relative debarbarisation of Europe had been completed, and a period in which universities, lawyers, and theologians were acquiring a status not unworthy of a civilised epoch, was a time at which the practice of referring disputes between rulers, potentates, and cities to impartial persons of high authority would almost inevitably grow. The records of the Italian cities and states show that not less than one hundred Italian arbitrations were undertaken in this century,[2] while the judgment of Popes, or of such eminent rulers as King Louis IX. of France, was sought freely by communities which had become involved in difficult disputes. English historians can produce the famous case of the arbitration conducted by St. Louis between his brother sovereign, King Henry III. of England, and the barons of that realm. The history of Eastern Europe produces instances as curious as the nomination of two bishops and a soldier as arbitrators between the Kings of Bohemia and Hungary.[3]

Although authorities claim to have detected a diminution in the number of arbitrations after the beginning of the fourteenth,[4] records of cases are still plentiful in succeeding centuries. One particularly interesting institution to modern eyes is the treaty which contains a clause defining, in advance of the disputes, the method by which they shall be adjudged. Venice and Genoa concluded such a treaty in 1235, under which the Pope was chosen as their arbitrator. In the "perpetual" peace of 1516 between Francis I. and the Swiss cantons arrangements for arbitration were made to cover the event of a dispute between French and Swiss citizens, as also between Swiss citizens and the King of France.

Treaties of peace made between two or more parties which had lately been at war were particularly apt to contain provisions for the reference of such matters as were still in dispute to the judgment of a neutral sovereign or of a court composed of an equal number of persons nominated by either side. Thus the Treaty of Vervins of 1598 provided for the arbitration of the Pope in the dispute which had arisen between the King of France and the Duke of Savoy concerning the succession to the marquisate of Saluzzo. The Treaty of Westminster signed between France and the government of Cromwell in 1655 provided for arbitration by the state of Hamburg in the calculation of damage suffered by either side since 1640.(5) On the other hand, the Anglo-Dutch peace of 1654 referred the question of certain losses suffered by English merchants in Denmark as a result of action by the Dutch to an arbitral commission of four; (6) and the long and embittered claim and counter-claim in the East Indies was referred to an arbitral commission of eight.(7) The peace concluded at Utrecht between England and France provided in Article 10 for one set of commissioners to decide the boundaries between Hudson's Bay and the French territories, and in Article 11 for another set to make decision on claims made by the subjects of one country against the other country's government in respect of raids and spoliation.

Modern arbitration is usually said to have had its origin in the arbitration proceedings undertaken in virtue of the treaty between England and the United States signed in 1794, and commonly known as the Jay Treaty. Certainly there is a striking contrast between the meagre tale of arbitrations to which resort was had during the eighteenth century, and that of the nineteenth century, in which between 1794 and 1900, according to Oppenheim,(8) no less than one hundred and seventy-seven must be reckoned. Under the Jay Treaty three matters were referred to joint commissions set up in virtue of the compact. Under its Article 5 an English commissioner, together with one appointed by the United States, succeeded in 1796 in agreeing upon the choice of a third member of their board. The three, after hearing extensive evidence and examining the maps of surveyors, agreed in 1798 upon a declaration and a map, in which position beyond dispute was given to the "St. Croix river," a loosely chosen term fixed by the negotiators of 1783 to define part of the future boundary between the British possessions and the United States. The two other arbitral commissions did not have such comparatively smooth sailing. That appointed by virtue of Article VI., to sit upon the whole question of the

CHAP. XIII.

judicial obstruction to the collection of debts, broke up amid high feeling in 1799; while that appointed under Article VII., to assess the damages complained of in consequence of British naval measures in the French war, though it did indeed conclude its labours in 1804, had to suspend its proceedings between 1799 and 1802.

Under the Anglo-American Treaty of Ghent two arbitrations were agreed upon—the first concerning itself with the disputed sovereignty over islands in the Bay of Fundy, the second dealing with the "north-eastern boundary," which had been inadequately defined in the treaty of 1783. For these arbitrations the treaty established the appointment of only two commissioners, one from either side. If these should prove unable to produce a united report, the matter at issue between them was to be referred to a neutral sovereign, or state, whose decision was to be final and conclusive. The matter of the islands gave little trouble, and a united report was furnished by the two commissioners in November 1817. The north-eastern boundary was not decided so readily. Although the proceedings dragged on from 1816 to 1822, agreement was not reached by the commissioners, who presented differing reports. The two governments, after a long and troubled interval, began in 1827 the consideration of the choice of the neutral arbiter. By 1828, after tedious negotiation, they had fixed on the King of the Netherlands and had agreed upon the material which should be presented to him in order to facilitate a judgment. In 1831 he gave his award. This, however, was not of a final character but merely recommendatory, and it was politely put aside by both parties to the dispute, who resumed negotiations. These were not conducted to a final conclusion until the signature of the Webster-Ashburton Treaty in 1842.

But before the fiasco of 1831 England and the United States had already successfully invoked the arbitration of a European ruler for the decision of a dispute. In 1822 the Tsar Alexander had made an award which had been accepted by both sides, and later in 1871 the German emperor was to arbitrate between the two countries in the Juan de Fuca boundary. It was perhaps rather the Genevan arbitration of 1871-1872 on the *Alabama* claims which provided the most instructive education in the methods, possibilities and advantages of arbitration. The two nations had agreed early in 1871 to refer a number of points to a joint High Commission. When the commission met, the Americans unexpectedly introduced a series of propositions which professed to define the duties incumbent upon a neutral "great maritime power," and claimed compensation for the violation of these "duties" by Great Britain during the course of the recent Civil War, or, alternatively, the reference of the question of liability to an agreed tribunal. The claims indeed had been anticipated, but not so the far-reaching propositions upon which they had been based. After much diplomatic effort had been expended within the joint commission, the American propositions, which without question extended far beyond the commonly understood duties of a neutral Power in 1861, were considerably amended in the Washington Treaty of 1871. In their amended form they were then adopted as an instruction to the tribunal of arbitration. This was to hold its sessions at Geneva, and was to contain, beside representatives of Great Britain and the United States, arbiters nominated by the Emperor of Brazil, the King of Italy, and the Swiss Confederation.

These arbitrators sat between 15th December 1871 and 14th September 1872. The proceedings were all but wrecked at the beginning by the American introduction of claims for indirect damage, as well as those for direct damage, which latter were in principle accepted. A grave crisis between the two governments lasted for several months, and proved, if the cases of 1794, 1814, and 1831 had not already done so, how carefully diplomats had need to define beforehand the precise limit of a tribunal's discretion. It proved that more undesirable consequences might be attached to a breach which arose before a tribunal and was public and advertised, than were produced when it took the more concealed form of a difference between the Foreign Offices. In this case the Anglo-American dispute was solved by a private diplomatic understanding that the tribunal itself would rule out the consideration of claims for indirect damage. This understanding materialised when the tribunal on 14th June issued its first decision, whereby the indirect claims were declared not to constitute a good basis for an award of compensation, even if there were to arise no disagreement between the governments as to the competency of the tribunal to admit the consideration of them. If the United States had here to make something of a surrender, Great Britain was destined to offer the final sacrifice, for the four non-British arbitrators awarded damages to the amount of fifteen and a half million dollars. Although this proved in the event to have been an

CHAP. XIII.

excessive figure and the British public was astounded by its size, the Cabinet resolved to accept the award despite the disagreement of their representative.

In the arbitration of 1893 over the fisheries of the Behring Sea, the tribunal, composed of one British, one American and five disinterested European representatives, gave a verdict which has been pronounced technically more defensible. In this case, however, national feeling ran less high and the arbitrators had a more easy task.

Another crisis arose between the United States and England in connection with the boundary of Venezuela. In its origin, a dispute between that country and British Guiana, interest was quickly provoked at Washington. In 1886 the ministry of Mr. Gladstone, then nearing its last days, had been preparing an agreement with Venezuela, under the terms of which the controversy was to have been submitted to the arbitration of a third state or states. The government of Lord Salisbury, however, adopted a somewhat stiffer attitude and insisted on the acknowledgment of a boundary line to be found in the British survey of 1848. In 1895 Olney, the Secretary of State, annoyed perhaps by a succession of obstructive or evasive answers suffered by the Department of State over this question since 1886, made the demand that the boundary question in all its fullness should be submitted to arbitration, and not merely such portions of the question as should have seemed to the British government suitable for such submission. Lord Salisbury replied with a paper which in effect constituted a lecture on the misapplication by Olney of the Monroe doctrine. Roused by the refusal to accept the doctrine as binding upon Great Britain, President Cleveland asserted on behalf of the United States, by virtue of the Monroe doctrine and because of its special geographical position, a right to decide the disputed boundary line. Feeling ran high in the United States, and could not be satisfied by Lord Salisbury's first offer, under which, except as regards such land as had been in *bona fide* occupation since the beginning of 1887, the decision would be placed in the hands of a tribunal of three persons, one to be appointed by England, another by Venezuela, and a third to be co-opted by the other two. The President insisted on unconditional arbitration, and obtained it in the treaty of 1897. A court of five was to be constituted under this compact. Two members were to be appointed to it by England, one by Venezuela, one by the United States. The fifth member, the Russian de

Martens, was co-opted by the other four. To a majority of this court the decision was confided, and it reached a decision, predominantly favourable to Great Britain, on 3rd October 1899. CHAP. XIII.

Arbitration, though not very frequently employed for the decision of political disputes between Powers in Europe during the nineteenth century, had been far from unknown on that continent. The two most familiar instances of a full political arbitration were perhaps that undertaken by President Macmahon between England and Portugal over Delagoa Bay in 1875, and that of the Pope between Germany and Spain on the subject of the Caroline Islands in 1885. In matters of less grave import there had been freer use of this method of appeasement. Statistics indicate that France employed it on 38 occasions, Germany on 16, Portugal on 14, Italy on 13, Spain on 11, Russia on 7, Holland on 6, Austria and Turkey on 5, Greece on 4, Switzerland and Norway-Sweden on 3, Belgium on 2, and Denmark on 1, but it has to be admitted that the issues in these cases were often of a trivial character.(9) Yet resort to arbitration was becoming in a sense habitual towards the end of the century, and a certain type of treaty was increasingly to be found which provided for it in advance. Thus there were seventeen Italian treaties which made provision for arbitration in the case of a sharp difference of opinion as to the application or interpretation of any point in their terms, at least as regards such clauses as dealt with commercial, shipping, or extradition matters. The commercial treaty between Portugal and Holland of 1894 was noteworthy as marking an even further development, for it was the first to provide, as between European Powers, that all the disputes arising between the parties, and not involving their independence, should be submitted to arbitration. Although a new feature in European treaties, such clauses were already to be found in treaties between the Powers of Latin America, which had indeed been engaged almost from the moment of their independence in inserting clauses in their treaties enjoining arbitration.

The Hague Conference of 1899 thus found a widely spread international custom of arbitration of some sort. It devoted a great part of its energies (10) to the regulation of it by the definition of its modes and scope. It gave to " the pacific settlement of international disputes " a special section among its conventions. A " Permanent Court of Arbitration " was erected at The Hague in order to furnish a body to which such Powers as had agreed on arbitration might instantly turn

CHAP. XIII.

for fit and proper arbiters. The "Permanent" court was indeed only "Permanent" as regards the place of its session and in having a fixed and continuous registry, for the judges were to be selected from a panel by the litigating parties on an agreed plan. It was laid down that to this panel each Power might nominate not more than four persons. Article XXVII. of the convention ventured to proclaim that the signatory Powers considered it their duty, should a serious dispute break out between any of their number, to remind the disputants that the "Permanent Court" was open to them.

Beside this measure a new international institution, not properly of arbitration, but rather of an interlocutory nature, was set up in the provision for commissions of inquiry. In disputes such as those arising from a difference of opinion as to facts which could be ascertained by local examination and which did not involve either the honour or the vital interests of the disputants, the signatories pledged themselves to the use of such commissions of inquiry. The Dogger Bank incident of 1904, which nearly provoked an Anglo-Russian crisis, indicated that the timely use of this institution could prevent the gravest consequences.

The Russian proposals on the subject of arbitration, as originally drafted, had been in one respect more drastic by far than the final convention agreed to. In the note explanatory of their draft the Russians had pointed out that in the sphere of international relations there existed extensive areas not properly considered political; and that, as regards these, the practice of submission to arbitration might well no longer rest on the free consent of the parties to a controversy, but be generally adopted as the compulsory rule. They argued that all states would gain by the adoption of such a rule. Their diplomatic machinery would be free to pursue ends admittedly political; and would be unfettered by the drudgery involved in business not indeed political, but often of a most contentious nature. If this were the argument addressed to the greater Powers, others were adduced by the Russian representatives which were calculated especially to attract the smaller. It was pointed out that under the system proposed legitimate claims would be more easily sustained and that unjustifiable demands would be more easily evaded. On these grounds the Russians proposed to class as arbitrable without option, so far indeed as they did not involve vital interests or national honour, the following types of international disagreement:—

(1) Disputes relating to pecuniary damages suffered by a state, or its nationals, as a consequence of illegal actions, or negligence, on the part of another state or its nationals.

(2) Disputes concerning the application or interpretation of

(*a*) postal, telegraph, railway or cable treaties: high sea regulations against collisions, conventions for the navigation of international rivers and interoceanic canals;

(*b*) conventions for the protection of literary, artistic and industrial property; those regulating money and measures; sanitary, veterinary or phylloxera conventions;

(*c*) conventions relating to inheritance, exchange of prisoners and reciprocal assistance in the administration of justice;

(*d*) boundary conventions, so far as the dispute were technical and not political.

The Russian proposal, as was obvious from its scope, was the result of international experience lasting over a century. The inevitable attempt was made at once by other countries to extend the Russian list of compulsorily arbitrable cases. Belgium, for example, proposed to add to the cases enumerated above all disputes arising from commercial or consular treaties: Italy suggested the addition of those which rose out of conventions relating to the free reciprocal aid of the sick and indigent, Holland those which concerned agreements as to the treatment of the sick and wounded in war. The first blow to the original proposal came from the United States, whose delegate, Mr. Holls, asked for the exclusion from the list of all treaties which referred to international rivers or interoceanic canals and monetary systems. The final blow came from Germany. In the session of 4th July the withdrawal of Articles IX. and X. of the Russian draft was demanded on the part of Germany by Dr. Zorn. These were the clauses which would have established compulsory arbitration and have defined its scope, so that the motion amounted to a direct negative. He said that Germany considered the time inopportune for an international agreement on any list of always arbitrable cases pending the accumulation of experience by the various nations in the working of the voluntary machinery which had been established.

CHAP. XIII.

The admirable draftsmanship of the convention for the "pacific settlement of international disputes" must have made considerable impression on the chancelleries of the Powers. Governments between whom relations were good began to sign special treaties of general arbitration as between themselves. Under these, differences "of a juridical order," to use the phrase commonly employed, if not settled by diplomatic methods, and if not involving considerations of vital national interest or honour, were to be settled by the arbitration of the Hague court. The first sign of improvement in the relations between France and England after the untoward events of 1898 was the arbitration treaty signed between them on 14th October 1903. Nine other treaties on somewhat the same lines were made by England before the end of 1905 with other European states. These treaties were all made for periods of five years. Though Anglo-American agreements for arbitration in individual cases had been prominent in the history of this problem, it proved more difficult to establish a general treaty between Great Britain and the United States. The reason is obvious. The federal nature of the constitution, and the strictly limited powers of the federal executive, made the government of the Republic as cautious of committing it to general and permanently binding international engagements as analogous, if not identical, considerations are now making the various constitutional advisers to the King in any one portion of the British Empire chary of attempting to commit any other portion of it, or the whole, to such engagements. Action is not impossible, but it is almost infinitely difficult. A very bold project was entertained on both sides of the Atlantic in 1897, but was brought to nought by the opposition of a minority in the Senate of the United States. At the time at which the Anglo-Venezuelan arbitration treaty was taking shape another and more general treaty was being drafted. By the treaty of 11th January 1897 all Anglo-American differences whatsoever were to be referred to arbitration; and no less than three different types of tribunals were adumbrated, each for a different purpose. That destined to settle cases of major dispute, such as those on territorial claims (the British-American dispute over the Yukon was ready for immediate reference) or national rights (the famous dispute over fisheries in the North Atlantic was typical of these), was to consist of a court of six persons composed of High Court judges appointed to the number of three by each party. A decision, to be authoritative, was to require a vote of at least five to one in its support. The previous history of arbitral disputes between the countries hardly suggested that the record of accomplishment under these conditions would be high. At any rate the treaty was rejected by the Senate, in which the required majority was not obtained. Jealousy for its treaty-making power, dislike of England, apprehension for the sanctity of the Monroe doctrine, and a quite perceptible fear lest there should be brought before the proposed tribunal the question of the unpaid financial obligations of certain southern states—all played their part in bringing about this decision of the Senate. And indeed no British-American treaty of arbitration was signed till 1908, while less ambitious treaties to the same end with other European states were wrecked because of constitutional disputes in the United States.

The question of compulsory arbitration, limited in the debates of 1899 to the small field above described, was given a broader scope in the debates of the Hague Conference of 1907. Even if the Russian draft proposals of 1899 had been successful, there would have been no general international treaty of compulsory obligation and no separate document embodying it. In 1907 the representatives of thirteen smaller nations openly advocated the preparation of such a document; and Sir Edward Fry from England, together with Mr. Choate from the United States, joined them. The Baron Marschall von Bieberstein, the German representative, stood out in voicing complete and continual opposition. Finally, an American project (11) for a general treaty of a kind was referred to a committee, the chief task of which was the definition of the class of cases to which it should apply. Thirty types altogether were proposed, but for the adoption of only eight types of cases was a majority obtained. The German and Austrian delegates voted consistently for the rejection of all the types suggested; the Norwegian, Dutch, Portuguese, and Serbian delegations voted with equal consistency, in the case of each type of issue, for adoption. As to the notion of a general treaty itself, the Germans and Austrians were hostile with equal persistence. Their argument was that, because honour, independence, and vital interest were reserved, and each nation was left to be its own judge whether these were involved in a dispute, the treaty became, or would become in practice, meaningless. They urged that the mere existence of a general treaty which was meaningless might prove positively harmful, in that it might discourage the tendency toward the signature of genuine two-Power treaties for compulsory arbitration. The fact that the delegation from the United States had made itself responsible for the proposal of a general treaty was, in view of the Senate's record in relation to arbitration, made the subject of several debating points by von Bieberstein and von Mercy. When the committee reported, a vote was taken in the commission itself. For the American proposal that compulsory arbitration should be adopted for juridical disputes and those arising from the application or interpretation of treaties (with vital interests, independence, honour, and the interests of third parties reserved), thirty-five states voted as against nine for rejection. For the proposal that compulsory arbitration should be adopted as regards certain types of disagreement (on a list afterwards to be drawn up), and without any reserved interests, the voting was thirty-three against eleven. For the proposal of obligatory arbitration without any reserve in the case of a list which had been prepared in the committee, thirty-one voted as against thirteen. In the face of minorities so considerable in number, and impressive in their composition, it was felt inexpedient to proceed further.

Since the American project for a multi-party agreement had been foiled at The Hague, the executive at Washington determined to conclude a number of separate two-party treaties. Ultimately an arrangement satisfactory to the Senate was reached, and in 1908 no less than twenty-four arbitration treaties, of which twelve were with European states, were ratified. Questions relating to vital interests, independence, and national honour were held in reserve; and each separate decision, as it arose, to refer a specific question to arbitration under the arbitration treaty was bound to be put in the form of a special treaty in order that the Senate might not be cheated of its right to a decision. The advantages gained then by the twenty-four agreements must seem to any student of American politics somewhat meagre, but they may have kept in the air the ideal of arbitration as an end to work for. Nor were the treaties of the United States either alone, or even foremost, in the inter-continental field. A series of Spanish treaties with the South-American states were signed in 1902 and 1904, while the Italo-Argentinian Treaty of 1898 had stipulated for the submission of all disputes to arbitration, making no reserve whatever.

That the treaties of 1908 were felt to be disappointing in the United States was evident from attempts made to complete or supplement them; and for a time that country became the centre at which the greatest efforts were apparent to broaden the limits of that practice of arbitration which had existed between 1902 and 1908. In 1911 President Taft ventured to negotiate treaties with England and France, under which disputes justiciable according to law or equity were to be referred to arbitration. But, although the prospects at one time seemed bright, senatorial apprehensions and national caution, which expressed themselves in renewed attempts to stake out reserved areas, produced an atmosphere in which the agreements were allowed to lapse. The approach to the subject of the next administration was from an angle suggested by the establishment at The Hague of machinery for the appointment of commissions of inquiry. Mr. Bryan succeeded in negotiating several treaties with the principal American and European states, whereby "all disputes of every nature whatsoever" which diplomacy had failed to solve were to be referred to international commissions of inquiry. These commissions were to contain five members, one national from each of the contracting Powers, one non-national nominated by each of them, and a fifth individual chosen by agreement. They were to report within a year of their inauguration, and within that period hostilities were strictly interdicted.

With the inauguration of the League of Nations arbitration passed into a new phase. The heart of the Covenant of the League of Nations lies in the obligation undertaken by all signatory states not to go to war unless they have first submitted the matter in dispute either to arbitration or judicial settlement or to an inquiry held by the Council. This is under the terms of Article XII., and in Article XIII. the nations subsequently agree to submit to arbitration or to judicial settlement a number of so-called juridical questions therein enumerated. Indeed, there are two novel features in the treatment of international disputes by those who framed the League. First, recognition is made of the difference between arbitration and judicial decision, organs being erected for both functions. Secondly, a great variety of treatment for such disputes is visualised. Thus the Council of the League may keep the matter in its own hands and try to bring the contesting Powers to agreement. It can in that process, if it choose, submit any dispute of a legal nature to the Permanent Court of International Justice, though the finding of the Court will have no force until it be endorsed by the Council. Or, while keeping the matter in its own hands, it can in a similar manner refer individual points to the Permanent Court for judicial decision. Or it may set up commissions of inquiry, *commissions pour établir les faits* in the manner of continental countries, or committees appointed *ad hoc*. In a word, great elasticity was preserved as regards method, but to some sort of arbitration of disputes the civilised nations did become solemnly pledged.

The League of Nations, as will be shortly seen, was under Article VIII. of its charter bound to take under consideration the problem of the reduction of national armaments. A permanent commission of expert advisers was appointed, and to this a temporary mixed commission, less expert in character, was added. Little progress was made, however, until M. de Jouvenel and Lord Cecil were included in addition by an Act of 1922. By the time the Fourth Assembly met in 1923 this commission had prepared a Draft Treaty of Mutual Assistance which embodied a system of mutual insurance among the nations by a series of reciprocal defensive alliances. The project was not enthusiastically received, and, after a speech by the English Prime Minister, Mr. Ramsay MacDonald, its place was taken by a protocol which aimed at the promotion of a feeling of security among the nations by rather different means. This was embodied in the protocol for the pacific settlement of international disputes. If the Draft Treaty of Mutual Assistance was predominantly a political, the protocol was predominantly a legal, document.(12) Compulsory arbitration was the essence of it, and what may have appeared to the reader of this book a divergence from the subject of the chapter to that of disarmament is justified by the fact that in seeking disarmament the Powers, led by MacDonald, found themselves once more face to face with arbitration.

The contents of the protocol in this respect are perhaps best described by saying that, instead of entangling every state in a joint European alliance against aggression, the protocol set out to define aggression, and found the test of a country's freedom from aggression in its readiness, or the reverse, to accept the existence of international mechanism for the drawing of disputes to arbitration without any loophole for escape from the necessity. Several separate reasons contributed to the rejection of the protocol by Great Britain, but first and foremost is the reluctance of that country, which has played such an honourable part in arbitration, to accept any compulsory obligation in the matter, even in the modified form which is covered by Ch. II. 36 of the Statute of the Court ("the optional clause"), and applies only to certain juridical disputes. Pressure has been brought, and will probably continue to be brought, upon successive governments to sign this clause, and refusal by British governments to do so has not been rendered less invidious by the announcement of the German Chancellor to the Eighth Assembly of the League that the German government will shortly subscribe to it. But those who have most closely studied recent British history will realise the necessity of reserving from the obligation to arbitration such questions as concern a nation's honour or its vital interest. A case in point will show the danger. In 1908 France practically demanded of the British government the reopening of a principal point supposed to have been settled by the Anglo-French Agreements of 1904 which led up to the formation of the *entente cordiale*. In effect, what was required was the exemption of French fishermen from the jurisdiction of Newfoundland courts. Now that Dominion had accepted the agreements of 1904 very reluctantly, for it was nearly affected; and did accept them only in return for a recovery of unrestricted sovereignty in its own waters. To Newfoundland the mother-country was bound by a solemn pledge, and France had been understood to have conceded terms satisfactory to Newfoundland. France, admitting that much had been conceded, thought that the concessions did not extend so far and asked for the submission to arbitration of the question of this interpretation of a treaty. It was a case, therefore, exactly covered by the optional clause of the statute of the Permanent Court. Great Britain for fear of an adverse decision, which would have involved a breach of faith with a Dominion, could not accept the French request. The government replied that this question constituted in a true sense a "vital interest," and was excluded from any obligation to arbitration. And, France not pursuing the matter, the controversy dropped. Federal states and empires as loosely knit together as the British are not in the position to sign clauses with such profound commitments in them.

CHAP. XIII.

The Treaty of Mutual Assistance yielded way to the protocol for the Pacific Settlement of Disputes. When the latter was out of the way the nations became once more profoundly interested in securing peace by a system of limited alliances. The most striking example was the Locarno Pact of mutual guarantee initialled by Germany, Belgium, France, Great Britain and Italy on 16th October. This pact marked a very

CHAP. XIII. definite advance in matters of arbitration over such models as the general arbitration treaties of 1903 or 1908. The embittered ex-enemies Germany and Belgium, and also Germany and France, " mutually undertook that they would in no case attack or invade each other or resort to war against each other " (Article 2; the treaty exceptions are printed in the note).[13] By Article 3 " all questions of every kind " were to be peacefully settled. When questions of right were in dispute the settlement was to be judicial, while " other questions "—presumably of policy—were to be remitted to a conciliation commission.[14]

Less spectacular, but representative of a type of treaty already growing in number and likely to multiply, was an agreement signed on 7th March 1925 by Switzerland and Poland.[15] This provided for the submission to arbitration of all disputes unsettled by the diplomats, reserving, not disputes which involved " vital interests, independence, or honour," to use the now historic phrase, but only those for which a special procedure had already been provided or those which " according to International Law come within the exclusive competence of the state." Of the validity of any plea under these reservations the Permanent Court of International Justice is to be the judge.

It is obvious that when the Arbitration Treaties of the 1903 or 1908 models come to be revised, there should be no objection to an " outlawry of war "—to use the picturesque phrase—as efficiently safeguarded as Article 2 of the Locarno Pact. But World-Powers, if they are to feel safe in abandoning the old reservation formula, whereby " vital interests, independence, or honour " might be pleaded in bar of arbitration proceedings under a general arbitration treaty, must have a greater power of reservation than that allowed in the Polono-Swiss Treaty of 1925. It is only necessary to think of the British position in the Suez Canal and the Sudan or the American in the Panama Canal and Central America to realise that World-Powers possessing well-defined political interests and rights outside the narrower spheres of " domestic " jurisdiction must not be left to fear that the signature of a new-model arbitration treaty will leave them exposed to the four winds of international attack under legal forms. In January 1928 the American government proposed in an arbitration negotiation to reserve not the old vague " vital interests, independence, or honour," but the more definite " (*a*) questions involving the interior politics of the Powers signatory; (*b*) questions involving a third Power; (*c*) questions to which the Monroe doctrine applies." Despite the scope of these reservations, fears lurked in some quarters that such a formula was still not safe enough, for did it not perhaps expose America to be dragged to arbitration, say on the question of the repudiated loans made from Europe to certain of the southern states? At the time of going to press it is too early for this book to discuss adequately the conversations which have taken place between France and the United States (April 1928). To say this is not to minimise their importance.[16]

Conclusion.—An examination of the history of arbitration during the last quarter of a century renders not unjustifiable considerable optimism with regard to the great future of this international institution. It is well to note, however, the reasons which the British government has put forward against the premature erection of a formally complete system of universal unconditional arbitration on all questions, together with arbitral awards, enforceable against all nations opposing them or even refusing their execution.

The British government's remarkable note of January 1928 was principally directed to show why such a completely water-tight system of arbitration as that foreseen by the famous Geneva protocol of 1924 should not be imposed on the society of nations until that society's usages had by gradual development adapted themselves to it. Thus on the question of sanctions the note pointed out, first, that all arbitration treaties (until the agreement at Locarno formed an exception) had had no sanctions outside their own terms. The submission of any question to an arbitration procedure under the treaty, and the execution of the award, had had no other security than the good faith of the parties. A sanction could only be obtained by putting the treaty under the guarantee of a strong third Power or group of Powers. What reason, it was asked, would induce such Powers to assume so heavy a responsibility? Only a real and vital interest would be sufficient. The Locarno Treaty, in which England and Italy had undertaken to guarantee a Franco-German and a Belgo-German arbitration and conciliation pact, was the unique instance of arbitration pacts so guaranteed. Yet it was essential to remember that England and Italy had a vital interest in the preservation of peace on the Rhine frontier, and, moreover, that their intervention in a Belgo-German or Franco-German crisis produced by the non-execution of the terms of the Locarno arbitration pacts had been made dependent on the decision of the Council of the League. Even though Italy and England had been willing thus to bind themselves to guarantee arbitration pacts peculiarly vital to them, they had found no imitators in other parts of the world. The inference from this part of the note, though not stated, was obvious. When all dangerous questions had been covered by similar arbitration pacts, suitably guaranteed by those Powers which were vitally interested in the maintenance of peace in the particular region or in the particular question concerned, the aims of the framers of the Geneva protocol would have been obtained—without the obvious danger of the complete breakdown of a system which might call upon Uruguay to enforce a Finnish-Esthonian arbitration award before Uruguay had become accustomed to undertaking to guarantee Paraguayan-Brazilian awards.

Further, the British note pointed out the danger of too completely abandoning the system of reserving certain types of dispute from the ordinary operation of arbitration procedure as fixed in general arbitration treaties. Though enthusiasts for the protocol would surrender all reserves and throw the decision of all disputes whatsoever upon an Arbitral or Conciliation Tribunal, the British note pointed out the *raison d'être* of the reserves. The system of reserves had been instituted because the responsible statesmen signing arbitration treaties had recognised that the public opinion of their nations could not be trusted to observe an unfavourable arbitral award on certain types of question. The spirit of international understanding would in time, perhaps, be developed to the point where nations could always be trusted to execute any award, and where their statesmen could conscientiously undertake to promise such action in advance. But it would take time and patience, and till then the water-tight, completely unreserved protocol system could not be safely adopted.

It is interesting to notice that both the Pan-American Conference of 1928 and the League's Preparatory Disarmament Commission seem to be committed to a strong recommendation of compulsory arbitration. The twenty-one American states are pledged to send jurists to a Washington conference at which an all-American convention is to be elaborated containing the minimum of reservations. The Security Committee of the Preparatory Disarmament Commission has recommended two model treaties A and B. Treaty A provides for either judicial decision or arbitral decision according as a dispute be justiciable or non-justiciable: Treaty B provides for a judicial decision in the former case, but the procedure of conciliation in the latter. CHAP. XIII.

NOTES

(1) The six volumes of Moore's *International Arbitrations* (1898) have provided the main material for the historical account of arbitration. The two volumes of Lapradelle and Politis, *Recueil des Arbitrages internationaux*, report some inter-European and other non-United States arbitrations which Moore did not print (1905). In the sincere enthusiasm for arbitration which ruled prior to 1914, the procedure of arbitrations proved a profoundly interesting subject for lawyers. There is an American work of 1911 by Robert C. Morris, entitled *International Arbitration and Procedure*, and an imposing German volume by Nippold (1907), entitled *Die Fortbildung des Verfahrens in Völkerrechtlichen Streitigkeiten*. The subject is much less important now than once seemed likely, owing to the activities of the Court of International Justice, under a fixed procedure, and the conciliation commissions acting under various International Treaties of Arbitration.

(2) J. B. Moore, *History and Digest of Arbitrations*, p. 4829.

(3) *Ibid.*, p. 4827.

(4) *Ibid.*, p. 4829.

(5) *Ibid.*, p. 4828.

(6) *Ibid.*, pp. 4834-4838.

(7) *Ibid.*, pp. 4838-4848.

(8) Quoting La Fontaine, *Histoire Sommaire et Chronologique des Arbitrages, Rev. de Dr. Int. et de Lég. Comp.* (2nd series), vol. x.

(9) The statistics are from Fried's *Handbuch der Friedensbewegung*, p. 192 (Leipzig, 1911).

(10) The volume of the Carnegie Endowment, entitled *Proceedings of the Hague Peace Conference, Conference of 1899*, contains a complete English translation of the official texts. Meurer's first German volume, *Das Friedensrecht der Haager Conferenz* (1905), gives a very full and methodical account of the Conference activities on arbitration. See also Dr. Pearce Higgins' *The Hague Peace Conferences*.

(11) Mr. Choate described his own activities in a little volume, *The Two Hague Conferences* (1913). A good general account of the debate may be obtained from Hull's *The Two Hague Conferences* (1908).

(12) Cf. Noel Baker's *The Geneva Protocol*, 1925; also Butler, *A Handbook to the League of Nations*.

(13) Germany and France, and Germany and Belgium, however, are not forbidden to fight in the case of—

1. The exercise of the right of legitimate defence, that is to say, resistance to a violation of the undertaking contained in the previous paragraph (*i.e.* not to attack) or to a flagrant breach of Articles 42 and 43 of the said Treaty of Versailles, if such breach constitutes an unprovoked act of aggression, and if by reason of the assembly of armed forces in the demilitarised zones immediate action is necessary.

CHAP. XIII.

2. Action in pursuance of Article 16 of the Covenant of the League of Nations.

3. Action as a result of a decision taken by the Assembly or by the Council of the League of Nations, or in pursuance of Article 15, paragraph 7 of the Covenant of the League of Nations, provided that in this last event the action is directed against a state which was the first to attack.

(14) It may be of interest to record the composition of a typical Committee of Conciliation—*e.g.* one under the Esthonian-German treaty (10th August 1925):—Professor Van Slooten, a member of the Dutch Supreme Court; O. Talas, former Minister of Justice in Finland; Westman, former Minister of Justice in Sweden; Ulnots, Esthonian professor; Wiedenfeldt (secretary), official.

(15) No. 1209. League of Nations Treaty Series.

(16) Since the book went to press a correspondence has taken place between the British Foreign Secretary and the U.S. Ambassador in London which has been published in the Command Paper 3109 (United States No. 1 [1928]). This carries the Franco-American discussions further and comments on them.

CHAPTER XIV

DISARMAMENT

The Limitation of Armaments—Humanitarian Restrictions in the Use of Arms.

The Limitation of Armaments.—After the Napoleonic wars the first authoritative suggestion for the general reduction of armaments came from the Tsar Alexander of Russia, who, in view of the suspicion aroused by his publication of the proposal for a Holy Alliance, suggested in a letter to Castlereagh a further European treaty which should be aimed at a general measure of disarmament. Castlereagh does not appear to have taken the Tsar's suggestion very seriously, for he was no doubt conscious of that monarch's pride in his immense army. Nevertheless, well aware of the apprehensions of both Austria and Turkey, he took the step of suggesting to the Emperor as a preliminary the reduction of his own forces. In a memorandum of 18th May he pointed out that the British navy had been reduced almost to the standard of 1792, that general disarmament by negotiation was no easy matter because of the difference in the circumstances and position of the several Powers, and that a Russian reduction, even if partial, would do much.(1) CHAP. XIV.

The problems of " disarmament " which arose in the course of intervention by European Powers during the Austro-Sardinian dispute of 1859 and the Austro-Prussian conflict of 1866 hardly concerned a permanent reduction of forces and would have involved merely what may be called an equal retreat on the part of the disputant states from their approach to a war footing. Real reduction of peace-time effectives was, however, in question between France and Germany in 1870, although no direct negotiation could be undertaken in view of the dangerous state of French and German popular opinion. England, which had been sounded by France in 1868 (2) with a view to a proposal by her of disarmament to Prussia, undertook this thankless task when a renewed appeal

CHAP. XIV.

from France was made in 1870. Clarendon, making his ground the wastefulness of standing armies, asked Bismarck in a confidential memorandum to advise a partial Prussian disarmament, and urged that he had reason to be confident that Napoleon III. would be willing to undertake a parallel reduction of his armaments. It was the moment at which the relation of Prussia and the North German confederation to the South German states was in its most delicate position. Bismarck rejected the offer. Owing to the Prussian Landwehr System a reliable comparison between the military strength of France and Prussia was, he contended, most difficult to draw. He emphasised the specially critical position of Prussia, centralised between three military empires, and professed that he hardly dared to show to his king the letter of Clarendon for he knew that it would be taken as nothing less than a British attempt to weaken Prussia. Clarendon indeed made yet another attempt upon Bismarck when he learned that there was talk in Paris of a reduction in the yearly intake of recruits. On this occasion he suggested a general disarmament. Bismarck laid this fresh proposal before the king, who, as he had foreseen, would not entertain the idea and thus cut short a somewhat unreal negotiation.

In 1899 a proposal was made to the states of the world by the Russian government, not indeed to undertake an immediate disarmament, but to confine themselves for a term of years to their existing forces. At the head of Mouravieff's programme for the first Hague Conference stood the discussion of "an agreement stipulating the non-increase, over a period to be agreed upon, of the present effective forces, by land and by sea, and of the war budgets connected with them." (3) The Powers were also invited to set about a preliminary study of the methods by which a possible reduction of the forces and the budgets might be effected in the future. Six other subjects for discussion were developed in Mouravieff's circular—subjects, one may say, of very different orders of importance and all tending to distract attention from the main business of the limitation of armaments, which was, after all, the proper occupation of the conference, and indeed the cause of such large support as had been forthcoming for the Tsar's project for international negotiation.

When the conference opened with this swollen and inadequately digested programme, the disarmament question was not referred separately (as experience has since made obvious it should have been) to a powerful committee of the plenary conference, predominantly political as regards its personnel. Associated with three other topics, it was referred to the first of the three commissions into which the conference divided itself. The three other topics which had been simultaneously committed, though not unimportant in themselves, were capable of being handled in technical fashion by naval and military experts. Accordingly the inevitable happened. The commission resolved further to divide itself into naval and military sub-committees which were in fact dominated by the professional members. In these circumstances the temptation was overwhelming to attack the more purely technical problems first, and to leave the portentously difficult political problem to the end.

Thus it came about that in a conference primarily convoked to consider methods of avoiding the increase of the armed forces of the states of the world, the central subject was not reached till the middle of the sessions, and then only in a subdivision of the conference. The ludicrously inadequate preparations made reaped their reward, for the weight of political interest among the delegates was concentrated on the arbitration proposals, where the ground had been much more carefully prepared. The only non-professional representatives from the great Powers on the disarmament commission were a professor from Munich, the French minister at The Hague, the ambassador in Berlin from the United States, a Russian, and a British civil servant. Thus neither Russia, England, Austria, Italy, nor Spain saw the matter apparently as one of first-class political importance, though it is true that Sir Julian Pauncefote, like M. Léon Bourgeois, did on occasion intervene.

The actual proposals laid before the commission were presented by Colonel Gilinsky of the Russian General Staff, and by Captain Scheine, the Russian naval attaché at Paris. Colonel Gilinsky's suggestions were extremely simple. He advocated the signature of an agreement, to be binding for five years, under which the increase of the active troops in the mother-country, not those in the colonies, was forbidden. The number of troops to be maintained under this agreement by all the Powers was to be defined. The military budgets, fixed in this manner, were not to be increased over the same period in any respect whatsoever. Captain Scheine's proposals were for a three-years agreement which should stipulate for the fixture of the naval budgets, the publication in advance of the total tonnage of the ships to be constructed, and the

CHAP. XIV. devotion of similar publicity alike to the number of officers and men upon the naval cadres and to the expense involved in the erection and maintenance of coast fortifications.

These proposals have been subjected in certain quarters to ridicule, probably because of their author's confession that, in excluding forces on colonial service from consideration, he had in mind his country's troops in Central Asia and Far Eastern territories. Chinese and Afghan contingencies were too real in the minds of the negotiators to have allowed them to treat with gravity offers encumbered by such reservations; and certainly disarmament proposals divorced from geography, strategy, or national policy can only waste men's time. And yet to-day, nearly thirty years after they were made, it is easier to be more just. Proposals for disarmament made since 1899 have not followed very different lines, though they may have varied in important details: and it has seemed to some, whose opinion has never been disproved, that there is value, where discussion, as in the case of disarmament, can easily be led over a vast terrain, in concentrating, as an initial step, upon some small part of the question, upon some unsatisfactorily small achievement, and in at least getting that part through first.

The *advocatus diaboli*, the opponent of disarmament proposals, has frequently been successful in enticing the unwary supporter of them to broaden the basis of discussion. The speech delivered on 25th June 1899 by the German representative, Colonel von Schwarzhoff, may be quoted as a case in point. He said:—

> "I think that the question of troops cannot be considered entirely alone, separated from the host of other questions to which it is almost subordinate. Such are, for example, the extent of public instruction, the length of active service, the number of established regiments, the troops in the army units, the number and duration of enrolments under the colours—that is to say, the military obligations of retired soldiers—the location of the army corps, the railway system, the number and situation of fortified places. In a modern army all such things are connected with each other, and form, together, the national defence which each people has organised according to its character, its history, and its traditions, taking into account its economic resources, its geographical situation, and the duty or duties which have devolved upon it. I believe that it would be very difficult to replace this eminently national task by an international agreement."

It is far from the intention of this treatise to suggest that

Colonel Gilinsky had chosen the right points upon which to concentrate. That he did concentrate was not in itself a fault. CHAP. XIV.

The situation produced by the development of opposition was met by the reference of the Gilinsky programme to a special technical committee of the military sub-commission, and that of Captain Scheine to a sister body. The military committee contained representatives of six great European Powers, of the United States, Sweden, and Rumania. After two meetings, it reported on 30th June to the full commission. Apart from Gilinsky, it had decided unanimously—

(1) that it would be very difficult to fix even for a term of five years the number of troops permissible, without regulating at the same time other elements of the national defence;

(2) that it could not think it less difficult to regulate by international agreement the elements of this defence, organised in each country upon different principles.

A majority of members believed that a more thorough study of the question by the governments themselves would be desirable. The Russian naval proposals, although revised, did not even reach the stage of consideration by a technical committee of the naval sub-commission. In the latter body itself the delegates of eight countries expressed various objections to the Russian plan. Captain Scheine gallantly rallied seven votes to a proposition which invited the delegates to obtain instructions from their governments such as might enable them before the end of the conference to express in a conclusive manner an opinion upon the project which he fathered. When this resolution, however, was reported to the full commission he had to be told by the President that he was "labouring under illusions" before he finally allowed the proposal for the limitation of naval armaments to be quietly and honourably buried beneath a suggestion inviting the governments to a profounder study of the problem.[4]

In the negotiations preliminary to the meeting of the second Hague Peace Conference of 1907 the United States and England laboured hard to have the question of disarmament included in the programme. The Russian government, however, which had issued the invitations and could control their form, did not accede to their wishes. It may have had private objections to any limitation of armament at the moment, for the wastage of the Russo-Japanese War had still to be replaced.

CHAP. XIV. Be that as it may be, the memory of the fiasco of 1899 and the known antipathy to the subject in Japan, Austria, and Germany were weighty enough deterrents to enthusiasm in themselves. When Sir Edward Fry, the British delegate, in moving a resolution at the fourth plenary session of the conference, discussed the increasing expenditure on armaments, the Russian leading delegate explained the absence of the subject from the agenda paper in these terms :—

> " It is believed that this question is not ripe for consideration if good results are to be obtained. It is undesirable to provoke discussions which, as is indicated by the experience of 1899, may only prove to be opposed to the object striven for in common, and may only accentuate discord between the Powers by causing irritating debates."

The Liberal ministry which in Great Britain assumed office in 1905 had already made a first bid for a general reduction of naval armaments [(5)] when it communicated to seven Powers its intention to remove one capital ship from its building programme, which had contemplated three, if it should find any readiness on the part of other Powers to do likewise. In the speech delivered on 17th August 1907 and referred to above, Sir Edward Fry announced another attempt on the part of the government to promote naval disarmament. It was willing to communicate each year to the Powers, who would do the same, its programme of new construction and the estimated expenditure involved. Such an exchange of information might, it was hoped, facilitate a consequent exchange of views between the governments on the reduction which might by common agreement be effected, for mutual confidence between governments was, over all matters of armament, a plant of tender growth. The mere act of taking the initiative was apt to expose a Power to misinterpretation of its motives. Indirect approaches such as that of Clarendon in 1870 were hardly satisfactory. It was a gain to make the interchange of views and programmes a matter of normal and constant procedure, in that this misconception might not arise. The idea was implicit in the suggestion of Captain Scheine. The British government was attempting to enrich diplomatic intercourse with a new mechanism.

The resolve of the German government to undertake a supplementary naval building programme, in addition to the standard programme already adopted, led in 1912 to renewed attempts on the part of England to negotiate a naval understanding. After some preparation of the ground by Sir Ernest Cassel and Sir Edward Goschen, Lord Haldane arrived in Berlin to initiate discussions, which in the nature of the case were not confined to armaments but embraced the political position in Europe as well as colonial differences. He rejected an offer of a ratio of 2 : 3 to be established between the German and English fleets, and insisted that, if Germany were to build to such an extent as to imperil the British position, England would adopt the line of laying down two keels to every one laid down in Germany. He suggested a delay in the execution of their supplementary programme, and even threw out a feeler as to a possible modification of their basic naval law. One has only to read the debate in the House of Commons on 3rd August 1914, which followed the famous announcement of Sir Edward Grey, to feel that the German statesmen may well have felt doubt as to the extent to which the British negotiators could rely upon the support which their followers would give them in making good their threats. The Imperial government might have made considerable concessions in return for a British promise of neutrality in the event of a European war in which Germany might become entangled. Fortunately, Haldane in Berlin and Grey in London followed the whole course of English foreign policy in the few previous years in abstaining from giving this. CHAP. XIV.

A one-sided and imposed limitation of armaments resulted from the Paris treaties of Versailles (Part 5), St. Germain (Part 5), Trianon (Part 5), and Neuilly (Part 4). It only differed from that imposed by Napoleon on Prussia in that in the preambles to the disarmament sections of these treaties the victorious alliance, which forced the limitation upon the defeated states, accepted in theory the eventual extension of such limitation to all states, though not necessarily, as is sometimes forgotten by those who have not carefully read the preambles, either upon a similar scale or upon a parallel plan. For the completion of this task Article VIII. of the Covenant of the League of Nations has provided an organ. The work done by the League upon the question of disarmament has been described at the end of the preceding chapter. The problem has been to create confidence.(6) Some have seen this most effectively accomplished by a system of alliances, which should give to the threatened state, if innocent, the knowledge that it would not at any moment have to defend itself alone. When practical difficulties were pointed out in numbers and the states discarded this idea, it has seemed to some that

CHAP. XIV. there was hope along the line of a general assumption by the nations of the duty to arbitrate in each dispute. Lastly, the place of the Treaty of Mutual Assistance and the later Protocol for the Settlement of Disputes was supplied by a less ambitious scheme for separate, but mutual and protective, alliances among the Powers for the preservation of peace and the promotion of confidence. Meanwhile, although the Preparatory Commission for a disarmament conference has had many formal meetings, the results may be described as disappointing.

Though the League of Nations had begun almost from its birth its patient attempt to prepare the way for a general limitation of armaments, the first great success in achieving a voluntary and agreed limitation came not from the League nor under its auspices but from a conference summoned in the old way by a Power outside the League, the United States.(7) The Washington delegates of 1921-1922 early recognised the hopelessness of achieving a success in the limitation of land armament. As it had been convoked with a special view to the appeasement of rivalry in the Pacific Ocean, largely naval in character, the conference was thus soon left free to confine its projects of limitation to naval armament, a ground where, from the success achieved, there is reason to suppose patient preparatory labour had been expended by the different national admiralties. The great success was scored with capital ships, which (with the exception of aircraft-carriers) were defined as those of over 10,000 tons or those carrying guns bigger than the 8-inch. Heavy and defined scrapping of existing capital ships was to be immediately undertaken by the United States, Great Britain, and Japan, but France and Italy were to be allowed their existing tonnage. A vessel allowed to remain in the fleets of the five Powers might be replaced by new construction when twenty years old, but no such new vessel was to have a displacement of more than 35,000 tons. No replacement (with certain specified exceptions) was to be begun before 12th November 1931, and then only such as should not violate the agreed maxima of 525,000 tons for the United States and Great Britain, 315,000 for Japan, and 175,000 for France and Italy. The treaty was to be valid until the end of 1936, but special modifications were to be permitted on the outbreak of a war in which any of the signatories should become engaged. A definite conference for possible revision was to meet after eight years. Other conferences were provided for in the event of one signatory's claiming that a material change of circumstances had occurred, or after the conclusion of a war in which one or all the signatories should have undertaken permitted departures from the normal treaty conditions.[8]

Another limitation success was obtained at Washington with a further class of ship, the aircraft-carrier. When, however, it was proposed to limit the auxiliary types of war-vessel in the same ratio as the capital ships of the battle fleets, the conference completely failed to achieve unity. France, for example, which was offered 30,000 tons for submarines and 150,000 tons for destroyers, flotilla-leaders, and small cruisers, asserted her need for a submarine tonnage of 90,000 and a tonnage of 330,000 for the other ships.[9] In these circumstances no results could be achieved, and nations were left to draft their own programmes of construction unfettered.

The Washington Conference, whose success in achieving a large measure of limitation had been mainly due to the excellent political understanding as to Pacific questions achieved simultaneously, was to be left unparalleled in the decade after the termination of the Great War, except for a relatively unimportant Central American Convention of 7th February 1923. A Moscow Conference of Baltic states, to which the Russian delegation presented a programme of military reductions which left the Russian army with 600,000 men, the Polish with 214,000, and other national forces in proportion, quickly broke down when the smaller states demanded political guarantees.[10] The 1924 conference of naval experts at Rome, which it was hoped would prepare the ground for a general diplomatic conference for naval disarmament, also broke down very quickly. Its plan for a universal clearly-defined limitation was much too ambitious, and would have failed in any case. The failure, however, was hastened by a Russian demand for a "capital" tonnage of 400,000 when the allotted programme tonnage was only 110,000.[11] The Geneva Three-Power Conference of 1927, despite its limited programme and the excellent political understanding between the participating Powers, also failed—well illustrating the extremely difficult character of the bargains to which Powers entering upon disarmament must submit. At Geneva, though both Britain and the United States accepted the principle of perfect equality and therefore equality of cruiser tonnage, Britain desired a larger number of smaller cruisers than the United States with its lack of coaling stations could profitably use. Britain, however, could not consent to a maximum figure for the total cruiser tonnage. That would

CHAP. XIV. have left America free to use all her tonnage for 10,000-ton cruisers, which are of very great use with battle fleets, while England would have been compelled to employ much of her tonnage for the smaller type of cruiser and so would be weaker in the battle-line than America. It has since transpired that the British delegates at Geneva made an offer to expand the Washington proposals still further by the adoption of three further suggestions: (*a*) maximum tonnage of capital ships to be 30,000 in replacing older vessels; (*b*) maximum calibre of marine artillery to be 13·5 inches; (*c*) no ship to be replaced for twenty-six years after completion. This offer was renewed at Geneva in March 1928.

Humanitarian Restrictions of Arms.—The use of poisoned weapons and the secret poisoning of water have been excluded from honourable warfare under civilised conditions almost from the memory of man.[12] The fighting men themselves by an almost tacit agreement declined to make their activity more grim, more fearful, and more treacherous by availing themselves of such agencies, which could only in the end produce a momentary advantage destined to be cruelly avenged by the enraged enemy. Strange to say, the old pike soldier and the men of sword and lance in the time of Bayard seem from somewhat the same sort of sentiment to have attempted to prevent the use of muskets on the battlefield. Bayard himself never spared a musketeer;[13] and the famous Marshal de Monluc, for whom the harquebus was "the devil's own invention," was not likely to have been prodigal of mercy to its carrier.

To pass, however, to the record of warfare waged under conditions familiar to recent generations, it is interesting to note that the movement against the explosive bullet, which produced the Declaration of St. Petersburg in 1869, was also rather a movement professionally military in character than undiscriminatingly philanthropic. Mere philanthropy would have chosen other phrases than "the technical limits at which the necessities of war ought to yield to the requirements of humanity," or "the adequacy of measures which disabled the greatest possible number of men without *uselessly* aggravating their sufferings or rendering their death inevitable."

The Hague Conference of 1899 met at an epoch in which chemical and mechanical invention was being applied to the making of war apparatus on a large and in some ways novel scale; it makes, therefore, a good starting-point for a discussion of the subject, particularly because the reasons for restriction were put on a basis of argument more thorough than had been seen before. The programme of Mouravieff proposed—

(*a*) the prohibition of the introduction into armies or navies of any new kind of firearm whatsoever, as well as of new explosives, or of any powder, more powerful than those in use, either for muskets or for cannon;
(*b*) the restriction of the use in military campaigns of the formidable explosives already existing: and the prohibition of the hurling of projectiles or explosives of any kind from balloons or by analogous means;
(*c*) the prohibition of the use in naval warfare of submarine torpedo-boats or plungers or of other similar engines of destruction: and an agreement not to construct in the future war-vessels made with rams.

During the discussion of the first topic among the military men on the first commission certain Russian proposals with regard to high explosives, field guns, and rifles failed to gain any acceptance as palpably resting on the Russian sense of inability in those respects to keep pace with the mechanical advance of the age. A warm discussion, however, arose over the "dum-dum" bullet, which General Ardagh, an English delegate, aided by the American Captain Crozier, ventured to defend against a large majority of opponents. Against savages, he stated, such a bullet producing a great shock "was necessary to stop an advancing soldier," nor was it designed with the aim of producing useless suffering. In the end a declaration was signed which was aimed against the employment of bullets which expanded or flattened easily in the body. All Powers present signed the declaration with the exception of the United States, England, and Portugal, but the two latter Powers announced their adherence in 1907.

In regard to the hurling of explosives from balloons, after a Dutch general had spoken of chivalry, a French general of the danger to non-combatants, and the Russian Colonel Gilinsky of the sufficiency of existing means of injuring one's country's enemies, the military sub-commission was only prevented from recommending the complete banishment of the practice from warfare by Captain Crozier, who was finally successful in restricting the recommendation of the prohibition to five years. This was signed by all the Powers represented at The Hague.

CHAP. XIV.

Warfare at sea was referred as a subject of study to the naval sub-committee of the first commission. Russian attempts to fix temporarily *maxima* limits to the size and strength of marine cannon and armour-plate were rejected because, as was pointed out, the project was not due to any consideration of humanity. It is interesting to note the importance attached by the first Hague Peace Conference to this, by no means the only, motive for disarmament. And in the light of it it is not surprising that a different fate awaited a proposal to prohibit " projectiles whose special object it was to diffuse asphyxiating gases." The then Captain Mahan of the United States navy put up a pertinacious struggle against the proposal. With the sureness of instinct, which never deserted that thoughtful officer, he had the sense of being in the presence of a subject more complicated than on the surface it seemed. His warning fell upon obdurate ears ; and the proposal became the subject of a declaration signed by all the Powers except the United States and Great Britain, which latter country acceded in 1907. The Russian proposal to lay submarine vessels under a ban was resisted by several of the small, and by two of the greater, Powers on the ground that they had an eminently defensive object, and, as such, were unsuitable as the subject of a declaration.

An elaborate proposal of the British in 1907 on the subject of submarine mines would have prohibited the use of floating mines and all those which did not immediately become harmless on breaking loose from their anchorage, would have forbidden a commercial blockade carried out through the agency of even allowable mines, and would have confined the laying of them to the territorial waters of belligerents, with the single exception of a ten-mile zone round naval forts. This was resisted by Admiral Siegel of Germany in the first sub-commission of commission III., and the subject formed the study of a special body which sat for two months. The rules, as finally elaborated, were disappointing to British eyes, and were indeed made more so by the subsequent French and German reservations to the rule which prohibited the use of mines for the sole purpose of interfering with commercial traffic. The declaration was limited in the first instance to five years ; but its authority was to endure after that period unless expressly repudiated by the Powers who had signed. There also figured on the agenda paper the subject of bombardments from the sea, which had figured also at the conference of 1899. It was very generally desired to restrict the naval bombardment of undefended and unfortified towns, but the extreme difficulty of producing a satisfactory definition for these adjectives presented itself at once, as, for instance, when Captain Ottley of the British navy asked that a town defended only by submarine mines should be excluded from the " undefended " class. Further difficulties were created by the need to allow the belligerent to take measures against unfortified places which had been made the centre of enemy stores or of a district under requisition for supplies. The final convention produced by the conference indicated that Great Britain, France, Germany, Spain, Japan, and China had reserved for themselves the right to bombard ports defended only by anchored and automatic submarine mines. This was the more emphatic in that the convention did allow the attacking force by sea to requisition stores and provisions by the threat of bombardment, and " in case of necessity " to bombard points of military importance even without notice. In case the bombardment should be in the nature of a surprise, it was laid down that the unfortified place should suffer the least possible inconvenience (!), and that special effort should be made to spare properly designated buildings, historic monuments, hospitals, and edifices devoted to religion or philanthropy.

As regards war in the air, the conference had indeed to face the possibility of a development in machines lighter than air, but the revolutionary possibilities of the aeroplane were generally as yet unvisualised. The British delegate, Lord Reay, won from a plenary session the extension of the prohibition passed by the first Peace Conference for a period of five years to one that should endure " until the end of the third, *i.e.* the next, Peace Conference." The French government must have had peculiar hopes of the results to be obtained from warfare by dirigible balloons, for its delegates first opposed any specific and permanent prohibition of the bombardment of unfortified towns from the air as unnecessary because already covered by the rules of land warfare; then argued for a temporary rather than a permanent prohibition; and lastly, refused to accept any limitation on hostilities in the air of any kind. Only twenty-seven of the forty-four delegates signed the declaration, and of the former number only fifteen saw their signature ultimately ratified by the home government.

The study of the proceedings of the two Hague Conferences not only provides ample illustration of the difficulty which

CHAP. XIV. lies in legislating, in a time of peace and in a detailed fashion, on the subject of the methods of warfare, it suggests an even more fundamental consideration. War is in the nature of things so brutal, and so brutalising, that the best meaning attempts to regulate it cannot succeed, and not infrequently merely readjust the incidence of its rigour in a manner which is as unfair as it is undesired. While the tendency was for hostilities to become more and more a conflict of two highly professional forces, each strictly under the control of authority, it was comparatively simple to elaborate a nice code of military practice, almost as simple as to alter the rules of fencing or the game of tennis. The idea of the "nation in arms" was a step on the road towards the obliteration of the distinction between soldier and civilian. The development of air warfare following on the conception of the starvation blockade has all but completed the process. The readiness of women to play a combatant part has introduced another complication. It is less easy nowadays than it used to be to draw a clear-cut distinction between combatant and non-combatant. Rude common sense is readier to see readjusted more equitably the risk to life and comfort between the individual on the esplanade at Scarborough and the individual in Flanders mud. The weak and helpless both in Flanders and at Scarborough may still be placed in a separate category and treated as exceptional, but it is no longer postulated that every civilian is in the same position as the babe at the breast, or that a tunic alone constitutes a soldier. This generation, in the mercy of God, will not see war waged again as it was waged between 1914 and 1918, and there will be at first a reaction in the rules of warfare to earlier models. But the old theory has been challenged, and old conditions, if they reappear, as they may do for a time, will not endure in permanence.

Meanwhile, *post bellum* legislation on the practice of war was attempted at Washington in 1921; and it was the work of men under the dominance of the experience of the recent war. The British government strongly advocated a proposal to banish the submarine from warfare. It had of course proved itself a formidable weapon against the nation with surface supremacy; and it was hailed as only natural that the state which had been all but brought low by its use should seek to expel it from civilised warfare. Yet experience had provided the British delegation with ample proof to sustain the thesis that as a mode of war it was inhumane to merchant seamen and a danger to all neutrals, much more convincing proof, indeed, than had been in the possession of Captain Ottley when at The Hague he had moved for the condemnation of the floating mine. The United States, France, Italy, and Japan were unanimous in rejecting the British case; and all that could be won was the recognition of "the practical impossibility" of conducting submarine warfare against commercial ships in accord with the accepted rules of International Law as to visit, search, and the safeguarding of the lives of crew and passengers in the case of the destruction of the ship which carried them. As a result the Powers present bound themselves to forbid the use of submarines as destroyers of commerce as between themselves in war, and to invite adherence to this rule on the part of other Powers. There was already, however, a weakness in any treaty which used such vague language; and in any case, as the treaty of February 1922 was not ratified even by all the signatory nations, its position in International Law is at the least precarious. CHAP. XIV.

At Washington also an attempt was made to reassert the principle laid down in 1899, which forbade the use of "asphyxiating or deleterious" gases. The treaty of February 1922 in its fifth article pledged the five Powers among themselves to refrain from the use not only of such gases but of analogous liquids. It is doubtful whether the treaty has received or will receive a sufficient number of ratifications to make it authoritative. The investigations at present being carried out into the possibility of producing gases, effective and momentarily deleterious yet ultimately not destructive, have proceeded so far, and the opinion of publicists as to the effect and nature of gas warfare is so far from settled, that there has already been some reaction from the attitude of wholesale condemnation. The movement in the matter is unlikely to be precipitate, though the Geneva protocol of 1925 forbidding the use of asphyxiating and toxic gases and bacteriological means of warfare has now obtained the recognition of France, Russia, and Italy.

NOTES

(1) See *Camb. Hist., For. Policy*, vol. ii. pp. 17-19 (Alison Phillips).
(2) *Ibid.*, vol. iii. pp. 23-24 (C. R. M. F. Cruttwell).
(3) Circular, 11th Jan. 1899.
(4) The story of the first Hague Peace Conference may be read

CHAP. XIV. in the English of Holts, the French of Mérignhac, and the German of Meurer. The works of J. B. Scott, Pearce Higgins, and Hull deal with the two conferences. There appeared in 1920, under the aegis of the Carnegie Endowment, an English version of the Proceedings of the Hague Conference of 1899.

(5) See Gooch in *Cambridge History of British Foreign Policy*, vol. iii. p. 352.

(6) See *The Problem of Security*, by Wheeler Bennett and Langermann.

(7) A journalistic and "human" account of the Washington Conference was written by H. G. Wells (1922).

(8) The treaty is printed in Noel Baker's *Disarmament.*

(9) See Mowat's *History of European Diplomacy* (1914-1925), p. 232.

(10) See J. Wheeler Bennett, *Reduction of Armaments*, pp. 149-150.

(11) Toynbee's *Survey for 1924*, pp. 77-80.

(12) Cf. Walker, *History of the Law of Nations*, pp. 56, 315.

(13) *Ibid.*, p. 190.

CHAPTER XV

THE CONCERT IN POLITICAL ACTION [1]

THE GREAT POWERS, GREECE AND BELGIUM. THE GREAT POWERS AND THE COLLAPSE OF THE OTTOMAN EMPIRE. THE GREAT POWERS AND THE CRIMEAN WAR. THE PROPOSED ITALIAN CONGRESS OF 1859. THE POWERS AND THE LEBANON. THE PROPOSED POLISH CONGRESS OF 1863. THE SCHLESWIG-HOLSTEIN CONFERENCE OF 1864. THE PROPOSED CONFERENCE OF 1866, AND THE CONFERENCES OF LONDON OF 1867 AND 1871. THE CONFERENCE OF CONSTANTINOPLE OF 1876-1877. THE CONGRESS OF BERLIN: THE POWERS AND THE EXECUTION OF THE DECISIONS OF THE CONGRESS. THE CONGRESS AT CONSTANTINOPLE ON EGYPT. THE CRISIS AND PROPOSED CONFERENCE OF 1908. THE CONGO CONFERENCE OF 1884. THE CONFERENCE OF MADRID, 1880, AND OF ALGECIRAS IN 1906. THE CONFERENCE OF AMBASSADORS, 1912-1913: THE PROPOSED CONFERENCE OF 1914. THE PEACE CONFERENCE AND THE PEACE TREATIES OF 1918-1919. THE GENOA CONFERENCE. THE LAUSANNE CONFERENCE.

The Great Powers, Greece and Belgium.—GREECE.—The rise of the power of orthodox Russia, hope of an approaching attack upon the relatively weakening Turkey, and a stirring of national sensitiveness and religious feeling combined to produce the sudden and savage revolt of the Morean Greeks in April 1821. The Turks, incensed by massacre and butchery unprovoked by any special action of their own, replied with atrocities as violent as those of the Greeks. Turkish reprisals did not prevent the spread of the rebellion to the central Greek areas, north of the Gulf of Corinth, and to many of the Aegean Islands. They did bring appreciably nearer a war with Russia, where popular feeling was profoundly moved by the news of such action as the hanging of the Patriarch of Constantinople in his robes, and the executions of the Archbishops of Adrianople, Salonica, and Tirnova. The Tsar was only restrained from war by the appeal from Austria and England that he should not bring about a fatal breach in the moral unity of Europe by precipitate action on behalf of the Greeks, whose most recent behaviour, they

CHAP. XV.

CHAP. XV.

took care to point out to the Tsar, was only a manifestation of the general spirit of European revolution. Thus Russian action on behalf of the rebel Christians was deferred until the Congress of Verona should have met: and, after that congress had produced no satisfactory result, was deferred again until it was seen what could be produced by negotiations undertaken on behalf of Russia by the British ambassador at Constantinople. The Turks for their part knew well how to play a waiting game in diplomacy and, despite the resourceful measures of Strangford, the British minister, were able to avoid the surrender of any vital diplomatic position. They were hopeful of recovering the military supremacy in the Greek war, and of thereby at one stroke removing the possibility of decisive European intervention.

The Emperor Alexander, perhaps justly impatient, then began to demand the summons of a special European congress to consider the Greek question. In a circular note to the Powers of January 1824 he proposed that the Greek principalities should be guaranteed by the five great Powers, and that this decision should be imposed by them upon the Sultan. The Greek territory contemplated in these proposals included Crete and Epirus. Canning manœuvred for a whole year to avoid any such congress, and finally in December took his stand upon the point that the imposition of this settlement was distasteful alike to the Turks and to the Greeks. In 1825, therefore, the conferences of the allies upon the Greek question were held without the assistance of the British. Metternich had made up his mind that the three principalities visualised by the Tsar should not become areas of exclusive Russian influence such as Wallachia and Moldavia already seemed. Instead, therefore, of his permitting the Austrian representative to accept the sanction of a Russian mandate to impose the Emperor Alexander's scheme upon Turkey, he ventured upon the risk of suggesting the notion of full independence for an Hellenic kingdom. On rejection of this idea by Russia, the Austrians, aided by the French, declined to consider forcible intervention. The Tsar, deeply mortified by what he considered the ungrateful attitude of Metternich, suspended the conferences in May, and for the rest of his life, which was prematurely closed in December, was undoubtedly considering the project of armed intervention by Russia despite the absence of European support.

The need for some sort of European interposition between the rebels and the Sultan, if the Greeks were to survive in any form in the European community, was becoming plain during the course of the year 1825. In the beginning of the preceding year it had indeed seemed that the establishment of a *de facto* independence was certain, and that consequently the accordance of legal independence could not be long delayed. The Turks, however, had in the meantime secured the intervention of the Pasha of Egypt with his powerful forces. Crete had been reconquered in 1824, and in February 1825 an Egyptian force, landing in continental Greece, had begun a career of victory which rumour suggested might well be crowned by the compulsory evacuation of the Greek survivors and the replacement of them by the African subjects of the Egyptian Pasha. The danger of the extinction of the Greeks on the continent was increased when the Egyptian operations in the Morea were supported by Ottoman operations which, during 1826 and 1827, were vigorously conducted north of the gulf of Corinth.

CHAP. XV.

After the death of Alexander I. Canning determined upon decided action in order to stave off the prospect of a declaration of war by Russia upon Turkey, a course of action likely to put not only the Greek, but the whole Near Eastern, situation out of control. The Duke of Wellington was sent to the new Tsar Nicholas with the proposal that British mediation between Greece and Turkey should be approved, or, if this idea should be rejected, that Russia and England should jointly undertake mediation. From this dramatic visit issued the protocol of 4th April 1826. British mediation between Greece and Turkey (and between Russia and Turkey) was to be proposed to Turkey first, and was to be succeeded by the adoption of a joint Anglo-Russian policy, if it were to be rejected. It was agreed that Greece should remain under Turkish suzerainty, but that it should secure a considerable amount of internal freedom, tempered however by the retention of a Turkish share in the appointment of officials. The territorial limits of Greece were left to subsequent negotiation with Turkey. Austria, France, and Prussia were to be invited to accede to these arrangements and to the final Greek settlement, and to join with Russia in its guarantee.

The specific demands made by Russia upon Turkey at the Ackerman Conference imposed some delay, but late in the year the protocol was communicated to the other great Powers. Austria and Prussia proved unreceptive, but France showed a desire to co-operate should the protocol be converted into a treaty. The drafting of this proved difficult, but the instrument was signed on 6th July 1827. One condition in the treaty was the closing of an immediate armistice between the Greeks and the Turks, an armistice to be enforced within a month (later shortened to a fortnight) by the prevention of "all collision between the contending parties." The duty of impeding hostilities between the belligerents was laid upon the British, French, and Russian fleets in the Mediterranean, which acted under the supreme command of the British Admiral Codrington. These fleets were compelled to confine their action to the prevention of Turkish expeditions against Greece, for while the Greeks had accepted the armistice, the Turks had refused it. Later, renewed Turkish atrocities in the Morea caused the allied admirals to sail in battle formation into the presence of the Turco-Egyptian fleet with the intention of demanding the instant cessation of Turkish devastations. In the bay of Navarino, and with the fleets thus stationed, an unforeseen battle was joined which resulted in the virtual annihilation of the Turco-Egyptian fleet. The ensuing Russo-Turkish War of 1828-1829 and the French military expedition of 1829 to the Morea finally reduced the recalcitrant Turks to the necessity of accepting the resolutions of the three Powers with respect to Greece. Article 10 of the Treaty of Adrianople between Russia and Turkey secured Turkish adhesion to the three-Power treaty of 1827, and to a later instrument of March 1829, which had decided that Greece should secure a wide extension of territory beyond the Gulf of Corinth bounded by the Arta-Volo line, and that it should be governed by a princely house, Christian and hereditary.

The final form of the Greek kingdom and its territorial limits were still to be the subject of much debate between the three Powers. England under the ministry of the Duke of Wellington, being fearful of the expansion of Russian influence in the Mediterranean, tended to insist at once that Greece should be small and in a position of complete independence of the Porte. Accordingly, the protocol of 3rd February 1830 provided for a reduction of Greek territory to the Thermopylae-Aspropotamus line. The hereditary throne was in the same month accepted by Leopold, Prince of Coburg, a prince who had close connections with the British royal family. He was at a later stage so much oppressed by a feeling of despair at the inadequate boundaries allotted to Greece, and the seeming hopelessness of introducing a European régime into that still very barbarous country, that he renounced the crown in May 1830 and left the three Powers with a solution to their problem still to be found. The vigorous administration of Capodistrias, the Hellenic president, allowed them to delay their next decisions without provoking a catastrophe. There was a change of government in England, and by the protocol of 26th September 1831 the Powers widened the dominions of Greece once more by adopting the Arta-Volo boundary. A European prince as hereditary sovereign and a loan to the new state were promised. The assassination of Capodistrias in October and the great and rapid development of anarchy now induced the three Powers to act with greater celerity than had been their practice till that point. A Bavarian prince was selected by the three Powers for the Greek throne in February 1832: arrangements were made to provide the new kingdom with a guaranteed loan of two million four hundred thousand pounds and a Bavarian force of troops. The Greeks were induced to accept the new arrangement, and King Otho of Greece appeared among his subjects in February 1833.

The new King of Greece proved in the event to have too few of the qualifications called for by his exigent position. Independent Greece certainly made some progress between the years 1833 and 1862, but the monarchy contributed little positive statesmanship to the solution of the many problems of Greece, and was at times the cause of actual harm. The thirst for territorial expansion, the continuance of brigandage, and the careless handling of financial questions gave the three protecting Powers legitimate cause for anxiety. In 1862 King Otho was dethroned by his own people, and the three protecting Powers watched with some disquiet Greek efforts to provide themselves with another dynasty. After some hesitation they renewed among themselves their agreements of 1827 and 1830, under which members of the reigning families of France, Russia, and Great Britain were excluded from the Greek throne. Despite the announcement of this resolution to the Greek Government, the Greeks elected the English Prince Alfred to the throne by an overwhelming majority.

England could not accept the election on behalf of this prince, but resolved to make a real effort to secure an efficient dynasty and some satisfaction, though only by peaceful means, for Greek territorial aspirations. It promised to Greece the Ionian Islands on the condition that the fortifications of Corfu were destroyed and the whole islands were recognised as neutral areas by the great Powers. In return for

CHAP. XV.

this concession Greece was to uphold constitutional monarchy and accept a king who should rule according to British principles. The throne was first offered to the widower King-Consort of Portugal, Ferdinand of Saxe-Coburg-Gotha, but it was refused. Another refusal came from the reigning duke, Ernest of Saxe-Coburg-Gotha, who was somewhat scrupulous as to the abdication of King Otho, the need for which he doubted, and who desired to retain his German principality. The Archduke Maximilian, the brother of the Austrian emperor, was also sounded, but declined the throne owing to his scruples concerning the rights of the fugitive King Otho. England finally had resort to the Danish royal family, and procured the candidature of the seventeen-year-old Prince William, who was elected on 30th March 1863 as King George I.

The three protecting Powers thereupon undertook some responsibility for the new system thus erected. On 27th May they declared that they were freed by the action of the Greeks from the pledge which they had given to King Otho, but that they intended to continue their interest in the maintenance of Greek tranquillity. On 5th June they recognised the election of King George I., made some efforts to secure him a private income, and undertook that the King's successors were to profess the Orthodox faith. Finally, the three Powers declared that the crowns of Denmark and Greece were never to be united, and undertook the task of securing approval for the new order from the rest of the states of the world. On 14th November the five great Powers consented to the transfer of the Ionian Islands to the Greek kingdom, and laid down the conditions of transfer in a protocol. The special "European" position of Greece was again affirmed in the Treaty of London, signed on 29th March 1864, which declared Greece, including the Ionian Islands, an independent constitutional monarchical state ruled by King George, guaranteed by Russia, France, and Great Britain, and possessed of the islands of Corfu and Paxos, which latter were under the perpetual condition of neutrality. The rights of the three Powers were notably revived in 1916, when England, France, and Russia supported M. Venizelos in his constitutional struggles with King Constantine, and were pleaded in justification of the allied landing in Salonica.

Belgium.—One of the most important changes produced in the map of Europe by the Congress of Vienna was the reunion under the house of Orange of the Catholic Netherlands with the Dutch provinces, after a political separation of nearly two hundred and fifty years. This kingdom of the United Netherlands was intended by the allies of 1814-1815 to be one of Europe's strongest bulwarks against French aggression, and no special difficulty was foreseen in the task undertaken by the house of Orange, that of welding Belgians and Dutch into a solidly based and stable state. The Belgian provinces had belonged to Spain, Bavaria, the Emperor, and Napoleon in turn, so that it was hard to predict what its mixed population of Walloons and Flemings would have decided had the country been allowed to enjoy the privilege of self-determination. Though it soon became apparent that among several classes of the Belgians considerable discontent was felt with the bureaucratic and military arrangements in the joint kingdom, which were alleged to favour the Dutch, few could have prophesied that the Belgo-Dutch union would come to an end within fifteen years of its foundation. Towards the end of 1829 relations between the Dutch king and his Belgian subjects began to take a more dangerous turn; and there were signs that Belgian unrest was not at all disapproved in Paris, where hopes were probably entertained in certain quarters of territorial gains at the expense of the Netherlands, and where, in other circles, anything in the shape of a revolution against a monarch, albeit in this case a most industrious, well-meaning, and enlightened monarch, became the object of sympathetic enthusiasm to a genuine but fanatical body of professed republicans.

The Church, always powerful in Belgium, was profoundly dissatisfied with the liberalising tendencies, especially in educational policy, displayed by the King, but the actual impulse to the Belgian revolt came from the July revolutionaries in Paris, who had overthrown the elder branch of the Bourbons and placed the Orleanist branch upon the French throne. Rioting broke out in Brussels on the evening of 25th August; and although order was quickly restored, the Belgians took the opportunity in the end of demanding from their king the separation of Belgium from Holland. There was some talk of the appointment of the King's eldest son, the Prince of Orange, as viceroy of Belgium for his father. On 23rd September the entry of Dutch troops into Brussels before any definite arrangement had been come to in regard to the future government of Belgium provoked a real revolution, which forced the retirement of the Dutch troops from the city after

CHAP. XV.

barricade fighting. The provisional Belgian government, which claimed now to speak for the entire population, proclaimed the independence of the Belgian provinces and made arrangements for the holding of a congress at which the nature of the future form of government would be decided.

On 5th October King William of the Netherlands called upon the five great Powers to defend the work of the Congress of Vienna. He hoped to secure British armed help in erecting once more the united kingdom which had been a specifically British creation at Vienna, and he knew he could rely upon Russian and Prussian and perhaps Austrian sympathy. In the existing state of affairs at Paris a foreign or even a successful Dutch intervention in Belgium might well have brought about the entry upon the scene of the French armies, for the various parties which disputed for control in Paris could combine in a wish to break down the settlement of 1815 and to restore the boundaries of 1802. Accordingly British diplomacy determined to attempt a settlement by means of the mediation of a conference of the five Powers called at London. The British Foreign Office therefore began its work on 4th November, and soon arranged an armistice, which was later supplemented by the withdrawal of the Dutch and Belgian forces to the opposite sides of an agreed line. It next made an effort to divert the Belgian National Congress, then drawing up a constitution in Brussels, from an attempt to sever in perpetuity the dynastic connection with Holland. A message was sent to Brussels expressing the opinion of the allied Powers that the exclusion of the house of Orange from the Belgian throne would endanger European peace and injure Belgian relations with other states. The possibility of an armed occupation of Belgium by the allies, and an enforced partition, was held out to frighten the Belgians into the acceptance of the Powers' will. The Belgians, incensed by this action, adopted in their convention the exclusion of the house of Orange by a large majority. At this juncture their cause was assisted by the outbreak of the Polish revolution, which prevented Russia, and to a less degree Austria and Prussia, from venturing upon any very practical step to mark their strong sympathy with the Orange claim. In these circumstances Palmerston, the new British foreign secretary, took a firm line of his own, and it was not a little due to his initiative that in a protocol of 20th December all five Powers accepted the principle of future Belgian independence; while in a further protocol of 10th January 1831 the Powers decreed that Holland was in future to have as its territorial limit the boundary of 1790, that Luxemburg was to remain in the possession of the Orange family, and that the remainder of the united kingdom of the Netherlands was to form the Belgian state. This state was, however, to be neutralised; the five Powers were to guarantee its integrity and its perpetual neutrality. The later protocol of 17th January, known as the Eighteen Articles, divided the national debt of the joint kingdom, assigning nearly one-half to Belgium. Some compensation for this oppressive allocation was to be obtained by the Belgians, who were to enjoy all the rights which the Dutch enjoyed of trading with the colonies of Holland.

The Dutch did not, as the Belgians definitely did, decline these terms. Relying upon French sympathy, the Belgian National Congress proceeded to offer the Belgian throne to the Duke of Nemours, the second son of Louis Philippe. This was in truth to play with fire, for a French acceptance would have plunged Europe into war. That England was once more the possessor in Palmerston of a shrewd and firm negotiator for her foreign affairs, was shown to the world when Louis Philippe was wise enough to refuse for his son the proffered crown. The Belgians after a space were brought to the conviction that a modification of the terms arranged by the Powers might be more easily arranged if choice were made of a king acceptable to them. Leopold of Saxe-Coburg-Gotha, who had declined the crown of Greece in 1830, was approached by the Belgians. They hoped that his election might secure the favourable modifications in the terms of settlement which they desired. Leopold, with the wisdom which seldom failed him, declared himself ready to be the Belgian king if, and only if, the Belgians would accept the terms which the great Powers offered. It needed, however, an ultimatum from the conference and a steadily growing conviction of their complete isolation in Europe to bring the Belgians to reason. On 4th June Leopold was elected king, and delegates were sent to London for the double purpose of procuring his acceptance and for bargaining with the London Conference. This was now willing to make some concessions to Belgium, which were embodied in a protocol of 26th June.

It was the turn now of the Dutch to refuse the findings of the conference. The original terms, as to the apportionment of the debt, were demanded by the Dutch from the Powers and from Belgium. After some weeks the armistice arranged by

CHAP. XV.

the Powers in November 1830 was denounced, and there began from Antwerp on 2nd August a Dutch advance into Belgian territory which provoked a corresponding entry of the French, who had been summoned by the Belgians to their aid.

The real, but quickly surmounted, peril threatened to the peace of Europe by the French delay in evacuating Belgium after the Dutch had withdrawn, caused Palmerston and the conference to grapple once more with the obstinate problem which had produced the trouble. A new set of terms—the Twenty-four Articles—was completed by the conference, and was handed to the Dutch and Belgian representatives in October. Only parts of Limburg and Luxemburg were assigned to Belgium; and though the Scheldt below Antwerp was placed for the purpose of pilotage and buoying under joint Belgo-Dutch supervision, ships coming in from the sea and destined to Antwerp were to pay Dutch tolls. The Twenty-four Articles, although they were less favourable to Belgium than the Eighteen Articles had been, were accepted by Belgium in November 1831, but rejected by Holland in the following month. Throughout the greater part of 1832 the Dutch king obstinately declined to surrender Antwerp, and claimed that maritime communication with Belgium through the Scheldt was legally impossible, since the separation of Belgium from Holland automatically closed the Scheldt, according to the terms agreed upon at Münster in 1648.

The patience of the conference was now exhausted, and on 1st October it was determined that something drastic must be done to break the Dutch king's obstinacy. Russia, Prussia, and Austria, although prepared to accept the idea of the application of economic pressure, were not prepared for such military action as could alone have compelled an evacuation of Antwerp. On 22nd October England and France agreed on an attack against the city and a blockade of the Dutch ports. The garrison of Antwerp surrendered on 22nd December, but not until May 1833 did the Dutch king bind himself to permit free navigation of the Scheldt and the Meuse and to abstain from hostilities until a Belgo-Dutch treaty had been arranged.

The conference then made with great patience another attempt to procure a Belgo-Dutch agreement to regulate the mutual relations of these two Powers, but gave up the attempt after several months of negotiation had proved that, even if Belgium and Holland could have been induced to agree on the twenty-four points, the partition of Luxemburg, which would need the assent of the German confederation and the house of Nassau, would still have stood in the way as an obstacle. Delay, however, was hardly now a constant peril to European peace, for the King of Holland had bound himself to refrain from armed attack, and there could thus be no incitement to the French party of *mouvement* or excuse for the despatch of French troops across the border. The King of Holland did not decide upon an acceptance of the Twenty-four Articles until March 1838, and there was then some difficulty in securing from the Belgians the surrender of the Dutch portions of Limburg and Luxemburg. The pressure of the united Powers, and some lightening of the Belgian share in the payment to the holders of the public debt of the Netherlands, brought a reluctant Belgian assent to the Twenty-four Articles, which were finally enshrined in the public law of Europe in the treaty of 19th April 1839. Perhaps the most important single provision signed on that day was that according to which Belgium was to join Switzerland and Cracow in the ranks of the "neutralised" states and to be guaranteed in that position by the great Powers. This remained its international condition until 1919. In that year, as a result of the European War, Belgium obtained an unfettered independence and the treaty of 1839 was cancelled.

The Great Powers and the Collapse of the Ottoman Empire.— Mehemet Ali, the Pasha of Egypt, who had thrown his army and fleet into the scale against the Greeks in 1824, became involved in a dangerous dispute with his suzerain, the Sultan, after the final defeat of the Turkish cause in 1829. He was dissatisfied with the government of Crete, which had been awarded to him, holding it to be an insufficient payment for his exertions; and he seized the opportunity of a quarrel with the Pasha of Acre to extend his government into Southern Syria (1831-1832). The Sultan declared the Pasha and his son and general, Ibrahim, to be rebels, and ordered his army to attack their forces. A first battle at Homs, resulting in an Egyptian victory, led to the fall of Antioch and Aleppo; and a second battle, resulting in still another Egyptian victory, led to a further northward advance towards the passes of the Taurus mountain range. The forces of Ibrahim next marched into the interior of Asia Minor, where at Konieh in December 1832 they overthrew another Turkish army. This left the way to Constantinople open before them.

CHAP. XV.

The Turkish Sultan now looked to the great Powers to save him from destruction at his vassal's hands. Appeals were made to England and to France; but when these were found to produce no immediate result, resort was had to the Russian Tsar, who showed surprising alacrity in sending his fleet to the Bosphorus and in landing troops from Sebastopol, first on its eastern shore and later on the European side. The presence of Russian forces near Constantinople was unwelcome alike to France, England, and Austria. The French were especially agitated by the Russian propinquity to Constantinople. After failing to effect their dislodgment by a protest, the French ambassador began an energetic effort to promote peace between the Egyptians and the Turks, an alternative means by which a Russian withdrawal from the Bosphorus might have been peacefully secured. The French influence, which was especially strong both at Alexandria and in the Egyptian camp at Kutaya, combined with English and Austrian influence, which was weightier at Constantinople as being comparatively pro-Turkish, succeeded in procuring the acceptance of terms by both sides, and thus put an end to the war and the growing danger of European complications. It was agreed that Mehemet Ali should add to his other governments Syria and Adana. So ran the Peace of Kutaya, which was signed on 10th April, but which was not ratified by the Sultan until later.

The Russian troops were withdrawn from the Bosphorus soon after the Sultan's ratification of the Convention of Kutaya. Russia, however, did not fail to turn to profit the gratitude of the Turks and their new feeling of dependence upon the Russian Tsar. A Russo-Turkish treaty of defensive alliance was signed at Unkiar Skelessi. This was valid for eight years, but renewable. Each Power was to furnish help to the other, both in the case of foreign war and in the event of any other peril to its peace and security. Terms of such a character really implied the infeudation of the Turkish to the Russian empire, which now became charged with a virtual protectorate over the Ottoman dominions, since it was bound to supply Russian troops by sea or land upon the Sultan's request.

The special danger of the treaty, which in the published form still retained the plausible appearance of equal alliance, was truly revealed in a secret article, which quickly came to the knowledge of England and France, and was, indeed, not to be kept secret long. In order to spare the Sublime Porte the cost and inconvenience of furnishing material aid in the event of a Russian claim for its assistance, the Russian Court announced its contentment with such aid as was represented by the closing of the Dardanelles to all foreign vessels of war. Russia would in this way become impregnable to naval attacks or demonstrations effected by fleets from the Mediterranean; while it might safely be presumed that Turkey, as an ally, would not refuse Russian ships permission to sail in and out of the Dardanelles. English, French, and even Austrian dislike of Russia's new position was patent, and there could be no doubt that a Russian attempt to avail itself of these novel and special treaty rights and duties would be met with formidable resistance. Happily for European peace, the Russian Tsar Nicholas showed no reluctance to surrender the special Russian position when a new Ottoman crisis aroused the general concern of the great Powers.

In the spring of 1839 the relations between the Sultan Muhammad and his powerful Egyptian vassal, never really friendly after the events of 1832-1833 and for long growing worse, were approaching breaking point. The five Powers, apprised of the imminence of war by the massing of Egyptian troops at Aleppo, and of Turkish troops on the Upper Euphrates, counselled peace both at Cairo and Constantinople, proposing in identical notes the erection of an hereditary pashalic of Egypt to be held by Mehemet Ali and his descendants. Palmerston had, indeed, suggested a conference of the five Powers at London, but was unable to secure general interest in his suggestion.

The Turkish Sultan, meanwhile, eluded the pressure of the Powers by sending a secret order to his commander to advance. His troops were decisively defeated on 24th June. The danger in the Near East was increased by the death of the Sultan on 29th June and the desertion of the Turkish fleet to the Egyptians. The five ambassadors at Constantinople resolved to prevent a settlement on the extravagant conditions of the Egyptians, conditions palpably lacking in the elements of permanence. They presented a joint note on 27th July announcing the certainty of agreement among the five Powers, and requesting that no final decisions should be reached without them. But such unity of the great Powers on the Eastern question was not so easily come by as the ambassadors had assumed. The worst dangers of the situation were avoided by the resolution of the Russians not to avail themselves of the possibilities open to them under the

CHAP. XV.

Treaty of Unkiar Skelessi. It had quickly become obvious that the despatch of a Russian fleet to the Bosphorus, in the manner adopted in 1833, would almost certainly lead to a Franco-Russian war, while even a renewal of the treaty of 1833 would envenom the situation. If Russia quickly resolved upon an attitude inoffensive to the majority of other great Powers, the same was not true of France. There public sentiment had become profoundly moved in favour of Mehemet Ali, the idol of St. Cyr and the favourite of the Parisians, insisting that the settlement of the Near East should make the most generous provision for the Pasha of Egypt. For almost a year the debate continued among the great Powers. Metternich and the Prussians objected to Mehemet Ali as a rebel. Palmerston refused to divide the Ottoman empire, whose integrity was necessary, he claimed, to the equilibrium of three continents, and Russia was committed in honour by the treaty of 1833 to the support of the Ottoman dynasty.

The information that the French were promoting a separate Turco-Egyptian negotiation at Constantinople induced Palmerston, who had made London the centre of the Near Eastern conversations of the Powers, to take action which, being offensive to French dignity, might easily have led to a European explosion. Together with representatives of Austria, Russia, and Prussia, he drew up the Treaty of London of 15th July 1840, which fixed the terms which were to be offered by the Sultan to his Egyptian vassal. Egypt was to be an hereditary pashalic in the line of Mehemet Ali, and, at the special request of the Austrian and Prussian ambassadors, concerned at the European danger which might arise out of French resentment at terms too uncompromising, it was agreed that the governorship of Southern Syria should remain with Mehemet for his life. If Mehemet did not accept the offer of the Powers within ten days, it was agreed that he should lose the offer of Southern Syria; if he delayed his acceptance for more than twenty days, that he should forfeit everything. The special Russian position acquired at Unkiar Skelessi was tacitly surrendered in virtue of other provisions. The coercion of Mehemet Ali by blockade, and the defence of Constantinople for the Sultan, were to be, not a Russian operation, but one undertaken by the four Powers. Further, the special danger in the secret article of Unkiar Skelessi, which provided for the opening of the Dardanelles to Russian warships, was avoided by a reaffirmation of the traditional

Ottoman rule that the Dardanelles were to be closed to non-Turkish warships so long as the Porte was at peace.

French statesmen were furious when they were informed that so important a treaty had been made without consulting them or inviting their signature. Patriotic Frenchmen saw the revival of a four-Power alliance like that of 1814 directed against France, and in their resentment were inclined for some time to meditate a challenge to the whole settlement of Europe as it had been fixed in 1815. The caution of Louis Philippe and Guizot, rather than the hot and sanguine temper of Thiers, was destined to decide French policy after nearly three months of great peril to European peace. The resolute temper of the four Powers was not without its effect on the French decision to attempt to re-enter the concert on the Near Eastern question. Prussia had shown a firm resolution to maintain the Rhine barrier. Russia was prepared to defend Constantinople from an advance of the Egyptian forces, and the British Mediterranean fleet, in co-operation with Austrian units, had already achieved marked successes on the Syrian coast, where, by its capture of Syrian coast towns and its encouragement of dangerous revolts against Egyptian authority, it was imperilling the Egyptian line of communications.

Palmerston, whose decision to force the French to desist from their unreasonable claims on behalf of Mehemet Ali had been the direct cause of the crisis, did not desire or expect war, though he would not have refused a challenge. Indeed, he had read the political conditions which obtained in Paris with accurate shrewdness. But when a false move on the part of the Sultan of Turkey gave the French the opportunity to re-enter the European discussions on the Near East, and with authority, Palmerston was by no means averse to showing a conciliatory temper. The Sultan had declared the Pasha of Egypt to be deposed on 14th September, and on 9th October a French note was delivered in London demanding his retention of the government of Egypt. A reconciliation of the five Powers on this basis was to prove the easier in view of the exploits and diplomacy of the British naval commander in the Mediterranean, Sir Charles Napier. This commander's capture of the powerful fort of Acre early in November had finally compelled the Egyptian armies to begin a withdrawal from Syria in view of the dangerous threat to their contact with Egypt. Later in the same month the admiral, stationing his fleet before Alexandria, had extorted

CHAP. XV. a convention from Mehemet Ali whereby that pasha undertook to withdraw his claims to all provinces other than Egypt and to restore the Turkish fleet, which had been treacherously surrendered to him in 1839. In return he was to obtain the hereditary pashalic of Egypt for his family.

The final French reconciliation with Europe was also helped by the replacement of the ministry of Thiers by a cabinet in which the portfolio of Foreign Affairs was held by the more pacific Guizot, summoned in October 1840 from London, where he had been in close contact with Palmerston. Mehemet Ali undertook to make formal submission to the Sultan; and the Porte, at the request of the now united Powers, cancelled his edict of September deposing the Egyptian pasha, and even decreed that the pashalic of Egypt should be hereditary in the latter's family. The Near Eastern situation thus established was taken under the virtual protection of the Powers, when all five of them signed the treaty of Mehemet Ali with his suzerain, and agreed, in another instrument signed in July 1841, to recognise the Dardanelles and Bosphorus as closed to foreign ships of war (provided Turkey were at peace).

The Great Powers and the Crimean War.—That the danger to European peace threatened by the developments in the Near Eastern situation during the years 1832-1841 had been overcome without the outbreak of a European war, had been largely due to the unusual fact that the ruler of Russia had shown not the slightest inclination to profit from Ottoman embarrassment by making claims for Russian territorial advancement or for the expansion of those Christian "liberties" contractually under the special aegis of Russia. Russian ambition had indeed taken the grander, if less immediately profitable, course of adopting the Sultan as a dependent ally; but even this specific result of the Treaty of Unkiar Skelessi had been surrendered later to the general European Concert. But if Russia had surrendered the special advantage gained by Unkiar Skelessi, the Russian Chancery still preserved earlier Russo-Turkish treaty clauses, which were in their way capable of uses dangerous to Turkey and provocative to the other great Powers. The Treaty of Kutchuk Kainardji of 1774 had made the Sultan promise to protect the Christian religion in his dominions, and was always available to justify a Russian intervention on behalf of at least the Orthodox subjects of the Turks. By the Treaty of Adrianople, Moldavian and Wallachian prosperity was "guaranteed" by Russia; while another Russo-Turkish arrangement of the same date provided for the removal of Turkish civil and military influences from those territories. CHAP. XV.

Russia intervened decisively in Moldavian and Wallachian affairs during the revolutionary troubles of 1848 by marching in troops to suppress disorder in both provinces. Turkish military co-operation had been very properly invited; and as Austria was in no position to resent Russian action, which might in other times have led to a crisis, the Russian military occupation of the "principalities" (ending after two years) was terminated without danger. It was to be a later Wallachian and Moldavian occupation, however, undertaken for the purpose of securing a re-definition, and incidentally a formidable expansion, of Russian claims on behalf of the Orthodox, which led to the situation of 1853, from which there proved to be no other outlet but war. After several minor crises between the Porte and Russia from 1849 to 1852, Prince Menschikoff had been sent to Constantinople early in 1853 with a series of demands, among which the most formidable was that in which the Tsar pressed for the revision of the terms of the Treaty of Kutchuk Kainardji. By that instrument of 1774 the Sultan had indeed bound himself "to protect the Christian religion and its churches," but had not authorised Russian intervention on behalf of the Christians. The new Russian claim was virtually for an instrument whereby Russia would be established as the official protector of Greek Christians—an instrument which would furnish the Tsar the opportunity, should he desire it, of interfering in every detail of Ottoman administration. Turkish recalcitrance, fortified by British and French encouragement, resisted the bullying of Menschikoff, and was strong enough to reject the draft of the treaty which he proffered on 5th May, an instrument under the terms of which the ancient existing rights of Ottoman Orthodox Christians were to be ensured for ever. This treaty was considered dangerous by all the four non-Russian ambassadors from the great Powers at Constantinople, in that it gave to Russia a special position in the Ottoman empire. Even Menschikoff's later revised demand, not now for a formal treaty, but for an official note to the Russian government declaring the Sultan's intentions towards the Orthodox Church, was rejected by the Turks; and not without encouragement. Thereupon Menschikoff left Constantinople on the 21st May. His master, after

CHAP. XV.

making one further attempt to force the Ottoman government to accept the note of Menschikoff, ordered on 22nd June the occupation of Wallachia and Moldavia as guarantee for the maintenance of the rights of Orthodox Christians in Turkey.

The other four Powers, disliking in varying degrees the Russian measure of force, were resolved to procure a Russian withdrawal from the principalities by means of mediation between the Tsar and the Sultan. They hoped to win a concession from the Turks which, while not dangerous in itself, would save the Tsar's face and permit him to order a withdrawal without loss of dignity. Discussions took place in the several capitals, but those at Vienna proved most decisive.

On 28th July, Count Buol, the Austrian minister, sent to the Russians a note which contained the terms suggested for a declaration to be made by the Sultan on the subject of the Greek Orthodox Church in Turkey. This declaration had been drawn up by the Austrian minister in consultation with representatives of England, France, and Prussia, and was thought by all four Powers to provide the best possible termination to the Russo-Turkish dispute. The Tsar had, but the Turks had not, been given an opportunity to express views during the drafting of the note. Accordingly, the declaration which was recommended to the Sultan for publication contained such contentious phraseology as the "active solicitude [of the Emperors of Russia] for the maintenance of the immunities and privileges of the Greek Orthodox Church in the Ottoman empire," and the Sultan's promise to remain faithful "to the letter and spirit of the stipulations of the treaties of Kainardji and Adrianople relative to the protection of the Christian religion." The draft declaration was accepted without amendment by the Tsar, but the Porte asked for several alterations, which were one and all intended to secure and to stress the independent and exclusive authority enjoyed over his Christian subjects by the Sultan. The Turkish amendments were rejected for this very reason by the Tsar, despite the pleas of the four Powers, anxious to make an end of a dangerous situation. The Tsar, too, was further influenced by the feeling that it was beneath his dignity to accept amendments dictated by the Turks in a document which already represented a retreat on his part from the position which had been assumed by Prince Menschikoff. To make the matter more complicated, England and France now left the four-Power Concert and, declining to join in further pressure upon the Turks, pressed instead upon the Tsar the acceptance of the Turkish amendments.

The Turks, encouraged by the proximity of the British and French fleets, and anxious to inflict a great humiliation upon the Tsar, or to force him into a war in which they believed they would have the English and French as allies, now took action which threatened to remove the Russo-Turkish dispute altogether from diplomatic control. An ultimatum was despatched to the Russian commander in Wallachia and Moldavia ordering him to evacuate those nominally Turkish principalities within sixteen days. The ultimatum was rejected almost as soon as it had been received, and a state of war between Russia and Turkey opened on 23rd October. On 22nd October the British and French fleets passed the Dardanelles to undertake the defence of Turkey against Russian attack. The Tsar, who did not desire a war with France and England as well as with Turkey, announced that his forces would not attack the Turks. The Turks, however, crossing the Danube, themselves attacked the Russians and goaded them into the decision to take offensive measures. The ensuing Russian naval attack, made by the Sebastopol fleet upon the Turkish squadron stationed at Sinope, and resulting in the total destruction of the Sultan's ships on the 30th November, provoked French and British action which made war almost inevitable. The French and British fleets then entered the Black Sea in January 1854 with instructions to force the Russian fleets back into port.

The diplomats of the four Powers stationed at Vienna did not even then despair of achieving a peaceful settlement. At the end of December they drew up a second note, which the Porte was induced to accept, but which the insulted Tsar, who had but just received the news of English and French measures in the Black Sea, rejected. Austria tried to stave off a Franco-British declaration of war upon Russia by offering co-operation in the despatch of a summons to the Russians requiring them to evacuate the principalities within a fixed limit of time. England and France, however, without waiting to co-ordinate their plans with Austria, despatched an ultimatum to Russia, which, remaining unanswered, produced at the end of March declarations of war from Paris and from London.

Though war was already in progress, the diplomats at Vienna did not cease their co-operation in the attempt to

CHAP. XV.

secure the Russian evacuation of the principalities, occupation of which was a cause for legitimate anxiety to Austria, and offensive to Prussia and to the Germanic confederation, as bringing the Russians to the mouth of the Danube. If Austria and Prussia were quite ready to sign protocols with the other two belligerent Powers of the Vienna conferences, they showed very great reluctance to undertake an enforcement of the evacuation of the principalities by military measures. Austria at length formally summoned Russia on 3rd June to undertake this evacuation, and the Russian commanders, whose siege of Silistria was not progressing too well, were, after an interval, given the order to withdraw from the principalities, which were forthwith occupied by the Austrians for the remainder of the war under a special Austro-Turkish convention.

The original cause of the war had now been removed, no direct contact between Russian and Turkish armies on the European front existed any longer, and peace should apparently have been very easy to make. Nicholas had, however, provoked a very dangerous temper in England and France, which refused to be satisfied by a return to the position of 1852. Instead they insisted on the need of finding permanent safeguards for the Ottoman empire and of ending for ever Russia's special claims to intervene in Turkey. Austria was not unwilling to follow upon this road, while Prussia, in danger of a complete and perilous isolation, was at least willing to listen in conference, though not always ready to sign conditions. In August 1854 diplomatic conferences of the four Powers at Vienna again elaborated conditions to be despatched to St. Petersburg for the settlement of the Near Eastern dispute—conditions, however, for which Prussia refused at the moment to accept responsibility.

The Four Points outlined at Vienna in August 1854 made demands upon Russia which involved humiliation hardly at that point justified by the military position. The Russian protectorate over Wallachia, Moldavia, and Serbia was to be abolished; freedom of navigation was to be established in the mouths of the Danube (which had been in Russian occupation since 1829 and had been deliberately left in a neglected condition); the treaty of July 1841 concerning the Dardanelles and the Black Sea was to be revised in the interests of the European balance (forecasting the end of Russian Black Sea Supremacy); and finally the Tsar's claim to a protectorate over Ottoman Christians, of whatsoever rite, was to be abandoned.

The Tsar refused to discuss the Four Points until four months of Anglo-French military pressure and an increasing Austrian readiness to make open cause with the two allies had broken his stubborn pride and permitted him in November to accept the formulae of Vienna as a basis of discussion.

Next a conference was assembled at Vienna in March at which detailed negotiations began though the war continued. Prussia was excluded as being unwilling to bind itself to make war upon Russia should the negotiations fail. The special difficulty of the conference arose out of Franco-British insistence that the Russian Black Sea fleet should be altogether suppressed by treaty provision—an extreme demand which Russia altogether declined, and which Austria considered unreasonable enough to justify in June 1855 the disbandment of the conference, and its abandonment of the Anglo-French alliance.

The end of the war was produced by another Austrian intervention in December 1855. Austria, after negotiations with France and England, produced a set of conditions—going considerably beyond the Four Points—the prompt acceptance of which by Russia was demanded on pain of a rupture with Austria. Russian consent was notified just before the expiry of the ultimatum on 16th January, and arrangements were completed for the holding of a conference at Paris.

The Congress of Paris, which opened on 25th February, was the most important assembly which had gathered since the Congress of Verona. Austria, France, Great Britain, Russia, and Turkey were full members, and Sardinia, which had participated in the war against Turkey, was invited to share such congress business as concerned itself. Prussia was excluded from the opening negotiations at the special wish of England, which disliked her pro-Russian attitude, and could of course urge that she had not been a belligerent or a mediator. When the revision of the " Straits " Convention of 1841 was undertaken, however, after the first articles had been settled, the entry of Prussia into the congress became necessary, for that Power had been a signatory. The business undertaken by the congress covered a wide area of international relations. Territorial topics did not bulk very largely in the discussions, for the principle of the return of occupied territory had been early conceded. The only territorial change undertaken in the map of Europe was the cession to Moldavia by Russia of a strip of Bessarabia, a cession which removed Russia from the mouths of the Danube. A British proposal to inquire into

CHAP. XV.

the state of the populations which inhabited the districts east of the Black Sea was inspired by a desire to check Russia's expansion in Asia by according a recognition of the independence of Caucasian populations either already fallen, or soon about to fall, under Russian power. It might have led to an interesting opening of the Central Asian question if the French could have been persuaded to take it seriously. As it was, nothing was done in this direction except that provision was made for the delimitation of the Asiatic frontier between Turkey and Russia.

An important omission of the treaties of 1815 was rectified when the Sublime Porte was admitted into the European Concert and recognised as sharing in the advantages of the public law of that continent. Each signatory of the treaty of 20th March engaged to respect Turkish independence and territorial integrity; and all united in undertaking to treat as a matter of general concern any attempt to alter either. The Powers, while they recognised the high value of the Sultan's decree "recording his general intention towards the Christian population of his Empire," declared that it would not give them singly or jointly a right to interfere in the internal affairs of Turkey. A provision specially intended to secure Turkey from unjust coercion was one which stipulated that, if any of the signatories were involved in differences with the Porte, such differences were to be referred to the mediation of the remaining signatories before measures of force were undertaken. The new European status of Turkey was to be shown even in the substitution of new two-party treaties, covering such subjects as trade and commercial relations, for the old Turkish unilateral decrees.

The suzerainty of the Porte over the semi-independent principalities of Wallachia and Moldavia was preserved. The congress, under Turkish and Austrian pressure, did not allow the then very fashionable ideas of nationality to dictate a union between the two Rumanian provinces. A measure of respect was, however, to be paid to the popular will in the two principalities. Their final form of administrative organisation was not determined at the congress, but was to attend upon the wishes to be expressed by the Moldavian and Wallachian populations. Such a settlement was notable as being the first admission by an International Congress of the principle of the consultation of the popular will in territorial alterations. The special Russian protectorate was abandoned, and the guarantee of the immunities and privileges of the two principalities was assumed by all the signatory Powers. The principalities, together with Serbia, were to possess their own non-Turkish forces, though Serbia was still to admit a Turkish garrison.

Napoleon III. of France had had ideas much more revolutionary than these for the disposal of the principalities, and might, had he had his way, have converted the congress into an Assembly for the national redistribution of European boundaries. Acutely sensitive as he was to Italian discontent, he would probably have favoured the absorption of the principalities into the Austrian system, if thereby he could have procured the evacuation of Lombardy by Austria. Failing to secure any Austrian approval for such revolutionary proposals, he had characteristically shown his devotion to the principle of nationality by urging the union of Wallachia and Moldavia into a Rumanian state under an hereditary monarch.

The ability of Russia to undertake aggressive measures against Sweden was weakened by a convention elaborated by the congress and appended to the main treaty. The Aaland Islands, dangerously near Stockholm, though they were allowed to remain with Russia, were to be disarmed. This was not a novel type of stipulation in International Law, for international treaties had already provided in the past for the dismantling of specific fortresses such as those on the Franco-Belgian border or of naval bases such as Dunkirk. Disarmed islands, it is true, were in a somewhat different category, as they could still facilitate the operations of fleets in a wide extent of sea otherwise less easily navigable. As such their capacity for mischief has been obvious to strong naval Powers. It is noteworthy that it was Great Britain which was responsible for the disarmament of Corfu and of Paxos in 1864, and for the dismantling of Heligoland in 1919.

A completely novel device introduced by the Paris Congress was the "neutralisation" of the Black Sea. By this was meant the banishment of all armament from off its waters and coasts. It was, of course, primarily intended to weaken the attacking power of Russia, for if the Russian Sebastopol fleet should once have been banned by International Law, the danger to Constantinople from the sea would have permanently ended. A grander air was given to the device by the proclamation of the opening of the waters and ports of the Black Sea to the merchant fleets of all nations, and the banning from its coasts of all maritime and military arsenals.

CHAP XV. Special exceptions of a minor character were made to this last general rule. A convention appended to the treaty of 30th March arranged for Russian and Turkish police flotillas, while the body of the treaty itself allowed the signatory Powers to despatch two light vessels each to the Danube.

Another innovation of the Paris Congress was the form of the new International Commission which was charged with the management of the Danubian mouths. The mouths of the Danube, while in Russian hands, had been grossly neglected, and the river had not played the part in the system of communication in South-Eastern Europe which might have been expected. The engineering works which were necessary at the estuaries were put in charge of an International Commission, not composed of representatives of riparian Powers exclusively, but of those of France, England, Prussia, Russia, Austria, Turkey and Sardinia. It was, indeed, intended that the International Commission should hand over its jurisdiction to a Danube Riverain Commission, also provided for in the treaty, as soon as its works should be completed. The works took much longer to finish than had been expected, and, even when they had been completed, the Powers showed such reluctance to allow a valuable and authoritative commission to lapse, and its work to be inherited by a probably less efficient riparian body, that the commission, with extended authority, has survived substantially unaltered to the present day.

After the main treaty had been signed on 30th March, the plenipotentiaries did not separate, but remained together for the transaction of further business. Unusually liberal arrangements were negotiated, even before the exchange of ratifications, in such matters as the resumption of commercial relations, the ending of the blockade, and the hastening of military evacuations. It was in the session of 8th April, however, that the congress took on the full aspect of an international areopagus. Comte Walewski then brought forward, besides certain maritime proposals, the four specially pressing difficulties of current international politics—the Austrian and French occupation of portions of the papal states, the Neapolitan scandals, the Franco-British occupation of Greece, and the inability of the Belgian government to repress conspiracies against the ruling house of France. Clarendon was given the opportunity of condemning Neapolitan abuses, Cavour of speaking in bold terms of the evil consequences of Austrian policy in Italy, the Russians of showing their desire to associate once more with France and England in the control of Greece, and the Prussians of airing their grievance in regard to the "revolutionaries" of Neuchâtel. Another small state in addition to Neuchâtel was introduced into the proceedings, when Cavour defended Sardinian policy in respect of the Prince of Monaco. It was in the later session of 14th April that Clarendon advanced his proposal—already enshrined in the treaty as far as the Eastern question was concerned—that states engaged in disputes should always invoke mediation before they had recourse to war. He was unable to win from the congress more than a mild resolution recommending to quarrelling states the use of the good offices of a friendly Power.

The congress, however, during its latter period was principally concerned to undertake some re-definition of International Maritime Law as it affected neutrals in war. Only the well-known objection of Great Britain had prevented that subject from entering the discussions at Vienna. At Paris, Great Britain and its maritime rival, France, were alike agreed that the concessions they had made to neutral commerce during the course of the war just ending should be made an immutable part of the Law of Nations. Accordingly, the famous declaration was drawn up by which privateering was abolished, neutral goods were freed from capture on enemy vessels, and enemy goods on neutral vessels (save contraband of war); and blockades were required to be maintained by forces effectively preventing access to the coasts of their enemy.

The Proposed Italian Congress of 1859.—In January 1859, from events which took place in Paris and Turin, the intelligent surmised that a Franco-Sardinian alliance might very shortly challenge Austria's dominance of the Italian peninsula. Great Britain worked hard to maintain the threatened peace, and Lord Derby's government, after elaborating four points which might serve as a basis of Austro-French agreement, offered Lord Cowley's services to France as a mediator between it and Austria. They were accepted, and Lord Cowley undertook some delicate negotiations with Austria on the basis of these four points. In March the situation assumed new characteristics when Russia proposed a congress of the four Powers on the Italian question. This proposal was quickly adopted by England with the limiting condition that discussion should be confined to the four points. These provided for French and Austrian evacuation of the papal

CHAP. XV.

states, the improvement of administration in those areas, an Austrian undertaking to refrain from attack upon Sardinia, and Austria's surrender of her treaties of 1847 with Parma and Modena, by which Austrian intervention had been pronounced permissible for the restoration of order. Austria would almost certainly have prevented the approaching war by accepting the congress on the British conditions. It decided, however, to add conditions of its own, and the Austrian point of view may be studied in Buol's communication to England of 29th March 1859, and the Austrian ultimatum of 19th April. It insisted on a preliminary Sardinian disarmament, and refused to allow the congress to effect any territorial changes or to admit to its councils Italian states not directly affected by its labours, aiming by this last condition at the exclusion of Sardinia. After Austrian negotiation with England, both Powers professed readiness to substitute general disarmament for special Sardinian disarmament as a condition of the congress, though Austria insisted on special guarantees against France. The Austrian plan to exclude Sardinia also caused Austro-British differences.

On 18th April the British ministry made a new and remarkable proposal. It was suggested that a military commission, not part of the congress, should undertake the supervision of a general and simultaneous disarmament, so necessary if the congress atmosphere were to be one fit for effective negotiations. The diplomatic congress itself was to be one of the five great Powers ; but the Italian states were to sit with the plenipotentiaries of the Powers on the receipt of an invitation. The British proposal, so far as the first point was concerned, planned a wholly new departure in international relations, but one which, in view of the achievements of the five Powers, seemed by no means beyond their reach. As far as the second point was concerned, the proposal seemed the best way to reconcile the claims of the great Powers and the small, and to establish a practical co-operation between them in the establishment of international policy. The Congress of Laibach—also mainly concerned with Italian affairs—had already established a precedent for the practice now proposed by the British government.

It was most unfortunate for the development of international polity that a brusque ultimatum from Austria to Sardinia prematurely provoked a war and prevented the holding of a congress which might have given the European

Concert a unique opportunity to develop self-confidence, and to extend the range of its administrative practices. The military commission would certainly have acquired some technical knowledge of the problem of disarmament, while the congress itself, once gathered, would probably have had to formulate a programme for administrative and constitutional reform, to be established within the Italian states, or possibly even to erect an Italian confederation. Wise men have maintained that United Italy was made too quickly.

Even after the war had been opened, the idea was still universally current that a European congress would be necessary to render valid such changes as had been agreed upon in principle among the belligerents. Such changes would have directly affected the territorial settlement of Italy made in 1815, which had been the collective work of Europe. The English ministry, disappointed by Napoleon's Treaty of Villafranca with Austria, claimed for the congress of Powers more than the mere privilege of ratifying the stipulations of Villafranca, and refused to enter a congress except upon terms. Belligerents, who had expended money and blood in a war, were not likely to allow inactive neutrals, however powerful, to dictate to them their terms of peace. Accordingly, only after the final terms of Austro-French peace had been signed at Zurich did Austria and France, finding that part of their plans for Italy had miscarried, resolve on the summons of a congress, the business of which was to be the pacification of Central Italy, not the revision of the results of the war which more especially concerned themselves. Invitations were sent to the three neutral Powers and to the three Italian potentates still in their capitals, the Kings of Sardinia and Naples and the Pope. The congress, however, was destined never to meet. The Pope (and Austria) required from France a promise that a plan put forward in an inspired pamphlet, *The Pope and the Congress*, should not be laid before the congress. This plan proposed to restrict the papal sovereignty to the territories in the immediate vicinity of Rome, but to secure this reduced sovereignty by the guarantee of the great Powers. When Napoleon declined to commit himself, both Austria and the Pope refused attendance at the congress; and Napoleon, who was to be its host in Paris, and who was by then revolving schemes which made its convocation a disadvantage, was able to adjourn it indefinitely.

CHAP. XV.

The Powers and the Lebanon.—On 29th May 1860 in the mountainous Lebanon district of Syria, a region whose disorder had attracted the attention of Europe since 1842, a massacre more notable than usual was perpetrated by the Druses, a local semi-pagan Muhammadan sect, upon the Christian Maronites. The French ministry almost at once proposed the despatch of a five-Power commission to the scene of the troubles. When the news of a new massacre of Christians at Damascus followed upon that reported from the Lebanon, the Powers accepted the French suggestion and even authorised a French landing of troops at Beyrut. The Commission of Inquiry investigated, reported and secured from an Extraordinary Turkish Commission despatched from Constantinople the execution of some exemplary punishments.

The commission next sat upon the reorganisation of the administration of the Lebanon with a view to the prevention of similar trouble in the future. Rival French and British schemes were proposed to this end. The French scheme desired the separation of the Lebanon province from Syria under a Maronite governor, appointed for life, and only to be dismissed by the Sultan with the consent of the Powers. The British scheme would have set up a governor of Syria appointed with the approval of the Powers for a term of years. Both schemes looked dangerously like the beginning of a policy of separating autonomous areas, even in Asia, from the main Ottoman body and were opposed by the Turks. These, however, were forced to concede something. They accepted a Christian governor for the Lebanon, who was to be appointed for three years and to be only removable for misconduct. Mixed courts and administrative councils, representing the different communities, were to be part of the new machinery of government.

The Proposed Polish Congress of 1863.—On the 21st January 1863 there broke out a national uprising of the Poles against Russian government in the "Congress kingdom." This central Polish area had been handed over by the European Congress of 1815 to the Tsars of Russia, who were to rule within its limits as constitutional kings of Poland. Mutual incompatibility had combined to make the congress plan unfeasible, and constitutional rule was formally suppressed by Nicholas after he had put down a formidable Polish revolt in 1831. Napoleon III., who shared his uncle's sympathy for the Poles, would have liked, had he dared, to bring the Polish question before the congress of 1856. When the insurrection of 1863, therefore, took on formidable dimensions, he proposed a European congress, after a preliminary consideration of other plans. Austria and England were moved by the Polish situation into a measure of co-operation with Napoleon, and all three Powers resolved to present "identic" notes at St. Petersburg on 17th April.

Russia's power was by no means as seriously endangered as it had been in 1831, when the Poles had possessed a national army. Russian statesmen had the further knowledge that an intervention by arms was unlikely. Accordingly, the Russian minister Gortchakoff in his replies to the diplomatic representation of the three Powers, though courteous, was never exactly yielding. The revolt, too, in spreading outside the limits of the congress kingdom and enlisting the support of the Polish minorities of Lithuania, Volhynia, Podolia and the Ukraine, made the task of the would-be foreign mediators more difficult. Russia had already questioned their legal rights to make representations even in regard to the congress kingdom, and.was now plainly infuriated by the Polish insurrections in the Russian border provinces.

Gortchakoff parried the first demand for a congress by asking that not Poland alone, but all subjects of international interest should be open for discussion. He was, of course, playing for time to enable a military suppression of the revolt. He was also prepared for a bargain in certain circumstances. If he could have regained the right of arming in the Black Sea, he might have been prepared to make concessions in the Polish kingdom. The three Powers, despite the obvious Russian ill-will, persisted with their efforts at mediation and at the assembling of a congress. In notes presented simultaneously at St. Petersburg on 17th June they asked for an armistice, an amnesty, the restoration of the constitution of 1815, and the assembly of a conference of the eight states, signatories of the *Acte final* of 1815. The request for an armistice and an eight-Power congress was rejected by the Russians. The specific propositions put forward with regard to Polish affairs (the Six Points) were not formally accepted, although Russia indicated its desire to undertake discussion of Polish affairs with Prussia and Austria. The diplomatic rebuff was complete. Napoleon was still willing to make another suggestion to England, but one which could not fail to be offensive. He suggested a

CHAP. XV.

congress to deal with Europe as a whole, the treaty of 1815 being regarded as having lapsed. Napoleon was fond of indulging in large schemes for the revision of the political map of Europe. The time had not yet come, however, when states assembled not after a war but in ordinary times of peace, were prepared to handle such delicate and ambitious business. Napoleon's suggestion was therefore rejected by England, the only Power, other than Napoleonic France and newly created Italy, in the least likely to be accessible to such an order of ideas.

The Schleswig-Holstein Conference of 1864.—On 8th May 1852, a treaty, previously considered by a conference of ambassadors at London, was signed between Denmark on the one side, and Austria, France, Prussia, Great Britain, Russia and Sweden on the other, Sweden being associated with the great Powers owing to its geographical propinquity to the Danish dominions. The purpose of the treaty as stated in the preamble was "the maintenance of the integrity of the Danish monarchy, as connected with the general interests of the Balance of Power in Europe." The special dangers threatening the integrity of the Danish monarchy were the separation of the German Duchies of Holstein and Schleswig from the Independent Danish kingdom by the operation of a different rule of succession to that employed within the kingdom. Accordingly, the treaty settled the Danish succession upon Prince Christian of Glücksburg and his male issue, and arranged for further co-operation between the King of Denmark and the other signatory Powers in the event of the extinction of the Glücksburgs.

The settlement of 1852 ignored the increasing difficulties of reconciling the entirely German population of Holstein and the predominantly German population of Schleswig to the centralising policy of a Copenhagen government, which, even if it admitted Holstein's German character, was impatient of attempts to limit its control of Schleswig or to frustrate the ambition of incorporating the duchy in the kingdom. It was Danish national ambition which, despite engagements taken in 1851-1852 with Austria and Prussia, provoked the crisis of 1862-1863 by disregarding both the very special connection of Schleswig with Holstein and the resolute dislike of the large majority of Schleswigers for the merging of the traditional individuality of their province in a unitary Danish kingdom. On 30th March the Danish government in a proclamation announced by implication the inclusion of

Schleswig in the constitutional arrangements foreseen for the Danish state proper, and maintained its resolution in a subsequent explicit announcement of 28th September, which concerned a change of constitution for Denmark and Schleswig.

When Austria, Prussia and the German confederation showed every intention of employing force against Denmark, if that country should persist in its policies for Schleswig, the remaining Powers, who had for fifteen years been vexed and perplexed by the problem of the Danish monarchy, saw the need of redoubled diplomatic energy. On 5th November 1863 Napoleon III. (who had the Italian and Polish problems in mind as well as that of Schleswig) proposed a congress for the settlement of all European difficulties. The Danish king accepted the idea of a congress, but England and Austria declined it, while Prussia made difficulties. On 31st December 1863, Russell appealed for a conference to be held at London or Paris between the Powers signatories of the treaty of 1852. On 11th January 1864 the Danish government asked all the signatory Powers of 1852 to meet in conference, and offered serious guarantees that the German objections to recent Danish proceedings would be met. The German confederation, however, declined to accept anything less than the immediate abolition of the Dano-Schleswig constitution, and since this was never offered by the Danish government, military "execution" upon Schleswig was undertaken on 1st February 1864, and resulted in a formal Germano-Danish war.

When the war had begun, English diplomacy redoubled its efforts to bring about an agreement, first for an armistice between the combatants, and then for a conference between the signatories of the treaty of 1852 (which provided for the maintenance of the integrity of the Danish monarchy). An agreement for an armistice could not be obtained; and while the conference was successfully gathered in London on 28th April, the only formula for the agenda on which it had been possible to obtain agreement was one which spoke indefinitely of the restoration of the blessings of peace to Northern Europe. At the conference British influence was strongly employed to produce an agreement on an armistice. Though the Danes disliked to surrender their strongest weapon—the blockade of North Germany—as a condition of an armistice, a short armistice to run (for about a month) until 12th June was accepted by the belligerents. Such a period would cer-

CHAP. XV. tainly serve to test the likelihood of any successful issue of the conference, and, if such issue seemed likely, would almost certainly be extended.

The armistice secured, the future of the Schleswig-Holstein duchies was immediately brought into the discussion by a Prussian proposal for the complete independence of the duchies, and by a later Austro-Prussian proposal for the erection of the united duchies into a single state under the Prince of Augustenburg. The English now introduced a compromise plan, fairer to the Danes, and one which had the approval of France and Russia. Lauenburg, Holstein and South Schleswig were to be separated from the remainder of the Danish monarchy, but their final political destiny was to be arranged with their consent. The remainder of the Danish monarchy, including almost certainly a portion of Schleswig, would obtain a guarantee of its independence from the great Powers. This independence would be additionally secured by a proposal that no fortresses or war-posts should be permitted in the dominions separated from the Danish monarchy, a proposal which, perhaps, bore evidence of the British tendency to demilitarise at every opportunity, partly from a genuine sentiment of humanitarianism, and partly for prudent military reasons—those of hindering in advance a German domination of the Baltic.

The British proposal (except in the matter of disarmament) met with a favourable reception from the German Powers, and was accepted in principle by the Danes. Dangerous differences, however, broke out between the Germans and the Danes on the frontier line to be traced between those portions of the Danish monarchy destined to be separated and the remainder. The armistice was prolonged for a fortnight in order to permit further negotiation. The English, when the danger of a resumption of the war seemed close, appealed for an agreement between Austria, Prussia and Denmark. It urged the designation of a friendly Power which should be commissioned to trace a frontier line to run between that proposed by the Germans and that proposed by the Danes. The Danes were foolish to reject this proposal, whose acceptance would have weakened the position of the German Powers at the conference. Their plenipotentiary was further prevented by his instructions from doing anything to welcome a French proposal which would have decided the fate of mixed German-Danish districts in Schleswig on the basis of votes taken in the communes. The Danes having thus assumed the main responsibility for the breakdown of the conference, the termination of the armistice found them engaged once more in the Germano-Danish war, the issue of which could no longer be subjected to any serious European control or supervision.

The Proposed Conference of 1866 and the Conferences of London of 1867 and 1871.—In the early months of 1866 the diplomats of Europe were occupied by the growing tension of Austro-Prussian relations, and the resulting serious increase in the armaments of Austria, Prussia and Italy, a Power which would almost certainly be a Prussian ally in a war against Austria. Clarendon, the British Foreign Secretary, offered English mediation in March 1866 and was eager to associate France and Russia in the work. A proposal for disarmament was brought forward and Bismarck was induced to accept a Prussian reduction of strength parallel to Austrian reduction, which was to be undertaken, however, not only on the Prussian frontier but on the Italian also. Clarendon had preferred an attempt to produce an accommodation by the proffered mediation of the three great Powers neutral to the conflict. Napoleon, however, for whom congresses had not yet lost their charm, despite the failure of his several attempts to muster one since 1856, proposed a congress, procured the assent of England and Russia, and issued invitations on 24th May.

The members of the congress were to be the parties in dispute, Austria, Prussia and Italy, the German confederation which was vitally affected by the Austro-Prussian differences, and the three remaining great Powers. The aim of the congress was to be settlement by diplomatic means not only of the Austro-Prussian differences concerning the final disposition of Schleswig and Holstein, but also of two other European questions of great difficulty—the "Italian dispute," by which the Austrian occupation of Venetia was indicated, and secondly, the pressing problem of suggested amendments to the German Federal Constitution, a question which had been long and bitterly discussed among the German governments and populations. The interference of non-German Powers in this last subject might have been justified by the citation of the fact that the actual German Federal Constitution was the work of the congress of 1815, or possibly by proof that Germany itself was incapable of producing the necessary amendments by peaceful means. The less offensive course was chosen of justifying what

CHAP. XV. measure of European discussion was to be undertaken by alleging considerations in connection with the Balance of Power.

Not only had a sufficient programme been thus laid down for the congress, but a plan had already come under view by which the three Powers contemplating war might be appeased. Clarendon approved a plan by which Prussia would annex Schleswig and Holstein and cede Silesia to Austria, which Power would in turn cede Venetia to Italy. A congress which should be able to effect such a territorial redistribution without a war would indeed be writing a startling chapter in history. It is impossible to refrain from the reflection that it was in the highest degree optimistic to believe that Prussia or Austria would be willing to undertake troublesome and humiliating territorial modification merely for the purpose of general European convenience. Bismarck was already planning a magnified Prussia, while Austria was determined not to emerge from the situation with less of territory or European influence than before.

The promoters of the congress had not ventured to insist on general demobilisation as a condition of its inauguration. The utmost that could be done in this direction was to express in the invitation a hope that military measures would not be pushed further. In these circumstances Prussia and Italy were able to agree to enter the congress without conditions. Austria, afraid to put much reliance on European regard for her inviolability as a necessary preliminary to a Balance of Power, and fearing that the changes to be proposed in Germany and Italy would be at her expense, either territorially or from the point of view of prestige and influence, laid down preliminary demands which made futile all hope of a successful negotiation. The congress was forbidden to consider any plans which would yield to any of the invited states additions of territory or influence. Such a limitation of the activities of the congress was, perhaps, designed by the Austrian statesmen to show Germany and Europe that greed and desire for power were the special attributes of the Prussians or Italians. Events indicated that Austria might have been wiser to enter a congress where Russian, English, French, and German federal interest would have been employed to wrest for her some compensation for an Italian annexation of Venetia, now manifestly inevitable.

The Austro-Prussian War of 1866 resulted in the magnified power of Prussia and in consequence of Italy. Both were

Napoleon's neighbours, which consideration made it imperative for him to win some gain for France, if his prestige at home and abroad were not to suffer. The celerity with which the Prussian generals had gained their victory in the summer had entirely frustrated Napoleon's hopes of intervening with authority and of winning, as the armed mediator, either Rhenish or Belgian territory. In February 1867 French policy was concentrated on obtaining the small Duchy of Luxemburg by purchase from its sovereign, the King of the Netherlands. The statesmen of the other great Powers were apparently not averse to the achievement of a small gain by Napoleon which would help him to keep his Empire peaceful. For this, however, it was necessary that no premature revelations should arouse such a Prussian or German national outcry as should force Bismarck to act against his private opinion and to oppose Napoleon's acquisition. The Prussian and German outcry would be grounded on Prussia's treaty right to garrison the fortress of Luxemburg, and on the fact that the Duchy of Luxemburg had been a member of the German confederation of 1815.

The French ambitions in Luxemburg were revealed to the German nation by a question put in the North German Parliament. They produced a state of excitement in Germany which compelled Bismarck to oppose Napoleon's annexation, and forced the King of the Netherlands to withdraw from his consent to the sale of his duchy. Franco-German feeling was now dangerously inflamed, and Austria, England and Russia were alike anxious for a peaceful termination of the crisis. When the French emperor professed himself as only anxious to secure the Prussian withdrawal from Luxemburg, and Bismarck offered a Prussian withdrawal if the grand duchy were neutralised under a guarantee of the great Powers, the issue seemed a plain one. A conference was called in London to provide the necessary European consent to the neutralisation of Luxemburg, a conference to which the new kingdom of Italy was convoked as a sixth great Power, and which was attended by Belgium and Holland in virtue of their signature of the instrument of 1839 which had last defined the status of the whole of the Low Countries. The conference drew up a treaty which provided for Prussian withdrawal from the fortress of Luxemburg, the destruction of its fortifications, and the retention by the King of Holland, as grand duke, of the lowest number of troops necessary for the maintenance of order. The duchy was to be perpetually

CHAP. XV. neutral, its neutrality being taken under the collective guarantee of all the Powers which signed the treaty, except Belgium. This solution of the Franco-Prussian difficulties, though producing a temporary pacification, did little to remove the deeper causes of European malaise. Had the conference been permitted to consider the Austrian proposal which Beust advanced (2) in the earlier stage of the crisis, and under which Belgium receiving Luxemburg would have ceded to France in return the frontier which it held in 1814, a much easier European situation might have resulted. Again, as in 1866, the relative impossibility of inducing any state, even the weakest, to consent to a shifting of boundaries merely for the sake of general European convenience prevented such a solution. Belgium had resisted the Austrian proposal and had found support in England.

The Franco-Prussian War of 1870 gave Russia the opportunity of making public its discontent with the humiliating conditions which had been imposed upon it by the Treaty of Paris in 1856. Owing to the opening disasters of the war against Prussia, France had lost the power to co-operate with England in naval action against Russia, while England was scarcely likely to undertake a war alone. Accordingly Gortchakoff, in a circular of 29th October, declared that the Tsar, while adhering to the general principles of the Treaty of Paris, no longer held himself bound by the restrictions imposed upon his sovereign rights in the Black Sea. He claimed that the violation of other clauses of the Treaty of Paris had been tacitly permitted by the Powers, as when Wallachia and Moldavia had been allowed to unite under Prince Charles of Hohenzollern; and that *de jure* the clauses which affected Russian interests could not be admitted to be binding while others had been violated. Further, he urged that Russia could not depend for its security on the fiction of the neutralisation of the Black Sea.

Gortchakoff's arguments were of the thinnest kind. No real violation of the neutralisation of the Black Sea could be pointed to in justification of his attack on this "fiction," while the violation of the Rumanian settlement of the Treaty of Paris was the work not of the signatories but of the Rumanian people, who had undertaken no obligation under that instrument. England tried to gather a European opposition to the Russian declaration, but failed to find useful support in any quarter. Gortchakoff, somewhat surprised by the warmth of British resistance, was willing to allow that his circular expressed for the moment nothing but the Russian theoretical attitude, and Bismarck's mediation led to the consent of England to enter a conference pledged to consider Russian claims and proposals "without bias." Turkey tried to obtain an assurance that the conference discussion would be limited to the Black Sea question, while France, on the other hand, attempted to place the Franco-German peace terms upon the agenda.

The conference of signatories of the Treaty of Paris was gathered in London in January 1871. It produced a preliminary protocol, declaring that no Power could undertake to liberate itself from treaty engagements, or to modify treaty stipulations, except with the consent of the other contracting states. In giving some satisfaction to the British desire to uphold the binding character of treaties, this declaration totally ignored the principal difficulties of the subject, with which, indeed, it was neither fitted nor instructed to deal. The principal difficulties underlying the Anglo-Russian differences were concerned with those treaties which had been accepted in the first instance only under duress, and for which there was no longer the means of enforcement; and with those others which, though accepted voluntarily in the first instance, had become obsolete or unduly oppressive to one side, and from which a release was refused by the other contracting parties. Much greater development of the international outlook and of international institutions was necessary before a conference of diplomats could deal more than formally with the ultimate problems which had been raised by the circular of Gortchakoff.

After the signature of the protocol the conference proceeded to deal with the specific Russian demands. Clauses X., XIII., and XIV. of the Treaty of Paris, which had ordained the "neutralisation" of the Black Sea, were abrogated by common agreement. In order to provide some compensating security for Turkey, the conference modified the régime of the passages into the Black Sea. The rule was fixed that foreign ships of war should be denied a passage. Nevertheless, Turkey was permitted to admit the warships of allied and friendly Powers when the Sultan should judge such action necessary in order to secure the execution of the Treaty of Paris of 1856.

The Conference of Constantinople of 1876-1877.—In 1875 a Christian revolt in Herzegovina and Bosnia, which showed signs of involving Serbia, Montenegro, Bulgaria, and even

CHAP. XV.

Crete, made plain to Europe that the Near Eastern settlement of 1856 stood in need of revision. Acting together, Russia, Austria, and Germany composed the Andrassy Note at the end of the year, and obtained for it the support of the remaining great Powers. The note proposed to the Sultan the establishment of complete religious liberty in Bosnia and Herzegovina, the abolition of the farming of taxes, the devotion of the money raised by direct taxes to provincial purposes under the control of provincial representative bodies, the constitution of a special mission (half Christian, half Muhammadan) to preside over the actual introduction of the reforms, and finally the improvement of the situation of the rural classes by the grant to them of state lands lying waste. The Andrassy Note was followed by the Berlin Memorandum of 13th May 1876, again produced by the "three Eastern Powers." To the Berlin Memorandum, which proposed a two months' armistice between Turkey and the rebels pending the application of the principles of the Andrassy Note, England refused the consent which she had given to the note of Andrassy. The Balkan situation, already sufficiently troubled, threatened to become altogether unmanageable when Serbia and Montenegro entered the war (July-August) and when the news of the Bulgarian massacres, committed by Turkish irregulars, reached the outside world. Though Turkey was able to win successes against Serbia after she had repressed Bulgarian discontent, the British ministry after the Bulgarian atrocities was no longer content merely to protect Turkey from undue pressure by other Powers. The ministry forced the Turks to concede an armistice, and, eager to prevent the Russians from taking charge of the situation as they had in 1828, procured the issue of invitations for a conference of the Powers which had been signatories of the treaty of 1856. A conference at Constantinople had obvious advantages. The plenipotentiaries would be in closest contact with the Near Eastern situation, and the Porte could not but be impressed with the unity of purpose of Christian Europe.

The English and Russian plenipotentiaries, Salisbury and Ignatieff, both came to the conference in December 1876 with very definite proposals. Between the 12th and 22nd December the non-Turkish plenipotentiaries laboured to produce a joint scheme for recommendation to the Turks—a scheme necessarily reconciling the British and the Russian ideas. On 23rd December the full conference opened with the entry of Turkish representatives and with the submission to them of the joint recommendation of the Powers. For four weeks the vain endeavour was made to induce the Turks to accept the moderate proposals of the plenipotentiaries, much modified in the desire to facilitate Turkish acceptance. The Turks objected not so much to the rectification of the frontier granted to Montenegro and Serbia, as to the proposal both that Bosnia, Herzegovina, and Bulgaria should obtain governor-generals approved by the Powers and nominated for five years, and that the introduction of a wide range of administrative, constitutional, financial, and judicial reforms in these provinces should be supervised by two commissions of control, appointed by them.

Though the Turkish government allowed the conference of Constantinople to disperse without result, England was not yet ready to abandon the Turks completely to Russian attack. After making the suggestion that the chancelleries should give the Sultan a year of grace in which to execute his promises of reform, Great Britain consented to sign the London protocol of 31st March, drawn up by the Russians Ignatieff and Schuvaloff, and approved by the Concert. The protocol informed the Turks that a failure quickly to improve the condition of Christians in their European provinces would lead the Powers to take common decisions on behalf of the Christian populations and the general peace. Immediate negotiations with Russia on the subject of demobilisation were urged upon Turkey. When Turkey refused this protocol, Russia was able to declare war without immediate fear of European complications.

The Russo-Turkish War of 1877 was terminated by the Treaty of San Stefano of 3rd March 1878. Great Britain had strong objections to the arrangements made in that treaty, and these were expressed with masterly power in Lord Salisbury's circular note of 1st April. Salisbury had a strong legal position in the fact that the Treaty of San Stefano, made only between Russia and Turkey, altered the arrangements of the Treaty of Paris made between Russia, England, France, Prussia, Austria, Sardinia, and Turkey. He therefore could claim that any of the clauses of San Stefano which altered the Paris arrangements needed the approval of all the signatories of 1856. Beyond this general position Salisbury urged detailed objections to various provisions of the San Stefano treaty. The "Greater Bulgaria" of that treaty was criticised as an outpost of Russian political and commercial

CHAP. XV. influence in the Aegean and in the Black Sea, while its frontiers were shown to sever the Turkish capital from the Albanian, Slavic, and Greek provinces which still remained Turkish. The Bessarabian and Batum annexations were opposed as still further increasing Russian influence throughout the Black Sea territories, the annexation of the Armenian fortresses as subordinating the whole population of that province to Russian influence, the gain of Bayazid as arresting European trade through Trebizond to Persia, and the indemnity arrangements as giving Russia the power to extort either further territorial gains or a complete subordination of Turkish policy to that of Russia.

Even before the signature of San Stefano the Austrian statesman Andrassy had foreseen the inevitability of a European gathering to approve the alteration of the arrangements of 1856. He had suggested a conference at Vienna, and had received general European approval for such a meeting. Later, when the full importance of the crisis under discussion stood revealed, the Russian Gortchakoff suggested a congress of leading Foreign Ministers, and Berlin was chosen for its seat. There was considerable Anglo-Russian argument concerning the authority of the congress. England desired the admission of the absolute freedom of the congress to decide upon all the San Stefano clauses which should be deemed to depart from the arrangements of 1856. Russia, however, refused to bind itself to anything more than an admission that each country was at liberty to raise whatsoever question it desired, and reserved the right of objecting to any proposed discussion. The Anglo-Russian difficulties were overcome when the two nations agreed on 30th May to the general principles of a revised settlement arranged between Salisbury, the English Foreign Minister, and Schuvaloff, the Russian ambassador in London. The congress could now assemble with an assurance that business would not be blocked from the outset by the advancing of irreconcilable proposals.

The congress was a meeting of Russia, Austria, Turkey, England, France, Italy, and Germany under the presidency of the first plenipotentiary of the German empire, Bismarck. Rumania, Greece, Serbia, and Montenegro had no representation, but the Greek and Rumanian governments, who for obvious reasons could not allow Slavic Russia to present their case, were allowed to state their views through delegates invited to address the assembled nations.

The congress, which sat between 13th June and 13th July—the date of the Treaty of Berlin—made another attempt to settle the Near East without weakening Turkey too far or overturning the balance of European power. Two Slavic communities were admitted into the European company of full sovereign states—Serbia and Montenegro. Both had their territories increased, but Serbia, which had been denied an outlet to the sea, and Montenegro, a state of no very great size, were yet hardly in a position to exercise their full independence and were bound to pass into the sphere of influence of the adjacent great Powers, Austria and Russia. Nothing, perhaps, illustrated this fact better than the Austrian right to police Montenegrin waters. Rumania also received an acknowledgment of its independence, but was compelled most unwillingly to exchange an important strip of Bessarabia, ceded to Russia, for the Dobrudja received from Turkey. It too, therefore, was exchanging the old nominal suzerainty of Turkey for the political influence of the two great Powers. Greece, which had not, like the three other states, fought against Turkey, was allowed to urge large territorial claims on the mainland and to press for the cession of Crete. The congress consented to press upon the Sultan the acceptance of frontier rectifications in Thessaly and Epirus, and to secure the Sultan's consent to the conscientious application in Crete of the Organic Statute of 1868, suitably amended.

Several new portions of the old and undifferentiated mass of European Turkey acquired a new international status. Bosnia and Herzegovina were to be occupied and administered by Austria under Turkish suzerainty. The Sandjak of Novi Bazar was to be garrisoned by Austrian troops, though Turkey retained full sovereign rights over it. The Russian plan of a greater Bulgaria was given up. The new Bulgaria was to be bounded by the Black Sea, the Danube, Serbia, and the Balkans. It was to be an autonomous principality under Turkish suzerainty, with a prince elected by the population and confirmed by the Porte with the assent of the Powers. An assembly of notables at Tirnova, in which all sections of the population were to be adequately represented, was to draw up a form of government. Provisionally a Russian commissioner, acting under the supervision of Turkey and the Powers, was to direct the administration. A new and artificial unit, Eastern Rumelia, was created south of the Balkans. Here the Sultan's troops were to be admitted

CHAP. XV.

to guard the frontier, but the principle of administrative autonomy and a local militia was established. Administration was to be under a Christian governor-general, nominated for five years by the Porte "with the consent of the Powers." The general principles of organisation were to be established by a European commission acting with the Porte. In Rumania (Article 44), in Montenegro (Article 27), in Serbia (Article 44), and lastly in Turkey (Article 62), there was to be full religious liberty for all, and no person was to suffer in his political or civil rights or in his capacity for public employment because of his creed. Further, Macedonia and all the parts of European Turkey not already differentiated by special institutions were to witness the labour of special commissions containing a large local element and charged with the elaboration of provincial constitutions on the model of the Cretan *règlement*. It is on these last religious and constitutional clauses, together with the special Armenian stipulations, soon to be mentioned, that any claim must be rested that the Congress of Berlin, no less than the Congresses of Vienna and Paris, was conscious of its grander duties as a "Parliament of humanity." In Asia, Turkish Armenia passed for the first time under the legal shelter of stipulations embodied in a general international treaty. Suitable amelioration and reforms in the Armenian provinces were to be executed by the Sultan, and the Circassians and Kurds were to be restrained. The Turkish reforms were to be notified to the Powers who were deputed to supervise them. Russia received Ardahan, Kars, and Batum. Great Britain's compensation for these Russian gains in Asia had already been provided before the congress. By a convention of 4th June with the Sultan, England was to receive the administration of Cyprus.

The Congress of Berlin did not attempt, therefore, legislation of the novelty and scope of that undertaken by the Paris congress. It is true that the Paris congress had undertaken no great territorial or governmental change, while that of Berlin had admitted three new members to the society of sovereign states, had made arrangements for the organisation of a new semi-sovereign area, Bulgaria, and a new autonomous area, Eastern Rumelia, and had ordained special conditions for Bosnia, Herzegovina, Novi Bazar, Crete, and Armenia. Nevertheless, it is difficult to avoid the feeling that the plenipotentiaries at Berlin formed a harder, perhaps a more fully disabused, assembly than those at Paris. Clarendon's readiness to surrender traditional British practices at sea and his pure zeal for the adoption of compulsory mediation must be compared with Beaconsfield's concentration on British imperial interests ; Bismarck's realism with Napoleon's humanitarianism ; the antique and not uncommendable straightforwardness of the Russians of the régime of Nicholas, who were still good Europeans, with the new trickiness and heightened nationalism characteristic of the school of Gortchakoff. Even the greatest mistake of the Paris congress was at least partly brought about by a naïve and humanitarian confidence in the ability of the Turks, even though they were Muhammadans, to produce and operate a constitutional system of government which would make possible the continued submission of peaceful and contented Christian citizens. Even the " hardness " of the men of 1878, however, was not allowed to take a wholly " realistic " form. The European diplomats knew that the dreams of the men of 1856 had proved to be but illusions, and yet they allowed Macedonia, Crete, and Armenia to continue under complete Turkish control, the maltreated victims of the theory of a balance of power.

The Powers and the Execution of the Decisions of the Congress.—At Berlin Greece had received no complete awards of territory, but the Powers had agreed to recommend large rectifications of frontier in Thessaly and Epirus. The Greeks, who had secured the special championship of France, were eager to interpret the rectifications recommended as giving them an absolute claim to large gains ; but the Sultan naturally took an exactly opposite view. Direct Turco-Greek negotiations, extending over nearly two years, proved quite fruitless, and, the intervention of the Powers becoming plainly necessary, the despatch of an international commission to the disputed frontier was recommended by England. This was not undertaken, but a conference of ambassadors was assembled at Berlin a little later, which made recommendations to the Greek and Turkish governments. Since the Turks declined acceptance of the Berlin recommendations, a new and more authoritative interposition became necessary. Plenipotentiaries assembled at Constantinople in February 1881, and produced, after negotiation with the Turkish government, the advice that Thessaly should be ceded to Greece, together with a smaller part of Epirus than had been originally recommended. This proved acceptable to both nations. A first Greek

CHAP. XV.

attempt to alter this settlement in 1886 was repressed by a five-Power blockade.

The Treaty of Berlin had provided that the Montenegrins should hand over the port of Dulcigno to the Turks. This they did, but they failed to add to their territorial gains, some of which had been projected at the expense of Albania, owing to the stout resistance of the Albanians themselves. The Berlin conference of June 1880 decided that Dulcigno with a small extent of sea-coast should be returned to Montenegro. The Powers enforced the recommendation of the ambassadors by a naval demonstration off the coast in question and by the display of a readiness to seize Smyrna.

If the Sultan decreed a local constitution for Crete in October 1878, as had been provided for in the Treaty of Berlin, he showed less regard for other European areas in which administrative reforms should have been undertaken under Article 23. Conditions in the Armenian provinces, where the Porte was pledged to reform not only by the general Berlin Treaty but by the Turco-Russian Treaty of San Stefano and the Anglo-Turkish Convention of 4th June 1878, led to international remonstrance at Constantinople. Identical notes from the Powers were presented on 11th June 1880; and when these proved barren of effect, a joint note of strong remonstrance was presented. There European insistence ended.

The Congress at Constantinople on Egypt.—In 1876 the careless and extravagant management of Egyptian finances by the Khedive Ismail, who was deeply involved in debt to European bondholders, led to the first European interference in the internal affairs of Egypt. The Khedive on 2nd May was compelled by France to set up the *Caisse de la Dette publique*, which was to be controlled by commissioners from France, Austria, Italy, and England. Increasing pressure from Europe during the succeeding years, justified on the ground of Egyptian indebtedness, produced a dangerous temper in the Egyptian army and among the populace, which in 1882 seemed to threaten not only the financial interests of the foreign bondholders but also the very lives of the foreign residents in Egypt. The English and French governments had already in February contemplated the submission of the Egyptian position to the Powers, and on 2nd June issued invitations for a conference at Constantinople. The Turkish government objected to the conference, but the other Powers agreed. A dangerous and bloody riot in Alexandria on

11th June and the existence of an exceedingly strained atmosphere in Cairo, from which city the Khedive was compelled to flee, induced England and France to open the conference on 23rd June, even without Turkish assistance.

The conference on 6th July invited the Sultan to intervene in Egypt on condition of maintaining the legal *status quo* and of limiting the Turkish occupation to three months.[3] The Turks first objected to the imposition of any conditions at all, and, after active English intervention had taken place at Alexandria on 11th July, offered on 19th July to send troops if the English would first evacuate Egypt. This condition made no appeal to the English ministry, which had already resolved on playing an active though not exclusive part in the pacification of Egypt and in the protection of the Suez Canal. The conference of Constantinople, which would have had an important rôle had the restoration of order been undertaken by the Turks, was only dangerous when England, though unseconded by France or Turkey, resolved even single-handed to restore order in Egypt. Since the restoration of order was not to be accomplished in the conditions foreseen at the opening, the conference was allowed to break up on 14th August.

The Crisis and Proposed Conference of 1908.[4]—In October 1908 the delicate diplomatic balance of the European world was violently disturbed by the Austrian annexation of Bosnia and Herzegovina and the Bulgarian proclamation of independence, since both actions altered the European position as fixed by the Berlin decisions of 1878. England, which had compelled Russia in 1870-1871 to seek the authority of a European conference before undertaking reversals of the 1856 decisions, quickly insisted on the need for a congress or conference. France and Russia were ready to co-operate with her in requiring the submission of the Austrian and Bulgarian measures to a conference of the signatories of the treaty of 1878. Turkey, which had been robbed of the suzerainty of vast areas, together with Serbia and Montenegro, which had received no compensation for a readjustment of the legal position in the Balkan peninsula very much to their disadvantage, could not but hope that a congress would secure them some compensation, if not a complete reversal of the Austrian and Bulgarian policies.

While the basis for English, Russian, and French co-operation in the presumed future conference was being arranged, the Austrian government was examining its attitude towards

CHAP. XV.

the conference which it regarded as the pet project of England and Russia. A conference whose liberty of discussion and decision had not been bartered away beforehand would in Austrian eyes present tempting opportunities to extort concessions and compensations from Austria. Receiving the assurance of German support, the Austrian government declined to enter such a conference. Only a conference whose programme met the Austrian wishes, and in which the Bosnian annexation would have been collectively authorised but not debated, would have received Austrian participation. By December, Isvolsky, the Russian Foreign Minister, had been compelled to beat a retreat to the position in which he conceded the annexation in principle before the meeting of the conference, and asked merely for discussion between the Cabinets beforehand. When Turkey consented to accept compensation in cash by a private arrangement with Austria, and Serbia was denied all territorial gain, the work left to the European conference would have been little more than a humiliating confirmation of Austrian measures. Accordingly the conference was avoided, the great Powers agreed to recognise the Bosnian annexation by declaration, and Serbia, which had taken up a violent anti-Austrian attitude, was half-forced, half-persuaded into an admission of past misbehaviour, and a promise of better conduct in the future.

The Congo Conferences of 1884 and 1890.—The notable efflux from Europe of colonising energy upon the African continent during the last two decades of the nineteenth century remained without general European regulation, except for that undertaken by the Berlin Conference of 1884-1885, and by the Brussels Conference of 1890. The immediate cause of the summons of the Berlin Conference was an Anglo-Portuguese Treaty of 1884, which undertook to secure to the two contracting parties the rights of control and police in the lower waters of the Congo. France and Germany protested with particular energy, and Bismarck announced his intention of summoning an international conference to settle the whole question of the Congo. To the Berlin Conference were summoned the great European Powers, the United States, Spain, Portugal, Belgium, Holland, Denmark, Sweden and Norway, and Turkey. The conference was to establish liberty of trade in the Congo, undertake the internationalisation of the Congo and Niger rivers on the Danube model, and define the technique to be adopted by Powers in any future occupation of African territory.

Proceedings opened on 15th November 1884 and were not closed until 26th February, when an *Acte général* was signed. Liberty of commerce to all flags was conceded throughout the Congo basin and the absence of all discriminatory import duties was assured. Powers which owned territory, or influence, within its defined bounds were pledged to protect and improve the position of the native population, to encourage religious, charitable and scientific institutions, and to co-operate in the suppression of slavery and the slave-trade. A praiseworthy attempt to banish war from the Congo territories was made in Article 12, which bound the signatories, in the event of a dispute, to have recourse to mediation ; and in Article 11, which bound the signatories, in the event of the outbreak of a war, to use diplomatic endeavours to secure the freedom of the Congo territory from operations of war. An international commission for the navigation of the Congo was erected, while, in the case of the Niger, France and England bound themselves in their respective territories to carry out a policy of non-discrimination between all traders and flags. Finally, in order to prevent colonial disputes in Africa, any Power taking possession of territory, or assuming a protectorate on that continent, was to send a notification of the fact to the other signatories of the General Act, so that existing claims might be asserted. Further, any Power undertaking the occupation of territory had the duty of establishing a sufficient administrative authority to protect existing rights.

The Brussels Conference contained delegates of the Powers represented at Berlin, and of the additional African governments of the Congo Free State and Zanzibar. Though summoned primarily to arrange measures against the African slave-trade, the conference was disturbed and delayed by the Italian attempt to secure indirect recognition of its claim to exercise protection over Abyssinia, and by the repercussions of an Anglo-Portuguese dispute concerning the national character of the country between Angola and Mozambique. When the conference was able to proceed on its real labours it evolved a highly detailed plan of dealing with the slave-trade, both on land and on sea, which the signatories undertook to execute. An international bureau was to be established at Zanzibar which was to centralise information and to supply it to the different governments and locally to naval officers. Consideration was given to naval action against suspected slaving ships in the Red Sea, the Persian Gulf, and throughout a wide extent of the Indian

CHAP. XV.

Ocean. Very serious restrictions were established upon the importation of arms and liquor, calculated, if left uncontrolled, to contribute to the downfall of the African races. An additional organ, concerned with the execution of the measures decided on at Brussels, was to be established in the Special Bureau attached to the Belgian Foreign Office.

The fact that all the Powers which had signed the Congo Act of 1885 were present at Brussels gave the Free State of the Congo a necessary opportunity to ask for a higher customs rate than had been stipulated for at Berlin in 1885. That government had found itself unable to raise a sufficient revenue.

Conference of Madrid, 1880.—In 1861 Spain had secured by treaty with Morocco a specially privileged position for Spanish subjects and protégés, in 1863 France had secured a similar treaty, and soon the concession was claimed and enjoyed by all nations possessing with Morocco a treaty which contained a most-favoured-nation clause. The sometimes unwise extension by foreign consulates of the grant of protection led to strong Moroccan objections to the whole practice, and even to the rejection of the right of the foreign governments to protect naturalised citizens of Moroccan origin. The Spanish government early in 1880 resolved to invite a conference to make decisions upon the problem; and a conference was assembled composed of the Prime Minister of Spain, a Moroccan delegate, and the representatives in Madrid of Austria, Belgium, France, Germany, England (acting for Denmark also), Italy, Holland, Portugal, Sweden and Norway, and the United States. After sixteen sessions the conference completed a convention which defined the rights of foreigners resident in Morocco, regulated the protection which foreign diplomats and consuls might accord to their employees, and fixed a principle to govern the status of Moroccans naturalised abroad and living once more in Morocco. The Madrid signatories had established a right by international usage to be invited to any further international conferences on the subject of Morocco.

In 1905, after the Anglo-French accord of the previous year had handed over the greater part of Morocco to French influence, French preparations for the establishment of a virtual protectorate began. In February a French mission to Fez presented a substantial list of changes, including military reforms, which were desired by Paris, and began negotiations. On 31st March the whole assumption of the establishment of a

French quasi-protectorate was challenged by Germany when the Kaiser, landing from his yacht, made reference in his speech to the "equal rights" of all the Powers, the "sovereignty" of the Sultan and the "independence" of Morocco. The arrival of a German mission in Fez on 13th May encouraged the Sultan to resist the French proposals, and to summon to Tangier a conference of the signatories of the Madrid Convention of 1880. The idea of the conference was undoubtedly German, and it was intended to render impossible the execution of the French designs. Moreover, the attendance of France in a Moroccan conference upon equal terms with other Powers could hardly fail to be humiliating. Nevertheless, it was impossible to go on with the Moroccan plans, or to use military force against the Sultan, unless a war with Germany were desired. The French Cabinet decided therefore to permit the Foreign Minister, Delcassé, to resign rather than to allow him, by his steadfast opposition to the conference, to bring a Franco-German war upon the country. Negotiations with Germany were begun in order to gain from that country the greatest possible concessions as a condition of French attendance at the conference.

In July both England and France agreed to the holding of a conference, and in September a Franco-German agreement was reached by which the place of meeting of the conference was altered to Algeciras, and various principles for the future organisation of Morocco were accepted in common.

The Conference of Algeciras opened on 16th January 1906. The institution of a state bank and the creation of a modern police force, the improvement of Moroccan harbours and the acceptance of the principle that public works should be executed by the lowest bidder, were excellent subjects for international action; but France was anxious to secure resolutions which should enable her to maintain her leading position and to improve it, while Germany was anxious that no decisions should be taken at the conference which should virtually instal France in a protectorate. The Moroccan police force proved the subject of the principal contest, for the Power which established its control over that body would command the principal armed force in Morocco. After a long crisis the mediation of the American delegate, White, produced a Franco-German compromise. The Moroccan police, commanded by a Moroccan, were to be trained by French and Spanish officers, and to be inspected annually by a Swiss. This was virtually a French triumph, especially when these

CHAP. XV. conditions were read together with such significant decisions as that giving the regulation of the Customs Act, and of the arms traffic on the Algerian border, to France and the Moroccan Sultan, and that on the Riff border to Spain and the Moroccan Sultan.

The Conference of Ambassadors, 1912-1913.—In August 1912 Count Berchtold, the Austrian minister, proposed to the Powers an exchange of views concerning the Balkans. He feared that Bulgaria, Serbia, and Greece might take violent action because of the local liberties about to be granted to the Albanians. He recommended that representations should be made to the Balkan States to show them that the Turkish measure was the beginning of a policy conceived in the interests of all nationalities, and that therefore they should keep the peace. Meanwhile, Turkey was to be supported in the new direction of her internal policy.[5] The Bulgarian, Greek, and Serbian governments showed much concern lest their diplomatic and military preparations against Turkey should be wasted.[6] No common European measure proved possible until the delivery of joint notes at the Balkan capitals and in Constantinople was authorised in October. By that time the common action taken was too late. The Balkan States refused to be coerced; they sent their own ultimata to Turkey, and on 18th October declared war, though the Powers had assured them they would be allowed to gain no Turkish territory. After the opening Turkish disasters European discussion ceased to centre on the old Turkish problem of the administrative reforms which it might be desirable to effect in European areas inhabited by Christians. In view of the great victories of the Balkan allies, the Powers were occupied by thoughts of the future of Adrianople, Salonika, Constantinople, and Albania, as also of the extent of sea-coast which should be allotted to Serbia.

The centre for the European discussion of the fate of such territories as should be detached from Turkey was London. There plenipotentiaries from the belligerents gathered in December, and there a conference of ambassadors of the Powers, under the presidency of the British Foreign Secretary, attempted to control the negotiations and decisions. The centre of European danger was not now, as in 1856 and in 1878, the Black Sea and the Straits, but the Adriatic. Austria and Italy alike were resolved to prevent the growth of a new Adriatic Power in Serbia, Austria even at the cost of war with Russia. The conference of ambassadors, therefore, gave its main concern to the limits of Albania and to the future status of that country. Austria desired Janina, Ochrida, Prizren, and Skutari to be included in the new state, while Greece, Montenegro, and Serbia had the strongest desire to partition the whole country, and had received a measure of support from Russia for more moderate claims. The most acute danger lay in the reluctance of Serbia to depart from the Adriatic, which Serbian troops had reached at Durazzo and San Giovanni di Medua, and in Montenegro's hesitation to surrender its hopes of acquiring Skutari. The pressure from the united Powers, fearful of the outbreak of a general war if Austrian troops undertook an independent expulsion of Serbs and Montenegrins from the Adriatic coast, induced the Montenegrin evacuation of Skutari (5th May) and the Serbian departure from Durazzo (6th May). A further success of the great Powers was gained when the preliminary Treaty of London of 30th May was signed by the belligerents under considerable pressure. By this treaty all Turkish territory west of the Enos-Midia line except Albania was divided among the Balkan allies—Crete was ceded to Greece, and the problems of Albanian and the Aegean Islands were remitted to the Powers. Yet the great Powers proved unable to prevent a further Balkan war in connection with the Turkish spoils,(7) and the Balkan peace of Bukharest (10th August 1913) was made without their supervision and almost in their despite. Albania, however, was in their hands. On 29th July the conference of ambassadors reached a common decision concerning its fundamental law, and on 11th August fixed its southern frontier. Another threat of force from Austria with resultant pressure from all the Powers was, however, necessary before the Serbians could be induced on 20th October to depart from Albanian territory as it had been fixed by the London Conference. An allotment of most of the Aegean Islands to Greece was made on 13th February 1914.

The Proposed Conference of 1914.—The London Conference of 1912-1913, though unable finally to control the fate of the Balkan States, had at least served the purpose of keeping the Powers in constant and in direct contact during times of the sharpest crisis, and had assured the presence of ample mediating influence when events had exacerbated the suspicion or resentment of one side or the other. When on 24th July 1914 another grave European crisis was provoked by an Austrian ultimatum to Serbia, which was barbed with a

CHAP. XV.

time limit, Sir Edward Grey endeavoured to meet the enormous dangers which he foresaw to European peace by advocating the assembly of another conference of ambassadors. The ambassadors of France, Germany, and Italy, it was proposed on 24th July, were to join him in mediation between Austria on the one hand, and Serbia and Russia on the other, and all military preparations were to be suspended meanwhile. The German government declined the conference as constituting an uninvited and unauthorised court of arbitration. On 31st July, when Austrian troops were already engaged in Serbia, and general mobilisations were about to begin, a joint diplomatic mediation by the four Powers was again proposed from London to Berlin, though not in so definite a shape as in the proposal of 24th July. The four Powers were to offer to Austria full satisfaction from Serbia, and to Russia the full maintenance of Serbian sovereignty. War operations and military preparations were not to be advanced further. The situation was now, however, beyond redemption. Military preparations were at different stages in different countries, and could not be maintained so, and a peculiar difficulty of the position was that the interposition of a conference of ambassadors between a small Power and a great could hardly fail to be a blow to the dignity and prestige of the stronger nation.

The Peace Conference and the Peace Treaties of 1918-1919.[8]—The fighting in the Great War of 1914-1918 was brought to a standstill by the Bulgarian armistice of 29th September, the Turkish of 30th October, the Austrian of 3rd November (supplemented by the Hungarian Convention of 13th November), and the German of 11th November. All these armistices were granted on such terms, and in any case involved such conditions, as made it impossible for the defeated Powers to contemplate a renewal of hostilities. In point of fact, they were really surrenders at discretion to the victorious alliance. The statesmen of this victorious alliance gathered to draft their treaties and to plan a new world-order in the early days of 1919. Their conference—which differed from previous peace conferences in that it did not include representatives of any of the Powers of the defeated alliance—was formally opened on 18th January. The formal division of the allied Powers into those with general interests and those with particular interests quickly showed that the great allies had assumed the task of drafting the treaty settlements in their main outlines, and that the smaller

Powers would be largely confined to the task of urging their principal ambitions upon the notice of their greater associates, whose earlier Council of Ten (until 24th March) and later Council of Four were for five months principally occupied with the decisions to be enshrined in the German treaty. CHAP. XV.

A German peace delegation, which had been summoned to the conference, received a draft treaty from the President, M. Clemenceau, on 7th May, at a special meeting at which all the allied delegations were represented. At this meeting the German first plenipotentiary, Brockdorff-Rantzau, took the only opportunity which was furnished to the Germans orally to address their late enemies. After that formal meeting the Germans were allowed, however, to address written observations to the allies and associates, but were never admitted to oral discussion. The German attempts to secure modification of the treaty by written negotiations were terminated by an allied ultimatum of 22nd June, which required a promise to sign the treaty—a little amended here and there since 7th May—before twenty-four hours had passed. The promise was made in time, and the treaty was signed on 28th June at Versailles.

The incomplete draft treaty with Austria, which had been in preparation since the latter half of April, was handed on 2nd June to the Austrian delegation which had been waiting since 14th May. Though some of the dominating figures departed from Paris with the signature of the German treaty, a Council of Five composed of Lansing, Balfour, Pichon, Tittoni and Clemenceau still waited behind to direct the remaining Allied Conference and to conduct the treaty negotiations with the enemy states. The Council of Five, however, did not enjoy the authority of the Council of Four; it had to face a determined revolt of the exasperated smaller Powers directly concerned in the Austrian treaty, as well as a copious stream of literature from the Austrian delegation. It only forced through the Austrian Treaty of St. Germain-en-Laye on 10th September.

In regard to Hungary, the Council of Four had already almost completely fixed the permanent frontiers to be allotted to that state by 13th June when a public announcement as to its borders with Czecho-Slovakia and Rumania was made. First the communist régime of Bela Kun, then the Rumanian invasion, and finally the fall of Kun's movement, these and the time necessary to introduce a new political order in Hungary, all defeated a prompt handling of the Hungarian

CHAP. XV. treaty, which the Peace Conference had originally hoped to negotiate simultaneously with the Austrian. Nevertheless, it was possible for the "Five" to draft the territorial clauses of a Hungarian treaty on the basis of the decisions of the Council of Four, and the non-territorial clauses on the general model of the Austrian treaty. Finally, when a Hungarian coalition was erected in November 1919 a Hungarian delegation was asked to come to Neuilly to receive the treaty. When he received the allied draft on 16th January 1920, Count Apponyi—the head of the delegation—took his opportunity of emulating the exploit of the German Brockdorff-Rantzau, and among other things reprobated the refusal of discussion by the allies. Written Hungarian observations on the draft were permitted, and an allied reply to these was sent on 4th May, with the announcement of a few minor concessions and the demand for a notification of acceptance of the treaty within ten days. This was sent in time, and the Treaty of the Trianon was signed on 4th June 1920.

Events had placed the Hungarian treaty later in time than the Bulgarian. A Bulgarian delegation had arrived in Paris at the end of July to receive a treaty. After waiting for five weeks the Bulgarian delegation sent a series of observations to the Supreme Allied Council protesting against some of the supposed terms of the Bulgarian treaty. The Bulgarians finally received the treaty on 19th September, made their formal reply on 24th October, received the announcement of a few concessions on 3rd November, and signed the treaty on 27th November. The Bulgarian treaty, as finally signed, was substantially the work of the "Five."

The treaties of peace drafted by the Paris Conference contained many remarkable and novel clauses. An international union of unique political authority, the League of Nations, was created. A new "colonial" system was organised for the government of enormous areas of non-European territory at the disposal of the conference. An international labour office was set up. Immediate extensive plebiscites were ordered in Silesia, Schleswig, East Prussia, and Klagenfurt, and others were contemplated after stipulated intervals at Smyrna, in the Saar Valley, and in East Galicia. A wholly new form of government was organised for the difficult frontier areas of Danzig and the Saar Valley. Thorough demilitarisation was imposed upon Germany, Austria, Hungary, and Bulgaria as a preliminary to a general reduction of armaments.

The Peace Conference, however, probably undertook no task which was more difficult than the elaboration of its minority treaties or minority clauses. The minorities which specially needed protection in 1919 were not so much the "religious" minorities, with whose fate in the Balkans Western Europe had already been concerned at the Congress of Berlin, but rather the new linguistic and national minorities which found themselves enclosed in novel and superfervid nationalistic states. The Jewish minority in Poland—at once linguistically, nationally, and religiously sundered from their fellow-citizens—were the people whose case first suggested the problem of international guarantee to the Peace Conference.[9] When once the idea of special protection had been accepted, its application to all racial or national minorities was inevitable. The Polish, Czech, Yugo-Slav, Rumanian, Greek, Austrian, Hungarian, and Bulgarian governments (but not the German or Italian) all assumed minority obligations intended to safeguard, not only the civil and political position of individual members of the minorities, but also the equitable claims of these minorities to some measure of state recognition and support as cultural communities, especially in the realm of education. An important task was allotted to the new international union, the League of Nations, when the minority provisions accepted by so many states were placed under its guarantee and the right to take action in the event of violation was bestowed upon its Council. The Council has fulfilled this duty with tact and effectively. Into what minute details of administration it has sometimes been led to descend may be instanced in Polish Upper Silesia, where the German minority is specially influential. The Polish government found itself required to provide German schools for children who were sometimes known to be of Polish speech. The League furnished a Swiss examiner, who examined the children and determined whether they were to be classed as of German speech or not. The Permanent Court of International Justice, another new international institution to be established in close connection with the League, was assured of large jurisdiction in disputes over minority difficulties between Powers, members of the Council, and Powers bound by minority obligations (cf. Article 69, Treaty of St. Germain).

Relatively minor sides of the activities at Paris are represented in the Convention of St. Germain, which on 10th September revised the General Act of the Congo Conference.

CHAP. XV.

Another convention of the same date dealt with the liquor traffic in Africa, abrogated the liquor sections of the Brussels Act of 1890, and imposed stricter conditions. A third convention of 10th September dealt with the traffic in arms, and a fourth, the International Air Convention, was signed on 13th October 1919.

A Turkish delegation had been summoned to Paris as early as June 1919, and had secured an opportunity to state a case to the Council of Ten on 17th June. The Turkish peace, however, was not substantially advanced by the arguments of the delegation, which withdrew after a short stay. The allies' plans for Turkey were of the most sweeping character, but the drafting of a treaty could not even be begun until the great question of Constantinople and the Straits had been decided. Until President Wilson's breakdown in September an American mandate for that region had been under contemplation as a possibility, though not perhaps by any one familiar with the principles of the foreign policy of the United States. After President Wilson's virtual elimination had compelled England and France to take the onus of a final decision upon themselves, there were prolonged negotiations between London and Paris which resulted in the decision of February 1920, that Constantinople should remain Turkish. At the San Remo Conference of April 1920 the internationalisation of the Straits, a French mandate for Syria, and British mandates for Palestine and Mesopotamia were finally decided. Further, inter-allied meetings at the house of Sir Philip Sassoon in Lympne (15th-16th May and 20th June) enabled other experts on the Turkish situation to be examined from the point of view of a definitive treaty. The Turkish Treaty of Sèvres was forced upon the Sultan's government, virtually imprisoned in Constantinople, by an ultimatum of 19th July. Though the delegates of the Turkish Sultan at Sèvres were authorised to sign the treaty on 10th August, the Turkish Nationalist army gathered by Mustapha Kemal in Anatolia recognised no other instrument than the Turkish National Pact. In the result the Sèvres treaty, proving inexecutable, was superseded by the Peace Conference of Lausanne.

The Genoa Conference of 1922.(10)—The Genoa Conference was convoked by the governments represented in the Supreme Allied Council, and by the associated Belgian Government, largely for the purpose of re-establishing principles of order in matters of currency, finance, transport, and trade, which all over Europe and the world were either disordered or even, in some cases, in utter chaos. Other principal purposes of the conference, which was intended to be a gathering of the first rank and dignity, were to put European peace on a firm basis, and associate Russia once more with the normal economic life of the world by establishing a principle for the settlement of its debts at once satisfactory to European creditors and acceptable to the Communists. All the European Powers were represented, together with the British Dominions and Japan. Financial, transport, and economic commissions were quickly set up to deal with the technical sides of the conference's business. The Russian negotiations were handled by a special political commission dominated by the leading European statesmen and politicians and their financial and economic advisers.

The Financial Commission was able to draft for presentation to the main conference resolutions on currency, the flight of capital, exchange, and credits; the Economic Commission presented resolutions on such matters as customs tariffs, import and export prohibition, the most-favoured-nation clause, and the treatment of foreigners in the conduct of business. The Transport Commission could do little save recommend the work done at the Transport Conference at Barcelona, and point out the vital need to bring European railways back to the stage in which they had been in 1914. As resolutions, of course, all these reports were wasted. Europe had certainly not yet come to the stage at which a nation could be indicted for not balancing its budget, debasing its currency, neglecting its railway service, or favouring the trade of its friends against that of its ex-enemies by refusing or limiting or misinterpreting "most-favoured-nation" clauses in its commercial agreements.

The Political Commission had a task of admitted difficulty. A draft treaty with Russia, prepared by the experts, was indeed ready at the beginning of May, but it represented principally Italo-British views, and was rejected by France and Belgium even before the Russian refusal to sign had been notified. The British and Italian governments, who were resolved to secure some shred of success for the conference, managed to obtain a supplementary conference of experts at The Hague, where another attempt, doomed from the beginning, was to be made to secure a financial agreement with Russia. The only gleam of actual political success was obtained in connection with this conference. A pact of non-

CHAP. XV. aggression, to run for four months after the Hague conference should have ended, associated Russia and Germany with the Powers of the League.

The Lausanne Conference of 1923.—The Lausanne Conference differed materially from the Paris Conferences which produced the treaties of Versailles, St. Germain, Trianon, Neuilly, and Sèvres. Those treaties had been made with governments incapable of resisting the will of the victorious alliance. The Turkish Nationalists of 1922-1923 had found powerful friendship in Russia and interested sympathy in France and Italy. They had routed a great Greek army, had torn up the Treaty of Sèvres by seizing Smyrna, and at the armistice negotiations of Mudania, where they obtained the promise of Eastern Thrace, had consented to provisional arrangements for the neutral zone of the Straits until the final settlement should be established by the Peace Conference. The very venue of that conference, for which the Turks had proposed Smyrna and the allies Venice, but which was finally fixed in neutral Lausanne, was not insignificant when contrasted with the treaties of 1919 and 1920 in suburban Paris.

Any treaty to be negotiated with Turkey would necessarily have had to cover a very large number of points vital to international society—capitulations, "the open door," minorities, the Straits, Armenians, and the full Turkish recognition of the exceedingly important ex-Turkish mandatory areas of Syria, Palestine, and Irak. Minor but still important matters, like the future of the Patriarchate of Constantinople, of the old Superior Council of Health, and of the old control of Turkish customs created in the interests of the Turkish bondholders, also awaited decision. One problem was soon taken out of the hands of the Lausanne negotiators. A questionable principle was readmitted into international life when the Turco-Greek Convention of 30th January 1923 on the exchange of populations made obligatory the Turkish emigrations from Greek territory and the Greek from Turkish. Lord Curzon had opposed it, aided by all the other Powers, but the Young Turks were not to be denied. A welcome exception from the general rule was made for the Greeks of Constantinople and the Moslems of western Thrace.

On capitulations Lord Curzon, who had begun stiffly, could obtain nothing better than a promise that the Turkish laws would be redrafted by "neutral" legal experts, not chosen from the Hague tribunal. On the question of minorities, for whom he had demanded treaty provisions superior to those of Versailles—that is, a board of control in Constantinople, freedom of movement, and the right to purchase exemption from military service—Lord Curzon accepted some Turkish pledges and a promise that Turkey would join the League of Nations and so place its minorities under the Council. In the matter of the Straits, Ismet after some demur accepted a Straits Commission to be composed of representatives of Great Britain, France, Italy, Japan, Greece, Rumania, Russia, Bulgaria, and Jugo-Slavia, neutral zones, and a normal régime of full liberty for all ships, modified only by the concession, made to the Black Sea Powers, that no naval force was to enter the Black Sea in numbers greater than those of the navy of the most powerful local maritime Power. The chairman of this commission being a Turk, there have been complaints that its activities are neutralised by his action, supported by Turkish officials. A more serious dispute than any that arose on other questions was caused by the Turkish demand for Mosul in the Irak mandated area. Lord Curzon's offer of the remission of the decision as to the boundary between Irak and Turkey to the Council of the League was ultimately accepted by Ismet in the event of a failure to settle the matter by negotiation within nine months. No agreement was reached, and the question came before the Council of the League in September 1924. After a Turkish attempt to force an issue by an armed invasion, which was repelled by the Air Force, the League proceeded to give further attention to the dispute, which after long delay was finally settled by the acceptance by Turkey in 1926 of the League's decision, which was very largely in favour of Great Britain,

Negotiations broke down on 4th February 1923, were renewed on 24th April, and were finally ended on 14th July with the signature of the treaty and annexed conventions. The most noteworthy features of the final treaty were perhaps the annexed conventions—the Thracian convention, that of the Straits, and the commercial convention. Both in the Straits and Thracian conventions very large demilitarisation was arranged. In Thrace the Turco-Bulgarian and Turco-Greek frontier areas, to a depth of thirty kilometres on each side, were demilitarised, and some of the worst dangers of Balkan disturbance were thus removed. Defined demilitarised zones were also provided on both shores of the Dardanelles and

CHAP. XV. Bosphorus and in various Greek and Turkish islands in the Aegean and the Sea of Marmora. Constantinople itself, with its limited garrison of twelve thousand, its arsenal and naval base, was the main exception allowed in the demilitarisation of the Straits. It was agreed that Turkey, when belligerent, was to have the right of barring the passage of the warships of her enemies through the Straits. Ordinarily the warships of Powers not riparian on the Black Sea were only to enter that sea in numbers not in excess of those of the most powerful littoral navy, but the right of a belligerent was not to be prejudiced by that limitation. The execution of the convention was to be supervised by an International Commission.(11)

The capitulations were abolished, but some security for foreigners was provided by the Turkish pledge to employ for a minimum period of five years a number of European lawyers, and by the retention of the jurisdiction of the foreign national courts for cases of personal status. The other limitation of sovereignty which had caused such heartburning to the Turks—the pre-war limitation on the customs tariff—was also almost completely abolished. The freely-adopted Turkish tariff of 1st September 1916 was made the rule, with a provision for alterations according to variations in the rate of exchange. Yet even this was only to bind Turkey at most for five years.

The main treaty, besides fixing the frontiers, the Turkish debt, and subordinate questions like those concerned with rights and interests of property, had abolished the Sanitary Council of Constantinople, had established for the minorities left in Turkey liberal principles, whose execution was placed under the guarantee of the League of Nations, and had registered Turkish acceptance of the mass of international conventions on which so many vital economic interests of the whole world had long been based.

NOTES

(1) No claim to contain the results of independent investigation can be made for this chapter, which is based largely on the *Cambridge History of British Foreign Policy*. The attempt, however, has been made to stress the origin, purposes, methods, ambitions, and failures of "concert action." It is, of course, impossible to follow "concert action" into all the different fields over which it was exercised (*e.g.* Crete or China).

(2) Friedrich Ferdinand Graf von Beust, *Aus drei Viertel-Jahrhunderten*, ii. p. 126.

(3) Debidour, *Histoire diplomatique* (1878-1904), p. 63.

(4) Pribram's *Austria's Foreign Policy*, 1908-1918, pp. 27-33.

(5) Cf. Siebert, *Entente Diplomacy and the War*, p. 353.

(6) Cf. *ibid.*, pp. 356-357.

(7) Though the great Powers had secured the signature of all the belligerents to the treaty of 30th May, Bulgaria was dissatisfied with the allocation of Salonika to the Greeks and of Central Macedonia to the Serbs.

(8) For the peace settlements after 1918, the *History of the Peace Conference* (ed. Temperley) has been used.

(9) See Goodhart, *Poland and the Minority Races*.

(10) There is a readable account of this conference by Saxon Mills.

(11) It would perhaps be over optimistic to hope that this represents the final solution of the international problem of entry to the Black Sea, a problem which already in the ancient world had caused such a war as that between Rhodes and Byzantium (220 B.C.), and has faced the world in its modern form since Peter the Great's capture of Azov in 1696. If the Western Powers be not altogether pleased with Turkey's interpretation of the Straits Convention, Russia on its side may be presumed to be in no way cordial towards a settlement which would admit a British or French fleet of equal numbers to its own in any crisis. This may explain why Russia has recently been accused of having deliberately attempted to mislead the Commission as to the strength of its naval forces in the Black Sea. (See *Annual Report*, Straits Commission, 1928.)

CHAPTER XVI

THE CONCERT IN ECONOMIC ACTION

COMMUNICATIONS. THE ADAPTATION OF INTERNATIONAL LAW IN THE MATTER OF CABLES AND AIRWAYS. INTERNATIONAL RIVER COMMISSIONS. THE OPENING OF ARTERIAL RIVERS TO GENERAL NAVIGATION. INTER-OCEANIC CANALS. OTHER CONVENTIONS. LABOUR CONVENTIONS BEFORE THE WAR. THE INTERNATIONAL LABOUR ORGANISATION.

CHAP. XVI.

Communications.—The commercial treaties of the seventeenth and eighteenth centuries had promoted commerce by safeguarding and assuring the position of the foreign merchant and by guaranteeing the security of his property; by authorising the establishment of consulates; by introducing the most-favoured-nation clause; and by providing some surety against the consequences of war. Those of the early nineteenth century had removed some of the remaining hindrances to commerce, which were caused by such restraints as the old colonial system or differentiated port dues; and this tendency of effort had been furthered by the international adoption of such principles as those of the freedom of navigation upon international rivers. The men of the later nineteenth century were faced by a vastly widened area of international commerce and communication. Indeed, it soon became taken almost as axiomatic that conveniences desired by all could be laid upon a much surer foundation if they were laid not upon a two-party, as hitherto, but on a much wider international basis. There was, of course, nothing novel in the idea. The development of the same attitude of mind in the grand affairs of Europe has already occupied the attention of the reader. The advent of the industrial revolution, with all its consequences in European life, was to call for the application of that attitude of mind to what, without any disparagement of them, it is convenient to term the petty affairs.

This it was which led to the signature of the international postal convention of 1874, the international telegraphic convention of 1875, the convention of Brussels for the publication of customs tariffs of 1890, and the convention of Berne in the same year for the regulation of international railway transport and goods traffic over a large part of the European continent.(1) All these conventions set up international unions, each with a membership of many states, founded administrative offices charged with the application of the general principles which the convention had laid down, and stipulated for the regular summons of congresses, at which the work of the union might be discussed or extended and at which amendments might be made in the original convention itself. There were many other international agreements of the kind—that for the protection of submarine cables in 1884, or the radio-telegraphic convention of 1906. One made in 1909 dealt with the international circulation of motor vehicles in Europe, while the international air convention of 13th October 1919 established the international air commission under the League of Nations. Some important rules to govern traffic by sea were given international validity by virtue of the Brussels conventions of 1910, which dealt with collisions, rescue, and salvage; while railway traffic was subject not only to the regulation of the original convention of 1890 but to subsequent conventions drawn up in 1893, 1895, 1898, and 1906, as also to special conventions of 1886 and 1907 concerned with the standardisation of railway material.

Before passing to another side of the subject it is worth devoting some attention in particular to the postal convention, which founded the first of the great international unions and the first administrative office, thus providing a model which was in its main features copied in all subsequent creations. It had been found that the method of procedure by two-party treaties in this matter had in fact resulted in the keeping of foreign postage rates much higher than was either necessary or advantageous. After pressure which emanated from men of business interest and from enlightened administrators, a postal congress, attended by the representatives of twenty-two states, was gathered, and the postal union was founded, the constitution of which was outlined in a convention. Later, the administrative details which arose out of it were embodied in a *règlement* which was amended in several respects in 1878. Arrangements were made for the establishment of three separate organs. A congress of plenipotentiaries was to meet every five years, or at other times upon the demand of two-thirds of the constituent states.

CHAP. XVI.

Each state was to be allowed one vote, and a majority of the states might proceed to amend the convention or the *règlement*, subject to the subsequent ratification of the member states. But there was also provision made for another deliberative organ, the so-called conference of delegates (of postal administrations), which was charged with the handling of minor questions. This could be summoned on the demand of two-thirds of the number of postal administrations. Finally, there was erected a permanent bureau at Berne, which was to work under the supervision of the Swiss postal union. This was to be supported by the member states of the union according to the class in which they were placed at their entry. There were seven of these classes, the lowest paying one, the highest twenty-five, units of contribution, the Swiss government being charged with the conduct of negotiation with new entrants as to their classification.

The Adaptation of International Law to this System of International Conventions.—It is not without interest to trace the process by which the principles of International Law were elaborated in conformation with the two new media of communication which were made available in the fifty years which preceded the war of 1914-1918. The subsoil of the sea came into question in connection with cables, the air in connection with wireless telegraphy and aircraft. As regards the former, it could hardly be pleaded that an analogy with the ocean itself was directly available, owing to the difficulty which lay in the application of the clear-cut distinction, made where the sea was concerned, between the territorial waters and the high seas. Was the jurisdiction of a government over a cable to end with the three-mile limit and, if so, who was to prevent and punish damage done to a cable under the high seas, that no-man's area? The Government of the United States,[(2)] in a programme prepared for a projected cable conference in 1864, proposed that wilful damage done to a cable which underlay the high seas should be assimilated to piracy and made punishable as such by any state signatory of the proposed convention. At the same time it ventured a further proposal to exclude all cables from the operation of war. By 1884, at which date an international agreement was finally signed, discussion had elucidated the question, and, it may be added, a sense of humour had reasserted itself. Great Britain had objected to an exclusion of cables from the operation of a war at sea, so that the convention was perforce restricted to peace-time conditions. Moreover, so far as human damage was to be anticipated, it was realised that the carelessness of navigators in approaching cable ships, of fishermen, and the owners of other cables, was more to be feared than intention to cause malicious damage, so that rules were provided which aimed primarily at the careless neglect of stated precautions.

Common-sense was also put under requisition gradually as regards the law of the air. On the subject four principal theories had started in competition.[3] There was the old doctrine, familiar from the use to which Grotius had put it in writing of the sea, that elements common to all were incapable of being possessed in complete dominion. Applied to the air in the nineteenth century, this theory might have been held to constitute the air space not only over the sea but over all land as well, an international domain as free as the high seas. Some theorists put forward a modification of this doctrine which, while it preserved as a principle the freedom of the air, would have permitted to subjacent states the exercise of a certain authority for the purpose of self-preservation up to a certain height. This fanciful suggestion faded into a third, which claimed for subjacent states full sovereignty over their air space up to a given height: and here the notion of the *portée de canon* associated with the name of Bynkershoek in connection with the limitation of territorial waters was disinterred and put to use. Lastly, as was maintained with stout good sense from the beginning by writers such as Sir Erle Richards, von Liszt, and Hazeltine, there was the theory that a state's sovereignty over its air space extended "from the soil to the sun."

No authoritative international decision was taken as between these doctrines before the outbreak of the war of 1914. In the wireless conventions of 1906 and 1912 it proved possible, without proceeding to a definition of the right of each state to interrupt foreign waves, to make arrangements based on practical considerations. That of 1912 contained in its Article VIII. the important provision that wireless transmission stations should be so organised as to reduce interference with other states to a minimum. Other articles made arrangement for the interchange of messages between all coastal stations and ships and between ship stations, for prompt attention to messages of distress, and for the transmission of messages by wireless telegraphy. In the sphere of aerial navigation it was significant of the time at which the congress was held that the discussion was from the first very largely

CHAP. XVI.

dominated by the consideration of the possibilities for espionage by air in war and even in time of peace. When the war came neutral states were quickly awakened to their danger not only from espionage but from the dropping of bombs and from the landing of aeroplanes by accident. Accordingly, there was a marked impetus to the assertion of complete authority to prevent the flight of belligerents through neutral air space ; and for these and other reasons less and less was heard of the specious analogy with the belligerent right of innocent passage through territorial waters. The flying convention of October 1919 reached in the end a definite conclusion that every state possessed "the complete and exclusive sovereignty in the air space above its territory and its territorial waters." This was, however, tempered by the general admission of a freedom of innocent passage to the private aircraft of contracting parties. The sovereignty of the state was made the more evident by the admission in Article V. of its right to prohibit navigation in certain areas and to fix the "airways" for flight over its territory. Further, a right was sanctioned in all states to forbid entirely the flight of foreign public aircraft without special authorisation ; and the populations to be flown over were additionally protected by a general agreement reached in Article XXVII. that foreign aircraft should carry no explosives or ammunition, should possess a certificate of air-worthiness, and should be flown only by pilots of certificated competence (Articles XI.-XIV).[(4)] Since October 1919, nations have on more than one occasion upheld their right under this convention to the sovereignty of their own air. Germany has held up the development by Imperial Airways (the British air line) of its European routes, and Persia in 1927 held up the development of a weekly air service from Cairo to India. The German objections were removed by a treaty with Great Britain signed in the course of 1928.

International River Commissions.—It is right to add here to the list of those international commissions concerned with transport and communications the international river commissions. The central commission of the Rhine, constituted in virtue of the Treaty of Vienna, was still only composed of the representatives of the riparian states, despite the importance of the river to the trade of the world. When the Treaty of Paris took from under Russian control the Danube mouths, which had been grossly neglected, it also provided the means by which not only the mouths but the whole course of the river should play their proper part in the system of communication of South-Eastern Europe. The considerable engineering work which was required to clear the mouths of the Danube was placed under the charge of a European commission composed of persons representing Austria, France, Prussia, Russia, Sardinia, Great Britain, and Turkey; but the actual navigation on the river was placed in the hands of a riparian commission, which was to take over the management of the mouths when the European commission had finished its labours. This last, however, proved much too valuable an instrument for Europe to surrender lightly, and its authority was renewed, as its scope was simultaneously extended, by later international agreements. At the end of the war of 1914-1918, after a pause and temporary management, the European commission, despite some protest of the riparian nations, was re-established.(5) The Conference of Berlin in 1885 produced the not very happy international commission for the Congo, while the peace treaty of Versailles in 1919 established international commissions for the rivers Elbe and Oder.

The Opening of Arterial Rivers to General Navigation.—More important perhaps than this small list of international commissions for the control of rivers, most of which conventions indeed owed their origin to special circumstances, was the liberation of the navigation on many arterial rivers all over the world from the control of exclusively riparian interests. The principle, proclaimed at Vienna, that commerce and navigation on all international rivers should be free, was but reluctantly admitted by the riparian nations of Europe, and carried no weight in South, or even in North, America, where the British only in 1871 put the use by the United States of the St. Lawrence River on a contractual footing, and then but in exchange for navigation rights on the Yukon, Porcupine, and Stickine.

The opening to all flags of such rivers as the Uruguay in 1852, the Amazon in 1867, the Orinoco in 1869, the Parana in 1885, or of the Congo and of the Niger in 1885, meant that the commercial development of important tracts of territory, not easily reachable except by river, was to be begun much more quickly than it would have been if the riparian, and sometimes even non-maritime, Powers had retained a harmful monopoly for themselves, or if the riparian, even though maritime, Powers had not been stirred to activity by competition.

Inter-Oceanic Canals.—The nineteenth century, however, was to see greater miracles than the legalised presence of

CHAP. XVI.

European and American flags far up the South American rivers, the Yangtse, or the Niger. The Suez Canal was built to shorten the sea distance from Europe to the Middle and Far East, and the Panama Canal to provide the Atlantic and Pacific coasts of America with rapid coastal communication. Despite the international interests involved, the Suez Canal was built by a French company and opened entirely under Egyptian control; and until 1888 no general international instrument regulated the right to admission and passage of merchant vessels and of warships, both those of Powers at peace and of Powers at war. During the Russo-Turkish War of 1877-1878 the British government feared the possibilities of a Russian attack upon the canal, nominally of course in Turkish territory, and became aroused to the danger of leaving the canal in the vague position which under International Law it held. Only in 1888, however, after critical negotiations, could the six great European Powers, together with Holland, as possessing its East Indian colonies, Spain, as owning the Philippines, and Turkey, come to an accord in the Suez Canal convention of October 1888. Then it was decided that the canal should never be put under a blockade; that it should always be open alike to vessels of war and to merchantmen; that all hostilities, even though Turkey were to be a participating belligerent, should be prohibited in the canal, in the ports of access, or in waters within a radius of three marine miles; that belligerent men-of-war should obtain no provisions or equipment during their passage through the canal; and that the representatives of the signatory Powers in Egypt should watch over the execution of the convention.

It did not prove so easy for a commercial company to construct the Panama Canal as it had been in the case of that at Suez. During the fifth decade of the nineteenth century English and American influence in Central America had been engaged in a struggle for control of a possible route in Nicaragua for the canal; but in 1850 the Clayton-Bulwer treaty put an end to rivalry, and each Power undertook to refrain from the occupation of any part of Central America, from the construction of fortifications designed to command the entrances to a canal if built, and from the acquisition of special advantages in trans-isthmian navigation not shared by the other party.(6) The Clayton-Bulwer treaty did not free the path for the construction of the canal to the extent which had been hoped. Instead of a neutralised Nicaraguan canal, erected under joint Anglo-American auspices, the French Panama Canal Company, under a concession from the Government of Colombia, attempted to achieve a work which would have owed nothing to either the United States or the British capitalists. The first attempt, which ended in disaster and was abandoned in 1891, left matters as they were. The United States was not free to proceed alone unless it could liberate itself from the agreement signed in 1850. In 1901 the Hay-Pauncefote treaty between England and the United States removed the obstacles to an American construction of the canal, but retained the general principles of neutralisation laid down by Clayton and Bulwer, now to be interpreted in the light of the Constantinople agreement of 1888 concerning the canal at Suez. The Anglo-American treaty of 1901, however, was not reinforced by a collective guarantee of the Powers, nor was any general international responsibility assumed for the conditions of navigation, as had been the case in 1888. The Panama Canal was only to be distinguished in status from that of Corinth or of Kiel by the conditions of the Hay-Pauncefote treaty of 1901 with Great Britain and by those of the Hay-Varilla treaty of 1903 with Panama, a state which had come into existence as a separate body from Colombia under the patronage of the United States and under circumstances which evoked no little criticism. A subsequent dispute arose in 1913 between Great Britain and the United States over the alleged discrimination in favour of American vessels which the latter country was supposed to be contemplating in the matter of tolls. The dispute, however, was composed by the conciliatory attitude of President Wilson, which made it clear that no such discrimination was for the time contemplated. It is held by some writers that the United States has broken the Hay-Pauncefote treaty in fortifying the canal.

Other Conventions.—Communication and transport were not the only commercial interests which it was sought to foster by international conventions. A number of states using the metric system entered into the Paris convention of 1875 for the institution of an international office of weights and measures. Two partial monetary unions were also founded in Europe, the Latin union of 1865 and the Scandinavian union of 1873. A more ambitious attempt to reach agreement on the holding of an international monetary convention in 1892 failed to produce result, although the United States and Mexico were associated with all the important European

CHAP. XVI.

Powers, except Russia, in the attempt. In view of the development of world-wide markets a proposal for a convention to enable inventors and proprietors of trade-marks to claim world-wide rights and protection was first made in 1883, and an international office at Berne was established for its administration. A similar convention for the protection of writers and artists was made at Berne in 1886, and under it an international union and offices were erected of a similar type to those erected under the convention of 1883 for the protection of industrial property. The vine-growing countries of Europe produced the phylloxera conventions of 1878, 1881, and 1889, by the execution of which they hoped to stay the ravages of *Phylloxera vastatrix*. The need of measures to stem the spread of cattle disease produced, if not a general convention, at least a great number of all but identical two-party treaties which dealt with such subjects as the disinfection of cattle trucks and the competence of veterinary surgeons at the frontiers. Birds useful to agriculturalists were protected by the very widely signed European convention of 19th March 1902, and the extinction of the North Pacific seal-fishery was prevented by the four-Power convention of 7th July 1911. The general interests of agriculture had already been made the object of the convention for the creation of an agricultural institute in Rome. And this does not in all probability exhaust the list of international conventions which, large or small in scope, sane or pragmatical in nature, reveal an important tendency of European development during the last century.

Labour Conventions before the War.—When so much was being attempted by international action in the realm of communications, commercial property, artistic achievement, and health, it is not to be wondered at that, by the beginning of the last quarter of the nineteenth century, industrial conditions should take on an international aspect. States industrially advanced, like England and Germany, had made laws and regulations which partially controlled the conditions of work in factories, and were designed to protect factory workers, particularly women and children, and those of all sexes and ages engaged in specially dangerous operations. The simplest way of procuring some protection for women workers was to forbid their employment on night work in factories or in specially laborious occupations such as those carried on beneath the surface in mines. Children could be protected by enacting an age, or educational, limit prior to the attainment of which they might not enter a factory, or by restricting their hours of labour while they were of tender years. The whole range of factory and industrial workers engaged upon dangerous work might be guaranteed a restricted normal working week, and the conditions under which they worked might be carefully controlled. Advances like these, and the further reform demanded by philanthropists and workers, could not be carried very far in one country without causing apprehension to employers and exporters that the effect of such measures on their costs of production would be so to increase them as to give a powerful advantage to competitors in states which had not introduced such a system of national regulation. It was indeed possible to answer that industrial concessions made in one country to the labouring classes would before long be demanded by those of all other countries which were on anything resembling the same level of culture; but even if such an answer were to prove correct on an ultimate view, which was at least open to question, its comfort was small in the immediate prospect. Thus from industrialists in "advanced" countries and from reformers in "backward" countries arose the desire to see a general commitment of all countries to a uniform plan of factory and labour regulation. CHAP. XVI.

It was Switzerland which took the first step in convoking an international conference on labour. In 1881 it approached the governments at Paris, Berlin, Vienna, Rome, London and Brussels with a view to obtaining their co-operation in the international regulation of labour. None of the governments were at that time ready for such a project. In the next few years, however, the Reichstag and the French Chamber were the scene of arresting debates on the subject; Adler of Freiburg and Brentano of Leipzig wrote voluminously and not without effect; while the trade-union movement warmed increasingly towards the notion. Accordingly, in 1889, the Swiss Federal Council sent a new circular note which suggested that the time might be ripe for the regulation in some degree of Sunday, female and child labour by international agreement. The only Power, approached on this occasion, which indicated its entire dissent was Russia.

Although the Swiss government, proceeding slowly and cautiously, had drawn up a tentative programme and had indeed issued the invitations for a conference to meet at Berne in May 1890, it decided to alter its plans and to make way for a more powerful state. The young Emperor, about to break with Bismarck and anxious to reconcile German labour,

CHAP. XVI.

had resolved to enter the field in February 1890. The negotiations were rapidly pushed forward with the Powers of Western Europe to secure the attendance of official delegates at Berlin in order to discuss the labour of women, children and young persons, Sunday work and mining. The conference was accepted and all the industrial states of Europe, with the exception of Russia, sent delegates to the proceedings which lasted from 15th March to 29th March 1890.

The field of labour conditions was at the time altogether a novel one for an international conference, and there can be little wonder that its final protocol consisted not so much of binding engagements as of recommendations. Children, it suggested, were to be protected by exclusion from factories until they had reached the age of ten in southern countries and twelve in others, and the attainment of a certain educational standard was also deemed a desirable prerequisite. Children below the age of fourteen were not to work for more than six hours a day, and an interval of half an hour at least was to divide the working hours into two portions. They were not to be employed at night or on Sundays, and they were not to be admitted to unhealthy or dangerous occupations save exceptionally and under special protection. Children between the ages of fourteen and sixteen were also to be excluded from Sunday and night work, but the daily maximum was fixed at ten hours of work a day, to be broken up by one and a half hours at least of break. Exceptions, however, were to be allowed.

Though the governments admitted that "restrictions" were desirable for children of this age engaged in particularly unhealthy or dangerous industries, they did not venture on a definition of the restrictions. For boys between sixteen and eighteen it proved to be impossible to do anything except to express the desirability of protecting them by the adoption of a maximum day and measures relative to Sunday and night work. Women and girls were to be protected from night work and were to enjoy a maximum day's work of eleven hours, broken by intervals amounting at the least to one hour and a half. Exceptions were to be allowed but, on the other hand, restrictions were recommended for particularly unhealthy and dangerous occupations in their case. After childbirth women were not to enter a factory until at least a month had elapsed.

A Sunday's rest was specially recommended for the protected classes of workers, and was suggested as the general rule for all other industrial workers. Exceptions were to be admitted in the case of industries necessarily continuous or those which furnished the public with the necessities of daily life; for those which were only seasonally active or which were dependent upon the irregular action of natural forces. Even here, however, one Sunday's rest in every two was recommended, and the precaution was taken of recommending an international understanding as to the classes of exceptions to be admitted to the general rule of Sunday rest.

The mining industry was the subject of a special section of the protocol. The minimum age for work beneath the surface was progressively advanced to fourteen years (twelve for the southern countries), while women were to be entirely excluded from underground operations. In the case of particularly unhealthy mines a restriction of hours was advised. The health and safety of miners were to be protected by every possible means and under the supervision of the state. The competence and experience of the engineers were to be officially tested and the relations between them and the miners were to be close. A progressive development of insurance against sickness, accident, old age, and death was enjoined. Finally, strikes were to be avoided by agreement between employers and employed that they would abide by arbitration whenever direct negotiation broke down. The execution of all these measures was to be supervised in each state by special governmental officials who were to issue reports upon conditions of labour. These reports, together with labour statistics and the texts of relevant laws or labour ordinances, were to be exchanged between the governments.

It was to be fifteen years before the summons of a new labour conference. In 1905 fifteen European states were represented at a meeting at Berne, which had been called largely in order to abolish night work for women engaged in industry, and to ban the use of white phosphorus in the manufacture of matches. The draft of the convention on phosphorus was not difficult to prepare: it was otherwise with that on the other more controversial subject. It was considered first necessary to define the industrial undertakings which might be counted as affecting world conditions and be therefore properly subject to international regulation. These were finally fixed at the limit of such firms as employed ten labourers or more. Then it was essential to obtain a definition of the phrase "industrial undertaking," and, in the event, factories, mines, and quarries were admitted, while purely

CHAP. XVI. agricultural or commercial enterprises were excluded. In the selected industries once more the general principle was adopted that women were not to work at night except in cases a list of which was to be fixed. It was then found essential to define "night work"; and it is surprising perhaps that the assembled wisdom of the delegates did not adumbrate the task of defining the word "woman." Night was fixed finally as a period of eleven hours' duration, which was in all cases to contain the hours between 10 P.M. and 5 A.M., but which might, as regards the other four hours, be varied according to national custom. Finally, the list of permissible exceptions to this ruling was drawn up and included extreme necessity or the prevention of loss owing to the deterioration of materials. The fact that a trade might be influenced by the seasons was held to justify a night's work of ten hours throughout an annual period of sixty days. Finally, certain states and industries were to be allowed special intervals for the adaptation of their laws and system to the new conditions. These draft conventions of 1905 were put into definite form at a diplomatic conference in 1906, and were submitted for signature and subsequent ratification.

The Swiss government called another labour conference in 1913, submitting in its invitation a programme which proposed the prohibition of all night work by young persons and the determination of the working hours suitable for those under sixteen and for women. With respect to young persons the same definition both of the phrase "industrial undertaking" and "night work" was adopted as had been chosen in 1906, though exceptions were to be allowed for European coal and lignite mines, for bakeries, as well as for industrial enterprises in colonies and states outside Europe. Night work was then to be forbidden absolutely to all under fourteen, and generally to all under sixteen save in the stated exceptions. In the case of glass works, rolling mills and forges the exclusion of boys from night work was made subject to an optional postponement for ten years at the will of individual governments. The convention which defined the working day for women forms an interesting example of international co-operation. A ten-hour day or a sixty-hour week, of which no day was to be longer than ten and a half hours, were adopted as alternative maxima. Periods for rest were prescribed, the first of which was to come not more than six hours after the day's work had begun. Times of employment might be extended in such cases as those in which the public interest demanded it, in cases of *force majeure*, under which phrase was contemplated the deterioration of material or the operation of the weather; and the restrictions were made elastic in this way in all seasonal occupations and in any industry under exceptional circumstances. Differing maxima for overtime were fixed for the general seasonal industries, for the exceptional fish, vegetable, and fruit establishments, and for houses manufacturing bricks, tiles, clothing, feather articles, fashion articles, and artificial flowers. Normal extensions of the working day were not to affect young workers under sixteen years of age. Both conventions as drafted were to have been submitted for final signature to a diplomatic conference which was appointed to meet at Berne on 3rd September 1914. The outbreak of the European war made such a consummation impossible.[7]

The International Labour Organisation.—At the conclusion of the War of 1914-1918 the work thus interrupted was resumed, but machinery for its continuous development was provided under the auspices of the League of Nations. Separate from, but attached to, the more familiar machinery of the League there was erected an international labour organisation. This consisted of a permanent bureau at Geneva and an annual public conference which has been held at various centres in different countries, starting in 1919 at Washington. The disturbed condition of the labour market and the existence of forces which it may be hoped are abnormal have rendered work less fruitful than might otherwise have been the case. But a respectable amount has been accomplished; and it can hardly be otherwise than a gain to have had put upon a permanent footing a body, supported by almost all the nations, which has already accumulated an invaluable body of experience. The international labour conferences are able to recommend to the various governments resolutions which reach over the whole field of employment; and they have done so on the vexed questions of an eight-hour day, the employment of women and children, the conditions of employment at sea and in agriculture, the weekly day of rest, the employment of white lead in painting, emigration, factory inspection and other kindred subjects.[8] The participating governments are not bound to do more than lay the recommendations before their legislatures. It is not without interest that the first advisory opinion handed down by the court of International Justice on 31st July 1922 concerned the method of nomination by a govern-

CHAP. XVI. ment of delegates to the international labour organisation; while the second declared that the competence of that body did extend to the conditions of employment in agriculture, though it did not extend to the consideration of the organisation of that greatest of all industries, or of questions as to the method of agricultural production.

NOTES

(1) Classic text-books like those of Ullmann, de Louter, and Oppenheim will all be found to have made the attempt to deal adequately with these newer sides of international activity. It was Pradier-Fodéré, however, who had earlier used his erudition and industry to force a way for the new non-political matter into the classic presentation of International Law. The public international unions have found their own historian in Reinsch. Professor J. L. Brierly in an article on "International Law as a Subject of Education," in the *Journal of the Society of Public Teachers of Law* for 1926, makes many suggestive remarks on the aspect of International Law as a branch of what Professor Pound would call "social engineering."

(2) Pradier-Fodéré's treatment of the subject of submarine cables will be found exhaustive, and needs only to be supplemented by the information that the allies of 1914-1918 treated German-owned cables as liable to the full rigour of the laws of war at sea.

(3) The abundant pre-war literature issued on the question of the law properly applicable to international relations in the air was effectively summarised by Hazeltine in his *Law of the Air*. As early as 1910 a *Revue Juridique Internationale de la Locomotion Aérienne* was founded.

(4) Cheney Hyde's closely packed but clear and concise presentation of International Law as revealed in American treaties and official American documents has here been used. It will be found profitable in other sections of International Law, such as those about to be discussed—international rivers and interoceanic canals.

(5) It is, of course, Rumania whose sovereignty is somewhat diminished by the special position of the European commission of the Danube. In 1927 the "World" court did not support Rumanian contentions which would have diminished the commission's authority both in scope and geographical extent. For the details of the international régime on the Rhine and the Danube, J. P. Chamberlain's recent work may be consulted.

(6) The Clayton-Bulwer Treaty of 1850 and the Hay-Pauncefote Treaty of 1901, with accounts of the circumstances attendant on their negotiation, are very fully treated in American Diplomatic Histories and in British Diplomatic Histories of the scope of the *Cambridge History of Foreign Policy*.

(7) B. E. Lowe's *The International Protection of Labour* is a very meritorious account of the whole movement described in this section.

(8) One of the most important services of the Labour Bureau has been the collection and, where possible, the publication of considerable masses of information and statistics on subjects of the type outlined in the text for which international action is being proposed.

CHAPTER XVII

SOME TYPES OF TREATIES IN THE NINETEENTH CENTURY

Some Types of Treaties in the Nineteenth Century. Treaties with Eastern Nations. Extradition Treaties. Treaties of Social Philanthropy. Health Conventions. International Scandals. Rebus sic stantibus.

Some Types of Treaties in the Nineteenth Century.—The mechanical advances of the nineteenth century, allied with development in the art and technique of government, enabled states gradually to undertake many types of international engagement, and to enter upon many kinds of international activity which, alike in their nature and their number, would have appalled the statesmen of the previous century. In 1785 von Ompteda only found twenty Prussian treaties in existence of which but one was non-political.(1) For the years 1874 to 1883 alone de Martens printed between eight hundred and nine hundred treaties of which the vast majority were non-political.(2) Some of these engagements, novel in their form, were patient of expansion into international conventions to be signed by many parties; and, though avowedly planned in many cases to supersede or supplement some older series of two-party treaties, they had often started in the two-party form themselves. Thus before the final adoption of the convention for the protection of industrial property there had been a large number of agreements between two parties aimed at the same result, the Franco-Russian Treaty of 1870, for example, the Franco-German of 1873 and the Franco-Italian of 1874. Similarly, the international protection of literary and artistic property, now regulated by a convention between the nations, had been from as early a date as 1840 undertaken in two-party treaties, of which that between Austria and Sardinia in 1840 and that between France and Sardinia in 1843 are early examples. CHAP. XVII.

Despite the emergence of many new types of non-political treaty, those which concerned commerce and navigation were

CHAP. XVII.

still perhaps by far the most important non-political instruments negotiated. The Dutch had been during the seventeenth century the foremost negotiators of such treaties, and early therefore set the fashion of separating their political relations with other states from relations more fitly to be controlled in agreements specially commercial. The earlier treaties between states had contained a medley of clauses—those of alliance, those governing war or peace conditions, clauses of guarantee, customs clauses, clauses relating to private trade and merchants, commercial clauses, and those dealing with the rights of neutrals or with the protection of foreign merchants. All such clauses the Dutch then gathered up into their special treaties of commerce: and the leading maritime nations soon imitated them. Even in the later half of the eighteenth century, however, there were grave gaps in the chain of commercial treaties. It has been already pointed out, for example, that in 1780 Prussia, Sweden and Russia possessed no treaties of commerce with France, and that all these three Powers, and Denmark also, possessed no treaties of commerce with Spain. Russian trade with France, Russian ships, Russian travellers and merchants were subject to the normal operation of the French municipal law as it related to alien commerce and to alien persons. When dispute over neutrality in 1780 and the subsequent years gave a fresh fillip to the negotiation of commercial and navigation treaties, it was inevitable that the experience of more than a century should make them more finished than had been the earlier types. Thus Article IV. of the Franco-Russian Treaty of 1787 contained a most-favoured-nation stipulation under which Frenchmen and Russians were to enjoy the privileges of the most-favoured-nation in one another's land. Article V. permitted the establishment of a consular system. Articles X., XI., and XII. made special trading concessions to Russian trade with France and to French trade with Russia in regard to specified materials, while Article XLVI., coming after a long string of clauses which dealt with matters so diverse as neutral privileges, the treatment of enemy persons and goods at the outbreak of war and bankruptcy procedure, fixed the duration of the treaty as one of twelve years.

During the nineteenth century treaties of commerce and navigation lost none of their importance, though there was a tendency to supplement them by consular treaties, which went into detail over consular powers and privileges, and by jurisdictional treaties, which defined minutely the legal capacity of foreign persons and companies, the authority of foreign judgments and documents, and questions of like nature. Commerce and travel entered increasingly on an international scale, and the clauses of such treaties paved the way for both. Among the western nations great importance was attached to the ability to secure "most-favoured-nation clauses" in all commercial treaties even if only in an attenuated form. A state which omitted to obtain the grant of those conditions might well see in every field the conclusion of special tariff bargains to the detriment of its export trade by its various competitors, and yet not possess the right to claim similar treatment for itself. Thus Germany in Article XI. of the Treaty of Frankfort at the end of the Franco-Prussian War compelled France on reciprocal terms to grant it most-favoured-nation treatment in respect of any advantages of commerce or communication granted to England, Belgium, Holland, Switzerland, Austria and Russia. Although this stipulation was made in a treaty of peace, it did as a matter of fact fix the basis of commercial relations between France and Germany until 1914.

Germany, of course, lost its most-favoured-nation status in the French markets when the outbreak of war in 1914 cancelled the effects of the Treaty of Frankfort. In 1920, therefore, German goods, unprotected by any treaty stipulations, would be exposed to the full rigour of the French tariff maximum and the additional severities of French measures of restriction or prohibition of imports. Germany did not disguise its eagerness once more to acquire most-favoured-nation status, a consummation which, after most difficult negotiations, was obtained in a treaty of August 1927. A denial of most-favoured-nation treatment constitutes in effect a declaration of a "tariff" war, of which there have been several devastating instances.

Many states have desired to make exceptions for one reason or another to the grant of full most-favoured-nation treatment to every government with whom a commercial treaty is concluded. Some have desired to make an especially close commercial bond with states which are in close physical proximity, in strong political sympathy, or even merely sentimentally allied. The preference allowed to British goods by some of the British self-governing dominions is well known, and was in the case of Canada the source of a long German-Canadian tariff "war." In Article VIII. of the present commercial treaty between Spain and Finland both

CHAP. XVII. parties are to be seen making special exceptions to the grant of most-favoured-nation treatment to one another. Finland excepts the special treatment allotted to its neighbour and political associate, Esthonia, while Spain excepts special concessions granted to Portugal, Spanish Morocco, and the Spanish-American republics.

A nation which has granted all its fellows most-favoured-nation treatment — even with reservations — may find its bargaining powers limited. If it seeks to promote its commercial interests by a further bargain with one of their number by which a lower duty to enter its markets is offered (in return, of course, for some concession), it will find that in virtue of their possession of most-favoured-nation clauses in their commercial treaties all the other governments will demand the same concession unconditionally—that is, without offering the same terms which the co-negotiator of the bargain had promised. The United States long struggled against this overwhelmingly accepted position in Europe, maintaining that such nations as possessed a treaty which contained this clause were to enjoy any subsequent favour granted to other nations " if the concession was freely made, or upon the same conditions if the concession was conditional." This interpretation would appear, latterly, to have been surrendered.

Some governments have found a way of discriminating between the identical products of two countries, both possessing commercial treaties with the most-favoured-nation clause and both therefore entitled to the same treatment. It is to be presumed that when this has been done corresponding value has been received from the country which has benefited by this somewhat unfair procedure. The Economic Conference of 1927 reported in this regard " that it is above all necessary to avoid tariff sub-headings [in the national tariff law] which do not refer to articles of a different nature and which are merely intended to discriminate between articles of different origin," and further that " any customs classification should be as objective as possible, lest it should become a means of discriminating to the prejudice of any country or of specialising tariffs to the advantage of any country."

Another type of clause, and a somewhat novel one, which can increasingly be found in the commercial treaties of the nineteenth century, is one which in matters of navigation or port administration provided for equal treatment as between national and alien, thus marking in a sense the end of the navigation laws of the old model, which restricted the amount of trade open to foreigners and discriminated against their ships.(3)

A previous paragraph has already alluded to the fact that in the nineteenth century commercial negotiation was interesting itself mainly in tariff-bargaining. The grant of ordinary sailing, establishment, mercantile, and legal rights to foreign merchants, which the Dutch negotiators had been so concerned to have registered in their seventeenth-century commercial treaties, had now become axiomatic (4) not merely for the metropolitan countries but even for the colonial domain. Only in the backward countries of the Muhammadan world and in the Far East did matters of this kind require the special attention of the commercial negotiator, who elsewhere concentrated his main effort in promoting his national exporting industries, seeking for them an opening in foreign countries on better terms than those allowed by the general tariff scales. The very remarkable Anglo-French treaty of 1786, negotiated for England by Eden, had early seemed likely to open a corpus of commercial treaties sensibly lowering the barriers to international trade at the frontiers. That destiny, however, was reserved more completely for the impressive Anglo-French treaty of 1860, negotiated with so much prudence and tact by Cobden and received with so formidable a volume of discontent from powerful interests in France. England from the beginning announced that the tariff reductions awarded nominally to French goods would be granted to the goods of all nations, while France offered terms just as favourable as those conceded to England to any nation willing to make a similar commercial treaty. This was a sensible advance on the precedent of 1786, when, if no "peculiar" advantages had been asked for by either contractant, the benefits of the treaty were yet confined to the two participants.

The difficult character of true international tariff negotiations—affecting so many interests real or supposed in either country—was already evident from the agitation of powerful English interests in 1786 and of similar French interests in 1860. Though commercial treaties with elaborate tariff stipulations are now incomparably more frequent than in 1860, they are not to be negotiated with any more facility. Only recently, critical Franco-German negotiations have taken years to mature (1924-1927), and Polono-German agreements have had to be signed for a single province of the whole com-

CHAP. XVII.

mercial field (timber, November 1927), because the general bargaining was so long-drawn-out as to leave no other alternative to both governments. Cobden spent from 18th October 1859 to 29th January 1860 in procuring his preliminary treaty, and from 10th April to 5th November in obtaining his supplementary conventions, which definitely fixed the French tariff scales for English goods.[5]

Treaties with Eastern Nations.—A special class of treaty, made by the Western Powers with Eastern states, has been mentioned and discussed above, but still needs some treatment, because it was through the medium of such treaties that "extra-territoriality" and "tariff limitation" were introduced into large areas of the Eastern world, and by their means these areas were first incorporated into the fabric of organised humanity. The institution of extra-territoriality had originally grown up in Turkey under voluntary grants made by the powerful Sultans of the sixteenth and seventeenth centuries. These grants permitted the European consuls of those states possessed of "capitulations" to exercise jurisdiction over their fellow-nationals. Further, the European merchants of the "capitulation Powers" were guaranteed a low and definite tariff. A glance at the second volume of Hertslet's *Commercial Treaties* will reveal the nature of the English capitulations as they were laid down in the Anglo-Turkish treaty of 1809.[6] By the nineteenth century the consular rights in Turkey had been extended from what seems in the first place to have been a mere right of the consuls to decide disputes between their fellow-nationals, and a right to be present at the criminal trial of any one of them, to a full and complete civil and criminal jurisdiction over their countrymen, as well as action in defence of their privileges, property, and law. A similar system, both with respect to jurisdiction over foreigners and in matters of the tariff, was arranged by treaty with nations which were opened up to the commerce of the world during the nineteenth century—that is, with Japan in 1858, with China in 1842, with Morocco in 1856, with Siam in 1855, and with Persia in 1857, to speak of British action only.

The relevant stipulations in the Anglo-Japanese treaty of friendship and commerce may be given as typical of numerous similar treaties. All questions of property and person between British subjects were to be determined under British jurisdiction. British subjects guilty of a crime in Japan were to be tried by their consul or by an authorised functionary: disputes between Japanese and British subjects were to be decided by the consul sitting jointly with Japanese authorities: absconding or recalcitrant debtors, if of British nationality, were to be brought to justice by the British authorities or forced to meet their debts. Finally, in an annex to the treaty, shipping duties were fixed and a tariff schedule was laid down. Imports were divided into the free class, the highly important 5 per cent. class, the 20 per cent. class, and a 35 per cent. class, which last consisted of intoxicating liquor. Export duty was to be 5 per cent., but bullion was excluded. The treaty was to be valid for fourteen years at least. Then a revision "with a view to the insertion of such amendments as experience shall show to be desirable" was to be attempted on the demand of either party.(7) Nothing was provided for the case of a disagreement between the parties either as to the desirability, or the nature, of the revision: nor was there any mention of a termination of the treaty, so that there was at least a defensible case for the view that a Japanese denunciation, should Japan fail to obtain an acceptable revision, would not be binding on the other party and would not obtain the abrogation of the treaty.

Thus these treaties did in effect, if not in theory, impose a limitation of sovereignty upon the Powers which were constrained to sign them. Turkey was unable to shake off the system of capitulations until 1923. Japan with the goodwill of Great Britain and the United States, and after a formidable demonstration of its military power, obtained the necessary relief by 1898, although even at that date it did not obtain full tariff autonomy, for which it had to wait until 1911. China, whose treaties had conceded navigation rights upon the Yang-tse-Kiang (8) as well as the usual capitulatory and tariff rights, had long formed the desire to imitate Japan, and obtained at the Washington Conference of 1921 a practical agreement from the Western Powers in principle, but circumstances have prevented the success of such ambitions. Meanwhile, China can draw some satisfaction from the fact that more favourable consideration was obtained for the Chinese case at the conference at Washington in 1921 than was accorded to Japan in the conferences at Tokyo in 1874 and 1882. Indeed, the first offer which a settled government in China would have before it for consideration would almost certainly be one from the capitulation Powers to discuss the whole question in a most sympathetic spirit. Siam by tact and good management has been able to win liberation from similar restraints, in its case in a fashion less

CHAP. XVII.

stormy than that which characterised the Turkish negotiations. Perhaps the result has been a little less complete.(9)

Extradition Treaties.—The nineteenth century witnessed a rapid development in the signature of two-party extradition treaties. These provided for the return of all those accused of stipulated classes of crime from another country to the native scene of their misdeeds. Up to the eighteenth century a British criminal under common law, who had succeeded in escaping to a foreign country, might feel comparatively safe. Princes indeed did sometimes ask one another for the surrender of their criminal subjects, but in such cases the crime had usually been of a political character, it might be of rebellion or political plotting. English history, for example, can furnish the well-known instances of Henry VII.'s successful demand for the De la Pole pretender from his enforced guest, the Duke of Burgundy, in 1506, and the negotiations conducted by Charles II. with Denmark and Holland for the surrender of the fugitive regicides.(10) This older conception of extradition was still to be found in the nineteenth century despite the hold which in that century the right of asylum had acquired. Thus in 1834 Russia, Prussia, and Austria, bound by a common fear of constitutionalism and of revolt in Poland, engaged to give up to one another political criminals charged with high treason, *lèse majesté*, or rebellion, while it is well known that the Austrian and Russian demands on Turkey for the extradition of the Hungarian rebels of 1849 provoked a grave international crisis.

During the eighteenth century, however, the idea of extradition was coming to be associated with other types of offenders than political. Vattel (11) mentions the fact that all the states of Switzerland were prepared to compel even their own subjects to appear before alien Swiss courts, not merely on the serious criminal charges but on those of a character much less grave. Outside Switzerland, however, progress had been slower. In the first half of the eighteenth century not a few "cartels," negotiated as between states, are to be found which make provision for the extradition of deserters, of refractory conscripts, or even of smugglers. But even here the offenders are semi-political, at least in the sense that their punishment is of direct concern to the state as a measure of military or financial administration. Although there were a few earlier anticipations, such as some interesting arrangements reached between Denmark and Brunswick in 1732 and 1744, it may truly be said that it was only in the second half of the eighteenth century that states became generally concerned for the punishment of their fugitive criminals in common law; and Beccaria's (*d.* 1795) observation that the assurance that there was no place of refuge for crime would be the best way of preventing it, may possibly explain their growing zeal.(12). By the end of the eighteenth century France had established regular and reciprocal relations of extradition with all the countries on its borders (13) except, somewhat naturally, England, though this country also was included upon the signature of the Treaty of Amiens in 1802. The types of crime to which official opinion at the end of the eighteenth century wished to see extradition extended are indicated best, perhaps, by the survey of a few of them. In 1766 a treaty between France and Württemberg gives a list which includes, beside deserters, "brigands, malefactors, robbers, incendiaries, murderers, assassins, vagabonds." Spain and Portugal in 1778 provide for the mutual surrender of deserters and those coining and smuggling. "Crimes of state, assassination, poisoning, falsification of public documents, coining, and theft with violence" figure in the Franco-Swiss treaty of 1798; but the Treaty of Amiens, between England on the one side and France, Spain, and Holland on the other, mentions only "murder, forgery, and fraudulent bankruptcy."

It was only in the course of the nineteenth century, however, that states bound themselves to the handing over of fugitive criminals not only with one or two of their immediate neighbours but with the greater part of the civilised nations of the world. It was early found that it was convenient to put the contract for extradition into a separate treaty. The rota of crimes, the specification of the requisitory procedure necessary to obtain the person of a criminal, the details of the reservations made by the contracting government, came in time to attain considerable bulk. The Anglo-American extradition engagements of 1842 were indeed capable of being compressed into one clause (14) of the Webster-Ashburton treaty; but though this was not incongruous where the list of the crimes concerned totalled merely seven, it could hardly be deemed suitable where, as in the case of the extradition treaty made by Spain with Germany in 1878, they totalled forty-three.

During the nineteenth century strong sympathy was aroused with the subjects of countries who were struggling for constitutional or national "liberty," and the principle of political "asylum" was maintained by certain countries, such

CHAP. XVII. as Great Britain, the United States, and Belgium. Several treaties of extradition contain clauses which specifically excluded offences of a political character from the list of crimes for which extradition would be granted. Of this Article VI. of the Anglo-German treaty of 1872 forms an example. Some argument developed in the later decades of the nineteenth century as to whether those fugitives who had attempted to assassinate a foreign ruler should not become liable to extradition. Attempts directed at the third Napoleon and against the Russian autocrats made the question a real one; and certain of the states of Europe, including Belgium and Holland, showed a readiness to commit themselves, for various motives, to the exclusion from the benefit of political asylum of the murderers of royal persons. A later difficulty arose from the activities of various types of anarchists who were bent upon outrages directed rather against the whole social order itself than against any particular "oppressor" or class of "oppressors." Should the plea that a bomb had been exploded in the hope that it would bring an end to the existing social order protect an anarchist from surrender to an injured government which had perhaps seen several of its citizens "murdered"? Many lawyers were not enamoured of a principle of asylum which could be pushed so far.

It is worthy of observation that the extradition accorded in nearly all treaties which concern the subject is one of aliens and not of nationals. In the case of many European states their constitution or their penal code or their special laws of extradition prevent the executive Power from according the extradition of its subjects in a treaty. The United States and England have taken a different view. England, though its usual practice is to concede a reciprocity of treatment, has on the other hand made at least one treaty, that with Spain in 1878, in which the surrender of British subjects has been contemplated without the according of reciprocity by the other side. Great Britain has also surrendered subjects whose extradition might have been refused under the conditions of the treaty by which it was bound.

Treaties of Social Philanthropy.—International benevolence toward the working classes was not confined to the operation of the Berne conventions. There were numerous two-party treaties, especially as between neighbouring states, which dealt with such matters as the provision of relief to distressed subjects of the one state in the territory of the other. Other treaties provided for the reciprocal accord of legal aid to poor persons in case of necessity or for the reciprocal grant of medical aid. One novel feature was introduced in the treaty between Belgium and Luxemburg which was signed on 15th April 1905, and the terms of which have been copied in other treaties.[15] It established the general principle that an alien labourer was not to be denied the benefit of the accident legislation of the country in which he lived.

A much more comprehensive type of treaty, in which protection is given to foreign labour, is represented by the Franco-Polish convention of 1920, a necessary complement to the treaty of immigration and emigration signed by France and Poland in September of the previous year. Workers' pensions, accident indemnities, sickness, invalidity, and unemployment insurance, were all comprehended, as well as the less novel medical aid. But there were still further stipulations which concerned such matters as the right of the foreign immigrant to share in the national provision for the protection of labour and health, even his right to acquire small holdings and to share in the direction of mutual-aid societies. Another agreement, between France and Czecho-Slovakia, gave special facilities to the foreign labourer for the transfer of his savings.[16]

Health Conventions.[17]—A new area for international action was broken into for the first time in the nineteenth century in the shape of the conservation of health. Advance in medical knowledge and skill was so marked that by the end of the first quarter of the century it was clear that the state would soon be entering the field of preventive medicine, and undertaking to an ever-increasing degree the supervision of such important factors of physical well-being as drainage and the supply of water. It is not to be wondered at, then, that in such circumstances some action would be taken against the importation of dangerous diseases, when infectious, from parts of the world in which both dangerous and infectious diseases raged unchecked. The plague, indeed, which as early as the fifteenth century had called out special measures of quarantine at Venice, Genoa, and Marseilles, was lying hidden for the time. Yellow fever, however, reached Spain from the Antilles in 1821, and Asiatic cholera reached Europe in 1831. The first outbreak led to the famous French sanitary law of 3rd March 1822 and the establishment of the "cordon sanitaire" of the Pyrenees. The visitation of the

CHAP. XVII.

cholera caused no little panic, and some of the "contagionists" would have committed their countries to theories which threatened to limit seriously the possibilities of international communication. The international institution which did result from the cholera panic proved to be the "superior council of health of Constantinople," formally established in 1839 as the agency by means of which the European Powers which had seaports endeavoured to control the transmission of infectious diseases from the Turkish ports. An "international sanitary council" was also set up at Tangier in 1840. Later, when the traffic through the Rea Sea had been proved to be a special source of danger, the improved "maritime sanitary and quarantine council" was set up in Alexandria in 1881. The Bucharest council of sanitation for the Danube, which acted at the mouths of the Danube, and a council for Persia set up in Teheran, may also be noted.

The first international conference on the subject of public health was summoned to meet at Paris in 1851, and occupied itself with the drafting of a convention which was almost entirely concerned with the regulation of quarantine precautions and procedure. This convention remained unratified save as between Sardinia and France, so that, when another epidemic of cholera in 1865 had ravaged the Near East and the south of Europe, the need for new deliberations on an international scale was widely felt.[18] Apart from a constant need of vigilance at the Red Sea, there were two more aspects of the problem of cholera which were specifically European. No arrangements had up till then been entered into (or were indeed to be made till 1893) for prompt notification by an affected state to all other governments of an outbreak of cholera in its jurisdiction. Accordingly, it was possible for the disease to be carried from Mecca to Suez, from Suez to Alexandria, from Alexandria to Marseilles and thence into the heart of Europe, all because the authorities at these points were without proper liaison and did not apparently realise the danger of the delay which marked their movements. The lack of organisation and the consequent uncertainty led to another disastrous result for Europe. Many states, in order to protect themselves, took drastic measures of quarantine with regard to ships on which cholera was definitely established or even only suspected. Greece, for example, in 1865 proclaimed a quarantine period of twenty days. The commercial losses and the private peril or inconvenience caused by measures of this kind, taken indiscriminately against a large volume of shipping, are obvious; and Great Britain, the great shipping and commercial Power, after some experiments with quarantine in the 'thirties, refused to adopt general quarantine measures for itself and protested against their use by other nations. This attitude, as well as much inherent difficulty in the question, involved delay in reaching a common international arrangement with regard to the classification of merchandise into disease-carrying and innocent varieties and the treatment of infected goods and ships. In fact, a final and approximately complete sanitary code was not produced till 1903.

Yet the conference at Constantinople in 1866 made some valuable recommendations, including such measures as the establishment of a strong international authority at the entry of the Red Sea and the interruption of maritime communication between the Arabian ports and Egypt. It even emphasised the need of preventive sanitary measures in India. The Vienna conference in 1874 desired to establish a permanent commission for sanitary research work; advocated the establishment of an international authority in Persia on the same lines as those already at work in Turkey and Egypt; and declared against the practicability of establishing quarantine ashore. The conference at Rome in 1885 modified maritime quarantine. The international treaties of Venice in 1892, of Dresden in 1893, and of Paris in 1894 were still occupied with the fight against cholera. The last-named established rigorous surveillance over the pilgrim ships, and entrusted its conduct to a special committee of the sanitary council at Constantinople, which was properly equipped.

A little later the plague, dreaded but thought extinct, began a new career in Bombay, and many governments propounded joint measures to meet it. At Venice in 1897 a conference drafted various measures which were adopted. It was, however, the conference at Paris in 1903 which was to produce a measure which contained the first really ambitious international regulation till then attempted against epidemic disease. This convention was signed by twenty states, and contained one hundred and eighty-four articles. The council at Constantinople was reorganised and allotted seventeen members, of whom four were always to be Turks; that at Alexandria was allotted eighteen, of whom four were to be Egyptian; and a new central office at Paris was established. A year before the Paris conference the American

CHAP. XVII. states had organised a Pan-American sanitary conference, and in 1905 had produced an American convention designed to check the ravages of yellow fever, cholera, and plague.

It has been a quiet and yet effective activity of the League of Nations to carry on and to perfect the world's work for the world's health. Each national department of health finds its efforts co-ordinated with (1) the Health Committee of the League, (2) the Permanent Committee of the *Office international d'Hygiène publique* (a pre-existing body) acting as the advisory health council of the League, and (3) the Health Section of the Secretariat of the League under a medical director. The health organisation, whose work is done at a cost to the League of £40,000 a year, and with the aid of substantial contributions from the Rockefeller foundation, has been concerned with the following objects :—

(1) The collection and circulation of particulars of the prevalence and spread of epidemic disease, partly through a new centre established at Singapore; and provision of assistance in emergency, at the request of governments affected, in coping with formidable epidemics which overrun national boundaries.

(2) The preparation and revision of international agreements on questions of health.

(3) The standardisation of the potency and the method of preparation of vaccines and similar therapeutic substances used for the prevention and cure of disease.

(4) A comparison of experience and statistics relating to widely prevalent diseases such as cancer, malaria, and tuberculosis.

(5) The interchange of visits between public-health officers serving in different countries.

International Scandals.—(*a*) THE SLAVE TRADE.—It has already been shown that the British government had been successful in winning from the Congress of Vienna a general declaration against the traffic in slaves. That government also attempted to secure from the subordinate conference of maritime Powers, which sat in London from 1816 to 1819, decisions which would make the enforcement of the suppression of this trade a real possibility. This attempt broke down, partly for the reasons indicated above, partly because demands for the general permission of a "right of search" in certain quarters of the sea frequented by "slavers" proved unpalatable to some of the great Powers, even on a basis of reciprocity. If Spain and Portugal permitted themselves to be half-bribed and half-cajoled into an acceptance of this controversial right, the four great Powers of the continent of Europe were not to be persuaded until 1841. In that year was made the famous quintuple treaty of the five great Powers, and even this was left unratified by France, which, smarting under the treatment of Palmerston, was drifting further and further away from England during the last few years of the Orleanist régime. In this agreement reciprocal right of search was permitted in a certain zone of the East Atlantic. Not until 1862 did the United States accept the same principle in a two-Power treaty with Great Britain. France in 1845 contracted a rather narrower agreement with England than had been suggested in 1841, and it was left to a less controversial period and to less ruffled statesmen to bring that country into line with more effective policies.

In the last quarter of the nineteenth century attention was turned from the west coast of Africa to the east and to the interior, where slave trade and caravans were part of the order of existence. The Congo conference of 1885, which laid down the conditions for the European development of a large section of Central Africa, forbade any territory therein to be used as a market or road for the slave trade. All Powers which possessed any land within the boundaries concerned were instructed to use every available means to suppress slavery and the sale of slaves. The conference held at Brussels in 1889-1890, in the hundred articles of which its *acte final* consisted, pledged the signatory Powers not only to energetic measures in detail against the trade on land, but to arrange for naval measures against the "dhows" which carried on the trade in the Indian Ocean, and this on the condition of what was practically a reciprocal right of search. Two offices—the international maritime bureau at Zanzibar and the bureau at the Brussels Foreign Office—were given important functions. The regulations thus promulgated were supplemented by special treaties such as the Anglo-Egyptian agreement of 21st November 1895. It may be noted in passing that this Brussels act contained provisions against the traffic in arms and in liquor as carried on in large African zones which were defined. Thus an overseas traffic in slaves became, so far as is known, a thing of the past. That slavery has been stamped out is perhaps too

CHAP. XVII. much to hope. Something not greatly unlike slavery drew the attention of the League of Nations to Abyssinia in 1925-1926. Sir Harcourt Butler, a recent Governor of Burma, had to embark in 1925 on an interesting campaign of considerable duration to put an end to slavery among the remoter tribes of Upper Burma. In 1927 attention was directed to the Sierra Leone protectorate, where slavery survived in the native territories. Owing to the strong agitation immediately begun, local legislation was secured by the British authorities under which affranchisement was to take place in January 1928.

(*b*) North Sea Fisheries.—The protection of the fishermen of the North Sea from the liquor traffic of the bumboats was undertaken in a convention of the interested Powers in November 1887. The right of search was reciprocally granted to the cruisers of the signatory Powers.

(*c*) White-Slave Traffic and Obscene Literature.—Two-party treaties on the subject of the white-slave traffic, such as the Germano-Dutch of 1889, preceded international action by more than a decade. The first international conference met in Paris in July 1902, and a convention, which sketched out administrative measures consequent on its decisions, was adopted on 18th May 1904. A convention directed against the related evil of the publication and interchange of obscene literature was adopted by many states in 1910. Both matters have occupied the attention of the League of Nations, which conducted an inquiry and issued in 1927 an exhaustive report upon the former. The two sections of this report were recognised as comprehensive, and it may be hoped that the deduction drawn by the experts of the League of Nations as to the connection between licensed houses and the existence of the traffic in women will affect national police codes.

Rebus sic stantibus.—It has been remarked more than once that the early European treaties were undifferentiated in type. Almost all of them were of a political character, being for the most part treaties of peace, alliance, or guarantee. Even in the eighteenth century the special treaty of commerce and navigation, or of friendship and navigation, was still uncommon. The Methuen treaty between England and Portugal, signed in 1703, or the Eden treaty between England and France of 1786, would probably rank as the boldest attempts up to the date of their conclusion made in the regulation of tariffs. And if the eighteenth century could show Sweden, Russia, and Denmark all without a commercial treaty with Spain in 1780, it must be remembered that even in the nineteenth century the United States did not sign its first treaty with Portugal until 1840, or with Belgium and Switzerland till considerably later.

Early treaties of peace, alliance, or guarantee were almost uniformly made without any provision for the limitation of their duration, so that, even when a treaty was not professedly "perpetual," its duration might well become indefinite. There are obvious reasons why a treaty of peace, concluded after the termination of a war and containing territorial provisions, should be unlimited in time. Stability in frontiers is the basis of international society. Yet even treaties of friendship or nominal alliance, such as the Anglo-Danish of 1670 or the Anglo-Swedish of 1661, were not bounded by any stipulation as to their endurance. Accordingly, when Sweden protested against the maritime policy of England in 1780, the British government was able to point to the Anglo-Swedish treaty made more than a century before and of course in an age of utterly different international circumstances. Although Denmark obtained a fresh treaty in 1780 which "explained" the treaty of alliance and commerce signed in 1670, and in a manner somewhat less onerous for Denmark, Sweden did not obtain a similar "explanation" until the convention of 25th July 1803. The Anglo-Dutch agreement for a perpetual alliance of defence, which was made in 1678, was destined to prove even more onerous for the less bellicose party. While the policy of Holland coincided with that of England, consisting first in opposition to Louis XIV. and later in resistance to any European disturbances calculated to disturb the peace and quiet of the Continent, the "maritime" Powers were generally found acting "defensively" together. In the Franco-British war of 1755-1763, however, the States-General were perpetually arousing the most vehement British animosity by refusing to consider the war as "defensive" on Great Britain's part, and by declining, therefore, to furnish up to six thousand troops—as they were bound to do by the treaty of 10th February 1716—since they maintained that the *casus foederis* had not arisen.[19] Even deeper was the British disgust when the States declined to furnish aid to England during the war of the American Revolution, despite the fact—satisfactorily established in British eyes—that France and Spain were aggressors. It was this feeling which

CHAP. XVII. led first to the suspension by Britain of the Dutch "privileges" recognised in Anglo-Dutch treaties made in 1674. Later, inflamed by the report of the opening by the Dutch of negotiations with the American colonies, the British gave the order for "general reprisals against Dutch commerce." (20)

It was not altogether without reason, then, that "time-clauses" began to be added to the other clauses of such treaties as admitted them naturally. There is an early example of a definite limitation of time in the treaty of alliance drawn up by Spain and Holland on 30th August 1673,(21) in which twenty-five years were stipulated as the period of the alliance. The allies of Chaumont in 1814 had grown but slightly more cautious, despite the experience of one hundred and fifty years, when they fixed at twenty years the duration of their treaty. This was, however, some improvement in technique in comparison with that of the perpetual alliances or permanent guarantees exemplified in the *pacte* of the Bourbon family in 1761.(22) It was not feasible for even royal families, closely related and apparently possessing common interests, to be sure that any possible eventuality would find them in the identical frame of mind in which they signed. In this case it was proved to be so to the detriment of Spain less than thirty years later, when the French Bourbons failed them, not through lack of will but through loss of control over French affairs.

The nineteenth and twentieth centuries saw many reasonable attempts to define the duration of treaties; and it is noteworthy, perhaps, that these were made in times of peace, when juster notions rule. This was increasingly the case towards the end of the century. Thus the famous Austro-German alliance, first concluded in a treaty of 1879, was drawn up for a five-years period, and was renewed from time to time until 1903. Even though it then took on the character of an indefinite understanding, the precaution of the participating Powers was made evident by the provision that either party could, under certain conditions, denounce it. The triple alliance between Germany, Italy, and Austria was also signed for a five-years period in 1882; while the league of the three emperors, formed twice between 1881 and 1887, was signed for terms of three years. If the Franco-Russian military convention, finally accepted by the Tsar in December 1893, appears not to have been characterised by similar precautions, at least the Anglo-Japanese alliance of 1902 was not indefinite, but was concluded for a period of "at least five years."

In other important treaties of a political nature a similar caution was shown. The arbitration treaty made by Great Britain with various countries between 1903 and 1905 was concluded for a period of five years; and such a treaty of extradition as that made with Germany in 1872 allowed either party to terminate it by a notification which would bring all obligations to an end after the lapse of six months. The Washington treaty of 1922 favoured a longer period than these, for its obligations were fixed to endure until 1936. Nevertheless, the statesmen who drew it up had learned something from the experience of the previous century, and resolved to take every precaution to remove all possible excuse for non-compliance on the part of the signatories. A conference of the signatory Powers, it was arranged, could be procured by any Power which claimed "a material change of circumstances"; and every contingency was frankly faced which might be produced at a subsequent date by a war involving one or more of the states which had signed the treaty. Lastly, it was arranged to hold a conference as early as five years after ratification in order that amendments, if such were suggested, might be considered. It is true, moreover, that obligations stretched over a much greater period of time than that arranged at Washington have been accepted in agreements as to debt payments and in reparation treaties between the former allies.(23)

Treaties of commerce—and this is true of those which contained any special concessions in the operation of a tariff over and above the conventional clauses on navigation or mercantile matters—were marked from an early date by a time limit. Yet it is interesting to note that perhaps the most famous tariff treaty of the eighteenth century was made in perpetuity despite the vast interests at stake. By the Methuen treaty England promised the admission of Portuguese wines into England at only two-thirds of the duty charged for French wines at their admission, while the Portuguese undertook to remove the prohibition on the importation of British woollens. These obligations were to bind not only the reigning sovereigns of the two countries but also their successors, and were to be valid for ever.(24) The *pacte de famille* of 1761, which in its twenty-fourth article contained the most important promise by France and Spain that they would treat the other country's ships and merchandise exactly as if they belonged to nationals, was made for an equally indefinite period. In the Anglo-Russian treaty of

CHAP. XVII. friendship and commerce of 1766, however, although it contained in its Articles XI. and XII. important stipulations as to war and neutrality, and in its Article XXIV. a tariff agreement to apply to British wool, the contracting parties provided that while peace, friendship and good understanding between them was to last for ever, the treaty itself should run only for twenty years. And yet they slipped into something which resembled an apology for thus fixing a term. "As it is usual," says Article XXV., "to fix a certain time for treaties of commerce the above high contracting parties have agreed that this one shall last for twenty years. . . . After the expiry of this term they will be able to agree on a renewal and prolongation."

Even if nations had no special tariff favours to bestow in their commercial treaties—and it was often the only bait which drew nations to brave the tedious effort of long negotiation—there was always at least the most-favoured-nation clause to be won, a practice of war mild for the neutrals to be secured, stipulations as to port charges to be made, not to mention clauses of a beneficent nature with regard to aubaine, détraction, emigration or bankruptcy. The maritime controversies of the eighteenth century seem to have made nations more conscious of the extent of their commitments in such treaties of commerce as had been signed without a limit. If the French treaty made with Hamburg in 1769 was still for twenty years' duration, the commercial treaties after 1760 tend to be made for shorter periods. Thus the treaty between Prussia and the United States was concluded for ten years; the Austro-Russian treaty of 1785 for twelve years; the Anglo-French treaty of 1786 for twelve years, and this last contained elaborate tariff stipulations for a great variety of merchandise. The pages of de Martens contain very many other treaties dating from this period and marked by the same features. Eighty years later such treaties as the Anglo-Russian of 1859 or the Franco-British of 1860 were still concluded for a limit of ten years; and the Franco-Russian of 1857 had even shortened that limit to six. The short term has difficulties of its own, though it may minimise the likelihood of a plea of "change of circumstance" upon the part of a nation which is loth to execute its obligations. The shorter the period the less likely are the industries of a country to adjust themselves to the new conditions or to gain by them. And some treaties signed recently have been signed for a time absurdly short.(25)

The Russo-Norwegian treaty of 1925 was made for three years and, if allowed to retain its validity beyond that period, was to be terminable at a year's notice on either side. In view of the fact that the Soviet government was a party, the terms of the treaty are comprehensible. But the Franco-Hungarian treaty of 1925 was designed to last a year in the first instance, and could be denounced after a twelvemonth on two months' notice. The Franco-Spanish treaty of the same year contained no provision as to time, but was voidable after notice of only two months. Perhaps the uncertain state at the time of European trade and of the European exchanges lay behind this diplomatic jerry-building.

It is, however, the territorial clauses of treaties, and those which impose servitudes, which have been the most fruitful cause of international dispute. A treaty of peace is of its nature made for an indefinite period. It was often proclaimed officially as such, and a fine old formula lingers in the ear—the "perfect and perpetual" peace. Frontiers cannot be fixed for a ten years' period and be left to waver when that time is past, if peoples on the border are to retain their poise. Yet it is equally difficult to fix a frontier in perpetuity; and, if it be arranged with apparent success, it may prove only to have been accomplished through the application of a *force majeure* or the inertia of exhausted disputants, in neither of which is to be found a solid basis. In 1856, by the treaty of Paris, Russia was brought to accept the neutralisation of the Black Sea: in 1878 Turkey was still protected from the inevitable consequences of the war which had recently ended, and Macedonia with Crete were left in its hands. In International Law there was no legal method by which a challenge could be pressed home against such arrangements. For neither denunciation by a single Power of any particular treaty, or clause in it, nor the recourse to war, could be considered a legal method. The release of Russia in 1871 from its treaty obligations in connection with the Straits produced the expression of opinion that the revision of treaties depended upon the consent of the original parties to them. What can be easier then, in facing the problem of "perpetual" but obsolete or unwise treaties, than to provide that in all drafts of treaties in the future a clause should be inserted to ensure that the signatory Powers should meet at a fixed date, or from time to time, or on request, to consider the question of revision? So it might well be argued, and the practice at Washington in 1922 or that of the French and

CHAP. XVII.

Hungarian commercial signatories in 1925 might be pleaded in support of this solution. Reflection will show its inadequacy. If Russia was freed in 1871 from its liability, this was due in the first place to the fact that France, one of the Powers which had imposed that liability, was at the time incapable of action, and that England was not prepared to undertake a costly war alone. Thus even if the victors in a war should consent to insert in their treaty a clause arranging for a later meeting to consider its operation, the vanquished would be unlikely to obtain revision of the treaty at that meeting, unless the political equilibrium had meanwhile changed. Even so, it may be confidently asserted that a revision, undertaken without a war, would have to be bought dearly. Though of course in 1878 they were not vanquished nations, it was perhaps because they knew the price which they would have to pay for a revision of that treaty that in 1908 Austria-Hungary and Bulgaria declined to take their admittedly weighty case to a conference of the signatories of the Treaty of Berlin. The Treaty of Locarno between Poland and Germany makes clear the difficulty which lies before Germany if it is to secure any peaceful revision of the Polish frontier. Despite the German acceptance of the French and Belgian frontiers, and the demilitarised Rhenish zone, which it lacks the strength and therefore the will to challenge, Germany was required to declare "that respect for the rights established by treaty or resulting from International Law is obligatory on international tribunals," and "that the rights of a state cannot be modified save with its consent." The first declaration hardly makes attractive for Germany an appeal to an institution like the Permanent Court of International Justice or even to the Council of the League itself; while the latter would prevent it denouncing or perhaps even challenging the present frontier unilaterally. That may be wise for the moment, but is it not once more to attempt the impossibility of a perpetual peace? Nations have learned by very diverse experience, and from very different points of view, that this is an impossibility, Russia with the Treaty of Paris of 1856, Austria and Bulgaria with the Treaty of Berlin, the United States with the Clayton-Bulwer treaty, Japan with the capitulation and tariff agreements, which the conferences at Tokio in 1874 and 1882 failed to perpetuate. Is a solution to be found for those cases in which treaties, indefinite as to limit of time or avowedly permanent, have become intolerably burdensome by providing for the examination of their terms by parties other than, or in addition to, those immediately interested in their maintenance or abolition ? The initial attempt to work towards the establishment of such an institution is to be found in Article XIX. of the League of Nation's charter. CHAP. XVII.

NOTES

(1) De Louter, *Droit international positif*, vol. i. p. 512.

(2) These were international, not Prussian treaties.

(3) In 1816 the first Anglo-American agreement was concluded by which there was to be complete reciprocity of treatment for British vessels in American ports and American vessels in British (home) ports. In 1822 special British measures against Dutch, Prussian and Russian commerce were withdrawn.

(4) That the price of such conditions is eternal watchfulness was made obvious by the findings of the Economic Conference of 1927. Recommending the immediate conclusion of bilateral agreements and the eventual signature of a general international convention on the subject of " the Economic and Fiscal Treatment of the Nationals and companies of one country admitted to settle in the territory of another," the conference urged the necessity of bearing in mind :—

(*a*) Equality of treatment with regard to conditions of residence, establishment, removal, and circulation, between foreigners admitted to a state and the nationals of that state.

(*b*) Conditions of carrying on trade, industry, and all other activities by foreign persons and enterprises.

(*c*) Their legal status.

(*d*) Their fiscal status.

(5) Morley's *Life of Cobden*, caps. xxix-xxxii.

(6) Hertslet, *Commercial Treaties*, vol. ii. pp. 346-77.

(7) For the text of the Treaty cf. Martens, *Nouv. Rec. Gén.*, vol. xvi., ii., pp. 426-39.

(8) Article 10, Treaty of 1858.

(9) The abolition of capitulations in Persia is promised in the Anglo-Persian treaty announced May 11, 1928, and France in the course of 1927 indicated to Persia its readiness to consider changes. How long the system can stand in Egypt—where its abuses have been denounced for years—is doubtful, but the very large European interests entrenched in that country, and the large European populations dwelling there, make the approach to revision difficult. See Cmd. Paper of British Government 3050. The Tangier situation will be considered by the four-Power conference summoned for 1928.

(10) In 1660.

(11) *Op. cit.*, bk. ii. cap. vi.

(12) Quoted by De Louter, *Droit international positif*, vol. i. p. 301.

(13) Pradier-Fodéré, quoting Billot, *Traité de l'Extradition* (1874).

(14) Article 10.

(15) B. E. Lowe, *The International Protection of Labour*.

(16) Lamas, *Traités internationaux de type social*, 1924 (a South-American work), pp. 223-4.

CHAP. XVII. (17) The subject is ably if shortly treated in Woolf's *International Government*. Pradier-Fodéré will be found to have given the subject minute attention. Readers of *Eothen* will recall Kinglake's experiences with Turkish quarantine.

(18) The cholera and typhus epidemics raging in Eastern Europe from 1919 to 1922 reintroduced the problem to the modern world. In May 1920 the League set up an Epidemic Commission which began work in Poland, and extended its activities to Latvia and Russia. When the sanitary cordon maintained by the Russian border states was broken in the autumn of 1921, Poland and the League co-operated to summon the Health Conference of Warsaw (March 1922). A plan of attack upon the epidemic scourges, especially in Russia, was outlined, and a draft convention was signed, an interesting feature of which was the constitution of the League's health section as arbiter in international epidemic disputes. Though sadly hampered by lack of money the League's effort was fruitful not only in Russia but in Greece, where new epidemic dangers were imported by the refugees from Asia who bore cholera, typhus, smallpox, and typhoid with them. Considerable precision has been reached. On 20th July 1927 cholera was suspected at Basrah, and on 23rd July two definite cases were treated. The alarm was given, and when the passengers by the Basrah-Cairo Air Line reached Egypt they found themselves treated as "suspects."

(19) D. J. Hill, *A History of European Diplomacy*, vol. iii. pp. 525-526.

(20) J. B. Scott, *The Armed Neutralities*, pp. 330-5.

(21) De Garden, *Traités de Paix*, vol. i. pp. 94-5.

(22) Martens' *Recueil de Traités*, vol. i. pp. 16-21.

(23) Many of these envisage annual payments made over a period of more than sixty years.

(24) The Methuen treaty was not abrogated for more than a century.

(25) On this subject the Economic Conference of 1927 expressed itself in no uncertain voice. One of its recommendations was "that states should conclude their commercial treaties for as long a period as possible, and should follow, in this regard, the policy practised by a large number of countries before the war."

CHAPTER XVIII

THE LEAGUE OF NATIONS

THE LEAGUE OF NATIONS. THE LEAGUE AND NON-MEMBERS. ARBITRATION AND JUDICIAL PROCEDURE. NON-POLITICAL SERVICES OF THE LEAGUE. CONCLUSION.

CHAP. XVIII.

The League of Nations.—It will be clear from what has been written in previous chapters that if any special feature distinguished the life of the nineteenth century it was the important rôle played by political conferences. Even after the break-down of the attempt to govern by Areopagus the Concert of the great Powers still exercised a special authority, more particularly in the conditions which followed the dissolution of the Turkish Empire, but also in many other European difficulties. The relation of the great Powers to the smaller, but influential and strongly established, states provided a problem which was never eliminated throughout the century. A reasonable temper displayed on most occasions by the great Powers worked wonders in postponing a crisis. All the Italian states had been invited to the Congress of Verona: Sweden had been invited to associate itself with the guarantee of the Danish monarchy in 1852: Sardinia had had a place at the Peace Conference of 1856: Belgium and Holland were present by invitation at the Luxemburg Conference of 1867: Spain was encouraged to take the lead at the Conference of Madrid in 1880: while in the important conference on the question of the Congo at Berlin in 1884-1885 the whole number of states which were internationally active might be said to have participated, for, in addition to the six great European Powers, the United States, Spain, Holland, Portugal, Turkey, Sweden, Norway, Denmark and Belgium were represented. An even more liberal attitude marked the Hague Conferences, for at the first the Balkan States, Switzerland, Luxemburg, Japan, Siam, China, Mexico and Persia were admitted to share for the first time in important international deliberations of a political order; while at the second all the South and Central American republics, even those of the

Caribbean, were participants. If the secondary states were thus frequently called into international councils on political matters, they were even allowed to take the lead in matters not properly political, more especially if these were of a nature not strongly contentious. The reaction of this upon public and expert opinion was intense and effective. Switzerland, for example, had played a prominent part in convening the Red Cross Conference at Geneva in 1864, and was the seat of several international bureaux. The Belgian government had brought together the Slavery Conference of 1889-1890, and the American republics had already gathered in the Pan-American conferences. Is it to be wondered that public sentiment, even when concerned with political questions, for a time followed that recurrent will-o'-the-wisp, the notion of the equality of states?

The Hague Conferences, based in some degree on this delusion, revealed the fact that even in a universal political Assembly the influence and experience of the great Powers would inevitably lead to their domination of the proceedings. In fact, both conferences were guided at critical moments by self-constituted groups predominantly composed of delegates from the greater Powers. Recalcitrancy on the part of the smaller Powers at the second Peace Conference, and their obstinate adherence to a theoretical position, led to the collapse of the projected plans for the creation of a Court of Arbitral Justice. Both for this and for the proposed International Prize Court the great Powers had felt compelled to champion an allotment of influence to each state commensurate in some measure with its position in the international arena. For the Court of Arbitral Justice the judges to be nominated by the great Powers were to sit throughout the whole of the projected twelve-year cycles. Those nominated by the Powers next in rank would sit for ten out of the twelve years; those by the third-class Powers for four years; and those by fourth-class Powers only for two years. The nominees of the Powers of the fifth class would sit but for one year. For the International Prize Court, after a totally different scheme had been considered and rejected, a similar design was finally felt to be most feasible.

The War of 1914-1918 supervened, and in reaction, as has been shown above, considerations of reality swung public opinion too far in an opposite direction. In contrast with the proceedings of the Peace Conference stood out the creation of the League of Nations, the work pre-eminently of

Lord (Robert) Cecil, President Wilson and General Smuts. No longer was the world to wait, as had been the case in the previous century, for the emergence of a political crisis, before an attempt was made to meet in council for the solution of it : no longer was the refusal of a few, or even of one, of the great Powers to accept a suggested programme for discussion to prevent the meeting of an urgently needed international conference. It is true that the two Peace Conferences of The Hague had already laid the basis of a habit of international discussion. The intervals between meetings, however, had been proved to be too long, and as the institution itself had no definite treaty basis it was at the mercy of malevolence. The conferences, so it seemed to men of this way of thinking, were under the old dispensation able enough to undertake the careful and conscientious examination of definite fissures in the international body politic, but they were in their very nature most unlikely to accumulate the experience to detect, still less to check, the forces which lay as a cause behind the fissures. International society needed some such instrument as was provided in the conferences at The Hague, but even more urgent was its need for a new and revised form of the Concert of the Powers, one always in session and always on the watch for the premonitory symptoms of disease. Hence the experiment in preventive medicine provided for a delicate Europe in the League of Nations.

The final form adopted at Paris for the political organs of the League comprised an Assembly, representative of all the member states, which should meet on a basis of equality among them ; and a Council, in which the great Powers were assured of direct and permanent representation and the smaller Powers of representation through the periodical election, from among their number, of states designated to act in the Council by the side of the great Powers. The Assembly, thus created, did much more than replace the Hague Conferences, for it was intended to meet more frequently, and to have a wider range of authority. In its constitution it permitted the inclusion of self-governing Dominions nominally under the sovereignty of their mother-country, and never before included in the most representative gatherings of this kind. The structure of the Council represented a bold attempt to associate the smaller states with the great Powers in the work, half-political and half-administrative, which was certain to be needed in the world after the war.

CHAP. XVIII.

And it was the Council which soon showed itself as the vital factor in the success of the League of Nations, though to say this is not to underestimate the importance of Assembly meetings. The earliest of the peace treaties had provided it with immediate tasks in the Saar district and in the city of Danzig. Later, agreements conferred upon it special tasks of importance connected with the safeguarding of minorities in Central and Eastern Europe, and in Asia. In addition, its charter entrusted the Council with the general duty of the formulation of plans for general disarmament and for the constitution of a Supreme Court of International Justice. Further, the Council was in each case to define "the degree of authority, control, or administration" to be exercised in mandated areas by the mandatory Powers. Finally, such controversial matters as the possible German absorption of German-speaking Austria, or the investigation of disarmament in Germany, were put under the jurisdiction of the Council, beside a variety of economic matters.(1) In these circumstances it was to be expected that the original proportion established within the Council, that of five great to four small Powers, would be speedily questioned despite the fact that the absence of the United States from the beginning reduced the antithesis from one of five to four to one of four to four. With the gradual establishment of peace conditions the dictatorship of the four great Powers was increasingly questioned. The result, perhaps inevitable, of this movement was the increase of the "non-permanent" members of the Council from four to six by the Assembly in 1922, so that a new proportion of four great Powers to six secondary Powers was thereafter established. It is of course a question, to which very different answers may be returned, as to whether in international or say in European affairs the proper proportion between the influence exercised by the great and small Powers respectively is one of four to six (or, as was later fixed, one of five to nine). It is no doubt possible that the respective weight of great and small Powers is a varying factor: that it differs in times of quiet and of crisis, in regions civilised and semi-civilised, and so forth. It will suffice here to point out, what is not always recognised by enthusiastic supporters of the League, that a fundamental change has twice been made in its nature since 1919; and that on the face of it—for in diplomacy things are not always what they seem—the change has been in the direction contrary to the teachings of recent experience.

But granting that the proportion of 1922 as between great and secondary Powers was satisfactory, or that the changes would be offset by considerations which it is not easy to draw up in formal clauses, the system still proved open to objection from many different angles. Continents like the Asian or the African, sub-continents like the South American, and even particular groups like the Little Entente or the Dutch-Scandinavian "neutrals," desired constant representation in the Council, and soon found no assurance that the elections in the Assembly would produce it, unless the number of conciliar seats could be considerably increased. Then the smaller secondary Powers, the least able to rally Assembly votes, complained that the principle of the equality of states demanded that every government should be guaranteed an opportunity of Council membership. They pointed out—instancing such examples as the constant re-election of Belgium, blessed with powerful connections—that the principle of election was not sufficient by itself to secure a fair measure of rotation of Council seats among the secondary Powers. It would have to be weighted with some further principle of non-eligibility for an agreed period after the tenure of a conciliar seat. But this would threaten the interests and dignity of a group of leading secondary Powers, already resentful of their subordination in the international order below the "permanent" Powers, and barely to be prevented from voicing dangerous demands. Thus there was the unique position of Spain, whose traditional prestige, and strong position in Latin-American regard, made it all but impossible to contemplate its exclusion from the Council. There were other restive countries, such as Brazil, conscious of a magnificent future close at hand and the imminent eclipse by it of certain of the reputed great Powers of the day. There were feverish Poland and enigmatic China.

It was certain, therefore, that when the Powers in control of the Council needed to approach their fellow-members of the League in order to obtain authority for a change in the composition of the Council, they would be compelled to accept a considerable enlargement of the number of "non-permanent" seats which would give some security for the representation of all the political groups or areas. Further, the question of a limited measure of rotation would have to be dealt with by making some provision for the temporary non-eligibility of secondary Powers retiring from a Council seat. Finally, either a new constitutional class would have to be created

CHAP. XVIII. within the League to meet the special position of Spain and Brazil—a class exempted from the non-eligibility provisions applied to other Powers—or there would be the greatest danger of the resignation of important Powers. The crisis came in the winter of 1925-1926, a time at which the Locarno group of Powers were anxious to have Germany represented on the Council with a permanent seat. Spain and Brazil, elected members, demanded permanent seats also as the price of their consent, and Poland, less exigent, reduced her demand to a requirement that she should enter the Council by arrangement at the same time as Germany, though not on the same permanent basis. The extraordinary Assembly of 1926 failed to establish agreement within the League despite the ingenuity displayed in compromise proposals. Spain and Brazil withdrew from the work of the League, and the remaining secondary Powers were able to arrange satisfactory terms with the great Powers during the ordinary sessions of September 1926. Germany was admitted to a permanent seat, but as the great Powers had thus increased to five in number, the secondary Powers were to have nine conciliar seats. In every future year three secondary Powers were to be elected to the Council, each for a three-years period. Ordinarily there was to be no re-election, but a state might, on its own demand, be voted eligible for re-election by a two-thirds majority of the Assembly, such a decision being possible at any time. The Assembly was thus given the power of denominating, if it so wished, its own "quasi-permanent" members of the Council, and provision was made at the elections in 1926 for the possibility of declaring three elected states re-eligible immediately. Spain and Brazil, however, did not choose to avail themselves of this compromise, which was designed, in fact, to put them in a privileged position, so that Poland was left alone in the solitary grandeur of a Power specially designated as eligible for re-election—and that, three years before it would find it necessary to apply again for a Council seat.

The pressure of the lesser Powers had increased the membership of the Council to fourteen and made it inconveniently large. A further danger to the League is represented by the necessity to which the Council is subjected of making its decisions either unanimously or, in the vital subject of international dispute, unanimously but for the vote of that member, or those members, of the Council directly concerned in the dispute. The provision was defensible so long as the Council remained small and so long as the opinion of mankind was content to contemplate certain matters as impatient of adjustment even by the League. "Granted the desire to agree," runs the official commentary on the Covenant, "which the conception of the League demands, it is believed that agreement will be reached, or at least that the minority will acquiesce. There would be little practical advantage, and a good deal of danger, in allowing the majority of the Council to vote down one of the great Powers." This is a wise saying, the implications of which are too often disregarded by those who are eager to fill up the gaps of the Covenant and by those who, in the words of one commentator, wish to regard the League as a unitary machine automatic in construction and not as dependent on the initiative and co-operation of the component states. But it is less applicable to a body of fourteen members than it was to one of eight. There remains, therefore, a dilemma. If the unanimity rule be maintained, there is more than a chance that the Council will wither in the nations' hands. If it be abolished, there is more than a chance that in the outvoting of the greater Powers contact will have been lost with reality. It should be noticed that in section 213 of the Treaty of Versailles, and in analogous paragraphs of the other treaties of peace, the allies in a matter of vital concern to themselves have departed from an insistence on unanimity. A majority only of the Council was fixed as necessary to order an inquiry in the defeated countries on questions affecting, it appears, the fulfilment of the provisions for disarmament. Will this mechanism be copied, and will it work ? The Council contemplated by the allies in 1919 was not the Council of 1927.

And yet a great virtue in the League has been the provision in an instant of an authoritative international conference to deal with any dangerous dispute as it arises between states. Before the war there is abundant evidence of the difficulty which lay in the mere constitution of such a conference. Just a report to the Secretary-General of the League of the existence of a dangerous dispute makes it his duty to arrange a complete inquiry, and that of other states to acquiesce. His usual recourse is to the Powers represented on the Council, who in the most urgent cases may be summoned by the president to an extraordinary meeting. It is interesting to speculate on the handling by such a body, had it existed, of the Italian dispute of 1859, or of the tangled relations

CHAP. XVIII. between Austria, Prussia, and Italy in 1866, or indeed of the agenda proposed for the ambassadors' conference at London in 1914. In cases of fundamental importance even an extraordinary meeting of the Assembly can be convoked, though it seems unlikely that, save to give dramatic support to a decision of the Council by a solemn public expression of international sentiment, the convoking of such an assembly would fulfil a useful purpose, for it would hardly make a satisfactory tribunal of first instance. Meanwhile, it is an undoubted fact that the frequent attendance of statesmen of the rank of Sir Austen Chamberlain, M. Briand, and Herr Stresemann, together with the permanent chiefs of their departments, such as M. Philippe Berthelot and Sir Ronald Lindsay, has made the League, in the words of *The Times*, less of a happy hunting-ground for cranks or faddists, and more of an arena for serious discussion.[2]

One important class of dispute between the nations has been excluded from the decision of the organs of the League —that which embraces differences with regard to matters which, according to International Law, are solely within the domestic jurisdiction of one party to the dispute. Thus a controversy over tariffs or an export tax, a difference concerning the law of immigration, or a dispute concerning provocative increases in military, naval, or air forces, cannot be considered by the Council if one party to the dispute establish the plea of "domestic jurisdiction." This is a large admission; and it appears doubtful whether there would not be a case for the removal from the investigation of the Council, under this plea, of a large proportion of the issues provocative of international controversy. The Council is in the end the judge before whom the plea must be established; and it is possible that a series of decisions on the part of the Supreme Court of International Justice may materially assist it to make logical and reasonably acceptable decisions. Here again its resolutions would need at present the unanimous vote of all the Council members except those concerned in the dispute, and once more the dilemma which is hinted at above is within the range of possibility.

The League and Non-Members.—In the political conditions which existed at the inauguration of the League of Nations, membership was looked on as a privilege not to be showered on states indiscriminately or to be hawked about with importunity in the couloirs of diplomacy. The allied and associated Powers assumed membership for themselves and invited many important neutral states, such as Spain, Switzerland, Sweden, Chili, and the Argentine, to adhere as original members. Other states needed election by a two-thirds majority of the Assembly, and were required to give a guarantee that they would perform their international obligations and accept the regulations of the League as touching their armed forces and their armaments. In such circumstances as these, in which it might be presumed that the former enemy states and Soviet Russia would be excluded for some time and that other states might be either unwilling to accept the limitations inherent in membership or, having assumed them, might avail themselves of the legal method provided in the Covenant to liberate themselves, it seemed advisable to constitute some procedure by which disputes between members and non-members, and even those between non-members exclusively, might pass under the supervision of the Council. The procedure established was an invitation from the Council, on the occasion of a dispute, to non-members requesting them to accept the obligations of membership *ad hoc*. Refusal on one side so to accede, if it were followed by a declaration of war against a member of the League, was to be met by the League's united action. A refusal from both parties to a dispute was still to leave the Council authorised to prevent hostilities and to promote a settlement. It is this part of the Covenant which has been pleaded by countries like Russia as evidence of the hostile encirclement of the League's diplomacy. Could or would it be employed against the United States ?

Arbitration and Judicial Procedure.—The arbitral and mediatory action of the Council was primarily intended to be called out in cases which were first-class political disputes, such as were not of a justiciable nature, and which states were undesirous of submitting to the ordinary type of arbitration. On the face of it the Council could not be expected to devote its time to the elucidation of, say, the meaning of a disputed clause in a commercial treaty, or even to the tracing of a disputed frontier where the frontier line was dependent on the interpretation of disputed documents or treaty clauses. For such matters the well-established practice of arbitration existed. Members of the League undertook to refer the appropriate types of disputes either to a process of arbitration or to the more novel process of a judicial settlement. The special organ provided for this last process was to be the Permanent Court of International

 Justice, with the preparatory work for the erection of which the Council was charged. A statute was approved in 1920, and by September 1922 sufficient ratifications were registered to bring it into operation and to permit of the election of the judges. The court's first task was to draw up its own rules of procedure.

The full force of those difficulties caused by the theoretical controversy over the equality of states had been ingeniously avoided in the statute, though in 1907 they had been sufficient to wreck the proposed plans for the Court of Arbitral Justice. The dispute could in 1922 be avoided by making use of those international institutions already in operation—the Council, the Assembly, and the Hague bench of arbitrators. Nominations for judgeships were made by the "national groups" of the Hague bench, and, in the exceptional case of a member of the League possessing no "panel," there was provision made for the conduct of nomination by other and analogous efforts. The bench was then formed by the election of the Council and the Assembly, voting separately but constrained to agree upon an identical list of judges, and by absolute majorities. The "equality" of states had not been neglected in the processes of nomination, and was further secured by the participation of the Assembly in the election. Yet some special and legitimate security had been given to the interests of the great Powers by the requirement that the Council on which they were so strongly represented should participate in the election on equal terms with the Assembly.

The Court quickly gained a wide measure of international support, as is sufficiently proved by the large number of general international instruments, or two-party treaties, which provide in advance for the submission of differences, very diverse in their nature, to the decision of the Court. Among the general conventions which refer differences to the Court may be noted the Barcelona Convention of 1921 on the freedom of transit and the régime of international waterways, the Geneva Convention of 1923 on the international régime of railways, and that on the international régime of ports. The peace treaties of Versailles, St. Germain, Neuilly, and Trianon and the minority treaties had referred certain categories of dispute to the Court, even before it had been established: while the mandates conferred upon certain allied Powers also made provision for reference to the Court in cases of dispute concerning their interpretation and application. Commercial treaties and treaties of arbitration are increasingly making use of the provision of a final recourse to the Court. A large jurisdiction is assured to the Court under the famous "optional clause" of the statute, which has already been discussed. This clause, already accepted by several states, including Germany, gives to the Court jurisdiction as between two states which have undertaken its obligations when any dispute shall arise concerning

(1) the interpretation of a treaty;
(2) any question of International Law;
(3) the existence of any fact which, if established, would constitute a breach of international obligation;
(4) the nature and extent of the reparation to be made in the event of such a breach.

Reasons which have caused some states to hesitate before committing themselves to the compulsory litigation involved in this "optional clause" have already been explained in a previous chapter (see p. 405).

A further activity for the Court was constituted in the original charter of the League, and consists in the giving of advisory opinions to the Council or the Assembly on any point referred to it. Experience has already shown that the Court can do useful work by giving an opinion on the legal part of any dispute before the Council.

The classes of action open for the League and its organs in the course of an international dispute are thus seen to be manifold. What, finally, is the guarantee given by the League to a member state which, despite its readiness to submit a dispute to arbitration, judicial procedure, or examination by the Council or the Assembly, may have been attacked either before such process has been begun, during the "reasonable" period of its course, or before three months have elapsed from the date of the arbitral award, judicial decision, or the publication of the report of the Council or the Assembly? All the member nations are solemnly pledged to coerce the nation which breaks its obligations by such an attack; and further, to prevent all intercourse with the nationals of such a state, a not very remote hint of the possible recourse to a blockade by land and sea. More vaguely the Council is charged with the examination of the military, naval, and air aspects of such a situation, and with the making of recommendations to the member states as to the armed forces which will be required of them in the defence of the League. It was the unsuitability of the Council for such a purpose which was alleged by the various states when in a different connection they rejected the treaty of mutual assistance. No state has been pledged in advance to undertake any specific armed operation; and should the occasion arise for the employment of troops or ships, there is likely enough to be much hurried negotiation as to the despatch of contingents, or even total refusal on the part of the more timorous states which border on the breaker of the Covenant. The staff work for a combined operation to be carried out in any given direction, against any given foe, under any given conditions, might well make the brain of a Moltke reel. Therefore it is not surprising to find that, in discussions during the meeting of the Assembly in 1922 on the subject of Article X. of the Covenant, several nations made it perfectly clear that, while they were ready to show the utmost respect for the recommendations of the Council in regard to the defence of a state unlawfully attacked, the adoption of military measures without an independent examination of the situation was entirely a different thing. It is noteworthy that member states have promised one another "mutual financial and economic" support in measures undertaken in support of the League, but that, too, is not the same as to undertake the measures instantly and acting for themselves. An actual crisis will find much hurried negotiation proceeding between several cabinets and the League Council on such matters as temporary advances of money and the loan of military supplies.

Non-Political Services of the League.—The League, besides the directly political work represented in the Council, the Assembly, the Court, and the conferences convoked for the consideration of disarmament and security, has largely taken from off the shoulders of individual states the labour of preparing and initiating international conferences for the consideration of pressing matters of a non-political nature. Labour conferences (and even emigration and immigration studies) have of course been made the special work of the International Labour Office. The Financial Committee of the League has done invaluable technical work for the Council in connection with the loans which saved Austria, Hungary, Danzig, and Greece from complete financial collapse and large populations from suffering, anarchy, and revolution. Further, the Committee's important studies of such difficult subjects as double taxation and fiscal evasion have some use for every national finance ministry.

Prima facie the Economic Committee of the League should have found even more work to hand than the Financial Committee, for the whole problem of the removal of unnecessary obstructions to international trade falls within its sphere. Here, however, advance proved most difficult to attain. To begin with, international action on such matters as export taxes, the lowering of tariff walls, and the ending of export and import prohibitions could hardly be considered by many serious statesmen until the chaotic currency conditions of the period 1919-1926 were in some measure under control. Even then the very thought of general international action has had to meet the resistance of large classes in every state. However, by the end of 1925 conditions seemed sufficiently encouraging for the appointment of a Preparatory Committee to make ready for a world conference. Throughout 1926 the Preparatory Committee, as the agent of the League and in co-operation with such pre-existing organisations as the International Chamber of Commerce and the Institute of Agriculture, was drawing up its plans. In May 1927 an International Conference was gathered.

It is impossible to cover all the recommendations of the conference even in the section of it which dealt with Commerce—one only of the three fields of its activity, the other two being Industry and Agriculture. Two sub-sections of the conference's Recommendations on Commerce may be taken as showing the range of its discussions. Section III. of the conference's report on Commerce is placed under the general heading of Commercial Policy and Treaties. Of this section, sub-section 1 is entitled Tariff Levels and sub-section 3 Export Duties. The detailed recommendations made under the heading of Tariff Levels run as follows :—

(1) That nations should take steps forthwith to remove or diminish those tariff barriers that gravely hamper trade, starting with those which have been imposed to counteract the effects of disturbances arising out of the war.

(2) That states should proceed to the conclusion of commercial treaties on lines and under conditions calculated to ensure the attainment of the aims mentioned herein.

(3) That in future the practice of putting into force, in advance of negotiations, excessive duties established for the purpose of bargaining, whether by means of

CHAP. XVIII.

tarifs de combat or by means of general tariffs, should be abandoned.

(4) That the Council of the League of Nations should be requested to instruct its Economic Organisation to examine, on the basis of the principles enunciated by the present conference, the possibility of further action by the respective states with a view to promoting the equitable treatment of commerce by eliminating or reducing the obstructions which excessive customs tariffs offer to international trade.

The recommendations of sub-section 3 on Export Duties are :—

(1) That the exportation of raw materials should not be unduly burdened by export duties or any other taxes, and that, even in cases where such duties or taxes are justified by fiscal needs or by exceptional or compelling circumstances, they should be as low as possible.

(2) That, in any case, export duties on raw materials should never be imposed for the special purpose of subjecting foreign countries using such materials to an increased burden which will place them in a position of unfair inferiority as regards the production of the finished article.

(3) That export duties on raw materials, whether levied for revenue purposes or to meet exceptional or compelling circumstances, should never discriminate between different foreign destinations.

(4) That the above principles apply equally to export duties on articles of consumption.[3]

A remodelling of the Economic Committee, or the addition to the League's equipment of a new advisory economic body, which should meet periodically and contain personalities of the greatest economic reputation and importance, was loudly called for as the only possible preparation for a real campaign to carry out the resolutions of the Economic Conference of May 1927. The Council and the Assembly showed themselves responsive to these complaints and suggestions, and the year 1928 should see the calling into being of an organ of the League at once more authoritative and urgent in the sphere of commerce than had been the older Economic Committee. CHAP. XVIII.

Another technical organisation of the League is that for Communications and Transit, which finds its *raison d'être* in Article XXIII. of the Covenant, by which members of the League promise to make provision to secure and maintain freedom of communication and transit. To advise the Council and Assembly in the technical details involved in railway, river, canal, and port administration there is the committee nominated according to an approved plan from the ranks of officials in various national ministries of public works.[4]

Conclusion.—To prophesy the future of the League is an undertaking foreign to the intention of this work, as foreign as it would have been to attempt, what has been performed elsewhere, an account in detail of its mechanism and its activities. It may, however, be permitted to ask whether any one supposes that, should the nations be engulfed in the agony of another world war, there would not be at the end of hostilities a return to an organisation not very different from that at present existing. It becomes, therefore, not so much a question of the survival of the League of Nations, as of the form in which it will survive. For undoubtedly there exist two schools of thought. The first sees the League as a unitary and an automatic organ. Something, it would say, has been created in the world which political scientists may find it hard to define, but which stands apart from the state system of Europe as that has been known up to the present. It is detached, permanent, supervisory, and protective: it can have a policy and standards of its own; it can win victories and suffer defeats. But there is a second and somewhat different attitude towards the League. According to this the function of the League is mediatory. Action by the League can at the most but represent the crystallisation of a readiness to agree among the states which have recourse to it. Only when that readiness can be induced can fruitful activity result: hence the insertion in its constitution, on more than one occasion, of obligatory unanimity. It is easy to score points against the contestants on either side. The truth is that the constitution of the League is neither that of a super-state nor that of ancient Poland, which abhorred minority dissent. Perhaps it is essential that both extreme conceptions should be avoided by theorists if the League is not to sustain a mortal blow.

CHAP. XVIII.

The officials and supporters of the League are faced with a double problem, that of stimulating respect for the authority of the League without inflicting an injury upon the sentiment of national patriotism. For them this is a problem in diplomacy and is one of judgment; for who can deny that before now diplomatic tact has proved itself a constructive force? It took nearly sixty years to bring the state of Massachusetts to final judgment in the Supreme Court of the United States. It was not the magnification of its office by the Bench which produced this result: rather it was due to a growing confidence in the discretion of the Court. Thus, by analogy, to wait upon unanimity may be the surest way in the long run of adding to the authority of the League.

The League of Nations has shown that it knows well how to display discretion. In the matter of the protection of minorities it has not proved so irksome as was expected by countries like Poland, Rumania, and Czecho-Slovakia, which contain minority populations composed of races formerly dominant. Intransigent adversaries of the new states in Europe have not been permitted to use the machinery of the League for purposes of sabotage; and governments quickly realised that the League intended to put no unnecessary obstacles in the way of the organisation of administrative machinery which should be as efficient as that which it had had to replace. Conversely, nationalistic parties were firmly resisted in any attempt to use the power of the state for the production of quick results in the policy of "assimilation."

Some criticism has been directed against the League for its handling of the system of mandates. Colonial administrators are not infrequently men who like plain speaking, but the causes of criticism go deeper than this. The last fifty years have seen a revolution in the colonial policy of European countries. The prosperity of the indigenous peoples now takes a foremost place in any apology for colonial possession. As a novel point it has tended to overshadow other, and equally valid, points of justification for the possession of colonial territory. What wonder, then, that in the earlier years of the League's history there should be found those who have pressed too far the genuine readiness, displayed by the mandatory Powers, to admit limitation in some directions of their control of the mandated areas? Such limitation is considerable in the direction of the relinquishment of a privileged position for the capital, the trade or the land hunger of the mandatory's subjects *vis-à-vis* those of other Powers. There is a danger lest an inquisitorial attitude, pressed too far by the League in points of detail, should end in producing a situation in which the only Power penalised should be the mandatory Power. That is not to argue that alleged abuses, when serious, should not be probed to the bottom, or that the system of annual reports to the League should not be maintained. Both are obviously desirable. As a matter of fact, the Permanent Mandates Commission is not, unlike the International Labour Organisation, setting for the world a standard which is on the whole in advance of average practice. Territories not under the mandatory system are in many cases experiencing more striking development than the mandated territories, and are, moreover, themselves taking the lead in what may be termed "colonial philanthropy." Such at least would seem to be a legitimate deduction from a comparison of Morocco with Syria, of the British West African colonies with Tanganyika, or of Malaya with Iraq.

It has been argued by some that the failure to make tangible advance towards the reduction of armaments constitutes the most striking testimony to the futility of the League as at present constituted. It is true that the reduction of armaments was set most prominently before the new organisation as its initial task, and that at the end of nine years no progress has been made beyond preparatory discussion. Nations are still divided upon a question so rudimentary as that of the method by which degree of armament, or absence of armament, is to be measured. Those who have studied the epoch of the Hague Peace Conferences will remember the elaborate nature of the rules and regulations which were evolved over the whole field of International Law, both for war and for peace. The codifying spirit, undaunted even after the lessons of the war of 1914-1918, is still at work to-day. It expresses itself in a fever of endeavour to reach some all-embracing agreement for universal, if gradual, disarmament. Delay in attaining this end is attributed to an imperfection, of some sort or other, in the particular scheme under discussion, be it a scheme for disarmament itself or for the closely associated devices of compulsory arbitration, or of pacts for the insurance of security. Is it conceivable that the impediment lies, not in the schemes themselves, but in the League under the aegis of which they would be signed? Between individual nations in particular

CHAP. XVIII. circumstances it may well be possible to reach agreement to disarm, although at the same moment it may be impossible to expect from all the nations an acceptance of general commitments in the same direction upon the authority of an organisation not yet ten years old. As that organisation proves itself, this situation may well change; and thus in a sense the League, in carrying out its normal duties with efficiency, is solving the problem of disarmament. In a word, time is desirable alike for the League to create confidence and for mankind to realise fully the horror and the more equal incidence upon combatant and non-combatant of modern methods of warfare.

There remains the fact that Russia and the United States have no place for a League of Nations in their foreign policy. Far too much effort, mostly mischievous, has been expended in abuse of, or argument with, this attitude of mind. Abuse is an impertinence; while as for argument, there can be but one solid reason for adhesion to the League, the conviction self-engendered that it is better to be in than out. For the present, an impartial consideration of the question is likely to lead most Europeans to the conclusion that the United States and Russia, in their present state of mind, have much to lose, and little to gain, by admission to the League of Nations. Whether this be a final condition of affairs is a conundrum which may be left to future generations. The answer will in a large degree depend upon the conduct and achievements of the League itself, for no substitute can ever take the place of actual achievement as a means of propaganda. The future can be left to the future: in the present, well-wishers of the League can content themselves with the ardent desire that its policy may be rooted in the realities of politics, that its ideal may be one of reliance upon the rule of law, and that its machinery may continue to bring into intimate contact the statesmen of the European countries. These are the lessons of history: they are held out for the enlightenment of this age by the Age of the Prince, the Age of the Judge, and the Age of the Concert.

NOTES

For a critical account of the League and an estimate of its possibilities, see the second edition of Butler, *A Handbook to the League of Nations*.

The effect of the existence of the League on the law and practice of nations is well brought out in the latest editions of the well-known text-books. There is a concise account in Birkenhead's *International Law*, p. 54. CHAP. XVIII.

(1) Nothing reveals the importance of the Council better than an examination of the agenda prepared for one of its four annual meetings. The subjects to be considered at the meeting of 5th December 1927 included—

(*a*) A Lithuanian appeal against certain measures taken against teachers in the Vilna and Grodno districts of Poland.
(*b*) A number of matters adjourned from the September sessions, including the treatment of the property of Hungarian optants in Rumania and the provision of a Polish naval port at Danzig.
(*c*) The question of expediting League decisions in the case of a crisis involving mutual aid under the Covenant.
(*d*) The annual nomination of the presidents of the committees of investigation for the control of disarmament in Germany, Austria, Hungary, and Bulgaria.
(*e*) The examination of a loan of nine millions to Greece and of the proposed rehabilitation of Bulgarian finance.
(*f*) The nomination of an advisory committee to follow up the application of the recommendations of the International Economic Conference of 1927.
(*g*) The proposal to reduce the annual number of Council sessions.

In addition to these subjects, mentioned in the agenda circulated among the member-states some time in advance of the meeting, the members of the Council almost of necessity undertook some examination of the labours of the Preparatory Commission on Disarmament, whose sittings began on 30th November. Lastly, on the appeal of Germany some minority school difficulties in Polish Silesia were added to the list of subjects to be considered by the Council.

(2) Though text-books have treated the recognition and succession of states and have tried to establish legal principles for international practice in the case of both, it must be admitted that governments have regarded them almost entirely from the political view of expediency. The treaty of France with U.S.A. in 1778, or the varying attitude of nations to Soviet Russia, proves this as regards recognition. In the matter of succession different wars and different cessions have produced quite different settlements. Even in treaties made in such similar circumstances as those of Versailles, St. Germain, and Trianon there appear different rules of fiscal succession, imposed partly from political reasons. The League of Nations may introduce a greater uniformity of practice.

(3) The whole of the conference's report, with commentary from its principal members, will be found printed in a volume entitled *The Economic Consequences of the League*, issued by the Europa Publishing Company.

(4) Before the war Switzerland had been the only nation entirely dependent on its neighbour's ports and railways for overseas trade, but competition among these secured it from injustice. The peace

of 1919 added Czecho-Slovakia, Austria, and Hungary to the list of portless countries, while Russia, Poland, and Serbia may be said to suffer from inadequate coast-lines. Special concessions were imposed on Germany as to port arrangements in the interests of Czecho-Slovakia. It can, however, be understood why the transit section of the League has more than an academic interest for these countries.

A good, concise account of the League's work in transit and communications is given in Maurice Fanshawe's *Reconstruction*.

INDEX

B

C

D

E

T

U

Y

Z

Printed in Great Britain by T. and A. Constable Ltd.
at the University Press, Edinburgh

www.ingramcontent.com/pod-product-compliance
Lightning Source LLC
LaVergne TN
LVHW091516200926
848483LV00005B/430/J
* 9 7 8 1 5 8 4 7 7 2 1 5 6 *